W9-CBJ-547

Handbook for
Conducting Research
on
Human Sexuality

Handbook for Conducting Research on Human Sexuality

edited by

Michael W. Wiederman
Columbia College

Bernard E. Whitley, Jr.
Ball State University

 LAWRENCE ERLBAUM ASSOCIATES, PUBLISHERS
2002   Mahwah, New Jersey   London

Lawrence Erlbaum Associates, Inc., Publishers
10 Industrial Avenue
Mahwah, New Jersey 07430

Cover design by Kathryn Houghtaling-Lacey

Library of Congress Cataloging-in-Publication Data

Handbook for conducting research on human sexuality / edited by
Michael W. Wiederman, Bernard E. Whitley, Jr.
p.   cm.
Includes bibliographical references and index.
ISBN 0-8058-3437-0
1. Sexology—Research.   I. Wiederman, Michael W.   II. Whitley, Bernard E.
HQ60.H353   2001
306.4'07'—dc21   01-040185
                                                                CIP

Books published by Lawrence Erlbaum Associates are printed on acid-free paper,
and their bindings are chosen for strength and durability.

Printed in the United States of America
10 9 8 7 6 5 4 3 2 1

Contents

PART III: DATA ANALYSIS

PART IV: INTERPRETING RESULTS

PART V: SPECIAL ISSUES

1

▼▼▼▼▼▼▼

A Preview: The Unique Nature of Sexuality Research

Michael W. Wiederman
Columbia College

Bernard E. Whitley, Jr.
Ball State University

What determines whether people are sexually attracted to men, women, or both men and women? What factors influence people's decisions to engage in relatively safe versus risky sexual practices? Are school-based sexuality education programs effective? Is viewing sexually explicit media harmful? There are several possible approaches to answering these and other questions about human sexuality, one of which is through empirical research. Recently some writers have questioned whether empirical research on sexuality is useful, or even possible, arguing that the socially constructed nature of both sexuality and research makes objectivity unattainable (e.g., Simon, 1996). However, the existence of the Society for the Scientific Study of Sexuality (SSSS), the International Academy of Sex Research, and the World Association of Sexology indicates that there are many professionals invested and engaged in empirical research on sexuality.

Behavioral and social scientists have been especially prolific in producing research on human sexuality. At least four academic journals are devoted to publishing the results of social and behavioral scientific research on sexuality (*Archives of Sexual Behavior, Canadian Journal of Human Sexuality, Journal of Psychology and Human Sexuality, The Journal of Sex Research*), and several other scholarly journals regularly publish research articles on specific facets of the behavioral and social aspects of human sexuality. These topics include sexual dysfunction and therapy (e.g., *Journal of Sex Education and Therapy, Journal of Sex & Marital Therapy, Sexual and Marital Therapy, Sexual Dysfunction*), intimate relationships (e.g., *Personal Relationships, Journal of Marriage and the Family, Journal of Social and Personal Relationships*), gender roles, gender identity, and sexual orientation (e.g., *Journal of Gay, Lesbian, and Bisexual Identity; Journal of Homosexuality; Sex Roles*), and HIV and AIDS (e.g., *AIDS and Behavior, AIDS Care, AIDS Education and Prevention, Journal of HIV/AIDS Prevention & Education for Adolescents and Children*).

What are the professional backgrounds of the people carrying out this empirical research on sexuality? There is no simple answer to that question. One of the hallmarks of sexuality research is its multidisciplinary nature. Traditionally, those studying sexuality from behavioral or social scientific perspectives have been trained in a more general field, such as psychology, sociology, or anthropology. This tradition has led to distinct advantages and disadvantages for sexual science, particularly with regard to research methodology (Reiss, 1999). Sexual scientists often come well prepared to carry out the research methods promoted within their discipline of origin, but may be less familiar and comfortable with methods from other disciplines. Similarly, they may be unfamiliar with the methodological issues unique to sexuality research. Because there are few formal programs for training sexual scientists per se, researchers must learn how to conduct sexuality research through individual mentoring and trial and error. Neither method is particularly efficient, which may explain the apparently slow progress of sexual science as a field. In 1990, Paul Abramson, then editor of *The Journal of Sex Research*, published an article in that journal entitled "Sexual Science: Emerging Discipline or Oxymoron?" In his commentary, Abramson emphasized the relatively crude nature of the methods used in sexuality research.

There seems to be a need for a handbook covering the methodological issues inherent in sexuality research. There have been past attempts to bolster dissemination of information on research methodology within sexual science. For example, in 1986, a special issue of *The Journal of Sex Research* (Volume 22, Issue 1) was devoted to methodology in sexuality research. C. E. Jayne, the editor of that special issue, noted the need for the field to take a broad perspective on the state of methodology; however, she was disappointed to find that the articles submitted for publication in the special issue each addressed a narrow aspect of a specific methodological question. Again in 1999, a special issue of *The Journal of Sex Research* (Volume 36, Issue 1) was devoted to research methodology. However, just as happened more than a decade earlier, the articles in that special issue were primarily reports of empirical research on very specific methodological issues.

Social and behavioral scientists who conduct research on human sexuality find themselves faced with research questions that entail conceptual, methodological, and ethical issues for which their professional training or prior experience may not have prepared them. This handbook is intended to provide guidance to graduate students and professionals interested in the empirical study of human sexuality from behavioral and social scientific perspectives. Some of the issues addressed in this volume are inherent in social scientific research in general; others are specific to research on human sexuality.

In several ways, conducting sound research on human sexuality entails special considerations. For example, perhaps because of the multidisciplinary nature of sexuality research, the role of theory has been inconsistently used to guide research and often has been entirely absent (see chap. 2). With regard to measurement of sexuality variables, some phenomena can be observed (see chap. 6) or captured through instruments designed to gauge psychophysiological response (see chap. 7). Each of these methods entails special issues to consider. However, the most common method of measuring sexual phenomena is through self-report, and there are a host of issues to consider when using self-report instruments (see chap. 3).

Of course it is important to consider the overall design of a particular sexuality study (see chap. 4). Also, given the sensitive nature of sexuality research, methods of recruiting research participants can have profound effects on results (chap. 5). Certain methods of collecting data, such as focus groups (see chap. 8), diaries (see chap. 9), and policy capturing (see chap. 10), have been underutilized yet hold promise. Each method also includes particular advantages and disadvantages that need to be carefully weighed. Occasionally, researchers are interested in examining cultural products that bear on sexuality, such as texts (see chap. 14) or visual representations meant to be erotic or sexually arousing (see chap. 15). Few behavioral and social scientists have been trained in how to empirically examine such materials.

Regardless of the form of data researchers gather, there are particular issues involved in the statistical tests performed on the data. Often the analyses of interest involve comparing groups (see chap. 11) or uncovering relationships between and among variables (see chaps. 12 & 13). Although many people find the statistical aspects of research design difficult to follow or anxiety-provoking, we encourage readers not to overlook chapters 11, 12, and 13; each was written to be accessible to readers who have only a basic background in statistics.

Once sexuality researchers have gathered and analyzed their data, they are faced with the issue of what their results mean. There are certain traps that must be avoided when interpreting research findings, especially when the topic is sexuality (see chap. 16). Placing findings into the context of the broader research literature, or reviewing and integrating the existing research literature, presents special challenges (see chap. 17).

Sexuality is unique in that the topic is sensitive and heavily influenced by culture. Accordingly, when conducting research on sexuality, it is important to consider the effects of culture or placing research findings within a cross-cultural context (see chap. 18). Within and between cultures, there is great diversity when it comes to sexuality. An accurate understanding of human sexuality must include examination and appreciation for that diversity (see chap. 19). Due to the sensitive nature of sexuality research, there are also ethical and sociopolitical factors to consider (see chap. 20). Because sexuality researchers conduct their work in social and organizational contexts, this volume also addresses issues related to the causes and consequences of a career in sexuality research (see chap. 21).

In attempting to construct a useful methodological guide for sexuality researchers, we are indebted to the professionals who volunteered their time and expertise to write the chapters in this volume. They represent psychology, sociology, anthropology, epidemiology, and family science, as well as a range of topics of expertise. By sharing each writer's knowledge in this public forum, our hope is that other sexuality researchers will find their work easier and more rewarding.

REFERENCES

Abramson, P. R. (1990). Sexual science: Emerging discipline or oxymoron? *The Journal of Sex Research, 27,* 147–165.
Jayne, C. E. (1986). Methodology in sex research in 1986: An editor's commentary. *The Journal of Sex Research, 22,* 1–5.
Reiss, I. L. (1999). Evaluating sexual science: Problems and prospects. *Annual Review of Sex Research, 10,* 236–271.
Simon, W. (1996). *Postmodern sexualities.* New York: Routledge.

FOUNDATIONS OF RESEARCH

2

▼▼▼▼▼▼▼

The Need to Integrate Sexual Theory and Research

David L. Weis
Bowling Green State University

In 1998, the *Journal of Sex Research* became the first sexological journal to publish a special issue devoted to the use of theory in sexuality research (Weis, 1998c). This collection of articles demonstrated the continuing development of sexual theory, but it also served to highlight the general lack of connection between research and theorizing in sexual science. In his 1981 presidential address to the Society for the Scientific Study of Sexuality (SSSS), Ira Reiss (1982) issued a challenge to the field to improve research by focusing on the general goals of science, particularly the development of empirically grounded theory. For Reiss, theoretical explanations comprise the heart of science. Such explanations are what scientists do. This is a view shared by Kerlinger (1979), who argued that the very purpose of science is theory.

In effect, the status of any specific scientific area can be evaluated by an examination of the state of theory in that area of study. This chapter represents an attempt to evaluate sexual theory critically. Compared with many other areas of scientific inquiry, it is fair to suggest that sexual theory is still in its infancy—both because relatively little sexuality research is oriented to testing theoretical hypotheses and because few empirically tested theories with conceptual precision have yet to emerge. Eventually, I assess the use of scientific theory in sexuality research, compare the use of theory in sexuality research to other areas of scientific investigation, and urge a greater integration of sexual theory and research. However, first I present a conceptualization of scientific theory in general. This perspective includes a definition of *theory* and related terms, a brief review of recent criticisms of what has come to be known as the positivist tradition of science, a description of the components of theory, and a set of criteria for evaluating theories.

METATHEORY – CONCEPTUALIZATIONS
OF SCIENTIFIC THEORY

Klein and Jurich (1993) argued that it is useful to pause occasionally and reflect on the work performed in any scientific field. They recommended a process of analysis and evaluation, an inventory of the field, taking stock. This involves, among other tasks, the assessment of research methods and theoretical models. This is an attempt to analyze and explain the field, including an identification of its strengths and weaknesses. Klein and Jurich emphasized the critical character of this evaluation. They used the term *metatheory* to describe the theoretical aspects of this process and defined it as "theorizing about the nature of theory" (p. 32). Metatheoretical analyses include several related activities: (a) identification of major schools of thought or theoretical perspectives, (b) critical evaluation of the meanings and structure of past and current theoretical explanations, (c) examination of theoretical trends, and (d) assessment of the rules for theory construction that have developed in the field (Doherty, Boss, LaRossa, Schumm, & Steinmetz, 1993; Klein & Jurich, 1993; Nye & Berardo, 1981).

A metatheoretical perspective is important to scientific theory in two ways. First, it helps us reflect on the meaning of theory in different contexts. In everyday conversation, the word *theory* is used to describe a hunch or set of untested ideas. Even many professionals use the term to describe speculative works that are not supported by empirical evidence. This meaning differs substantially from what scientists mean by the term. Second, a metatheoretical perspective helps us identify and evaluate different types of theory. Scientists have defined a variety of types of theory (e.g., axiomatic, causal, set-of-laws) and have outlined different approaches to constructing theory (e.g., theory-then-research, research-then-theory, causal modeling; for a discussion of how research results can be used to construct theory, see chap. 16, this volume). In fact, a number of conceptualizations or definitions of theory have been proposed (Doherty et al., 1993). As one example, Mullins (1973) presented an unusual approach to metatheory by organizing sociological theories by the intellectual leaders of a theoretical approach and the graduate programs that subsequently trained students in that theory.

The most widely shared perspective has been a view that has come to be known as the *positivist approach*. In this tradition, scientific theory is viewed as a logically interrelated series of propositions that are used to specify the empirically meaningful relationships among a set of concepts (Babbie, 1995; Burr, 1973; Kerlinger, 1979; Klein & White, 1996; Martindale, 1988; Marx, 1963; Nye & Berardo, 1981; Reynolds, 1971; Runkel & McGrath, 1972; Sjoberg & Nett, 1968). This lengthy list of references demonstrates that this particular definition of scientific theory has been widely shared for a considerable period of time.

Four dimensions characterize this positivist conceptualization of theory. First, science has a tradition of basing its claims on the results of observation and experimentation, which is aimed at explaining and predicting specified phenomena

(Babbie, 1995; Edwards, 1957; Marx, 1963; Reiss, 1982). In other words, scientific theory is subjected to empirical testing. Second, scientific theory is built around concepts, which have actually been described as the building blocks of theory (Babbie, 1995; Klein & White, 1996). A concept is an abstract, symbolic representation of an idea or a phenomenon (Babbie, 1995; Klein & White, 1996; Marx, 1963; Nye & Berardo, 1981; Reynolds, 1971). Because concepts are used to build theoretical explanations, issues of the clarity of definition, agreement among scientists about the meaning of the definition, and potential for measurement of the concept are always prime concerns (Klein & White, 1996).

The third dimension of this approach to theory concerns the use of propositions. Propositions constitute the heart of scientific theory. A theory is composed of a series of propositions, each of which is a statement of some association between concepts (Babbie, 1995; Klein & White, 1996; Marx, 1963; Nye & Berardo, 1981; Reynolds, 1971). Various kinds of relationships (e.g., existence, correlational, causal) can be specified (Klein & White, 1996; Reynolds, 1971), but the key component of scientific explanation is the specification of relationships among concepts in the form of propositions. Some authors maintain that the assumptions of a theory may also be considered an important component (Klein & White, 1996; Nye & Berardo, 1981). Assumptions can be distinguished from propositions by the fact that assumptions, in the case of the human sciences, are more likely to delineate a set of general human characteristics (i.e., humans are social beings), rather than specify a relationship between concepts. Assumptions also represent the underlying premises of the theory, and they are frequently untested.

Finally, theories are designed to explain particular phenomena. No single theory is intended to explain everything in the universe or about human beings. Rather, scientific theory is intended to use a designated set of concepts to explain a particular set of phenomena (Klein & White, 1996). To cite just one example in the realm of sexuality, the concept of sexual scripting and its focus on social interaction were designed to explain social influences on sexuality in various situations (Gagnon & Simon, 1973). There is probably a good deal about human sexual behavior that sexual scripting theory was never intended to explain, and there is no corresponding conceptual apparatus to explain other phenomena. The term *mini-theory* has been used to describe theories intended to explain specific, particular phenomena. Perhaps the classic example of a mini-theory in sexuality is *The Social Context of Premarital Sexual Permissiveness* (Reiss, 1967).

Some authors (Burr, 1973; Burr, Hill, Nye, & Reiss, 1979; Nye & Berardo, 1981) have suggested that scientific theory can also be constructed through the use of explanatory or causal models. Typically, in this approach, little attention is paid to identifying underlying assumptions or defining variables in a conceptual way. Rather, researchers move directly to measuring variables and testing propositions (hypotheses; Nye & Berardo, 1981). Examples in the area of sexuality research include causal models of sexual coercion (Allgeier, 1987) and child sexual abuse (Finkelhor, 1984).

Criticisms of the Positivist Philosophy

This positivist approach has been traced in the social sciences through Karl Popper and Max Weber back to the works of Comte in the early 19th century (Babbie, 1995). Most scientific research reports in the United States reflect a positivist approach (Doherty et al., 1993). Babbie (1995) argued that the positivist philosophy was built on three primary assumptions: logical empiricism, rationality, and objectivity.

There have been critics of positivism throughout its history. However, there has been a sharp increase in attacks on this metatheoretical approach in recent decades. Postpositivist or postmodernist critics have challenged the premises underlying positivism, particularly the notion that value-free, universal, objective, and rational research can be conducted and that general human theories can be constructed (DeLamater & Hyde, 1998; Doherty et al., 1993; Simon, 1996). Postmodernists have stressed the contextual (i.e., sociocultural) process of science and the multitude of meanings associated with human experience. With respect to sexuality research and theory, this applies both to the populations and phenomena studied and the professional activities of sexual scientists.

Whereas postmodernists have generally criticized positivism for its focus on a value-free, objective science, relatively few have directly challenged the empirical base of science (Martindale, 1988; Reiss, 1982). As a rule, postmodernists have not rejected the collection or analysis of empirical data (Doherty et al., 1993; Simon, 1996). In addition, postmodernists have been more inclined to criticize the weaknesses of positivism than they have to recommend alternative approaches or solutions to those problems.

In response to such criticisms, several authors (Babbie, 1995; Doherty et al., 1993; Martindale, 1988) have argued that positivists have not denied or ignored the influence of values on objectivity, but have sought to minimize their impact. Certainly there is little question that what we observe and conclude are shaped by what we already believe (Babbie, 1995). At the very least, scientific theorists need to recognize the contextual nature of science and the multiplicity of meanings assigned to the phenomena studied.

It seems premature to predict how this dispute will be resolved. DeLamater and Hyde (1998) provided a general summary of the essentialist and social constructionist disputes, which can be seen as one element of the more general positivist versus postmodernist conflict. The concept of Kuhn paradigms may be relevant here. Kuhn used the concept in two ways to describe both the idea of a single grand theory in a discipline (Babbie, 1995) and the idea of a universally recognized, ideal theory (Martindale, 1988). Postmodernism represents a challenge to the positivist paradigm, perhaps its greatest challenge to date. Many regard the two paradigms as incompatible. This has led to a loss of consensus as to what constitutes optimal theory and scientific methods. There is a sense of rivalry, and even hostility, between advocates of the two camps. However, precisely such disputes lead to new syntheses. We may yet find ways of satisfying the traditional positivist concerns over scientific rigor and the postmodernist focus on subjective meaning. Some authors have already begun to move in this direction (Doherty et al., 1993; Thomas & Roghaar, 1990).

The Notion of Conceptual Frameworks

As with many fields, no single paradigm has yet to emerge in sexual science. This is so both in the sense of a single grand theory of sexuality or an ideal theory universally accepted by sexual scientists. This is due, only in part, to the positivist–postmodernist disputes. In fact, few theoretical perspectives of sexuality fully meet the standards of the definition provided earlier of theory as a set of systematic, interrelated, and empirically grounded propositions specifying relationships among concepts. In their assessment of theory in family studies, Nye and Berardo (1981) reached similar conclusions about the state of theory in that field. They employed the term *conceptual framework* to describe the state of family theory.

A conceptual framework is a group of concepts employed as a classification scheme, the specification of a set of definitions delineating a few aspects of reality. A conceptual framework can be seen as a developmental precursor of theory (Nye & Berardo, 1981). The term can be used to describe a line of inquiry with defined concepts and a corresponding set of underlying assumptions. The concepts might be integrated into some meaningful configuration, but a systematic set of propositions has yet to emerge. Klein and White (1996) suggested that a conceptual framework can be seen as a vocabulary of shared definitions of concepts. In this view, a conceptual framework serves as a guide to the focus of inquiry and is broader, but less precise, than a theory.

Nye and Berardo (1981) believed that the construct of a conceptual framework was a useful device for creating more refined definitions of important concepts, organizing and testing possible propositions, and fostering theoretically meaningful research. They saw a conceptual framework as a stage that could lead to more fully developed theories. Klein and Jurich (1993) noted that there is some controversy about whether the notion of conceptual frameworks actually advances theoretical development.

A debate by sexual scientists about the relative merits of using conceptual frameworks to guide research and theory might well be desirable. It would represent a form of self-examination and criticism in which sexual scientists have rarely engaged. To the extent that sexuality research is oriented toward theoretical concerns, it would be fair to conclude that most such research has employed conceptual frameworks. In fact, this notion of conceptual frameworks was used as the organizing principle in the special issue of the *Journal of Sex Research* devoted to theory. Most of its articles are reviews and critiques of existing conceptual frameworks with some established history (Weis, 1998c).

Criteria for Evaluation of Theory

The discussion to this point on positivist and postmodernist perspectives and the debate about the utility of the conceptual framework approach to theory construction highlight the diversity of metatheoretical perspectives on science. There are numerous approaches to defining theory and various strategies for theoretical development. Against this background, it is exceedingly difficult to specify a set of criteria for evaluating various theories or conceptual frameworks that is suitable for all metatheoretical perspectives. Some time ago, I presented a list of criteria for evaluating theory that attempts to synthesize the positivist and postmodernist positions (Weis, 1998b). That list is presented in Table 2.1.

This particular set of criteria is not original. In compiling it, I used the work of several authors (Babbie, 1995; Doherty et al., 1993; Marx, 1963; Nye & Berardo, 1981; Reynolds, 1971). Moreover, some criteria may actually conflict with one another. For example, the idea that a theory should be abstract or independent of time and space considerations may well conflict with the idea that a theory should recognize its own sociocultural context. The criteria are presented here in the hope of

TABLE 2.1
Criteria for Evaluation of Theory

Adequacy of Conceptual Apparatus
  Level of abstraction—independence of time and space
  Recognition of human pluralism
  Acknowledgment of context surrounding phenomenon
  Clarity of conceptual definitions
  Intersubjective agreement among scientists
Adequacy of Theoretical Explanations
  Richness of ideas generated
  Parsimony—simplicity of explanations
  Internal consistency—logical rigor
  Clarity of assumptions and propositions
  Ability to predict phenomena of concern
Level of Empirical Support
  Potential for validation—testability
  Amount of research generated
  Level of congruence with empirical data
  Level of validation
  Acknowledgment of limits and inconsistencies
  Openness to change and modification
  Level of generalizability
General Metatheoretical Characteristics
  Acknowledgment of values and ethical considerations
  Scientific utility—advances understanding of phenomena
  Potential for human intervention and social policy
  Ability to combine subjective human experience and scientific rigor

stimulating dialogue among sexual scientists. I see it as a starting point—a place where we can begin examining this question: What makes a sound sexual theory?

THEORY IN SEXUALITY RESEARCH

These metatheoretical issues—including definitions of scientific theory, the post-modernist reaction to the positivist tradition, the possible utility of employing conceptual frameworks to make advances in sexual theory, and the specification of criteria for the evaluation of theory—are relevant to sexual scientists. They raise fundamental questions about the very nature of sexuality research, the practices of sexual scientists, and the future direction of sexual theory. To what extent has research on sexuality been informed or guided by theory? What kinds of sexual theory have been developed? Is there a tradition of metatheory in sexual science? What role, if any, have professional organizations played in fostering the development of sexual theory?

Perhaps the most basic point is that no general tradition of asking such metatheoretical questions has emerged in the field of sexuality research. In one of the few attempts to assess these concerns empirically, Ruppel (1994) conducted a content analysis of a sample of articles published in *The Journal of Sex Research* and *Archives of Sexual Behavior* from 1971 to 1990. He rated the articles as to length, sexual topic, grant support, type (e.g., data report, theory development), discipline of the first author, methods of data collection, nature of sample, theoretical orientation, statistical techniques, and assumptions made by the authors. Ruppel reported that three fourths of the articles published in this period were primarily categorized as data reports. Roughly one fourth of the articles appearing in *The Journal of Sex Research* were primarily concerned with theory development, but only 6% of the articles in *Archives of Sexual Behavior* were classified as theory-development works. Of course, the authors of some articles coded as data reports could have claimed to have utilized a theoretical perspective or discussed findings in terms of an existing theoretical model. However, fully 53% of the articles in *Archives of Sexual Behavior* and 31% of the articles in *The Journal of Sex Research* were coded as containing no theory whatsoever. Only 30% of the articles in both journals had a discussion of specific theoretical issues. Finally, Ruppel reported that there had been an increase in the percentage of articles concerned with theory in some way in *The Journal of Sex Research*, but not *Archives of Sexual Behavior*, from 1976 to 1985.

Allgeier (1984) reported, in a separate content analysis of the 253 articles appearing in *The Journal of Sex Research* and *Archives of Sexual Behavior* between 1980 and 1983, that only 2% could be classified as presenting a theoretical model. This estimate may be considered low because any article with data-collection and statistical analyses was placed into another category. However, Allgeier concluded that the majority of research published in these journals has been descriptive, rather than theoretical. She noted that tests of what she called *explanatory inferences* or *theoretical models* were fairly rare.

These studies depict a tendency of the sexological journals to publish data reports, which are descriptive and atheoretical. Even when specific hypotheses are tested, they are rarely derived from, or designed to test, theoretical propositions. However, these studies tell us little about the kinds of sexuality articles that are published in other disciplines. Although I suspect that the same patterns will be evident, it is possible that sexuality articles published in journals in such fields as biology, psychology, and sociology are more likely to have been theoretical. This possibility should be tested.

Another aspect of this situation is the fact that the field has generally been rather unconcerned with the development of a metatheoretical perspective for sexual science. In other words, sexual scientists have rarely paused to take stock of the state of sexual theory. Of the 25 theoretical works identified as classics by Weis (1998b), only Geer and O'Donohue's (1987) could be considered a metatheoretical analysis. In his analysis of publication trends in *The Journal of Sex Research* and *Archives of Sexual Behavior* during the previous two decades, Ruppel (1994) found few research articles with a theoretical base, and he failed to find a single article on metatheory.

This point can be illustrated with a comparison to other areas of research. Three areas seem useful in this regard. The first two—psychology and sociology—are traditional academic disciplines that are defined by their broad focus of study. Like sexual science, no single paradigm has ever emerged, and no single theory has ever come to dominate either discipline. However, a tradition of metatheoretical analysis and evaluation extends to the earliest periods of the 20th century (Burgess, 1926; Cooley, 1902; Parsons, 1950; Waller, 1938; Watson, 1925). Marx (1963) suggested that this may be considered a critical approach to theory construction and refinement. This trend has continued in psychology (Baldwin, 1967; Gergen, 1993; Shaw & Costanzo, 1982; Swensen, 1973) and sociology (Cook, Fine, & House, 1995; Fine, 1993; Giddens & Turner, 1987; Martindale, 1988; Turner, 1978).

Comparisons can also be drawn to family studies. As with psychology and sociology, no paradigm has ever emerged in this field. However, like sexual science, it is a fully multidisciplinary field devoted to the study of a substantive focus. Although it was once dominated by family sociologists, it eventually saw the emergence of several professional organizations. As with the professional organizations in sexuality, members are drawn from a variety of professions, and professional journals in the family field reflect this multidisciplinary perspective. Thus, it shares much in common with sexual science.

Klein and Jurich (1993) argued that a tradition of self-examination in the family studies field extends to the 1920s, citing Burgess (1926) as an example. Nye and Berardo (1981) were more critical and argued that no tradition of metatheory, the systematic construction and evaluation of theory, existed in family studies prior to 1960. However, since that time, a rich tradition of metatheory has emerged (Boss, Doherty, LaRossa, Schumm, & Steinmetz, 1993; Burr et al., 1979; Christensen, 1964; Nye & Berardo, 1981). In contrast, Klein and White (1996) maintained that systematic theory building in the family field began around 1950. This early period, which they called the *conceptual frameworks phase*, ended in the mid-1960s with the publication of the *Handbook of Marriage and the Family* (Christensen, 1964) and the first edition of Nye and Berardo's (1981) anthology on conceptual frameworks. This was followed by a period of formal theory construction, which lasted until 1980, culminating with another anthology to assess the state of theory (Burr et al., 1979). Klein and White described the 1980s and 1990s as a pluralistic period with at least one metatheoretical classic publication (Boss et al., 1993). Taken together, these publications demonstrate an ongoing commitment by family scholars to examine developments in family theory.

Sexual scientists have never developed a comparable tradition of metatheoretical review and criticism. Although numerous authors have presented specific sexual theories, few general reviews of sexual theory and even fewer critical evaluations of the status of sexual theory have been published. Geer and O'Donohue (1987) provided one of the notable exceptions. They edited a collection of 14 essays reviewing and summarizing various theoretical and disciplinary perspectives. Included were evolutionary, phenomenological, developmental, sociocultural, learning, cognitive, social scripting, and psychoanalytical frameworks. Also included were essays summarizing theoretical issues in such disciplines as theology, history, feminism, anthropology, sociology, and physiology. Geer and O'Donohue indicated that they had tried to be inclusive. They did not provide a specific definition of theory or select perspectives by a system of metatheoretical criteria. Instead, they tried to include the broadest group of perspectives possible. Given the state of sexual theory and the lack of a metatheoretical tradition in sexual science at the time, this approach was both understandable and laudable.

However, this anthology also illustrates the general lack of a metatheoretical perspective in sexual science. Although Geer and O'Donohue briefly discussed several criteria for evaluating theory, they did not use these criteria to evaluate the various perspectives or ask their contributing authors to provide a systematic evaluation. One result is that many chapters can be described as advocating a particular perspective, rather than providing a critical review and assessment.

This analysis can be extended to the activities of professional organizations. Beginning in the 1960s, the National Council on Family Relations (NCFR) has sponsored a theory construction workshop as a part of their annual conventions. Its goals have been to foster dialogue about theory and facilitate the development of new and refined theory. The organization also created a Research and Theory section of membership. Since 1970, a decade review issue has appeared every 10 years in the *Journal of Marriage and the Family*, published by NCFR. The decade review series has always included an assessment of developments in theory in the previous decade. Comparable activities have never been sponsored by sexuality organizations.

Available evidence supports the view that relatively little sexuality research has been derived from theoretical premises or designed to test theoretical hypotheses. In addition, no general tradition of metatheoretical analysis has emerged in sexuality journals or organizations. However, a full assessment of the development of sexual theory must acknowledge that there have been major theoretical works. In my prior analysis of the current state of sexual theory (Weis, 1998b), I provided a list of 25 classic theoretical works. These works document that sexual scientists have developed and published a variety of theories. These theoretical works have advanced our understanding of sexuality, and several are notable for their integration of theory and research (e.g., Allgeier, 1987; Byrne, 1977; Finkelhor, 1984; Reiss, 1967). However, it is also interesting to note that many of the more prominent sexual theories have remained essentially untested by research (Freud, 1957; Gagnon & Simon, 1973; Maltz & Borker, 1983). While recognizing the importance of these contributions, it is still the case that, too often, theorizing about sexuality has been separated from the research process.

The publication in 1998 of a special issue of *The Journal of Sex Research*, devoted to theory in sexuality research, was merely a first step toward the development of a metatheoretical tradition in sexual science and an endorsement of greater integration between sexual theory and research (Weis, 1998c). The articles collected in that issue were certainly not the final or definitive statement about sexual theory. Nonetheless, the issue was an important attempt to examine and critique the theories sexual scientists use, identify the components of such theories, assess the level of empirical support for various theories, and evaluate the current status of sexual theory. In my concluding article (Weis, 1998a), I provided a set of recommended readings for 39 theoretical perspectives and evaluated 23 of those perspectives by the criteria presented in Table 2.1. Much of that concluding article was devoted to a discussion of what I believe are two of the greatest challenges facing sexual scientists: (a) the need to refine the conceptualization of the theoretical constructs used by sexual scientists, and (b) the importance of building and testing explanatory models. In the present chapter, I stress two other concerns. One is the need, that I have noted throughout, to establish a metatheoretical tradition in sexual science, and the other is the need for sexual scientists to more fully integrate theory and research.

COMBINING THEORY AND RESEARCH

To address this issue of integration, I present three examples drawn from the sexuality literature. These examples were chosen precisely because they reflect different degrees of integration between theory and research. In this chapter, I do not have the space to provide a truly systematic metatheoretical analysis. Instead, I simply explore how such integration is an important component of such analyses and how sexual scientists need to move in this direction.

Autonomy Theory of Premarital Sexual Permissiveness

One of the better examples of a sexual theory that is highly integrated with research is the Autonomy Theory of Premarital Sexual Permissiveness from sociology (Burr, 1973; Reiss, 1967). Reiss began by studying the premarital sexual attitudes (permissiveness) of students and adults across the United States. The results were used to generate the earliest form of the theory. At this stage, Reiss (1967) presented a general theoretical summary statement and a series of seven specific propositions reflecting aspects of the general statement. Without reviewing the propositions in their entirety (see Burr, 1973; Reiss, 1967; Reiss & Miller, 1979), the summary statement was that the greater the level of autonomy in a courtship group and the greater degree of permissiveness in sociocultural groups (institutions), the greater would be the permissiveness of individuals. As just one illustration, we would expect greater permissiveness in a culture where young people are free to select their own dating partners, their own sexual partners, or both.

The theory stimulated a great deal of research to test the original propositions, and the results were used to revise the theory (see Burr, 1973; Reiss & Miller, 1979). Reiss and Miller (1979) decomposed the theory by identifying explicit and implicit concepts and further specifying the interrelationships among concepts. Little subsequent research or revision has occurred in the years since. Reiss and Miller suggested that the theory might well extend to other areas of heterosexual permissiveness, such as marital or extramarital sex. This suggestion has gone largely untested. We might also question whether permissiveness toward homosexual relations and other sexual practices could be explained with the same concepts. Finally, although Reiss has always been explicit in his claim that the theory was designed to explain attitudes, questions remain about how sexual behavior might relate to permissiveness and the social forces associated with it.

Learning Theory

A second example can be taken from learning theory (psychology), a theory that is generally integrated with research results. There is considerable evidence that various patterns of behavior, including sexual behavior, are learned in the classical and operant conditioning processes (Hogben & Byrne, 1998). Much of the research on conditioning extends back to the early decades of the 20th century. Eventually, what has come to be called *social learning theory* emerged to explain forms of learning that did not fit in either the classical or operant conditioning perspectives (Bandura, 1977, 1986; Bandura & Walters, 1963). For example, social learning theorists have identified the concept of modeling and demonstrated its utility in explaining behavior. There was recognition that, in addition to classical

and operant conditioning, individual differences in personality, cognition, and affect mediate environmental cues in shaping behavior. This perspective has been
shown to relate to the development of sexuality among children, adolescent sexual and contraceptive behavior, health-related sexual behavior, and coercive sexual behavior (Hogben & Byrne, 1998).

There is, however, little consensus about how to conceptualize or measure this
individual mediation. Various conceptualizations have been proposed (reward expectancy, cognition, motive, cognitive competency, self-efficacy, and affect) as
internal factors that influence how individuals respond to their environment
(Hogben & Byrne, 1998). One of the more fruitful lines of research has been the
Affect-Reinforcement Model proposed by Byrne (1977). Here the affective reactions to sexual stimuli (or events) are seen as reinforcing (positive affect) or punishing (negative affect), which in turn establishes expectancies for the future.

This perspective could be used to formulate a series of hypotheses in a relatively new research area: affective reactions to the first intercourse (Schwartz,
1993; Sprecher, Barbee, & Schwartz, 1995; Thompson, 1990; Weis, 1983). As far
as I know, no studies of first intercourse have ever used a social learning perspective to generate hypotheses or interpret results. This area seems particularly relevant because the experience of first intercourse is popularly seen as a major life
transition and because, at first glance, it might appear to establish contingencies
for subsequent sexual interaction. However, I know of no studies that have shown
that affective reactions to the first intercourse are significantly related to the outcomes of later sexual encounters or relationships. Moreover, although social
learning theory would view such affective reactions as reinforcing, this would be
only part of a complex set of contingencies. Subsequent sexual experiences might
well be related to changes in one's expectations about intercourse, changes in
partner, exposure to new models, and so forth.

Working in the other direction, we might ask what would be related to variations in affective reactions to the first intercourse. Here, exposure to relevant
models, expectations about what intercourse will be like or the discrepancy between expectations and actual events, and patterns of reinforcement and/or pun-
ishment for prior noncoital sexual behavior would all fit within this perspective. I
might add that the relevant set of expectations could well include items that are
not directly sexual in the sense we typically think. For example, some persons
might well believe that sex is a useful way to achieve popularity or status, keep a
boyfriend or girlfriend, establish intimacy, or relax. Numerous studies could be
designed to test such speculations, and the results might well inform our understanding of sexual development through adolescence.

Social Scripting Theory

My third example is what has been described as sexual (social) scripting theory.
The perspective was introduced by Gagnon and Simon (1973) and has been
widely used since (Gagnon, 1990; Simon, 1996; Simon & Gagnon, 1987). I previ-

ously reviewed the history and use of the concept (Weis, 1998a). That summary is not presented again here except to note that the use of the theater as a metaphor may be viewed as an extension of the dramaturgical school of symbolic interactionism (Goffman, 1959; Mead, 1934). Gagnon and Simon (1987) indicated that they employed scripting as a conceptual tool to examine sexual conduct (which includes both the specific behaviors involved and the multitude of meanings assigned to them), rather than seeking to build an explanatory theory. Basically, this perspective maintains that humans use a set of guidelines or beliefs (i.e., a script) in directing behavior and ordering experience in the same way that an actor uses a script on the stage. The script is the actor's construction of stage reality. In effect, social scripts are used to define and organize what Berger and Luckmann (1966) called the reality of everyday life both spatially and temporally.

The concept has been used primarily as a vehicle for discussing substantive issues. Little effort has been directed at identifying possible explanatory correlates of internalized scripts, which may be seen as cognitive organizations of beliefs, perceptions, and meanings associated with some particular referent (Weis, 1998a). In discussing the general lack of empirical research, I proposed one possible explanatory model (Weis, 1998a). I suggested that scripts are internalized by individuals through a series of interrelated processes that comprise an individual response to human experience. Scripts are formed as people try to make sense out of the world by cognitively assimilating and organizing personal experiences. This basic process is influenced by reinforcement, modeling, rehearsal opportunities, and symbolization (the acquisition of the meanings of symbols). Each of these processes, in turn, occurs within a particular social environment. This social environment limits or establishes a social boundary surrounding script internalization.

Again, space does not allow a full examination of the perspective, but portions of the model can be used to illustrate its use in sexuality research. I proposed that, among other concepts, reinforcement and rehearsal influence the internalization of social scripts (Weis, 1998a). Because I have already discussed the issue of reinforcement, I now focus my comments on the role of rehearsal. Since the earliest days of the theory (Mead, 1934), symbolic interactionists have maintained that learning does not always conform to reinforcement contigencies. Gagnon (1977) noted that, even with all of the cognitive elements of a script formulated, a person must still rehearse or practice the script, which provides an opportunity to test the script.

Returning to the issue of first intercourse, we can question whether these concepts have any relevance. As with social learning theory, where there is little consensus about how to conceptualize a person's internal processing of stimuli, there is no consensus within sociology about how to measure an internalized social script. One approach might be to argue that a measure of affective reactions to a stimulus event is a general indicator of a script. Certainly scripts are more than simple evaluative judgments. We might, then, question what constitutes rehearsal for sexual intercourse. One direct (explicitly sexual) form would seem to regard an act of intercourse as a fairly complex series of sexual activities, which in the United States have typically included hugging, kissing, french kissing, petting, and oral sex—what adults later call *foreplay*. In fact, I showed that just such a measure of rehearsal is related to affective reactions to first intercourse for a group of college females (Weis, 1983). Less direct, but perhaps important, forms of rehearsal might include meeting potential sexual/romantic partners, self-presentations to potential partners, flirtation, dating, "going" with a partner, and so forth—what adults later characterize as *relationship formation* or *seduction*. In both cases, we would expect that persons with the greatest rehearsal experience to have more positive reactions to first intercourse. Questions about the social situations or personal characteristics that promote opportunities for rehearsal also remain.

Of course, questions remain as to whether reinforcement and rehearsal would have separate main effects or would interact with each other in relation to affect, but it is important to note that symbolic interactionists would predict that rehearsal would operate independently of patterns of reinforcement. To provide just one example, many Americans anecdotally report that, when they first learned of the existence of french kissing, they were initially disgusted by the prospect of inserting their tongue into someone's mouth. However, many tried the practice and eventually became fond of it. Exactly how this process occurs is still largely an open empirical question.

GUIDELINES AND SUMMARY

The discussion of rehearsal serves as a bridge to the major themes of this chapter. To a large extent, theory is learned as you use it in conjunction with research. Perhaps the most basic guideline is to start with the recognition that the field of sexuality will benefit from a greater integration of theory and methodology. Your own research will become more precise and critical. So, to quote a recent Nike slogan: "Just do it." We would expect that, as you gain more experience integrating research and theory, you will improve at it. Other suggestions include:

1. Remember to use theory critically, rather than as an advocate of a particular theory.
2. Read about various theories. Anthologies are useful in this regard. Weis (1998a) has provided suggested readings for 39 theoretical frameworks relevant to sexuality research.
3. Read and learn more about metatheory (sometimes also listed under "Philosophy of Science").
4. Ask theory-based research questions. Thousands remain to be tested.

5. Recognize that theoretical concepts and variables are two sides of the same coin. Practice developing operational definitions for concepts and transforming variables into abstract concepts.

6. Similarly, practice translating propositions into testable hypotheses and research results into theoretical propositions.

7. Recognize that the results of atheoretical research may well involve variables that could be included in several theories.

8. As with the discussion on first intercourse, explore how different theories might be used to explain the same sexual phenomena.

9. Build a consideration of theoretical issues and concerns into the planning stages of research.

10. Practice interpreting research results in terms of various competing theories.

11. Get in the habit of assessing research you read metatheoretically. What does this study tell us about theory?

12. In your research, test relationships that are predicted by theory.

13. Build a network or group of people who share these concerns and meet regularly to consider these issues. If you talk about interesting topics and interesting questions, it might even be fun!

As sexual scientists seek to improve the general character of the theories they use and the research they conduct, one challenge for the future is to reduce the disengagement between the two that has characterized the past. As just one final example of the type of metatheoretical questions we need to examine as a field, little is known about why most sexuality research is atheoretical or why sexual scientists select the theories they use. Why do certain theories appeal to certain researchers or disciplines? Certainly the selections reflect some preference or perspective. Postmodernists would insist that these choices are not made at random and probably reflect values that may well affect the outcome of research (Simon, 1996). Among the many challenges we face, we need to examine why sexual scientists use the theories they use.

SUGGESTED READINGS

For a separate discussion of metatheoretical analysis, see Klein and Jurich (1993). There are numerous anthologies available that review and assess theories within a discipline or field of study. Weis (1998a) provides suggested readings for 39 theoretical frameworks in biology, psychology, and sociology. One source that is helpful in creating a historical perspective of the development of theory in the 20th century is Boss et al. (1993). For a review of how various theories might be employed in sexuality research per se, see Weis (1998c). Finally, the best single source describing a theoretically based research program, including a systematic assessment of empirical evidence and revision of the theory, is Reiss and Miller (1979).

REFERENCES

Allgeier, E. R. (1984, April). *State of the science: Sex research—Contrasts and complements.* Paper presented at the annual conference of the Eastern Region of The Society for the Scientific Study of Sex, Philadelphia, PA.

Allgeier, E. R. (1987). Coercive versus consensual sexual interactions. In V. P. Makosky (Ed.), *G. Stanley Hall Lecture Series* (Vol. 7, pp. 9–63). Washington, DC: American Psychological Association.

Babbie, E. (1995). *The practice of social research* (7th ed.). Belmont, CA: Wadsworth.

Baldwin, A. L. (1967). *Theories in child development.* New York: Wiley.

Bandura, A. (1977). *Social learning theory.* Englewood Cliffs, NJ: Prentice-Hall.

Bandura, A. (1986). *Social foundations of thought and action.* Englewood Cliffs, NJ: Prentice-Hall.

Bandura, A., & Walters, R. (1963). *Social learning and personality development.* New York: Holt, Rinehart & Winston.

Berger, P. L., & Luckmann, T. (1966). *The social construction of reality: A treatise in the sociology of knowledge.* New York: Doubleday.

Boss, P. G., Doherty, W. J., LaRossa, R., Schumm, W. R., & Steinmetz, S. K. (Eds.). (1993). *Sourcebook of family theories and methods: A contextual approach.* New York: Plenum.

Burgess, E. W. (1926). The family as a unit of interacting personalities. *The Family, 7,* 3–9.

Burr, W. R. (1973). *Theory construction and the sociology of the family.* New York: Wiley.

Burr, W. R., Hill, R., Nye, F. I., & Reiss, I. L. (Eds.). (1979). *Contemporary theories about the family: Vol. 2. General theories/theoretical orientations.* New York: The Free Press.

Byrne, D. (1977). Social psychology and the study of sexual behavior. *Personality and Social Psychology Bulletin, 3,* 3–30.

Christensen, H. T. (Ed). (1964). *Handbook of marriage and the family.* Chicago: Rand McNally.

Cook, K. S., Fine, G. A., & House, J. S. (Eds.). (1995). *Sociological perspectives on social psychology.* Boston: Allyn & Bacon.

Cooley, C. H. (1902). *Human nature and the social order.* New York: Charles Scribner's Sons.

DeLamater, J. D., & Hyde, J. S. (1998). Essentialism versus social constructionism in the study of human sexuality. *The Journal of Sex Research, 35,* 10–18.

Doherty, W. J., Boss, P. G., LaRossa, R., Schumm, W. R., & Steinmetz, S. K. (1993). Family theories and methods: A contextual approach. In P. G. Boss, W. J. Doherty, R. LaRossa, W. R. Schumm, & S. K. Steinmetz (Eds.), *Sourcebook of family theories and methods: A contextual approach* (pp. 3–30). New York: Plenum.

Edwards, P. (Ed.). (1957). *The encyclopedia of philosophy* (Vol. 7). New York: Macmillan.

Fine, G. A. (1993). The sad demise, mysterious disappearance, and glorious triumph of symbolic interactionism. *Annual Review of Sociology, 19,* 61–87.

Finkelhor, D. (1984). *Child sexual abuse: New theory and research.* New York: The Free Press.

Freud, S. (1957). Three essays on sexuality. In J. Strachey (Ed. and Trans.), *The standard edition of the complete psychological works of Sigmund Freud* (Vol. 7, pp. 123–243). London: Hogarth Press. (Original work published 1905)

Gagnon, J. H. (1977). *Human sexualities.* Glenview, IL: Scott Foresman.

Gagnon, J. H. (1990). The implicit and explicit use of the scripting perspective in sex research. *Annual Review of Sex Research, 1,* 1–43.

Gagnon, J. H., & Simon, W. (1973). *Sexual conduct: The social sources of human sexuality*. Chicago: Aldine.

Geer, J. H., & O'Donohue, W. T. (Eds.). (1987). *Theories of human sexuality*. New York: Plenum.

Gergen, K. J. (1993). Theory in historical context. In H. V. Rappard, P. J. van Strien, L. P. Mos, & W. J. Baker (Eds.), *Annals of theoretical psychology* (Vol. 8, pp. 245–248). New York: Plenum.

Giddens, A., & Turner, J. (Eds.). (1987). *Social theory today*. Stanford, CA: Stanford University Press.

Goffman, E. (1959). *Presentation of self in everyday life*. New York: Doubleday.

Hogben, M., & Byrne, D. (1998). Using social learning theory to explain individual differences in human sexuality. *The Journal of Sex Research, 35*, 58–72.

Kerlinger, F. N. (1979). *Behavioral research: A conceptual approach*. New York: Holt, Rinehart & Winston.

Klein, D. M., & Jurich, J. A. (1993). Metatheory and family studies. In P. G. Boss, W. J. Doherty, R. LaRossa, W. R. Schumm, & S. K. Steinmetz (Eds.), *Sourcebook of family theories and methods: A contextual approach* (pp. 31–67). New York: Plenum.

Klein, D. M., & White, J. M. (1996). *Family theories: An introduction*. Thousand Oaks, CA: Sage.

Maltz, D. N., & Borker, R. A. (1983). A cultural approach to male–female miscommunication. In J. J. Gumperz (Ed.), *Language and social identity* (pp. 195–216). New York: Cambridge University Press.

Martindale, D. A. (1988). *The nature and types of sociological theory* (2nd ed.). Prospect Heights, IL: Waveland.

Marx, M. H. (Ed.). (1963). *Theories in contemporary psychology*. New York: Macmillan.

Mead, G. H. (1934). *Mind, self, and society*. Chicago: University of Chicago Press.

Mullins, N. C. (1973). *Theories and theory groups in contemporary American sociology*. New York: Harper & Row.

Nye, F. I., & Berardo, F. M. (Eds.). (1981). *Emerging conceptual frameworks in family analysis* (rev. ed.). New York: Praeger. (Original work published 1966)

Parsons, T. (1950). The prospects of sociological theory. *American Sociological Review, 15*, 3–16.

Reiss, I. L. (1967). *The social context of premarital sexual permissiveness*. New York: Holt, Rinehart & Winston.

Reiss, I. L. (1982). Trouble in paradise: The current status of sexual science. *The Journal of Sex Research, 18*, 97–113.

Reiss, I. L., & Miller, B. C. (1979). Heterosexual permissiveness: A theoretical analysis. In W. R. Burr, R. Hill, F. I. Nye, & I. L. Reiss (Eds.), *Contemporary theories about the family: Vol. 1. Research-based theories* (pp. 57–100). New York: The Free Press.

Reynolds, P. D. (1971). *A primer in theory construction*. Indianapolis, IN: Bobbs-Merrill.

Runkel, P. J., & McGrath, J. E. (1972). *Research on human behavior: A systematic guide to method*. New York: Holt, Rinehart & Winston.

Ruppel, H. J., Jr. (1994). *Publication trends in the sexological literature: A comparison of two contemporary journals*. Unpublished doctoral dissertation, Institute for the Advanced Study of Human Sexuality, San Francisco, CA.

Schwartz, I. M. (1993). Affective reactions of American and Swedish women to their first premarital coitus: A cross-cultural comparison. *The Journal of Sex Research, 30*, 18–26.

Shaw, M. E., & Costanzo, P. R. (1982). *Theories of social psychology*. New York: McGraw-Hill.

Simon, W. (1996). *Postmodern sexualities*. London: Routledge.

Simon, W., & Gagnon, J. H. (1987). A sexual scripts approach. In J. H. Geer & W. T. O'Donohue (Eds.), *Theories of human sexuality* (pp. 363–383). New York: Plenum.

Sjoberg, G., & Nett, R. (1968). *A methodology for social research*. New York: Harper & Row.

Sprecher, S., Barbee, A., & Schwartz, P. (1995). "Was it good for you, too?": Gender differences in first sexual intercourse experiences. *The Journal of Sex Research, 32*, 3–15.

Swensen, C. H., Jr. (1973). *Introduction to interpersonal relations*. Glenview, IL: Scott Foresman.

Thomas, D. L., & Roghaar, H. B. (1990). Postpositivist theorizing: The case of religion and the family. In J. Sprey (Ed.), *Fashioning family theory: New approaches* (pp. 136–170). Newbury Park, CA: Sage.

Thompson, S. (1990). Putting a big thing into a little hole: Teenage girls' accounts of sexual initiation. *The Journal of Sex Research, 27*, 341–361.

Turner, J. H. (1978). *The structure of sociological theory* (rev. ed.). Homewood, IL: Dorsey.

Waller, W. (1938). *The family.* New York: Dryden.

Watson, J. B. (1925). *Behaviorism.* London: Kegan Paul, Trench, Trubner.

Weis, D. L. (1983). Affective reactions of women to their initial experience of coitus. *The Journal of Sex Research, 19*, 209–237.

Weis, D. L. (1998a). Conclusion: The state of sexual theory. *The Journal of Sex Research, 35*, 100–114.

Weis, D. L. (1998b). The use of theory in sexuality research. *The Journal of Sex Research, 35*, 1–9.

Weis, D. L. (Ed.). (1998c). Special issue: The use of theory in research and scholarship on sexuality. *The Journal of Sex Research, 35*, 1–124.

3

▼▼▼▼▼▼▼

Reliability and Validity of Measurement

Michael W. Wiederman
Columbia College

A scientific discipline is only as solid as its methods of measurement. To draw meaningful conclusions from scientific data, those data must be generated using measures that are both reliable and valid. This chapter provides a brief overview of measurement reliability and validity and how these concepts are typically assessed in sexuality research.

Sexuality researchers may use psychophysiological measures of sexual arousal (see chap. 7, this volume), direct observation of behavior (see chap. 6), or evaluators' judgments of text (see chap. 14) or visual stimuli (see chap. 15) to generate data. Each of these methods entails specific issues with regard to reliability and validity, which are addressed in the respective chapters. However, sexuality researchers typically rely on self-reports from research participants, and such self-reports are vulnerable to a number of sources of error and bias (Baker & Brandon, 1990). Accordingly, in addition to discussing reliability and validity, I also briefly review the research literature regarding several important factors influencing self-reports.

RELIABILITY OF MEASUREMENT

A measure is said to be reliable if it is consistent, or stable, or dependable in its measurement (Anastasi & Urbina, 1997; Kerlinger, 1986; Whitley, 1996). Theoretically, if one could administer a highly reliable measure multiple times simultaneously with the same research participant, one would obtain the same results each time. In this theoretical case, if the results varied across administrations of the instrument, the measure would be said to contain some degree of unreliability. Why might this occur? With imperfect measures and imperfect respondents, there will be some random factors that influence scores on the measure (e.g., inconsistent interpretation of some test items, carelessness or inattentiveness by the test taker). These factors are collectively referred to as *random error in measurement*. Scores on a highly reliable measure contain less random error than do scores on a less reliable measure.

In the hypothetical case in the preceding paragraph, reliability was assessed by administering the same measure multiple times simultaneously to the same respondent. Of course, in reality this cannot be accomplished, so researchers must rely on less direct ways to assess reliability. Although there are several ways to assess reliability in measurement (Anastasi & Urbina, 1997), this chapter focuses on three of the most commonly used methods: test–retest reliability, internal consistency of scales, and inter-rater reliability.

Test–Retest Reliability

In attempting to assess the reliability of self-reported behavior, researchers may ask for the same information at two or more separate points in time (e.g., Carballo-Dieguez, Remien, Dolezal, & Wagner, 1999) and then compare each respondent's answers to assess the degree to which those answers are consistent (i.e., reliable) across time. Such consistency is typically calculated as a correlation coefficient or percentage agreement between the two scores taken from the two points of assessment. In some instances, the information is asked for at two separate points in the same questionnaire or interview, whereas in other instances, the information is asked for during separate assessment sessions, sometimes spaced up to months apart. Each approach entails advantages and disadvantages.

For example, suppose researchers wished to assess the reliability of responses to the question, "With how many partners have you had vaginal intercourse during the previous 12 months?" An investigator who asks the question during two separate interviews, each conducted 3 months apart, is not asking about the same reference period, so there is likely to be some discrepancy between the reports gathered during each session because the respondents may have had changes in their sexual experience. In the second interview, the researcher could attempt to specify "in the 12 months prior to the previous interview," but it is unclear (and doubtful) whether respondents would be able to effectively draw boundaries in their memories around the span of time the researcher designates as of interest (note that the time span probably does not correspond to any meaningful demarcation in respondents' lives).

Sexuality researchers could circumvent this problem by assessing the number of partners at two different points in the same interview. However, a high degree of consistency might simply indicate that the respondents were able to accurately recall their first response over the relatively short span of the interview. Sexuality researchers often take a compromise approach by measuring sexual experience during two separate assessment sessions, each spaced closely enough together (e.g., 2 weeks) to minimize the likelihood of actual differences in the respondents' behavior between the two points yet spaced far enough from one another to minimize the effect of directly recalling one's earlier answer.

Sexual behavior or experience is often measured with single interview or questionnaire items. With regard to theoretical constructs, however, multiple-item scales are often used because such scales are generally more reliable than single-item measures. Single-item measures are relatively more vulnerable to measurement error because such error is more concentrated, or more liable to affect the final overall score, than multiple-item measures. For example, suppose two researchers measure attitudes toward condom use—one uses a single item, whereas the other uses a 10-item scale designed to measure the same construct. If a respondent is careless in responding to the single-item measure or if it contains ambiguous language, the measurement error introduced will have a tremendous effect on the value ascribed to that respondent. In the case of the 10-item measure, the effect of careless responding to a few items, or ambiguous wording in some items, will be watered down when a single score is generated across the items (some of which are better items than the problematic ones). Therefore, the 10-item scale will demonstrate greater reliability relative to the single-item measure.

To assess test–retest reliability of scales, one would administer them to the same individuals at two points in time; the correlation between the two sets of scores would indicate the test–retest reliability of the measure. Such an index of reliability is inappropriate, however, for tests measuring constructs that are, by their nature, unstable. For example, suppose researchers developed a self-report inventory of sexual arousal. Although sexual arousal may entail a component best conceptualized as a trait (i.e., some individuals tend to experience more frequent or intense sexual arousal than do others), certainly a large component of sexual arousal involves the individual's current state (i.e., situational variables are probably most prominent). Accordingly, we might expect a fair degree of variation in sexual arousal across situations. The researcher's inventory might in fact be highly reliable, yet appear to be unreliable because the influence of situational variables such as stimuli present during testing, the respondents' levels of fatigue or stress, respondents' recent sexual activity, and other factors that vary between testing sessions results in low correlations between administrations.

Regardless of whether a self-report scale measures a state or trait variable, generally the longer the span of time between the two administrations, the lower the test–retest correlation (Anastasi & Urbina, 1997; Kerlinger, 1986). Accordingly, Anastasi and Urbina (1997) advocated that "the interval between retests should rarely exceed six months" (p. 92). Because test–retest reliability requires repeated access to the same sample, as well as the ability to match responses from the repeated sessions, researchers typically rely on alternative measures of reliability.

Internal Consistency of Scales

The most common index of reliability for sexuality-related scales appears to be the coefficient of internal consistency (typically Cronbach's alpha), which is derived from the mean correlation between scores on all possible halves of the measure (Kerlinger, 1986). In other words, one could split any multiple-item scale into two sets, with half the items in one set and the other half of the items in the other set, and calculate the correlation between scores on the two halves. Because there are multiple ways the sets could be generated, the internal consistency coefficient is based on averaging the results obtained across all possible pairs of sets. Spearman (1904) was among the first to use the internal consistency of a scale as a measure of the scale's reliability. He reasoned that if the items in a scale all measure the same latent construct, responses to those items should display substantial covariation. If responses to a set of scale items are not highly related to one another, then those items presumably are not measuring the same construct (and hence the scale has low internal consistency).

Generalizability of Internal Consistency Estimates. A common statement regarding scale reliability in published reports of sexuality research fits the following formula: "In a large sample [or in a previously published study], the X scale exhibited a high degree of reliability with an internal consistency coefficient of .86." Typically, such authors refer to their scale (or subscale) as reliable and as measuring a single construct, mostly based on the acceptably high internal consistency coefficient. However, both conclusions may be inaccurate.

First, the internal consistency coefficient refers to the reliability of the data generated by the measure *in that particular sample* (Vacha-Haase, 1998). As Thompson and Snyder (1998) noted, "Put simply, *reliability is a characteristic of scores for the data in hand*, and not of a test per se" (p. 438; italics original). The internal consistency coefficient derived from a particular sample could be viewed as an estimate for the internal consistency coefficient found for the population from which the sample was drawn. Taking the mean internal consistency coefficient across several such samples would be an even better estimate. There will be sample-to-sample variations from this mean, sometimes very large ones. Hence, it is important that internal consistency coefficients be calculated each time a scale is used with a new sample. Only when researchers have access to numerous internal consistency coefficients for a particular scale, each of which was generated based on an independent sample from a larger population of interest (e.g., college students), might they be able to generalize from that set of coefficients to a conclusion about the scale's reliability in that population (Vacha-Haase, 1998).

This issue of internal consistency being a function of a particular sample rather than the measure per se has been amply illustrated with research findings. For example, self-report scales administered to individuals who are relatively high in private self-consciousness result in higher internal consistency coefficients than when the same scales are administered to individuals who are relatively low in private self-consciousness (Siegrist, 1996). One might speculate that this is because those who are relatively self-conscious might simply be more self-aware while completing the measures. However, Nasby (1989) demonstrated that individuals who score relatively high on private self-consciousness are probably more consistent in their responses to self-report instruments because they have a better articulated self-view that is temporally more stable. This explanation fits with earlier findings that more mature adults evidence higher internal consistency coefficients than do younger adults (McFarland & Sparks, 1985). Subsequently, Britt and Shepperd (1999) demonstrated that there are notable differences across individuals in how consistently those individuals respond to self-report measures according to how personally relevant the measures are. Those individuals for whom the measures are most personally relevant respond most consistently (have the highest internal consistency coefficients).

Another illustration of the conditional nature of a scale's internal consistency is the finding that the reliability of the individual items comprising scales tend to be higher when the items appear later rather than earlier within the scale (Knowles, 1988; Steinberg, 1994). That is, test items display greater reliability when placed later in the scale than they do when placed earlier. The first several items in a scale may serve to focus the respondents' attention on the construct (such as their relevant attitudes), such that respondents reply more consistently as they encounter additional test items in a particular measure. This phenomenon has important implications for the results of factor analyses in which the researchers make decisions or recommendations regarding which test items to keep versus discard.

Internal Consistency and Unidimensionality. The authors of many published reports of sexuality research (as well as other types of research) mistakenly imply that a relatively high internal consistency coefficient is evidence that the items are homogeneous and the scale or subscale is unidimensional. Unfortunately, this "wisdom" is often passed from mentor to student or simply gleaned from reading statements such as that previously mentioned, despite that several writers have explained why a high internal consistency coefficient is a necessary but far from sufficient condition for unidimensionality in a scale (Boyle, 1991; Cortina, 1993; Clark & Watson, 1995).

The problem stems from confusion over the difference between item *homogeneity* and item *interrelatedness*. Homogeneous items are those that all measure the same construct. Interrelated items are those whose scores are correlated with one another; they may or may not measure the same construct. The internal consistency coefficient is not a measure of item homogeneity and is a poor measure of item interrelatedness because its value is a function of the number of scale items as well as the degree of interrelatedness among them. A relatively large set of items (e.g., 30 or so) will have a high internal consistency coefficient as long as the correlations among the items are greater than 0 (Cortina, 1993). For example, a 30-item scale in which the average inter-item correlation is .12 will have an internal consistency coefficient of .81 (see Green, Lissitz, & Mulaik, 1977).

Perhaps even more problematic is the fact that, regardless of the length of the scale, the internal consistency coefficient will be high as long as the average intercorrelation among items is larger than 0, even if such an average inter-correlation derives from subsets of items that are highly related to one another but totally unrelated to the items in the other subsets. In other words, if a scale is composed of several subscales, each of which contains relatively homogeneous sets of items, the internal consistency coefficient for the entire scale will be high even when the subscales are unrelated to one another. Cortina (1993) demonstrated this fact with a hypothetical 18-item scale comprised of three distinct 6-item subscales. The average inter-item correlations within each subscale was .70, yet the correlations among the subscale scores were all zero. The result was an internal consistency coefficient of .84 for the entire 18-item scale. Based on misuse of the internal consistency coefficient, the user of the scale might mistakenly conclude that the scale is unidimensional.

What should sexuality researchers do instead of relying on the internal consistency coefficient as an index of item homogeneity? If the goal is to demonstrate that a particular scale is unidimensional, researchers should perform factor analysis (see chap. 13, this volume, as well as Comrey, 1988; Floyd & Widaman, 1995) and pay more attention to the inter-item correlations than to the overall internal consistency coefficient (Clark & Watson, 1995). The range and mean of inter-item correlations provide a straightforward measure of internal consistency that avoids the potential problems noted in the hypothetical case from Cortina (1993).

Is there reason to be concerned about whether purported unidimensional scales are indeed measuring only one construct? Misspecification of the number of factors comprising a scale has grave implications for the validity of relationships found between scores the scale and scores on measures of other constructs (Smith & McCarthy, 1995). For example, Wryobeck and Wiederman (1999) analyzed the factor structure of the 25-item Hurlbert Index of Sexual Narcissism (ISN) among a sample of male undergraduates. Hurlbert, Apt, Gasar, Wilson, and Murphy (1994) presented the scale as unidimensional, citing a high internal consistency coefficient, and advocated use of an overall score. However, Wryobeck and Wiederman (1999) found that 16 of the items comprised four distinct subscales, and that the remaining 9 items did not load clearly or consistently on any factors. They went on to show that, depending on the sexuality construct under consideration, some subscales were significantly related, whereas others were not. Simply using the overall scale score would obscure potentially important theoretical relationships between individual facets of the larger construct (sexual narcissism) and other sexuality measures (also see Carver, 1989).

Perhaps more surprising, Wryobeck and Wiederman (1999) found that the multiple correlation between various sexuality constructs and scores on the four subscales was as high, and sometimes higher, than the correlation between the sexuality constructs and the score on the 25-item ISN. How can this be when the full ISN contains all of the items comprising the four subscales? Part of the answer lies in the fact that sometimes a particular subscale score correlated negatively with the sexuality construct under consideration, whereas the remaining subscale scores correlated positively. In these cases, using the overall score resulted in a loss of predictive power. Also, the 9 ISN items that did not load on the four primary factors apparently were not related to the other sexuality constructs in consistent ways, resulting in the introduction of error variance when using the full 25-item ISN.

The extent to which the phenomenon discovered with the ISN applies to other commonly used measures in sexuality research is unknown. However, it is an important issue, as we see when discussing measurement validity.

Inter-Rater Reliability

Inter-rater reliability is most often used to assess the reliability of observations (see chap. 6) and judgments regarding stimuli (see chaps. 14 & 15). These applications are discussed in their respective chapters. Inter-rater reliability is sometimes used in sexuality research when comparing reports of the same phenomena from two or more respondents. For example, with regard to partnered sexual activity, researchers sometimes attempt to assess reliability by comparing reports from each member of an ongoing couple (e.g., Carballo-Deguez et al., 1999). Relevant questions might be: To what degree do sexual partners agree in their self-reported frequency of sexual intercourse? To what extent do partners agree that each of several sexual behaviors did or did not occur? Depending on the nature of the data, a sexuality researcher might attempt to answer these questions by computing kappa (for nominally scaled data), weighted kappa (for ordinally scaled data), or the intraclass correlation coefficient (for dimensionally scaled data). Calculation and interpretation of these statistics are discussed in Ochs and Binik (1999) and Siegel and Castellan (1988).

What Constitutes Adequate Reliability

Having discussed the primary methods by which sexuality researchers assess reliability of measurement, we are still faced with the issue of what constitutes adequate reliability. Unfortunately, answering that question is a somewhat subjective process. Although previous writers have provided guidelines or general rules regarding acceptable numerical values for each type of reliability coefficient (e.g., see Cicchetti, 1994; Whitley, 1996), such a judgment requires consideration of the individual measure and the context in which it was used.

For example, when evaluating the magnitude of test–retest correlations, one should consider them in light of the degree to which the measured construct is proposed to be stable, as well as the length of time between the two points of measurement. For internal consistency coefficients, one should consider the number of items comprising the measure as well as whether the measure is considered to assess a unidimensional construct. If so, such unidimensionality can be better assessed by examining the factor structure of the scale items or the item-total correlations (range as well as mean correlation). For inter-rater reliability, what constitutes adequate reliability may vary as a function of the use to which the data are put. If the data of concern are generated by one rater or reporter, for example, a higher standard may prevail than if the data for analysis are comprised of a composite measure constructed across numerous raters. In the latter case, some degree of unreliability across particular individual raters will wash out when data from multiple raters are combined. In the case of using data from a single rater or reporter, however, unreliability can have dramatic effects on results.

VALIDITY OF MEASUREMENT

We can only measure that which can be observed. However, sexuality researchers are commonly interested in variables such as sex guilt, sexual anxiety, and sexual esteem, which cannot be directly observed. Such variables are referred to as *hypothetical constructs*.

To assess hypothetical constructs, researchers typically create self-report scales intended to indirectly measure the construct of interest. Such measures may include items based on past or current behavior or attitudes toward a referent. The goal of the scale developer is to create a set of items that reflect the construct being measured. The theory underlying the scale development process is that the hypothetical construct influences people's responses to items such that higher scores on the scale represent higher (or lower) levels of the construct. To the extent that this relationship between item responses and the hypothetical construct actually exists, the researcher can infer that those responses are indicative of the respondents' underlying degree of sex guilt, sexual anxiety, or sexual esteem, for example. That is, the strength of the hypothetical construct is inferred from the strength of the respondents' answers to the items that comprise the measure. Is this an accurate inference?

Measurement validity refers to the degree to which a measuring instrument accurately assesses what it is intended to measure (Foster & Cone, 1995; Whitley, 1996). I noted earlier that random error in measurement results in decreased reliability. The principle that reliability is a necessary but insufficient condition for validity points to the importance of evaluating measurement reliability when assessing validity of an instrument (Whitley, 1996). If a measure is unreliable, it contains a high degree of random error and so, by definition, cannot be a good measure of a construct. However, a measure can be highly reliable, yet demonstrate a low degree of validity. This may occur because the source of low validity in measurement is systematic error. Responses to a measure may be a function of systematic factors other than what the measure is intended to assess. In essence, the measure may be assessing, perhaps even consistently (reliably), some construct or phenomenon other than that intended. For example, responses to the items may be influenced by the respondent's attempts to portray the self in a socially desirable light.

Assessing Validity

In general terms, researchers assess the validity of a measure by examining relationships between responses on the measure and other variables and considering the pattern that emerges (Foster & Cone, 1995; Whitley, 1996). A valid measure should demonstrate substantial and predictable relationships with some variables (convergent validity) and a lack of relationship, or very modest relationships, with others (discriminant validity). The variables used to demonstrate convergent validity might entail a behavioral or group membership criterion or scores on measures of other, related theoretical constructs. Discriminant validity would be demonstrated by a lack of relationship to theoretically unrelated variables. For example, scores on a measure of negative sexual attitudes should be positively related to avoidance of sexual stimuli as well as scores on other scales measuring negative sexual attitudes (indicating convergent validity), yet not be related to scores on measures of particular personality variables such as conscientiousness (indicating discriminant validity).

Ideally, evidence for convergent validity should entail different methods of measurement. For example, evidence for convergent validity of a self-report scale of negative sexual attitudes should include demonstration of predictable relationships with group membership (e.g., in a fundamentalist religious sect) and behavior (e.g., avoidance of sexually explicit stimuli), as well as perhaps physiological response (e.g., autonomic nervous system arousal in response to sexually explicit words) and cognitive processing (e.g., relatively greater difficulty remembering sexually explicit stimuli presented in a laboratory setting). If evidence for convergent validity comes only from other measures based on self-report, one is left wondering whether the resulting correlational relationships simply reflect shared method variance (i.e., relationships based on the notion that individuals tend to be consistent in the general ways they respond to self-report scales, regardless of the content of such scales). If only self-report measures are used to assess the validity of a measure, it is imperative to demonstrate discriminant validity using self-report instruments as well (Foster & Cone, 1995).

When assessing validity, the issue of what constitutes substantial and predictable relationships for convergent validity, or a lack of relationship or modest relationship for discriminant validity, can be ambiguous. For example, does a correlation of .12 between scores on two measures of sexual-esteem constitute validity evidence even if the correlation is statistically significant due to high statistical power in the particular study? What about a correlation of .32 between scores on two measures that theoretically should be unrelated, even if this correlation is not statistically significant due to low statistical power? Is the fact that two groups (e.g., an intervention group and a control group) display a small yet statistically significant difference with regard to scores on some measure evidence of the validity of that measure? Unfortunately, these are questions often left to individual researchers to answer. My recommendation is to pay considerable attention to effect size when assessing convergent and discriminant validity.

As with reliability, researchers should keep in mind that the demonstrated validity of a measure may apply only to the samples and uses that have been investigated. In other words, it is dubious to proclaim unconditional validity for a measure whose validity has not been assessed under a variety of conditions. "Because of the conditional nature of validation, it should rarely be assumed that an assessment instrument has unconditional validity. Statements such as '. . . has been shown to be a reliable and valid assessment instrument' do not reflect the conditional nature of validity and are usually unwarranted" (Haynes, Richard, & Kubany, 1995, p. 241). The validity of a measure may also change over time as the construct it measures evolves with additional research and conceptual modification (Haynes et al., 1995). Accordingly, the validity of measures must be reestablished over time.

In the end, evaluating the validity of a measure is a somewhat subjective process of weighing the evidence for both convergent and discriminant validity, and entails evaluating multiple sources of evidence. Ideally, conclusions as to a measure's validity are drawn on the basis of numerous relationships demonstrated between the measure and other constructs (these being assessed using a variety of methods) involving data from several different, recent samples.

Breadth of Measurement and Validity

Although a scale is ideally both highly reliable and valid, tension can arise between satisfaction of these two goals, particularly when attempting to measure a broad theoretical construct. The issue has to do with the appropriate breadth of measurement for a particular research question. As an example, consider the construct of *erotophobia-erotophila* as measured by the Sexual Opinion Survey (SOS; Fisher, Byrne, White, & Kelley, 1988). The construct was defined as a disposition to respond to sexual stimuli along a negative–positive dimension of affect and evaluation. Certainly such a broad construct has many different specific manifestations. The issue then became creating a set of test items that represents the domain of responses covered by the erotophobia-erotophilia construct. The resulting SOS is comprised of 21 items and is one of the most widely used self-report measures in sexuality research. Still the question remains, how valid is the SOS?

The question of measurement validity is somewhat misleading in the current context because the answer depends on the intended use of the scale. First, as noted earlier, a scale such as the SOS must be reliable if it is to be valid. In that regard, it is interesting to note that Fisher et al. (1988) reported relatively high internal consistency coefficients (.82 to .90) among samples of college students. Recall, however, that such coefficients are strongly influenced by the number of items, and in this context, a 21-item test is relatively long. Also, the relatively high internal consistency coefficients do not tell us anything about the degree to which the SOS is unidimensional. Indeed, researchers have reported that the SOS is comprised of multiple factors, despite also finding high internal consistency coefficients (Gilbert & Gamache, 1984; Rise, Traeen, & Kraft, 1993). Fisher et al. (1988) explained that "it is possible that the use of subscale rather than total scores will yield more precise relationships" (p. 130) with other variables of interest. So, are the subscales or the entire SOS more valid measures of erotophobia-erotophilia?

Again, the answer to this question depends on the way the researcher wishes to conceptualize the constructs and use the measure. Previous writers have pointed out the potential advantages and disadvantages associated with using a summary index of a proposed construct as opposed to the individual factors comprising that construct. For example, Carver (1989) noted that using a summary index results in easier computation and communication of results (see also Hull, Lehn, & Tedlie, 1991). However, there are some serious potential costs to such an approach—primarily the risk of losing important information (Carver, 1989; Mershon & Gorsuch, 1988; Smith & McCarthy, 1995).

This loss of information can take two forms. First, theoretically relevant variables may be differentially related to the facets of the proposed construct. In such a situation, correlating the summary index with these variables would leave the facet relationships unknown (e.g., Smith & Reise, 1998). Conversely, a nonsignificant correlation between a summary index and another variable may mask significant facet correlations (e.g., when some of those facet correlations are positive and others are negative, and hence cancel each other out when combined; see Wryobek & Wiederman, 1999). Second, combining across facets can lead to a loss of information when two or more facets have an interactive relationship with another variable, perhaps with no main effect for any of the facets (Carver, 1989; Smith & McCarthy, 1995). Because interactions are multiplicative effects, they cannot be represented by a summed index.

In the end, the researcher attempting to measure a broad theoretical construct is potentially faced with a paradox. A test could have high reliability because its developer discarded any items that did not load highly on the single primary factor. The result would be a highly reliable unidimensional scale, yet one that may assess only a narrow facet of the larger theoretical construct. The problem, then, is that "maximizing internal consistency almost invariably produces a scale that is quite narrow in content; if the scale is narrower than the target construct, its validity is compromised" (Clark & Watson, 1995, p. 316). Taken to the extreme, a test developed using this approach would end up being highly reliable but consisting of items that are simply slightly reworded versions of each other.

In contrast, a test could have been developed taking a different approach, attempting to sample as broadly as possible from the items that fall into the domain covered by the theoretical construct. As Clark and Watson (1995) noted, "a scale will yield far more information—and, hence, be a more valid measure of a construct—if it contains more differentiated items that are only moderately intercorrelated" (p. 316). Although such an approach would result in a more valid measure of the construct, the measure's internal consistency would be lower because the individual items will be less strongly related to one another. In this case, it is likely that the overall measure will be comprised of multiple factors.

The issue of whether to use scores from an overall index of a construct or the individual subscales comprising that index is salient whenever sexuality researchers study broad theoretical constructs. For example, previously published measures of sexual motivation (Hill & Preston, 1996), sexual attitudes (Hendrick & Hendrick, 1987), sexual assertiveness (Morokoff et al., 1997), and sexual self-esteem (Zeanah & Schwartz, 1996) all consist of multiple factors. Researchers should examine their needs in using the scale and provide a rationale for their choice of considering overall summary scores versus subscale scores. For example, when a researcher wishes to examine the components or correlates of these constructs, consideration of the subscale scores may be most appropriate. Conversely, if an overall measure of the broader construct is of interest, such as in the context of statistically controlling for sexual assertiveness or sexual self-esteem in a multivariate analysis, then using the overall summary score may be most appropriate. In either case, the researcher is still left with the issue of assessing the validity of the measures.

FACTORS INFLUENCING THE RELIABILITY AND VALIDITY OF SELF-REPORTS

Regardless of whether a sexuality researcher employs single questions or multiple-items scales, respondents' sexual experiences and attitudes are considered sensitive information, so researchers typically must rely on self-reports from research participants (Weinhardt, Forsyth, Carey, Jaworski, & Durant, 1998). Such self-reports are vulnerable to a number of sources of error and bias that can adversely affect reliability and validity of measurement (Baker & Brandon, 1990). This section briefly reviews the most prominent sources of error and bias in self-reports in the context of sexuality research.

Participant Factors

When researchers ask people about their sexuality, either through interviews or questionnaires, there are several factors that can influence responses. Of course, one of those factors is the respondent's actual sexual attitudes or experiences (whichever one is being asked about), and ideally this would be the only factor affecting responses. If this were the case, researchers could be sure that people's responses to their questions reflected those respondents' actual attitudes or behavior (i.e., that the measures were valid). Unfortunately, researchers have documented that participants' responses are affected by several factors besides their attitudes or experiences (Catania, 1999; Catania et al., 1993; Weinhardt et al., 1998).

Memory and Recall. Suppose researchers presented the following question to respondents: "With how many different partners have you had vaginal intercourse during your lifetime?" Who would most likely be able to provide an accurate response? Probably those respondents who have never had vaginal intercourse, or who have had one, two, or three partners, would easily be able to recall the exact number of partners.

Now consider a respondent who in actuality has experienced vaginal intercourse with 16 partners over a span of 30 years. Some of these partners were long-term relationship partners and some were casual sexual affairs or "one-night stands." Imagine that this respondent first had vaginal intercourse at the age of 17 and is now 47 years of age (a sexual history spanning 30 years). Suppose that this person has been married since age 29 and has not had sexual intercourse with anyone outside of marriage. This person accumulated 15 of the 16 partners between the ages of 17 and 29—a period that ended 18 years ago! How likely is it that, when confronted with the posed research question, this individual will be able to recall exactly 16 partners, especially when the respondent will probably only spend a few seconds arriving at an answer?

The example in the previous paragraph involved remembering distinct experiences (sexual activity with a new partner) that occurred over a 30-year time span. Consider a second type of example: "How many times during the past 12 months have you used your mouth to stimulate a partner's genitals?" Here the respondent is asked to recall experiences over a much shorter span of time, but each of the experiences to be recalled is unlikely to be distinct. We can imagine that someone who had not performed oral sex during the past year or so would easily produce an accurate response (0 or "none"). However, what about respondents who have had several partners, or who have had only one partner with whom they have had an ongoing sexual relationship, over the previous year? Certainly it is unrealistic to expect that these respondents could remember each instance of oral sex, even if highly motivated and given enough time to try.

How do respondents produce answers to questions about their sexual behavior when it is impossible to recall and count every actual instance of the behavior? In the end, most respondents estimate their experience, and respondents do so in different ways depending on the frequency and regularity of the behavior about which they are being asked (Brown, 1995, 1997; Conrad, Brown, & Cashman, 1998; Croyle & Loftus, 1993). For example, in response to the number of sex partners question, respondents with several partners are liable to give a round, "ball-park" estimate (Brown & Sinclair, 1999; Wiederman, 1997). Indeed, respondents with more than about 10 partners typically provide numbers that end in 0 or 5 (e.g., 10, 15, 25, 30, 50, 75, 100).

Considering responses to frequency questions such as the aforementioned oral sex question, it appears that people who have had numerous such experiences go through a cognitive process to arrive at an estimate (Brown, 1995, 1997; Conrad, et al., 1998; Jaccard & Wan, 1995). The thinking of one hypothetical respondent might go something like this: "Well, my partner and I typically have sex about twice a week or so, and I perform oral sex about half of those times. There are 52 weeks in a year, so I guess I performed oral sex about 50 times during the previous 12 months." Notice that this cognitive process is liable to occur in the course of just a few seconds and that the respondent does not even attempt to remember each instance because to do so is impossible. How accurate the resulting estimate is depends on how regularly the respondent engages in the behavior as well as the accuracy of his or her recall (or estimation) of that typical frequency (Downey, Ryan, Roffman, & Kulich, 1995; Sudman, Bradburn, & Schwartz, 1996). Minor exceptions (e.g., that week the respondent was on vacation, was ill, or was fighting with the partner) are typically not factored in when arriving at global estimates.

It is probably the case that individuals have a more difficult time recalling particular behaviors (e.g., condom usage) over longer rather than shorter periods of time (Thompson, Skowronski, Larsen, & Betz, 1996). All else being equal, researchers should have more faith in responses to the question "Did you use a condom during your most recent experience of vaginal intercourse?" than in responses to the question "How often did you use condoms during the previous 12 months?" In responding to this latter question, an individual who recently has been using condoms consistently might tend to overestimate condom usage for the past year compared with someone who had used them quite regularly but who has been lax over the past few months. In actuality, both individuals might have had the same condom usage rates over the past year, but their more recent experiences bias their estimates for the longer time span.

Some questions that sexuality researchers pose to respondents contain an element requiring location of an event or behavior in time. For example, "At what age did you first engage in self-stimulation of your genitals?" Unfortunately, it does not appear that human memory contains a component having to do with remembered time per se. That is, people use different methods for trying to locate a remembered event in time, and these methods may be prone to distortion, particularly as the event becomes more distant in time (Friedman, 1993). In the end, researchers should be cautious of the absolute accuracy of answers respondents provide about events that occurred several years ago or when the individuals were very young, regardless of the nature of the events (Henry, Moffitt, Caspi, Langley, & Silva, 1994; Thompson et al., 1996).

Degree of Insight.   In addition to asking questions that rely on respondents' memories, sometimes sexuality researchers ask respondents to answer *why* questions. Note that these questions may not actually contain the word *why*, but yet they ask for some degree of introspection as to motives or decision making nonetheless. For example, "What factors led to your decision to have sexual intercourse the first time with your most recent partner?" Similar questions may explicitly ask why the respondent did something: "Why did you fall in love with your most recent partner? Why did you break up with your most recent partner?" Such questions not only demand recall but also a great degree of insight into one's own motives and the factors that led to particular emotions and decisions. However, people apparently do not have good insight into these mental processes (Brehmer & Brehmer, 1988; Nisbett & Ross, 1980; Nisbett & Wilson, 1977), and this is especially likely to be true with complex feelings and decisions.

When asked questions about their motives or decisions, people readily provide responses: "He was the kindest person I had ever met"; "We were no longer communicating and just grew apart." These are typical answers people might give to the questions about falling in love and breaking up in the previous paragraph, yet it is doubtful that they capture all of the complexity that went into the experience of falling in love or the potentially difficult decision to end a meaningful relationship. People apparently provide such answers based on stereotypes or beliefs they hold regarding the causes of relationship events (Baldwin, 1992, 1995; Knee, 1998).

These stereotypes or beliefs may or may not accurately reflect what occurred within the respondent's individual life, and hence have implications for the validity of self-report information about one's relationships. Because people's beliefs about romantic relationships in general affect how each person perceives his or her actual relationship partner (Baldwin, 1992, 1995; Knee, 1998), any questions or measures that rely on respondents' memories or perceptions of how things used to be within the relationship are vulnerable to distortion. Over time, as couples develop a history together and construct stories to make sense out of that history, their recollection of earlier events, feelings, and perceptions within the relationship tend to be influenced by the stories (LaRossa, 1995; McGregor & Holmes, 1999). Research based on such measures may lead to results that are questionable if taken at face value.

Placebo and Expectancy Effects.   If sexuality researchers ask people about their behavior or attitudes subsequent to some intervention or notable event, respondents are liable to provide answers commensurate with their expectations for how their attitudes or behavior should have changed. For example, when people believe they have participated in an intervention that should affect their behavior, they tend to report such improvements in their behavior even if there has not been any such improvement (Dawes, 1988). One explanation of this phenomenon is that people often do not remember precisely what their attitudes or behavior were prior to the intervention, so it is possible to recall that things were better (or worse) than they were because of the assumption that an intervening experience must have had some effect. These *expectancy* or *placebo effects* have been studied most in regard to drug trials and psychotherapy outcome (Critelli & Neumann, 1984; Horvath, 1988; Quitkin, 1999), yet the phenomena have important implications for sexuality researchers relying on self-reports. For example, when people participate in a sex education program, they may report (and honestly believe) there has been at least some improvement in their behavior, regardless of whether the intervention was effective.

Response Sets. It appears that respondents vary systematically in their tendency to provide certain responses regardless of the content of the items (Austin, Deary, Gibson, McGregor, & Dent, 1998; Greenleaf, 1992). That is, some people tend to use the extreme ends of a scale provided for response, whereas others may tend to gravitate toward the middle of such scales (or at least avoid using the end points).

Similarly, some respondents may tend to agree with survey items (acquiescence response bias), seemingly regardless of the content of such items. In an attempt to address this form of potential response bias, some researchers advocate inclusion of reverse-scored items so that respondents will be prompted to consider both positively and negatively worded items. However, it is difficult to construct positively and negatively worded items that are equivalent. For example, Snell and Papini (1989) constructed a self-report measure of sexual preoccupation and included both positively and negatively worded items. Examples of each include "I think about sex more than anything else" and "I hardly ever fantasize about having sex." After reverse scoring the second item, would one expect comparable scores on each item? If they are both measuring the same phenomenon, the answer should be "yes." However, Wiederman and Allgeier (1993) found that the positively and negatively worded items each comprised their own factors in data collected from college student respondents. Apparently, respondents did not equate an absence of sexual preoccupation as synonymous with an absence of sexual thoughts and fantasies.

Social Desirability Response Bias. Some respondents in sexuality studies distort their responses, consciously or unconsciously, to present themselves in a positive light (Nicholas, Durrheim, & Tredoux, 1994; Siegel, Aten, & Roughman, 1998; Tourangeau, Smith, & Rasinski, 1997). For example, if a respondent who has had several sexual partners believes that greater sexual experience is something to be proud of, she or he may tend to overestimate the lifetime number of sex partners. Conversely, if a respondent feels ashamed of something sexual from his or her past, the respondent may not remember or admit this experience in an interview or on a questionnaire. Researchers refer to these types of distortion as *social desirability response bias*, and it has been a long-time bane of the sexuality researcher's existence (Meston, Heiman, Trapnell, & Paulhus, 1998; Wiederman, 1997).

Almost without exception, the potential impact of social desirability response bias has been tested by examining correlations between scores on sexuality measures and the Marlowe–Crowne measure of socially desirable responding (Crowne & Marlowe, 1964). This instrument is purported to measure the respondent's general tendency toward unrealistically positive self-presentation. There has been debate as to what the Marlowe–Crowne scale actually measures, and space limitations prevent me from going into the potential conceptual problems associated with the measure (see Paulhous, 1991). I simply note one possibility that appears to have been overlooked in previous research.

Calculating a simple correlation between scores on a sexuality measure and a measure of social desirability response bias is based on the assumption that socially desirable responding exhibits a linear relationship across individuals. However, it is possible that individuals vary with regard to what is considered socially desirable when it comes to sexual attitudes and experiences. Such differences may be related to gender, life stage, and membership in various subcultures. Thus, within a given sample (e.g., male and female college students), some respondents who are prone to social desirability response bias may minimize reports, whereas other such individuals may exaggerate their reported attitudes and experience. In such a case, the net result would be lack of a statistically significant correlation between scores on each sexuality measure and scores on the measure of socially desirable responding. Obviously, the lack of relationship in this case would be an artifact of testing for a linear relationship and ignoring the possibility of a curvilinear one.

Research Method Factors

So far, the forms of measurement error I have focused on involve factors related to the respondent. There are, however, aspects of the research itself that may result in measurement error and hence compromised reliability and validity of measurement.

Question Wording and Terminology. To elicit respondent's self-reports, researchers must rely on words, either spoken or printed, to form the questions (Binson & Catania, 1998; Catania et al., 1996). The problem is that any time words are used, there is the possibility for misunderstanding. Can researchers be sure that the words used in an interview or questionnaire have the same meaning to all respondents as they do to the researchers? Researchers often take great care in choosing the wording for questions, sometimes pilot testing the items prior to conducting the study. However, it is easy for different meanings to arise (Huygens, Kajura, Seely, & Barton, 1996). Consider the following questions:

How many sex partners have you had during your lifetime?

How often have your and your partner engaged in sex during the past month?

Have you ever forced someone to have sex against their will? (Or, have you ever been forced to have sex against your will?)

How often do you experience sexual desire?

How frequently do you masturbate?

Respondents generate answers to these types of questions quite readily, especially if a scale is provided to indicate frequency. However, respondents may interpret the meaning of certain words in a variety of ways. In the first three questions, what does the term *sex* mean? Heterosexual respondents are liable to interpret *sex* to mean vaginal intercourse. To many such individuals, if there was not a penis moving around inside a vagina, there was no sex. However, others will interpret *sex* to include oral or manual stimulation of the genitals (Sanders & Reinisch, 1999).

What about lesbian women (Rothblum, 1994)? Heterosexual definitions of *sex* rely on the involvement of a penis, and episodes of sex typically are marked by ejaculation from that penis. If a heterosexual couple is asked the second question ("How often have your and your partner engaged in sex during the past month?"), the response will likely be based on the number of times the man ejaculated after having been inside his partner's vagina, regardless of the number of orgasms the woman did or did not have. Lesbian respondents may arrive at an answer to the same question in a variety of ways, yet one may ask whether the question would even have meaning for most such respondents (Rothblum, 1994).

In the preceding list of questions, how might the terms *partners, forced, sexual desire*, and *masturbate* be interpreted by different respondents with different histories, different upbringings, different religious values, and so forth? Does *partners* include every individual with whom one has had any sexual contact, or only those individuals with whom one also shared an emotional relationship? How strong does the experience of *sexual desire* have to be to count? What about a fleeting sexual thought or fantasy? What qualifies as *force* in a sexual situation?

This last question may elicit images of physical restraint and forcing one's body on an uninterested partner, and certainly most respondents would include such experiences in their definition of *forced sex*. Generally, these are the kinds of experiences that researchers are interested in when studying rape. However, because many respondents may not have had such an experience, some may tend to take a more liberal definition of *forced*. Ross and Allgeier (1996) had college men individually complete a questionnaire containing several commonly used questions having to do with forcing or coercing women into having sex. Afterward, each respondent was individually interviewed to find out how each had interpreted the meaning of the words used in some of the questions. Interestingly, there were a variety of ways the men interpreted what was meant by each question, and some of the interpretations of the questions had nothing to do with physical force. There is also variation in how research participants interpret response choices to sexuality questions; thus, two respondents giving the same answer may mean different things (Cecil & Zimet, 1998; Wright, Gaskell, & O'Muircheartaigh, 1997).

The last question in the list of sample questions has do to with masturbation. I intentionally chose this term to demonstrate that some sexual words probably elicit a stronger emotional reaction than others. Imagine respondents being confronted with "How frequently do you masturbate?" versus "How frequently do you stimulate your own genitals for sexual pleasure or release?" Might the second question be perceived as less threatening and easier to answer? What if the question had been preceded with a statement about masturbation being a common experience? Researchers have shown that referring to a particular behavior (e.g., masturbation) as relatively common leads respondents to be more likely to admit having performed the behavior themselves (Catania et al., 1996; Raghubir & Menon, 1996).

Response Choices. Earlier I noted how people are unlikely to be able to recall every instance of their sexual behavior. So, if asked how frequently they engage in some form of sexual expression, those respondents who have had the experience are liable to provide a quick estimate. If researchers provide response choices for such question (e.g., "once per week, twice per week, 3 to 5 times per week, more than 5 times per week"), participants may use those response choices to generate their estimate or to determine what is normal (Schwartz, 1999). Consider respondents who believe they are average with regard to sexual experience. If so, they may tend to use the middle response choice on the assumption that the researchers know something about how frequently the experience occurs and designed the response choices so that a middle response represents the average. Consequently, these hypothetical respondents might choose "3 times per month" in one questionnaire because that is the middle response, yet if given another questionnaire containing the same question, might choose "5 times per month" because that is the middle response choice in the second questionnaire.

Even the response choices respondents are given can influence the data they provide. Researchers typically provide respondents with a response scale anchored from *never* to *always* with regard to condom use (Sheeran & Abraham, 1994). It is easy to imagine that there is variation across respondents in how each interprets intermediate points on the scale, such as those that might be labeled *rarely, occasionally, sometimes,* or *frequently.* However, even with regard to the more definite terms *always* and *never,* there is apparently individual variation in how these terms are applied to condom use. Cecil and Zimet (1998) found that a substantial proportion of college student respondents interpreted using condoms 18 or 19 times out of 20 as *always* and using condoms once or twice out of 20 times as *never.*

Context and Order Effects.   When people respond to questions in a question-naire or interview, they do not respond to each question in a vacuum. As such, the questions surrounding a target question may influence responses to that particular item. For one, people's answers to the target question may be influenced by their responses to related questions within the questionnaire or interview, coupled with a desire to be consistent in their own behavior or viewpoints. There is even evidence that at least some people go back and change responses to earlier items in a self-administered questionnaire to make them more consistent with later responses (Schwartz & Hippler, 1995).

Respondents also consider the questions surrounding a particular question when trying to determine what the researchers mean by the question (Schwartz, 1999; Sudman et al., 1996). If respondents are asked to rate their degree of satisfaction with their relationships, and that question is preceded by a series of questions about sexual relationships they have experienced, respondents are liable to interpret the satisfaction question as referring to their sexual relationships. In contrast, if the same satisfaction question is preceded by a series of items having to do with family relationships, respondents might be more likely to assume that the satisfaction question has to do with familial relations.

Context effects can also influence how people evaluate their attitudes or feelings (Council, 1993). Because respondents typically provide the first appropriate answer that comes to mind (Ottati, 1997), previous questionnaire or interview items may influence responses to a current question because those previous items call to mind particular experiences, attitudes, or feelings. To take a concrete example, suppose that researchers ask respondents to rate their overall satisfaction with life. If this item is preceded by several items having to do with the quality of the respondent's sexual functioning and relationships, how the respondent feels about his or her sexuality is then liable to color how he or she rates overall satisfaction with life (Marsh & Yeung, 1999), perhaps inflating the correlation between sexual satisfaction and satisfaction with life.

Conditions and Procedures.   Apart from the questions asked, the scales used, and the context in which those items are embedded, researchers may affect respondents' answers by the conditions under which they ask participants to respond (Catania, 1999; Kaplan, 1989). Imagine asking respondents to answer questions about their first sexual experiences and asking respondents to answer such questions either when alone or in the presence of a relationship partner. Under what circumstances would respondents feel most comfortable and free to answer openly and honestly?

As a general rule, people are more comfortable and more willing to admit personal, potentially embarrassing information about their sexuality when they are completing an anonymous questionnaire compared with when they believe others have access to their answers (Sudman et al., 1996). The important factor is whether the respondents believe that others might see or hear their answers, not necessarily whether others actually could. All else being equal, people are probably most likely to admit to masturbation or extramarital sex when completing an anonymous questionnaire compared with answering the same questions posed in a face-to-face interview. Accordingly, some research has shown that people are more likely to provide sensitive sexual information when interviewed by a computer program compared with a human interviewer (Gribble, Miller, Rogers, & Turner, 1999; Turner et al., 1998). Asking sensitive questions in front of family members or a group of peers would likely result in even lower rates of admitting particular sexual experiences compared with a stranger.

The context in which respondents generate answers to sexuality questions may also influence their mind set and hence their responses. In a fascinating example, Baldwin and Holmes (1987) randomly assigned college women to two conditions, each involving visualization of the faces of two people known to the participant. In one condition, the women were asked to picture the faces of two acquaintances on campus, whereas in the other condition, participants were asked to visualize the faces of two older members of their own family. All of the women were subsequently presented with the same sexual story and asked to rate their response to it. Interestingly, those women who had been asked to visualize family members rated the sexual stories less positively than did the women in the other condition. Why? Although we cannot be sure, it is likely that the internal "presence" of the family members led the women to respond more in line with what would be expected by the family members. In a sense, the women's responses were distorted (perhaps unconsciously) by what they had focused on prior to providing their ratings. These findings have implications for sexuality data that are generated when respondents are in the presence of significant others, or perhaps are alone but in the presence of stimuli that bring to mind significant others.

In summary, there are numerous issues that sexuality researchers need to consider regarding measurement reliability and validity. The process of constructing a meaningful and sound interview schedule or a questionnaire is a complex one. Because sexuality researchers typically rely on respondents' self-reports, the various potential influences on those self-reports should be considered both when designing research and interpreting the results.

SUGGESTED READINGS

With regard to basic issues related to measurement reliability and validity, Anastasi and Urbina (1997), Kerlinger (1986), and Whitley (1996) each provided easily understood discussions. Weinhardt et al. (1998) provided a succinct review of the numerous studies published between 1990 and 1995 on the reliability and validity of self-report measures of sexual behavior, and their Table 1 provides a useful overview of the advantages and disadvantages of each type of assessment mode (e.g., mail survey vs. telephone interview). With regard to reviewing the numerous potential influences on self-reports, the most comprehensive discussions revolve around research on nonsexual topics, although such work has direct implications for sexuality research. Accordingly, Thompson et al. (1996) provided a fascinating review of research, including their own, on the factors affecting autobiographical memory. Schwartz and Sudman (1994) also provided an excellent collection of chapters, by authors from various disciplines, on the topic of autobiographical memory and the validity of retrospective reports. Finally, Sudman et al. (1996) reviewed the cognitive processes and influences involved in responses to survey questions and highlighted many of the conclusions with examples from their own numerous studies.

REFERENCES

Anastasi, A., & Urbina, S. (1997). *Psychological testing* (7th ed.). Upper Saddle River, NJ: Prentice-Hall.

Austin, E. J., Deary, I. J., Gibson, G. J., McGregor, M. J., & Dent, J. B. (1998). Individual response spread in self-report scales: Personality correlations and consequences. *Personality and Individual Differences, 24*, 421–438.

Baker, T. B., & Brandon, T. H. (1990). Validity of self-reports in basic research. *Behavioral Assessment, 12*, 33–51.

Baldwin, M. W. (1992). Relational schemas and the processing of social information. *Psychological Bulletin, 112*, 461–484.

Baldwin, M. W. (1995). Relational schemas and cognition in close relationships. *Journal of Social and Personal Relationships, 12*, 547–552.

Baldwin, M. W., & Holmes, J. G. (1987). Salient private audiences and awareness of the self. *Journal of Personality and Social Psychology, 52*, 1087–1098.

Binson, D., & Catania, J. A. (1998). Respondents' understanding of the words used in sexual behavior questions. *Public Opinion Quarterly, 62*, 190–208.

Boyle, G. J. (1991). Does item homogeneity indicate internal consistency or item redundancy in psychometric scales? *Personality and Individual Differences, 3*, 291–294.

Brehmer, A., & Brehmer, B. (1988). What have we learned about human judgment from thirty years of policy capturing? In B. Brehmer & C. R. B. Joyce (Eds.), *Human judgment: The SJT view* (pp. 75–114). New York: Elsevier.

Britt, T. W., & Shepperd, J. A. (1999). Trait relevance and trait assessment. *Personality and Social Psychology Review, 3*, 108–122.

Brown, N. R. (1995). Estimation strategies and the judgment of event frequency. *Journal of Experimental Psychology: Learning, Memory, and Cognition, 21*, 1539–1553.

Brown, N. R. (1997). Context memory and the selection of frequency estimation strategies. *Journal of Experimental Psychology: Learning, Memory, and Cognition, 23*, 898–914.

Brown, N. R., & Sinclair, R. C. (1999). Estimating number of lifetime sexual partners: Men and women do it differently. *The Journal of Sex Research, 36*, 292–297.

Carballo-Dieguez, A., Remien, R. H., Dolezal, C., & Wagner, G. (1999). Reliability of sexual behavior self-reports in male couples of discordant HIV status. *The Journal of Sex Research, 36*, 152–158.

Carver, C. S. (1989). How should multifaceted personality constructs be tested? Issues illustrated by self-monitoring, attributional style, and hardiness. *Journal of Personality and Social Psychology, 56*, 577–585.

Catania, J. A. (1999). A framework for conceptualizing reporting bias and its antecedents in interviews assessing human sexuality. *The Journal of Sex Research, 36,* 25–38.

Catania, J. A., Binson, D., Canchola, J., Pollack, L. M., Hauck, W., & Coates, T. J. (1996). Effects of interviewer gender, interviewer choice, and item wording on responses to questions concerning sexual behavior. *Public Opinion Quarterly, 60,* 345–375.

Catania, J. A., Turner, H., Pierce, R. C., Golden, E., Stocking, C., Binson, D., & Mast, K. (1993). Response bias in surveys of AIDS-related sexual behavior. In D. G. Ostrow & R. C. Kessler (Eds.), *Methodological issues in AIDS behavioral research* (pp. 133–162). New York: Plenum.

Cecil, H., & Zimet, G. D. (1998). Meanings assigned by undergraduates to frequency statements of condom use. *Archives of Sexual Behavior, 27,* 493–505.

Cicchetti, D. V. (1994). Guidelines, criteria, and rules of thumb for evaluating normed and standardized assessment instruments in psychology. *Psychological Assessment, 6,* 284–290.

Clark, L. A., & Watson, D. (1995). Constructing validity: Basic issues in objective scale development. *Psychological Assessment, 3,* 309–319.

Comrey, A. L. (1988). Factor-analytic methods of scale development in personality and clinical psychology. *Journal of Consulting and Clinical Psychology, 56,* 754–761.

Conrad, F. G., Brown, N. R., & Cashman, E. R. (1998). Strategies for estimating behavioural frequency in survey interviews. *Memory, 6,* 339–366.

Cortina, J. M. (1993). What is coefficient alpha? An examination of theory and applications. *Journal of Applied Psychology, 78,* 98–104.

Council, J. R. (1993). Context effects in personality research. *Current Directions in Psychological Science, 2,* 31–34.

Critelli, J. W., & Neumann, K. F. (1984). The placebo: Conceptual analysis of a construct in transition. *American Psychologist, 39,* 32–39.

Crowne, D. P., & Marlowe, D. (1964). *The approval motive: Studies in evaluative dependence.* New York: Wiley.

Croyle, R. T., & Loftus, E. F. (1993). Recollections in the kingdom of AIDS. In D. G. Ostrow & R. C. Kessler (Eds.), *Methodological issues in AIDS behavioral research* (pp. 163–180). New York: Plenum.

Dawes, R. M. (1988). *Rational choice in an uncertain world.* New York: Harcourt Brace Jovanovich.

Downey, L., Ryan, R., Roffman, R., & Kulich, M. (1995). How could I forget? Inaccurate memories of sexually intimate moments. *The Journal of Sex Research, 32,* 177–191.

Fisher, W. A., Byrne, D., White, L. A., & Kelley, K. (1988). Erotophobia-erotophilia as a dimension of personality. *The Journal of Sex Research, 25,* 123–151.

Floyd, F. J., & Widaman, K. F. (1995). Factor analysis in the development and refinement of clinical assessment instruments. *Psychological Assessment, 7,* 286–299.

Foster, S. L., & Cone, J. D. (1995). Validity issues in clinical assessment. *Psychological Assessment, 7,* 248–260.

Friedman, W. J. (1993). Memory for the time of past events. *Psychological Bulletin, 113,* 44–66.

Gilbert, F. S., & Gamache, M. P. (1984). The Sexual Opinion Survey: Structure and use. *The Journal of Sex Research, 20,* 293–309.

Green, S. B., Lissitz, R. W., & Mulaik, S. A. (1977). Limitations of coefficient alpha as an index of test unidimensionality. *Educational and Psychological Measurement, 37,* 827–838.

Greenleaf, E. A. (1992). Measuring extreme response style. *Public Opinion Quarterly, 56,* 328–351.

Gribble, J. N., Miller, H. G., Rogers, S. M., & Turner, C. F. (1999). Interview mode and measurement of sexual behaviors: Methodological issues. *The Journal of Sex Research, 36,* 16–24.

Haynes, S. N., Richard, D. C. S., & Kubany, E. S. (1995). Content validity in psychological assessment: A functional approach to concepts and methods. *Psychological Assessment, 7,* 238–247.

Hendrick, S., & Hendrick, C. (1987). Multidimensionality of sexual attitudes. *The Journal of Sex Research, 23,* 502–526.

Henry, B., Moffitt, T. E., Caspi, A., Langley, J., & Silva, P. A. (1994). On the "remembrance of things past": A longitudinal evaluation of the retrospective method. *Psychological Assessment, 6*, 92–101.

Hill, C. A., & Preston, L. K. (1996). Individual differences in the experience of sexual motivation: Theory and measurement of dispositional sexual motives. *The Journal of Sex Research, 33*, 27–45.

Horvath, P. (1988). Placebos and common factors in two decades of psychotherapy research. *Psychological Bulletin, 104*, 214–225.

Hull, J. G., Lehn, D. A., & Tedlie, J. C. (1991). A general approach to testing multifaceted personality constructs. *Journal of Personality and Social Psychology, 61*, 932–945.

Hurlbert, D. F., Apt, C., Gasar, S., Wilson, N. E., & Murphy, Y. (1994). Sexual narcissism: A validation study. *Journal of Sex & Marital Therapy, 20*, 24–34.

Huygens, P., Kajura, E., Seeley, J., & Barton, T. (1996). Rethinking methods for the study of sexual behaviour. *Social Science and Medicine, 42*, 221–231.

Jaccard, J., & Wan, C. K. (1995). A paradigm for studying the accuracy of self-reports of risk behavior relevant to AIDS: Empirical perspectives on stability, recall bias, and transitory influences. *Journal of Applied Social Psychology, 25*, 1831–1858.

Kaplan, H. B. (1989). Methodological problems in the study of psychosocial influences on the AIDS process. *Social Science and Medicine, 29*, 277–292.

Kerlinger, F. N. (1986). *Foundations of behavioral research* (3rd ed.). San Francisco: Holt, Rinehart & Winston.

Knee, C. R. (1998). Implicit theories of relationships: Assessment and prediction of romantic relationship initiation, coping, and longevity. *Journal of Personality and Social Psychology, 74*, 360–370.

Knowles, E. S. (1988). Item context effects on personality scales: Measuring changes the measure. *Journal of Personality and Social Psychology, 55*, 312–320.

LaRossa, R. (1995). Stories and relationships. *Journal of Social and Personal Relationships, 12*, 553–558.

Marsh, H. W., & Yeung, A. S. (1999). The lability of psychological ratings: The chameleon effect in global self-esteem. *Personality and Social Psychology Bulletin, 25*, 49–64.

McFarland, S. G., & Sparks, C. M. (1985). Age, education, and the internal consistency of personality scales. *Journal of Personality and Social Psychology, 49*, 1692–1702.

McGregor, I., & Holmes, J. G. (1999). How storytelling shapes memory and impressions of relationship events over time. *Journal of Personality and Social Psychology, 76*, 403–419.

Mershon, B., & Gorsuch, R. L. (1988). Number of factors in the personality sphere: Does increase in factors increase predictability of real-life criteria? *Journal of Personality and Social Psychology, 55*, 675–680.

Meston, C. M., Heiman, J. R., Trapnell, P. D., & Paulhus, D. L. (1998). Socially desirable responding and sexuality self-reports. *The Journal of Sex Research, 35*, 148–157.

Morokoff, P. J., Quina, K., Harlow, L. L., Whitmire, L., Grimley, D. M., Gibson, P. R., & Burkholder, G. J. (1997). Sexual Assertiveness Scale (SAS) for women: Development and validation. *Journal of Personality and Social Psychology, 73*, 790–804.

Nasby, W. (1989). Private self-consciousness, self-awareness, and the reliability of self-reports. *Journal of Personality and Social Psychology, 56*, 950–957.

Nicholas, L. J., Durrheim, K., & Tredoux, C. G. (1994). Lying as a factor in research on sexuality. *Psychological Reports, 75*, 839–842.

Nisbett, R. E., & Ross, L. (1980). *Human inference: Strategies and shortcomings of social judgment.* Englewood Cliffs, NJ: Prentice-Hall.

Nisbett, R. E., & Wilson, T. D. (1977). Telling more than we can know: Verbal reports on mental processes. *Psychological Review, 84*, 231–259.

Ochs, E. P., & Binik, Y. M. (1999). The use of couple data to determine the reliability of self-reported sexual behavior. *The Journal of Sex Research, 36*, 374–384.

Ottati, V. C. (1997). When the survey question directs retrieval: Implications for assessing the cognitive and affective predictors of global evaluation. *European Journal of Social Psychology, 27,* 1–21.

Paulhus, D. L. (1991). Measurement and control of response bias. In J. P. Robinson, P. R. Shaver, & L. S. Wrightsman (Eds.), *Measures of personality and social psychological attitudes* (pp. 17–59). New York: Academic Press.

Quitkin, F. M. (1999). Placebos, drug effects, and study design: A clinician's guide. *American Journal of Psychiatry, 156,* 829–836.

Raghubir, P., & Menon, G. (1996). Asking sensitive questions: The effects of type of referent and frequency wording in counterbiasing methods. *Psychology & Marketing, 13,* 633–652.

Rise, J., Traeen, B., & Kraft, P. (1993). The Sexual Opinion Survey scale: A study of dimensionality in Norwegian adolescents. *Health Education Research: Theory & Practice, 8,* 485–494.

Ross, R., & Allgeier, E. R. (1996). Behind the pencil/paper measurement of sexual coercion: Interview-based clarification of men's interpretations of Sexual Experience Survey items. *Journal of Applied Social Psychology, 26,* 1587–1616.

Rothblum, E. D. (1994). Transforming lesbian sexuality. *Psychology of Women Quarterly, 18,* 627–641.

Sanders, S. A., & Reinisch, J. M. (1999). Would you say you "had sex" if . . . ? *Journal of the American Medical Association, 281,* 275–277.

Schwartz, N. (1999). Self-reports: How the questions shape the answers. *American Psychologist, 54,* 93–105.

Schwartz, N., & Hippler, H. J. (1995). Subsequent questions may influence answers to preceding questions in mail surveys *Public Opinion Quarterly, 59,* 93–97.

Schwartz, N., & Sudman, S. (Eds.). (1994). *Autobiographical memory and the validity of retrospective reports.* New York: Springer-Verlag.

Sheeran, P., & Abraham, C. (1994). Measurement of condom use in 72 studies of HIV-preventive behaviour: A critical review. *Patient Education and Counseling, 24,* 199–216.

Siegel, D. M., Aten, M. J., & Roughman, K. J. (1998). Self-reported honesty among middle and high school students responding to a sexual behavior questionnaire. *Journal of Adolescent Health, 23,* 20–28.

Siegel, S., & Castellan, N. J. (1988). *Nonparametric statistics for the behavioral sciences* (2nd ed.). New York: McGraw-Hill.

Siegrist, M. (1996). The influence of self-consciousness on the internal consistency of different scales. *Personality and Individual Differences, 20,* 115–117.

Smith, G. T., & McCarthy, D. M. (1995). Methodological considerations in the refinement of clinical assessment instruments. *Psychological Assessment, 7,* 300–308.

Smith, L. L., & Reise, S. P. (1998). Gender differences on negative affectivity: An IRT study of differential item functioning on the Multidimensional Personality Questionnaire Stress Reaction Scale. *Journal of Personality and Social Psychology, 75,* 1350–1362.

Snell, W. E., & Papini, D. R. (1989). The Sexuality Scale: An instrument to measure sexual-esteem, sexual-depression, and sexual-preoccupation. *The Journal of Sex Research, 26,* 256–263.

Spearman, C. (1904). The proof and measurement of association between two things. *American Journal of Psychology, 15,* 72–101.

Steinberg, L. (1994). Context and serial-order effects in personality meaurement: Limits on the generality of measuring changes the measure. *Journal of Personality and Social Psychology, 66,* 341–349.

Sudman, S., Bradburn, N. M., & Schwartz, N. (1996). *Thinking about answers: The application of cognitive processes to survey methodology.* San Francisco: Jossey-Bass.

Thompson, B., & Snyder, P. A. (1998). Statistical significance and reliability analyses in recent *Journal of Counseling & Development* research articles. *Journal of Counseling & Development, 76,* 436–441.

Thompson, C. P., Skowronski, J. J., Larsen, S. F., & Betz, A. L. (1996). *Autobiographical memory: Remembering what and remembering when.* Mahwah, NJ: Lawrence Erlbaum Associates.

Tourangeau, R., Smith, T. W., & Rasinski, K. A. (1997). Motivation to report sensitive behaviors on surveys: Evidence from a bogus pipeline experiment. *Journal of Applied Social Psychology, 27,* 209–222.

Turner, C. F., Ku, L., Rogers, S. M., Lindberg, L. D., Pleck, J. H., & Sonenstein, F. L. (1998). Adolescent sexual behavior, drug use, and violence: Increased reporting with computer survey technology. *Science, 280,* 867–873.

Vacha-Haase, T. (1998). Reliability generalization: Exploring variance in measurement error affecting score reliability across studies. *Educational and Psychological Measurement, 58,* 6–20.

Weinhardt, L. S., Forsyth, A. D., Carey, M. P., Jaworski, B. C., & Durant, L. E. (1998). Reliability and validity of self-report measures of HIV-related sexual behavior: Progress since 1990 and recommendations for research and practice. *Archives of Sexual Behavior, 27,* 155–180.

Whitley, B. E. (1996). *Principles of research in behavioral science.* Mountain View, CA: Mayfield.

Wiederman, M. W. (1997). The truth must be in here somewhere: Examining the gender discrepancy in self-reported lifetime number of sex partners. *The Journal of Sex Research, 34,* 375–386.

Wiederman, M. W., & Allgeier, E. R. (1993). The measurement of sexual-esteem: Investigation of Snell and Papini's (1989) Sexuality Scale. *Journal of Research in Personality, 27,* 88–102.

Wright, D. B., Gaskell, G. D., & O'Muircheartaigh, C. A. (1997). How response alternatives affect different kinds of behavioural frequency questions. *British Journal of Social Psychology, 36,* 443–456.

Wryobeck, J. M., & Wiederman, M. W. (1999). Sexual narcissism: Measurement and correlates among college men. *Journal of Sex & Marital Therapy, 25,* 321–331.

Zeanah, P. D., & Schwartz, J. C. (1996). Reliability and Validity of the Sexual Self-Esteem Inventory for Women. *Assessment, 3,* 1–15.

Validity in Research[1]

Bernard E. Whitley, Jr.
Ball State University

The purpose of research is to allow scientists to draw valid conclusions about relationships between variables. In some cases, these relationships are hypothesized in advance of data collection on the basis of theory, previous empirical findings, or experience in applied settings. In other cases, interesting relationships emerge unexpectedly from data. In either type of situation, researchers must have confidence that they are drawing accurate—that is, valid—conclusions from the data. Cook and Campbell (1979) described four types of validity to which researchers should attend: internal validity, construct validity, statistical conclusion validity, and external validity. Two other forms of validity can be added to this list: theoretical validity (Cook, Gruder, Hennigan, & Flay, 1979) and hypothesis validity (Wampold, Davis, & Good, 1990). Table 4.1 defines these types of validity, listing them in the order in which I discuss them.

THEORETICAL VALIDITY

Although sexuality research only rarely tests hypotheses derived from theories (see chap. 2, this volume), when it does so it must provide a fair test of the theory. Some theories specify conditions that must be met for predictions made by the theories to be fulfilled. To have *theoretical validity*, a study testing hypotheses de-

---

[1] Adapted from *Principles of Research in Behavioral Science* by Bernard E. Whitley, Jr., Mayfield Publishing Company, 1996. Copyright 1996 by Mayfield Publishing Company. Adapted by permission.

TABLE 4.1
Types of Validity in Research

Type of Validity	Meaning
Theoretical	If the theory driving the research specifies conditions that are necessary for the independent variable to have an effect, was the research designed to meet those conditions?
Hypothesis	To what extent do research results reflect theoretically meaningful relationships between or among hypothetical constructs?
Internal	To what extent can one be certain that an observed effect was caused by the independent variable rather than by extraneous variables?
Construct	How well do the operational definitions of hypothetical constructs represent those constructs?
Statistical Conclusion	Are the correct conclusions being drawn about the the effect of the independent variable from the statistical analyses that were conducted?
External	To what extent can one be sure that the results of a study are replicable under other research conditions or that they are applicable outside the context in which the study was conducted?

rived from such a theory must meet the conditions the theory specifies as being necessary for the independent variable to have an effect on the dependent variable.

For example, in its simplest form cognitive dissonance theory (Festinger, 1957) holds that when people act in ways contrary to the attitudes they hold, they experience an aversive state called *cognitive dissonance*. Because cognitive dissonance is aversive, people are motivated to reduce it; one way of doing so is to bring attitudes and behavior back into alignment, such as by changing attitudes to be consistent with behavior or changing future behavior to be consistent with attitudes. However, as the theory has developed over time, it has been expanded to include a set of conditions that are necessary for cognitive dissonance to occur and to have its effects (Cooper & Fazio, 1984): The attitude-discrepant behavior must result in unwanted negative consequences, the person must take responsibility for the behavior, cognitive dissonance must be experienced as physiological arousal, and the person must see the physiological arousal to be a consequence of the behavior. If any of these conditions is absent, the effects predicted by cognitive dissonance theory do not occur. For example, giving research participants a tranquilizer, which reduces physiological arousal, prevents attitude change predicted by the theory (Cooper & Fazio, 1984). However, if the conditions are met, cognitive dissonance can have a considerable impact on behavior, including sexual behavior. Stone, Aronson, Crain, Winslow, and Fried (1994), for example, aroused cognitive dissonance in a sample of college students by pointing out to them the discrepancy between their endorsement of the value of condom use and their failure to use condoms. When presented with the opportunity to buy condoms using the money they had earned for participating in the study, 83% of the students in the cognitive dissonance condition made the purchase compared with 42% of the students in other conditions.

HYPOTHESIS VALIDITY

Meeting the conditions set by a theory for a proper test of hypotheses derived from it is necessary, but not sufficient, for an adequate test of the theory. As Wampold et al. (1990) pointed out, the hypotheses must adequately reflect the propositions of the theory. They coined the term *hypothesis validity* to represent the extent to which the results of tests of research hypotheses provide unambiguous information about the validity of the theory from which the hypotheses were derived.

> If a study has adequate hypothesis validity, the results will be informative about the nature of the relations [the theory proposes exist] between constructs; that is, the study will inform theory. If a study has inadequate hypothesis validity, ambiguity about the relation between constructs will result, and indeed less certainty about the relation may exist than before the research was conducted. (p. 360)

Wampold et al. (1990) described four criteria for hypothesis validity in re-search: consequential research hypotheses, clearly stated research hypotheses, congruence between research and statistical hypotheses, and specific statistical hypotheses and tests. Here I discuss the first two criteria; I discuss the other two later as aspects of statistical conclusion validity.

Consequential Research Hypotheses

A study can provide either a strong test of a theory by positing hypotheses that, if falsified, also tend to falsify the theory, or provide a weak test by positing hypotheses that, if not supported, pose little threat to theory. Consequential hypotheses provide strong tests of a theory by testing central propositions of the theory and pitting competing theories against one another.

Testing Central Propositions. Some propositions that a theory makes about relationships between variables are central to its validity: If those propositions are shown to be false, those findings call the entire theory into question. Other propositions are more peripheral: The theory can stand, albeit with modification, if the propositions are shown to be false. Therefore, research that tests hypotheses derived from central propositions of a theory provide the most useful information about the validity of the theory. For example, a central proposition of cognitive dissonance theory is that inconsistency between attitudes and behavior leads to an aversive psychological state, that is, cognitive dissonance. If research had shown that attitude–behavior inconsistency did not arouse dissonance, then the entire theory would have fallen. As it happened, that central proposition stood the test of research, but tests of other, less central propositions indicated the necessity of modifying the theory to include the conditions for its effectiveness discussed earlier.

Pitting Competing Theories. When the results of a well-designed study in which the data are properly analyzed are consistent with the predictions made in the research hypotheses, one can conclude that those results support the theory being tested. However, the fact that a set of results is consistent with predictions derived from a particular theory does not necessarily mean that the theory provides the best explanation for the phenomenon under study: The same pattern of results could be consistent with explanations provided by other theories. A strong test of a theory requires not only that the theory under consideration be supported, but also that competing theories be ruled out as explanations for the observed data. Therefore, research that pits competing theories against one another is preferable to research that tests a single theory. For example, Wulfert and Wan (1995) compared the degree to which three competing theories could predict safe-sex intentions and condom use. The theories were the health belief model, which emphasizes the perceived risks and benefits of health-related behaviors; the theory of reasoned action, which emphasizes the influences of attitudes and social norms on behavior; and social cognitive theory, which emphasizes self-efficacy and the expected consequences of behavior. Wulfert and Wan's results provided the best support for the social cognitive model.

Clearly Stated Research Hypotheses

Clear research hypotheses explicitly state the expected relationships between the variables being studied, whereas ambiguous hypotheses simply state that a difference will exist between groups or that two variables will be correlated. For example, "Women will score higher than men on sex guilt" and "There will be a negative correlation between level of sex guilt and sexual behavior" are clear hypotheses, whereas "There will be a gender difference in sex guilt scores" and "Sex guilt will be related to sexual behavior" are ambiguous. Clearly stated hypotheses provide strong tests of theory by establishing explicit criteria by which the theory can be judged: Either women score higher than men (supporting the theory) or they do not (falsifying the theory); the correlation is either negative (supporting the theory) or not (falsifying the theory). With the ambiguous hypotheses, there is no way to determine whether the results support or contradict theory. As Wampold et al. (1990) wrote:

> In one sense ... research [based on ambiguous hypotheses] cannot fail, because some relation between variables will be "discovered" even if the relation is null (i.e., no relation). In another sense, the research will always fail because the results do not falsify or corroborate any theory about the true state of affairs. (p. 363)

INTERNAL VALIDITY

The concept of *internal validity* represents the extent to which researchers can feel certain that the results of a study are due to the effects of the independent variable rather than the effects of extraneous variables. This section briefly discusses a few of the factors that can threaten the internal validity of a study: history, testing, instrumentation change, and participant selection.

History

History refers to events that occur outside the research situation while the research is being conducted that affect participants' responses on the dependent measure. For example, Greene and Loftus (1984) conducted a study in which university students read a story about a trial that included eyewitness testimony and gave their opinions about whether the defendant was guilty or not guilty. They collected their data over the course of a semester; part way through the semester, an incident in which a man was mistakenly identified as a criminal received wide publicity in the city where the university was located. Greene and Loftus found that fewer of their participants made guilty judgments during the time that the incident was publicized compared with students who participated before and after the publicity. A follow-up experiment provided evidence that it was the publicity that caused the drop in guilty judgments. An analogy for sexuality research might be the effect of televised safe-sex ad campaign on research on factors affecting condom use. Because events outside the research situation can affect participants' responses, researchers must be aware of events that could affect their data and check to see if such an effect is present.

Testing

Much research is directed at testing the effectiveness of interventions for changing personal characteristics, such as attitudes, intentions, or behavior patterns. One way to conduct such research is to pretest participants on the dependent variable (i.e., the characteristic to be changed), conduct the intervention, posttest participants on the dependent variable, and examine the amount of change from pretest to posttest. A testing problem arises, however, when taking the pretest affects scores on the posttest independently of the effect of the intervention. For example, people might try to keep their responses consistent across different administrations of a measure or try to "do better" on the posttest than they did on the pretest. The simplest way to deal with testing confounds is not to give a pretest; for example, pretesting is usually not necessary when research participants are randomly assigned to conditions of the independent variable (see chap. 12, this volume).

If a pretest is necessary or desirable, the presence and degree of testing effects can be assessed by using what is known as a Solomon four-group experimental design (e.g., Braver & Braver, 1988). As its name indicates, the Solomon four-group design requires four sets of research participants (see Fig. 4.1): two control conditions, one with a pretest and one without, and two experimental conditions, one with a pretest and one without. If a simple testing confound exists, the posttest means of Groups 1 and 3 in Fig. 4.1 will differ: Because the only way in which these groups differ is in whether they received a pretest, a difference in the posttest means indicates that the pretest affected performance on the posttest. The presence of a more complex testing confound can be detected by comparing the differences

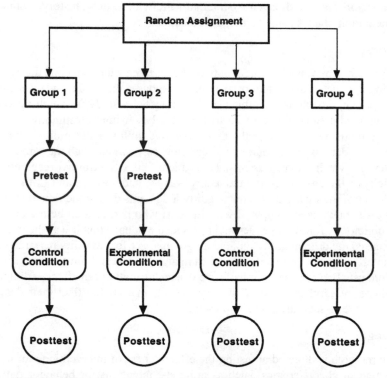

FIG. 4.1.   The Solomon four-group design: A difference in the posttest means of
Groups 1 and 3 indicates a simple testing confound: Responses on the posttest differ
because of a pretest. Unequal differences in the posttest means of Groups 1 and 3
versus Groups 2 and 4 indicate a complex testing confound: The effect of the pretest
is different in the experimental and control conditions. From *Principles of Research
in Behavioral Science* (p. 210), by Bernard E. Whitley, Jr., 1996, Mountain View,
CA: Mayfield. Copyright 1996 by Mayfield. Reprinted with permission.

in the posttest means of Groups 1 and 3 (the control conditions of the experiment)
with the difference in posttest means of Groups 2 and 4 (the experimental conditions). If these differences are not equal, then pretesting combines with the effect of
the experimental manipulation to affect posttest scores: The pretest has different effects on the posttest performance of the experimental and control groups. Either
form of testing confound calls into question the internal validity of the research.

Instrumentation Change

Instrumentation change occurs when the measure used to assess the dependent
variable changes over time, leading to artificial differences in scores at different
points in time. Instrumentation change can take several forms. Mechanical and
electrical measuring devices can go out of calibration as they are used, resulting in

cumulative inaccuracies. Although this problem is probably less severe with modern solid state electronic devices than it was in the days of electromechanical instrumentation, battery-powered instruments can go out of calibration when their batteries weaken. A solution to this form of instrumentation change is to periodically test any apparatus that might be subject to it.

Another form of instrumentation change occurs when observers change the classification that they give a behavior as they gain experience. This problem can be prevented by using clearly defined coding categories and by carefully training coders. A similar problem can occur with self-report measures: People might interpret the meanings of questions differently as time passes. For example, sexual dysfunction that appears to be severe at the start of a treatment program may be perceived as less severe later—not because the problem has changed, but because the client's criterion for judging severity has changed. This can happen in group therapy when a client, after hearing about others' problems, decides, "My problems aren't as bad as I thought."

Finally, the content of measures might change over time. For example, I reviewed a research report on changes in college students' attitudes toward homosexuality over a period of several years. The first 2 years the questionnaire was administered, the attitude questions referred to "homosexuals," whereas in the other 2 years, the questionnaire referred to "lesbians and gay men." The results of the study show that attitudes became less negative over time. However, because people interpret the terms *homosexual* and *lesbians and gay men* differently (e.g., Kite & Whitley, 1996), there was no way to determine whether the results were due to actual attitude change or to the change in the measurement instrument.

Selection Threats

Selection threatens the internal validity of research when participants in one condition differ systematically from those in another condition. Here I briefly consider three forms of selection bias: nonrandom assignment of research participants to the conditions of a study, use of preexisting groups in research, and mortality.

Nonrandom Assignment. A clear example of a selection problem is having only men in one condition of a study and only women in another condition. Although researchers are careful to avoid such obvious selection biases, others can slip in unnoticed. For example, a selection bias occurs when researchers allow participants to volunteer for the experimental condition of a study or when they use people who volunteer for research as the experimental group and use data from nonvolunteers as the control condition. These procedures can result in a selection bias because people who volunteer for research differ on a number of characteristics from those who do not (see chap. 5, this volume).

Data collection procedures can also lead to selection biases. For example, collecting all the data for one condition of an experiment before collecting the data for the other condition can cause a selection confound as well as opening the door for a history confound if people who participate early in the data collection period differ from those who participate later.

Preexisting Groups. Selection biases can also arise in research conducted in natural settings when researchers must assign preexisting natural groups, rather than individuals, to experimental and control conditions. For example, in a study evaluating the effectiveness of a school-based sexuality education program, the students in one school in a district might be designated the experimental group and those in another school, the control group. Selection bias is a problem in these situations because people are not randomly assigned to natural groups. Sometimes people choose to join a group, sometimes the group chooses them, and sometimes they are assigned to a group by a decision maker, such as a school administrator. In any of these cases, the choices and assignments are probably not random, but are based on the characteristics of the people involved. Consequently, when utilizing preexisting groups as experimental and control groups, it is essential to ensure that the members of the groups are as similar as possible on relevant characteristics, such as age, knowledge, experience, and so forth.

Mortality. Mortality refers to people dropping out of a study while it is being conducted. In longitudinal research, if only people with certain characteristics drop out, such as the participants whose behaviors put them at greatest risk of HIV infection in a study of safe-sex behaviors, the results of the study apply only to those people whose characteristics match those of the "survivors." In group-comparison research, differential mortality occurs when people in one condition of the study are more likely to withdraw from the research than are people in other conditions. For example, consider a hypothetical experiment testing the effects of viewing sexually explicit movies on sexual behavior over a 14-day period. Participants in the experimental condition watch sexually explicit films each day, whereas participants in the control condition watch films with no sexual content. Participants keep a diary of their sexual behavior. Five percent of the experimental participants withdraw from the research, compared with 48% of the control participants, with the dropouts complaining that the films they have to watch are boring. The researchers find that the experimental participants report higher levels of sexual behavior than do the control participants. However, because the control participants who finish the research are those people willing to watch the control films, they might be different from the experimental participants in their psychological make-up. Consequently, there is probably a confound between participants' characteristics and the condition in which they must complete the study.

There is no solution to the problem of differential mortality. Researchers can try to determine if survivors and dropouts in the high-dropout condition differ on any demographic characteristics or on variables assessed during a pretest. If they do, these differences can be taken into account when interpreting the results of the research by comparing the survivors with the members of the other group who have similar characteristics. If there are then differences between the groups on the dependent variable, the independent variable probably caused them. However, the results of the study would apply only to people with characteristics similar to those of the survivors in the high-dropout condition. Also, if differential mortality does not occur until after some time into the data collection period, data collected before mortality became a problem would not be affected by selection. For example, if none of the control participants in the hypothetical sexually explicit film study dropped out until the eighth day, the data from the first week would present no selection problem.

CONSTRUCT VALIDITY

Many of the variables of interest to sexuality researchers are abstract in nature: personality traits, attitudes, belief, sexual orientation, and so forth. To conduct research with these abstract concepts or hypothetical constructs, researchers must put them into concrete form by measuring or manipulating them. Such measures and manipulations of hypothetical constructs are their operational definitions; *construct validity* deals with the degree to which operational definitions adequately represent hypothetical constructs. Even if a study has excellent internal validity, if construct validity is lacking, one cannot be certain whether the operational definitions used are true reflections of the hypothetical constructs of interest. Consequently, construct validity assists the researcher in confidently making the inference that is the primary goal of research: that the relationships found between the operational definitions reflect the relationships that exist between the hypothetical constructs. This section discusses four types of threats to the construct validity of research: confounds, validity of manipulations and measures, inadequate conceptualization of constructs, and use of single operational definitions and narrow stimulus sampling.

Confounds

A confound exists when two variables are combined so that the effect of one cannot be separated from the effect of the other. Three types of confounds can threaten the construct validity of research: natural, treatment, and measurement.

Natural Confounds. The combination of the variables of biological sex and interest in certain topics is an example of what might be called a *natural confound*: In nature, some variables tend to be associated with certain other variables. For example, people who share demographic characteristics such as age, sex, and ethnicity have undergone a common set of experiences associated with those variables, leading them to have some common attitudes, values, and other characteristics. Because of such natural confounds, when demographic variables are used as independent variables in research, one can almost never be sure whether group differences found on the dependent variable are due to the demographic variable, such as biological sex, or to a confounded variable, such as the results of sex-role socialization.

Treatment Confounds.   Treatment confounds occur when the manipulated independent variable (or treatment) in an experiment is confounded with another variable or treatment. For example, having a female experimenter conduct all the experimental sessions and a male experimenter conduct all the control sessions would result in a treatment confound. Although participants in each condition should have been exposed to only one treatment (i.e., the conditions of the independent variable), they actually received two combined treatments (condition of the independent variable and sex of experimenter).

More subtle confounds can creep into research and sometimes remain undetected until subsequent researchers look at the topic from a new perspective. Research on sex differences in persuasion provides an example of a subtle confound. Studies of this topic typically find that women are more likely than men to change their expressed opinions in response to persuasive messages. Eagly and Carli (1981) showed, however, that these findings result from a confound between sex of research participant and interest in the topic of the opinions used in the research. The research frequently used topics such as professional sports, which men found more interesting than did women. Because the variables of sex and level of interest were confounded, there was no way of knowing which variable was related to attitude change.

Confounds can also sometimes emerge in the process of conducting the study. For example, if the experimental condition requires equipment that is in short supply and the control condition does not, the researcher might have people participate individually in the experimental condition and in groups in the control condition. Although this procedure makes data collection easier and faster than having people in the control condition participate individually, it also confounds treatment with the social context of research participation. If differences between the experimental and control conditions are found, are they due to the independent variable or to participating alone versus in a group?

Researchers must be very careful to avoid treatment confounds when designing and conducting research. The critical question to ask is: Do the participants in the experimental and control conditions have *exactly* the same experiences in *exactly* the same physical, social, and temporal environment except for the manipulation of the independent variable? If the answer is "no," then a treatment confound exists and must be eliminated.

Measurement Confounds. Confounds can occur in the measures used to assess dependent variables as well as in independent variables. A measurement confound occurs when a measure assesses more than one hypothetical construct. For example, many self-report measures that are designed to assess depression also assess anxiety (Dobson, 1985). Consequently, one does not know if a high score on such a measure represents high depression, high anxiety, or both. Measurement confounds, which are shown by the lack of discriminant validity in a measure, often result from natural confounds between the constructs being assessed. For example, a high degree of anxiety might be a natural concomitant of depression. However, because measurement confounds, even natural measurement confounds, obscure the relationship between an independent variable and the dependent variable that one is interested in, only measures high in discriminant validity should be used in research. When measurement confounds cannot be avoided, statistical techniques, such as partial correlation analysis, sometimes can be used to separate the effects of the confounded variables.

Validity of Manipulations

Perhaps the most familiar meaning of the term *construct validity* is in the context of measurement (see chap. 3, this volume). However, in experimental research, it is equally important to attend to the construct validity of the manipulations used to operationally define independent variable. For example, if a rescarcher wants to assess the effects of viewing sexually explicit films that include images degrading to women, the images in those films must be perceived by the research participants as degrading and the images in the control film must be perceived as not degrading. The construct validity of a manipulation is tested by means of a manipulation check. The manipulation check tests the convergent validity of the manipulation by checking it against measures of the construct and by ensuring that participants in different conditions of the experiment are experiencing different levels or conditions of the independent variable. For example, participants in the degrading film condition of such a study should rate the film they see as more degrading to women than participants in the control condition rated the film they see. A manipulation check should also test the discriminant validity of the manipulation by ensuring that it manipulates only the construct that it is supposed to manipulate. For example, the two films in the example study should be rated as equally sexually arousing.

Manipulation checks can be made at two points in the research project. The first point is during pilot testing, when the bugs are being worked out of the research procedures. One of the potential bugs is the effectiveness of the manipulation. It is not unusual to have to tinker with the manipulation to ensure that it has the intended effect and only the intended effect. Manipulation checks can also be made during data collection to ensure that all participants experience their condition of the independent variable as intended. However, if manipulations checks are made only concurrently with data collection, it is too late to alter the manipulation if problems are discovered unless the researcher is willing to stop data collection and start the research from the beginning. Researchers can also use manipulations validated in other research (e.g., Cowan & Dunn, 1994). However, they can still use a manipulation check because the validity of a manipulation can sometimes vary from one participant population to another.

Inadequate Conceptualization of Constructs

Development of valid operational definitions requires a clear understanding of the hypothetical constructs in question. Some constructs are more easily conceptualized and so lend themselves to clearer operational definition; other constructs can be difficult to conceptualize because they have multiple meanings, have multiple facets, or can be operationally defined at more than one level of analysis. The complexity of such constructs is problematic because it may be inappropriate to generalize conclusions across the different aspects of a construct.

Constructs Having Multiple Meanings.   When collecting data, researchers often use common-language terms to facilitate participants' understanding of the questions being asked. However, common-language terms often have multiple meanings, and the particular meaning that a term has for a particular participant can affect that person's response. Similarly, when using such terms, different researchers may conceptualize them differently, leading to apparently contradictory results.

Consider, for example, the construct of childhood sexual abuse. Roosa, Reyes, Reinholtz, and Angelini (1998) pointed out that researchers' operational definitions of childhood sexual abuse vary along three dimensions: the sexual behaviors included in the definition, the ages of the victim and perpetrator, and the relationship of the victim and perpetrator. For example, some researchers ignore differences among forms of abuse, grouping victims of such diverse acts as unwanted touching and forced intercourse into a single category, whereas other researchers distinguish between as many as six forms of abuse. The operational definition of child ranges from 10 years of age or younger to 16 years of age or younger, and some researchers include abuse by friends or boyfriends, whereas others do not. Using data from a single sample, Roosa et al. (1998) found that incidence rates of childhood sexual abuse differed by as much as 300% depending on the operational definition used. Other concepts used in sexuality research can also be conceptualized in multiple ways. Researchers must therefore carefully consider what they mean by the terms they use, explicitly define them in research reports so their meaning is clear to others, and interpret their results in context of the meanings they assign to avoid unwarranted generalizations.

Multifaceted Constructs. Carver (1989) defined *multifaceted constructs* as those "that are composed of two or more subordinate concepts, each of which can be distinguished from the others and measured separately, despite their being related to each other both logically and empirically" (p. 577). An example of a multifaceted construct is attitudes toward homosexuality. LaMar and Kite (1998) conducted a factor analysis of items drawn from several published scales of attitudes toward homosexuality and found eight correlated factors, four parallel factors for lesbians and gay men: condemnation/tolerance, morality, contact, and stereotypes.

Because the facets of a multifaceted construct are correlated, the distinctions among the facets are sometimes ignored, and the construct is treated as if it were unidimensional. For example, one could combine scores on LaMar and Kite's eight factors into a single scale measuring attitudes toward lesbians and gay men. Although there are circumstances when it can be appropriate to combine across the facets of a multifaceted constructs (see Carver, 1989), doing so can lead to erroneous interpretation of research results: When the facets of a multifaceted construct are combined into a general index, useful information can be lost. For example, LaMar and Kite (1998) found varying patterns of gender differences in ratings of lesbians and gay men on the four attitude factors: Men were more negative toward gay men than toward lesbians on the condemnation/tolerance and morality factors, whereas women made similar ratings of lesbians and gay men on these factors; men were more negative about contact with gay men than about contact with lesbians, but the reverse was true for women; and although men endorsed stereotypes of both lesbians and gay men more strongly than did women, there was no difference in stereotype endorsement by gender of the attitude target for either male or female respondents. If all eight factors had been combined into one attitude scale, or even if the four factors for lesbians and the four factors for gay men each had been combined into separate scales, the different patterns of response would not have been found. Therefore, unless researchers are certain that the combined score on a construct and the scores on all the facets have the same relation to a dependent variable, they should test both the combined score and the facet scores to derive the most accurate information from the data.

Constructs Having More Than One Level of Analysis. Some hypothetical constructs can be conceptualized at more than one level of analysis. Consider again attitudes toward lesbians and gay men. Research on this topic sometimes assesses attitudes toward lesbians and gay men as social groups, using items such as "The increasing acceptance of gay men in our society is aiding in the deterioration of morals" and "If a lesbian approached me in a public restroom, I would be disgusted" (LaMar & Kite, 1998, p. 192). Other research assesses attitudes toward lesbians and gay men as individuals, presenting participants with vignettes describing the characteristics of a particular lesbian or gay man, or having them interact with someone they believe to be a lesbian or gay man (see Kite & Whitley, 1998, for examples of these studies).

Distinguishing among different levels of analysis is important because the findings of research conducted at one level may not generalize to another level. For example, the typical gender difference found for attitudes toward lesbians and gay men considered as social groups is only occasionally found for attitudes toward lesbians and gay men considered as individuals (Kite & Whitley, 1998). Researchers must therefore carefully consider possible distinctions among levels of analysis for a construct and interpret their results in context of the level they use in their research to avoid unwarranted generalizations.

Single Operational Definitions and Narrow Stimulus Sampling

When conducting research, investigators are usually interested in the general effects of hypothetical constructs on other hypothetical constructs rather than the specific effect of one operational definition on another. However, in many studies, researchers use only single operational definitions of the variables they are studying or only a single stimulus from a population of possible stimuli that could be used to represent a particular hypothetical construct. Such use of single operational definitions and narrow stimulus sampling leaves no way to determine the extent to which the results of the study reflect the general relationships between the hypothetical constructs under study or the unique relationships between their operational definitions.

Single Operational Definitions. Any operational definition consists of a combination of true score—which accurately represents the hypothetical construct—and error. Consequently, each operational definition has its own advantages in terms of the aspect of true score that it captures and limitations in terms of its errors of measurement. When researchers use multiple operational definitions, the advantages of one can compensate for the limitations of another, thereby improving the overall quality of measurement. For example, latent variables modeling (see chap. 14, this volume) uses confirmatory factor analysis to identify the common true score components (the latent variables) of multiple measures of hypothetical constructs and then analyzes the relationship between the latent variables. Similarly, multivariate analysis of variance (MANOVA; e.g., Weinfurt, 1995) analyzes the effect of one or more independent variables on a set of interrelated dependent variables, such as multiple measures of a construct. Because multiple operational definitions capture the essence of a hypothetical construct better than any single operational definition, researchers should use them whenever possible.

Stimulus Sampling. The term *stimulus* refers to the person, object, or event that represents the operational definition of a condition of the independent variable and to which research participants respond. For example, in a study of the effects of sexual images that are degrading to women, the independent variable is degrading imagery, its operational definition might be a scene containing such imagery from a sexually explicit film, and the stimulus would be the particular scene to which research participants respond. When the independent variable is a hypothetical construct, it can very often be represented by any number of stimuli. In the degrading imagery study, for example, the concept of degrading sexual images could be represented by any of a large number of scenes.

Although there are many constructs that can be represented by multiple stimuli, most research dealing with such constructs uses only one stimulus to represent each condition of the independent variable, such as one film scene containing degrading imagery and one scene without degrading imagery. If the research results in a difference between the conditions, a problem arises in interpreting the findings: Although the outcome could have been due to the effects of the hypothetical construct being studied, they could also be due to the unique features of the stimulus used (Maher, 1978; Wells & Windschitl, 1999). In the degrading imagery study, for example, are the participants responding to the general construct of degrading imagery—the intended independent variable—or to the unique characteristics of the particular scene used as its operational definition, such as the actors, sequence of events, and so forth? That is, are the research participants responding to the general characteristic of degrading imagery or to the unique characteristics of how degradation is portrayed in that one scene? There is no way to answer this question if only a single stimulus is used to represent each condition of the independent variable.

The question would have an answer, however, if each research participant responds to a set of stimuli that provides a sample of the possible stimuli that can represent the conditions of the independent variable. For example, one could have participants in each condition of the experiment view four scenes rather than just one. With multiple stimuli per condition, it becomes possible to treat stimuli as a random variable in an analysis of variance (ANOVA) design and separate the variance in the dependent variable due to specific stimuli, such as the scenes used to portray degradation, from the variance due to the hypothesized construct represented by the stimuli, such as the concept of sexually degrading imagery. This form of ANOVA is extremely complex (e.g., Fontenelle, Phillips, & Lane, 1985). However, because it separates irrelevant stimulus variance from the relevant variance due to the hypothetical construct, it provides a more valid test of the effects of the independent variable than would the use of a single stimulus per condition.

STATISTICAL CONCLUSION VALIDITY

Having collected relevant data, researchers test their hypotheses statistically. That is, they convert their research hypotheses into statistical hypotheses, such as "The mean of the experimental group will be larger than the mean of the control group," apply statistical tests to determine if the data support the hypotheses, and use the results of the statistical test to determine the validity of the research hypotheses. Because the statistical test is applied to data from a sample drawn from a population of interest rather than from the entire population, the results found in the sample might not accurately reflect the true state of affairs in the population. Statistical conclusion validity refers to the accuracy of the decisions researcher make about how well the results found in their sample represent the relationships in the population between the variables being studied. A Type I error occurs if the researchers conclude that a relationship exists in the population when, in fact, it does not; a Type II error occurs if the researchers conclude that a relationship does not exist in the population when, in fact, it does. This section discusses three threats to statistical conclusion validity: testing the wrong statistical hypothesis, using multiple statistical tests, and sources of Type II errors.

Testing the Wrong Statistical Hypothesis

No matter how well designed a study is, its statistical analysis is meaningless if the proper statistical hypothesis is not tested. A common problem of statistical inference arises when a study includes more than two conditions of the independent variable. The statistical test for multiple group studies, ANOVA, tests the hypothesis that at least one of the possible comparisons between groups is significant, but cannot reveal which comparison that is. ANOVA is therefore an *omnibus test*: It tests everything at once. However, as Rosenthal and Rosnow (1991) pointed out, researchers are almost never interested in everything at once; rather, they are interested in comparisons between specific groups. Consider, for example, the results of a hypothetical study comparing the change in sexual satisfaction of people undergoing couples counseling, individual counseling, and no counseling (the control group). The people in the couples counseling group improve an average of 5.8 points on the outcome measure, those in the individual counseling group improve an average of 4.2 points, and those in the control group improve an average of 1.4 points. An ANOVA of the scores in the three groups presents a statistically significant result, so there is definitely a difference somewhere among those groups. However, the results of the omnibus test do not tell the researchers which means differ from each other.

If the researchers have a clear hypothesis specifying which group should improve the most, the way to test for the specified differences is through the use of planned comparisons of means that test the specific differences between means that are of interest to the researchers. For example, if the researchers propose that the couples counseling clients should improve more than either of the other two groups, they could test the differences between the couples counseling mean and the mean of the individual counseling and the mean of the other group. If both tests are statistically significant, the hypothesis is supported. If the researchers had tested the weaker hypothesis that there would be some difference among the groups, they would have to use a post hoc test such as Tukey's HSD test.

Note that the wrong approach for the researchers to take would be to test the difference between the couples counseling mean and the combination of the other two means. Although this test superficially represents the research hypothesis, it contains a potential pitfall: If the control group mean is low enough, the average of it and the individual counseling could be sufficiently smaller than the couples counseling mean to result in a statistically significant difference even if the couples counseling and individual counseling means did not differ significantly. In such a case, the researchers would conclude that their hypothesis had been supported when in fact it had not because the couples counseling mean differed only from that of the control group not from the mean of the individual counseling group.

Multiple Statistical Tests

Researchers frequently use multiple dependent variables in their studies either because they expect the independent variable to affect several dependent variables or because they are using multiple measures of their dependent variable. Although the use of multiple dependent variables can increase the hypothesis and construct validity of the research, it can threaten statistical conclusion validity if the researchers use multiple statistical tests to analyze the data, such as by conducting (in the simplest case) separate t tests for each of the dependent variables.

The threat can take two forms (Wampold et al., 1990). First, ambiguity over the meaning of the results arises if the outcomes of the statistical tests are inconsistent, some being statistical significant and others not. If some outcomes support the hypothesis (and through it, the theory) being tested and others do not, does this constitute evidence in support of the theory or evidence against it? The second threat is Type I error rate inflation. For any one statistical test, the probability of making a Type I error is set at a particular level (the alpha level), usually .05. However, when multiple statistical tests are employed, the probability of making one or more Type I errors is $1 - (1 - alpha)^c$, where c is the number of tests (e.g., Kirk, 1982). Thus, the overall Type I error rate for five statistical tests is .23 rather than .05, and there is no way of knowing which of the test results represent Type I errors and which do not.

Two solutions exist for this problem. One is to use a multivariate analysis, examining the effect of the independent variable on a dependent variable conceptualized as the aggregate of the dependent measures rather than separately examining the effect of the independent variable on the individual measures (e.g., Weinfurt, 1995). Note, however, that MANOVA cannot be used to control Type I error rate in the sense of first conducting a MANOVA and, if it is statistically significant, interpreting each of the univariate ANOVAs (see Weinfurt, 1995, pp. 262–264, for a discussion of this issue). The second solution is to interpret each statistical test separately, but to control the Type I error rate by using a more stringent alpha level. A simple way to do this is to divide the desired overall Type I error rate, such as .05, by the number of statistical tests. Thus, a researcher conducting five statistical tests would set alpha at .01 for each test. Alternatively, some statistics books provide tables of t values corrected for multiple statistical tests (e.g., Kirk, 1982, pp. 843–845). This solution has the drawback of lowering the statistical power of the analysis and so requires a larger sample size than the MANOVA solution.

Sources of Type II Errors

Null results, that is, finding no difference between groups or no relationship between two variables, is not an uncommon outcome in research. However, a number of factors can result in a null other than the lack of a true relationship between the variables being studied. Here I discuss some of those sources of Type II errors and the conditions under which it would be appropriate to accept the null hypothesis of no difference or no relationship.

Measurement Problems. The relationship between two variables conceptualized as hypothetical constructs is their true score correlation; the correlation found between operational definitions of those constructs is called the *observed correlation*. The observed correlation is an estimate of the true score correlation; its value is not necessarily equal to that of the true score correlation. All else being equal, the more reliable the measures of the two variables, the closer the observed correlation will be to the true score correlation. As the measures become less reliable, the observed correlation will underestimate the true score correlation. For example, with a true score correlation of .55 and two measures with reliabilities of .80, the maximum possible observed correlation is .44. Researchers must therefore use the most reliable available measures when conducting correlational research. The same principle applies, of course, to experimental research. However, because the reliability of a carefully manipulated independent variable should approach 1.00, the attenuation of the observed relationship relative to the true score relationship is greatly reduced. Nonetheless, an unreliable measure of the dependent variable can lead to underestimates of the size of its relationship to the independent variable.

Another problem—restriction in range—occurs when the scores of one or both variables used to compute a correlation coefficient have a range of values that is less than the range of scores in the population. Restriction in range reduces the correlation found in a sample relative to the correlation that exists in the population. This reduction occurs because, as a variable's range narrows, the variable comes closer to being a constant. Because the correlation between a constant and a variable is zero, as a variable's sampled range becomes smaller, its maximum possible correlation with another variable will approach zero. It is therefore important for researchers to check their data for any restrictions in the sample range relative to the population range. College students are an example of a subpopulation with a natural restriction in age range, with most students being 18 to 22 years old. Correlations between age and other variables may therefore be deceptively low when college students serve as research participants.

Low Statistical Power. Statistical power is the probability of correctly deciding that an independent variable had no effect. The power of a statistical test depends on several factors, including the alpha level chosen for the test, the size of the effect that the independent variable has on the dependent variable, and the size of the research sample. The operational definition of effect size depends on the statistical test, but a commonly accepted standard is that a small effect to be equivalent to a correlation of .10 between the independent and dependent variables, a medium effect to be equivalent to a correlation of .30, and a large effect to be equivalent to a correlation of .50 (Cohen, 1992). Unfortunately, most behavioral science research has inadequate statistical power. For example, Rossi (1990) found that research published in four major psychology journals in 1982 had an average statistical power of only .17 for small effects, .57 for medium effects, and .83 for large effects. This means that if an independent variable has only a small effect on a dependent variable, researchers are not detecting that effect 83% of the time, and when an independent variable has a medium effect, researchers are not detecting it 43% of the time.

One way for researchers to improve the likelihood of detecting the effect of an independent variable is by conducting high-power research; one way of achieving statistical power is by having an adequate sample size. To determine sample size, researchers must answer four questions. First, what is the critical effect size for their study—the effect size they are trying to detect with the research? There are several approaches to answering this question. One approach is for the researchers to decide on the smallest effect that they consider to be important to the theory or application that your research is testing. For example, setting the critical effect size at $r = .25$ says that any correlation smaller than .25 is equivalent to a correlation of zero for the purpose of answering the research question. A second approach to deciding on the critical effect size is to use the average effect size found in previous research using the independent and dependent variables being studied; mean effect sizes for a body of research can be calculated using meta-analysis (see chap. 18, this volume). Finally, lacking any theoretical, applied, or empirical basis for setting a critical effect size, researchers could simply use a medium effect size and probably be fine. For example, Lipsey (1990) found that the average effect size found across 186 meta-analyses of research on mental health and educational interventions fell in the middle of the medium range.

The second question to answer is: What alpha level should be used? The smaller the alpha (e.g., .01 vs. .05), the lower the statistical power will be and the larger the sample needed to achieve a given level of power. By convention, most research involves an alpha set at .05. The third question is: Should a one-tailed or two-tailed statistical test be used? A two-tailed test has less power than a one-tailed test, and so requires a larger sample size to achieve a given level of power. The final question is: What level of power is required? Generally speaking, the higher the power, the better. One would certainly want power to exceed .50, giving a better than 50% chance of detecting an effect; Cohen (1992) suggested a level of .80.

Given the answers to these questions, one can consult any of several sources that provide tables of the sample sizes required for different levels of statistical power (e.g., Cohen, 1988; Kraemer & Thiemann, 1987; Lipsey, 1990). A sample of a particular size represents a trade-off between ease of data collection—smaller samples are easier to deal with in terms of time and money than are larger samples—and protection against making a Type II error—larger samples provide more protection than do smaller samples. However, as Kraemer and Thiemann (1987) pointed out:

> The smaller the sample size, the smaller the power, i. e., the greater the chance of failure. . . . If one proposes to [use] a sample size of 20 or fewer subjects, one must be willing to take a high risk of failure, or be operating in an area in which the critical effect size is large indeed. (p. 27)

Combining Facets of a Multifaceted Construct.   I noted earlier that combining across the facets of a multifaceted construct can obscure the true relationships among variables. It can also lead to Type II errors. If one facet of a construct has a positive correlation with a variable and another facet has a negative correlation, combining the facets may result in the two correlations canceling each other. For example, Johnson, Brems, and Alford-Keating (1997) examined the relationship between religious beliefs and attitudes toward homosexuality. The correlation between beliefs and scores on the overall attitude scale was $r = .10$, which was not statistically significant. However, the correlations between religious beliefs and three components of the attitude scale, which they called *proximity*, *rights*, and *beliefs*, were $r = .24$, .09, and $-.25$, respectively. Researchers should therefore examine the facet-level correlations for a multifaceted construct before combining across the facets.

Heterogeneity of Research Participants.   As discussed later, having a group of research participants that is diverse in terms of gender, ethnicity, and other characteristics contributes to the external validity of the research. However, such diversity can also be a problem: If these characteristics are correlated with the dependent variable in the research, the variance of the scores will be increased. Because the denominator (the error term) in the calculation of statistical tests such as the *t* test is a function of the variance of the scores on the dependent variable, greater variance leads to smaller values for the test statistic and so to a lower likelihood of meeting the criterion for statistical significance. There are two possible solutions to this problem. One is to keep the participant sample as homogeneous as possible, which has the disadvantage of making the external validity of the results more difficult to assess. The second solution is to ensure that enough members of each group are represented in the sample to treat group membership as an independent variable in a factorial design (see chap. 12, this volume). This procedure removes variance due to group membership and the group by independent variable interaction from the error term, resulting in a more sensitive statistical test.

Overlooking Curvilinear Relationships.   Some statistics, such as the correlation coefficient r and the t test, assume that the relationship between two variables is linear; that is, that scores on one variable increase or decrease steadily as scores on the other variable increase. If there is a curvilinear relationship between two variables, for example, if scores on one variable rise and level off, or rise, level off, and then fall as scores on the other variable increase, statistics that assume linear relationships will not accurately represent the relationship between the variables. For example, Hynie and Lydon (1996) noted that much of the research on the correlation between sexual attitudes and contraceptive behavior obtained null results, so they hypothesized that the relationship might be curvilinear rather than linear. They found a nonsignificant correlation of $r = .02$ between sexual attitude scores and consistency of contraceptive use. They also found that adding a curvilinear term for sexual attitudes to a multiple regression analysis (see chap. 13, this volume) explained 25% of the variance in contraceptive behavior: Women with extremely negatively and extremely positive sexual attitudes were less consistent in their use of effective contraception than were women with moderate sexual attitudes. As these findings illustrate, unless there is evidence that a relationship between two variables is linear, researchers should consider the possibility of a curvilinear relationship.

Accepting the Null Hypothesis

Occasionally a researcher obtains null results despite theoretical and empirical evidence suggesting that the research hypothesis should be supported. Under such circumstances, one should require very strong evidence that the independent variable did not, in fact, have an effect (e.g., Shaughnessy & Zechmeister, 1990). If the study were well designed, had sufficient statistical power, and other possible sources of Type II error can be ruled out, three other factors can provide evidence supporting a true null result. One factor is that the study resulted in a very small effect size; the closer it is to zero, the less likely it is that the independent variable had an effect. The second factor is consistency with other research that produced null results. However, given that studies finding null results are rarely published (Greenwald, 1975), research providing evidence for the convergent validity of null results might be difficult to find. Finally, replication research can provide evidence to confirm the null result. Such replications should not only give the independent variable a fair chance of having an effect and so overturn the initial null result, but should also bend over backward to give the independent variable an opportunity to have an effect; in essence, the deck should be stacked as much in favor of the research hypothesis as good research procedures allow. If the independent variable still has no observable effect under even the most favorable conditions, it probably has no effect at all (Mook, 1983).

EXTERNAL VALIDITY

The concept of external validity can be expressed as a question: Are the findings of a study specific to the conditions under which the study was conducted, or do they represent general principles of behavior that apply under a wide-ranging set of conditions? Cook and Campbell (1979) identified two aspects of external validity. One aspect they referred to as *generalizing across*, which refers to the question of whether the results of a study pertain equally to more than one setting, population, or subpopulation, such as to both men and women. The other aspect they called *generalizing to*, which refers to the question of whether the results of a study pertain to a particular setting or population, such as sex offenders. In this discussion, these two aspects of external validity are referred to as *generalizability* and *ecological validity*, respectively. Vidmar (1979) suggested that external validity has three components: a structural component that is relevant to both generalizability and ecological validity, and functional and conceptual components that are more relevant to ecological validity. These components, which are the focus of this section, are defined in Table 4.2.

The Structural Component

The structural component of external validity is concerned with the method by which a study is carried out, including factors such as the setting in which the study is conducted, the research procedures used, and the nature of the participant sample. The findings of a particular study are high on the generalizability aspect

TABLE 4.2
The Structural, Functional, and Conceptual Components of External Validity

Component	Focus	Issue Addressed
Structural	Methodology	Are the results of research consistent across variations in settings, procedures, populations, and so on?
Functional	Psychological processes	Are the psychological processes that operate in research settings similar to those operating in applicable natural settings?
Conceptual	Research question	Is the research question under investigation one of importance in the applicable natural setting?

Note. From *Principles of Research in Behavioral Science* (p. 469), by Bernard E. Whitley, Jr., 1996, Mountain View, CA: Mayfield. Copyright 1996 by Mayfield. Reprinted with permission.

of external validity to the extent that they remain consistent when tested in new studies that use different methods. That is, studies that test the same hypothesis should get reasonably similar results regardless of differences in settings (e.g., laboratory or field), research procedures (e.g., operational definitions), and research participants (e.g., college students or factory workers). Research findings are high on the ecological validity aspect of external validity to the extent that they can be replicated in a particular natural setting, using the procedures that are normally used in that setting and with the people who are usually found in the setting. A large number of structural factors can influence the external validity of research (e.g., Whitley, 1996, chap. 14). This discussion focuses on three of the most commonly discussed: research setting, participant samples, and research procedures.

The Research Setting.   Laboratory research has often been criticized, with some justification, for its artificiality, which is often equated with a lack of external validity, especially ecological validity (e.g., Argyris, 1980; Sears, 1986). However, an often overlooked aspect of this issue is that conducting research in a natural setting is no guarantee of its external validity (e.g., Banaji & Crowder, 1989). That is, any research carried out in a natural environment is done so in a particular setting, with a particular set of participants using a particular set of procedures, just as in laboratory research. Therefore, the results are no more or less likely than those of a laboratory experiment to apply to other settings (either natural or laboratory), participants, or procedures. As Oakes (1972) noted regarding participant populations, "*any* population one may sample is 'atypical' with respect to some behavioral phenomenon. But the point is that we cannot really say a priori what population is 'more typical' " (p. 962; italics original). Banaji and Crowder (1989) suggested that generalizability and ecological validity are independent dimensions of research and gave examples of natural setting studies with low generalizability and of artificial setting studies with high generalizability.

Convenience Sampling.   Most sexuality research uses convenience sampling; that is, participants are chosen on the basis of availability rather than on the basis of representativeness of the population as a whole or of a particular subpopulation. The most convenient participants for most researchers are college students (e.g., Wiederman & Hurd, 1999), which has led to the assumption that the results of such research are ungeneralizable to other populations (e.g., Sears, 1986). As Sears noted, late adolescents are different from the population in general and from specific populations of interest to many applied researchers. College students are not even representative of late adolescents in general. To the extent that the participants in research are different from the population to which the results of the research might be applied, the research is low on the structural aspect of ecological validity. Because only a relatively small amount of research is intended to be applied solely to college students, their use as research participants is often taken as an a priori indicator of low ecological validity.

Although the most ecologically representative participant sample consists of people from the natural setting of interest, these people are not always available for research. However, for some research, an alternative strategy may be to carefully select college students for similarity to the people in the natural setting of interest. Gordon, Slade, and Schmitt (1986), for example, suggested employing research participants with demographic, personality, and interest profiles as similar as possible to those of members of the natural setting population or using older, nontraditional students as research participants.

Restricted Sampling. Sometimes participant samples are restricted to one category of persons, such as men, people of European descent, or young adults (see chap. 20, this volume). For example, in a content analysis of research published in *The Journal of Sex Research* and *Archives of Sexual Behavior*, Wiederman, Maynard, and Fretz (1996) found that, although 87% of the studies had included White participants, only 46% had included African-American participants, 25%, Latino participants, and 19%, Asian participants. The age of participants is also frequently restricted: Wiederman and Hurd (1999) found that the most common sample in research published in *The Journal of Sex Research* consisted of college student participants. However, men and women are about equality represented in sexuality research, with 79% of studies including male participants and 67% including female participants (Wiederman et al., 1996, unpublished data). Thus, it may be difficult to generalize much of psychological research across subpopulations because of the predominance of White college students as research participants. Nonetheless, sexuality research may be more inclusive in terms of participant characteristics than some other areas of behavioral science, such as psychology (Gannon, Luchetta, Rhodes, Pardie, & Segrist, 1992; Graham, 1992).

Volunteer Participants. People who volunteer for research differ on a number of characteristics from those who do not volunteer (see chap. 5, this volume), potentially limiting the generalizability of results to people with similar characteristics. Even when people are required to participate in research, as are many introductory psychology students, elements of volunteerism remain. People are generally allowed to choose from several experiments, and certain types of people are attracted to certain types of studies. For example, men are more likely to volunteer for studies on *masculine* topics such as power and competition, and women for *feminine* topics such as revealing feelings and moods (Signorella & Vegega, 1984). People who volunteer for sex research are more sexually experienced and have more liberal sexual attitudes than nonvolunteers (e.g., Strassberg & Lowe, 1995). Because participants can withdraw from research after they learn about the procedures to be used, they can *devolunteer*. Wolchik, Braver, and Jensen (1985), for example, found that volunteer rates for sex research dropped from 67% to 30% for men and from 38% to 13% for women when the procedures required some undressing. These problems point out the importance of reporting participant refusal and dropout rates and of taking the characteristics of survivors into account when interpreting the results of a study. Those results may only apply to people with certain characteristics.

Research Procedures. Argyris (1980) and others have contended that the setting, tasks, and procedures of laboratory experiments are artificial and therefore do not generalize to real-world phenomena. Sears (1986) suggested that much of this artificiality derives from dependence on college students as research participants, which leads researchers to use artificial, academic-like tasks that differ considerably from those that most people perform in natural settings. In addition, laboratory research requires participants to take a short-term time perspective on tasks; unlike natural situations, participants generally suffer no consequences for mistakes or harm done to others (Fromkin & Streufert, 1976). When participants interact with people other than the experimenter, these people are usually strangers—confederates of the experimenter or ad hoc groups of other research participants—rather than members of natural acquaintance networks. The demands of experimental control may require artificial means of communication between subjects, such as intercoms or the observation of a videotaped stimulus person rather than face-to-face interaction. Such artificial conditions could elicit artificial responses from research participants.

Another aspect of procedural artificiality is that dependent measures are often assessed in ways that are highly artificial and restrictive to the participants' behavior. For example, in the typical laboratory experiment on the effect of viewing violent pornography on men's aggression toward women, a female confederate "angers and provokes" (Fisher & Grenier, 1994, p. 32) the male participant before he watches a pornographic film. Afterward, the participant is instructed to administer electrical shocks to the confederate when she makes mistakes on a task. Fisher and Grenier noted that the restriction on participants' behavioral options to punishing the confederate limited the ecological validity of the previous research because in most naturally occurring situations people have the opportunity to either avoid confrontation or talk out their differences. In a variation on the standard paradigm, Fisher and Grenier provided their participants with two options in addition to giving the shock: speaking with the confederate and having no further interaction with her. Only 14% of the participants chose to administer the shock, contradicting the results of much previous research.

Artificiality is not without its advantages, however. For example, experiments can dissect a complex, naturally occurring variable into its component parts to determine which of the components is crucial to the variable's relationship with another variable. This finer grained knowledge increases our understanding of the relationship and may help to tie it into a theoretical network (Mook, 1983). Thus, by constructing a set of videotapes that independently manipulate the sexual and violent content of films, researchers can estimate the degree to which sexual and violent content each affect responses such as aggression.

The Functional Component

The functional component of external validity addresses the question of the extent to which the psychological and social processes that affect behavior in the research situation are similar to those that affect behavior in the natural situation. Jung (1981) cited experimental research on the effects of TV violence on aggressive behavior as an example of research that is relatively low on functional verisimilitude. Although the experiments are high on the structural component of external validity because they use real TV programs, the experimental requirement of random assignment of participants to conditions undermines the functional component. Random assignment is designed to balance individual differences across groups. However, if individual differences determine who does and does not watch violent TV programming in natural situations, the experiment no longer accurately models the natural process, and functional verisimilitude is lost. One such factor related to watching violent TV programs is trait aggressiveness. People who have a history of aggressiveness prefer violent TV programs to nonviolent programs (Bushman, 1995). A similar criticism could be made of studies of the influence of sexually explicit films on aggression: Realistic films are shown under unrealistic conditions.

The Conceptual Component

The conceptual component of external validity deals with the question of the degree to which the problems studied in research on a topic correspond to problems found in the natural situation. The conceptual component is therefore especially important for researchers who want their work to be applied to real-world problems. If the researcher's conceptual system does not match that of the policymakers or others who are expected to implement the research in the applied setting, the results of the research will not be used. Ruback and Innes (1988) suggested two ways in which the research conceptions of researchers and policymakers differ. The first difference is found in policymakers' need for research involving independent variables that they can change. These variables, which Ruback and Innes called *policy variables*, may or may not be the most important determinants of behavior in a situation. However, they pointed out, if a variable cannot be changed, knowledge about its effects cannot lead to policy changes. Researchers more often focus on variables that can be manipulated in the laboratory, which Ruback and Innes called *estimator variables*. However, these variables are not useful to policymakers because there is no way that policymakers can control them. For example, in terms of factors affecting condom use, a person's attitudes toward condoms is an estimator variable because policymakers cannot control it. However, the availability of condoms can be controlled, and so it is a policy variable.

The second difference is in what Ruback and Innes (1988) referred to as the utility of the dependent variables used; that is, the degree to which the behavior studied is of direct interest to the policymaker. For example, sex educators may be more interested in students' sexual behavior than in the students' perceptions of their parents' beliefs about sexuality, which may be of greater interest to the researcher because of its empirical or theoretical importance. Ruback and Innes' analysis suggests that, for research to be high on the conceptual component of external validity, it must be high on both the number of policy variables investigated and the utility of the dependent variables.

Relationships Among the Components of External Validity

The structural, functional, and conceptual components of external validity are not entirely independent of one another; all three are necessary to accurately model a natural situation. One aspect of this interdependence is illustrated by Hendrick and Jones' (1972) distinction between chronic and acute manipulations of independent variables. Chronic manipulations are those found in natural situations and that often result from an accumulation of small effects over time, have been experienced for some time, and are expected to continue into the future; examples are anxiety, self-esteem, and stress. However, experiments normally involve acute manipulations, which result from a single event, occur relatively suddenly, and end with the research situation; in fact, ethical considerations require that they end then. For example, the use of threat of electric shock to manipulate sexual performance anxiety in the laboratory constitutes an acute manipulation of such anxiety. Acute manipulations thus lack structural verisimilitude because of their time-limited nature. This time limitation may, in turn, call other aspects of ecological validity into question.

Conceptual verisimilitude questions the equivalence of long- and short-term anxiety at the construct level and finds that they are probably not equivalent (e.g., Spielberger, Vagg, Barker, Donham, & Westberry, 1980). Functional verisimilitude questions whether the processes involving long- and short-term anxiety are equivalent and finds that they are probably not (e.g., Millman, 1968). One threat to external validity may therefore imply others. Conversely, conceptual verisimilitude may require structural verisimilitude; for example, the study of policy-relevant variables may often be practical only in natural settings.

RELATIONSHIPS AMONG THE TYPES OF VALIDITY

Although this discussion addressed each of the types of validity separately, it is important to note that they are interrelated (Cook & Campbell, 1979; Wampold et al., 1990). Internal validity, construct validity, theoretical validity, and statistical conclusion validity all function to assist the researcher in avoiding false conclusions about the effects of an independent variable. Internal validity allows the researcher to rule out the influence of factors other than the independent variable, construct validity ensures that manipulations and measures are not contaminated with irrelevant factors (confounds), statistical conclusion validity safeguards the accuracy of inferences drawn about populations from samples, and theoretical validity provides theories with a fair opportunity to be tested. Hypothesis validity, in requiring explicit hypotheses, clearly delineates the statistical tests to be conducted and the expected outcomes of the tests, allowing the researcher to draw valid conclusions about whether the hypotheses were supported. Construct validity and external validity assist the researcher in making appropriate generalizations about the results of the research.

All six types of validity are therefore important to drawing valid conclusions from research; however, it is impossible to simultaneously maximize all types of validity in any one study (McGrath, 1981). This problem is perhaps most clearly illustrated by the tension between internal and construct validity on the one hand, which call for strict control over the research situation and thereby result in a high degree of artificiality in the research, and external validity on the other hand, which has naturalism in research settings and procedures as one of its foci.

Because of the conflicting demands among some forms of validity, researchers must choose which are the most important for the research they want to conduct and then design their studies to maximize the more important forms of validity for a given study and optimize the others. For example, based on Cook and Campbell's (1979) analysis, basic and applied researchers might give different priorities to the types of validity. Because basic researchers are most interested in determining causal relationships among variables, their order of priority might be internal validity, theoretical validity, construct validity, hypothesis validity, statistical conclusion validity, and external validity. In contrast, applied researchers are often most interested in the effectiveness and generalizability of treatments, so their order of priority might be internal validity, external validity, construct validity of effects (dependent variables), hypothesis validity, statistical conclusion validity, construct validity of causes (independent variables), and theoretical validity.

Despite the differences in these priorities, Cook and Campbell (1979) remarked that, although there will be a trade-off between them, internal validity should take precedence in research design. Whether the research is being conducted to test a theoretical proposition in a laboratory setting or test the effectiveness of a treatment in a natural setting, the researcher's basic goal is to draw valid conclusions about the effect of the independent variable. It is only by being able to rule out plausible alternative explanations for effects—that is, by maintaining appropriate standards of internal validity—that the researcher can achieve this goal. No matter how well the research meets the criteria for the other types of validity, its results are useless if one cannot be confident of the accuracy of the conclusions drawn from them.

SUGGESTED READINGS

The definitive work on internal, construct, statistical conclusion, and external validity is, of course, Cook and Campbell's (1979) book, and Kazdin (1992) provided an excellent discussion of their application to intervention research. Both sources also discuss threats to validity not included in this chapter. Wampold et al. (1990) provided an introduction to the concept of hypothesis validity, Carver (1989) discussed the ramifications of multifaceted constructs, and Wells and Windschitl (1999) discussed the question of stimulus sampling. Kazdin (1992) provided a thorough discussion of manipulation checks, and Whitley (1996) included an extensive discussion of external validity. Cohen (1992) provided a brief introduction to the concept of statistical power, and Kraemer and Thiemann (1987) and Lipsey (1990) provided guidelines for calculating the sample size needed to achieve a given level of statistical power. Finally, Grimm and Yarnold (1995) compiled a set of very readable introductions to understanding various multivariate statistics.

REFERENCES

Argyris, C. (1980). *Inner contradictions of rigorous research*. New York: Academic Press.

Banaji, M. R., & Crowder, R. G. (1989). The bankruptcy of everyday memory. *American Psychologist, 44*, 1185–1193.

Braver, M. C. W., & Braver, S. L. (1988). Statistical treatment of the Solomon four-group design: A meta-analytic approach. *Psychological Bulletin, 104*, 150–154.

Bushman, B. J. (1995). Moderating role of trait aggressiveness in the effects of violent media on aggression. *Journal of Personality and Social Psychology, 69*, 950–960.

Carver, C. S. (1989). How should multifaceted personality constructs be tested? Issues illustrated by self-monitoring, attributional style, and hardiness. *Journal of Personality and Social Psychology, 56*, 577–585.

Cohen, J. (1988). *Statistical power analysis for the behavioral sciences* (2nd ed.). Hillsdale, NJ: Lawrence Erlbaum Associates.

Cohen, J. (1992). A power primer. *Psychological Bulletin, 112*, 155–159.

Cook, T. D., & Campbell, D. T. (1979). *Quasi-experimentation: Design and analysis issues for field settings*. Chicago: Rand McNally.

Cook, T. D., Gruder, C. L., Hennigan, K. M., & Flay, B. R. (1979). History of the sleeper effect: Some logical pitfalls in accepting the null hypothesis. *Psychological Bulletin, 86*, 662–679.

Cooper, J., & Fazio, R. H. (1984). A new look at dissonance theory. *Advances in Experimental Social Psychology, 17*, 229–262.

Cowan, G., & Dunn, K. F. (1994). What themes in pornography lead to perceptions of the degradation of women? *The Journal of Sex Research, 31*, 11–21.

Dobson, K. S. (1985). The relationship between anxiety and depression. *Clinical Psychology Review, 5*, 307–324.

Eagly, A. H., & Carli, L. L. (1981). Sex of researcher and sex-typed communications as determinants of sex differences in influenceability: A meta-analysis of social influence studies. *Psychological Bulletin, 90*, 1–20.

Festinger, L. (1957). *A theory of cognitive dissonance*. Stanford, CA: Stanford University Press.

Fisher, W. A., & Grenier, G. (1994). Violent pornography, antiwoman thoughts, and antiwoman acts: In search of reliable effects. *The Journal of Sex Research, 31*, 23–38.

Fontenelle, G. A., Phillips, A. P., & Lane, D. M. (1985). Generalizing across stimuli as well as subjects: A neglected aspect of external validity. *Journal of Applied Psychology, 70*, 101–107.

Fromkin, L. H., & Streufert, S. (1976). Laboratory experimentation. In M. D. Dunnette (Ed.), *Handbook of industrial and organizational psychology* (pp. 415–465). Chicago: Rand McNally.

Gannon, L., Luchetta, T., Rhodes, K., Pardie, L., & Segrist, D. (1992). Sex bias in psychological research: Progress or complacency? *American Psychologist, 47*, 389–396.

Gordon, M. E., Slade, L. A., & Schmitt, N. (1986). The "science of the sophomore" revisited: From conjecture to empiricism. *Academy of Management Review, 11*, 191–207.

Graham, S. (1992). "Most of the subjects were white and middle class": Trends in published research on African-Americans in selected APA journals, 1970–1989. *American Psychologist, 47*, 629–639.

Greene, E., & Loftus, E. F. (1984). What's in the news? The influence of well-publicized news events on psychological research and courtroom trials. *Basic and Applied Social Psychology, 5*, 211–221.

Greenwald, A. G. (1975). Consequences of prejudice against the null hypothesis. *Psychological Bulletin, 82*, 1–20.

Grimm, L. G., & Yarnold, P. R. (Eds.). (1995). *Reading and understanding multivariate statistics*. Washington, DC: American Psychological Association.

Hendrick, C., & Jones, R. A. (1972). *The nature of theory and research in social psychology*. New York: Academic Press.

Hynie, M., & Lydon, J. E. (1996). Sexual attitudes and contraceptive behavior revisited: Can there be too much of a good thing? *The Journal of Sex Research, 33*, 127–134.

Johnson, M. E., Brems, C., & Alford-Keating, P. (1997). Personality correlates of homophobia. *Journal of Homosexuality, 34*(1), 57–69.

Jung, J. (1981). Is it possible to measure generalizability from laboratory to life, and is it really that important? In I. Silverman (Ed.), *Generalizing from laboratory to life* (pp. 39–49). San Francisco: Jossey-Bass.

Kazdin, A. E. (1992). *Research design in clinical psychology* (2nd ed.). New York: Macmillan.

Kirk, R. E. (1982). *Experimental design: Procedures for the behavioral sciences* (2nd ed.). Belmont, CA: Brooks/Cole.

Kite, M. E., & Whitley, B. E., Jr. (1996). Sex differences in attitudes toward homosexual persons, behavior, and civil rights: A meta-analysis. *Personality and Social Psychology Bulletin, 22*, 336–353.

Kite, M. E., & Whitley, B. E., Jr. (1998). Do heterosexual women and men differ in their attitudes toward homosexuality? A conceptual and methodological analysis. In G. M. Herek (Ed.), *Stigma and sexual orientation: Understanding prejudice against lesbians, gay men, and bisexuals* (pp. 39–61). Thousand Oaks, CA: Sage.

Kraemer, H. C., & Thiemann, S. (1987). *How many subjects?* Newbury Park, CA: Sage.

LaMar, L., & Kite, M. E. (1998). Sex differences in attitudes toward gay men and lesbians: A multidimensional perspective. *The Journal of Sex Research, 35*, 189–196.

Lipsey, M. W. (1990). *Design sensitivity*. Newbury Park, CA: Sage.

Maher, B. A. (1978). Stimulus sampling in clinical research: Representative design reviewed. *Journal of Consulting and Clinical Psychology, 46*, 643–647.

McGrath, J. E. (1981). Dilemmatics: The study of research choices and dilemmas. *American Behavioral Scientist, 25*, 179–210.

Millman, S. (1968). Anxiety, comprehension, and susceptibility to social influence. *Journal of Personality and Social Psychology, 9*, 251–256.

Mook, D. G. (1983). In defense of external invalidity. *American Psychologist, 38*, 379–387.

Oakes, W. (1972). External validity and the use of real people as subjects. *American Psychologist, 27*, 959–962.

Roosa, M. W., Reyes, L., Reinholtz, C., & Angelini, P. J. (1998). Measurement of women's childhood sexual abuse experiences: An empirical demonstration of the impact of choice of measure on estimates of incidence rates and of relationships with pathology. *The Journal of Sex Research, 35,* 225–233.

Rosenthal, R., & Rosnow, R. L. (1991). *Essentials of behavioral research* (2nd ed.). New York: McGraw-Hill.

Rossi, J. S. (1990). Statistical power of psychological research: What have we gained in 20 years? *Journal of Consulting and Clinical Psychology, 58,* 646–656.

Ruback, R. B., & Innes, C. A. (1988). The relevance and irrelevance of psychological research: The example of prison crowding. *American Psychologist, 43,* 683–693.

Sears, D. O. (1986). College sophomores in the laboratory: Influences of a narrow data base on social psychology's view of human nature. *Journal of Personality and Social Psychology, 51,* 515–530.

Shaughnessy, J. J., & Zechmeister, E. B. (1990). *Research methods in psychology* (2nd ed.). New York: McGraw-Hill.

Signorella, M. L., & Vegega, M. E. (1984). A note on gender stereotyping of research topics. *Personality and Social Psychology Bulletin, 10,* 107–109.

Spielberger, C. D., Vagg, P. R., Barker, L. R., Donham, G. W., & Westberry, L. G. (1980). The factor structure of the State-Trait Anxiety Inventory. In I. G. Saronson & C. D. Spielberger (Eds.), *Stress and anxiety* (Vol. 7, pp. 95–109). Washington, DC: Hemisphere.

Stone, J., Aronson, E., Crain, A. L., Winslow, M. P., & Fried, C. B. (1994). Inducing hypocrisy as a means of encouraging young adults to use condoms. *Personality and Social Psychology Bulletin, 20,* 116–128.

Strassberg, D. S., & Lowe, K. (1995). Volunteer bias in sexuality research. *Archives of Sexual Behavior, 24,* 369–382.

Vidmar, N. (1979). The other issues in jury simulation research: A commentary with particular reference to defendant character studies. *Law and Human Behavior, 3,* 95–106.

Wampold, B. E., Davis, B., & Good, R. H., III. (1990). Hypothesis validity of clinical research. *Journal of Consulting and Clinical Psychology, 58,* 360–367.

Weinfurt, K. P. (1995). Multivariate analysis of variance. In L. G. Grimm & P. R. Yarnold (Eds.), *Reading and understanding multivariate statistics* (pp. 245–276). Washington, DC: American Psychological Association.

Wells, G. L., & Windschitl, P. D. (1999). Stimulus sampling and social psychological experimentation. *Personality and Social Psychology Bulletin, 25,* 1115–1125.

Wiederman, M. W., & Hurd, C. (1999, November). *College student samples in published sexuality research: 1980–1997.* Paper presented at the annual meeting of the Society for the Scientific Study of Sexuality, St. Louis, MO.

Wiederman, M. W., Maynard, C., & Fretz, A. (1996). Ethnicity in 25 years of published sexuality research: 1971–1995. *The Journal of Sex Research, 33,* 339–342.

Whitley, B. E., Jr. (1996). *Principles of research in behavioral science.* Mountain View, CA: Mayfield.

Wolchik, S. A., Braver, S. L., & Jensen, K. (1985). Volunteer bias in erotica research: Effects of intrusiveness of measure and sexual background. *Archives of Sexual Behavior, 14,* 93–107.

Wulfert, E., & Wan, C. K. (1995). Safer sex intentions and condom use viewed from a health belief, reasoned action, and social cognitive perspective. *The Journal of Sex Research, 32,* 299–311.

DATA COLLECTION

5

▼▼▼▼▼▼▼

Sampling Considerations

Michael P. Dunne
Queensland University of Technology

Throughout the history of quantitative sexuality research, the validity of many studies has been questioned because the field has had difficulty reaching one of the basic requirements of any science: that, other things being equal, different investigators should reach consistent conclusions. Amid the lively debates about the meaning of results from sexuality research, one of the most justifiable criticisms concerns the ways in which samples have been selected and recruited. In this chapter, I review aspects of the history of sampling in sexuality research, describe standard methods for sample selection, and give examples where these have been applied. Finally, I discuss biases that arise from self-selection, and consider ways in which these problems can be minimized.

A BRIEF HISTORY OF SAMPLING IN SEXUALITY RESEARCH

Sexuality research evolved in fascinating directions during the 20th century (Nye, 1999). In many ways, the quantitative survey tradition lies at the dry end of a distribution of thinking about sexuality. However, it developed as a major focus of activity for many reasons; scientific determinism became increasingly strong, expanding democratization increased demand for knowledge about the lives of the general population, and the HIV/AIDS epidemic and other sex-related health problems introduced an important epidemiological imperative.

As with any social survey approach, one of the primary goals is to draw inferences from the sample to the population. Considering the collective effort from many surveys, however, the picture that emerges is more opaque than clear pri-

marily because estimates of the prevalence of important sexual events or characteristics vary widely. The problem is not that estimates vary—after all, diversity
makes life interesting—but rather that doubts arise when studies with ostensibly
similar questions and samples conducted at the same time produce quite different
estimates. Is this variation random, is it due to systematic methodological error, or
does it have meaning for the substantive research questions under consideration?

The gold standard in survey sampling is a random selection procedure in which
each person in the population has a known probability of being chosen. In this approach, variation in sample estimates can be understood quite clearly. We assume
that the estimates in any particular survey fall somewhere on a normal distribution
around, and occasionally on, the supposed true value. The direction and magnitude of sampling errors can be measured if we know the population parameters
(e.g., the true average age of first intercourse and its variance). Although these are
usually not known in advance, probability theory facilitates the calculation of
confidence intervals that allow us to evaluate the precision of estimates, and to
compare the extent to which a single sample estimate overlaps (or lies outside) the
range of estimates from other similar studies (Kish, 1965; Laumann, Gagnon, Michael, & Michaels, 1994; Thompson, 1997).

Generalizations about the sexual experiences, attitudes, and lifestyles of populations have been seriously hampered by ad hoc approaches to sampling. Samples
have often been used without regard to the limitations they place on statistical inference. Four of the most common problems are:

1. coverage error, in which significant proportions of the population are absent from lists used to draw the sample;
2. selection on the dependent variable, in which participants are chosen because of their sexual characteristics or from closely correlated attributes;
3. nonresponse error, in which individuals are lost after selection because of
   inaccessibility or refusal; and
4. measurement error, in which there is a difference between the true value
   and the sample mean due to imprecise or biased measurement.

The impact of the first two of these problems is illustrated through the following
examples of contentious issues in sexuality research (i.e., the rates of male homosexuality and childhood sexual abuse experiences among females). Nonresponse
error is discussed later in this chapter, and measurement error in sexuality research is considered elsewhere in this book (see chap. 3).

SELECTION BIAS IN ESTIMATES OF HOMOSEXUAL EXPERIENCE

The usual starting point for discussions of systematic sampling error in sexuality
surveys is the studies by Kinsey and colleagues from the 1940s and 1950s (see
Brecher & Brecher, 1986; Cochran, Mosteller, & Tukey, 1954; Laumann et al.,

1994). In Kinsey, Pomeroy, and Martin's (1948) landmark survey of 5,300 males, there was no systematic random sampling. Rather, 163 separate groups were approached, including college students and staff, seven groups of institutionalized males (juvenile delinquents, adult prisoners [including many male prostitutes], and one group of mental patients), and assorted others including high school students, speech therapy patients, conscientious objectors (for army service), hitchhikers, and people from three rooming houses. A serious limitation of the sample was the overreliance on college students. Kinsey estimated that about half of his personal histories were from people recruited following the attendance of "tens of thousands" of people at several hundred college and public lectures given by him and his colleagues (Cochran et al., 1954).

Kinsey's work was followed in the 1970s and 1980s by widely publicized studies that were based on very flawed sampling procedures (Hite, 1981; Janus & Janus, 1993). Those later researchers paid even less attention to representative selection and ignored the significant developments in sampling methods since the 1940s (Laumann et al., 1994). Hite (1981) and Janus and Janus (1993) relied on the worst types of convenience samples, such as readers of magazines, personal contacts of the researchers or their colleagues, and people who approached the researchers and asked to be included.

The extent of the bias that arises from convenience samples is clear from subsequent studies that have utilized more conventional sampling methods. For example, Kinsey's estimate of the proportion of males with any homosexual behavior during adolescence or adulthood (37%) is at least two to three times higher than most other estimates derived from random samples of the general population (ACSF Investigators, 1992; Johnson, Wadsworth, Wellings, & Field, 1994; Laumann et al., 1994). Similarly, Hite's (1981) estimate that 13% of men had a strong homosexual or bisexual preference is at least twice as high as any of the more recent surveys. When estimates in the Janus and Janus (1993) study were compared to similar measures in U.S. national social surveys based on random samples, there was considerable overestimation in the former study, especially for sexual activity among older people (Laumann et al., 1994).

Kinsey et al. (1948) argued that it was not feasible at the time to select a true random sample of the U.S. population, and that his decision to purposely select diverse subgroups (as well as his intensive interview techniques) produced estimates of sexual experience that were truly representative (Cochran et al., 1954). Of course, it is possible that Kinsey's estimates were a valid reflection of American society at that time, and that attribution of the differences to sampling bias is unjustified (after all, sometimes the normative sexual behavior of societies does appear to change at a remarkable rate). However, this appears unlikely. The nature of selection bias on estimates of the behavior of gay males has been convincingly demonstrated by Sandfort (1997), who used four contemporaneous samples of gay men in the Netherlands (see Table 5.1). One group was comprised of (a) gay men from a random sample of the general Dutch population (3.8% were clas-

TABLE 5.1
Comparison of Four Groups of Gay Males

	Sample Type			
Variable	Random (%)	Readers (%)	Member (%)	Gay Cohort (%)
In steady relationship?	71.4	60.8	80.6	61.2
Sexual contact outside primary relationship?	24.4	50.2	65.4	72.7
Regular partner have sex outside relationship?	43.4	69.6	NA	NA
Often have sex with casual partners?	17.5	28.7	NA	33.6

Note. NA = no data available. Random = random sample from the population, Readers = readers of gay/lesbian magazines, Member = members of a community-based gay group, and Gay Cohort = members of an existing health research cohort of gay men.

sifiable as homosexual), whereas the other three groups were (b) readers of a bi-weekly gay/lesbian magazine, (c) randomly selected members of a Dutch gay and lesbian organization, and (d) members of a cohort of gay men involved in a longitudinal health study. After adjusting for age differences, the four groups were compared on a number of measures of sexual relationships and behavior. As shown in Table 5.1, the differences between convenience samples and a random sample in the self-reported sexual experiences of homosexual men are obvious. It is also interesting to note the significant variability among the three different convenience samples, possibly indicating multiple sources of selection bias.

Selection of nonrepresentative samples has a deeper impact beyond error in simple prevalence estimates. Consider, for example, studies of genetic influences on sexual orientation. These behavior genetic surveys, based mainly on interviews with people who are twins, have reported rates of concordance for homosexual orientation among identical twins varying from 20% to 100%, which is an extraordinary range of estimates (Bailey & Pillard, 1991, 1995; Bailey, Dunne, & Martin, 2000; Kallmann, 1952, cited in McKnight, 1997; Whitam, Diamond, & Martin, 1993).

If a trait is mediated by genetic influences, identical twins (who share 100% of their genes) should be more similar than are pairs of fraternal twins (who share 50% of the genes). To date, some studies with reasonably large samples have found significantly greater similarity among identical twins, and it has been estimated that approximately 50% to 60% of the variance in homosexuality among samples of male and female twins may be due to genetic influences (Bailey & Pillard, 1991; Bailey, Pillard, Neale, & Agyei, 1993). Work such as this evokes keen public interest. However, biases in recruitment may strongly affect concordance rates and lead to overestimation of the strength of genetic influences. All of the studies cited earlier recruited twins through homophile networks, the gay press, and word of mouth. With such sampling strategies, it is likely that twins concordant for the trait are more likely to volunteer than are discordant twins, which could introduce subtle ascertainment biases that lead to overestimation of genetic influences (Kendler & Eaves, 1989).

In this respect, it is interesting that the only twin study of this issue that utilized a national sample of twins (4,901 volunteers in a health research cohort who also agreed to participate in a sexuality survey) revealed very low concordance for "nonheterosexuality" (i.e., the twins were not exclusively heterosexual on several Kinsey-scale psychological measures). Concordance rates were 20% for identical males and 24% for identical females (Bailey et al., 2000). These are among the lowest rates yet reported. Although the concordance among identical twin males exceeded that of nonidentical males, analyses of the heritability of homosexual orientation (broadly defined) in this study could not reject the null hypothesis of no genetic influence, which is the first large twin study to report such a finding. It appears that the two types of sampling methods tend to recruit twins with different degrees of homosexual feelings and fantasy, with twins from convenience samples being much more likely to be exclusively homosexual.

Clearly, selection bias creates a problem for inferences about some aspects of sexuality. However, this bias is not consistently observed in all areas, as is evident when we consider studies of the sexual abuse of women.

SELECTION BIAS AND ESTIMATES OF CHILDHOOD SEXUAL ABUSE

Among the numerous studies of childhood sexual abuse of women, estimates of the lifetime prevalence have been found to vary from 6% to 62% (Finkelhor, 1994; Mullen, Romans-Clarkson, Walton, & Herbison, 1988). Although some researchers have proposed a best average estimate of serious intrusive abuse of 20% (Finkelhor, 1994; Fleming, 1997), wide variation around that figure is a far more prominent feature of the research than is agreement on the proposed mean. This has evoked considerable political and scientific debate, including claims that opponents of women's health programs have used the uncertainty surrounding the estimates to hamper political and administrative support for prevention and treatment services (Lynch, 1996).

How much of this variability in reported childhood sexual abuse might be due to systematic biases in sampling, rather than random error? Although there are literally hundreds of prevalence studies with random population samples and different types of nonprobability and convenience samples, other methodological differences cloud comparisons (e.g., widely differing definitions of abuse, different response rates, varying recall periods, and wide ranges in ages of participants). Nevertheless, enough comparable studies are available to form clusters that differ systematically in term of sampling methods.

Finkelhor (1994) reviewed epidemiological data on the prevalence of childhood sexual abuse in 21 countries. Fifteen studies were based on random samples of the general population or student subpopulations, whereas six studies were based on nonrandom samples that varied in the extent of systematic recruitment and representativeness. The average prevalence of childhood sexual abuse reported by females from random samples was 20.9%, whereas the average from the nonrandom samples was 19%, which in this instance suggests that prevalence estimates are not seriously biased by nonrandom sampling strategies.

Many researchers have recruited female college students. Although sampling error has been minimized by studying entire subpopulations (e.g., all first-year students at a particular college) or through random selection, there is reasonable doubt as to whether the findings can be generalized to young people who are not students. Pilkington and Kremer (1995) reviewed 34 studies of women in general or college student populations in the United States, Canada, the United Kingdom, New Zealand, Norway, and South Africa. There was much methodological diversity and wide variation in quality. However, from the published data, I selected all studies that specified a response rate, a reference age for onset of abuse at 18 years of age or younger, and a definition of childhood sexual abuse that included contact and noncontact abuse. Thirteen studies were comparable on these criteria, including seven studies of the general population and six student samples. The average prevalence rates were remarkably similar in the general population samples (27.7%) and student samples (29.8%), which suggests that prevalence rates are not always discrepant in samples drawn from different segments of the population.

In an interesting study, Gorey and Leslie (1997) conducted an integrative review of 16 cross-sectional surveys from the United States or Canada that questioned samples of women about unwanted sexual experiences as a child or adolescent (this included 5 of the 13 studies I selected from Pilkington & Kremer, 1995). Again, Gorey and Leslie found considerable variation in the prevalence estimates. They identified seven methodological variables that might influence prevalence estimates, including breadth of definition of childhood sexual abuse, response rate, sample size, sampling method (random or convenience), type of sample (general or college), and geographic location (United States or Canada). Their regression model explained approximately 50% of the variance in prevalence estimates, but only two methodological variables were statistically significant: breadth of definition of childhood sexual abuse, and response rate (60% or more vs. less than 60%). Neither sampling method nor type of sample explained significant proportions of the variation in prevalence rates.

Together the findings suggest that deviation from random population sampling per se is not a major cause of the very large degree of variation among studies in prevalence estimates of childhood sexual abuse among females. At the very least, there is no obvious bias inherent in the use of college samples. However, this does not mean that all or most studies of childhood sexual abuse are likely to have minimal sampling biases. The work just mentioned was restricted to population-based

TABLE 5.2
Comparison of Childhood Sexual Abuse Experiences Among
a National Random Sample (Australia; Fleming, 1997) and
Health Clinic Clients (Brisbane; Ffrench & Dunne, 1999)

The Perpetrator . . .	Random	Health Clinic
Touched breast or genitals	8%	21%
Made girl touch his genitals	2%	9%
Attempted intercourse	3%	9%
Had intercourse	2%	4%

samples or generally well-conducted studies of large student groups. As a final example of the direction and magnitude of sampling biases, I compared data on childhood sexual abuse from a random sample of the Australian female population (Fleming, 1997) with a sample obtained from self-referred clients of clinics at a women's sexual and reproductive health center in one Australian city (Brisbane; Ffrench & Dunne, 1999). The two studies were comparable in many respects. Precisely the same questions and definitions of perpetrators were used, the sample sizes were comparable (Fleming; $N = 710$, Ffrench & Dunne; $N = 401$), and response rates were similar (Fleming; 65%, Ffrench & Dunne; 60%). Prevalence estimates for four key measures of abuse are shown in Table 5.2. Selection bias in the convenience sample appears to be quite strong.

Summary

Although many aspects of sampling contribute to nonrandom variation in sexuality surveys, two are especially important. First, convenience samples overestimate prevalence because they sample on the dependent variable. Consider that the Kinsey et al. (1948) sample was rich in college students. Although such samples are not necessarily biased, Kinsey relied to a large extent on volunteers who had attended lectures about sexuality, and only a small proportion of these (perhaps 1 in 10) were recruited into the study—mainly through self-referral. These men were probably much more likely than nonparticipants to have diverse sexual experiences. A similar problem is evident in the behavior genetic studies of twins recruited through gay media and social networks. The Brisbane sexual abuse study recruited women at a center specializing in sexual and reproductive health, and thus was sampling a group in which significant proportions may have had clinical problems resulting from, or related to, sexual abuse.

The second major source of bias is coverage error (Thompson, 1997). If participants are recruited from institutions such as prisons or psychiatric hospitals, it is unlikely that the distribution of various measures of recent sexual experience in those parts of a sample frame would overlap with the general population. Similarly, the Brisbane clinic survey would not represent (most probably) the majority of women who do not attend such clinics.

Criticism of convenience sampling is mainly concerned with limits to inference about the general population; it does not amount to a wholesale rejection of studies based on other than random samples. If social science relied solely on research designs that are free from selection bias, we would eliminate a vast portion of fruitful research, and sexual science in particular would have a very narrow focus. However, the sometimes difficult history of this field highlights the importance of careful choice in sampling designs so that they are appropriate to the questions and available resources.

MAKING DECISIONS ABOUT SAMPLE SELECTION IN SEXUALITY RESEARCH

As a researcher, consider these first-order questions: Do you want to generalize? If so, how broadly? Is your work exploratory, or do you want to test hypotheses? Are there special subgroups in the population that you want to study in detail? How rare are the phenomena of interest and how widely dispersed in the community? Answers to each of these questions will help determine the nature and size of your sample. Equally, survey sampling will be heavily influenced by answers to second-order questions such as: How much money, time, and expertise do you have? Is there an existing, valid population register from which you can select? What mode of interview or measurement do you prefer? How many people will agree to participate given the methods you have chosen?

Numerous different sampling methods have been applied in sexuality research, and I review the most prominent examples here. Although some methods are clearly superior to others, the appropriateness of each method for any individual study is a matter of judgment for the researcher. Answers to each of the prior questions can help determine the best option.

SAMPLING METHODS

Two primary classes of methods are used in sexuality research: *probability sampling* and *nonprobability sampling*. As was briefly mentioned, a probability sample has the essential characteristic that every person in a population has a known, nonzero probability of being included in the sample. If correct procedures are followed, randomness in probability samples allows valid inferences to be drawn about populations, and the precision of estimates can be determined. In contrast, a nonprobability sample can be defined most simply as one that does not have this essential feature, and hence there is no clear way of determining the reliability of estimates or the validity of generalizations (Kish, 1965; Levy & Lemeshow, 1997).

A practical reality of research in sexuality is that many types of people are elusive and specific sexual practices are rare. Even with large probability samples, recruitment of subgroups that comprise just 1% or 2% of the population would involve very large surveys that are prohibitively expensive. A third class of sampling methods, called *adaptive sampling*, has been developed; it combines elements of probability sampling with the ability to increase the likelihood that people with special characteristics will be sampled (Blair, 1999; Sudman, Sirken, & Cowan, 1988; Thompson & Seber, 1996).

Before describing the specific sampling designs, common terms need to be defined. *Target population (or universe)* refers to the entire set of individuals to which the findings of the survey are to be extrapolated. *Elementary units* are the individual members of the target population whose characteristics are to be measured. *Source or survey population* is the accessible part of the population from which a sample is to be drawn. Ideally this will be the same as the target population, but in practice the two do not completely overlap. *Sampling frame* refers to the list or computer file in which the elementary units are recorded. Ideally, each element in the population would be included, but often this does not occur. For example, the target population may include all residents in households, but the sampling frame may be a list of addresses through which each element is potentially accessible. In this case, an elementary unit is a person, but the *sampling unit* is the household. *Sampling fraction* is the proportion of the elements in the sampling frame selected for a sample (e.g., if there are 1,000 university students in a list, a sampling faction of 15% would involve selection of 150 individuals).

PROBABILITY SAMPLES

Simple Random Samples

For selection of sampling units to be truly random, every unit (e.g., person, household, telephone number) in the sampling frame should have an equal probability of being selected each time a unit is selected. This is called *unrestricted random sampling* (URS) and is the basis on which most statistical theory is built. However, in this method, there is always a possibility that the same units will be selected more than once. The preferred technique is to use simple random sampling (SRS), where units are selected without replacement. The standard error of estimates in SRS is calculated slightly differently from that in URS by including a "finite population correction" ($1 - n/N$), although if the population is large relative to the sample (as in many cases), then this correction approaches unity and can be omitted.

In SRS, all units in the sampling frame are assigned a number, and units are then chosen randomly. The best manual method is to use random number tables. Consider a small country that has an entire population of 100 physicians specializing in sexually transmitted diseases. Each doctor is numbered from 1 to 100, and the sampling fraction is set at 20%. The researcher could consult a table of random numbers, start at an arbitrary column, and select the first 20 unique two-digit numbers. The doctors with these numbers are selected for the sample. Although this procedure is easy for small studies, the manual processing is arduous and potential for error high if large samples are involved. If the task was to choose 500 general physicians from 10,000, then this is more easily achieved using random number selection functions available in standard software packages such as SYSTAT (Levy & Lemeshow, 1999).

Many SRS designs utilize multistage random sampling, which is necessary when the sampling units are locations (e.g., households) or telephone numbers. Consider household sampling: Once an element has been selected, found to be a valid residential address, and the residents are approached about participation, the first task is to determine the number of eligible people in the household (e.g., English-speaking adults between the ages of 18 and 69 years) and then to select a person for interview. Serious biases may be introduced if the residents make the decision about selection, as cultural factors may dictate, for example, that the oldest male be interviewed.

It is essential that the respondent be selected randomly from the total number of residents. In a British national sexuality survey, Johnson et al. (1994) used a modification of the standard Kish Grid (Kish, 1949). When contact was made, eligible residents were listed in descending order of age, and the interviewers used a grid in which a randomly selected number was provided for each possible number of eligible residents in a household. For example, for households with 2, 3, 4, 5, 6, or 7 eligibles, the person selected could be number 1, 2, 1, 4, 6, or 3. There is differential probability of selection of each individual in large versus small households, although this is handled quite easily during analysis by a weighting procedure that adjusts for household size. The weight in this case would be the reciprocal of the number of eligible people in the household. If the study were a telephone survey and there were multiple nonbusiness telephone numbers in the same household, the data are weighted by the reciprocal of the number of separate phone numbers (Czaja & Blair, 1995). Clearly, an important task for the researcher is to collect information in the interview that is sufficient to derive relevant weights.

Simple random sampling provides the most powerful approach in surveys because it is the only method in which it is possible to achieve unbiased estimates of the means, proportions, and variance (Kish, 1965; for a detailed explication, see Levy & Lemeshow, 1999). Despite the statistical power of the method, SRS has rarely been used in research with human populations primarily because of three issues. First, prior to developments in computing in the 1990s, the construction of exhaustive lists of members of populations was an arduous task, and true randomization of thousands of names or addresses was too inefficient. Second, although some technical difficulties in constructing lists have been reduced in recent years, there is no single sampling frame that can capture an entire population and facilitate the enumeration of each individual. Significant proportions of populations do not have telephones, stable addresses, official registration with government systems, and so forth. Finally, most surveys have many objectives apart from simple estimation of means and prevalence, and often there is special interest in subgroups, some of which are quite rare. SRS approaches offer little help in recruiting sufficient numbers of people in such groups.

I have been unable to locate any surveys related to sexuality that unequivocally satisfy the stringent SRS criterion—that each person in a population has an equal probability of inclusion and is chosen from a complete list of the population—although some studies approximate true randomness. For example, a national survey in France (ACSF, 1992) used a simple random selection of numbers from a national directory list, although as usual the sampling frame excluded people without telephones or those with silent numbers. In one city in New Zealand, and nationally in Australia, postal surveys have used name and address information from (compulsory) electoral rolls that are used in federal parliamentary elections (Fleming, 1997; Mullen, Martin, Anderson, Romans, & Herbison, 1996). If recently collated, these registers contain reliable information on 90% to 95% of the adult population, and it is possible to extract a simple random sample.

Systematic Random Sampling

Conceptually, systematic random sampling is very straightforward. The researcher begins with a list of the population (e.g., names in a telephone directory, students in a school, or patients in a hospital) and estimates the desired sample size, which in turn determines the sampling fraction and the sampling interval (k). The task then is to select every kth element down the list to derive the sample. For example, in a study of the sexual health caseloads of general medical practitioners in Queensland, Australia, Dunne, George, Byrne, and Patten (1995) used a list of all medical practitioners in the state. The list was constructed by a postgraduate medical education center and was believed to be the most valid list of practicing doctors in the state at that time. From 3,266 eligible physicians, we used a one-fifth sampling fraction, and hence selected every fifth doctor down an alphabetical list to extract a final sample of 653. Babbie (1992) suggested that this method is virtually identical to simple random sampling if the list is randomized beforehand. Other types of ordering, such as alphabetical lists, approach randomness. However, many lists are highly nonrandom. An example of the latter is medical record lists, which often are ordered by date of diagnosis or treatment, or patients are grouped in clusters by diagnosis or their treating physician. There may be systematic differences between early or late members of the list, or significant periodicity, where similar types of patients recur at regular intervals.

In the sampling process, randomness is enhanced by one essential step. The element in the first sampling interval must be selected randomly, usually by choosing a random number within that interval and starting from there. Selection then follows at the standard interval k. This type of systematic sampling selects elements that are more evenly spread over the population list than is usually obtained in simple random selection. Therefore, estimates have greater precision especially when populations are small.

Levy and Lemeshow (1999) suggested a method for obtaining a start point that always leads to an unbiased estimates of population parameters. A randomly chosen number j, which lies between 1 and N (population size), is divided by the sampling interval k, and the remainder in the resulting fraction is chosen as the start point. For example, if the list has 150 elements, the sampling interval is 5, 33 is randomly chosen, the start point is 33/5, or $6\frac{3}{5}$, then the start point is 3. If there was no remainder, we begin with the first k (i.e., 5 in this example).

A practical advantage of systematic random sampling is that it is not always necessary to have a complete list at the start of a study. In clinical studies, in particular, it is often desirable to sample from concurrently collected lists. The processes are the same, in that every kth element is selected as people enter the sampling frame, although in this case the start point must be derived from a random number between 1 and k because N is unknown. One drawback of the method is that the initial sampling fraction may be too high or low if there is a major change over time in the flow of people into research sites.

Stratified Random Sampling

So far I have discussed two random sampling methods that achieve the laudable goal of separating the researchers' preconceptions about the population from the processes by which elements are selected into the sample. Although there are obvious advantages to these approaches, they have several major limitations, including difficulty in adequately sampling rare individuals, and the fact that simple random sampling from lists can result in poor dispersion of elements across the sampling frame. Moser and Kalton (1971) cited an example of a simple random selection of towns in Britain that unfortunately had a highly disproportionate number of coastal towns, which, in the judgment of the researchers, would seriously hamper the generalizability of their findings. Dunne et al. (1994) had a similar experience when drawing a large sample of schools for a study of adolescents' sexual behaviors in Australia. In two of seven states and territories included in that study, approximately 85% of the schools were in metropolitan areas, which therefore underrepresented rural towns. When this occurs, one is tempted to redraw the sample so that it is "more representative." However, this breaches the spirit and the statistical assumptions of the random sampling process and introduces a possible bias if this judgment of the researcher is not formally incorporated into the design and analysis.

Stratified random sampling is designed to achieve a high degree of representativeness in samples, and it can ensure that numbers of people are adequate for statistical analysis both within and between strata. The researcher decides which strata of the population should be adequately represented, and then samples are taken randomly from within these strata. In population surveys, the stratification units often are geographic areas, gender, age groups, or ethnicity. Any variable could be used for stratification as long as there were good preexisting data on people with these special characteristics. A critical step is to decide whether the samples within strata are equivalent in size, directly proportional to the relative size of the strata to the total population, or at some point in between.

Proportional Stratification. In a national random-digit dialing telephone survey regarding sexuality in New Zealand, Davis, Yee, Chetwynd, and McMillan (1993) ensured geographic dispersion of their sample by dividing the sampling frame into 14 regions throughout the country that coincided with dialing zones. Within each zone, a sample of random numbers was generated, with the size of the sample of phone numbers within each region proportionate to zonal census data on the numbers of people ages 18 to 54 years. In this method, regional variation in population density does not confound the statistical analyses.

Disproportionate Stratification. The simplest example of this method is where the strata have equal size. For example, if high schools were the initial sampling unit in a national survey of adolescents, equal numbers of schools could be selected from within each state. In the United States, this would result in very great overrepresentation of schools in Alaska or North Dakota and underrepresentation of schools in California or New York. Nevertheless, a benefit of this method is that it produces sufficient data within each stratum for comparative analyses between strata.

In the Australian survey of schools mentioned earlier (Dunne et al., 1994), we were required for political reasons to achieve representation from small states. Rather than select equal numbers of schools in each state, we truncated the ratio in population size. The true ratio of population size in the largest to smallest state was approximately 22 to 1, and we preserved some of this relativity by choosing a ratio of 4 to 1. In subsequent analyses of the full sample data, the estimates were weighted to adjust for differential probability of school selection in each state.

Levy and Lemeshow (1999) summarized three major advantages of stratification over simple random sampling. First, stratification can increase the precision of population estimates. Second, it is possible to determine the precision of estimates within individual strata, which can increase the usefulness of the data for analysis within regions (often an important political issue in large-scale studies). Third, stratified sampling is no more difficult to achieve than simple random sampling, and there is little to lose because the standard errors rarely will exceed those obtained from latter method.

Cluster Sampling

As we have seen, sampling is reasonably straightforward if elements can be chosen from existing lists. In practice, this is often not feasible. For example, if we want to sample adolescents who attend school, then an exhaustive list of schools is relatively easy to construct, but an accurate, complete list of students is not. Similarly, research with people who attend sexual health clinics within a country or state could utilize existing lists of clinics, but not of the primary elements (clients). In these circumstances, representative samples are best achieved through the initial random sampling of groups of elements (clusters), followed by selection of elements within these clusters.

Procedures for cluster sampling vary because populations differ in complexity. Sometimes direct access to individuals can be achieved immediately following cluster selection. Often individuals are located within clusters that are part of larger clusters, and these in turn may be subunits of larger clusters. The simplest approach, simple one-stage cluster sampling, is where clusters are selected randomly, and then all individuals within clusters are invited to participate in a study. When this is not feasible (e.g., if clusters are very large), then simple two-stage cluster sampling is used, in which clusters are randomly sampled, lists of all elements within clusters are obtained, and random samples from within each list are drawn.

In practice, these simple approaches to cluster sampling are rarely used because the clusters are dissimilar in important ways. For example, high schools vary in size; if we took a simple random sample of schools throughout a state, the likelihood of selecting large urban schools would be the same as that for small rural schools. Hence, the probability that any individual in the sampling frame is chosen for the survey would be greater for those from smaller than from larger schools. This could introduce a systematic bias if the sexual experiences of rural and urban adolescents differ. A further limitation is that the precision of estimates (means, proportions, etc.) is poor if a researcher incorrectly assumes that clusters have equivalent size (Levy & Lemeshow, 1999).

These problems are minimized through cluster sampling with probability proportional to size (PPS), where the likelihood of cluster selection is adjusted for the number of elements within each cluster. In large-scale surveys, especially those that require face-to-face contact with respondents, cluster sampling with PPS is the most efficient way to achieve a sample that is truly representative of the population while minimizing biases that arise due to systematic underrepresentation or overrepresentation of people in particular types of clusters (Laumann et al., 1994). This method is illustrated with the following two examples.

In the U.S. National College Health Risk Behavior Survey, the aim was to survey a representative sample of college students and enrich the sample with Latino and African-American students so that patterns in health-risk behaviors of ethnic minorities could be analyzed (Brener, McMahon, Warren, & Douglas, 1999). The first stage sampling frame included all 2- and 4-year colleges in the United States.

From this list, 148 institutions (clusters) were selected from 16 strata formed on the basis of the relative percentage of these ethnic minority students, and presidents of these colleges were approached for their cooperation. Once this was achieved, the colleges provided lists of all undergraduate students ages 18 years and over, and simple random samples were taken.

In the British National Survey of Sexual Attitudes and Lifestyles, the aim was to recruit a representative sample of people ages 16 to 59 years for a face-to-face, in-home interview (Johnson et al., 1994; Wadsworth, Field, Johnson, Bradshaw, & Wellings, 1993). There were three major stages in which clusters were sampled:

1. The initial clusters were 1,000 wards (i.e., regions) selected from 93 stratification cells that were constructed to ensure geographic diversity. These wards differed in terms of population density, and hence probability of selection of individual wards was weighted for the number of addresses.
2. Within each ward, clusters of addresses were chosen. Fifty consecutive household units were systematically chosen from lists of addresses after a starting address was randomly chosen from the ward.
3. Once the household was identified, clusters of eligible residents were identified, and a single individual from within each cluster was randomly selected for interview.

The most serious limitation of cluster sampling is that standard errors of estimates often are higher than those obtained from simple random sampling (Levy & Lemeshow, 1999). This occurs because units chosen within clusters are often more homogeneous than a purely random selection. For example, residents within geographically small clusters of households tend to be similar to one another in many important characteristics. This problem is most serious if the samples are small. However, if we consider alternatives such as simple random selection of all addresses in an entire region, then the costs involved in travel by researchers to each selected location would be prohibitive. This becomes more important in studies with broad sampling frames (e.g., a state or entire country), with costs per contact reduced through the use of multiple-stage cluster sampling.

NONPROBABILITY SAMPLING

Nonprobability samples are those in which all individuals in a population do not have a known, nonzero, and equivalent probability of selection. Consequently, such samples are a major source of bias and error in inferences about sexual characteristics of populations. Despite this fact, they remain popular for a variety of reasons primarily because of their convenience. There are three main types of nonprobability sampling.

Convenience Sampling

Simply stated, this method is the most convenient and usually the least expensive in terms of time and money. Some examples include selection of individuals from groups of college students, clinic attenders, volunteers from media advertisements, and members of organizations related to sexuality. There can be little doubt that an edifice of knowledge built on studies of people who are easy to contact would be very shaky. Nevertheless, perusal of the prominent research journals in sexuality, such as the *Archives of Sexual Behavior* and *The Journal of Sex Research*, reveals that the clear majority of empirical papers during the 1990s that attempted to describe sexual characteristics of different groups were based on samples not selected randomly or systematically from the general population.

This situation is likely to continue because of the following: First, there is a strong phenomenological tradition in sexual science, with a primary aim to study diversity rather than generalize to larger populations. Second, sexuality research is sensitive, and it is often easier to obtain cooperation from groups with which the researcher has personal contact and some influence (e.g., college students, clinic patients, members of other social groups) than from randomly selected individuals. Third, certain sexual characteristics are rare, and people with those characteristics cannot be efficiently recruited from the general population. Finally, funds for sexuality research usually are inadequate for population-based studies.

Few would argue that there are inherent weaknesses in inferences drawn from convenience samples, especially if the focus is on estimating simple parameters, such as means and variance, and then generalizing these to the entire population. However, a case can be made that studies using nonprobability samples are valuable if the primary focus is on associations between the various characteristics under study (Brecher & Brecher, 1986). For example, a convenience sample of women recruited through a health clinic may show convincing evidence of associations between a history of unprotected sex with multiple partners and risk of cervical cancer. If this phenomenon were found repeatedly in different studies using similar types of convenience samples from clinics, the validity of the observation can be established quite strongly and sound generalizations made. If possible, this could be verified by studies using large-scale probability samples, but this is not necessary. In the case of studies of cervical cancer and sexual history, many descriptive epidemiological studies of convenience samples produced data so convincing that it contributed to virological causal hypotheses and eventually to the development and trial of vaccines to prevent this cancer.

Quota Sampling

Quota sampling is a method designed to achieve representativeness without resort to random or systematic selection. One begins by reviewing demographic information about the population. For example, census data could be used to assess population diversity in gender, age, ethnicity, employment status, educational level, income, geographic dispersion, family structure, home ownership, and so forth. A matrix is constructed to reflect the numbers of people in the population who fit into defined cells, such as the number of individuals who are female, 18 to 30 years old, Latino, and employed, or the number of individuals who are male, low-income, single parents, between the ages of 30 and 50 years. The more variables in the matrix, the more specific and smaller the cells.

Once the proportions of people in the population with various characteristics are known and a desired sample size has been chosen, these proportions determine the numbers of people to be recruited for each cell in the sample. Each interviewer is assigned a quota of people of each demographic type, and participants are purposively recruited until the required number for each cell is achieved, using many and varied (and often the most convenient) sources for recruitment. If we think of the cells as strata in the population, quota sampling might best be described as stratified sampling when selection within strata is nonrandom.

Quota sampling is often used in opinion polls and marketing research, but is not common in academic sexuality surveys, although some examples include studies of sexual networks among low-income men and truck drivers in Thailand (Morris, Podhisita, Wawer, & Handcock, 1996) and a study of experiences of marital violence and rape among British women (Painter & Farrington, 1998). The former researchers set quotas in three provinces and in different age bands, whereas the latter researchers set quotas for representation across 10 geographic regions.

There are several distinct advantages of quota sampling (Cummings, 1990; Moser & Kalton, 1971). First, it is possible to achieve broad representation at relatively lower financial cost than that found in probability surveys. Second, quota sampling is administratively easier because, if a particular person targeted for the survey refuses or cannot be contacted easily, the interviewer looks for a replacement with the same characteristics rather than making further attempts to recruit the initial individual (i.e., response rate is not a major concern). Third, quota sampling is more feasible than probability sampling for rare or difficult-to-reach populations because interviewers can utilize convenient social networks or onsite recruitment in particular areas (e.g., locations where gay men or adolescents typically congregate).

Quota sampling also has two major disadvantages. First, it is not possible to estimate standard errors of the means and proportions derived from the sample. Second, there may be serious questions about the representativeness of individuals within cells. Selection biases that arise from convenience sampling are just as potent within subsamples as full samples. For example, there may be systematic differences between married women in rural areas who are victims of sexual violence who are reached by interviewers and those who are not. The essential problem is that control over selection of individuals is handed over to the interviewers rather than the principal researchers, and quality control may be difficult to achieve.

Snowball or Network Sampling

In this method, the researcher starts with an initial set of contacts and is then intro-duced to other people with similar characteristics, who in turn open up contact with people in further personal networks. It is particularly suitable for work with rare, covert, or highly elusive populations, or any individuals for which no popu-lation listing is possible. The primary assumption is that people with similar char-acteristics know each other (Czaja & Blair, 1995). For example, if the focus is on young, urban, non-English-speaking gay men who inject drugs, it is likely that groups of these men will coalesce to some extent because youth, ethnicity, sexual-ity, and drug use are all aspects of social cohesion. If a researcher was outside this culture, then initial access to the group would require contact with key informants, possibly reached through collaborative work with community-based groups. As long as rapport and a common purpose are established, primary informants might recommend the research project to others, and recruitment could extend success-fully until the networks are exhausted.

Snowball sampling was used in a study of 230 sex workers throughout Queensland, Australia (Boyle, Dunne et al., 1997; Boyle, Glennon et al., 1997). The context of the study posed challenges for any conventional survey technique. That state has a large land area and low-density population, sex workers make up a small proportion of the population, and sex work is a mainly covert activity (it was illegal at the time of the survey, and there was considerable uncertainty about the enforcement of recent major change to the laws regarding prostitution). Some sex workers were known to work in brothels and escort agencies in the major cit-ies, but it was believed that many others were working in tourism centers, on the street, and in rural areas. The broad aim of the study was to explore the nature and social context of sex work, with a particular focus on HIV/AIDS and other sexu-ally transmitted disease (STD) prevention.

In this specific case, the following steps were taken. First, the researchers de-veloped a collaborative relationship with a sex workers' advocacy group and with the state AIDS council. Second, the aims of the study were advertised in a sex workers' newsletter and a gay newspaper. Third, a research assistant with exten-sive contacts throughout the sex industry was employed. Fourth, interviews were conducted with people in personal contact with the research assistant and the col-laborators from the sex worker advocacy group. Each interviewee was asked to recommend the project to other sex workers and, if possible, to provide contact details. Each of these people in turn was asked to provide contact to other sex workers or to suggest possible recruitment sites. Finally, visits were made to se-lected sexual venues, and some otherwise unconnected street workers were ap-proached individually.

This process yielded a sample of 230 sex workers, of whom 87% were female, in five different cities or large regional centers. It is not possible to know the ex-tent to which this sample reflected the broader sex industry. There was some evi-dence of underrepresentation, given that no sex workers were recruited from small rural areas, and few (only 8 of 230) were primarily working on city streets, which appeared to the researchers to be a very small proportion. It is likely that inferences to the general sex worker population would be limited, at least in this case. However, snowball sampling does not necessarily produce unrepresentative samples, as can be seen in the next example.

Martin and Dean (1993) provided an interesting description of outcomes from snowball sampling when they recruited a community-based sample of gay men in New York City for studies related to HIV/AIDS. This is one of the few studies to compare the characteristics of people recruited by this method to those of people recruited by random sampling. In the late 1980s, convenience samples of gay men in New York City were recruited using five initial points of contact: gay social organizations, STD clinic patients, men who attended a gay pride festival, the friends of existing members of a small research cohort, and unsolicited readers of newspapers that published stories about the research. Together, these five groups of gay men comprised the initial cohort ($N = 291$).

After each of these volunteers was interviewed, they were asked to send information about the research project to friends or acquaintances who they knew to be gay. Martin and Dean (1993) recorded the source of each contact. When the next generation of recruits was interviewed, they were also asked to contact friends or acquaintances about the study. This procedure was followed throughout the study, and it was possible to identify up to five generations of men recruited through the snowball method from each of the five groups in the original cohort. In all, the original 291 men generated contact with an additional 455.

The snowball technique was more effective for some groups than others. The men originally recruited from gay organizations and the volunteers from media reports tended to generate proportionately more successful referrals than did men originally recruited through an STD clinic or a gay pride festival. In general, the men recruited from these networks were similar in terms of age, median income, education, and ethnicity, except for those recruited via the STD clinic, who were younger, poorer, and more likely to be from ethnic minorities.

Martin and Dean (1993) compared their final cohort of 746 gay men from New York City with two samples of gay men from San Francisco recruited through random probability sampling. Men recruited through snowball or probability sampling were remarkably similar in terms of age, race, and the extent to which they said they were "out of the closet" with family and friends. The only strong difference was that the New York men were more highly educated, and Martin and Dean suggested that could reflect differences between the cities rather than differences arising from the sampling methods. Therefore, it would appear that careful snowball sampling of difficult-to-reach groups sometimes can achieve samples comparable to those recruited through more expensive and time-consuming probability samples.

To conclude, it is important to note that the usefulness of network samples should not be judged solely by whether the final samples appear to be representative. Brecher and Brecher (1986) argued that a great deal of sexuality research derived from nonprobability methods has resulted in insights into associations between various phenomena and has allowed examination of the consistency (or uniqueness) of these association in diverse cultural groups. For example, in the Queensland sex worker study, we found a significant association between sex workers' degree of psychological distress and the extent to which they practiced unsafe sex with clients (Boyle, Dunne et al., 1997). This and other findings were similar to a study conducted with a snowball sample of sex workers in Puerto Rico (Alegria et al., 1994), despite that the sampling frames and research methods were quite different. The essential point is that the external validity of findings from such studies can be judged by the overall convergence of evidence from diverse sources.

ADAPTIVE SAMPLING OF RARE
OR DIFFICULT-TO-REACH POPULATIONS

A common difficulty facing sexuality researchers is to find a sampling method that facilitates contact with rare or elusive populations while minimizing both the biases inherent in methods that select participants on the dependent variable and the costs and other inefficiencies that arise from probability sampling. Adaptive sampling is one method for selecting a representative sample while maximizing the likelihood of capture of people with the relatively rare characteristics under study (Thompson & Seber, 1996).

The first phase of adaptive sampling begins with a random sample of the population, and data from early observations are used to guide the search for additional elements in later phases of recruitment (Blair, 1999). The essential premise is that people with like characteristics tend to cluster together, either in close geographic proximity or through social networks. The initial sample is stratified into cells, such as census districts. When a *hit* occurs (e.g., a screened household is found to contain people with certain characteristics), this indicates that contact with a larger cluster is possible. In a random digit dialing telephone survey that seeks ethnic groups, such as Russian immigrants in New York state, several hits in a defined residential area would suggest that further sampling of that area would be successful. However, if random dialing in some districts fails to detect any Russian immigrants, then canvassing in that area can be halted or reduced.

Blair (1999) provided a detailed description of adaptive sampling of gay men in San Francisco, Los Angeles, New York, and Chicago. Within these cities, secondary sources of data (e.g., concentrations of gay businesses, AIDS cases, census data on single males, etc.) were used to identify areas (strata) likely to contain large, moderate, and small concentrations of gay men. Random telephone screening of households in all strata in each city (Phase 1) found that the expected density of gay male households in each stratum was confirmed with reasonable accuracy. For example, of three geographic strata in Los Angeles, the expected prevalence rates of gay households were 23.1%, 8.7%, and 5.7%, and the actual prevalence following initial screening using random digit dialing was 16.3%, 8.0%, and 5.6%.

In Phase 2, Blair (1999) calculated the financial cost per household detected. Where this was high (i.e., in moderate density areas for gay households), further sampling was stopped in strata with lower expected prevalence, and the resources were re-allocated to strata with higher density and to those areas where the cost per case detected was moderate. Some broad strata were divided into high- and low-yield segments, with sampling discontinued in the latter. This approach maximized the yield of the target population and significantly reduced the cost per case.

Of course, this method has the potential to introduce sampling error in parameter estimates, as well as significant biases. Blair (1999) and Thompson and Seber (1996) described weighting procedures to adjust for differential probability of selection of individuals in large versus small clusters. One potential pitfall of this method is undercoverage bias that arises because some areas on the sampling frame are excluded due to high cost per case. Subsidiary studies comparing prevalence rates in simple random sampling and adaptive sampling are necessary to estimate the direction and magnitude of this bias. Nevertheless, this approach provides a way to initiate a study with probability sampling while maximizing efficiency by taking advantage of the natural clustering of people with relevant characteristics. This method should be applied in other areas of sexuality research and could offer a fruitful avenue for methodological studies.

SELF-SELECTION (PARTICIPATION) BIAS

The ways in which people are selected into samples influence, to a greater or lesser extent, the external validity of inferences from sexuality surveys. Hence, there are limits on generalizability from the sample to the population. An important and closely related issue is the extent to which self-selection can affect the internal validity of survey data. The likelihood that people will volunteer for sexuality research is strongly influenced by the mode of interview, the ways in which individuals within samples are approached, and other methodological factors. Every sexuality researcher must question whether the data from responders should be generalized to nonresponders. Self-selection (participation) bias arises when there are systematic differences in the sexuality of individuals who do, compared with those who do not, volunteer to participate in research.

In large-scale sexuality surveys, it is often found that between 30% and 40% of people selected for the sample are not successfully recruited, and published studies reporting participation rates of less than 50% are not uncommon. Nonparticipation is often due to direct, explicit refusal, although passive refusal (e.g., nonreturn of mail questionnaires and telephone messages or deliberately missing inhome appointments) is also substantial. Some of the reasons that people have for not participating, including reasons that some cannot be contacted at all, may be unimportant as far as sexuality is concerned. However, many researchers strongly suspect that the focus on sexuality is important (Bancroft, 1997).

The extent of the problem is illustrated with reference to research into the prevalence of childhood sexual abuse. In a study of a longitudinal, national research cohort of Australian adult twins, Dunne, Martin et al. (1997) asked people who volunteered for a general health survey a single question about forced sexual intercourse before age 18. At a different time, these same individuals were asked whether they would volunteer for a specific survey that "asked explicit questions about sexual attitudes and behavior." Volunteers for the sexuality survey ($n = 2,362$) were much more likely than people who explicitly refused ($n = 988$) to have reported forced sexual intercourse when questioned in the general health survey. Specifically, 6.6% of volunteers reported childhood sexual abuse, compared with 2.7% of refusers, which suggests that sexuality surveys may include an overrepresentation of people with childhood sexual abuse.

In their review of 16 cross-sectional surveys in the United States and Canada, Gorey and Leslie (1997) found that the average prevalence of childhood sexual abuse among women was much lower in studies with *good* response rates than among those with *poor* levels of participation. In surveys with response rates between 60% and 98%, the mean prevalence of childhood sexual abuse was 16.8%, but among surveys that achieved participation from between 25% and 59%, the prevalence was much higher, at 27.8%. In a logistic regression model, they found that the binary classification of good versus bad response rate accounted for 11% of the total variability in reported prevalence of childhood sexual abuse among the 16 studies.

A similar trend appears in the studies listed by Pilkington and Kremer (1995). Of 12 comparable surveys of childhood sexual abuse, 6 achieved participation from 70% or more of those selected for the surveys, whereas 6 recruited less than 70%. The average rate of childhood sexual abuse (combined contact and noncontact) in studies with high response rates was 20.2%, compared with an average of 33.3% in those with low participation rates. Refusal rates can vary in different studies for many reasons (Armstrong, White, & Saracci, 1992; Johnson & Copas, 1997). The main issue here is that studies that achieve low response rates appear to include proportionately more people with traumatic sexual histories. Gorey and Leslie (1997) suggested that people with troubled sexual histories might in part be attracted to sex surveys for reasons of catharsis or general help-seeking (see also Catania, 1997). It may also be that childhood sexual abuse is a nonspecific correlate of adult sexual experience and that people with most sexual experiences are most likely to volunteer for sex research. The extent of this bias may be most severe in surveys where the response rate is low.

In most population-based sexuality surveys, it is not possible to determine whether there are systematic differences between participants and refusers in their sexual experiences because we simply do not have any data on refusers. However, there is an increasing amount of methodological research into this issue, and in general these studies are consistent with the childhood sexual abuse examples cited earlier; that is, overestimation of prevalence of a wide range of characteristics is more likely than underestimation. Compared with refusers, volunteers have been found less often to be virgins, have had more sexual partners, be more interested in erotica and novel sexual practices, hold liberal sexual attitudes, and indicate higher sexual self-esteem and less personal sexual guilt (Bogaert, 1996; Catania, Gibson, Chitwood, & Coates, 1990; Dunne, Martin et al., 1997; Johnson & Copas, 1997; Strassberg & Lowe, 1995; Wiederman, 1999).

It is important to consider, however, that the direction and magnitude of participation bias may differ among various strata in the population. Reluctance to volunteer is not uniform across different gender, age, geographic, and ethnic groups, and it may be that the reasons for nonparticipation, including unwillingness to disclose sexual information, also differ (Johnson & Copas, 1997). For example, in a survey of women's experience of violence, young women may be more likely than older women to volunteer. The younger women may be willing to participate in part because they want to talk about their violent experiences, whereas older women may refuse because they do not want to talk about it. The result would be overestimation of prevalence in young women and underestimation among older women.

Direct refusal to participate in social surveys is becoming increasingly common. In addition, there is a steady increase in technology that assists passive refusal. Barriers that protect privacy (e.g., silent telephone numbers, screening and blocking of unsolicited telephone calls, and security devices restricting entry to homes) make it difficult for sexuality researchers to establish personal contact and collect basic information on the full sample. At present it is not known whether people who choose to have such barriers systematically differ from those who do not with regard to their sexuality. It is becoming increasingly necessary to carry out experimental research into methods that increase participation.

TECHNIQUES TO MINIMIZE NONPARTICIPATION

Nonparticipation in health and social research can be reduced by careful attention to many aspects of survey procedures, and these have been reviewed in detail by Armstrong (1992); Catania (1997); Groves, Cialdini, and Couper (1992); and Kessler, Little, and Groves (1995). Generally, response is improved if individuals are given advance notice of the survey, interviewers are highly trained and experienced in establishing rapport, and (usually) interviewers are women (Johnson & Copas, 1997). It is especially important to tailor the demographic characteristics of the interviewers in ways appropriate to the ethnic and socioeconomic characteristics of the sample (Catania, 1997).

Government or university sponsorship remains an important factor in establishing credibility. However, the benefits of such affiliations are not uniform across different groups. In research with convenience samples of difficult-to-reach people, it is very useful to work closely with members of these groups to gain access and collaborative insights, and ultimately the cooperation of people who otherwise would not respond to approaches from officials.

An important practical question in sexuality surveys is: In what ways and for how long should we pursue people who are difficult to recruit? Biggar and Melbye (1992) and Laumann et al. (1994) found that concerted efforts to recruit initially reluctant or evasive individuals was successful in improving participation (e.g., Biggar & Melbye reduced nonresponse from 48%–27%). Interestingly, these studies revealed few differences between early and late responders, which, at one level, may indicate that participation bias is minimal. However, the fact that there was little correlation between sexuality and tardiness in response does not answer the question of whether the bias is strong among those who repeatedly refuse to participate regardless of incentives or other methods researchers may use to try to convince people to volunteer.

Kessler et al. (1995) raised the interesting point that concerted effort to increase participation rates may, paradoxically, increase the extent of bias. This would occur if the methods used to recruit difficult-to-reach people were more successful for some segments of the population than others, and if the sexual experiences of people in these segments were different from those who could not be recruited. In the case of sexual abuse research among samples of women, this bias might arise if younger women were significantly more or less responsive to persistent appeals than were older women. Another major complication is that persistent appeals to refusers, and perhaps those who passively evade the research team, may lead to complaints to ethics committees or institutions about the behavior of researchers. At some point, survey teams have to *let go* of reluctant individuals. Planning for the survey should include development and testing of decision rules, which usually involve classification of the firmness of the initial refusal and recording the number of unsuccessful contact attempts for people with whom no personal contact was established.

Postsurvey statistical adjustments for missing data can be used to estimate the effect of differential participation on prevalence estimates. Techniques involved in data imputation and hypothesis testing about the extent of biases are reviewed in detail by Kessler et al. (1995) and Kalton (1983). The key point is that it is possible to test various assumptions about the behavior of people who refuse. One strategy is to calculate confidence intervals for estimates (e.g., prevalence of sexual abuse) under the assumptions that nonparticipants are equivalent to participants, have zero experience, or are at some points in between. These figures can then indicate the likely precision of estimates.

CONCLUSION

Sampling considerations are a central part of quantitative sexual science. Research findings are often scrutinized and sometimes ridiculed because of doubts about the adequacy of sample selection methods and difficulties in measuring and controlling participation bias. Some critics (e.g., Lewontin, 1995) suggest that sexuality researchers naively or at least uncritically accept their data on face value, ignoring the context in which they are gathered and the numerous limitations. However, this is demonstrably not true when we consider the depth and complexity of methodological studies that have been conducted over the past several decades.

In the 21st century, sexologists face many technical hurdles in obtaining adequate samples especially because of changes over time in the population coverage of public databases and the feasibility of different interview modes (e.g., land-line telephones, households, and the Internet). However, we can also be optimistic that research will become easier as sexuality becomes a more recognized part of the self and society and a more legitimate topic for inquiry.

SUGGESTED READINGS

The emphasis in the sampling methods section of this chapter was on the application of methods in practice, rather than detailed analysis of underlying theory and statistical methods. For specialist texts on sampling, see Cochran (1977), Thompson (1997), and Thompson and Seber (1996). For a comprehensive treatment of theory and statistical methods involved in sampling, classic texts include Kish (1965) and Moser and Kalton (1971). Although these texts are now quite dated, their primary ideas remain entirely relevant to contemporary research. For an excellent recent text on statistical models and methods in sampling, see Levy and Lemeshow (1999). Sampling procedures for large-scale sexuality surveys are described very clearly by Laumann et al. (1994) and Johnson et al. (1994; see Appendix 2 for an excellent description of multiple-stage cluster sampling with PPS). Consult Sudman et al. (1988) for an overview of the issues involved in sampling rare or difficult-to-reach populations and various chapters following Bancroft (1997) regarding sampling issues for particular ethnic groups.

ACKNOWLEDGMENT

This chapter was primarily written while the author was a Visiting Research Fellow at the Department of Behavioural Sciences, University of Huddersfield, West Yorkshire, United Kingdom.

REFERENCES

Analyse des Comportements Sexuels en France Investigators. (1992). AIDS and sexual behavior in France. *Nature, 360*, 407–410.

Alegria, M., Vera, M., Freeman, D. H., Robles, R., Santos, M. C., & Rivera, C. L. (1994). HIV infection, risk behaviors and depressive symptoms among Puerto Rican sex workers. *American Journal of Public Health, 84*, 2000–2002.

Armstrong, B. K., White, E., & Saracci, R. (1992). *Principles of exposure measurement in epidemiology*. Oxford: Oxford University Press.

Babbie, E. (1992). *The practice of social research*. Belmont, CA: Wadsworth.

Bailey, J. M., Dunne, M. P., & Martin, N. G. (2000). Genetic and environmental influences on sexual orientation and its correlates in an Australian twin sample. *Journal of Personality and Social Psychology, 78*, 524–536.

Bailey, J. M., & Pillard, R. C. (1991). A genetic study of male sexual orientation. *Archives of General Psychiatry, 48*, 1089–1096.

Bailey, J. M., Pillard, R. C., Neale, M. C., & Agyei, Y. (1993). Heritable factors influence sexual orientation in women. *Archives of General Psychiatry, 50*, 217–223.

Bancroft, J. (1997). Introduction. In J. Bancroft (Ed.), *Researching sexual behavior* (pp. ix–xvi). Bloomington, IN: Indiana University Press.

Biggar, R. J., & Melbye, M. (1992). Responses to anonymous questionnaires concerning sexual behaviour: A method to examine potential biases. *American Journal of Public Health, 82*, 1506–1512.

Blair, J. (1999). A probability sample of gay urban males: The use of two-phase adaptive sampling. *The Journal of Sex Research, 36*, 39–48.

Bogaert, A. F. (1996). Volunteer bias in human sexuality research: Evidence for both sexuality and personality differences in males. *Archives of Sexual Behavior, 25*, 125–139.

Boyle, F. M., Dunne, M. P., Najman, J. M., Western, J. S., Turrell, G., Wood, C., & Glennon, S. (1997). Psychological distress among female sex workers. *Australian and New Zealand Journal of Public Health, 21*, 643–646.

Boyle, F. M., Glennon, S., Najman, J. M., Turrell, G., Western, J. S., & Wood, C. (1997). *The sex industry: A survey of sex workers in Queensland, Australia*. Aldershot: Ashgate.

Brecher, E. M., & Brecher, J. (1986). Extracting valid sexological findings from severely flawed and biased population samples. *The Journal of Sex Research, 22*, 6–20.

Brener, N. D., McMahon, P. M., Warren, C. W., & Douglas, K. A. (1999). Forced sexual intercourse and associated health-risk behaviors among female college students in the United States. *Journal of Consulting and Clinical Psychology, 67*, 252–259.

Catania, J. A. (1997). A model for investigating respondent–interviewer relationships in sexual surveys. In J. Bancroft (Ed.), *Researching sexual behavior* (pp. 417–436). Bloomington, IN: Indiana University Press.

Catania, J. A., Gibson, D. R., Chitwood, D. D., & Coates, T. J. (1990). Methodological problems in AIDS behavioral research: Influences on measurement error and participation bias in studies of sexual behaviour. *Psychological Bulletin, 108*, 339–362.

Cochran, W. G. (1977). *Sampling techniques*. New York: Wiley.

Cochran, W. G., Mosteller, F., & Tukey, J. W. (1954). *Statistical problems of the Kinsey report*. Washington, DC: American Statistical Association.

Cummings, R. G. (1990). Is probability sampling always better? A comparison of results from a quota and a probability sample survey. *Community Health Studies, 14*, 132–137.

Czaja, R., & Blair, J. (1995). *Designing surveys*. Thousand Oaks, CA: Pine Forge.

Davis, P. B., Yee, R. L., Chetwynd, J., & MacMillan, P. (1993). The New Zealand partner relations survey: Methodological results of a national telephone survey. *AIDS, 7*, 1509–1516.

Dunne, M. P., Ballard, R., Peterson, K., & Dunne, T. (1997). Stability and change in adolescents' sexual health-related knowledge, attitudes and behaviour in Queensland. *Venereology, 10,* 228–235.

Dunne, M. P., Donald, M., Lucke, J., Nilsson, R., Ballard, R., & Raphael, B. (1994). Age-related increase in sexual behaviours and decrease in regular condom use among adolescents in Australia. *International Journal of STD and AIDS, 5,* 61–67.

Dunne, M. P., George, M., Byrne, D., & Patten, J. (1995). The sexual health caseloads of general practitioners in Queensland. *Venereology, 8,* 71–75.

Dunne, M. P., Martin, N. G., Bailey, J. M., Heath, A. C., Bucholz, K. K., Madden, P. A. F., & Statham, D. J. (1997). Participation bias in a sexuality survey: Psychological and behavioural characteristics of responders and non-responders. *International Journal of Epidemiology, 26,* 844–854.

Ffrench, M., & Dunne, M. P. (1999). *The health status and support needs of women who have been sexually abused.* Unpublished manuscript, Queensland University of Technology, Brisbane, Australia.

Finkelhor, D. (1994). The international epidemiology of child sexual abuse. *Child Abuse and Neglect, 18,* 409–417.

Fleming, J. M. (1997). Prevalence of childhood sexual abuse among a community sample of Australian women. *Medical Journal of Australia, 166,* 65–68.

Gorey, K. M., & Leslie, D. R. (1997). The prevalence of child sexual abuse: Integrative review adjustment for potential response and measurement biases. *Child Abuse and Neglect, 21,* 391–398.

Groves, R. M., Cialdini, R. B., & Couper, M. P. (1992). Understanding the decision to participate in a survey. *Public Opinion Quarterly, 56,* 475–495.

Hite, S. (1981). *The Hite report on male sexuality.* London: MacDonald Futura.

Janus, S. S., & Janus, C. L. (1993). *The Janus report on sexual behavior.* New York: Wiley.

Johnson, A. M., & Copas, A. (1997). Assessing participation bias. In J. Bancroft (Ed.), *Researching sexual behavior* (pp. 276–287). Bloomington, IN: Indiana University Press.

Johnson, A. M., Wadsworth, J., Wellings, K., & Field, J. (1994). *Sexual attitudes and lifestyles.* Oxford: Blackwell Scientific Publications.

Kalton, G. (1983). *Compensating for missing survey data.* Ann Arbor, MI: Institute for Social Research.

Kendler, K. S., & Eaves, L. J. (1989). The estimation of probandwise concordance in twins: The effects of unequal ascertainment. *Acta Geneticae Medicae et Gemellologiae, Twin Research, 38,* 253–270.

Kessler, R. C., Little, R. J. A., & Groves, R. M. (1995). Advances in strategies for minimizing and adjusting for survey nonresponse. *Epidemiologic Review, 17,* 192–204.

Kinsey, A. C., Pomeroy, W. B., & Martin, C. E. (1948). *Sexual behavior in the human male.* Philadelphia: Saunders.

Kish, L. (1949). A procedure for objective respondent selection within the household. *Journal of the American Statistical Association, 44,* 380–387.

Kish, L. (1965). *Survey sampling.* New York: Wiley.

Laumann, E. O., Gagnon, J. H., Michael, R. T., & Michaels, S. (1994). *The social organization of sexuality.* Chicago: University of Chicago Press.

Lewontin, R. C. (1995, April 20). Sex, lies and social science. *New York Review,* pp. 24–29.

Levy, P. S., & Lemeshow, S. (1999). *Sampling of populations: Methods and applications.* New York: Wiley.

Lynch, J. P. (1996). Clarifying divergent estimates of rape from two national surveys. *Public Opinion Quarterly, 60,* 410–430.

Martin, J. L., & Dean, L. (1993). Developing a community sample of gay men for an epidemiological study of AIDS. In C. M. Renzetti & R. M. Lee (Eds.), *Researching sensitive topics* (pp. 82–99). London: Sage.

McKnight, J. (1997). *Straight science?* London: Routledge.

Morris, M., Podhisita, C., Wawer, M. J., & Handcock, M. S. (1996). Bridge populations in the spread of HIV/AIDS in Thailand. *AIDS, 10,* 1265–1271.

Mullen, P. E., Martin, J. L., Anderson, J. C., Romans, S. E., & Herbison, G. P. (1996). The long-term impact of the physical, emotional, and sexual abuse of children: A community survey. *Child Abuse and Neglect, 20,* 7–21.

Mullen, P. E., Romans-Clarkson, S. E., Walton, V. A., & Herbison, G. P. (1988). Impact of sexual and physical abuse on women's mental health. *Lancet, 1*(8590), 841–845.

Nye, R. A. (1999). *Sexuality.* Oxford: Oxford University Press.

Painter, K., & Farrington, P. (1998). Marital violence in Great Britain and its relationship to marital and non-marital rape. *International Review of Victimology, 5,* 257–276.

Pilkington, B., & Kremer, J. (1995). A review of the epidemiological research on child sexual abuse. *Child Abuse Review, 4,* 84–98.

Sandfort, T. G. M. (1997). Sampling male homosexuality. In J. Bancroft (Ed.), *Researching sexual behavior* (pp. 261–275). Bloomington, IN: Indiana University Press.

Strassberg, D. S., & Lowe, K. (1995). Volunteer bias in sexuality research. *Archives of Sexual Behavior, 24,* 369–382.

Sudman, S., Sirken, M. G., & Cowan, C. D. (1988). Sampling rare or elusive populations. *Science, 240,* 991–996.

Thompson, M. E. (1997). *Theory of sample surveys.* London: Chapman & Hall.

Thompson, S. K., & Seber, G. A. F. (1996). *Adaptive sampling.* New York: Wiley.

Wadsworth, J., Field, J., Johnson, A. M., Bradshaw, S., & Wellings, K. (1993). Methodology of the National Survey of Sexual Attitudes and Lifestyles. *Journal of the Royal Statistical Society, 156,* 407–421.

Whitam, F. L., Diamond, M., & Martin, J. (1993). Homosexual orientation in twins: A report of 61 pairs and three triplet sets. *Archives of Sexual Behavior, 22,* 187–206.

Wiederman, M. W. (1999). Volunteer bias in sexuality research using college student participants. *The Journal of Sex Research, 36,* 59–66.

6

▼▼▼▼▼▼▼

Behavioral Observation

Monica M. Moore
Webster University

Most people have been conducting behavioral observation all their lives: Sitting in cafés, walking in the park, or shopping for groceries all involve a good deal of *people watching*. Indeed, when new acquaintances hear about my research, which regularly involves making observations, they often comment about how lucky I am to people-watch for a living (I agree). Although the process of making observations may seem intuitively obvious to some people, in reality this *natural activity* involves learned skills that are necessary to generate valid data. Using those skills is what this chapter is about. I provide a brief look at the use of observation in human sexuality research, a discussion of the limitations and benefits of using the methods of behavioral observation in studying human sexuality, and an overview of the techniques used in observational research, including a consideration of ethical issues.

Behavioral observation is a very old form of research in the social and biological sciences. Other methodological experts (e.g., Babbie, 1998) have pointed out that people not considered social scientists, such as newspaper reporters, also employ these methods in the course of their work. Unlike newspaper reporting, however, scientific behavioral observation generates theory. Reporting is done with the aim of capturing the actions of people, whereas observational research, as one of the methods of science, must be held to the same standards as work conducted in the laboratory or data gathered through interviews, questionnaires, or case histories. Therefore, observers ground their observations in theory. Another difference between newspaper reporting and behavioral observation is the length of time available to reporters to construct their story, often made minimal by the pressure to meet a deadline and report a recent event or crisis. Field-workers are often able to spend weeks, months, or even years making observations to construct their story. The field-worker's story may differ from the reporter's in an additional key way. Rather than being made up of unusual newsworthy events, ethological observations often entail documenting the mundane and ordinary (Smith, 1991). Finally, the field-worker not only reports what people do (similar to a reporter) but, unlike a reporter, also tries to make sense of what people do by looking for patterns or the underlying reasons.

Sexuality is one aspect of human behavior that has long been the subject of observational research. Anthropologists routinely use behavioral observation as one technique (along with interviews) to learn more about cultures or subcultures other than their own, including sexual behavior as an aspect of culture. In this regard, several famous ethnographic accounts come to mind. Margaret Mead was one of the first ethnographers to openly discuss the sexual norms of other cultures, such as in her book, *Growing Up in New Guinea* (1930). Malinowski (1929) provided another early account when he detailed sexual behavior in the Trobriand society of Melanesia. Money and his associates (1970) spent many years studying the Yolngu on Elcho Island off the northern coast of Australia. By living among the Yolngu, observing them, and talking with them, Money and his group learned a great deal about sexual behavior in that culture. For example, nudity was acceptable from infancy into old age, and crying infants were soothed by adults masturbating their genitals. Indeed, masturbation was taught to girls before puberty. Sex play among children was no cause for concern, but merely amusing to the adult members of the group. Marshall and Suggs' (1971) *Human Sexual Behavior: Variations in the Ethnographic Spectrum* described sexual behavior in four cultures, some of which were repressive, others of which were more tolerant of sexual expression. Finally, Beach (1977) not only made comparisons across cultures, but also to animals in his book, *Human Sexuality in Four Perspectives*.

Ethnographers have also studied subcultures within American society, sometimes as participants and sometimes as observers. For example, Bartell (1970) conducted participant observation research on swinging when he and his wife attended swinging parties and had contact with swinging couples who had placed ads in newspapers. Other examples of participant observation research include the work of Douglas, Rasmussen, and Flanagan (1977), who went to nude beaches and observed interaction patterns; Story (1993), who also studied nudists; Petersen and Dressel (1982), who attended male strip shows as customers; and Humphreys (1970), who played the role of lookout while observing homosexual contacts in public restrooms. Examples of nonparticipant observational research on sexuality include the work of Warren (1974), who studied the gay community, and Prus and Irini (1988), who observed prostitution without taking on the role of prostitute or customer. Furthermore, some authors (e.g., Allgeier & Allgeier, 1995; McCammon, Knox, & Schacht, 1993) consider the research of Masters and Johnson (1966) to be observational, despite being conducted in the laboratory, often with the use of equipment for monitoring the physiological changes that constitute human sexual response.

Many methods used to study human sexuality result in data appropriately analyzed using quantitative methods. Observational research more typically yields qualitative data. For example, in my own research (Moore, 1985), I made observations of women in singles' bars and other dating contexts to document the nonverbal behaviors women commonly use to indicate their attraction to a particular man. Many people refer to this behavior as *flirting*, and it has been documented through the use of ethological observations by many investigators (Givens, 1978; Lockard & Adams, 1980; Perper, 1985; Scheflen, 1965). My dissertation research resulted in a catalogue describing 52 of these nonverbal behaviors. Of course, there are times when field research does involve the collection of quantitative data. I not only described nonverbal courtship behaviors, but also counted the number of times that women used them and, more recently, compared the nonverbal courtship behaviors of women to those of teenage girls (Moore, 1995). Knowing the frequencies for each group allowed me to see that girls not only used fewer of the behaviors in the original catalogue, but also used them less frequently than did women.

These examples of human sexuality research demonstrate the variety of observational techniques employed in field research. One form of observational research is ethnography, more commonly employed by anthropologists or sociologists. Wolcott (1973) defined *ethnography* as the science of cultural description. That is, ethnography is primarily a process that attempts to describe and interpret social expressions between people and groups.

Observational research can also take the ethological approach more often used by biologists or comparative psychologists. The ethological approach has three major attributes (Hinde, 1966). First, description and classification of behavior is necessary before analysis. Second, behavior cannot be properly studied without some knowledge of the natural environment in which that behavior is found. Third, questions about the evolution and biological function of behavior are as valid and important as those about immediate causation.

Although both ethnography and ethology rely on behavioral observations made in the field, ethnography more commonly results in a narrative, full of broad or macrodescriptions of people's behavior, and attempts to account for the immediate causes of behavior. Ethology may result in a narrative, a quantitative analysis, or both. Regardless of the form of data analysis used, the descriptions are made at the microlevel and ultimate causations are sought.

MEASUREMENT

Validity, Reliability, and Generalizability

Validity. Some of the most important measurement issues in any research project are validity, reliability, and generalizability. Validity concerns the extent to which measures actually capture what they purport to assess rather than assessing something else (see chap. 3, this volume). On the surface, nothing seems more natural when observing behavior than to believe that we are actually measuring what we think we are measuring. One aspect of the validity of observation measures is their predictive power, a form of criterion-related validity. Do they predict relevant criteria dependably? When I discussed at a conference the catalogue of women's nonverbal courtship behaviors my students and I had compiled, one man questioned whether we had truly identified flirting. His solution was an experimental test: train women in the use of the behaviors in the catalogue and send them into bars to see if they were more successful in attracting male attention than an untrained control group. Because I was uncomfortable with the manipulation of unsuspecting men for scientific purposes, I declined launching such a project. Still, I did want to satisfy my critics. In the social sciences, we often say that behavior is understood when it can be predicted, so I decided to use the number of nonverbal courtship signals as a predictor of male approaches. Indeed, the number of catalogued behaviors women engaged in turned out to be highly predictive of the likelihood men would approach them (Moore & Butler, 1989). This technique of establishing validity can be used in the investigation of other research questions.

Another way of validating a construct is to provide evidence for the function of a behavior. For example, one way I tried to provide evidence for the existence of flirting behavior patterns among women was to show that they had a specific function. To do this, I utilized two strategies recommended by Hinde (1975): consequential and contextual data. In the first case, Hinde argued that "statements about function are usually based on observations that the behavior in question has a certain consequence, and that that consequence appears to be a 'good thing' " (p. 9). Thus, in my work, the observation that female nonverbal courtship behaviors attract the attention of males is evidence that flirting functions to enable women to gain access to men. However, a further type of evidence is needed. Contextual evidence concerns correlations between behaviors observed and the environments in which they are seen (Hinde, 1975). If behavior is observed in an *appropriate* context (singles' bars) more frequently than in an *inappropriate* context (meetings where only women are present), another powerful argument for the function of nonverbal courtship signaling can be made. Taken together, these two forms of observational evidence help a researcher make a case for the why of the behavior she is observing.

Reliability. Assessing the reliability of behavioral observation systems is somewhat more straightforward than assessing validity. Reliability is a matter of consistency: Would you get the same result if you made the same observations again? Video and audio recordings, when appropriate, can help the observer achieve a high level of reliability. With recordings, the observer can later check to see if every occurrence of the behavior under study was captured. When using several observers, interobserver reliability scores can be calculated periodically. The following is one formula for calculating interobserver reliability (McGrew, 1972):

$$\frac{Agreements\,(observer\,A\,\text{and}\,observer\,B)}{Agreements + disagreements\,(A\,only) + disagreements\,(B\,only)}$$

Observers who do not meet a preset minimum standard (usually +.70) must then receive further training before being allowed to return to the field.

Generalizability.   *Generalizability* refers to the extent to which the findings of a study can be applied to other conditions, such as different settings, times, or participants. One aspect of generalizability is *ecological validity*—the degree to which the conditions under which research is conducted mimic the conditions found in the natural setting to which they are applied. In this regard, Babbie (1998) argued that field research seems to provide more ecologically valid measurements than those used in surveys or experiments, which can be superficial and artificial. In contrast, when making field observations, one is confronted with behavior directly, often in the environment in which that behavior typically occurs. The researcher is not relying on self-reports, which may be distorted through misremembering, impression managing, or outright lying (see chap. 3, this volume). Neither has the behavior been restructured by the constraints of the laboratory so that it bears little resemblance to what happens in the natural context.

Although behavioral observation is generally touted as having more ecological validity than does research done in the laboratory because the researcher connects with people in their natural environment, the specific demands of answering a particular question may mean that the mechanisms or systems a research team develops for a particular setting may not readily transfer to another environment or another research team. There are some observational systems that are designed for use on many different research problems, such as the Bales (1951) group interaction analysis approach, but many systems are created to measure specific variables limited to one project.

Furthermore, given the demanding nature of behavioral observation, many studies contain information about a limited number of people. In some cases, these individuals are drawn from an even more restrictive group, such as HIV-positive drug users living in New York City. It would be dangerous to generalize the findings from this sample to more rural populations or to individuals who are of a different ethnic background or age group than those observed.

Categories and Units of Behavior

One of the main tasks of the observer is to assign behaviors to categories. The categories should not overlap, yet there should be enough categories so that all behaviors can be classified. In some observational systems, this is not difficult, as when one is looking for the presence or absence of a particular behavior such as orgasm. In other systems, it is up to the researcher to generate categories that seem to capture all possibilities and then provide adequate operational definitions so that the behaviors observed can be classified appropriately. This is easier if the terms being defined are relatively concrete. In my own research, I categorized the behaviors in the nonverbal courtship and rejection catalogues according to the body parts involved: facial and head patterns, gestures, and whole body movements. There was little disagreement about which behaviors belonged in which categories. However, if one is dealing with ambiguous concepts or internal states that must be inferred from external actions, then the task becomes more difficult.

What units to use in measuring human behavior presents the observer with another dilemma. A researcher taking the molar approach relies on larger behavioral patterns as the units of observations, often using interpretation to record behaviors under a broadly defined umbrella. The molecular approach uses smaller segments of behavior as units of observation, often employing little or no interpretation as to what larger behaviors these segments constitute. In looking at observational studies of courtship, Perper (1985) used the molar approach, whereas I took the molecular approach. Perper conceptualized courtship as a series of phases involving the active participation of both partners through approach, turn, first touch, and the steady development of body synchronization. I described more specific nonverbal behaviors that may occur during these phases: glancing, lip pouting, hair flipping, smiling, palming, primping, caressing, and soliciting aid. If the observer can use small, easily observed, and recorded behaviors as units, reliability is likely to be quite high. The danger is that this reductive approach compromises validity, as the observer's findings bear little resemblance to the way overall behavior is enacted by people in the actual environment. The alternative is to use very broad definitions, encompassing many examples. Even with operational definitions of what kinds of behaviors make up this unit, it is likely that, if a number of observers are employed in the project, there will be problems with reliability.

To get around these issues, some researchers list a number of specific behaviors for all the observers to count. No others are recorded. Although a high degree of reliability will be achieved using this approach, it is probable that some relevant behaviors will be missed. If this is the case, the validity of the findings can be questioned. The behavioral observer is constantly trying to achieve balance between the demands of validity and reliability. A detailed description of how to construct categories is beyond the scope of this chapter. See the suggested readings for references to works on this topic.

PREPARING FOR FIELDWORK

Suppose you decide to covertly observe public displays of affection in city parks. Perhaps you prefer to observe streetwalkers in a major metropolitan area. In this section, I discuss a few of the preparations that should precede observations.

The first order of business, as with any research project, is to conduct a review of the relevant literature. This not only informs you as to what other researchers did previously, but may also give you ideas about how to conduct your project and sensitize you to difficulties you may encounter. It might be helpful to contact scientists who have previously conducted research on your topic because there may be things that you should be aware of that never made it into print. For example, in conducting observational studies of courtship behavior, I had to spend quite a bit of time canvassing singles' bars to ascertain the nature of their clientele and when they are most likely to be busy. It may help observers who are new to the field to know they need to build into the project time to preview the singles' bars in the area. With the advent of electronic mail, this kind of information exchange has become quite easy.

Making Initial Observations

Although you may set out to make observations with a fairly clear idea of what you hope to observe, it is a good idea to conduct a pilot study. Smith (1991) referred to this informal visit to the proposed research site as *casing*. By going into the field before deciding what to record, you may find new and exciting issues to investigate. I think this flexibility is one of the key advantages of observational research.

Furthermore, you may become aware of logistical issues that you had not yet considered. For example, through our own pilot studies, my colleagues and I found that certain nights at the bars around campus were poor candidates for observation; there were very few patrons. We also discovered that we were less likely to be discovered as researchers if observers worked in male–female pairs because singles do not pay much attention to people already coupled.

Initial Contacts

There are a number of ways to make an initial contact with those you hope to observe. In the example of studying public displays of affection, you simply have to find the appropriate parks on the appropriate days and show up. In the second case, observing prostitutes on the streets, things are more complicated. Taking on the role of complete participant means that you, too, would solicit customers. As a participant–observer or observer–participant, even if you do not trade sex for money, you must establish rapport with the people you observe. You might want to initially establish contact with one person in the hope that he or she could provide you entry into the group found on a particular street corner. In some settings, it may be easy to gain entry because the group has a role it needs filled. Humphreys (1970) found a way to study homosexual encounters in public restrooms by accepting the role of watchqueen or voyeur–lookout. In the case of making observations of a formal group, contacting those in leadership positions and obtaining their permission for the research is advisable. In formal organizations, it may also be necessary to assure the members that you will not be a threat to them or the organization. Some organizations may require a brief letter of introduction from the researcher that identifies his or her institutional affiliations and outlines the proposed research project.

Regardless of how you start, remember that initial impressions are important and that their influence is bidirectional. When establishing contacts for the street-walker study, the person you first meet is going to give you her perspective on the behavior under study. This perspective may or may not be shared by the other prostitutes on the street. Similarly, how you appear may greatly influence how easy it is to gain access to the other prostitutes. Imagine that you choose to first clear your presence with the police on the street. This may make it quite difficult for you to work effectively, given that you may be seen as a spy. Even if you initially gain the trust of those you hope to observe by first approaching the right person, trust establishment may be a long process, involving negotiation and renegotiation. Dalby's (1985) study of Japanese geisha illustrates how long it may take to find out about the secret lives of those observed for research. Although Dalby was allowed by the women she was observing to train as a geisha after 2 months in Kyoto, it was not until near the end of her 14th month there that she was trusted with the other geishas' deepest secrets.

In making contact with people you hope to observe, you may be pressured to divulge not only your role as a researcher, but also the goals of the project. How much to convey can be a tricky issue. Telling the people being observed everything may mean that they refuse to cooperate or that they change their behavior in your presence. Yet if you misrepresent the purpose of your project and are later discovered, that can mean a serious blow to the rapport you have worked so hard to establish. As discussed later in the section on ethical issues, in many cases it may be up to the observer to decide what is most appropriate to reveal.

Even when doing purely observational research in public places, it may be advisable to obtain permission from people in authority or those who control the research settings. In some cases, these individuals may limit what you can do, whereas in others, there may be few problems. I have routinely approached bar owners to get permission to observe in their establishments. In most cases, they have been completely cooperative. In a few instances, however, we have been denied permission to make observations because the owner feared that business might suffer if word got out that research was being conducted there.

Observer Roles

Once you have been to the field to conduct a pilot study and are ready to initiate the actual project, a decision must be made about the observational role you take. There are four typical field roles (Gold, 1969): complete participant, participant as observer, observer as participant, and nonparticipant observer. Each of these has its unique advantages and biases.

The *complete participant* conceals his or her observer role from the people observed and becomes a member of the group being studied. By concealing his or her purpose, the observer may gain access to information that might not be revealed if the group knew his or her true identity.

In addition to the issue of deception, several logistical problems are inherent in this approach. For example, many methodologists have questioned whether the complete participant role allows for adequate data collection procedures. This is because actively participating in activities may mean that the participant–researcher may be interrupted while recording observations or must reconstruct events from memory. Even when data collection proceeds as planned, there can be problems. If the researcher has become immersed in the activity being studied, it can be difficult to switch to a role (e.g., interviewer), necessary at a later point, that may be more conducive to data collection.

At the other end of the continuum is the *nonparticipant observer*. In nonparticipant observation, the observer remains apart from those being studied while making and recording observations. The observations may be conducted overtly, with people aware that they are being studied, or covertly, with people unaware that they are being observed. The latter approach is rarely used in the field unless the researcher has access to a secluded observational venue or can conduct public observations in such a way that people fail to notice the observer. In my own research in singles' bars, we were once offered the use of a room with a one-way mirror installed by the owner of the establishment presumably to watch over both employees and customers. However, opportunities such as this are rare in the field. Of course, the nonparticipant observer role does exist in the laboratory where the use of one-way mirrors and concealed recorders is common. One of the major problems with nonparticipant observation is that the researcher has to rely on describing the action taking place and cannot turn to the participants for their points of view regarding their own behavior.

Because of problems such as these, more typically one of the other two roles is used in behavioral observation: participant as observer or observer as participant. The *participant as observer* places more emphasis on participation than observation. An example of participant observation is the research done by Story (1993), who wrote about being personally involved in her research on nudism. Those being studied are generally aware that the researcher is, indeed, both participant and observer. Because of the latter characteristic, all of the problems generally encountered when people know they are being observed may come to the fore. The primary concern is that the people alter their behavior in the presence of the observer. It may also be the case that those being studied want the researcher, by virtue of her status, to intervene on their behalf when a problem arises in the setting being studied. The problem of what the researcher owes participants may arise when one of those observed asks for a favor. In this regard, a colleague who studies homeless women was asked both for money and help dealing with homeless men and their sexual harassment of her study participants.

When covert or overt contact with those being observed is minimally interactive, the *observer as participant* role is said to be employed. Here, a major problem is that the observer's contact with subjects is so limited. Because the observer is relying only on what is seen and does not interact with those observed, meaning can be difficult to interpret.

Stein's (1990) study of a pornographic bookstore may illuminate some of the limitations of the observer as participant role. The management made Stein promise that he would only observe in the capacity of a store clerk. His role as clerk severely limited what and when he could observe. Additionally, the quiet environment in the adult bookstore he observed presented barriers in terms of the use of data collection devices. (Stein had hoped to talk to bookstore users, but was not permitted to do so by the owner.)

Observer Training

Because there has not been much discussion of observer training in the literature, many observers are trained on the job, so to speak. In an early article, Bennett (1960) outlined his approach to training observers and indicated that dealing with the individual perspectives of the trainees must be a large component of training. After some basic technique training for the collection of data, he tried to make students aware of their unique ways of approaching the world by having them practice on ethnographic films. He claimed that, while doing this, students revealed their own particular approach to the world, with some focusing on sensory information (smells, tastes, etc.), some using many descriptors while others used few, and some injecting their own personal experiences. With these kinds of biases inherent in observers, training needs to include making observers aware of these problems before they move on to the research site.

Smith (1991) recommended that there be some means of simulating the use of the actual observational protocol in formal training sessions so that observers become familiar with the situations they encounter, the instrument(s) they use, and the sampling techniques they employ. For example, practice in estimating crowd size can be accomplished using films of mass gatherings of humans or even animal herds. Trainees may watch and record very simple observations before moving on to learn the researchers' more complex and precise classification system. Many trainers (e.g., Smith, 1991) suggest using consensus sessions in which the researcher meets regularly with observers to discuss problems and methods of coding. The more difficult the system of observation, the more training and supervision that may be needed.

Ethical Issues

Because of the types of roles in which field-workers may engage (participant, participant–observer, observer–participant, and nonparticipant), unique ethical issues arise. If the researcher identifies herself as such and explains her purpose—

as in, "I am writing my thesis on prostitution in Nevada and would like the opportunity to observe the selections customers make from among the women in the house"—then what is implied is not only that the researcher will observe, but also that those observations will result in some potentially publishable material (Agar, 1980).

The publication issue can be problematic because, in fieldwork, the potential for identifying who was studied is often much easier than in more anonymous types of social science research, where there are often large numbers of participants. Even if the researcher tries to disguise the identities of those observed, other individuals may discover who was involved, particularly if the group being studied was small. Also, in trying to disguise the identities of participants in any write-up of the observations, valuable material may be deleted or distorted. In some cases, the observer may feel ethically bound to show the group studied his or her final written report. A difficulty may present itself if group members want to change the report in significant ways, perhaps even disagreeing with the analysis, despite the researcher's attempts to protect anonymity.

If the researcher goes into the field in a covert fashion, another set of issues arises. Although the American Psychological Association (APA) considers observation of public behavior to be ethically acceptable, not all researchers agree with these guidelines. There is a presumption that people know that others may observe and record their public behavior. This belief, however, does not address that people are under scrutiny without having given permission for their participation in a research project. The privacy of those being observed for research purposes is invaded even when, in accordance with federal regulations, no identifying information about participants is recorded. Some researchers (Middlemist, Knowles, & Matter, 1977) observing public behavior see consent as having been given implicitly by people while they are in a public setting, whereas others (Steininger, Newell, & Garcia, 1984) still prefer to have informed consent obtained because they see scientific observation and recording of data as different from casual people-watching. Those in the latter camp also argue that, given the lengths laboratory researchers go to to acquire permission from participants, including allowing them to withdraw from the project at any time without penalty, field-workers should be held to the same or a similar standard.

A sticky problem for the observer of sexual behavior is arriving at an acceptable definition of *public setting*. Some sexual behavior takes place in truly private venues, such as the bedroom of one's home. Other sexual behavior takes place in ambiguously private places, such as public restrooms. Most people would agree that individuals expect to have privacy in a restroom. Although users of the facility may observe what goes on there, they are not recording these observations of what people assume to be private behavior.

Another issue can be the use of the observer's report by various bureaucracies. What should the researcher (who is observing illegal behavior, such as soliciting for prostitution or IV drug use) do if approached by governmental or law enforcement officials and asked to divulge the identities of those observed? This becomes a particularly difficult problem if the researcher has accepted money from governmental agencies. Although some researchers (e.g., Agar, 1980) believe that money can and should be accepted from any source, as long as the researcher controls the research process, others are uneasy about any strings being attached to their research. In reality, researchers do not have the right of privileged communication with participants in their research. Without a certificate of confidentiality granted through the National Institutes of Health's Office for the Protection from Research Risks (OPRR), an observer may have to turn over records or testify if subpoenaed.

All of these issues are raised without clear answers. In most cases, once researchers acquire approval from the human subjects research review panel at their institution, they are left to decide for themselves what feels comfortable in conducting their work.

METHODS IN ETHOLOGICAL OBSERVATION

Nonverbal courtship behavior has been described by several observers employing an ethological approach (Givens, 1978; Lockard & Adams, 1980; Moore, 1985; Perper, 1985). Ethology is an approach in which the emphasis is on description and classification of behaviors observed in the natural environment of the organism. Questions about evolution and function are considered as well as those about immediate function.

Sampling Behavior

Before using any system of observation in an actual research setting, one has to decide what and how to measure. Are all occurrences of the behavior to be recorded, or will specific behaviors be sampled systematically or randomly? If all occurrences of the behavior are to be recorded, then it might be advisable to use video or audio recording, particularly if the behavior is quite frequent. When the use of recording devices is not possible, then some type of shorthand system may be desirable to ensure that observers are able to capture all the behaviors exhibited. Babbie (1998) recommended the use of standardized recording forms, prepared in advance, when the observer knows that he or she is interested in observing a few specific behaviors. When the spatial characteristics of the research site are relevant, the use of gridded paper may make recording more systematic. Despite having prepared recording methods, the observer should not, however, be limited to those instruments and should reserve space for unexpected events that do not fit neatly into the formats described previously. It is the occurrence of such serendipitous events that give fieldwork its unique character.

If the researcher records a limited sample of behavior rather than all behaviors exhibited by the person, he or she must choose between event and time sampling. In event sampling, all examples of a particular class or type of behavior are recorded. Event sampling is particularly useful when observing behaviors that are infrequent or unusual; because the behavior is captured naturally, validity is not an issue. Also, because the individual exhibits the behavior in its complete form, the researcher does not have to make difficult decisions about the unit of behavior to record; he or she simply records the complete event as a whole.

Time sampling involves recording specific behavioral units at specific points in time. This can be accomplished in a systematic or random manner. In systematic sampling, behavior may be observed for 10 minutes at the beginning of each hour, whereas in random sampling, the 10-minute observation periods may be scattered randomly across several hours. The question being asked, as well as logistical issues such as number of observers available and access to the site, should help in deciding which sampling technique makes the most sense. Time sampling may mean that some rare occurrences are missed, but more often it also captures a representative sample of behavior because a larger span of time can be examined. Furthermore, the demands made on the research team are minimized.

Number of Individuals per Observation Session

If all occurrences of behaviors of interest are recorded for a particular individual during an entire sample period, that individual may be referred to as a *focal individual* (Altmann, 1974). Conversely, there may be a focal group or subgroup.

Alternatively, there may be no focal individuals because attention is focused on first one individual, then another, with the choice being determined on an ad lib basis. This approach is more likely to be employed when using event sampling. When focal individual sampling is used, the focal individuals are best selected randomly. The observer keeps track of the total amount of time during each observational session that the focal individual is in view so that calculations can be made about frequencies of occurrences for comparison across participants or sessions. When doing focal subgroup observation, it is important that the record be obtained when all individuals in the sample group are continuously visible throughout the sample period; otherwise it is difficult to make reliable comparisons to other subgroups. A record may be compiled that includes not only what the focal individual does, but also the behaviors directed to him or her by others. Then the observer can tell whether the focal individual is the actor or receiver of an action.

Sequential Analysis

Sequential analysis may be the method of choice when the observer wants to know about the nature of interaction sequences, rather than the behavior of an individual, as in focal individual sampling. This approach is invoked when antecedent–consequent events take place over a time period that may be missed if time or event sampling were used. A sample period begins when an interaction begins. During the sample, all behaviors under study are recorded in order of occurrence. The sampling process continues until the interaction sequence terminates or is interrupted. The next sample begins with the onset of another sequence of interactions. As can be seen from this description, this method allows the observer to obtain information about antecedent–consequence streams in social interaction that would not be discerned in focal individual sampling. One problem, however, may be defining the criteria for when a sequence begins and ends. Another problem arises when a sequence branches off in two directions perhaps because of the addition of a new member to the group (Altmann, 1974).

Rating Scales

After a researcher has a firm idea of what he or she wants to observe, he or she may then want to characterize the behaviors in some fashion. There are many possible rating scales that can be employed for this purpose, including category, numerical, and graphic types. The category rating scale presents the observer with several categories from which to select that best typifies the behavior being observed (e.g., dressed very seductively, dressed somewhat seductively, dressed moderately seductively, or dressed not at all seductively).

Numerical rating scales are the easiest to use and construct. They also provide the observer with numbers for statistical analysis. In the previous example, rather than use descriptive terms for seductive dress, numbers could be assigned (4 for *most seductive dress* to 1 for *least seductive dress*). An approach that combines the use of descriptive phrases with bars or lines is the graphic system. Both Kerlinger (1986) and Guilford (1954) regarded the graphic system as optimal because it fixes a continuum in the mind of the observer, suggests equal intervals, and is clear and easy to use.

Rating scales have inherent weaknesses. Because they are easy to construct, they are ubiquitous in social science research, often being used when there are better (even if more time-consuming) ways to answer a question. There are problems in the construction of the scale in terms of validity and subjectivity (see chap. 3, this volume). When the rater uses the scale during observation, several rating errors may come to the fore (Kerlinger, 1986). First is the tendency of raters to rate things favorably—the so-called *leniency effect*. Conversely, there is the error of severity, in which the raters provide low scores across the board. Perhaps the most general problem is that of the error of central tendency, whereby the rater avoids extreme judgments and uses the middle of the rating scale for most observations. According to Kerlinger (1986), this error is most likely to occur when the rater is unfamiliar with what is being rated.

Sociometry

Suppose that you want to know who is attracted to whom, as well as when there is a lack of reciprocal interest on the part of someone being selected by a potential partner. The use of sociometric analysis would provide you with a method of answering this question. *Sociometry* is actually a broad term covering a number of methods for gathering information on the selection, communication, or interaction patterns of organisms within a group (Kerlinger, 1986). It is commonly used as a mechanism for studying the attraction of members of groups and so is a very important analysis technique for sexuality research. Of the methods of sociometric analysis, sociometric matrixes are used most frequently by the behavioral scientist (for discussion of other sociometric techniques, see Ove, 1981; Fienberg & Wasserman, 1981).

A *matrix* is a rectangular array of numbers or other symbols. In a sociometry square, $n \times n$ matrixes are the norm, with n equaling the number of people in the group. Rows of the matrix are labeled i; columns are labeled j. Imagine that you have five people who are at a singles' bar. You observe them to see who they approach. Their approaches are choices. If, in your observations, you see that a group member has selected one other group member, the choice is represented by a 1. If a group member has not been observed to approach another group member, that choice (or nonchoice) is represented by 0. Analysis of the matrix determines who chose whom. With a simple matrix (and few group members), this is easy because there are only three possible observations. A simple one-way choice occurs when one person selects another, but that person rejects the approach. A mutual choice occurs when i chooses j and j reciprocates by choosing i as well. A no-choice situation occurs when neither of two individuals chooses the other.

The extent to which any member is chosen is easily seen by adding the columns of the matrix. One person can be determined to be popular if he or she is chosen by all of the group members. Conversely, a person is unpopular if not selected by anyone or if selected by relatively fewer persons in the group.

According to Altmann (1974), the technique of matrix completion is particularly suited to studies in which the basic problem of interest to the researcher is the direction and degree of one-sidedness in the relations of pairs of individuals within a group, but is not suited to many other types of questions about behavior. Altmann recommended that focal individual sampling generally be used instead because, through this method, a researcher can answer questions about asymmetry and other aspects of behavior as well.

ETHNOGRAPHY

The early works of Mead (1930) and Malinowski (1929), as well as the accounts offered by Humphreys (1970) and Dalby (1985), are considered ethnographic rather than ethological. This type of observational research entails observing and recording ongoing events of a particular group of people while one is at least somewhat of a participant. Observations tend to be narrative accounts describing all of the relevant information about group members, rather than sampled behaviors of a particular kind. Given how active people are and the range of activities in which they engage, this can be a demanding task. If that were not enough, a good ethnography requires another level of analysis (otherwise a video camera would suffice): that of discovering relationships and generating hypotheses about the underlying reasons for those things that the observer sees.

So that field-workers know what to observe, Smith (1991) recommended that ethnography be grounded in theory. That is not to say that fieldwork is not sometimes also used to test ways of organizing observations. Indeed, Smith argued that in most cases the field-worker is constantly comparing hypotheses derived from theory to the findings from the field to devise better explanations. Consequently, Smith characterized field research as having five stages: provisionalizing, monitoring, analyzing, routine mapping, and resolving.

Provisionalizing is the first stage of field research, when the scientist knows little (aside from library research) about the individual(s) being observed. Basic decisions must be made about the scope of the problems to study and how to go about doing so. According to Agar (1986), the field researcher assumes the role of learner in a world he or she does not understand.

The *monitoring, analyzing*, and *routine mapping* stages constitute a circular process. Once the researcher decides what events to observe, he or she watches the natural environment for their occurrence. Smith (1991) and Babbie (1998) both recommended using these guiding questions: Who did what? Who said what to whom? What was the context of what happened (along with notations of possible bias on the part of the observer)? This who, what, where, and when approach is also commonly used by police when gathering information about a crime or by reporters when gathering information for a report.

The process of analyzing permeates fieldwork. Smith (1991) recommended that the observer constantly ask the question, What happens when. . . ? Only by doing so will the observer be able to uncover the patterns underlying human behavior. By asking this question on leaving the field, the observer may reconsider what kinds of data to record when returning to the research setting.

Knowing what else, if anything, to observe may help the researcher in the fourth stage—routine mapping. Routine mapping is used to depict the ordering of events. In this regard, Smith (1991) recommended flow chart construction to ensure that the observer actually understands what is taking place. The chart may be very crude, but even a rough map may help the researcher discover alternative explanations to those being considered.

By using a circular model of monitoring, analyzing, and routine mapping, with each activity enhancing the other two, the observer more readily achieves resolution. Resolution comes about when the field-worker has moved from the discovery of hypotheses to the testing of hypotheses and is satisfied that more observations will not illuminate further understanding (Smith, 1991). Schatzman and Strauss (1973) spoke of this as *saturation*. At this point, the researcher is ready to move onto the development of higher order analysis, unveiling inferences and holding them out to the scholarly community for evaluation. The field-worker is prepared to produce the report that caps off any field study. A good narrative requires that the observer describe the physical setting in which the observations took place, take adequate notes throughout the process of collecting information about those being observed, and try to uncover the relationships among behaviors.

PROBLEMS IN DATA COLLECTION

Because behavioral observation is so demanding of the observer, many problems in data collection are traceable to that observer. A poorly trained observer or one who, although trained, is not meticulous about record keeping may produce data that do not adequately reflect what actually happened.

Cognitive Biases

Beyond the issue of training or poor methodology lies the problem of bias. Suppose, on the one hand, that an observer who is strongly hostile to gays is observing support systems in the gay community for those dying of AIDS. Expectations about what will be seen may affect people's observations (Fiske & Taylor, 1991). They interpret what they see in terms of what they expect to find. Researchers who dislike gay people may invalidate their findings if they are not careful to stick closely to the guidelines for behavioral observation. As noted earlier, Bennett (1960) recommended sensitizing observers to their unique biases as part of their training to help them control the effects of those biases. In addition, working with a colleague and collecting inter-observer reliability scores of behavioral ratings may uncover instances of biased observation.

Another source of bias is selective attention. Observers are confronted with a wealth of information in the field, so it can be extremely difficult for the behavioral observer to take in everything needed to process. Consequently, people tend to pay attention to individuals who stand out perhaps because they are dressed unusually or they constitute a minority in a group (Fiske & Taylor, 1991). As a result, observers may unknowingly focus selectively on certain individuals rather than on a representative sample of people. In my research on courtship signaling in women, it is easy to see how the results would have been biased had we not randomly selected the women to be observed, but instead had picked the most attractive individuals or those who were most pronounced in their bodily movements.

When people cannot take notes during observational research, they may experience reconstructive memory (Fiske & Taylor, 1991). That is, they may remember events not as they actually occurred, but in a way that makes sense to them. This happens because of the mental stories people construct to guide their behavior in unfamiliar situations and help them remember things. For example, a researcher who thought he or she knew how prostitutes solicited customers may later, when recording his or her observations, be guided by a stereotype obtained from films rather than what actually happened. To remedy this problem, the researcher should record behavioral observations as they occur if at all possible.

Finally, being immersed in the setting may mean that, across time, researchers lose the fresh perspective with which they came to the field. To avoid this, researchers should take breaks to reflect back on and analyze their field behavior. On returning to the field, it is more likely that observers will notice things that earlier might have been taken for granted.

Record Keeping

If at all possible, it is optimal to record observations as they occur. Sometimes this is easy because the observer is working in a setting in which seeing someone write is not unusual. When I observed the flirting behaviors of girls, playing the role of a mother at the mall or the skating rink allowed me to write down my observations under the cover of doing work while supervising my supposed children. Because my students and I work in dark, smoky bars when observing adults, we are able to use concealed audio recorders to collect data. In many instances, however, taking notes in an obvious fashion can be problematic. Similarly, the use of a video recorder, camera, or laptop computer may make it so obvious that research is being conducted that both the observer and those being observed will be uncomfortable. In these situations, the researcher has no choice but to record observations at a later time.

When observers must wait several hours to write down their observations, both the cognitive biases described earlier and typical forgetting may lead to inaccurate data. However, experience at doing fieldwork has led many researchers to develop strategies to aid in a more accurate reconstruction of events. Some of these strategies include recording observations in private to eliminate distractions, recording observations in the order that events occurred, and making an outline to organize observations before recording them (Bogdan, 1972).

Even when one can record while observing, Smith (1991) recommended observation periods of no longer than 15 minutes with an outside limit of 2 hours. This limitation is necessary because observing and recording can be extremely demanding for the observer rapidly surpassing the fatigue threshold. Smith additionally recommended that the field-worker record a wide variety of information, including use of physical space, nonverbal behavior, speech of actors, listener behaviors, actions of peripheral persons, and actions in peripheral settings. When looking at this extensive list, it becomes obvious why shorter periods of observation are desirable. With so many sources of information, even a short period of observation results in copious notes that have to be transcribed once the researcher leaves the field.

Next, the field-worker needs to compile from the field notes a more complete account of the day's activities. This is best done as soon as possible after leaving the field and certainly should be done the same day. There are various ways to organize this narrative. Some field-workers prefer to use essay format, whereas others make use of charts with columns for different kinds of material, perhaps dividing description from inference. Babbie (1998) recommended keeping a chronological record using a word processor. Numerous copies of the original can then be made for cutting up, writing on, and so forth. Because the observer relies on this narrative when writing the final report, it is important that it be as complete and precise as possible. For example, rather than saying a large number of people were present, the field-worker should make a numeric estimate. Similarly, the richer the detail in the daily narrative, the more the observer has to use in the final report. One may never use much of what is recorded, but it is better to have too much material than not enough; the field-worker cannot go back and reconstruct what happened with any degree of reliability. Finally, without a good ongoing diary, data analysis will be based on inadequate or superficial information.

Because it can be cumbersome to page through the daily narrative while analyzing data, the field-worker may employ different organizational strategies to increase efficiency. McCall and Simmons (1969) recommended the use of a different folder for various types of information, such as variables, hypotheses, and categories of behavior. I like to use large index cards, on which I describe each participant, his or her behavior, and responses made to him or her by others, because I can lay them out on the floor and easily reorganize them to look for routines. Schatzman and Strauss (1973) recommended separately labeled sets of notes according to whether they are observational, theoretical, or methodological. With the advent of personal computers, file management software makes it possible for the researcher to enter and store data, as well as to conduct analysis in ways that are less time-consuming than those of the past. Word processing systems permit searching notes for specific words or phrases, which can help in content analysis. A partial list of computer programs designed for qualitative research includes Ethnograph, Nudist, Aspects, Context, HyperResearch, Intext, and Top Grade (Babbie, 1998). Whatever strategy is used, the goal is to make sense of what is happening and see if anything is being overlooked.

Reactivity

When people know they are being observed, they may change their behavior. This is particularly true in the case of illegal behavior or behavior, such as sexuality, about which many people are uncomfortable. Consequently, many researchers choose the complete participant role or make nonparticipant observations covertly. Those who operate in a covert fashion argue that to divulge their presence would irreparably harm the research environment: People would behave in an unnatural manner and the project would be ruined. Heyns and Lippitt (1954), however, argued early on that, in reality, most individuals and groups adapt quickly to an observer's presence and behave as usual. With this in mind, it is advisable for observers to allow those being observed to habituate to their presence before collecting actual data for their project.

Influencing Events

Although the observer believes that he or she is reducing reactivity by choosing the complete participant role, such may not be the case. The researcher may change the behavior of those being observed simply by being present. In many cases, the researcher, being a new group member, receives a great deal of attention. In other instances, the group may select the observer to a position of leadership or influence. Consequently, the observer should try to minimize his or her influence as much as possible and be aware of possible influence when interpreting data.

Effects on the Observer

When the observer conceals his or her true purpose by becoming part of the group being studied, he or she may be faced with a variety of problems. First, unless one is a trained actor, it can be very difficult to remain *in role*. This is particularly true if the research project lasts months or even years. It can be very difficult to remain in character for a long period of time, particularly if the researcher's adopted role is in conflict with his or her actual values or lifestyle.

Furthermore, if the researcher is too self-conscious about being discovered by the group members, that anxiety may actually lead to his or her discovery. The researcher may inadvertently give him or herself away through a mistake in speech, dress, or behavior. In some instances, the slip may not be entirely unintentional, as the researcher wants to be revealed. It is not uncommon for covert participant observers to feel so guilty about deceiving and invading the privacy of those observed that they feel compelled to reveal their true identity to those in the group.

Because the participant observer immerses him or herself in the situation he or she is studying, he or she is in danger of *going native*, or adopting the attitudes and behaviors of the culture under study (Smith, 1991). This may lead to the observer interpreting his observations with a less detached view than that called for in science or, in the extreme situation, of data collection going out the window.

A final difficulty may emerge as the project ends. Exiting the research setting may be painful for both the observer and those she observed especially if the field-worker participated to a high degree in the behavior being studied. Host group members may feel abandoned and the observer may feel the pull of obligations built during the study. Finally, similar to a therapist, unless ties are maintained, field-workers must live with the fact that they are no longer privy to the activities of those they observed for so long. Their lives go on without the field-workers knowing the rest of the story.

EVALUATING AND INTERPRETING DATA

Many of the types of data recorded in observational research are easily analyzed. Quantitative data the researcher has collected can be represented by total absolute or relative (percentage) frequencies of observation. Duration of behavior is also analyzed quite easily. The researcher may report the total duration of some event or measure its relative duration with a mean or percentage of total time. The observer could calculate measures derived from these other numbers such as average duration per occurrence or rate of occurrence (Altmann, 1974).

When the observer has worked on an issue that is not captured by using any numbers whatsoever (ethnography), the data take the form of a narrative report. A good published account of observations is one in which the reader could work back to the actual field notes, but that also summarizes material in the field notes so that the reader does not have to view repetitive material. At times, the researcher may quote directly from field notes (to capture the essence of a particularly striking event), but more often the researcher condenses and synthesizes. It is also the job of the behavioral observer to provide analysis of what he or she has seen, illuminate patterns, and consider possible explanations for the behaviors observed.

Indeed, one of the major problems in behavioral observation is the observer. To a certain extent, this is a general problem in the social sciences because we are studying ourselves, rather than another species, which can bring a wide variety of biases into play. The observer is intimately involved in making both observations and inferences from those observations. He or she is immersed in the situation. Therefore, the strengths and weaknesses of the findings of any project rest squarely on the shoulders of the observer. It is making inferences that most stringently tests the creativity of the researcher; if one merely had to report what was observed, rather than also trying to make sense of it, any video recorder or reporter would suffice. The observer's powers of inference, bringing together the observations and potential underlying patterns, are what make for good observational research.

Of course, observation systems differ on the amount of inference required of the observer. Molecular systems require relatively little inference. The observer simply notes what the individual says or does. At a very basic level, the observer may simply be noting the presence or absence of a particular behavior, or counting its frequency. No inferences are made in such systems. However, most research projects involve some degree of structuring the findings for the reader.

In the middle of the continuum are the inferences used by the researcher to construct categories. In this case, it is the job of the observer to place the behaviors observed under overarching designations that seem to make sense of disparate behaviors. If the items grouped are relatively similar and unambiguous, there will be few problems with reliability.

Situations where a high degree of inference is required from the researcher are the most demanding. Probably the best examples come from situations in which the observer is dealing with an ambiguous concept such as *dominance* or trying to capture the measurement of something internal, such as love. The researcher has to provide some sort of operational definition. In the case of love, the amount of time spent in mutual gaze has been used (Rubin, 1970).

One of the most common errors in interpreting observational results is to overinterpret the data—either to generalize the results to a broader population than actually sampled or see a cause-and-effect relationship where there is merely correlation. I was very happy when the editors of *Semiotica* suggested adding a note to the effect that my research on nonverbal courtship behavior in women (Moore & Butler, 1989) had been done in a midwestern U.S. university community with mainly college-age individuals. It is unlikely that the same results would be obtained in another cultural context. Indeed, in talking to Karl Grammer (personal communication, May 5, 1999), I discovered that he and his students had tried to replicate my study in Austria only to find that women there did not employ many of the nonverbal behaviors commonly seen here in the United States. According to Grammer (as well as one of my contacts in the Netherlands), an interested woman merely goes to stand near the man she finds attractive, waiting for him to talk to her. There are none of the smiles, glances, and primping behaviors so central to American ways of flirting.

Field research is one scientific method where inductive logic is very important. In this regard, looking for similarities and differences is advisable. In searching out the former, you are looking for norms or universals. Do all the prostitutes dress seductively? If yes, you can ask why; what purpose does dress serve? Uncovering exceptions may allow you to see how deviations from the norm also serve a purpose and how those who are different in their behavior handle their nonconformity. Putting similarities and differences together can help you move to the thematic level and understand the thread or threads that tie together many of your observations.

SUMMARY AND CONCLUSION

Observational research has many uses. Researchers who do not routinely do field-work often find going to a natural setting and casually observing behavior to be instrumental in generating ideas for laboratory research. Similarly, the use of behavioral observation can be valuable for fruitful hypothesis generation for any type of research (field, survey, or laboratory). Employing behavioral observation as a research method can inform us about relationships and contingencies. Then we can test speculations about causation in the laboratory. Conversely, field observation can be used to test the generalizability of laboratory findings. This approach is definitely recommended to augment the use of questionnaires or interviews in which the researcher is relying on the perception and veracity of the informants. Of course, some kinds of research can only be done with naturalistic observation methods, such as when the researcher wants to know about the behaviors of individuals in their natural environments. Accordingly, behavioral observation deserves a place in the battery of methods used to study human sexuality.

SUGGESTED READINGS

There are many good books that outline methods of research for the social sciences. I find Babbie (1998) and Smith (1991, chaps. 9 & 10) particularly helpful. Altmann (1974) provided detailed discussions of sampling methods. A similarly comprehensive classic review of sociometric matrixes, with discussions of validity and reliability, can be found in Lindzey and Byrne (1968). Herbert and Attridge (1975) provided an excellent guide to constructing categories. A good resource for nitty-gritty issues in data collection and analysis is Lofland and Lofland (1995). For an in-depth look at qualitative field research, I recommend Shaffir and Stebbins (1991).

REFERENCES

Agar, M. H. (1980). *The professional stranger: An informal introduction to ethnography*. New York: Academic Press.

Agar, M. H. (1986). *Speaking of ethnography*. Beverly Hills, CA: Sage.

Allgeier, A. R., & Allgeier, E. R. (1995). *Sexual interaction* (4th ed.). Lexington, MA: D. C. Heath.

Altmann, J. (1974). Observational study of behavior: Sampling methods. *Behavior, 49*, 227–267.

Babbie, E. (1998). *The practice of social research* (8th ed.). Belmont, CA: Wadsworth.

Bales, R. (1951). *Interaction process analysis*. Reading, MA: Addison-Wesley.

Bartell, G. D. (1970). Group sex among the mid-Americans. *The Journal of Sex Research, 6*, 113–130.

Beach, F. A. (1977). *Human sexuality in four perspectives*. Baltimore: Johns Hopkins University Press.

Bennett, J. M. (1960). Individual perspective in fieldwork: An experimental training course. In R. N. Adams & J. J. Preiss (Eds.), *Human organization research* (pp. 431–442). Homewood, IL: Dorsey.

Bogdan, R. (1972). *Participant observation in organizational settings*. Syracuse, NY: Syracuse University Press.

Dalby, L. C. (1985). *Geisha*. New York: Vintage Books.

Douglas, J. D., Rasmussen, P. H., & Flanagan, C. A. (1977). *The nude beach*. Beverly Hills, CA: Sage.

Fienberg, S., & Wasserman, S. (1981). Categorical data analysis of single sociometric relations. In S. Leinhardt (Ed.), *Sociological methodology* (pp. 156–192). San Francisco: Jossey-Bass.

Fiske, S. T., & Taylor, S. G. (1991). *Social cognition* (2nd ed.). New York: McGraw-Hill.

Givens, D. (1978). The nonverbal basis of attraction: Flirtation, courtship, and seduction. *Psychiatry, 41*, 346–359.

Gold, R. L. (1969). Roles in sociological observation. In G. J. McCall & J. L. Simms (Eds.), *Issues in participant observation* (pp. 30–39). Reading, MA: Addison-Wesley.

Guilford, J. (1954). *Psychometric methods* (2nd ed.). New York: McGraw-Hill.

Herbert, J., & Attridge, C. (1975). A guide for developers and users of observation systems and manuals. *American Educational Research Journal, 12*, 1–20.

Heyns, R., & Lippitt, R. (1954). Systematic observational techniques. In G. Lindsey (Ed.), *Handbook of social psychology* (pp. 370–404). Cambridge, MA: Addison-Wesley.

Hinde, R. (1966). *Animal behaviour: A synthesis of ethology and comparative psychology*. New York: McGraw-Hill.

Hinde, R. (1975). The concept of function. In S. Bariends, C. Beer, & A. Manning (Eds.), *Function and evolution in behavior* (pp. 3–15). Oxford: Clarendon.

Humphreys, L. (1970). *Tearoom trade: Impersonal sex in public places*. Chicago: Aldine.

Kerlinger, F. N. (1986). *Foundations of behavioral research* (3rd ed.). New York: Holt, Rinehart & Winston.

Lindzey, G., & Byrne, D. (1968). Measurement of social choice and interpersonal attractiveness. In G. Lindzey & E. Aronson (Eds.), *The handbook of social psychology* (pp. 452–525). Reading, MA: Addison-Wesley.

Lockard, J. S., & Adams, R. M. (1980). Courtship behaviors in public: Different age/sex roles. *Ethology and Sociobiology, 1*, 245–253.

Lofland, J., & Lofland, L. H. (1995). *Analyzing social settings: A guide to qualitative observation and analysis*. Belmont, CA: Wadsworth.

Malinowski, B. (1929). *The sexual life of savages*. New York: Harcourt, Brace & World.

Marshall, D. S., & Suggs, R. C. (1971). *Human sexual behavior: Variations in the ethnographic spectrum*. New York: Basic Books.

Masters, W. H., & Johnson, V. E. (1966). *Human sexual response*. Boston, MA: Little, Brown.

McCall, G. J., & Simmons, J. L. (1969). *Issues in participant observation*. Reading, MA: Addison-Wesley.

McCammon, S., Knox, D., & Schacht, C. (1993). *Choices in sexuality*. Minneapolis, MN: West.

McGrew, W. C. (1972). *An ethological study of children's behavior*. New York: Academic Press.

Mead, M. (1930). *Growing up in New Guinea*. New York: New American Library.

Middlemist, R. D., Knowles, E. S., & Matter, C. F. (1977). What to do and what to report: A reply to Koocher. *Journal of Personality and Social Psychology, 35*, 122–124.

Money, J., Cawte, J. E., Bianchi, G. N., & Nurcombe, B. (1970). Sex training and traditions in Arnhem Land. *British Journal of Medical Psychology, 43*, 383–399.

Moore, M. M. (1985). Nonverbal courtship patterns in women: Context and consequences. *Ethology and Sociobiology, 6*, 237–247.

Moore, M. M. (1995). Courtship signaling and adolescents: "Girls just wanna have fun"? *The Journal of Sex Research, 32*, 319–328.

Moore, M. M., & Butler, D. L. (1989). Predictive aspects of nonverbal courtship behavior in women. *Semiotica, 3*, 205–215.

Ove, F. (1981). A survey of statistical methods for graph analysis. In S. Leinhardt (Ed.), *Sociological methodology* (pp. 110–155). San Francisco: Jossey-Bass.

Perper, T. (1985). *Sex signals: The biology of love*. Philadelphia: ISI Press.

Petersen, D. M., & Dressel, P. L. (1982). Equal time for women: Social notes on the male strip show. *Urban Life, 11*, 185–208.

Prus, R., & Irini, S. (1988). *Hookers, rounders, and desk clerks: The social organization of the hotel community*. Salem, WI: Sheffield.

Rubin, Z. (1970). Measurement of romantic love. *Journal of Personality and Social Psychology, 16*, 265–273.

Schatzman, L., & Strauss, A. L. (1973). *Field research: Strategies for a natural sociology*. Englewood Cliffs, NJ: Prentice-Hall.

Scheflen, A. E. (1965). Quasi-courtship behavior in psychotherapy. *Psychiatry, 28*, 245–257.

Shaffir, W. B., & Stebbins, R. A. (Eds.). (1991). *Experiencing fieldwork: An inside view of qualitative research*. Newbury Park, CA: Sage.

Smith, H. W. (1991). *Strategies of social research* (3rd ed.). Fort Worth, TX: Holt, Rinehart & Winston.

Stein, M. (1990). *The ethnography of an adult bookstore: Private scenes in public places.* Lewiston, NY: Edwin Mellen.

Steininger, M., Newell, J. D., & Garcia, L. T. (1984). *Ethical issues in psychology.* Homewood, IL: Dorsey.

Story, M. D. (1993). Personal and professional perspectives on social nudism: Should you be personally involved in your research? *The Journal of Sex Research, 30,* 111–114.

Warren, C. (1974). *Identity and community in the gay world.* New York: Wiley.

Wolcott, H. F. (1973). *The man in the principle's office: An ethnography.* Prospect Heights, IL: Waveland.

7

▼▼▼▼▼▼▼

Psychophysiological Measurement of Sexual Arousal

Erick Janssen
The Kinsey Institute/Indiana University

Sexual psychophysiology is an emerging discipline. The annual number of publications on sexual arousal has increased about 10-fold over the last 30 years. Paralleling this growth in output is a considerable expansion of the field in terms of its subject matter. Whereas initially researchers focused on the assessment and treatment of sexual deviations and disorders, psychophysiological methods are now being applied to an increasingly broad array of questions. The topics studied include the activation and inhibition of sexual arousal; the psychophysiology of sexual motivation, orgasm, and ejaculation; the effects of aging, hormones, and mood on sexual responsivity; the association between sexual preferences/orientation and sexual arousal; and the effects of exposure to erotica/pornography on sexual attitudes and behavior. On a more applied level, psychophysiological methods are used in the assessment of sexual offenders, diagnosis of sexual dysfunctions, and evaluation of treatment efficacy.

Sexual psychophysiology can be defined as the application of psychophysiological methods to the study of sexual arousal, with special emphasis on the interplay between subjective (cognitive and affective) and physiological determinants of sexual arousal (Rosen & Beck, 1988). However, what exactly is sexual arousal? The first English-language article in which the term appeared was published in 1942 by the eminent sexuality researcher Frank Beach. Interestingly, Beach (1942) referred to sexual arousal as a motivational construct, as did Whalen (1966), who, in an influential article on sexual motivation, used the words *arousal* and *motivation* interchangeably. It is not unlikely that the publications by Kinsey and his colleagues (1948, 1953), who used the term *sexual arousal* to describe the physiological changes resulting from sexual stimulation, and the work of Masters and Johnson (1966) changed the meaning of this term. Nowadays the term *sexual arousal* is understood to be related to the possible physiological and mental changes that occur in response to sexual stimulation.

Most people can probably describe an experience that characterizes certain features of sexual arousal. Still the multiple components potentially constituting sexual arousal, and the variable relationships among them, make it difficult to design a universal template that can be used to classify phenomena as sexual. To put it differently, we do not really know the necessary and sufficient conditions for labeling a response as sexual. Is the subjective feeling of sexual arousal sufficient for saying someone is sexually aroused? Is an erection of the penis, even if the man connected to it does not feel sexually aroused, a sufficient condition for labeling his state as sexual? Is it a necessary condition? Sachs (2000) presented 19 examples of verbal and operational definitions of sexual arousal. The diversity is striking. Some rely on the presence of a genital response in inferring a state of sexual arousal, others give primacy to an individual's subjective experience of arousal, and still others make the attribution dependent on the presence of sexual activity.

Sexual arousal can be conceived of as an emotion (Everaerd, 1988). As with other emotions, sexual arousal consists of physiological, psychological (cognitive and affective), and behavioral components, and the relationships among these components vary. This variability appears to be a basic characteristic of the "human sexual response" and critically determines the relevance of sexual psychophysiology. After all, why measure genital responses if these responses can (much more economically) be predicted from the feelings people report having?

A common finding in psychophysiological research is that correlations between subjective and genital responses are lower in women than in men (e.g., Laan & Everaerd, 1995). The discordant pattern most frequently found in women is that genital responses occur while subjective sexual arousal is low or absent. Although correlations are generally higher in men than in women, discordant patterns can also be found in men. For instance, several studies demonstrated that different experimental manipulations may modify genital response levels in men while not affecting their subjective sexual arousal (Janssen & Everaerd, 1993). Also, relationships between reported feelings and physiological responses have been found to be weaker in men with erectile problems than in sexually functional men. Janssen, Everaerd, van Lunsen, and Oerlemans (1994), for example, found that men with and without psychogenic erectile problems responded with equally strong erections to a sexual film that was combined with vibrotactile stimulation of the penis. However, the men with psychogenic erectile dysfunction reported having less strong erections and experienced lower levels of sexual arousal.

In view of the variability in physiological and subjective response patterns, it is arbitrary to give primacy to one response component over another in the definition and study of sexual arousal. More important is to further our understanding of the interplay between its subjective and physiological components. In my view, sexual arousal may, at this stage, be best approached as a complex triad of affective, physiological, and behavioral processes; the most fruitful approach to studying sexual arousal is to assess both subjective and physiological sexual responses.

HISTORIC BACKGROUND OF SEXUAL PSYCHOPHYSIOLOGY

Although sexual psychophysiology is young as a scientific discipline, awareness of and interest in the interrelationships between psychological and physiological sexual processes is clearly not unique to our time (Bullough & Bullough, 1977; Rosen & Beck, 1988). However, the first systematic attempts at establishing an understanding of the psychophysiology of sexual response should probably be dated to the first part of the 20th century, originating with writings on sexual physiology. Two medical texts produced in the 1930s were particularly influential. These were the marriage manual *Ideal Marriage* by Van de Velde (1926) and Dickinson's (1933) *Human Sex Anatomy*. These books described in detail the physiological processes that occur during sexual arousal. Dickinson pioneered the use of a glass tube to observe genital responses in women—a precursor to modern measurement techniques. These books predated the work of Alfred Kinsey and of William Masters and Virginia Johnson. In the preface to *Human Sexual Response* (1966), Masters and Johnson acknowledged the importance of Dickinson and Van de Velde to the history of sexuality research by declaring that they "first dared to investigate and to write of sexual physiology" (p. vii).

Kinsey and his colleagues, and later Masters and Johnson, provided the context that permitted further study of sexual arousal. Kinsey and his colleagues were among the first to provide an extensive description of the responses that occur during sexual arousal—an aspect of their work not often recognized by scholars. In *Sexual Behavior in the Human Female* (1953), they specified some 20 physiological changes that accompany sexual behavior, including blood pressure, peripheral blood flow, respiration, and central nervous system changes. Western society had just begun to digest Kinsey's work when Masters and Johnson (1966) published *Human Sexual Response*—a book in which they reported detailed observations on human sexual response in 694 individuals during both intercourse and masturbation. Masters and Johnson summarized their work by presenting a descriptive model of the human sexual response. That now well-known four-stage model of sexual response has been the stimulus for much psychophysiological research.

The publications of Dickinson (1933) and Masters and Johnson (1966) marked the beginning of laboratory approaches to the study of sexual arousal. The hallmark of this type of approach is the direct observation and measurement of bodily responses during actual sexual arousal (Rosen & Beck, 1988). In the case of Dickinson and Masters and Johnson, observation literally involved the use of cameras and other tools to visualize physiological changes. In addition to the fact that this type of methodology is invasive and potentially reactive, it does not easily lend itself to quantification. For this reason, the birth of sexual psychophysiology as a discipline is perhaps better assigned to the year the first psychophysiological measurement instrument was introduced (i.e., the first device with which genital responses could be quantified continuously). This device, a so-called *penile plethysmograph*, was described by Freund in 1963, three years prior to the publication of Masters and Johnson's book.

ANATOMY AND PHYSIOLOGY OF SEXUAL RESPONSE

Before presenting some models of sexual response and the methodologies used to measure sexual responses, those aspects of genital anatomy and physiology relevant to this chapter are briefly described.

Men

There are three cylindrical, spongelike bodies of erectile tissue in the penis: two corpora cavernosa and one corpus spongiosum. The three corpora contain small irregular compartments or vascular spaces separated by bonds of smooth muscle tissue. These bodies become engorged with blood during erection. The function of the corpora cavernosa is purely erectile. The corpus spongiosum (of which the glans is a part) also acts as a urinary conduit and an organ of ejaculation.

Erection is essentially a hydrodynamic manifestation, weighing arterial inflow against venous outflow. Many investigators believe that the driving force for the increase in blood flow to the penis is decreased vascular resistance in the corpora. A large number of studies have explored the role of corporeal smooth muscle tissue in this process. Cavernosal tissue is spongelike and composed of a meshwork of interconnected cavernosal spaces. The most plausible theory is that the cavernous smooth muscles of the corpora, which are in a tonically contracted state when the penis is flaccid, relax during the initiation of penile erection (Melman, 1992). This relaxation lowers the corporal vascular resistance and results in increased blood flow to the penis. Venous return is diminished by means of a passive occlusion of the penile veins against the tunica albuginea—a thick fibrous sheath that surrounds the corpora cavernosa.

The cholinergic, parasympathetic component of erection was long considered to be the primary efferent system for generating penile erection. More recent evidence, however, suggests that normal erection requires participation of the parasympathetic *and* the sympathetic and somatic nervous systems. In addition, researchers have begun to explore the role of nonadrenergic, noncholinergic neurotransmitters in erection. Ottesen et al. (1987) found that a vasoactive intestinal polypeptide (VIP) plays a role in the mediation of erection. Other studies have focused on the role of prostaglandins and nitric oxide. At present, although its synthesis and action in the penis is regulated by many other factors, nitric oxide is considered to be the principal mediator of corporeal smooth muscle relaxation (Burnett, 1997).

Women

The organ that has been the main focus of psychophysiological measurement in women has been the vagina. The vagina consists of a flat, scalelike epithelium, is surrounded by a sheath of smooth muscle, and has numerous transverse folds (Levin, 1992). The vascular system is supplied with an extensive anastomotic network throughout the vagina's length. During sexual arousal, vasocongestion (a pooling of blood) occurs, and vaginal lubrication is believed to result from vasocongestion raising the pressure inside the capillaries and creating an increase in transudation of plasma through the vaginal epithelium (Levin, 1992). This *vaginal lubricative fluid* initially forms sweatlike droplets that coalesce into a lubricative film covering the vaginal wall.

The sympathetic and parasympathetic divisions of the autonomic nervous system innervate the vaginal epithelium, blood vessels, and smooth muscle. The clitoris is innervated through the terminal branch of the pudendal nerve. Among the peptides located in the female genitals are nitric oxide and VIP. According to Levin (1998), the available data point to VIP as the possible major neurotransmitter controlling vaginal blood flow and lubrication. In his discussion on the role of nitric oxide, Levin concluded that, although nitric oxide has been strongly implicated as an essential neurotransmitter in penile erection mechanisms in men, there is, at this stage, no evidence that it is involved in the control of vaginal blood flow. Indeed, Hoyle, Stones, Robson, Whitley, and Burnstock (1996), in a study with pre- and postmenopausal women, failed to find nitric oxide synthase, the enzyme that manufactures nitric oxide, in approximately half of the women in their sample. The relative importance of VIP and nitric oxide, however, remains open to investigation.

Several psychophysiological studies in women have found that levels of subjective sexual arousal in response to sexual stimuli tend to remain stable across phases of the menstrual cycle. However, a more complex picture emerges for genital responses. Some studies have found stable response patterns across phases (e.g., Hoon, Bruce, & Kinchelow, 1982; Morrell, Dixen, Carter, & Davidson, 1984; Slob, Koster, Radder, & Werff-ten Bosch, 1990). Others have found higher response levels during the premenstrual rather than during the periovulatory phase (e.g., Meuwisen & Over, 1992; Schreiner-Engel, Schiavi, Smith, & White, 1981). Still others found complicated interactions between menstrual phases and the order of the phases tested (e.g., Slob, Ernste, & Werff-ten Bosch, 1991; Graham, Janssen, & Sanders, 2000). Among the factors that may have contributed to this lack of consistency are differences in the method used for determining cycle phase, experimental design, and participant characteristics (Hedricks, 1994). Although there is no consensus about the possible effects of menstrual cycle phase on sexual arousal, it is important to control for, or at the very least assess, participants' menstrual phase.

MODELS OF SEXUAL RESPONSE

Over the years, a number of models of sexual response have been described in the sexological literature. The amount of empirical support that existed at the time they were introduced varies, as does the extent to which they inspired new research and the development of therapeutic interventions. One of the first models of sexual response was introduced by Havelock Ellis in 1906. His two-stage model differentiates between a stage of building up sexual arousal (tumescence) and one of climactic release (detumescence). This model was extended by Moll (1908/1912), who described a "curve of voluptuousness" consisting of four phases: the build-up of sexual excitement (the ascending limb); a high, stable level of sexual excitement (the equable voluptuous sensation); orgasm (the acme); and the cessation of the sexual impulse (the decline), usually associated with a sense of satisfaction.

The Sexual Response Cycle

Although initially introduced as little more than a frame of reference, Masters and Johnson's (1966) four-stage model is probably the best known model of sexual response to date. The model, reminiscent of Moll's curve of voluptuousness, describes the genital and extragenital responses that occur in humans during sexual behavior. The phases are (a) excitement, (b) plateau, (c) orgasmic, and (d) resolution. Although few would dispute the impact of the Masters and Johnson model on subsequent research and therapy, it has been subjected to serious criticism. For one, the separation of sexual response into four discrete stages has been challenged (Robinson, 1976). The distinction between the excitement and plateau phases is especially problematic; there is no empirical support for a clearly identifiable plateau phase. Similarly, questions have been raised about the universality of the model (Tiefer, 1991). Another issue is of particular interest to the psychophysiologist: Masters and Johnson failed to adequately describe the methods they used to collect their data, and the physiological data were not quantified nor presented in a form that permitted evaluation by others. Finally, the studies were restricted to the observation of physiological changes; psychological factors are not considered in Masters and Johnson's model.

Kaplan (1977, 1979) proposed a modification of the Masters and Johnson model. In her three-stage model, the first stage is not sexual excitement but desire. Her second and third phases, excitement and orgasm, are similar to Masters and Johnson's first and third phases. Kaplan's model has played an influential role in the formulation of the American Psychiatric Association's diagnostic manuals since the Diagnostic and Statistical Manual of Mental Disorders (3rd ed. [DSM–III]; American Psychiatric Association, 1980).

Cognitive-Affective Models

Models of sexual response such as Masters and Johnson's suggest some preprogrammed sexual mechanism exists that is activated by adequate sexual stimulation (Janssen & Everaerd, 1993). Such models have the appealing property that they account for the experience, reported by many men and women, of sexual arousal being brought about in an effortless or spontaneous manner. They fail, however, to describe what exactly constitutes effective stimulation. In fact, Masters and Johnson's definition of the term is circular. Effective stimulation produces the response. How does one know what is effective stimulation? When a response occurs. Another problem with such models is that they do not provide an explanation for the many regulatory processes related to sexual arousal, nor do they account for the many variations in subjective experience of sexual arousal and the complicated variation in stimulus and response parameters from such models.

Although several other models relevant to sexual arousal have been proposed over the years (e.g., Bancroft, 1989; Byrne, 1977), I only discuss the few that are strongly based on psychophysiological research findings. One such model was proposed by Barlow (1986). In an impressive series of psychophysiological studies, he found experimental support for a number of factors differentiating men without sexual problems from men with erectile problems. Together, these findings provide the basis for his model, which emphasizes the interaction between autonomic activation and cognitive processes in the control of sexual arousal. Sexual response patterns are conceptualized as forming either a positive or negative feedback system, both starting with the perception of an explicit or implicit demand for sexual performance. This perception results in either positive or negative affective evaluations, both triggering autonomic arousal. This increase in autonomic arousal enhances attention for those features of the sexual situation that are most salient. Continued processing of erotic cues produces genital response and ultimately leads to sexual approach behavior. Continued processing of nonerotic issues (e.g., interpersonal consequences of not responding) interferes with sexual arousal and ultimately leads to avoidance behavior.

Barlow's model is based entirely on studies of men. Recently, Palace (1995a) presented a model based on studies in sexually functional and dysfunctional women. In her model, the summation of autonomic arousal and perceived and expected levels of genital response leads to an optimal sexual response. The model is based on studies showing that increased autonomic arousal and positive false feedback can enhance sexual responses in sexually functional and dysfunctional women (Palace, 1995b; Palace & Gorzalka, 1990, 1992). It should be noted that these studies lacked psychophysiological controls for autonomic response activation, involved heterogeneous patient groups, and used a controversial genital response measure (vaginal blood volume, which is discussed later). However, the studies by Barlow and colleagues were not flawless either. For example, in their studies on the effects of experimentally induced anxiety, no manipulation checks were used, and the effects of autonomic arousal on the focus of attention were never tested directly.

Interestingly, despite the differences in methodology and study populations, the two models have much in common. Both models emphasize the interaction between autonomic activation and cognitive processes in determining whether a response occurs, and both models highlight the importance of feedback. Palace emphasizes the relevance of expectations of sexual arousal, as does Barlow (as initial affective evaluations set the stage for further responding). Also, the actual effects of expectations as discussed by Palace seem closely related to the attentional mechanisms discussed by Barlow.

Conceptual Issues: Interactive Mechanisms

In constructing their models, both Barlow and Palace recognized the complexity of the interrelationships among response components, yet they essentially treated sexual arousal as a unified construct. Instances of discordance between genital and subjective responses, however, suggest that the components of sexual arousal are, at least to a certain degree, under the control of different mechanisms (Bancroft, 1989). Janssen, Everaerd, Spiering, and Janssen (2000) presented a model that highlights the interaction between automatic (unconscious) and controlled (conscious) cognitive processes and proposes that different levels of processing can differentially affect subjective and physiological sexual arousal. The model states that unconscious processes are relevant to explaining the automaticity of the genital response, whereas subjective feelings of sexual arousal are believed to be under control of higher level, conscious cognitive processing. Some initial support for the model is provided by studies exploring the role of unconscious processes in the activation of genital responses and sexual meaning in men (Janssen, Everaerd et al., 2000; Spiering, Everaerd, & Janssen, 2001). A basic assumption of the model is that sexual stimuli may convey more than one meaning. Thus, automatic and controlled cognitive processes may help explain differences in outcome in situations that convey sexual meaning (content or cues), whereas negative meanings that induce other emotions are activated simultaneously. Janssen, Everaerd et al. (2000) proposed that, in these situations, automatic processing of sexual meaning induces genital response, whereas controlled processing of negative meaning may result in nonsexual subjective experience.

GENITAL MEASURES OF SEXUAL RESPONSE

This section describes the measures that are used most widely to measure genital responses in men and women. The description, which is largely based on Geer and Janssen (2000) and Rosen and Beck (1988), focuses on measures of penile erection in men and vaginal vascular changes and labial temperature in women.

Female Genital Measures

Types of Measures. The most widely used technique to measure genital arousal in women is vaginal photoplethysmography. This method uses a photometer, developed by Sintchak and Geer (1975) and improved by Hoon, Wincze, and Hoon (1976), which is made of clear acrylic plastic and shaped like a menstrual tampon. Embedded in the probe is a light source. Light is reflected and diffused through the tissues of the vaginal wall and reaches a photosensitive cell mounted alongside the light source in the photometer. Changes in the electrical resistance of the cell correspond to changes in the amount of back-scattered light. It is assumed that a greater back-scattered signal reflects increased blood volume in the vaginal blood vessels (Levin, 1992). The vaginal photometer is designed so that it can be easily inserted by the participant. A shield can be placed on the probe's cable so that depth of insertion and orientation of the photoreceptive surface is known and held relatively constant (Geer 1983; Laan, Everaerd, & Evers, 1995). The photometer renders two signals. The first is the direct current (DC) signal, which is thought to provide an index of the total amount of blood (Hatch 1979), often abbreviated as VBV (vaginal blood volume). The second signal available from the photometer is alternating current (AC) coupled. This signal, the AC or vaginal pulse amplitude (VPA) signal, provides information on vaginal pulse wave and reflects phasic changes in the vascular walls dependent on pressure changes within the vessels (Jennings, Tahmoush, & Redmont, 1980).

Another measure, developed by Henson and Rubin (1978), involves the registration of labial temperature and is composed of three surface temperature probes designed to measure temperature changes from individually determined baselines. One of the thermistors monitors ambient room temperature. The other two thermistors are used to monitor changes in surface skin temperature. One is attached to the labia minora by means of a clip, and the other is attached to the chest and provides a reference temperature. Labial temperatures of 9 of the 10 participants in the Henson et al. study were shown to increase in response to their viewing an erotic film. Slob et al. (1990, 1991) also found an increase in labial temperature in the majority of participants during the viewing of erotic stimuli. Slob et al. (1990) compared women with and without diabetes mellitus and found initial labial temperature to be lower in the diabetic women than in the nondiabetic women. Apparent differences in responsivity between the two groups disappeared, however, when participants were matched on initial labial temperature.

A less commonly used measure, introduced in 1978 by Levin and Wagner, involves a probe that can be used to detect changes in oxygen pressure (pO_2) in the vaginal wall. This device consists of an electrode that is held on the vaginal wall by a partial vacuum generated in a suction cup. It is assumed that an increased volume of blood in the tissues will lead to greater amounts of oxygen perfused across the vaginal epithelium. Using this device, it is possible to determine the level of oxygen in the blood of the tissues located beneath the device. In addition, the device can be used to measure heat dissipation. This method uses as the dependent variable the amount of energy that is required to keep the temperature of a heated thermistor constant. The heated oxygen probe has proved to be of value in the advancement of our understanding of mechanisms of genital arousal in women (see Levin, 1992, for a review). Further, an advantage of the device is that it is relatively free of movement artifacts.

Levin and Wagner (1997) developed a method that allows for the quantification of their probe's output in absolute units of vaginal blood flow. Considering that other techniques (e.g., vaginal photoplethysmography) provide the researcher with only a relative index of blood flow, this is an important development in the measurement of female genital responses. Unfortunately, the method has its disadvantages, too. It is an expensive technique, the measurement procedure is relatively obtrusive, and duration of measurement sessions has to be kept within limits to protect the vaginal mucosa from being damaged by heat or by the suction needed to hold the device against the vaginal wall (Levin, 1992).

Validity of Measures.   Although both the VBV and VPA measures of the vaginal photoplethysmograph have been found to reflect responses to erotic stimuli, the exact nature and source of the two signals is unknown. The interpretation of their relationship with underlying vascular mechanisms is hindered by the lack of a theoretical framework and of a calibration method allowing transformation of the signals in known physiological events. At present, most researchers describe their findings in relative measures, such as mm pen deflection or change in microvolts.

The correspondence between the VPA and VBV components has been found to vary across studies (e.g., Heiman, 1976; Meston & Gorzalka, 1995). These findings have led to an exploration of the issue of which signal is the most valid (i.e., sensitive and specific) measure of sexual arousal. Geer, Morokoff, and Greenwood (1974), who found that only VPA increased contingent with the progression of an erotic film, concluded that VPA was the more sensitive measure. Heiman (1977) and Osborne and Pollack (1977) arrived at a similar conclusion— Heiman on the basis of the higher correlations she found between VPA and subjective arousal, and Osborn and Pollack on the basis of finding only VPA discriminated between responses to hard-core and "erotically realistic" stories. It could be noted, however, that this research support for the notion that VPA is the more sensitive measure is indirect. That is, such support relies on implicit assumptions about the relationship between vaginal blood flow and variables such as stimulus content and subjective arousal (i.e., that genital responses and subjective arousal should be strongly related).

Laan et al. (1995) were the first to test the sensitivity and specificity of the two measures concurrently. They investigated the specificity of the two signals by comparing responses of sexually functional women to sexual, anxiety-inducing, sexually threatening, and neutral film excerpts. In contrast to VPA, VBV was found to be sensitive to the sexual stimulus but not to the sexual-threat stimulus. However, participants did report feelings of sexual arousal to the sexually threatening stimulus. In addition, a striking difference between the two signals was that VBV, and not VPA, showed a marked decrease during the presentation of the anxiety stimulus, coinciding with an increase in skin conductivity and heart rate. These latter findings indicate that VBV is less specific to sexual arousal than is VPA. In general, the results demonstrate response specificity of vaginal vasocongestion to sexual stimuli.

A few studies have explored the relationship between labial temperature and vaginal blood flow measures. Henson and Rubin (1978) and Henson, Rubin, and Henson (1982) measured VBV and labial temperature in response to sexual films. Henson and Rubin (1978) found a very low, nonsignificant correlation between VBV and labial temperature. Further, only correlations between labial temperature and subjective arousal were statistically significant. On this basis, Henson and Rubin suggested that physiological changes in the labia might be more easily perceived by women than might intravaginal changes. Although vaginal responses tended to decrease more quickly after the sexual stimulus presentation ended, measurements from neither instrument returned to prestimulus baseline levels.

Several researchers have commented on the advantages and disadvantages of the vaginal versus labial devices. For example, Henson, Rubin, and Henson (1979) noted that ambient temperature control is a requirement for using the labial clip, but not for the vaginal blood flow measure. In contrast, movement artifacts are more common with the vaginal probe, and reliable measurement with the thermistor is not precluded by the menses. (As yet there are no published reports of vaginal photometer readings during menses.) Levin (1998) asserted that measurements with the photometer are easily invalidated because it slides easily over the lubricated epithelium, illuminating new areas of tissue. According to Levin, VBV seems especially affected by this phenomenon. It would seem that the shield, whose function is to stabilize probe placement, would protect against this artifact.

Another important difference between the two devices is that a common absolute unit of measurement is used (°C) with the labial clip, whereas changes in vaginal blood flow are relative. Thus, the values obtained during the recording of vaginal blood flow are dependent on the electronic circuitry and the level of amplification used. Further, it is not yet known to what extent factors related to individual variations in anatomy and to physiological characteristics, such as resting levels of vaginal muscular tone and vaginal moistness, may affect the amplitude of the signal (Geer & Janssen, 2000). Rogers, Van de Castle, Evans, and Critelli (1985), in a study on genital arousal during sleep, used a measure of integrated VPA and muscle-contraction pressure, which facilitated the detection of movement and muscle contractions. As Geer and Janssen (2000) concluded, it may prove valuable to extend the current design of the vaginal plethysmograph with an additional measure of muscle-contraction pressure and maybe also vaginal temperature.

TABLE 7.1
Characteristics of Three Genital Measures in Women

| | Genital Measure | | | |
| | Vaginal Photoplethysmograph | | | Heated Electrode Probe |
Characteristic	VPA	VBV	Labial Thermistor	
Understanding of underlying physiology	−	−	+/−	+/−
Known units/calibration possible	−	−	+	+
Sensitivity	+	+/−	+	+
Reliability	+/−	+/−	+	?
Specificity	+	+/−	?	?
Movement artifacts/muscle contractions	−	−	+/−	+
Return to baseline	−	−	−	+
Ease of use	+	+	+	−
Price	+	+	+	?

Note. The + sign indicates a positive rating; − indicates a negative rating; +/− indicates an intermediate rating; and ? signifies a lack of empirical data. Known units/calibration possible refers to the potential of measuring/transforming data in physiologically meaningful units. Reliability pertains to test–retest stability (e.g., Henson, Rubin, & Henson, 1979). Specificity refers to the measure being sensitive to sexual stimuli only. Ratings for movement artifacts/muscle contractions are reversed, with positive ratings indicating low sensitivity.

Table 7.1 summarizes characteristics of the vaginal photoplethysmograph, labial thermistor, and heated electrode probe.

Male Genital Measures

Types of Measures. The first instrument to continuously measure male genital responses was developed by Freund in 1963. This device, the air volumetric plethysmograph, uses the principle of volumetric plethysmography in which a body part is placed in a sealed container with air or fluid. Less widely used variants of this technique were described by Fisher, Gross, and Zuch (1965), who used water instead of air, and McConaghy (1974). Freund's plethysmograph is positioned by the experimenter, who places a sponge-rubber ring and a plastic ring with an inflatable cuff over the penis. A glass cylinder with a funnel at the top is then fitted over the other components, and the cuff is inflated with air. Changes in the size of the penis result in displacement of air, which can be detected by a pressure transducer. Volumetric devices can be calibrated and scored in terms of absolute penile volume. Also, volumetric plethysmography has the advantage of offering high sensitivity. A limitation of this technique, however, is that it does not allow for the determination of the source of change. For example, the device cannot be used to discriminate between changes in volume due to increases in penile length or penile circumference. In addition, the apparatus is relatively complex, cumbersome, and sensitive to temperature and movement artifacts.

Fisher et al. (1965) developed a measure known as a mercury-in-rubber strain gauge, which was adapted from a similar transducer used by Shapiro and Cohen (1965). The device consists of a hollow rubber tube filled with mercury and sealed at the ends with platinum electrodes that are inserted into the mercury. The electrodes are attached to a bridge circuit for connection to a polygraph or computer. The operation of the mercury-in-rubber strain gauge depends on penile circumference changes that cause the rubber tube to stretch or shorten, thus altering the cross-sectional area of the column of mercury within the tube. The resistance of the mercury inside the tube varies directly with its cross-sectional area, which in turn is reflective of changes in the circumference of the penis. Variations of the mercury-in-rubber gauge were described by Bancroft, Jones, and Pullan (1966), Jovanovic (1967), and Karacan (1969).

Another commonly used type of penile strain gauge is the electromechanical strain gauge developed by Barlow, Becker, Leitenberg, and Agras (1970). This device is made of two arcs of surgical spring material joined with two mechanical strain gauges. These gauges are flexed when the penis changes in circumference, producing changes in their resistance. The resistance changes are in turn coupled through a bridge circuit to a polygraph or computer. The electromechanical gauge does not fully enclose the penis. For this reason, it is more sensitive to movement artifacts and less suitable for studies on nocturnal penile tumescence (NPT) than the mercury-in-rubber gauge. However, mechanical strain gauges are quite sensitive and more rugged than their rubber counterparts.

Bradley, Timm, Gallagher, and Johnson (1985) first described an instrument designed to measure continuously penile circumference and rigidity. This device has been modified and is now commercially available as the Rigiscan Plus monitor. The Rigiscan consists of a recording unit that can be strapped around the waist or thigh. The device comes with software that allows two modes of measurement (which cannot be modified to accommodate variations in study design or measurement timing): It can operate ambulatory or be connected to a computer. It has two loops, one placed around the base of the penis and the other around the shaft just behind the glans. Each loop contains a cable that is tightened at discrete time intervals. Circumference is measured at 15-second intervals using a linear force of 1.7 Newton. The Rigiscan takes its first rigidity measure when a 20% increase in circumference is detected. This is repeated every 30 seconds. To measure rigidity, the loops tighten a second time after circumference is measured with a greater force of 2.8 Newton. The rigidity of a noncompressible shaft (i.e., no loop shortening to the higher force) is given as 100%. At present, although the Rigiscan is rather costly, it is probably the most widely used measure of male genital response.

Validity and Reliability.   Four studies have compared volumetric and circumferential measures. Freund, Langevin, and Barlow (1974) compared Freund's volumetric device with Barlow's electromechanical strain gauge, whereas McConaghy (1974), Wheeler and Rubin (1987), and Kuban, Barbaree, and Blanchard (1999) compared the volumetric device with a mercury strain gauge. In contrast to Freund et al. (1974), who found evidence for a higher sensitivity of the volumetric device, McConaghy (1974) and Wheeler and Rubin (1987) found the circumferential measure they used to be as sensitive as the volumetric device. McConaghy (1999) argued that the volumetric device is superior to penile circumference measures because shorter duration stimuli can be used to differentiate heterosexual and homosexual men using penile volume assessment (cf. Freund, 1963). However, this seems to particularly true for the classification of heterosexual men because more homosexual men have been correctly identified using a combination of longer duration stimuli (film excerpts) and strain gauges (cf. Sakheim, Barlow, & Beck, 1985). In the most recent study comparing the two measures, Kuban et al. (1999) found, similarly to Freund et al. (1974), that the volumetric device is more sensitive to changes in genital vasocongestion, but only at low response levels (i.e., below 10% of full erection).

The validity and reliability of the mercury-in-rubber and electromechanical strain gauges have been reasonably well established. Although only two studies thus far have explored and compared the properties of the two types of strain gauge in vivo, a number of laboratory simulation studies have shown that both gauges have linear outputs, high test–retest reliability, high stability over time, and minor sensitivity to temperature changes (e.g., Karacan, 1969; Farkas et al., 1979; Earls & Jackson, 1981; Richards, Bridger, Wood, Kalucy, & Marshall, 1985; Richards, Kalucy, Wood, & Marshall, 1990; Janssen, Vissenberg, Visser, & Everaerd, 1997). The mercury-in-rubber type of strain gauge is now also available in a version that is filled with an indium-gallium alloy, which is considered to be even less sensitive to temperature changes than is mercury (Richards et al., 1985).

Laws (1977) was the first to compare the two strain gauges in vivo. He found discrepancies in measurement with the two devices. Unfortunately, however, he obtained data from only one participant. More recently, Janssen et al. (1997) compared the two types of penile strain gauge, as well as two different methods of calibration, in a group of 25 sexually functional men. Typically, both gauges are calibrated (to allow the transformation of a relatively meaningless electrical signal to known units of circumference) using a graduated circular cone. The authors found that the electromechanical gauge showed greater circumference changes than did the other gauge when it was calibrated on a circular device. Circumference changes were identical, however, when an oval-shaped device was used to calibrate the two gauges. In addition, response patterns were very comparable on the individual level, with averaged correlations between the two gauges falling above .90.

A potential concern with the use of circumferential measures is the suggestion that penile circumference may show a slight decrease at the onset of sexual arousal, which may be incorrectly interpreted as a decrease in sexual response. Also, it has been noted that strain gauges may be unreliable at the upper end of the tumescence curve. These observations may represent a limitation if the measures are to be used for determining the full range of erectile capacity (Geer & Janssen, 2000).

The Rigiscan represents the first feasible attempt to measure rigidity continuously and has gained wide acceptance, particularly in clinical research settings. Nonetheless, several questions related to its validity and reliability have yet to be explored. For example, there are no data available on its test–retest reliability. Such reliability over long periods of usage is pertinent because, in contrast to strain gauges where routine calibration allows for the test of linearity over time and where replacement is viable, a Rigiscan monitor is typically used for a number of years (Geer & Janssen, 2000). The importance of developing a stable calibration method for the Rigiscan is underlined by the finding that different Rigiscan devices can record different degrees of rigidity (Munoz, Bancroft, & Marshall, 1993). Another question concerns the potential reactivity of the measurement. The extent to which the tightening of the loops may induce or modify sexual responses, either in the absence of or in interaction with experimental or clinical manipulations, has not yet been assessed. Furthermore, only one study to date has reported correlations between the Rigiscan's circumference and rigidity measures (Levine & Carroll, 1994). Here NPT responses for 113 nights were analyzed and the correlations between Rigiscan's measures of tip tumescence and rigidity, and base tumescence and rigidity were .87 and .88, respectively. Clearly, these correlations suggest that more research is needed to establish the value of measuring rigidity in addition to circumference, especially if one considers the differences in cost and amount of control researchers have over data acquisition using the two types of measures.

Table 7.2 summarizes the characteristics of the volumetric plethysmograph, the mercury and Barlow gauges, and the Rigiscan.

SELF-REPORT MEASURES OF SEXUAL AROUSAL

According to Mosher's (1980) involvement theory, subjective sexual arousal consists of awareness of physiological sexual arousal, sexual affects, and affect-cognition blends. Within the framework of this theory, Mosher, Barton-Henry, and Green (1988) developed a measure—the "multiple indicators of subjective sexual arousal"—that consists of three sexual arousal scales: ratings of sexual arousal, affective sexual arousal, and genital sensations. The ratings of sexual arousal scale consists of five items asking about sexual arousal, genital sensations, sexual warmth, nongenital physical sensations, and sexual absorption. A 7-point answer format is used to rate each item, with anchors such as *no sexual arousal at all* to *extremely sexually aroused*. The affective sexual arousal scale consists of five adjective prompts such as *turned-on* and *sexually excited*, which are rated using a 5-point scale, and the genital sensations scale is an 11-item checklist that participants use to indicate their highest level of genital sensations.

TABLE 7.2
Characteristics of Three Genital Measures in Men

Characteristic	Genital Measure			
	Volumetric Plethysmograph	Mercury/Barlow Strain Gauges		Rigiscan
Understanding of underlying physiology	+	+	+	+
Known units/calibration possible	+	+	+	+
Sensitivity	+	+/–	+	–
Reliability	+	+	+	?
Specificity	+/–	+/–	+/–	+/–
Nocturnal Penile Tumescence (NPT)	–	+	–	+
Movement artifacts	–	–	–	+
Return to baseline	+	+	+	+
Ease of use	–	+	+	+/–
Price	+	+	+	–

Note. The + sign indicates a positive rating; – indicates a negative rating; +/– indicates an intermediate rating; and ? signifies lacking empirical data. Indirect evidence for the three measures' specificity exists, but it has never been tested systematically. NPT (Nocturnal Penile Tumescence) refers to whether the device can be used to measure sleep-related erections. Ratings for movement artifacts/muscle contractions are reversed, with positive ratings indicating low sensitivity.

Although the Mosher et al. measure is one of the few self-report measures with known psychometric properties (see Mosher, 1998), it is rarely used in its original form. Most researchers use adaptations of this measure or comparable questions derived from the work of others (e.g., Heiman & Rowland, 1983; Henson et al., 1979). For example, whereas the genital sensations scale (Mosher et al., 1988) measures the experience of genital changes (e.g., vaginal lubrication) and orgasm in one single item, many researchers prefer to evaluate these experiences separately, using two or more questions. Also, in contrast to the Mosher et al. measure, in which participants simply indicate how aroused they felt during a stimulus presentation, many researchers ask participants to indicate both their strongest feelings of sexual arousal and how they felt most of the time (overall sexual arousal).

Wincze, Hoon, and Hoon (1976) were the first to describe a continuous measure of subjective sexual arousal: a lever capable of swinging through a 90° arc that participants could operate with one hand to indicate their degree of sexual arousal. Wincze, Venditti, Barlow, and Mavissakalian (1980) compared stimulus conditions in which the lever was and was not used and found that the continuous measure did not influence genital response levels. Other researchers (e.g., Janssen et al., 1997) have used a variant of this technique in which the lever is replaced by a horizontally placed slider (potentiometer). The slider is so calibrated that its position determines how many of 10 lights are illuminated. The lights can be placed in front of a television monitor so that participants need not look away from the screen when they are presented with a video excerpt.

Although rating scales and continuous measures have been found to yield roughly equivalent results (Steinman, Wincze, Sakheim, Barlow, & Mavissakalian, 1981), both approaches have advantages and disadvantages. The use of a continuous measure may not interfere with the activation of genital responses; however, it does require participants to monitor their response continuously and thus may lead to *spectatoring*—a heightened awareness of one's sexual performance (Masters & Johnson, 1970). Thus, the extent to which this measure affects response patterns in different participant groups (e.g., sexually functional vs. dysfunctional) could well vary, an issue that warrants more research. An obvious advantage of the continuous measure is that it allows for an evaluation of the relationship between subjective and genital responses throughout an entire stimulus episode. Peak levels of subjective sexual arousal assessed with continuous and discrete measures may be comparable, but when the peak occurs can be determined with continuous measures only. In addition, continuous measures allow for the calculation of within-subjects correlations, an index of the strength of the (temporal) relationship between the two signals for each individual participant. With physiological measures where calibration of the signal is not possible (e.g., vaginal photoplethysmography), within-subjects correlations may be more reliable and informative than between-subjects correlations. Finally, it should be noted that, although continuous measures are mostly used to assess sexual arousal, they may be used for the exploration of a number of other affective and cognitive processes, such as the experience of sexual desire or the presence of distracting thoughts.

One disadvantage of discrete measures of subjective sexual arousal is that they are retrospective in nature; participants answer questions about how they felt after completion of the stimulus presentation. This leaves the possibility that responses are constructed or modified post hoc, influenced by, for example, how one responded and was expected to respond (see chap. 3, this volume). An apparent advantage of rating scales, however, is that more than one question can be asked. In a short time, participants can rate their experience of sexual arousal, physiological changes, and other, sexual and nonsexual emotions and cognitions.

Whether one chooses to employ either a discrete or continuous measure, or whether one decides to use a combination of both, it is important to establish prestimulus response levels for both types of measure. Although this is considered a standard procedure in the measurement of physiological responses, where differences between baseline and evoked measures are used to index genital responses, it is not a common practice when it comes to the measurement of subjective sexual arousal. However, the same arguments for correcting for prestimulus intervals apply here. Due to the research context, presence of the measurement instruments, and anticipation of sexual stimuli, participants are likely to vary in their initial emotional state, including their experience of sexual arousal. The measurement of prestimulus levels will improve measurement precision because it allows for the computation of difference scores and other techniques to correct for initial response levels (e.g., analysis of covariance [ANCOVA]).

CONDUCTING PSYCHOPHYSIOLOGICAL EXPERIMENTS

This section discusses practical aspects of psychophysiological research on sexuality. Because of the nature of the information provided, the style of writing is more informal. Several of the issues covered in this section, and the suggested ways of dealing with them, have been, and continue to be, topics of discussion on *SexLab*, an e-mail listserve on methodological issues in psychophysiological sex research.

The Laboratory

Preferably, a psychophysiological laboratory unit consists of two rooms: one for the participant and one for the experimenter. Two rooms are preferred for several reasons, the most important being that participants should be provided with as much privacy as possible. Another reason to have two rooms is to minimize the influence of sounds and noises caused by equipment, slide carousals, and other experimental materials. Also, when training students and assistants in experimental procedures, you can talk with one another while collecting data from a participant without distracting him or her.

Yet another reason for using two rooms concerns standardization. The experimental situation should be as similar as possible for all participants. However, an experimenter's behavior can affect a participant's response (see the section on experimenter effects), and such influence is not a constant; that is, the experimenter's behavior is not uniform or consistent, but will vary from day to day, from experimenter to experimenter, and from participant to participant. Here is a paradox. On the one hand, you want participants to be comfortable, which means you are friendly, spend time explaining procedures, and answer questions. On the other hand, the experimenter is a potential source of confounding influences and preferably should not even be present in the lab. Researchers deal with the incompatibility of these objectives in different ways. Some prefer to tape all participant instructions for purposes of standardization. This may be fine with most participants because it may increase their sense of privacy. However, the advantage of using an intercom system to read instructions is that it allows you to check if participants understand the instructions.

Some researchers manage to create a relatively comfortable laboratory environment. Others, in particular researchers who work in clinical settings such as hospitals, are more constrained in their possibilities and sometimes have to conduct their research in a one-room lab. Creativity can help overcome many disadvantages. For example, goggles are being used in some laboratories to present participants with visual stimuli. If combined with headphones, working in a less-than-optimal experimental environment will be less important and less strongly affect participants' responses. More generally, it is important to keep in mind that, although no laboratory will resemble everybody's home, one does want to approach as closely as possible a natural or ecologically valid setting. The context in which one is presented with sexual stimuli can have effects on, if not on one's genital responses, how sexually aroused one feels (cf. Laan & Everaerd, 1995). Therefore, you want to create a pleasant atmosphere while respecting individual differences in taste and preference for decorations and furniture. Finally, the most important piece of furniture is the participants' chair. It is crucial to select a (reclining) chair that is comfortable. Participants are usually asked to stay seated for long periods of time, and sitting in an uncomfortable chair may not only affect how they respond, but may also increase the occurrence of movement artifacts.

Equipment and Instruments

Visitors to a sexuality lab tend to notice the presence of all sorts of unfamiliar, interesting looking equipment. In addition to computers, they may see amplifiers, filters, converters, cables, and a number of odd-looking devices. The technical principles of amplifiers and other equipment are not discussed here (however, see Cacioppo, Tassinary, & Berntson, 2000). Instead, more practical issues are considered.

Psychophysiological sexuality research does not, of course, start with a lab filled with equipment, but with questions you would like to answer. Hence, the types of devices, amplifiers, filters, and so forth you should use in your lab depends on your research questions. Researchers usually describe the systems they used in the Method section of their articles, thus it is a good place to learn what equipment is commonly used. You will find that the devices and systems vary from research area to research area (e.g., the Rigiscan is most often used in clinical research). When deciding what company from which to order, you will have to weigh several factors, including the price, quality, and user-friendliness of the equipment and software, as well as the services provided by the company. In general, multipurpose recording systems manufactured by companies such as Biopac, CPI, and Grass appear, especially in the longer run, to lead to higher levels of satisfaction than the specialized measurement systems that are available partly because of the wider range of possible applications and the more versatile software that comes with these systems.

The choice of what instrument to use to measure sexual arousal should be guided by questions about the instrument's sensitivity, specificity, and reliability. Does it measure what you want it to measure? Is it sensitive enough to detect the changes you expect? Requirements will differ if you want to measure effects of 3-second slide presentations or if you want to use 3-minute film clips. For research on men, you would not want to use the Rigiscan in the first case because it only takes measurements every 15 seconds. Instead, the Barlow gauge or a volumetric device may be more appropriate. Is the instrument you choose responsive to sexual arousal only, or may it be sensitive to the effects of an anger induction or exercise condition (e.g., due to movement artifacts) that you wish to use in this study?

Will you compare the effects of certain manipulations, stimuli, or drugs within or between subjects? For the latter approach, you might want to use or include a measure that uses an absolute scale (e.g., the labial thermistor) or one that can be calibrated. Between-subject comparisons using relative measures such as the vaginal photoplethysmograph are subject to potentially large but meaningless differences in absolute output levels, and therefore they require relatively large numbers of participants to achieve statistical significance. Individual variations in placement of the device and/or the anatomy and physiological characteristics of participants, such as resting levels of vaginal muscular tone and vaginal moistness, may all affect the amplitude of the signal.

There are also other practical issues to consider. Will participants have to place the device themselves or can you help with or at least visually check for correct placement? If you work with patients who are experienced with undergoing all sorts of medical tests, visually checking instrument placement may be experienced as less interfering and obtrusive than when you measure sexual responses to erotica in freshmen college students. Also, cost, shelf life, ease of calibration, placement, cleaning, and comparability with devices used in other published research need to be considered.

Calibration procedures allow raw data to be transformed to an absolute scale of, for example, circumference and are available and straightforward for some instruments. For mercury-in-rubber strain gauges, usually a graduated circular cone or circular discs are used to calibrate the signal, with steps ranging from anything like 85 to 160 mm circumference. Using more than two steps is essential because it allows you to evaluate the linearity of the instrument's output. The same approach can be used with other measures of genital response in men (e.g., the mechanical strain gauge), although more advanced procedures have been proposed (Janssen et al., 1997; Munoz, Bancroft, & Marshall, 1993).

As for measures such as the vaginal photoplethysmograph, calibration has proved to be a challenge. Hoon, Murphy, Laughter, and Abel (1984) developed a system to calibrate the signal of this device in terms of light reflectance units. They used a box consisting of two chambers—one side containing white 90% reflectance paper and the other containing 18% reflectance paper. Apart from the problem of not using three or more types of reflectance paper (the minimum required to estimate the linearity of the probe's output), there is the question of whether the reflectance levels they used adequately reflect what happens in the vaginal wall. Also, it is unclear whether white and gray (e.g., compared with different levels of red) papers are appropriate to use. Finally, using chambers differing in light reflectance only allows one to calibrate the DC component of the signal. A calibration method for the AC component of the probe requires a system that simulates the pulse signal measured in the vaginal wall. The development and validation of this type of calibration has yet to be achieved.

A note on the disinfection of measurement devices and lab hygiene in general seems appropriate because participants often ask questions about how the devices are cleaned. Although for many devices the use of bleach is sufficient, the majority of researchers follow more rigorous disinfection procedures. They do this not only to minimize the chance of transmitting infections or diseases, but also to communicate to participants that hygiene is taken very seriously in their laboratory. The Centers for Disease Control recommend, for reusable devices or items that touch mucous membranes (i.e., the cervix), a minimum of high-level disinfection. According to the guidelines for selecting disinfectants, published by the Association for Professionals in Infection Control and Epidemiology (Rutala, 1996), inexpensive household bleach (1:50 dilution) fits the criteria for high-level disinfection. Still many researchers use more expensive glutaraldehyde-based formulations (e.g., *Cidexplus* or *Cidex PA*) that are used in hospitals to sterilize, among others, catheters. Although these disinfectants are not more effective than bleach, informing participants that they are being used may lead participants to feel better protected and therefore more at ease during the experimental procedure.

Stimulus Selection

Once you have furnished and equipped your lab, and decided what measures you will use, you have to think about your independent variables. They include the sexual stimuli you present to the participants. However, you also have to decide on what neutral stimuli to use to determine physiological and affective baseline levels, what kind of instructions to give, the length of the stimulus presentations and the interstimulus intervals, and the number of stimuli, to list just a few of the relevant issues. I focus on the selection of sexual stimuli.

What makes a researcher so sure that a photo of a nude person or a video of two strangers touching each other's genitals will induce sexual arousal? In other words, what fits the definition of a sexual stimulus? An actual naked body? A pictorial representation of a naked body? A sexual thought or memory? A touch? Clearly any of these sometimes prove effective in eliciting sexual responses, but not always. Sexual videos are often used in psychophysiological studies, and that choice is based on the assumption that they, with few exceptions, will induce sexual arousal. Yet experimenters know from their own experience that that is not always the case. They do not, or at least not always, process the sexual information conveyed by the videos. Tactile stimulation of the penis is another example. It clearly can lead to the development of an erection. Sometimes a light stroke is enough, but most men do not get an erection when touching and holding their penis in a public restroom. What, then, determines whether a response occurs if the same stimulus can be an effective sexual stimulus under certain conditions but not others? Although this is a central question in studies comparing people with and without sexual arousal problems, a more or less conclusive answer is yet to be found. One element that research findings have pointed to as important is the role of cognitive processes (cf. Barlow, 1986). A stimulus leads to sexual arousal if it is processed in a sexual way—or, to put it differently, if attention is directed toward its sexual content or meaning.

Related to the question about the effectiveness of any specific stimulus or its intrinsic qualities, one should consider interpersonal differences; that is, differences in how people respond to potentially relevant stimuli (Bancroft & Janssen, 2000; Janssen, Vorst, Finn, & Bancroft, 2001). As clinicians know, almost all possibly effective sexual stimuli seem to fail for some people. For others, imagined or real stimuli are so salient and intense that they hardly feel in control of their responses to them. What does this mean? Well, for one, you would do well to assess individual characteristics; that is, dispositional variables (e.g., frequency of sexual behaviors, erotophilia–erotophobia, or sexual inhibition/excitation proneness) that may modulate responses and thus help you explain variability in response levels.

Although some stimuli are more likely to induce responses in large numbers of people than are others, a standard for sexual stimuli does not exist. It is not known exactly which tape, slide, film, story, or fantasy instruction is the most effective in inducing sexual arousal. However, certain things are known. Studies have shown that films generally lead to higher levels of sexual response than do stories, slides, or fantasy. Other studies have shown that stimuli with explicit sexual content lead to higher levels of sexual arousal in both men and women than do stimuli with more romantic and less explicit content (Laan & Everaerd, 1995; Janssen & Everaerd, 1993).

There are many more issues related to stimulus selection that could be discussed. One frequently asked question is whether subjects should be offered the opportunity to select their own sexual stimuli, perhaps from brief previews. Although this approach is alluring, the study will be less standardized. Also, it is not known what determines people's decisions for choosing a particular stimulus. Letting people choose their own sexual stimulus assumes that everyone is a good judge of what stimuli are effective in inducing arousal in them. In some situations, people may actually avoid selecting stimuli that might arouse them most. This may be particularly relevant if one is afraid a sexual response may expose you in a certain way (e.g., as having a psychogenic sexual problem, as being homosexual, or as being a sex offender).

Other issues are related to the choice of the intensity of a stimulus. Sometimes differences between groups will only show up with stimuli that are of moderate intensity. For example, when evaluating the effects of a manipulation of unknown strength (e.g., a drug, fragrance, or fantasy instruction), a strong sexual stimulus may override the effects of such a manipulation. In addition to such ceiling effects, floor effects can occur when the sexual stimulus used proves to be ineffective to induce sexual arousal in the majority of participants. One defense against ceiling or floor effects involves the usage of multiple (e.g., fantasy and film) or composite stimuli. As for the latter, film excerpts could be used that incorporate scenes reflecting different levels of intensity (e.g., 1 min of petting, 1 min of oral sex, and 1 min of sexual intercourse). This allows the researcher to analyze the data for effects of the manipulations they are interested in at various levels of sexual arousal.

Experimenter Effects

Everything present in the laboratory is part of the stimulus context. However, anything that is not too prominent can be considered a constant that should not interfere with the effects of the specific treatments or manipulations in which you are interested. Some variables are, however, more likely to have an effect on your findings than are others. One factor that needs to be considered is the role of the experimenter.

Experimenter effects, which have been studied widely in nonsexological research, have received surprisingly little attention in the sexuality laboratory. Examples from the general psychological literature indicate, for example, that an experimenter's expectancies about the results, and his or her attitudes and general behavior, can influence a study's findings (many of these effects have also been described under the term *demand characteristics*). For example, in a nonsexual psychophysiological study, Hicks (1970) found that different experimenter moods and behaviors produced different physiological results and subjective reports from research participants.

Clearly, if experimenter effects have been found in nonsexual research settings, they are, considering the sensitivities and taboos surrounding sexuality, likely to play a role in laboratory studies on sexual arousal. If one and only one experimenter conducts a study, that person could be considered a constant. However, the possibility exists that that one person can influence the responses of all participants in a consistent way that could work for or against the researcher's predictions. One unpublished study (Williams, Barlow, Mitchell, Prins, & Scharff, 1990) found that genital responses in sexually functional men were lower when the experimenter was a woman than when the experimenter was a man. Other than that, virtually nothing on the topic exists in the research literature, although several relevant and easily testable questions can be generated. For example, what are the effects of an experimenter's gender, sexual orientation, and sexual attitudes on the sexual responses of male and female participants who differ in their sexual attitudes and sexual orientation? Most research laboratories apply commonsense rules, such as male experimenters study men and female experimenters study women, but empirical support for this approach awaits research on the issue. For the time being, it is important to keep in mind the relevance of the potential influences of these factors. One modest protection against variations in experimenter behavior involves the use of a protocol—a manual describing everything that needs to be done during a study in a step-by-step fashion. Including suggestions of how to interact with a participant (e.g., offer your participant something to drink, ask whether he or she is comfortable) and written instructions (e.g., for how to fantasize or what to do when presented with a sexual stimulus) can help increase standardization and reduce experimenter effects.

Recruiting Participants for Psychophysiological Studies

How Many?   Statistical power is addressed elsewhere in this volume and in general can be easily applied to psychophysiological studies. Among the factors that influence statistical power are the design of the study (e.g., for psychophysiological studies, between- vs. within-subjects or repeated-measures designs), the measures and statistical tests used, the sample size, and, also of relevance to psychophysiological studies, the number and timing of measurements per participant. It may make a difference if you decide to compare a drug and a placebo in one group of participants (i.e., using a within-subjects or repeated-measures design) or in two groups, one receiving the drug and the other receiving the placebo (i.e., using a between-subjects design). In general, given a fixed sample size, repeated-measures designs have higher statistical power than between-subjects designs. However, power partly depends on the strength of the relationship between the observations (Levin, 1997). In addition to standard works on statistical power (e.g., Cohen, 1977; Kraemer & Thiemann, 1987), computer programs can be used for calculating sample size (e.g., nQuery Advisor, Elashof, 1995; GPOWER, Buchner, Faul, & Erdfelder, 1992) that are particularly helpful to psychophysiologists who use repeated-measures designs.

Volunteer Biases.   A number of studies have explored differences between volunteers and nonvolunteers for sexuality studies. They found differences in sexual experience, frequencies of sexual activity, sex guilt, exposure to erotic materials, and sexual attitudes (e.g., Bogaert, 1996; Morokoff, 1986; Plaud et al., 1999; Strassberg & Lowe, 1995; Wiederman, 1999; Wolchik, Braver, & Jensen, 1985). Some of these studies have specifically explored the influence of the degree of intrusiveness on participation rates and found (but not consistently) psychophysiological studies to be particularly susceptible to volunteer biases. Although it is obvious that we should not ignore the potential influence of volunteer biases, we should also be cautious in assuming that no valuable conclusions can be derived from psychophysiological data because they are obtained in selective groups of people. In the end, the question is not whether there are differences between volunteers and nonvolunteers, but whether these differences affect our inferences regarding the processes and mechanisms relevant to human sexual response (cf. Geer & Janssen, 2000). There is no definitive answer to that question because it is not possible to collect data from nonvolunteers; however, some thoughts and research findings may provide support for a somewhat more optimistic view on the credibility of our conclusions.

Although volunteers and nonvolunteers have been found to differ on a number of variables, the differences are generally small. Thus, it may be more relevant to explore whether the range of behaviors, attitudes, and experiences of volunteers is comparable to the range reported by nonvolunteers. For example, one might expect people who experience sexual problems or who have strong religious feelings not to participate in psychophysiological studies. However, there is no support for this expectation. For example, Wiederman (1999) found no differences between volunteers and nonvolunteers in religiosity. Similarly, Laan and Everaerd (1995), in a meta-analysis of six psychophysiological studies involving 289 women, found that a substantial proportion (22%) of participants had experienced some form of sexual abuse. They concluded that the threshold for participating in psychophysiological studies may be lower than expected. Clearly, Laan and Everaerd's findings indicate that the assumption that volunteer populations will only represent those who have had positive sexual experiences is not tenable, and they also suggest less bias than might otherwise be expected from those who would assume that only participants who like sex volunteer for research that involves genital measures.

Data Reduction and Analysis

I restrict the discussion of data reduction and analysis to a few of the more challenging and time-consuming issues that confront psychophysiological researchers after they have completed data collection (most of these issues do not apply to the Rigiscan because that device measures only once every 15 s). The first has to do with the removal of movement and other artifacts. Especially with penile circumference measures and the vaginal photoplethysmograph, the acquired data files may contain numbers that do not reflect real variations in genital blood flow. For example, with the vaginal photoplethysmograph, sudden strong fluctuations in the amplitude of the signal indicate a movement artifact. The same type of movement artifact can occur with the use of penile strain gauges. In most cases, the software that comes with the equipment allows you to either cut (e.g., Biopac) or ignore (e.g., CPI) these sudden changes in the signal. However, not only distinct body movements (e.g., sitting back in a chair), but also less conspicuous behaviors (e.g., tensing one's abdominal or pelvic muscles, or crossing one's ankles) can affect the photoplethysmograph's output (Carpenter, Janssen, & Graham, 1999), and these artifacts are not always as easy to detect. The best strategy for dealing with movement artifacts is therefore to try to prevent them. Providing a comfortable reclining chair and instructing participants to try not to move or tense their muscles, especially during stimulus presentations, can help reduce the number of movement artifacts considerably.

Once you have removed all clearly visible artifacts from the signal, you will have to extract numbers from it to enter into your statistical software. Most researchers will sample the signal of a plethysmograph or strain gauge at frequencies between 10 and 100 Hz, resulting in 10 to 100 numbers per second. Thus, some data reduction is clearly in order. In most published reports you will find that researchers work with (e.g., 5-, 15-, or 30-s) windows or epochs. That is, they will compute the average and/or maximum for a short window and then analyze these numbers using for example a repeated-measures ANCOVA or multivariate analysis of covariance (MANCOVA). If you presented participants with a composite stimulus, such as a video clip containing different sexual behaviors (e.g., 1 min of petting, 1 min of oral sex, and 1 min of sexual intercourse), you could condense the data into 15- or 30-second intervals and include stimulus intensity as a within-subjects factor in your statistical analysis.

One final issue concerns the specific variables you enter in your analyses—and it involves questions about data transformation (e.g., z-score), difference scores, covariates, and how to deal with blood flow levels or temperatures that do not return to a participant's original baseline level. Many of these issues are interrelated and a continuing topic of discussion among psychophysiological researchers. The most common way of operationalizing a sexual response is to subtract a person's baseline level from his or her response level. For example, if a man's penis has a circumference of 100 mm when it is flaccid and a circumference of 125 mm when he is presented with a sexual film, his response is 25 mm. In addition to using difference scores (in units of mV or mm pen deflection, or with calibrated signals; e.g., mm circumference), researchers can express genital responses in terms of percentage change. The problem with that approach, however, is that one has to ask subjects to obtain a full sexual response (e.g., through masturbation), which one can use as the maximal level (100%), and the reliability of this approach has not been established. As for unscaled measures, such as the VPA and VBV signals of the vaginal photoplethysmograph, sometimes researchers use z score transformations or an ANCOVA approach in an attempt to decrease between-subject variability in the absolute amplitude of the signal due to anatomical differences or variations in probe placement, but it is undecided to what degree these type of strategies improve the validity of one's findings.

With several measurement devices (in particular with those used with women), it has proved difficult, after the presentation of a sexual stimulus, to induce a decrease in the device's output that corresponds to the initial baseline. Although the use of variable interstimulus intervals or distracting tasks (e.g., a puzzle or counting backward from 1,000) may help to some degree, with devices such as the labial thermistor and the vaginal photoplethysmograph, more often than not blood flow or temperature will not return to its original baseline level in a substantial number of subjects. This clearly only poses a problem if you use a within-subjects design—that is, if you present all participants with heterosexual and homosexual slides. In a between-subjects design, in which you present every participant with only one stimulus, it does not matter whether their blood flow or temperature return to their original baseline level. Before you decide to use between-subjects designs only, be aware that there are problems with this type of design, too. It has lower statistical power, and, especially with measures that cannot be calibrated (e.g., the vaginal photoplethysmograph), there are more problems with comparing the effects of experimental manipulations or drugs. How to best deal with an incomplete return to baseline should at least partly depend on what the underlying physiological mechanisms are, which at this stage we do not know. One way researchers deal with this is to work with difference scores, using either the baseline that immediately precedes a sexual stimulus or the initial baseline. Another way would be to use absolute VPA levels (i.e., not working with difference scores at all), but that approach is problematic in that it fails to take into account constitutional differences (due to individual differences in anatomy, etc.), placement differences, or differences in amplification settings. At this stage, probably one of the preferred ways to deal with incomplete return to baseline is to use difference scores with the original baseline and include the baseline that preceded the second, third, and so on, sexual stimulus as a covariate in the analyses.

CONCLUDING REMARKS

Over the last 20 to 30 years, psychophysiology has become an important approach in studies on human sexuality. In addition to a continually growing number of studies on basic mechanisms of sexual response, an impressive body of practical information has accumulated, particularly related to the diagnosis of sexual dysfunctions and methods for the assessment of sex offenders. As is true for other areas of psychophysiology, however, future progress in laboratory research on human sexuality will prove to be contingent on methodological advancements. More than 10 years ago, Rosen and Beck (1988) noted that measurement approaches in sexual psychophysiology are based more on the availability and ease of use of particular transducers than on a sound understanding of the underlying processes of sexual arousal. Many of the concerns that Rosen and Beck raised are still relevant today. For example, they questioned the reliance on the vaginal photometer, pointing out that basic physiological studies (e.g., Wagner & Ottesen, 1980) "highlighted serious limitations in the vaginal photoplethysmograph as an adequate measure of genital engorgement" (p. 340). The introduction of new measures, especially measures of genital arousal in women, would indeed be a welcome contribution to the field of sexual psychophysiology. However, it should be recognized that, although the development and construction of a new measure may require creativity and effort, establishing its validity and reliability is a tedious and time-consuming process and, as a result, is often neglected. In fact, for several existing measures (e.g., the Rigiscan, the heated oxygen probe), validity or reliability data are still lacking. Similarly, whereas some innovative new measurement techniques have recently been proposed (e.g., vaginal PH and vaginal pressure-volume change; Berman, Berman, & Goldstein, 1999; axial penile rigidity, Udelson et al., 2000), the validation of these techniques remains to be established. Still, initiatives such as these are important and hopefully will lead to a stronger focus on the improvement and expansion of our methodology. The availability of sophisticated scanning techniques such as magnetic resonance imaging (MRI) and positron emission tomography (PET) may, through the insights they provide in anatomy and physiology at both central and peripheral levels (e.g., Weijmar Schultz, van Andel, Sabelis, & Mooyaert, 1999), prove to be beneficial to this process and facilitate the development of new measures of sexual arousal.

SUGGESTED READINGS

Two works that are highly recommended, one as a general introduction to the principles of psychophysiological inference and bioelectrical measurement and the other as an excellent overview of sexual psychophysiology, are the *Handbook of Psychophysiology* (Cacioppo et al., 2000) and *Patterns of Sexual Arousal* (Rosen & Beck, 1988), respectively. For a discussion of less widely used genital response measures (e.g., penile EMG and intravaginal temperature), see Geer and Janssen (2000). For a more extensive discussion of the anatomy and (peripheral and central) physiology of sexual response, see Andersson and Wagner (1995), Bancroft (1989), Levin (1992), McKenna (1998), O'Connell et al. (1998), and, of course, Dickinson (1933) and Van de Velde (1926).

REFERENCES

Andersson, K. E., & Wagner, G. (1995). Physiology of penile erection. *Physiological Review, 75,* 191–236.
Bancroft, J. (1989). *Human sexuality and its problems*. Edinburgh, UK: Churchill Livingstone.
Bancroft, J., & Janssen, E. (2000). The dual control model of male sexual response: A theoretical approach to centrally mediated erectile dysfunction. *Neuroscience and Biobehavioral Review, 24,* 571–579.
Bancroft, J., Jones, H. G., & Pullan, B. P. (1966). A simple transducer for measuring penile erection with comments on its use in the treatment of sexual disorder. *Behavior Research and Therapy, 4,* 239–241.
Barlow, D. H. (1986). Causes of sexual dysfunction: The role of anxiety and cognitive interference. *Journal of Consulting and Clinical Psychology, 54,* 140–157.
Barlow, D. H., Becker, R., Leitenberg, H., & Agras, W. (1970). A mechanical strain gauge for recording penile circumference change. *Journal of Applied Behavior Analysis, 6,* 355–367.
Beach, F. A. (1942). Analysis of factors involved in the arousal, maintenance and manifestation of sexual excitement in male animals. *Psychosomatic Medicine, 4,* 173–198.
Berman, J. R., Berman, L., & Goldstein, I. (1999). Female sexual dysfunction: Incidence, pathophysiology, evaluation and treatment options. *Urology, 54,* 385–391.
Bogaert, A. F. (1996). Volunteer bias in human sexuality research: Evidence for both sexuality and personality differences in males. *Archives of Sexual Behavior, 25,* 125–140.
Bradley, W. E., Timm, G. W., Gallagher, J. M., & Johnson, B. K. (1985). New method for continuous measurement of nocturnal penile tumescence and rigidity. *Urology, 26,* 4–9.

Buchner, A., Faul, F., & Erdfelder, E. (1992). *GPOWER, A priori-, post hoc-, and compromise power analyses for the Macintosh* [computer program]. Bonn, Germany: Bonn University.

Bullough, V., & Bullough, B. (1977). *Sin, sickness, and sanity, A history of sexual attitudes*. New York: Meridian.

Burnett, A. L. (1997). Nitric oxide in penis, physiology and pathology. *Journal of Urology, 157,* 320–324.

Byrne, D. (1977). The imagery of sex. In J. Money & H. Musaph (Eds.), *Handbook of sexology*. Amsterdam: Elsevier.

Cacioppo, J. T., Tassinary, L. G., & Berntson, G. G. (2000). *Handbook of psychophysiology*. New York: Cambridge University Press.

Carpenter, D., Janssen, E., & Graham, C. (1999). *Vaginal photoplethysmography artifacts*. Unpublished data.

Dickinson, R. L. (1933). *Human sex anatomy*. Baltimore: Williams & Wilkins.

Earls, C. M., & Jackson, D. R. (1981). The effects of temperature on the mercury-in-rubber strain gauge. *Journal of Applied Behavioural Analysis, 3,* 145–149.

Elashof, J. (1995). *nQuery Advisor* [Computer software]. Saugus, MA: Statistical Solutions.

Everaerd, W. (1988). Commentary on sex research: Sex as an emotion. *Journal of Psychology and Human Sexuality, 2,* 3–15.

Farkas, G. M., Evans, I. M., Sine, L. F., Eifert, G., Wittlieb, E., & Vogelmann-Sine, S. (1979). Reliability and validity of the mercury-in-rubber strain gauge measure of penile circumference. *Behavior Therapy, 10,* 555–561.

Fisher, C., Gross, J., & Zuch, J. (1965). Cycle of penile erection synchronous with dreaming (REM) sleep. *Archives of General Psychiatry, 12,* 27–45.

Freund, K. (1963). A laboratory method for diagnosing predominance of homo- or hetero-erotic interest in the male. *Behaviour Research and Therapy, 1,* 85–93.

Freund, K., Langevin, R., & Barlow, D. (1974). Comparison of two penile measures of erotic arousal. *Behaviour Research and Therapy, 12,* 355–359.

Geer, J. H. (1983). *Measurement and methodological considerations in vaginal photometry*. Paper presented at the meeting of the International Academy of Sex Research, Harriman, NY.

Geer, J., & Janssen, E. (2000). The sexual response system. In J. T. Cacioppo, L. G. Tassinary, & G. G. Berntson (Eds.), *Handbook of psychophysiology* (pp. 315–341). New York: Cambridge University Press.

Geer, J. H., Morokoff, P., & Greenwood, P. (1974). Sexual arousal in women, the development of a measurement device for vaginal blood volume. *Archives of Sexual Behavior, 3,* 6, 559–564.

Graham, C., Janssen, E., & Sanders, S. A. (2000). Effects of fragrance on female sexual arousal and mood across the menstrual cycle. *Psychophysiology, 37,* 76–84.

Hatch, J. P. (1979). Vaginal photoplethysmography: Methodological considerations. *Archives of Sexual Behavior, 8,* 357–374.

Hedricks, C. A. (1994). Sexual behavior across the menstrual cycle: A biopsychosocial approach. *Annual Review of Sex Research, 5,* 122–172.

Heiman, J. R. (1976). Issues in the use of psychophysiology to assess female sexual dysfunction. *Journal of Sex and Marital Therapy, 2,* 197–204.

Heiman, J. R. (1977). A psychophysiological exploration of sexual arousal patterns in females and males. *Psychophysiology, 14,* 266–274.

Heiman, J. R., & Rowland, D. L. (1983). Affective and physiological sexual response patterns: The effect of instructions on sexually functional and dysfunctional men. *Journal of Psychosomatic Research, 27,* 105–116.

Henson, D. E., & Rubin, H. B. (1978). A comparison of two objective measures of sexual arousal of women. *Behaviour Research and Therapy, 16,* 143–151.

Henson, D. E., Rubin, H. B., & Henson, C. (1979). Analysis of the consistency of objective measures of sexual arousal in women. *Journal of Applied Behavior Analysis, 12,* 701–711.

Henson, D. E., Rubin, H. B., & Henson, C. (1982). Labial and vaginal blood volume responses to visual and tactile stimuli. *Archives of Sexual Behavior, 11*, 23–31.

Hicks, R. G. (1970). Experimenter effects on the physiological experiment. *Psychophysiology, 7*(1), 10–17.

Hoon, P., Bruce, K., & Kinchelow, G. (1982). Does the menstrual cycle play a role in erotic arousal? *Psychophysiology, 19*, 21–26.

Hoon, P. W., Murphy, W. D., Laughter, J. S., Jr., & Abel, G. G. (1984). Infrared vaginal photoplethysmography: Construction, calibration, and sources of artifact. *Behavioral Assessment, 6*, 141–152.

Hoon, P. W., Wincze, J. P., & Hoon, E. F. (1976). Physiological assessment of sexual arousal in women. *Psychophysiology, 13*(3), 196–204.

Hoyle, C. H., Stones, R. W., Robson, T., Whitley, K., & Burnstock, G. (1996). Innervation of vasculature and microvasculature of the human vagina by NOS and neuropeptide-containing nerves. *Journal of Anatomy, 188*, 633–644.

Janssen, E., & Everaerd, W. (1993). Determinants of male sexual arousal. *Annual Review of Sex Research, 4*, 211–245.

Janssen, E., Everaerd, W., Spiering, M., & Janssen, J. (2000). Automatic processes and the appraisal of sexual stimuli: Toward an information processing model of sexual arousal. *Journal of Sex Research, 37*, 8–23.

Janssen, E., Everaerd, W., van Lunsen, H., & Oerlemans, S. (1994). Validation of a psychophysiological Waking Erectile Assessment (WEA) for the diagnosis of male erectile disorder. *Urology, 43*, 686–695.

Janssen, E., Vissenberg, M., Visser, S., & Everaerd, W. (1997). An in vivo comparison of two circumferential penile strain gauges: Introducing a new calibration method. *Psychophysiology, 34*, 717–720.

Janssen, E., Vorst, H., Finn, P., & Bancroft, J. (2001). *The Sexual Inhibition (SIS) and Sexual Excitation (SES) Scales: Measuring individual differences in the propensity for sexual inhibition and excitation in men.* Submitted for publication.

Jennings, J. R., Tahmoush, A. J., & Redmont, D. P. (1980). Non-invasive measurement of peripheral vascular activity. In I. R. Martin & P. H. Venables (Eds.), *Techniques in psychophysiology* (pp. 70–131). New York: Wiley.

Jovanovic, U. J. (1967). Some characteristics of the beginning of dreams. *Psychologie Fortschung, 30*, 281–306.

Kaplan, H. S. (1977). Hypoactive sexual desire. *Journal of Sex and Marital Therapy 3*, 3–9.

Kaplan, H. S. (1979). *Disorders of sexual desire.* New York: Brunner/Mazel.

Karacan, I. (1969). A simple and inexpensive transducer for quantitative measurements of penile erection during sleep. *Behavior Research Methods and Instrumentation, 1*, 251–252.

Kinsey, A. C., Pomeroy, W. B., & Martin, C. E. (1948). *Sexual behavior in the human male.* Philadelphia: Saunders.

Kinsey, A. C., Pomeroy, W. B., Martin, C. E., & Gebhardt, P. H. (1953). *Sexual behavior in the human female.* Philadelphia: Saunders.

Kraemer, H. C., & Thiemann, S. (1987). *How many subjects? Statistical power analysis in research.* Newbury Park, CA: Sage.

Kuban, M., Barbaree, H., & Blanchard, R. (1999). A comparison of volume and circumference phallometry: Response magnitude and method agreement. *Archives of Sexual Behavior, 28*, 285–318.

Laan, E., & Everaerd, W. (1995). Determinants of female sexual arousal: Psychophysiological theory and data. *Annual Review of Sex Research, 6*, 32–76.

Laan, E., Everaerd, W., & Evers, A. (1995). Assessment of female sexual arousal: Response specificity and construct validity. *Psychophysiology, 32*, 476–485.

Laws, D. R. (1977). A comparison of the measurement characteristics of two circumferential penile transducers. *Archives of Sexual Behavior, 6*, 45–51.

Levin, J. R. (1997). Overcoming feelings of powerlessness in "aging" researchers: A primer on statistical power in analysis of variance designs. *Psychology and Aging, 12*, 84–106.

Levin, R. J. (1992). The mechanisms of human female sexual arousal. *Annual Review of Sex Research, 3*, 1–48.

Levin, R. J. (1998). Assessing human female sexual arousal by vaginal plethysmography: A critical examination. *Sexologies, European Journal of Medical Sexology, 6*, 26–31.

Levin, R. J., & Wagner, G. (1978). Haemodynamic changes of the human vagina during sexual arousal assessed by a heated oxygen electrode. *Journal of Physiology, 275*, 23–24.

Levin, R. J., & Wagner, G. (1997). Human vaginal blood flow-absolute assessment by a new, quantitative heat wash-out method. *Journal of Physiology, 504*, 188–189.

Levine, L. A., & Carroll, R. A. (1994). Nocturnal penile tumescence and rigidity in men without complaints of erectile dysfunction using a new quantitative analysis software. *Journal of Urology, 152*, 1103–1107.

Masters, W. H., & Johnson, V. E. (1966). *Human sexual response.* New York: Little, Brown.

Masters, W. H., & Johnson, V. E. (1970). *Human sexual inadequacy.* New York: Little, Brown.

McConaghy, N. (1974). Measurements of change in penile dimensions. *Archives of Sexual Behavior, 3*, 381–388.

McConaghy, N. (1999). Unresolved issues in scientific sexology. *Archives of Sexual Behavior, 28*, 285–318.

McKenna, L. (1998). Central control of penile erection. *International Journal of Impotence Research, 10*, 25–34.

Melman, A. (1992). Neural and vascular control of erection. In R. C. Rosen & S. R. Leiblum (Eds.), *Erectile disorders, assessment and treatment* (pp. 141–170). New York: Guilford.

Meston, C. M., & Gorzalka, B. B. (1995). The effects of sympathetic activation on physiological and subjective sexual arousal in women. *Behaviour Research and Therapy, 3*, 651–664.

Meuwissen, I., & Over, R. (1992). Sexual arousal across phases of the human menstrual cycle. *Archives of Sexual Behavior, 21*, 101–119.

Moll, A. (1909). *Das sexualleben des kindes.* Leipzig, Germany: Vogel.

Moll, A. (1912). *The sexual life of the child.* New York: Macmillan.

Morokoff, P. J. (1986). Volunteer bias in the psychophysiological study of female sexuality. *Journal of Sex Research, 22*(1), 35–51.

Morrell, M. J., Dixen, J. M., Carter, S., & Davidson, J. M. (1984). The influence of age and cycling status on sexual arousability in women. *American Journal of Obstetric Gynecology, 148*, 66–71.

Mosher, D. L. (1980). Three dimensions of depth of involvement in human sexual response. *Journal of Sex Research, 16*, 1–42.

Mosher, D. L. (1998). Multiple indicators of subjective sexual arousal. In C. M. Davis, W. L. Yarber, R. Bauserman, G. Schreer, & S. L. Davis (Eds.), *Handbook of sexuality-related measures* (pp. 75–77). Thousand Oaks, CA: Sage.

Mosher, D. L., Barton-Henry, M., & Green, S. E. (1988). Subjective sexual arousal and involvement: Development of multiple indicators. *Journal of Sex Research, 25*(3), 412–425.

Munoz, M. M., Bancroft, J., & Marshall, I. (1993). The performance of the Rigiscan in the measurement of penile tumescence and rigidity. *International Journal of Impotence Research, 5*, 69–76.

O'Connell, H. E., Hutson, J. M., Anderson, C. R., & Plenter, R. J. (1998). Anatomical relationship between urethra and clitoris. *Journal of Urology, 159*, 1892–1897.

Osborne, C. A., & Pollack, R. H. (1977). The effects of two types of erotic literature on physiological and verbal measures of female sexual arousal. *Journal of Sex Research, 13*, 250–256.

Ottesen, B., Pedersen, B., Nielsen, J., Dalgaard, D., Wagner, G., & Fahrenkrug, J. (1987). Vasoactive intestinal polypeptide (VIP) provokes vaginal lubrication in normal women. *Peptides, 8*, 797–800.

Palace, E. M. (1995a). A cognitive-physiological process model of sexual arousal and response. *Clinical Psychology, Science and Practice, 2*(4), 370–384.

Palace, E. M. (1995b). Modification of dysfunctional patterns of sexual response through autonomic arousal and false physiological feedback. *Journal of Consulting and Clinical Psychology, 63,* 604–615.

Palace, E. M., & Gorzalka, B. B. (1990). The enhancing effects of anxiety on arousal in sexually dysfunctional and functional women. *Journal of Abnormal Psychology, 99,* 403–411.

Palace, E. M., & Gorzalka, B. B. (1992). Differential patterns of arousal in sexually functional and dysfunctional women: Physiological and subjective components of sexual response. *Archives of Sexual Behavior, 21,* 135–159.

Plaud, J. J., Gaither, G. A., Hegstad, H. J., Rowan, L., & Devitt, M. K. (1999). Volunteer bias in human psychophysiological sexual arousal research: To whom do our research results apply? *Journal of Sex Research, 36,* 171–179.

Richards, J. C., Bridger, B. A., Wood, M. M., Kalucy, R. S., & Marshall, V. R. (1985). A controlled investigation into the measurement properties of two circumferential penile strain gauges. *Psychophysiology, 22,* 568–571.

Richards, J. C., Kalucy, R. S., Wood, M. M., & Marshall, V. R. (1990). Linearity of the electromechanical penile plethysmograph's output at large expansions. *Journal of Sex Research, 27,* 283–287.

Robinson, P. (1976). *The modernization of sex.* New York: Harper & Row.

Rogers, G. S., Van de Castle, R. L., Evans, W. S., & Critelli, J. W. (1985). Vaginal pulse amplitude response patterns during erotic conditions and sleep. *Archives of Sexual Behavior, 14,* 327–342.

Rosen, R. C., & Beck, J. G. (1988). *Patterns of sexual arousal.* New York: Guilford.

Rutala, W. (1996). APIC guideline for selection and use of disinfectants. *American Journal of Infection Control, 24*(4), 313–342.

Sachs, B. D. (2000). Contextual approaches to erectile function and sexual arousal. *Neuroscience and Biobehavioral Review, 24,* 541–560.

Sakheim, D. K., Barlow, D. H., & Beck, J. G. (1985). Diurnal penile tumescence: A pilot study of waking erectile potential in sexually functional and dysfunctional men. *Sexuality and Disability, 4,* 68–97.

Schreiner-Engel, P., Schiavi, R. C., Smith, H., & White, D. (1981). Sexual arousability and the menstrual cycle. *Psychosomatic Medicine, 43,* 199–214.

Shapiro, A., & Cohen, H. (1965). The use of mercury capillary length gauges for the measurement of the volume of thoracic and diaphragmatic components of human respiration: A theoretical analysis and a practical method. *Transactions of the New York Academy of Sciences, 26,* 634–649.

Sintchak, G., & Geer, J. H. (1975). A vaginal plethysmograph system. *Psychophysiology, 12*(1), 113–115.

Slob, A. K., Ernste, M., & Werff-ten Bosch, J. van der. (1991). Menstrual cycle phase and sexual arousability in women. *Archives of Sexual Behavior, 20,* 567–577.

Slob, A. K., Koster, J., Radder, J. K., & Werff-ten Bosch, J. van der. (1990). Sexuality and psychophysiological functioning in women with diabetes mellitus. *Journal of Sex and Marital Therapy, 2,* 59–69.

Spiering, M., Everaerd, W., & Janssen, E. (2001). *Priming the sexual system: Automatic versus nonautomatic processing of sexual stimuli.* Submitted for publication.

Steinman, D. L., Wincze, J. P., Sakheim, D. K., Barlow, D. H., & Mavissakalian, M. (1981). A comparison of male and female patterns of sexual arousal. *Archives of Sexual Behavior, 10*(6), 529–547.

Strassberg, D. S., & Lowe, K. (1995). Volunteer bias in sexuality research. *Archives of Sexual Behavior, 24,* 369–382.

Tiefer, L. (1991). Historical, scientific, clinical, and feminist criticisms of "The Human Sexual Response Cycle" model. *Annual Review of Sex Research, 2,* 1–23.

Udelson, D., Park, K., Sadeghi-Najed, H., Salimpour, P., Krane, R. J., & Goldstein, I. (2000). Axial penile buckling forces vs Rigiscan radial rigidity as a function of intracavernosal pressure: Why

Rigiscan does noet predict functional erections in individual patients. *International Journal of Impotence Research, 11,* 327–339.

Van de Velde, T. H. (1926). *Ideal marriage, Its physiology and technique.* New York: Random House.

Wagner, G., & Ottesen, B. (1980). Vaginal bloodflow during sexual stimulation. *Obstetrics and Gynecology, 56,* 621–624.

Weijmar Schultz, W., van Andel, P., Sabelis, I., & Mooyaart, E. (1999). Magnetic resonance imaging of male and female genitals during coitus and female sexual arousal. *British Medical Journal, 319,* 1596–1600.

Whalen, R. E. (1966). Sexual motivation. *Psychological Review, 2,* 151–163.

Wheeler, D., & Rubin, H. B. (1987). A comparison of volumetric and circumferential measures of penile erection. *Archives of Sexual Behavior, 16,* 289–299.

Wiederman, M. W. (1999). Volunteer bias in sexuality research using college student participants. *Journal of Sex Research, 36,* 59–66.

Williams, D. M., Barlow, D. H., Mitchell, W., Prins, A., & Scharff, L. (1990, November). *The effects of experimenter gender and performance demand on sexually functional males.* Paper presented at the 24th annual convention of the Association for Advancement of Behavior Therapy, San Francisco, CA.

Wincze, J. P., Hoon, E. F., & Hoon. P. W. (1976). Physiological responsivity of normal and sexually dysfunctional women during erotic stimulus exposure. *Journal of Psychosomatic Research, 20,* 445–451.

Wincze, J. P., Venditti, E., Barlow, D., & Mavissakalian, M. (1980). The effects of a subjective monitoring task in the physiological measure of genital response to erotic stimuli. *Archives of Sexual Behavior, 9,* 533–545.

Wolchik, S. A., Braver, S. L., & Jensen, K. (1985). Volunteer bias in erotica research: Effects of intrusiveness of measure and sexual background. *Archives of Sexual Behavior, 14,* 93–107.

8

▼▼▼▼▼▼▼

Focus Group Methods

Peggy Y. Byers
Ball State University

Richard A. Zeller
Bowling Green State University

Bryan D. Byers
Ball State University

The focus group grew out of what Merton, Fiske, and Kendall (1956) referred to as a *focused interview*. It is traditionally defined as a well-designed discussion group that concentrates on a particular topic or topics, is facilitated by a trained moderator, and typically consists of 8 to 12 participants in a formal setting. Although the "definition of focus groups has very elastic boundaries," in an actual focus group, "there must be an effort to gather information through a focused discussion" (Morgan, 1998, p. 35). Morgan (1996) stated that focus groups have three essential elements: The goal is data collection, the group discussion is the source of those data, and the researcher's active role in creating the group discussion is acknowledged. The goal of a focus group is not necessarily to produce consensus, but to stimulate thinking and obtain a range of ideas, opinions, and explanations of experiences.

Focus groups provide several unique opportunities for sexuality researchers. First, they provide researchers the opportunity to see process in action (Goldman, 1962). That is, they provide a chance to observe transactions between and among participants, and how they respond and react to each other. Second, focus groups, through their candid discussions, also have the potential to expose latent attitudes, opinions, and behavior patterns (Pramualratana, Havanon, & Knodel, 1985). Ideally, a focus group closes the gap between a participant's initial perceptions of a topic and what he or she may have experienced (Merton et al., 1990). That is, the discussions can help participants clarify their positions and articulate their experiences more clearly. Morgan (1996) suggested that, "what makes the discussion in focus groups more than the sum of separate individual interviews is the fact that the participants both query each other and explain themselves to each other. . . . Such interaction offers valuable data on the extent of consensus and diversity among the participants" (p. 139). Third, Morgan and Spanish (1984) suggested that focus groups provide a unique source of qualitative data and can add to other qualitative or quantitative data collection strategies, thus making them useful in a variety of research areas. Focus groups are appropriate when the research is exploratory or preliminary, when the purpose is to gain insight into complicated behavior or motivation, when synergy or dynamics among the members is desired, or when the researcher places a high value on capturing open-ended comments from participants (Krueger, 1994).

Technical descriptions of focus groups can be found throughout the literature (see suggested readings at the end of this chapter). This chapter presents current thought on the focus group as a research design. It makes a case for the use of focus groups in sexuality research, briefly reviewing pertinent literature concerning background, method, validity, reliability, advantages, and disadvantages.

OVERVIEW OF FOCUS GROUP METHODS

To better appreciate the usefulness of focus groups in sexuality research, an understanding of the method's origination and theoretical framework are important.

Theoretical Framework

Lederman (1989) suggested that the focus group method rests on four fundamental assumptions:

1. People are a valuable source of information.
2. People can report on and about themselves, and they are articulate enough to verbalize their thoughts, feelings, and behaviors.
3. The facilitator who focuses the group can be used to generate genuine and personal information.
4. The dynamics in a group can help people retrieve forgotten information.

These assumptions provide guidelines for selecting situations in which the focus group is an appropriate and useful method for answering research questions and generating meaningful data. Thus, Calder (1977) distinguished among exploratory, clinical, and phenomenological approaches to focus group research.

Exploratory.   Calder (1977) suggested that the exploratory approach to qualitative research produces prescientific knowledge. This knowledge is not meant to have scientific status; it is meant to be its precursor, a foundation on which the researcher can build future studies. In this instance, the goal is to determine what participants believe to be important aspects of the topic under discussion.

The exploratory approach is useful when scientific explanation is desired, but researchers are uncertain about what is important. Grant (1993) suggested that some researchers initially use a focus group for purely exploratory purposes—a point echoed by Patterson (1989). After determining what the respondents see as important aspects of the topic at hand through initial exploration in the focus group, researchers may then develop theories that can be tested quantitatively or with additional focus groups. The focus group interview can be useful by itself as a self-contained method, or in conjunction with individual interviews, surveys, experiments, or participant observations (Grant, 1993; Morgan, 1988, 1993), all of which are amenable to the field of sexuality research. When focus groups are conducted as precursors to developing quantitative scientific knowledge, their purpose is to stimulate the thinking of researchers. When they are conducted in anticipation of gaining qualitative exploratory knowledge, they are facilitating the construct-generation process.

Clinical. Calder's (1977) second perspective, the clinical approach, suggests that focus groups should be used when researchers need to explore areas that are not amenable to direct observations. He claimed that this is a useful approach for obtaining information for clinical, or therapeutic, judgments. Because sexuality researchers generally do not have the advantage of direct observation, focus groups provide another avenue to obtain relevant data about sexual behaviors.

Phenomenological. In Calder's (1977) third perspective, the phenomenological approach, the researcher is attempting to understand and describe a particular experience. The goal is to understand how the participants experience the phenomenon, the most basic, underlying elements of the topic at hand; that is, to see the phenomenon as the respondents see it. This type of approach should be used when researchers are out of touch with their targeted participant group or participant groups are changing rapidly.

These three frameworks for conducting research provide the sexuality researcher with guidelines for determining when the focus group is an appropriate method. Focus groups provide a useful way of generating exploratory data where little are known beforehand, and a useful way of investigating topics such as sexuality that are generally not amenable to direct observation or paper-and-pencil surveys. Finally, they provide a useful way to gather data about the most basic human experience of the phenomenon under study.

From Theory to Method

Poole and McPhee (1985) suggested that the key links between theory and method are the "modes of inquiry" (hypothetico-deductive, modeling, and grounded) and the "modes of explanation" (causal, conventional, and dialectical). Together, these modes form nine templates, or types of research options. Each template contains different assumptions and standards of inference of proof. The grid of templates provides a general scheme from which researchers can select the most appropriate mode of inquiry depending on the type of explanation desired.

The focus group method is a grounded mode of inquiry and a conventional mode of explanation. As a grounded mode of inquiry, the focus group is a bottom–up approach to research, where scholars are actively developing concepts, hypotheses, and theoretical propositions from direct experiences with the data (Poole & McPhee, 1985). Presuming the independence of researcher and the participants in the research, conventional explanations assume the world is a *social product*, where the subjects actively regulate their behavior. This perspective seeks to explain why people react in a particular manner. As Byers and Wilcox (1991) stated, when this type of explanation is sought, the focus group method is useful. In this type of research, the investigator uses qualitative techniques to uncover conventions and how they are used. Validity rests primarily on the strength of the researcher's insight and techniques of discovery. This approach brings the researcher into the most intimate contact with the subject.

Methodological Assessment

The purpose for which a focus group is used determines, to a large extent, the degree to which reliability, generalizability, and validity become salient issues. If the group is conducted to ascertain information about a single case, these issues may not be very pressing. However, if the group is conducted for a broader purpose and more academic reasons, these issues must be dealt with appropriately.

Generalizability. Calder (1977) provided the most comprehensive discussion of generalizability, reliability, and validity as applied to focus groups. He suggested that, for exploratory purposes, generalizability is not a crucial issue because the goal of this approach is to generate ideas for scientific research or compare scientific explanations with everyday explanations. For the clinical approach, generalizability is more important. In this approach, the researcher is making scientific interpretations, and other researchers would like to know whether these interpretations hold true beyond the focus group participants. Generalizations can be assessed through subsequent research designed to test the clinical interpretation with a quantitative technique. Generalizability, for the phenomenological approach, can be assessed through follow-up quantitative research if necessary. Calder advised, however, that the phenomenological approach is predicated on sharing the experience of others; this is best done through personal contact.

Wells (1974) suggested that, because group interviews cannot be conducted with large portions of the population and it is therefore difficult to ensure random selection of participants, researchers must assume that what is being investigated is so uniformly distributed in the population that it does not matter much where one *dips* into the population for a sample. In addition, stratification can be used to ensure that important demographic and other variations in the population are reflected in the sample. Although quantitative surveys permit better estimates of generality of responses than do focus groups, they are a "poor substitute for even the vicarious experience" provided by focus group (Calder, 1977, p. 361). This point is particularly applicable to research on sexuality. Calder further suggested that conducting additional focus groups is the best way to establish generalizability given the phenomenological nature of focus group data. Also, it is not justifiable to assume that data are not generalizable simply because they come from a single focus group. As Lunt (1996) noted, "It may be as problematic to assume that findings for a particular category of [focus group] respondents do not generalize to other categories (or other times or places) as it is to assume that they do, as both assumptions are comparative" (p. 91).

Reliability. To optimize the reliability of focus group data, a general rule is to conduct focus groups until the researchers can be reasonably sure that the same information will be repeated, thus demonstrating the reliability of the information. This typically occurs after the fourth or fifth session. When the goal of focus group research is to ask "why" rather than "how many," to generate hypotheses rather than assert their representativeness, the question of reliability may be less important.

Validity. Calder (1977) suggested that to promote validity and objectivity, focus group moderators should refrain as much as possible from contributing to the discussion and monitor their actions carefully. Focus groups tend to suffer from inhibiting factors, such as social desirability response bias, as is often the case with other qualitative research methods. Goldman (1962) concluded that discrepancies between attitude expression and actual behavior are decreased in focus groups, implying reasonable validity of the method. Focus groups should possess content validity, which can be achieved by the moderator prompting the participants to cover the full range of meanings of the topic at hand (Lunt, 1996).

Further evidence for the validity of focus group data can be obtained through triangulation with other research methods. The blind spot of one research method is often the focus of another. Therefore, the wise researcher seeks to confirm insights derived using one method by using yet another method. This is the essence of validity. As Zeller (1993a) expressed it, "A valid phenomenon has been established when pressing the flesh, chasing the decimal point, and producing the effect all provide the same messages about the nature of the phenomenon" (p. 109). In other words, a phenomenon is validated when different methods of research reach the same conclusions. Focus groups contribute to validity because they allow a deeper knowledge of social phenomena than is available using the sample survey (Strauss, 1987).

The issues of generalizability, reliability, and validity are important in the focus group method to the extent that the researcher will apply the results to other populations. The goals of the research are also instrumental in determining the effects and importance of these three methodological concerns. Accordingly, depending on the goals of the research, focus groups represent advantages and disadvantages over other methods of data collection.

Advantages and Disadvantages of the Focus Group

Openness, flexibility, ability to handle contingencies, and efficient use of time are four distinct advantages to the focus group method. A well-moderated group encourages full and open expression of perceptions, experiences, and attitudes. Compared with surveys, the primary difference is the ability of the focus group to produce more in-depth information on the issue under discussion. Focus groups provide a different kind of information than is provided by verbal self-report. In a verbal self-report, the respondents simply provide information about themselves; however, in the focus group, participants react to the thoughts and ideas of others. When compared with individual interviews, the focus group is more adept at providing insights into complex behaviors and motivations (Morgan, 1996).

Focus groups are also typically more flexible than individual interviews, Wells (1974) asserted, as the moderator "works from a list of topics—listening, thinking, probing, exploring, framing hunches and ideas" (p. 134). When the purpose of the group is exploratory, the moderator has the flexibility to adapt to the group and build on issues uncovered through the process of group dynamics, rather than following a strict interview guide. The interaction in a focus group produces an emergent set of ideas that would not be forthcoming if the participants were interviewed separately.

The ability of focus groups to handle contingencies is another advantage. They allow the researcher to discover and explore linkages between ideas that would go untouched in a sample survey (Wells, 1974). The moderator has the opportunity to ask for clarification of vague responses, generally not an option for survey researchers. Moreover, it is possible to explore important issues other than those listed on a questionnaire that may arise in the course of the group discussion.

A fourth advantage involves time. Eliciting responses from 8 to 12 respondents in a focus group lasting 1 to 2 hours is more efficient than interviewing the same number of people individually. A final advantage is the interpretability of data. Although the data usually contain a wide range of responses (Kover, 1982), identification of issues and reasons that participants hold positions on those issues is usually clear on careful analysis. Moreover, as Morgan (1996) suggested, the researcher has the "ability to ask the participants themselves for comparisons among their experiences and views, rather than aggregating individual data in order to speculate about where or why the interviews differed" (p. 139). This provides valuable insight when interpreting the data. The group often stimulates recall and makes salient important but forgotten personal details. Provision of basic exploratory information is another advantage of such data. When little is known in advance of investigation, the focus group may provide a basis for formulating further questions (Zeller, 1986).

In summary, focus groups are far less labor intensive than traditional qualitative methods such as participant observation. Thus, they are a relatively efficient method for obtaining insight into sexual attitudes and behaviors. The focus group method does, however, have some disadvantages. A series of three or four focus groups lasting over a weekend could easily cost $2,500 or more depending on moderator's fee, facility rental, video/audio recording and transcribing, coding, data analysis and interpretation, and participant incentives. Grant (1993) pointed out, however, that focus groups still may be less expensive than other forms of opinion research. For example, Twiggs (1994) noted that small focus groups conducted at facilities already available to the researcher, such as classrooms, could cost as little as $400.

A second disadvantage may be participants' conformity to social norms. Social desirability response bias (Crowne & Marlow, 1964), or respondent motivation to provide socially acceptable responses that conform to group norms, is somewhat greater in a group than in the anonymous process of survey questionnaire completion. Self-selection on the part of the participants is another potential problem. It is important to remember that the respondents are volunteers who may be more extroverted, outgoing, and more sociable than the average individual. In addition, as in any research setting, the presence of the moderator or researcher may affect the discussion. Morgan (1996) noted that, "the moderator's efforts to guide the group discussion [may have] the ironic consequence of disrupting the interaction that [is] the point of the group" (p. 140).

A final weakness is the range of topics available for a focus group. For example, some topics may be off limits for certain participants because the presence of others reduces their willingness to talk abut their attitudes and experiences regarding those topics. Although Morgan (1996) claimed that sensitive topics such as sexuality may be inappropriate for the focus group method, this has not been supported by empirical investigations. In fact, work with focus groups on the sensitive topic of romantic marital jealousy shows the opposite effect (Yuhas, 1986). Yuhas found that with homogeneous groups, members were very outspoken about the topic. Some participants even suggested that the discussion was somewhat cathartic.

USING FOCUS GROUPS IN SEXUALITY RESEARCH

Although there are costs and benefits associated with any methodological approach, one may most effectively use the focus group method in sexuality research by being aware of its disadvantages while capitalizing on its advantages. This section offers some strategies for achieving that goal.

Advantages and Disadvantages for Sexuality Research

Focus groups are useful in sexuality research because there is much information that sexuality researchers want and need that is unavailable using other methods. The most common method for obtaining information is the sample survey. The sample survey has some major strengths, including, but not limited to, the following:

1. Items can be constructed to speak directly to the research questions of the investigator.
2. Using a well-designed sample and well-developed statistical tools, the results of the survey can be generalized to populations in the millions from samples in the hundreds with known margins of error.
3. Reliability and validity estimates are obtainable.
4. Sample surveys are usually relatively cost-effective on a per-respondent basis.

These are major advantages, and the preference for the sample survey capitalizes on them. The General Social Survey (GSS) conducted regularly by the National Opinion Research Center (NORC), for example, asks, "About how often did you have sex during the last 12 months?" Response categories range from *not at all* to *more than 3 times per week*. Careful coding and analysis can yield mean scores that can be categorized by demographic variables (e.g., age and race) and correlated with others (e.g., church attendance, political view, and income). Most respondents are quite willing to answer this question using a response from among the categories provided.

The sample survey suffers from some serious disadvantages that limit its application in sexuality research. For example, in answering the question quoted earlier, some may simply guess, others may exaggerate, and others may minimize their level of sexual activity (see chap. 3, this volume). That is, there is a legitimate question about the validity of the responses to this item. Not having an objective validity criterion (e.g., video cameras focused on the respondents 24 hours per day), we cannot unequivocally establish the true value of this measure. More problematic is the measurement of sexual activity outside of marriage. For example, the GSS asks, "Have you ever had sex with someone other than your husband or wife while you were married?" Because of the norm of sexual fidelity to one's marital partner, this question literally begs for a socially desirable response (Wiederman, 1997). Indeed, that sexual activity with someone other than one's spouse is called *cheating* is evidence of the socially undesirable nature of an affirmative answer to this question.

Finally, survey research on human sexuality may suffer from the fact that the sample survey is at its best when asking *top of mind* questions, but not when asking questions that involve complex and intense emotional feelings (Zeller, 1993a).

Sexual activity is replete with such deep feelings. The identification of questions that can accurately elicit the roles played by trust, lust, loyalty, opportunity, and deceit in an intense mixed-motive sexual activity is a major challenge. Indeed, in our experience, attempts by survey researchers to measure important dimensions of sexual behavior and attitudes are often intellectually unsatisfying. Not only may researchers suspect that the answers to questions about sexual attitudes and behaviors reflect social desirability response bias, but they also suspect that respondents may utilize a *boilerplate* set of responses that technically answer the questions without really answering the questions (Zeller, 1993b). This lack of satisfaction with survey data may therefore be due to the gut-level feeling that something important was going on between the partners that the survey items failed to measure.

Because of these potential problems with survey data, sexuality researchers should seek out alternative research strategies that provide contexts in which the researcher can come to insights about sexual attitudes and behaviors. To get past barriers preventing serious communication with an outsider on an intimate topic, researchers must cast off the highly structured survey that allows people to make only limited, emotionless responses. They must seek a venue through which they can discover the deeper meanings and motivations of intimate activities that respondents are usually reluctant to divulge. This research approach calls for a different kind of data.

The desired data will reveal attitudes and behaviors that cannot be elicited from questionnaire items. Were it not for ethical, legal, and logistic limitations, the researcher may choose to observe sexual activity and discuss its meaning and interpretation with the participants in close temporal proximity with the sexual event. When these activities take place in a public arena, such observation is legitimate and possible (see chap. 6, this volume). Indeed, observation may be the only way to identify and quantify the cues used to indicate sexual interest (e.g., Moore, 1985, 1995; Moore & Butler, 1989). Next best, the researcher may prefer to be a "mouse in the corner" overhearing discussions on the topic across the backyard fence, at the bowling alley, at the coffee clutch, at the bar, and at the game. The problem presented by such discussion is that, in many of these circumstances, the mere presence of an outsider may substantially alter the conversation.

All of this suggests that focus groups may provide crucial information to sexuality researchers possibly unavailable from other research methods. Focus group research provides in-depth information with a much richer and varied quality than is often available from other methods. In a sense, focus group research allows the investigator to set the agenda without setting the agenda (Zeller, 1993b).

Conducting Successful Focus Groups for Sexuality Research

There are some basic procedures that help the researcher obtain valid and reliable data from a focus group discussion. This section provides several essential ingredients, or issues to consider, for achieving a successful focus group for sexuality research.

A Clearly Understood Objective.   Establishing an objective is the first thing the sexuality researcher should do. The researcher needs to determine whether the focus group is part of an ongoing research project or if it is self-contained. This determines how salient the issues of generalizability, reliability, and validity are. Also, the researcher should have a clearly defined goal, or desired outcome, of the focus group discussion. The concepts to be investigated should be clearly defined, and the number of topics should be kept small so that each can be discussed in some detail. The research objectives can help determine, to a large extent, how the researcher addresses the other focus group design elements.

Structure.   Groups can be more or less structured based on the level of moderator involvement (Morgan, 1996). A group can be more structured with regard to questions, so that the moderator controls the topics discussed. It can also be more structured with regard to managing the group dynamics, with the moderator controlling participation. A key factor in defining the degree of structure is the number of questions the moderator asks (Morgan, 1996). The degree of structure imposed by the moderator should be determined by the goals of the research. If the goal is to generate new knowledge, then the degree of structure may be minimal. However, if the goal is to obtain information on some specific questions regarding the topic at hand, more structure may be necessary (Morgan & Krueger, 1998).

Standardization.   The extent to which identical protocols for questions and procedures are used in every group for a particular research endeavor is an issue to consider (Morgan, 1996). For example, each group's questions may be somewhat different from the previous group, taking advantage of what has been learned from earlier groups. This approach typifies the grounded orientation some focus group applications may take. Alternatively, a project could consist of a fixed set of questions and procedures for use in all focus groups. Morgan (1996) concluded that, although the tendency of most social scientists is to utilize a fixed set of questions and procedures, the decision should ultimately "be based on a conscious assessment of the advantages and disadvantages of standardization with regard to the goals of the particular project" (p. 142).

Moderator Influence.   The moderator should begin the discussion by inviting honest and open dialogue, and guiding the discussion only when necessary. The moderator will keep the group clearly focused and on task if specific information is needed, or he or she may allow the group to divert from the topic and talk about what the participants think is important when a broad range of information is needed.

A common source of bias in focus group research is the moderator leading the participant, in the sense that the moderator may unintentionally provide cues that lead participants to make statements they believe the moderator wishes to hear regardless of whether the participant believes them. The researcher wants to provide a give-and-take context within which participants feel free to express their thoughts and feelings about the phenomenon under study. However, in establishing that context, the moderator may give off subtle cues. Indeed, the moderator may need to give off such cues to be taken seriously in the focus group interaction situation.

Environment. Focus groups are sometimes conducted via video conference with television monitors, remote control cameras, and digital transmissions rather than in a room with a researcher behind a one-way mirror. Video conferencing allows for individuals who otherwise would be unable to travel to the session to observe the process and gain valuable insight (Heather, 1994). The majority of focus groups are held in formal settings such as a conference room or research lab. However, there are instances where a more informal setting may be appropriate. This decision must be based on the goals of the research. Regardless of the physical environment, the moderator should ensure a psychological environment of confidentiality of participant responses and open discussion, especially with a sensitive issue such as sexuality.

Recruitment of Participants. Successful focus group research requires a sufficient number of qualified participants. The researcher should decide on the characteristics of the individuals to be targeted for focus group selection. Although any one group should be homogeneous (referred to as *control characteristics*), some characteristics (referred to as *break characteristics*) may differ from group to group (Morgan, 1993). Consider, for example, demographic characteristics. Although any one group should be homogeneous in, for example, sexual experiences, different focus groups should be comprised of members of different ethnic groups. This procedure helps determine patterns of responses particular to different segments of the population (Grant, 1993), as well as promote open discussion because it is usually easier for people to talk openly within a group whose members have similar experiences.

Morgan (1996) referred to this technique as *segmentation* and noted that it helps build a comparative dimension into the project, including the data analysis. Recent practice has moved away from traditional sampling techniques to using "naturally occurring groups of like-minded people" (Lunt, 1996, p. 82). However, the composition of any group should be based on the goals of the research.

A screening guide is typically utilized for determining which group a participant should be assigned to. The guide, serving as a script for the recruiter, would contain questions to assess important break and control characteristics. This procedure ensures that the participant possess necessary experiences and demographic characteristics as they pertain to the topic under investigation.

The dispositions of the participants and the expectations that they bring with them to the focus group discussion are of crucial importance. Some people are reluctant to divulge the nature of their sexual attitudes and behaviors to others, whereas other people have no such reluctance. The conventional wisdom in focus group research is that only people who have expressed a willingness to talk about sexual behavior and attitudes should be included in focus group discussions. The critic will point out, quite legitimately, that the dispositions of those who are willing to talk about their sexual practices will differ from the dispositions of those who are not willing to talk. This problem is not limited to focus group research (see chap. 5, this volume). Indeed, just as an ethical focus group researcher will not invite to a focus group people who do not wish to discuss intimate features of their sexuality, so an ethical survey researcher will not pry opinions out of reluctant respondents. Social research is always characterized by a lack of information on those unwilling or unable to provide that information.

Focus group researchers want each group to consist of similar people who share the same culture. Members of homogeneous groups are similar in terms of the usual demographic categories of sexuality, age, race, and so forth. More important in sexuality research, however, participants need to have similar sexual experiences. Participants may be more open to discussion if they know they are among others who have had similar experiences. Borrowing from a previous example, suppose that a sexuality researcher wishes to explore the topic of extramarital sexual affairs. The resulting focus groups should be composed of same-sex participants, all of whom have engaged in extramarital sexual affairs. If even one participant has not engaged in such a sexual liaison, that fact alone may be sufficient to defeat a productive discussion. This occurs because the focus group participant who had never had such a relationship may offer the opinion that extramarital sexual relationships are immoral. The other participants might then reassess their willingness to describe their experiences for fear that the sexual moralist will brand them as immoral. In this situation, little discussion of value should be expected.

Group Size.   Groups should consist of at least 3, but no more than 10 to 12 participants. Morgan (1996) suggested that relatively smaller groups are more appropriate for sensitive and emotional issues, such as sexuality, giving more time for each participant to discuss his or her experiences with the research topic. Larger groups are more appropriate for neutral topics, which generate lower levels of psychological involvement. The researcher may thus obtain a wider variety of responses when the group is appropriately small or large.

Determining the Number of Groups.   Break characteristics, as mentioned earlier, should be kept to a meaningful minimum with at least one focus group per break characteristic. This allows the researcher to make comparisons between and among the groups. An effective rule of thumb is to be aware of repeated information. A sufficient number of groups should be conducted until the data become saturated; that is, until no new information is forthcoming (Morgan, 1996). The greater the diversity among the groups, the more groups will be needed to reach this saturation point.

The Moderator's Role. A successful focus group in sexuality research is a group in which the participants discuss the issues that the moderator wishes to raise without the moderator overtly raising those issues. This does not happen automatically; indeed, any of a wide variety of factors can prevent this from happening. Moreover, it does not happen without an agenda and a moderator who is responsible for directing the discussion.

A moderator can either make or break a focus group, particularly one discussing a sensitive topic such as sexuality. During the discussion, other members of the research team may serve as observers behind a one-way mirror. Their role is to monitor and take notes on participants' nonverbal reactions to the discussion. They may also suggest additional questions for the moderator and identify statements that may need further exploration or clarification arising from the discussion. However, it is the moderator who approaches the focus group with a topic outline or interview guide, specifying the issues that need to be raised in the group to answer the research questions. Usually these issues begin with generic wide-ranging questions and become more focused as the discussion proceeds (hence, the name *focus group*). However, in successful focus groups, after the moderator introduces the topic, provides an introduction, and begins to probe for discussion, generally group members begin to talk among themselves about the topic under investigation.

Often these discussions address issues that appear on the moderator's topic outline guide, but have not yet been introduced into the discussion. When this occurs, the moderator should resist the temptation to drag the discussion back to the question next specified on the topic outline guide. Instead, the moderator, and any observers, should be aware that the focus group is operating properly because the participants have now taken control of the agenda. The moderator's role at this point is to screen out irrelevant parts of the discussion and keep the attention focused on the issues in the topic outline guide that the participants have raised. In this way, the moderator ceases to be the central player in the unfolding drama. Instead, the moderator becomes a minor player in the interaction, and the focus group comes to resemble the interaction that takes place at the bar, the bowling alley, and across the backyard fence.

There are a number of technical duties and environmental issues that the moderator typically sees to in addition to facilitating the discussion. For example, these consist of ensuring that all the equipment such as the tape recorder and/or the video recorder are functioning properly. Light refreshments are usually provided for the participants, along with an honorarium for their participation. The room must be comfortable with chairs preferably arranged around a table, and name tags with first name only should be provided. The moderator should welcome participants as they arrive and direct them to the refreshments and any seating arrangement that may be in place. The moderator facilitates the discussion and brings it to a close by thanking the individuals, answering any remaining questions they may have, and debriefing the participants.

If the principle investigator is moderating his or her own focus groups, there are special issues to keep in mind. One may not speak solely of disadvantages, however, because there are certain advantages to the principle investigator conducting the groups. As for advantages, the principle investigator is probably the most knowledgeable individual concerning the research problem under investigation. Second, the investigator, given this intimacy of understanding and knowledge, may be the best positioned person to probe for additional information during focus groups that a less knowledgeable moderator may not have the insight to pursue. Finally, by having the principle investigator as the moderator, the journey from data collection, to coding, and then to analysis is not as long. That is, if the principle investigator is the moderator, additional insight and understanding may be added to each of these phases.

Although there are potential advantages to this situation, there are also clear disadvantages. As mentioned earlier, having the principle investigator serving as the moderator may produce bias during the data collection phase. Demand characteristics and researcher expectations may be more at issue. Also, and not unrelated to the last point, a focus group that is the product of the principle investigator serving as the moderator may be more susceptible to critique and criticism on validity issues. This latter point should be of particular concern to the focus group researcher because issues of validity are common criticisms of focus group methods.

Facilitating Discussions of Sensitive Topics

Zeller (1993b) articulated three principles designed to enhance the value of the discussion of a focus group on a sensitive topic such as sexuality:

1. The methodological principle of reactivity should be used on the screening guide to stimulate the thinking of the participants during the days prior to the focus group session itself.
2. To increase the acceptable range of self-disclosure on the part of the participants, the moderator should use the communications principle of "sufficient but not excessive self-disclosure."
3. The social-psychological principle of legitimization should be used to ensure that the participants see a wide diversity of thoughts, opinions, and descriptions as acceptable within the context of the group discussion.

We discuss these three principles in turn.

Reactivity. The term *reactivity* refers to the process of measurement changing what is being measured. In the classic documentation of reactivity, Star and Hughes (1950) showed that a publicity campaign was effective for those who had been asked about the topic in question prior to the campaign, but was ineffective for those who had not been asked these questions prior to the campaign. Those who were asked about the topic prior to the campaign were sensitized to receiving and encoding the information from the campaign, whereas the others were not.

Although reactivity is usually viewed negatively, as a threat to validity, it can be viewed positively, in the context of focus groups, as a method to get participants to think about the topics of discussion before the discussion takes place. Indeed, reactivity can be used to enhance the value of information obtained from focus group participants. That is, when the focus group participants are recruited, they can be asked a series of questions that serve two purposes. First, these questions serve to screen out those who do not meet the inclusion criteria. Second, these questions serve to stimulate the thinking of those who are invited to participate in the focus group. This latter function is particularly valuable for sexuality researchers. Sexuality topics are emotionally charged. If focus group participants have a few days to think about the sexual issues that are the topic under discussion, they can organize their thoughts. Then during the subsequent focus group session, they are better able to articulate their ideas.

Self-Disclosure. This refers to how much one reveals about one's attitudes and behaviors in what settings. Self-disclosure can be used to enhance the willingness of focus group participants to reveal intimate details of their sexual encounters. The moderator can provide some details of his or her own sexual encounters as a way to stimulate the focus group participants to reveal their own sexual experiences. However, self-disclosure must be used with care: Either an excessive level or an inadequate level of self-disclosure inhibits such discussions. (See Zeller, 1993b, for a discussion of strategies to maximize the positive impact of self-disclosure on the quality of data produced by focus groups.)

Legitimization. This is the process by which people engaging in normatively proscribed behavior come to feel comfortable about revealing such behavior. Consider the situation in which a sexuality researcher wishes to find out the reasons and motives people have for engaging in extramarital intercourse. Survey research data suggest that such behavior is relatively infrequent. In the 1996 GSS, 19% of respondents indicated that they had had sex with someone other than their husband or wife while they were married (Wiederman, 1997). Moreover, large proportions of people believe that such behavior is "always or almost always wrong" (Wiederman, 1997). When a focus group researcher faces this situation, the initial and perhaps fatal challenge is to get the participants to talk candidly about a matter that is relatively infrequent and normatively proscribed. If such talk is not made legitimate, the focus is unproductive.

The introductory remarks made by the moderator can be used to legitimate the discussion of normatively proscribed topics. For example, the moderator may say:

> We are here to discuss sexual activity. Specifically, we are here to discuss extramarital sexual experiences. You have been recruited to participate in this focus group because you have acknowledged that you have engaged in extramarital relations at some point in your married lives. [This tells participants that they are in a group where everyone has engaged in extramarital sexual relations.] Because this is a sensitive topic, let us stick to first names, and we request that you do not talk outside this room about who else was here and what they might have done. [This requests confidentiality among participants.] I will ask each of you to introduce yourself and tell us something about you. Let me start with myself. . . .

The moderator then introduces him or herself and describes a behavior he or she has engaged in relevant to the discussion. The moderator starting the discussion legitimizes it; that is, if the moderator can talk of his or her extramarital sexual encounters, the participants can too. Of course, the moderator must set an appropriate level of self-disclosure. At the same time, the discussion needs to move to sensitive areas with some speed because there is usually only a 90-minute or so window within which the researcher can find out some very intimate things about the participants.

Analysis of Focus Group Data

According to the *analysis continuum* developed by Krueger (1998), analysis of focus group data begins with collecting and presenting the raw data, describing the data through quotes and paraphrasing, interpreting the data, and, finally, making recommendations and drawing final conclusions. To this end, focus group data can be analyzed through either a qualitative or quantitative content analysis. However, the researcher should be cognizant of using qualitative criteria to meet qualitative research goals and quantitative criteria to meet quantitative research goals. That is, because the purpose of qualitative research is to gain insights, an analysis design that puts the focus on insight is in order. Similarly, because the purpose of quantitative research is generalization from a sample to a population, an analysis design that puts the focus on estimation, confidence intervals, and statistical significance tests is in order.

Just as it is risky to look to quantitative research for insights, it is risky to look to qualitative research for estimation, confidence intervals, and statistical significance tests. Hence, reports of what percentage of the participants said this or that in the analysis of focus group data run the risk of using quantitative criteria to evaluate qualitative research. The researchers should assure themselves that the analysis design does not inadvertently employ a technique ill-suited for the research technique they are using. The choice depends on the purpose of the study;

the goal is to assemble what was said in the groups into meaningful units that can answer the research questions and meet the goals of the researchers.

The standard method for analyzing focus group data is to construct a verbatim transcript from which participant statements about particular issues raised in the focus group can be categorized. However, if the purpose of the focus group is purely exploratory, transcript summaries may be substituted for verbatim transcripts. Notes from observers provide more information about the discussion and a context in which to frame participants' statements.

As Knodel (1993) noted, a considerable amount of subjective judgment is involved when analyzing and interpreting the data. Statements must be interpreted within the larger context of the discussion. At least two analysts should conduct these analyses without communicating with each other so that inter-rater reliability estimates for the resulting categories can be assessed. That is, another researcher looking at the same data should arrive at the same conclusions (Krueger, 1998). This inter-rater agreement is a critical safeguard against inadequate and incorrect analyses. When dealing with subtle messages and themes, a reasonable research practice is to acknowledge different interpretations between the raters when drawing conclusions.

The researcher must devise a useful coding scheme. To do this effectively, the researcher may need to read the transcripts numerous times. This process may include physically marking transcript margins using a meaningful system. For example, the researcher may want to code according to the group, a certain demographic characteristic such as age or gender, individual research questions, individual discussion guide questions, consistently emerging topics of interest, and any other analytically distinct units. Coding in these ways helps the researcher identify related statements, themes, and issues.

The next step is to discover any emergent patterns. This occurs as the researcher continually returns to the coded transcripts and observer notes looking for related statements, phrases, ideas, words, reactions, and so forth. The coded transcripts are cut apart and pasted back together into meaningful categories after coding. Categories or segments are generally organized around the research questions and the discussion guide questions. Often, however, topics emerge through the discussion enough to be recognized as a meaningful category for analysis. Effective analysis is directly related to the quality of questions asked in the discussion. These questions are the backbone of the study (Krueger, 1998). The researcher cannot assume the responses of interest will only come from the words the participants used to answer the questions. Although words are the core, the effective analyst must also consider the behaviors and actions of the participants. Things such as posture, body language, and tones of voice, which could be documented either through observer notes or a video recorder, should also be considered in the analysis (Krueger, 1998).

Knodel (1993) suggested constructing a large chart or table referred to as an *overview grid*. The grid provides a descriptive summary of the content of the discussions. Topic headings would be one axis of the grid and session identifiers would be another. The cells would contain brief summaries of the content of the discussion for each group concerning each topic, as well as other related information deemed useful. Topic headings could be the research questions, discussion guide questions, and other emerging topics. Comparisons and contrasts can be made within and among groups. The grid is a useful way of looking at a large amount of information. It also allows the researcher to look for relationships and themes that may be missed by looking at the coded transcripts in smaller chunks, as would be seen from the computer monitor.

As an example, in her analysis of romantic marital jealousy, Yuhas (1986) transcribed the taped discussions. She then wrote verbatim text on separate index cards for each meaningful statement. The cards were coded by group, member, and type of statement represented (e.g., intentional provocation of jealousy, emotional response to the feelings of jealousy, etc.). The index cards were then sorted into a number of different piles to develop the most meaningful categories and interpretation of the data. The themes represented by each pile were developed to answer her research questions. The cards were also arranged into piles of related issues arising from discussion that were not addressed in her research questions. The cut-and-paste function of a word processor is valuable for this purpose, as well as its indexing and macrofunctions. There is also a variety of software programs available for use such as Ethnograph, Qualpro, and Hyperqual.

Applications of the Focus Group Method to Sexuality Research

There are numerous applications of the focus group technique in sexuality research. A brief computer search revealed published focus group research on sexual attitudes and behavior in several different countries including Brazil, Cameroon, Haiti, Thailand, Costa Rica, Kenya, China, and Nigeria. The range of topics of focus group research on sexuality included marriage (e.g., Pramualratana et al., 1985); sexually transmitted diseases, HIV, and AIDS (e.g., Deering, 1993); and sexual intercourse, intimacy, and pregnancy (e.g., Harris, 1998).

These and other published articles illustrate the wide variety of applications for focus groups in the area of human sexuality and indicate that the focus group is particularly well suited to researching difficult topics in difficult settings where the sampling and interviewing constraints of the survey method are inappropriate. At the same time, however, the review revealed some uses of focus groups that appear to ignore the strengths and weaknesses of the technique. Specifically, some authors appear to cast their results in exclusively quantitative rather than qualitative terms. The appropriateness of this decision rests on the specifics goals of the research.

We remind the reader that the focus group is particularly well suited to gaining insight about a topic, but is not well suited for the generalization to a larger population inherent in percentages and regression slopes. Some authors may also use focus groups as a pretext for articulating their own ideological positions and fashion their data to support those positions. The potential for this kind of data biasing is one of the weaknesses of focus groups; people who use it for this purpose undermine its value for those researchers who wish to glean genuine insight from focus group research. However, the promise and track record of the application of focus groups in sexuality research is wide and deep; it is limited only by the creative imaginations of researchers and the variety of sexual attitudes and behaviors that constitute the domain of sexuality research.

SUGGESTED READINGS

For those interested in learning more about the general characteristics, features, and uses of focus groups, we highly recommend *The Focus Group Kit* (Morgan & Krueger, 1998). This six-volume collection contains separate handbooks on topics such as planning focus groups, developing questions, and moderating focus groups. We also suggest Greenbaum (1993), Krueger (1994), and Stewart and Shamadasani (1990) as general and definitive works on focus groups. For further direction in analysis of focus group data, Knodel (1993) provided some useful suggestions, as did Bertrand, Brown, and Ward (1992). Although there are many sources of information on applying the focus group method to specific disciplines and perspectives, perhaps one of the best is Templeton (1994). Last, Wilkinson (1999) discussed the use of focus groups as a feminist research method.

REFERENCES

Bertrand, J. T., Brown, J. E., & Ward, V. (1992). Techniques for analyzing focus group data. *Evaluation Review, 16,* 198–209.

Byers, P. Y., & Wilcox, J. R. (1991). Focus groups: A qualitative opportunity for researchers. *The Journal of Business Communication, 28,* 63–78.

Calder, B. J. (1977). Focus groups and the nature of qualitative marketing research. *Journal of Marketing Research, 14,* 353–364.

Crowne, D., & Marlow, D. (1964). *The approval motive.* New York: Wiley.

Deering, M. J. (1993). Designing health promotion approaches to high-risk adolescents through formative research with youth and parents. *Public Health Reports, 108,* 68–77.

Goldman, A. E. (1962). The group depth interview. *Journal of Marketing, 26,* 61–68.

Grant, B. C. (1993). Focus groups versus mock trials: Which should you use? *Trial Diplomacy Journal, 16,* 15–22.

Greenbaum, T. L. (Ed.). (1993). *The handbook of focus group research.* New York: Lexington.

Harris, J. (1998). Urban African American adolescent parents: Their perceptions of sexuality, love, intimacy, pregnancy and parenting. *Adolescence, 33,* 833–844.

Heather, R. P. (1994). Future focus groups. *American Demographics, 16*(1), 6.

Knodel, J. (1993). The design and analysis of focus group studies: A practical approach. In D. Morgan (Ed.), *Successful focus groups: Advancing the state of the art* (pp. 35–50). Newbury Park, CA: Sage.

Kover, A. J. (1982). Point of view: The legitimacy of qualitative research. *Journal of Advertising Research, 22,* 49–50.

Krueger, R. A. (1994). *Focus groups: A practical guide for applied research* (2nd ed.). Beverly Hills, CA: Sage.

Krueger, R. A. (1998). *Analyzing and reporting focus group results.* Beverly Hills, CA: Sage.

Lederman, L. (1989, November). *Assessing educational effectiveness: The focus group as a technique for data collection.* Paper presented at the annual meeting of the Speech Communication Association, San Francisco, CA.

Lunt, P. (1996). Rethinking the focus group in media and communications research. *Journal of Communication, 46,* 79–98.

Merton, R. K., Fiske, M., & Kendall, P. (1956). *The focused interview.* Glencoe, IL: The Free Press.

Merton, R. K., Fiske, M., & Kendall, P. (1990). *The focused interview* (2nd ed.). New York: The Free Press.

Moore, M. M. (1985). Nonverbal courtship patterns in women: Context and consequences. *Ethology and Sociobiology, 6,* 237–247.

Moore, M. M. (1995). Courtship signaling and adolescents: "Girls just wanna have fun"? *The Journal of Sex Research, 32,* 319–328.

Moore, M. M., & Butler, D. L. (1989). Predictive aspects of nonverbal courtship behavior in women. *Semiotica, 3,* 205–215.

Morgan, D. L. (1988). *Focus groups as qualitative research.* Beverly Hills, CA: Sage.

Morgan, D. L. (Ed.). (1993). *Successful focus groups: Advancing the state of the art.* Beverly Hills, CA: Sage.

Morgan, D. L. (1996). Focus groups. *Annual Review of Sociology, 22,* 129–152.

Morgan, D. L. (1998). *The focus group guide book.* Beverly Hills, CA: Sage.

Morgan, D. L., & Krueger, R. A. (Eds.). (1998). *The focus group kit* (Vols. 1–6). Beverly Hills, CA: Sage.

Morgan, D. L., & Spanish, M. T. (1984). Focus groups: A new tool for qualitative research. *Qualitative Sociology, 3,* 253–270.

Patterson, A. H. (1989). Trial simulation: Testing cases with mock juries. *The National Law Journal, 11,* 26–28.

Poole, M. S., & McPhee, R. D. (1985). Methodology in interpersonal research. In M. L. Knapp & G. R. Miller (Eds.), *Handbook of interpersonal communication* (pp. 100–170). Beverly Hills, CA: Sage.

Pramualratana, A., Havanon, N., & Knodel, J. (1985). Exploring the normative basis for age of marriage in Thailand: An example from focus group research. *Journal of Marriage and Family, 41,* 203–210.

Star, S. A., & Hughes, H. M. (1950). Report on an educational campaign: The Cincinnati plan for the United Nations. *American Journal of Sociology, 55,* 355–361.

Strauss, A. L. (1987). *Qualitative analysis for social scientists.* London: Cambridge University Press.

Stewart, D., & Shamadasani, P. (1990). *Focus groups: Theory and practice.* Newbury Park, CA: Sage.

Templeton, J. F. (1994). *The focus group: A strategic guide to organizing, conducting and analyzing the focus group interview.* Chicago: Probus.

Twiggs, H. F. (1994). Do-it-yourself focus groups: Big benefits, modest cost. *Trial, 30,* 42–117.

Wells, W. D. (1974). Group interviewing. In R. Ferber (Ed.), *Handbook of marketing research* (pp. 133–140). New York: McGraw-Hill.

Wiederman, M. W. (1997). Extramarital sex: Prevalence and correlates in a national survey. *The Journal of Sex Research, 34,* 167–174.

Wilkinson, S. (1999). Focus groups: A feminist method. *Psychology of Women Quarterly, 23,* 221–244.

Yuhas, P. L. (1986). *Romantic marital jealousy: An exploratory analysis.* Unpublished doctoral dissertation, Bowling Green State University, Bowling Green, OH.

Zeller, R. A. (1986). *The focus group: Sociological applications.* Unpublished manuscript, Bowling Green State University, Bowling Green, OH.

Zeller, R. A. (1993a). Combining qualitative and quantitative techniques to develop culturally sensitive measures. In D. G. Ostrow & R. C. Kessler (Eds.), *Methodological issues in AIDS behavioral research* (pp. 96–116). New York: Plenum.

Zeller, R. A. (1993b). Focus group research on sensitive topics: Setting the agenda without setting the agenda. In D. L. Morgan (Ed.), *Successful focus groups: Advancing the state of the art* (pp. 167–183). Newbury Park, CA: Sage.

9

Dear Diary: A Useful But
Imperfect Method

Paul Okami
University of California–Los Angeles

> *I never travel without my diary. One should always have something sensa-*
> *tional to read on the train.*
>
> —Oscar Wilde (cited in Coxon, 1988)

After more than 100 years of scientific and scholarly work in the field of human sexuality, the present volume is one of the very first concerned primarily with research methodology. Although there are a number of probable reasons that a volume such as this one is a rarity, undoubtedly one reason is that there is precious little variance in methodology to be found among such investigations. Even when we are able to venture tentatively into the world of direct observation and measurement, we find our results compromised by volunteer bias (Plaud, Gaither, Hegstad, Rowan, & Devitt, 1999) or primitive measurement instruments (Kuban, Barbaree, & Blanchard, 1999; McConaghy, 1999). Thus, human sexuality is a presumably scientific field dominated by a single methodology: We ask some people what they do and hope that their memories are working and they are telling the truth.

I am not the first to point out that research participants' memories are faulty, they may lie like thieves, and communication styles of investigators and participants are often mismatched (Abramson, 1992; Clement, 1990; Cochran, Mosteller, & Tukey, 1954; Lewontin, 1995; Wiederman, 1997). Of course, this is not the entire picture. Sometimes memories do work, truths (or at least facts) are told with candor, and researchers and participants sometimes communicate well with each other. The problem with survey methodology lies in discerning which set of circumstances apply in a given study. Usually survey data are simply accepted uncritically, with unspoken hopes that all is well. Even when attempts are made to demonstrate the reliability of data, these efforts typically do not also include attempts to establish the validity of data (Berk, Abramson, & Okami, 1995). As sexuality researchers have been made painfully aware in the age of AIDS, where mathematical modeling for epidemiology is often attempted on data of questionable quality, reliable data are not necessarily valid data. The fact that responses on a questionnaire administered today closely match responses on a questionnaire administered 6 months ago is no indication of the degree to which responses on either occasion are accurate.

There is another problem with survey methodology that goes beyond questions of veracity. Shweder (1991) complained that surveys are conducted within a presumed transcendent realm wherein the effects of context and idiosyncratic or culturally specific meanings are controlled or eliminated. Thus, qualitative data, which unquestionably bear on questions of private and/or volatile matters such as sexuality, are ignored in most of our investigations.

What is a reasonable response to this problem? First, we need to display greater modesty in our assertions of fact based on survey research. Moreover, as pointed out by Fortenberry, Cecil, Zimet, and Orr (1997), there is no single gold standard for valid measurement of sexual behavior. Thus, we must also display modesty in assertions made about our instruments. Last, we must find methods that function responsibly within our ethical and cultural restraints to obtain human sexuality data that complement survey data or, in certain cases, perhaps improve on them. One such method is the participant sexual diary.

DIARY AS METHOD

Diaries have always been effective as literary devices and have also been useful as sources of historical data (Plummer, 1983). However, prior to the 1970s, their place in the behavioral sciences was, with a few exceptions, limited to case studies. When research in substance abuse began to proliferate during the 1970s and 1980s, the participant diary became more commonplace as researchers attempted to circumvent drug users' well-known tendency to underreport use, simply forget details of use, or both (e.g., Fuller, Bebb, Littell, Houser, & Witschi, 1972; Poikolainen & Karkkainen, 1983).

The story is similar for sexuality research. Alfred Kinsey (1948) used the diary of at least one "boy lover" as data on child sexuality for his initial study during the 1940s, and other sexuality investigators experimented with the diary method over the years (e.g., Reading, 1983; Spitz, Gold, & Adams, 1975; Udry & Morris 1967). However, it was not until the emergence of AIDS that epidemiologists and others began to use the diary method in earnest to study sexual behavior (e.g., Berk et al., 1995; Coxon, 1994; Leigh, Gillmore, & Morrison, 1998).

One wonders why sexuality researchers waited as long as they did to fully explore this method. Intuitively, diaries seem a good choice for collecting sexual data. As Coxon (1994) pointed out, large numbers of people have kept diaries at some point in their lives, and diaries are often used to confide intimate details of a person's life. Although diaries may take structured and unstructured forms, there is no necessity for a set sequential ordering of items, allowing room for idiosyncratic modes of processing and recalling information. This possibility for open-ended reporting inherent in the diary format make it ideal for collecting qualitative as well as quantitative data. Moreover, diaries may be written in the participant's own natural language, circumventing problems of communication between investigator and participant. Such problems may be prodigious, invalidating not only single investigations, but seriously compromising meta-analyses as well. For example, Coxon (1988) suggested that meanings ascribed to important terms such as *sexual partner* vary significantly among the populace. Additionally, in taking the investigator out of the picture to some extent, diaries reduce reactivity and demand characteristics.

Perhaps the most important potential benefit of the diary lies in its concurrent nature. Although in a technical sense diary data are elicited retrospectively, the period of recall can be very short: several minutes or hours. Problems of faulty reporting that arise as a consequence of forgetting, telescoping, or other cognitive errors (e.g., participants' confusing average with modal behaviors) are therefore ameliorated, and variations in behavior over time may be recorded. These characteristics accord diary studies a prospective quality (Leigh et al., 1998; McLaws, Oldenburg, Ross, & Cooper, 1990), and details of specific events—missed in retrospective aggregation—may be recorded (Fortenberry et al., 1997).

Finally, research participants seem to prefer the diary method over recall instruments. For example, McLaws et al. (1990) found that 86% of their sample of homosexual men preferred the diary method, compared with 14% who preferred the standard recall questionnaire.

Do the theoretical advantages of the diary format add up to actual increases in reliability and validity over retrospective questionnaire and interview methods? Interestingly, relatively few studies have tested this proposition (Abramson, 1988; McLaws et al., 1990). Indeed, a number of researchers favoring the diary format have applied to their method the same unsupported presumption—that all is well—that I attributed to researchers who use survey instruments (cf. Berk et al., 1995; Coxon, 1994; Fortenberry et al., 1997).

Despite the apparent benefits of the diary format, there are reasons for caution. According to Leigh et al. (1998), potential threats to reliability and validity in diary studies include:

1. attrition and nonrepresentativeness of samples resulting from the increased time and effort involved in participation, as well as the intimately detailed nature of data participants are asked to report;

2. carry-over effects including fatigue and reactivity;
3. compliance issues, including failure to fill out diaries within the prescribed time frame.

Diaries also involve recording highly sensitive, sometimes stigmatized, material in detail. Therefore, problems of confidentiality may emerge (Fortenberry et al., 1997). Some participants might be less willing to record sexual events in detail than to simply provide frequency estimates, offer qualitative rankings, and so forth.

Moreover, the diary format does not circumvent a basic problem of survey research: Apart from autoerotic behaviors, sexuality involves more than one person. The diary expresses the viewpoint and experience of only one person: the research participant. Sexuality investigators have sometimes found that a participant's account of a dyadic experience has been flatly contradicted by the presumed partner (Coxon, 1988).

There is another potentially serious weakness in the diary format expressed in the following entirely true anecdote. I carried out a diary study of sexual behavior at the University of California, Los Angeles, in 1992 as part of my graduate training (Berk et al., 1995). A number of years later, after the study had been published, I met a young woman in a social situation. When she discovered that I was a sexuality researcher and had attended her alma matter, she proceeded to describe a *sex experiment* that she had participated in while a student to fulfill a class requirement for research participation. The experiment involved keeping diaries of sexual behavior! I was on the verge of blurting out the amusing fact that I was the one who had designed and carried out that study when she gleefully proceeded to recount how she and several of her friends had not only participated, but had made up wildly exaggerated or flatly untrue accounts for their own amusement and had recorded them in their diaries.

How many friends were there and were they the only participants to exaggerate? I will never know. Did this invalidate our findings? Maybe. I take comfort in the fact that our findings converge on those of similar investigations using different methodologies, but it certainly does give one pause.

VALIDITY AND RELIABILITY

One problem with attempting to validate the diary method is that there is no objective way to determine empirically what has actually occurred in the sexual situation being recorded. The closest one could come to such validation probably would be to use procedures similar to those used by Udry and Morris (1967), who collected urine specimens from women to test for sperm content. However, this method is specific to coital activity involving heterosexual females who do not use condoms and simply answers the question of whether coitus with male ejaculation did or did not occur. Thus, as Fortenberry et al. (1997) suggested, the real question becomes one of convergent validation. If diary and retrospective data converge, then confidence in each method is strengthened. However, if they do not converge, one is left having to chose which instrument's estimates to favor.

In terms of reliability, whereas test–retest procedures may be administered for recall instruments, they are only relevant to the diary format if one assumes that sexual behavior is stable over time—a questionable assumption for sexually active populations. When reliability is assessed at all—which is rarely—reliability estimates for diary instruments typically are computed in this way, comparing two different weeks of diary entries for test–retest stability (e.g., McLaws et al., 1990). Moreover, as noted by Graham and Bancroft (1997), comparisons are usually made by averaging scores across groups rather than individuals. Neither averaging across groups nor test–retest procedures based on assumptions of stability of sexual activity over time are ideal for drawing inferences regarding reliability. In contrast, Coxon (1994) defined test–retest reliability more literally and perhaps more accurately, suggesting that it is not possible to assess reliability of the diary method with regard to the sexual activities recorded. Instead, he assessed reliability of diary coding procedures among his research assistants.

In any event, reports of attempts to offer comparisons between the reliability and validity of diary method and conventional retrospective methods are equivocal. In a cross-national study of the effects of steroidial contraceptives on women's sexual interest and activity in the Philippines and Scotland, Graham and Brancroft (1997) compared self-report ratings given in retrospective interviews with daily diary ratings for each participant. Agreement between the two sets of ratings was assessed using weighted kappas, and the target time period was identical for the diary and retrospective interview methods. Although high-frequency events measured by diary recording were consistently underreported in the questionnaire, these investigators reported good agreement between diary and interview methods for frequency of sexual activity (weighted kappas = .71 in the Philippines and .67 in Scotland), but very low agreement between the two methods for frequency of sexual interest (weighted kappas = .03 in the Philippines and .32 in Scotland). Results suggest that women from these samples consistently underreported sexual interest—sometimes strikingly so—in the retrospective interview as compared with the diary, even given the probable increase in accuracy of the retrospective report as a consequence of having kept a diary for the target time period. Despite the general picture of disagreement between diary and questionnaire methods found by these investigators, they concluded in their discussion section that good agreement existed between the methods. This conclusion was based entirely on findings for lower frequency events involving sexual activity.

In a somewhat similar study, Reading (1983) used Pearson r to measure concordance between retrospective and diary methods over a 3-month period in a sample of male volunteers. These correlations were high for measures of frequency of intercourse, moderate for measures of frequency of sexual thoughts and frequency of masturbation, and low for measures of frequency of morning erections. However, in all cases, the retrospective interviews reported lower frequencies of events. Although it is not possible to determine empirically which estimates were closer to the truth, it is reasonable to favor larger estimates if they are reported very close to the time of occurrence of the event (Berk et al., 1995; McLaws et al., 1990; but see Catania, Gibson, Chitwood, & Coates, 1990, for another view).

Reading (1983) also compared diary and retrospective interview methods for assessing qualitative data. His participants were asked to rate satisfaction (sexual and otherwise) with their current relationship and intensity of pleasure and desire experienced during sexual activity. Correlations were moderately high for measures of satisfactions with their relationship, but low (and sometimes negative) for intensity of desire and pleasure. Although the relatively higher correlations for measures of satisfaction may appear encouraging, Reading pointed out that higher correlations on overall measures of relationship satisfaction may well represent a confounding effect of volunteer bias rather than an equivalence of measures. Men unsatisfied with their relationships would have been unlikely to volunteer for this experiment. Virtually all of the men rated their relationships as generally satisfying, and they did so in the diary as well as the interview formats. Thus, the correlations between diary and survey instruments were high for this measure.

Finally, Reading (1983) assessed agreement of dichotomous measures of the occurrence of various sexual problems. Concordance for these measures was quite low, and Reading concluded that dichotomous items fail to "reflect behavior adequately." However, this result, along with other findings of this study, may simply reflect the failure of retrospective measures to reflect behavior adequately.

Fortenberry et al. (1997) studied concordance between diary and retrospective questionnaire data in a sample of adolescent girls attending a clinic for the treatment of sexually transmitted diseases. These investigators found that a greater number of coital events were recorded by diary than questionnaire, particularly when frequencies were high. This finding of decreased recall accuracy for high-frequency events replicated findings of Berk et al. (1995) and McLaws et al. (1990). Disparity between diary and questionnaire reports were also found for substance-related coital events and condom-protected events, although lack of concordance for the latter was described by investigators as not as severe for this variable than for the former two. This greater concordance for condom-protected events, however, may have occurred for two reasons. First, a substantial number of respondents used condoms all the time, so these people were essentially estimating an event that never occurred (i.e., nonuse of condoms). Therefore, their recall task was similar to that given respondents who are sexually inactive, but who are asked to estimate the numbers of partners with whom they had sexual intercourse over a specified period. Second, Fortenberry et al. (1997) used ordinal categories to characterize condom use as reported in the diaries (e.g., less than 20% of the time, between 21% and 40%, 41% and 60%, etc.). If a person reported condom use in the diaries 82% of the time, but reported condom use *all of the time* on the questionnaire, that person's reports were counted as being in total agreement.

Although agreement between methods for number of partners was strong in this study, replicating some earlier findings (e.g., Berk et al., 1995), as with the other studies very few sexual partners were reported. The median number of partners reported by both methods was one. Few commentators have expressed concern about respondents' ability and willingness to report accurately that they had sexual intercourse with only one partner. This is because of the relatively socially sanctioned nature of single-partner sexual activity and because recalling a single partner accurately is a simpler task than recalling several or many such partners. Once again, despite substantial lack of agreement between diary and questionnaire methods for most of their variables, Fortenberry et al. (1997) maintained that agreement between the two methods was "consistent" and "reassuring" (p. 247).

Coxon (1994) attempted to assess reliability and validity of diary and questionnaire instruments using a sample of homosexual men as part of an AIDS research project (Project SIGMA). Using linear regression analysis, Coxon found that, taken as a whole, his respondents consistently overestimated sexual activity in the retrospective questionnaire as compared with the diary. This perhaps counterintuitive result was not commented on. Instead, the investigator continued to make explicit his assumption that diary estimates for high-risk activities should be more accurate than interview methods, given that social desirability factors would constrain respondents from reporting all of their experiences of unsafe sex.

Berk et al. (1995) conducted a factorial experiment among university freshmen, testing a diary format versus recall questionnaire (including various methods of memory enhancement). We found a very high—nearly perfect—correspondence between the two recording methods for number of sexual partners; but again, the vast majority of these college freshman had no partners or one partner during the test period—not a very taxing recall assignment. However, there was disparity between the methods for reporting types of sexual activity. As with Coxon's (1994) study, we found substantially higher estimates of frequency of sexual intercourse using the questionnaire format than had been recorded in the diaries for the same time period. Specifically, for every act of vaginal intercourse recorded in the diaries, there were 1.3 acts of vaginal intercourse recalled on the questionnaires. However, this result occurred primarily as the result of men's reports. Although women overestimated very slightly (using the diary as the criterion), men overestimated substantially. This is consistent with intuitive expectations for men to exaggerate their sexual activity (Wiederman, 1997).

Without dwelling morbidly on my confidence-shaking experience with the former research participant (recounted earlier), it may be that her revelations actually strengthened our findings that there was a tendency to overestimate frequency of sexual intercourse on retrospective questionnaires. If my unwitting informant's behavior was actually widespread among the study participants, and therefore diary estimates were skewed in the direction of higher frequency, honest diary accounts would have resulted in a figure even more removed from that of the questionnaires, making the magnitude of the effect that much greater.

McLaws et al. (1990) attempted to compare recall and diary measures for reliability and validity in a sample of 30 sexually active homosexual men. They found that the methods corresponded fairly well for infrequent sexual practices, but not for practices engaged in with high frequency. In particular, respondents tended to underreport higher risk activities on the recall instruments. Whereas McLaws et al. reported poor test–retest reliability for the diary method as compared with the questionnaire method, they arrived at this viewpoint by comparing frequencies for the first 2 weeks of the test period with frequencies for the last 2 weeks. As suggested previously, the assumption imbedded in this method of testing reliability for diaries—that sexual behavior is stable over time—is questionable. The authors acknowledged this point to some degree, but proceeded to discount the possibility that the sexual behaviors of their sample of men were not stable across the study time period, doing so on the basis of the stability demonstrated in the recall instrument. They did not consider the possibility that the stability of recall reports may have resulted from heuristics used by the respondents that may have leveled or otherwise averaged recall estimates (e.g., Hornsby & Wilcox, 1989). They ended their report by explicitly endorsing the recall questionnaire method over the diaries "at least where reliability is concerned" (p. 279).

Leigh et al. (1998) studied the co-occurrence of alcohol use and sexual activity in a sample of adolescents and young adults. They found what they termed a *strong correlation* between the diary and recall instruments. However, drinking as recorded in diaries, especially frequent drinking, was underreported on the recall instrument by approximately 39%, and sexual activity was overreported in the adolescent sample by 46%. Moreover, among the adolescents, those who engaged in sexual intercourse more frequently than twice a week were more likely to overreport than those who engaged in sexual intercourse less than twice a week, in keeping with the general tendency for high-frequency activities to be more vulnerable to memory distortion.

In summary, this brief review of reliability and validity studies suggests an equivocal pattern of results that does not confirm the general superiority of the diary format over recall instruments. Moreover, if it is true that diary estimates are superior, it is not at all clear whether recall instruments in general tend to elicit underreporting or overreporting. One cheerful result of this review, however, is that many low-frequency sexual events are probably reported with reasonable accuracy in questionnaires.

Despite many substantial discrepancies between diary and recall data in the studies reviewed here, several of the authors of these articles continued to insist that the two methods had *good agreement*, were *strongly correlated* and consistent with each other, that their results were *reassuring*, and so forth. At first this seems somewhat mysterious. However, on closer inspection, it raises an important issue: How close do we expect—or, more to the point, need—agreement to be?

It may be that some researchers' inaccuracy alarms are calibrated to a higher threshold for activation than some others as a consequence of their research questions. For example, epidemiologists seeking to create mathematical models of the natural history and transmission patterns of various sexually transmitted diseases understandably seek a high degree of accuracy in data collection (Berk et al., 1995). The same might be said of those who are interested in raising sexual science as a field to a higher standard than previously has been the case (see chap. 21, this volume). In these instances, a response of *all the time* is quite a different animal from reports of *between 82% and 100% of the time*. However, many research questions entail a wider envelope of acceptable accuracy. Do men and women differ on measures of intrinsic sexual interest? Which group experiences more sexual guilt—Catholics or Jews? How many women experience multiple orgasm?

DIARY FORMATS AND PROCEDURES

Diary Styles

If a diary format is to be chosen, the style of the diary instrument is an important consideration. Two general styles of diary have been used: checklist and open ended. Under these basic categories are variations based on specific research questions. For example, if one is interested in only a very few variables—for example, the occurrence of anal intercourse, the use of condoms, and the number of partners—a brief checklist may be self-administered each day with only three boxes to fill in or check. Because the task is simple and completion quick, such an instrument promises high compliance rates, little missing data, and few memory distortions, in addition to other advantages of the diary method in general. Moreover, checklists are easily and accurately coded. With open-ended diaries, coding represents a potential migraine.

If one is interested in more than a few variables, checklists are still an option. Again there is an advantage in terms of coding and missing data, but as the checklist grows in size, some of the advantages over the open-ended format are lost. An unwieldy checklist instrument, or an instrument that alternates checklists and Likert-format scales, may become boring, confusing, or take too long to complete; hence, accuracy may be compromised.

If qualitative data are sought, one may take advantage of the diary format's ability to tap events in the participant's natural language by using an open-ended style. This format may also be useful if many variables are of interest. Participants may be instructed to recount instances of sexual activity in their own words, from the beginning of the experience to its completion (it is, of course, important to operationally define *beginning* and *end* of an experience), being sure to include information pertaining to the variables of interest. Participants may also be asked to describe their feelings, reactions, and so on. Although this method allows for collection of rich qualitative data, such data can be very difficult to code, and missing response to certain items may be a problem. For example, lack of a participant's mention of some activity will be coded as if the activity did not occur, when, in fact, the participant simply forgot to write it down. This is not the same as the participant having forgotten that the event occurred, but it has the same quantitative consequences. Having used the open-ended format for my first diary study (Berk et al., 1995), I have promised myself that I would only use checklists and Likert scales in the future unless qualitative data are of primary importance to the research question.

A mixed open-ended or checklist (or Likert) format may be the best choice for many projects. Variables for which quantitative accuracy is most important may be assessed in a checklist, leaving room for participants to record open-ended material. If only a few variables are of interest, data for the same variables may be elicited using both methods—an excellent strategy for cross-checking accuracy.

Procedural Issues

There are certain procedural questions specific to the diary format regardless of the research design being used. Primary among these are the issues of collection method and daily compliance. By definition, the dairy is completed without investigator supervision, so one has no way of knowing whether the diaries have been filled out at the appropriate times. For example, if the diaries are collected on a weekly basis, what is to prevent busy (or lazy) participants from waiting until the end of the week to fill out the entire week's entries, much like a student waiting to the final possible night to complete a term paper?

One way around this problem is to have respondents fill out their diaries for the previous day in the presence of an investigator on a daily basis. The problems with this approach, however, are numerous and probably obvious. First, one has lost the concurrent quality of the study, and length of recall period becomes an issue. Second, this method could only work in a clinic or university setting, where participants have the leisure to stop by an office at a specified time. Third, filling out a diary form in the presence of an investigator introduces reactivity, thus defeating a central purpose of the diary method.

As a partial solution to these problems, an *audio diary* might be reported daily instead of a written one. Each participant can call the investigator's voice mail on a daily basis, identify him or herself (perhaps with a code number), and recount the days sexual activity in a prearranged format. This addresses the daily compliance and prospective/retrospective issues, but still introduces some potential reactivity and necessitates daily transcription, introducing greater risk of measurement error during transcription and coding.

An easier method would be to have participants complete their diaries and send them to the investigator on a weekly basis by mail in stamped envelopes supplied to them. Similarly, they might drop the diaries off on a weekly basis at a specified location. Although this method certainly improves on daily compliance compared with waiting until the end of the month (e.g., Kunin & Ames, 1981) or the end of the study test period to collect all the diaries, one is still left with the possibility that participants might wait until the end of the week to fill out a week's worth of diaries. To ask participants to mail their diaries in on a daily basis solves that problem, but is expensive for the investigators, unwieldy for both investigator and participant, and would probably result in the problem of attrition in such a study. I am not aware of any investigation that has utilized this approach. Still I suppose one might consider it. Reading (1983) used a 3-day mail-in period, which seems like a reasonable compromise. Ideally, each participant would be supplied with a locked, slotted box and a time clock.

A new possibility exists with the advent of the Internet: Diaries may be e-mailed. This is a simple procedure that solves the problem of respondents not filling out their diaries in a timely manner. With some preparation, it also allows the respondent to remain anonymous. Clearly, this is a promising procedure.

Interestingly, despite the importance of collection interval and collection method, relatively few reports of diary studies mention how and when the diaries were collected. This information is of importance in evaluating research reports.

SUMMARY

Measurement of sexual behavior is still at a primitive stage. Retrospective surveys and other forms of investigator-administered self-report instruments are still the dominant modes of data collection. The diary is a useful, but imperfect, method of data collection that may improve on these methods under certain circumstances. It may reduce problems of recall and reactivity, allow for idiographic data to be collected within a nomothetic design, and allow quasi-prospective research to be conducted with relative ease and low expense. Diary studies may reduce communication problems between investigator and participant by using the participant's natural language for data collection. Finally, people seem to prefer diaries over questionnaires.

Nevertheless, diaries may present numerous compliance problems, and there are no easy methods to control for failure. Diaries may encourage lying in ways that questionnaires do not, and they produce underestimates or overestimates of sexual behavior depending on circumstances and sample properties.

SUGGESTED READINGS

Several previous publications provide guidance or examples regarding the use of diaries as a method of data collection in sexuality research. Coxon (1988) discussed relevant issues, as did Reading (1983). Examples of diaries used to collect data on sexual activity include Coxon (1994), Reading (1983), Spitz et al. (1975), and Udry and Morris (1967). Studies involving empirical comparison between diary and recall methods of data collection include Berk et al. (1995), Fortenberry et al. (1997), Graham and Bancroft (1997), Leigh et al. (1998), and McLaws et al. (1990).

REFERENCES

Abramson, P. R. (1988). Sexual assessment and the epidemiology of AIDS. *The Journal of Sex Research, 25*, 323–346.

Abramson, P. R. (1992). Sex, lies, and ethnography. In G. Herdt & S. Lindenbaum (Eds.), *The time of AIDS* (pp. 101–123). Newbury Park, CA: Sage.

Berk, R., Abramson, P. R., & Okami, P. (1995). Sexual activities as told in surveys. In P. R. Abramson & G. Herdt (Eds.), *Sexual nature, sexual culture* (pp. 371–386). Chicago: University of Chicago Press.

Catania, J. A., Gibson, D. R., Chitwood, D. D., & Coates, T. (1990). Methodological problems in AIDS behavioral research: Influences on measurement error and participation bias in studies of sexual behavior. *Psychological Bulletin, 108*, 339–362.

Clement, U. (1990). Surveys of heterosexual behavior. *Annual Review of Sex Research, 1*, 45–74.

Cochran, W. G., Mosteller, F., & Tukey, J. W. (1954). *Statistical problems of the Kinsey report on sexual behavior in the human male*. Washington, DC: American Statistical Association, Committee to Advise the National Research Council Committee for Research in Problems of Sex.

Coxon, A. (1988). "Something sensational . . ." The sexual diary as a tool for mapping detailed sexual behavior. *Sociological Review, 36*, 353–367.

Coxon, A. (1994). Diaries and sexual behaviour: The use of sexual diaries as method and substance in researching gay men's response to HIV/AIDS. In M. Boulton (Ed.), *Challenge and innovation: Methodological advances in social research on HIV/AIDS* (pp. 125–148). Bristol, PA: Taylor & Francis.

Coxon, A. P. M., Coxon, N. H., Weatherburn, P., Hunt, A. J., Hickson, F., Davies, P. M., & McManus, T. J. (1993). Sex role separation in sexual diaries of homosexual men. *AIDS, 7*, 877–882.

Fortenberry, D. J., Cecil, H., Zimet, G. D., & Orr, D. P. (1997). Concordance between self-report questionnaires and coital diaries for sexual behaviors of adolescent women with sexually-transmitted infections. In J. Bancroft (Ed.), *Researching sexual behavior* (pp. 237–249). Bloomington, IN: Indiana University Press

Fuller, R. K., Bebb, H. T., Littell, A. S., Houser, H. B., & Witschi, J. C. (1972). Drinking practices recorded by a diary method. *Quarterly Journal of Alcohol Studies, 33*, 1106–1121.

Graham, C. A., & Bancroft, J. (1997). A comparison of retrospective interview assessment versus daily ratings of sexual interest and activity in women. In J. Bancroft (Ed.), *Researching sexual behavior* (pp. 227–236). Bloomington, IN: Indiana University Press.

Hornsby, P. P., & Wilcox, A. J. (1989). Validity of questionnaire information on frequency of coitus. *American Journal of Epidemiology, 130*(1), 94–99.

Kinsey, A. C., Pomeroy, W., & Martin, C. (1948*). Sexual behavior in the human male*. Philadelphia: Saunders.

Kuban, M., Barbaree, H. E., & Blanchard, R. (1999). A comparison of volume and circumference phallometry: Response magnitude and method assessment. *Archives of Sexual Behavior, 28*, 345–359.

Kunin, C. M., & Ames, R. E. (1981). Methods for determining the frequency of sexual intercourse and activities of daily living in young women. *American Journal of Epidemiology, 113*(1), 55–61.

Leigh, B. C., Gillmore, M. R., & Morrison, D. M. (1998). Comparison of diary and retrospective measures for recording alcohol consumption and sexual activity. *Journal of Clinical Epidemiology, 51*, 119–127.

Lewontin, R. C. (1995, April). Sex, lies and social science. *New York Review of Books*, pp. 24–29.

McConaghy, N. (1999). Unresolved issues in scientific sexology. *Archives of Sexual Behavior, 28*, 285–318.

McLaws, M. L., Oldenburg, B., Ross, M. W., & Cooper, D. A. (1990). Sexual behaviour in AIDS-related research: Reliability and validity of recall and diary measures. *The Journal of Sex Research, 27*, 265–281.

Plaud, J. L., Gaither, G. A., Hegstad, H. J., Rowan, L., & Devitt, M. K. (1999). Volunteer bias in human psychophysiological sexual arousal research: To whom do our research results apply? *The Journal of Sex Research, 36*, 171–179.

Plummer, K. (1983). *Documents of life*. London: Methuen.

Poikolainen, K., & Karkkainen, P. (1983). Diary gives more accurate information about alcohol consumption than questionnaire. *Drug and Alcohol Dependence, 11*, 209–216.

Reading, A. E. (1983). A comparison of the accuracy and reactivity of methods of monitoring male sexual behavior. *Journal of Behavioral Assessment, 5*(1), 11–23.

Shweder, R. A. (1991). *Thinking through cultures: Expeditions in cultural psychology*. Boston: Harvard University Press.

Spitz, C. J., Gold, A. R., & Adams, D. B. (1975). Cognitive and hormonal factors affecting coital frequency. *Archives of Sexual Behavior, 4*, 249–263.

Udry, J. R., & Morris, N. M. (1967). A method for validation of reported sexual data. *Journal of Marriage and the Family, 29*, 442–446.

Wiederman, M. W. (1997). The truth must be here somewhere: Examining the gender discrepancy in self-reported lifetime number of sex partners. *The Journal of Sex Research, 34*, 375–386.

10

Policy Capturing

Michael W. Wiederman
Columbia College

Although many research questions in sexual science have to do with behavior, some sexuality research is focused on people's judgments or decisions. In these cases, there is frequently an emphasis on why people make the choices that they do or the factors influencing those decisions. Examples include studies of mate selection criteria, the conditions under which a condom would be used, decisions as to whether sexual activity would take place within a dating context, or the contextual factors influencing likelihood of engaging in extramarital sex. Note that although each of these examples involves behavior, the focus of study in each is decision making. Similar to studies focused on sexual behavior, the norm in these cases is to directly ask respondents about motives or the stimuli influencing their decisions, and the resulting responses are taken at face value.

Unfortunately, several problems exist with asking individuals to report on the factors that affect their own decisions and judgments. Researchers have convincingly shown that humans typically do not have good insight (or, many times, any insight at all) into the various influences involved in their decision-making processes, although respondents typically believe that they do (e.g., Brehmer & Brehmer, 1988; Nisbett & Ross, 1980; Nisbett & Wilson, 1977). Despite objectively poor insight, people routinely report on the factors that went into their judgments or decisions. How can this be?

It appears that, when asked to comment on their own mental processes, which are impossible to observe, respondents typically generate reports of motives and cognitive influences based on a sort of folk psychology as to what motives and factors are most plausibly at work. For example, self-reports on preferences and influences regarding intimate relationships may be tapping into individuals' relationship schemas (Baldwin, 1992) or beliefs about relationship development and processes (Fletcher & Kininmonth, 1992), rather than actual influences on relationship decisions. In other words, what researchers end up measuring are people's beliefs about what influenced their judgment or decision. Sometimes these beliefs coincidentally correspond to the actual influences, whereas other times they do not.

From a research standpoint, ideally the investigator would have the power to manipulate stimuli or conditions in people's lives and observe the resulting effects on their decisions and judgments. If I send a man with red hair to approach a particular female for sex, how does she respond? If I take the same male and change only his hair color (now blonde), how does the woman respond to his request? Assuming that only hair color changed from Trial 1 to Trial 2, any difference in the woman's response could be attributed to the man's hair color. Obviously, researchers do not have the ability to perform such experiments, especially when one wants to consider multiple variables and their possible interaction. Hence, researchers would more typically ask women, "To what extent does a man's hair color influence your decision to have sex with him?" Respondents provide answers, but the accuracy of those answers is dependent on, among other things, the degree of insight about the stimuli that influence their decision to have sex with particular men.

POLICY CAPTURING

Is there a way researchers can circumvent some of the inherent problems with introspection when studying the stimuli influencing people's sexual judgments and decisions? One can answer in the affirmative if one finds analogue laboratory conditions an acceptable research methodology. For example, given a specified judgment or decision-making task, one could manipulate or measure particular variables of interest and evaluate how variation in these variables is related to corresponding variation in the respondents' actual judgments or decisions. One such method for doing this is referred to as *policy capturing*.

The term *policy* has come to be used in the field of human judgment and decision making to refer to "the factors used in making a judgment and the relative weighting thereof" (Ullman & Doherty, 1984, p. 179). Within that context, the term *policy capturing* refers to "studies that analyze judgments made on the basis of multidimensional stimuli by means of a linear model" (Brehmer & Brehmer, 1988, p. 78).

Methodology

In a policy-capturing study, the respondent is given a relatively large set of scenarios, each of which is composed of several stimuli, and the respondent is asked to make a judgment in response to each scenario (Stewart, 1988). The numeric values corresponding to each level of each stimulus (cue) within each scenario are then entered into a multiple regression equation to predict the respondent's judgments. In this way, the relative importance of each cue in the respondent's judgments can be quantified. The regression equation (see chap. 12, this volume), with its indexes of the relative weight given to each variable (e.g., standardized beta weights), represents the individual's judgment policy. Although the standardized regression coefficient is the most commonly used index of the weight an individual gives to factors in making a decision, alternative measures of the relative importance of the cues do exist (Stewart, 1988).

To be more specific, the analysis of individual policies involves treating each respondent's judgments as a separate sample. This is why a relatively large number of scenarios must be presented to each respondent, as such a number must be large enough to permit multiple regression analysis of the individual's judgments by regressing the judgments on the cues (Brehmer & Brehmer, 1988; Stewart, 1988).

For the sake of illustration, consider a task in which the respondent makes a series of judgments in response to 60 different scenarios, each of which consists of five cues (and each cue has several levels with corresponding numeric values). The respondent's judgment in response to any given scenario can be represented by Y_s. For each Y_s there are five predictor scores, one for the level associated with each of the decision cues provided in the scenario. The 60 Y_s values are regressed on the five cues. The multiple correlation (R) between the cues and the Y_s is a measure of how predictable (consistent) the respondent's judgments are, given the cues provided. Linear relationships, nonlinear relationships, and interactions among cues can be tested, as would be the case in other types of multiple regression analyses (Stewart, 1988).

Although this approach is inherently ideographic in nature, it is possible to aggregate individual policies to characterize the policies for a group of respondents (nomothetic approach), such as comparing men's and women's policies. However, the aggregation should occur only after the individual policies have been generated (see Hammond, McClelland, & Mumpower, 1980, pp. 117–119; Stewart, 1988, p. 52, for discussion of this issue).

How many scenarios should be used? Although there is no one answer (Brehmer & Brehmer, 1988), a general rule to ensure statistical stability is at least 10 scenarios per cue. Hence, if a researcher is asking participants to make judgments in response to scenarios comprised of five different stimuli, at least 50 scenarios should be used (see Stewart, 1988). Greater numbers of scenarios should be used if the researcher (a) expects relatively unreliable judgments by respondents, (b) uses cue that are intercorrelated, or (c) analyzes hypothesized interactions among cues. Frequently, a greater number of scenarios is used to allow for assessment of reliability (consistency) of respondents' judgments by including some duplicate scenarios. That is, including a relatively small subset of duplicate scenarios embedded within the larger set allows one to correlate judgments across identical scenarios (sort of a test–retest reliability check).

Aside from including duplicate scenarios, the overall R value does give some indication of the reliability of the judgments. Multiple correlations of .7 to .9 are common in policy-capturing studies (Stewart, 1988), and a relatively high value (e.g., .8 or greater) is indicative of reliable judgments.

A relatively low R value is open to several different interpretations. It may be that the respondent was inconsistent in responding due to carelessness or a rushed approach to the task. However, if the stimuli presented to respondents for judgments contain information not controlled or measured by the experimenter (e.g., the use of photos as stimuli when not all characteristics of the photographed object have been quantified by the researcher), it is possible that the R value is relatively low because the respondent was basing his or her judgments on some quality not assessed by the researcher (and hence not included in the regression equation). This is less of a concern when the stimuli consist of written scenarios created by the researcher in which each aspect has been either measured (as one of the relevant cues) or held constant across scenarios. Another possible, although less likely, reason for a relatively low R value involves the respondent using a nonlinear configuration of the variables (cues) in arriving at judgments (Stewart, 1988).

An Example

Recent policy-capturing studies having to do with sexually intimate relationships include those by Boon and Sulsky (1997), who examined attributions of blame and provision of forgiveness in romantic relationships, as well as Finkelstein and Brannick (1997), who investigated college students' decisions to engage in sexual intercourse. Similarly, Wiederman and Dubois (1998) examined college students' choices regarding short-term mates. Because I am most familiar with that study, I present it in some detail to illustrate use of the methodology in sexuality research.

In Wiederman and Dubois (1998), we were interested in testing evolutionary hypotheses regarding gender differences in preferred characteristics for short-term sexual partners. Specifically, would men and women place differential values on the characteristics physical attractiveness, financial resources, generosity, prior sexual experience, current relationship status, and desired relationship status when evaluating potential short-term sexual partners? We constructed written descriptions of 50 hypothetical short-term sexual partners, each of which contained information about the six variables (cues) listed earlier. Each of these variables, or cues, had five levels, with a corresponding numeric value (1–5) associated with each level (see Table 10.1). Note that the numbers 1 to 5 were used to correspond with the ordinal nature of the five levels of each cue. Alternatively, we could have asked a group of the respondents' peers to rate the degree to which each level of the cue represented the construct, and then used these ratings as the values corresponding to each level of each cue.

TABLE 10.1
Levels for Each of the Six Cues Used by Wiederman and Dubois (1998)

Cue	Levels
Physical attractiveness ("When it comes to physical attractiveness, this woman is . . .")	1. very unattractive; some people might consider her ugly.
	2. below average, but not terrible looking.
	3. average looking; not really attractive or unattractive.
	4. above average; appealing to look at.
	5. extremely attractive; some people might think she is a model.
Financial resources ("Financially speaking, she . . .")	1. is rather poor and does not have money for things beyond the bare necessities.
	2. earns enough money to get by, but sometimes has difficulty making ends meet.
	3. earns an average amount of money compared to other women.
	4. earns a healthy salary and can afford some of the extras in life.
	5. earns a lot of money, and in most cases she can afford the best.
Generosity ("Regardless of her financial situation, this woman . . .")	1. is very stingy and refuses to spend her money on a dating partner.
	2. is reluctant to share and does not frequently spend her money on a dating partner.
	3. does not mind spending her money on a dating partner.
	4. is rather free with money she spends on a dating partner and frequently gives gifts.
	5. is very generous with her money and often splurges on nice gifts for her dating partner.
Sexual experience/interest ("With regard to sexual experience, this woman has had sex . . .")	1. only a few times with one partner and does not really care that much for sex.
	2. with two different partners and thinks that, although sex is "O.K.," it is not that important.
	3. with five different partners and finds sex moderately enjoyable.
	4. with ten different partners and is excited about sex with a new partner.
	5. with more than twenty partners, is very comfortable being sexual, and believes that when it comes to sex, "more is better."
Current relationship status ("Right now she is . . .")	1. not dating anyone.
	2. dating a few men on a casual basis.
	3. dating one man for whom she cares, but is also dating other men.
	4. dating only one man for whom she cares, but would be open to dating other men.
	5. "going steady" with just one man.
Desired level of commitment ("Regardless of her current relationship status, this woman . . .")	1. is not really interested in an ongoing relationship with just one partner.
	2. would not refuse an ongoing relationship with the right man, she is just not actively looking for such a relationship.
	3. is interested in the possibility of forming a serious relationship with the right man.
	4. would very much like to find a serious relationship that she could be sure would last.
	5. is looking for a potential spouse and hopes to get married before long.

To begin, we (Wiederman & Dubois, 1998) constructed a shell for the scenarios, into which the corresponding level of the cue could be interjected. Following is the shell we used for male respondents (an analogous version was used for female respondents).

> When it comes to physical attractiveness, this woman is _____. Financially speaking, she _____. Regardless of her financial situation, this woman _____. With regard to sexual experience, this woman has had sex _____. Right now she is _____. Regardless of her current relationship status, this woman _____.

After constructing five verbal descriptions for each cue (see Table 10.1), each corresponding to increasing levels or degrees of the characteristic, we randomly generated a value (1–5) for each cue for each description (scenario). In other words, Scenario 37 might consist of a hypothetical short-term sexual partner who is described as having Level 3 physical attractiveness, Level 5 financial resources, Level 1 generosity, and so forth. By randomly generating the level of each cue for each scenario, the cues were not significantly correlated, thus eliminating the potential problem of multicolinearity among the predictor variables (cues) in the regression analyses (Brehmer & Brehmer, 1988). Of course, sometimes a researcher might want the cues to be correlated to mirror real-world conditions (Brehmer & Brehmer, 1988; Stewart, 1988). Note that mathematically there were 15,625 possible scenarios ($5 \times 5 \times 5 \times 5 \times 5 \times 5$). Thus, the 50 used in the study represented a random sample of that larger population of scenarios. The following is a single example of the 50 scenarios presented to respondents, in this case, describing a potential female partner:

> When it comes to physical attractiveness, this woman is above average; appealing to look at. Financially speaking, she is rather poor and does not have money for things beyond the bare necessities. Regardless of her financial situation, this woman is reluctant to share and does not frequently spend money on a dating partner. With regard to sexual experience, this woman has had sex with a total of 5 different partners and finds sex moderately enjoyable. Right now she is "going steady" with one man for whom she cares. Regardless of her current relationship status, this woman is looking for a potential spouse and hopes to get married before long.

College student respondents rated the desirability of each depicted short-term sexual partner using a 7-point scale. These ratings were then regressed onto the values for the 50 sets of six cues to derive a cognitive policy for each respondent. When the subsequent policies were aggregated across individuals, analyses of variance (ANOVAs) were performed on the standardized beta weights. Interestingly, only two of the six hypothesized gender differences emerged with regard to policy capturing preferences for short-term sexual partners. That is, men and women differed in the relative value placed on only two of the six cues when making judgments about the desirability of short-term sexual partners. However, when asked at the end of the task to rate how important the respondent believed each of the six characteristics were in determining his or her judgments, there were gender differences with regard to five out of the six.

Having data on the policy-capturing value placed on each of the cues, as well as the self-reported value placed on each of the cues, allowed us (Wiederman & Dubois, 1998) to assess the degree of insight respondents had into their own cognitive policies. Interestingly, only with regard to physical attractiveness was there a statistically significant relationship between the policy-capturing and self-reported importance placed on the characteristic (cue). In other words, respondents who placed the most importance on the physical attractiveness of potential short-term sexual partners did report placing the greatest value on physical attractiveness. Otherwise respondents displayed a complete lack of insight overall into the partner characteristics that influenced their judged desirability.

We (Wiederman & Dubois, 1998) concluded that, had we only used the typical self-report methodology, the evolutionary hypotheses would have been supported, as had been the case in previous studies using such methodology. However, our findings from the policy-capturing methodology resulted in different conclusions. It may be that direct questioning regarding the characteristics most valued in short-term mates results in responses based on gender stereotypes.

Strengths and Weaknesses

As previously mentioned, the primary strength of policy-capturing methodology is the ability for the researcher to directly assess the relative effects of various stimuli (cues) on an individual's judgments. Accordingly, the researcher is not relying on respondent insight regarding which stimuli had the greatest impact, but rather is measuring the impact each stimulus had on the respondent's judgments. Respondents can still be asked for such introspection, which would then allow the researcher to compare the individual's policy-capturing, cognitive policy with that reported by the individual respondent (i.e., one can assess how much insight the individual has into his or her own policy).

That the methodology allows for ideographic analysis is another strength. Rather than simply assessing general differences between groups, one can examine each research participant's cognitive policy. Thus, true investigation of individual differences and possible correlates of those individual differences is possible (see Wiederman & Dubois, 1998). Rather than simply concluding that one group differs from another, variables that may determine who among the two groups is responsible for the apparent group difference can be examined.

Relying on introspection regarding motives for past behavior limits one's effective sample to those individuals who have engaged in the behavior. However, it may be of theoretical interest to compare the cognitive policies of experienced individuals with those who have not engaged in the behavior. An advantage of policy capturing is that one need not have experienced the depicted situation to be able to make a decision or judgment. For example, if one were studying potential influences in people's decisions to use a condom during vaginal intercourse, traditional methodology might result in asking respondents who have had coitus to recall the most recent experience and to report why a condom was used or not. Policy capturing allows the researcher to compare virgins and nonvirgins with regard to the impact of the variables contained in the scenarios, and any differences to emerge may have important implications for promoting condom use during first coitus.

An additional advantage of the policy-capturing methodology is that it allows the researcher a relatively high degree of control over the stimuli presented to respondents (especially when written scenarios are used). This strength is also one of the primary weaknesses of the methodology. It is possible that the stimuli presented to respondents are not representative of real-world stimuli encountered in the described situation, or that the researcher has failed to present the most relevant stimuli (Brehmer & Brehmer, 1988). If an important cue is not included in the study, its value in making judgments may go undiscovered.

To avoid such a possibility, researchers using a policy-capturing methodology frequently survey or interview the group from whom respondents will be sampled first to inquire about the most salient cues in the judgment task (Stewart, 1988). The researcher could also observe people actually engaged in making the judgments in their real lives in an attempt to determine the most important stimuli. Classic works of fiction, mass media depictions, and clinical experience all provide possible sources of information for generating ideas about the most relevant factors involved in the particular judgment or decision-making task. Hence, a researcher interested in using policy capturing to assess the decision to end a marriage might first survey therapists who work with distressed couples, interview recently divorced individuals, and study accounts of divorce in magazines, television, and novels to determine the factors that appear to be most important in the decision to divorce. The resulting stimuli could then be included in scenarios presented to respondents.

A related weakness of the policy-capturing methodology involves the potential artificial nature of the stimuli presented to research participants. The stimuli may be representative of those encountered in the real world, but the mode of presentation may deviate significantly from that encountered in naturalistic settings (Brehmer & Brehmer, 1988). In this case, the judgment task is artificial and may result in judgments potentially not representative of those made in actual situations. How well do the stimuli presented to respondents, which typically involve a written description, photograph, or both, compare to the actual sensory stimuli encountered in the real-life analogue? How well do *paper people* compare with real people as stimuli on which to base a judgment? These are important questions and concerns to consider when conducting policy-capturing research (Brehmer & Brehmer, 1988).

All of this is not to say, however, that policy-capturing studies must involve written scenarios. For example, college students have reported in focus groups that extraneous stimuli such as the age, physical attractiveness, and dress of potential sex partners influenced whether the respondent judged that person a risk for HIV infection (Williams et al., 1992). One could test this possibility by having college students rate the physical attractiveness, perceived age, degree of provocative dress, and so forth of a series of photographed individuals. A subsequent sample of college students then could rate each photographed individual with regard to perceived risk for HIV infection. Substantial correlations between the two ratings would support the idea that college students rely on particular extraneous cues for safety from HIV.

Another weakness of the methodology involves the very nature of the research task. Respondents are typically presented with 50, and sometimes upward of 100, scenarios, photos, or other depicted cases and asked to make a decision or judgment about each. The task can become tedious or boring, and maintaining respondent interest may be a concern. One possible solution is to break the task into more than one session (Stewart, 1988). I have had students express concern that using a policy-capturing methodology might result in respondents eventually skimming cases looking for the information that is most relevant to them rather than carefully reading each scenario or examining each photo. One can hope that research participants would be invested in the study and read every word or notice every detail. However, such is not always the case. When presented with standard questions regarding personal attitudes and behavior, hurried responding is liable to result in unreliable and potentially inaccurate responses. However, in responding to scenarios in a policy-capturing study, if the respondent has identified the one or two cues that are salient for determining his or her judgments, then focusing only on that information is not as problematic and is liable to result in reliable judgments across scenarios.

As with any form of research requiring self-report, there is also the possibility of hypothesis guessing on the part of the respondent in policy-capturing studies. After reading several of the scenarios, the respondent is liable to notice the variables that are being manipulated (and it is likely that the respondent was told in the instructions which characteristics would vary). The extent to which such knowledge affects the respondent's tendencies to affirm or disconfirm the expectations he or she believes the researcher holds remains an unknown but possible problem.

CONCLUSION

Policy-capturing methodology is far from perfect, and there are several inherent weaknesses. Of course, it is applicable only when the focus of study is the *why* underlying judgment and decision making (or, more appropriately, the stimuli influencing judgments or decisions). When this is the case, it allows a direct assessment of the external factors that influence individuals' judgments—a quality that is particularly attractive given that humans apparently have little insight into their own mental processes (Gibbons, 1983). Also, based on research involving non-sexual judgments, it appears that there is much individual variation in what cues people use, how much insight each respondent has into his or her cognitive policy, and so forth. Policy-capturing methodology allows for examination of these and other individual differences. Whether, and in what ways, it can be adapted to the myriad questions posed by sexuality researchers awaits further consideration.

SUGGESTED READINGS

Previously published guides to policy-capturing methodology are scarce, as are applications to sexuality-related topics. Policy capturing is certainly an under-utilized method in sexuality research. For those contemplating such a study, Brehmer and Brehmer (1988) and Stewart (1988) provided readable orientations to the methodolgy involved in policy capturing. Hammond et al. (1980) provided an earlier account of some of the methodological issues, particularly within the context of other approaches to measuring judgments and the decision-making process.

ACKNOWLEDGMENT

An earlier version of this chapter was published as: Wiederman, M. W. (1999). Policy capturing methodology in sexuality research. *The Journal of Sex Research, 36*, 91–95.

REFERENCES

Baldwin, M. W. (1992). Relational schemas and the processing of social information. *Psychological Bulletin, 112*, 461–484.

Boon, S. D., & Sulsky, L. M. (1997). Attributions of blame and forgiveness in romantic relationships: A policy-capturing study. *Journal of Social Behavior and Personality, 12*, 19–44.

Brehmer, A., & Brehmer, B. (1988). What have we learned about human judgment from thirty years of policy capturing? In B. Brehmer & C. R. B. Joyce (Eds.), *Human judgment: The SJT view* (pp. 75–114). New York: Elsevier.

Finkelstein, M. A., & Brannick, M. T. (1997). Making decisions about sexual intercourse: Capturing college students' policies. *Basic and Applied Social Psychology, 19*, 101–120.

Fletcher, G. J. O., & Kininmonth, L. A. (1992). Measuring relationship beliefs: An individual differ-ences scale. *Journal of Research in Personality, 26*, 371–397.

Gibbons, F. X. (1983). Self-attention and self-report: The "veridicality" hypothesis. *Journal of Per-sonality, 51*, 517–542.

Hammond, K. R., McClelland, G. H., & Mumpower, J. (1980). *Human judgment and decision mak-ing: Theories, methods, and procedures*. New York: Praeger.

Nisbett, R. E., & Ross, L. (1980). *Human inference: Strategies and shortcomings of social judgment.* Englewood Cliffs, NJ: Prentice-Hall.

Nisbett, R. E., & Wilson, T. D. (1977). Telling more than we can know: Verbal reports on mental processes. *Psychological Review, 84,* 231–259.

Stewart, T. R. (1988). Judgment analysis: Procedures. In B. Brehmer & C. R. B. Joyce (Eds.), *Human judgment: The SJT view* (pp. 41–74). New York: Elsevier.

Ullman, D. G., & Doherty, M. E. (1984). Two determinants of the diagnosis of hyperactivity: The child and clinician. In M. Wolraich & D. K. Routh (Eds.), *Advances in behavioral pediatrics* (Vol. 5, pp. 167–219). Greenwich, CT: JAI Press.

Wiederman, M. W., & Dubois, S. L. (1998). Evolution and sex differences in preferences for short-term mates: Results from a policy capturing study. *Evolution and Human Behavior, 19,* 153–170.

Williams, S. S., Kimble, D. L., Covell, N. H., Weiss, L. H., Newton, K. J., Fisher, J. D., & Fisher, W. A. (1992). College students use implicit personality theory instead of safer sex. *Journal of Applied Social Psychology, 22,* 921–933.

DATA ANALYSIS

11
▼▼▼▼▼▼▼

Group Comparison Research[1]

Bernard E. Whitley, Jr.
Ball State University

Group comparison research involves comparing the mean scores of two or more groups of research participants on one or more dependent variables. The groups could be formed in any of three ways: The researcher could randomly assign research participants to groups, such as the experimental and control groups in a true experiment; the researcher could assess scores of members of preexisting groups, such as students in two classrooms who received different sex education interventions; or the researcher could group participants on the basis of some personal characteristic, such as gender, sexual orientation, or personality. As shown in Table 11.1, the manner in which participants are formed into groups is one of three characteristics—manipulation of the independent variable, assignment of participants to groups, and control over extraneous situational variables—that define the three types of group comparison research: true experiments, quasi-experiments, and nonexperimental studies. This chapter begins with a brief review of some relevant statistical concepts and then discusses issues related to each of these types of research and variations on the basic designs in terms of the number of conditions of the independent variable and the number of independent variables used in the research.

A NOTE ON STATISTICS

Statistics and research design are closely related: Proper research design allows researchers to collect valid data and statistics help researchers interpret those data.

[1]Adapted from *Principles of Research in Behavioral Science* by Bernard E. Whitley, Jr., Mayfield Publishing Company, 1996. Adapted with permission by Mayfield Publishing Company.

TABLE 11.1
Characteristics of True Experiments, Quasi-Experiments,
and Nonexperimental Studies

Research Design	Characteristics	Strength of Causal Inferences
True experiment	Manipulated independent variable	High
	Participants are randomly assigned to conditions of the independent variable	
	Other potential influences on the dependent variable are tightly controlled	
Quasi-experiment	Manipulated independent variable	Moderate
	Participants are members of preexisting groups but not randomly assigned to groups	
	Groups are randomly assigned to conditions of the independent variable	
	Variable control over other potential influences on the dependent variable	
Nonexperimental study	Measured independent variable; therefore participants cannot be randomly assigned to conditions of the independent variable	None
	Variable control over other potential influences on the dependent variable	

Many of the statistical tests most commonly used in group comparison research, such as the t test and analysis of variance (ANOVA), are parametric statistics. Parametric statistics operate by dividing (or partitioning) the variance in the dependent variable scores into two pieces: variance caused by the independent variable and variance caused by everything else in the research situation.

Consider, for example, research on the effect of watching a violent sexually explicit film on men's aggression toward women. In a typical experiment, a female confederate angers a male participant before he watches a sexually explicit film that contains violence (experimental condition) or a film that is sexually explicit but nonviolent (control condition). Afterward, the participant is instructed to administer electrical shocks to the confederate when she makes mistakes on a task. Considering all of the participants in the research, both those in the experimental group and those in the control group, there will be variance in the number of shocks they administer: Some men will administer many shocks, some will administer a few, and some will administer a moderate number. If watching violent sexually explicit material does affect aggression, some of the variance in shocks will be due to the independent variable. On the average, people in the violent condition will administer more shocks than people in the nonviolent condition. This variance in the dependent variable that results from the independent variable is called *treatment variance*.

Not all of the variance in the number of shocks will be due to the independent variable. Some will be due to differences among participants. For example, some men will be more inherently aggressive and so administer more shocks than do low aggressive men regardless of whether they view a violent or nonviolent film; some men will be more vulnerable to the effects of viewing violence of any sort and so administer more shocks in the violent film condition than their counterparts in the nonviolent film condition. Variance in the dependent variable can also result from random measurement error and slight unintentional variations in how the experimenter treats each participant. For example, an experimenter who is having a bad day might be less patient with that day's research participants, perhaps speaking abruptly and appearing to be irritated, thereby annoying those participants more than the participants with whom the experimenter interacts on good days. This increased annoyance could cause participants to administer more shocks.

From a statistical point of view, all variance in the dependent variable not caused by the independent variable is error variance. The magnitude of a parametric statistical test, such as the F value in ANOVA, represents the ratio of treatment variance to error variance. Consequently, the magnitude of a test statistic increases as the treatment variance increases and the error variance decreases. The larger the magnitude of the test statistic, the less likely it is that the results of the experiment were due to chance factors (the errors represented by the error variance) and the more likely it is that they were due to the effect of the independent variable; in other words, the results are more likely to be statistically significant. Therefore, two goals of research design are to increase the impact of the independent variable (and so increase the treatment variance) and reduce the error variance (and so increase the ratio of treatment variance to error variance). The rest of this chapter discusses ways of achieving these goals in group comparison designs.

TRUE EXPERIMENTS

The true experiment is the gold standard of research design. In a true experiment, researchers take complete control of the research situation: They manipulate the independent variable to establish conditions that will test the research hypothesis, randomly assign participants to conditions of the independent variable, and control other aspects of the the research situation to ensure that only the independent variable influences scores on the dependent variable. In its simplest form, the experiment has two conditions of the independent variable—an experimental condition and a control or comparison condition. If there are differences in the mean scores of participants in the experimental and control conditions, the high degree of control exerted by experimenters allows them to conclude that the independent variables caused the difference in mean scores because that control has ensured that only the independent variable had an opportunity to affect scores on the dependent variable. Because this degree of control exists in true experiments, only true experiments allow the researcher to conclude with a high degree of confidence that the independent variable caused any observed changes in the dependent variable. This section discusses two aspects of true experiments: characteristics of a good manipulation and ways of controlling extraneous (error) variance in the research situation.

Characteristics of a Good Manipulation

Three characteristics of a good measure are construct validity, reliability, and sensitivity (see chap. 3, this volume). Similarly, the procedures used to manipulate an independent variable should be characterized by construct validity, reliability, and strength. In addition, a manipulation must be salient to participants.

Construct Validity. Whenever a manipulation is intended to operationally define a hypothetical construct, researchers must be sure that the manipulation accurately represents the construct. For example, if research participants write essays to manipulate their moods, how do the researchers know that participants' moods actually changed in the ways that the researchers intended them to change? Just as it is necessary to ensure the construct validity of measures, it is necessary to ensure the construct validity of manipulations. The construct validity of a manipulation is tested by means of a manipulation check. The manipulation check tests the convergent validity of the manipulation by checking it against measures of the construct, thus ensuring that participants in different conditions of the experiment experience different levels or conditions of the independent variable. For example, participants who view a sexually aggressive film should perceive it as containing more aggression than participants who view a control film that is low in aggressive content. A manipulation check should also test the discriminant validity of the manipulation by ensuring that it manipulates only the construct that it is supposed to manipulate. For example, both film scripts should be equally sexually arousing, otherwise degree of aggression is confounded with degree of sexual arousal (see chap. 4, this volume).

Manipulation checks can take two forms, which can be used either separately or together. One way to conduct a manipulation check is by interviewing research participants after data have been collected, asking them questions that determine whether the manipulation had the intended effect. For example, if researchers were trying to manipulate the degree to which participants perceived a confederate as physically attractive, the researchers could ask participants about their perceptions of the confederate as part of a postexperimental interview. If the manipulation was successful, participants should describe the confederate in ways that are consistent with the condition of the independent variable they were in. The other way to conduct a manipulation check is to include as part of the research dependent variables that assess the construct being manipulated. This kind of manipulation check can be made at either or both of two points in the research project. The first point is during pilot testing, when the bugs are being worked out of the research procedures. For example, Bauserman (1998) sought to examine the attitudinal effects of egalitarian, sexist, and aggressive sexual materials, and conducted a pilot study to ensure that the materials he selected were perceived accordingly.

Manipulation checks can also be made during data collection to ensure that all participants experience the independent variable as intended. For example, Fisher and Grenier (1994) sought to assess men's attitudes toward women as a function of exposure to three types of sexually explicit videos: nonaggressive, aggressive with a positive outcome (the woman in the appears to enjoy the aggressive active), and aggressive with a negative outcome (the woman responds with pain and distress). In addition to the attitudinal dependent variables, the researchers included measures of participants' perceptions of the degree to which the women enjoyed the activity portrayed in the video they saw and of how violent the video was. Statistical analysis of participants' responses showed that men in the negative outcome condition perceived the female character's enjoyment to be less than did participants in the positive outcome and nonaggressive conditions, indicating that the manipulation worked as intended. The effectiveness of the violence manipulation was also supported. However, if manipulation checks are only conducted concurrently with data collection, it is too late to fix manipulation problems unless one is willing to cease data collection and restart the research project.

Researchers sometimes omit manipulation checks because previous researchers have used a manipulation successfully. However, it is always wise to include a manipulation check because the validity of manipulations, like that of measures, can vary across participant samples.

Reliability. Reliability of manipulation means consistency of manipulation: Every time a manipulation is applied, it is applied in the same way. If a manipulation is applied reliably, every participant in a given condition of the experiment experiences it in essentially the same way. High reliability can be attained by preparing detailed scripts for experimenters to follow and rehearsing experimenters and others involved in the manipulation, such as confederates portraying research participants, until they can conduct every condition of the experiment correctly and consistently. Low reliability entails low validity; no matter how valid a manipulation is in principle, if it is not applied reliably, it is useless.

Strength. A strong manipulation is one in which the conditions of the independent variable are sufficiently different from one another to affect behavior differentially. Consider a hypothetical experiment in which the researcher is interested in the effects of the number of therapy sessions in a sexual dysfunction treatment program. The researcher hypothesizes that more sessions result in more improvement than fewer sessions. The researcher tests the hypothesis by having half of the participants in the experiment receive 10 therapy sessions and the others 12 sessions. It would not be surprising to find no difference in performance between the groups because the difference in the number of sessions is not large enough to have an effect on sexual functioning.

Strong manipulations are achieved by using extreme levels of the independent variable. The sexual dysfunction treatment study, for example, might use 4 versus 12 sessions to have more impact on behavior and so increase the amount of treatment variance in the dependent variable. Although it is desirable to have a strong manipulation, there are two factors to consider in choosing the strength of a manipulation. One consideration is realism: An extreme manipulation might be unrealistic. For example, it would be unrealistic to use 1 versus 100 therapy sessions as the conditions in the treatment outcome experiment: People almost never recive so few or so many treatment sessions. A lack of realism has two disadvantages. First, participants might not take the research seriously and so provide data of unknown validity. Second, even if there were no internal validity problems, it is unlikely that the results would generalize to any real-life situations. The second consideration is ethical: An extreme manipulation might cause undue harm to research participants. For example, there are ethical limits to the amount of stress to which a researcher can subject participants.

There is an exception to the general rule that stronger manipulations are better for obtaining differences between conditions on the dependent variable. Sometimes the relationship between the independent and dependent variables is curvilinear. Under such conditions, the largest differences in behavior will show up not when the two extreme conditions are compared, but when the extremes are compared to a moderate level of the independent variable.

Salience. For a manipulation to affect research participants, they must notice it in the context of everything else that is happening in the experiment. A salient manipulation stands out from the background, and it is sometimes necessary to put a great deal of effort into establishing the salience of a manipulation. For example, Landy and Aronson (1968) conducted a study to determine whether people react more strongly to evaluations of them made by another person if they think that person is especially discerning, that is, especially skilled in deducing the personality characteristics of other people. The researchers manipulated how discerning the other person appeared to be by having him or her perform a task in the presence of the participant that was designed to show either the presence (experimental condition) or absence (control condition) of discernment. But how could the researchers be sure that the participants noticed how discerning the other person was? They "told the subject that 'degree of discernment' was an aspect of the confederate's behavior that was of particular interest to them; asked the subject to rate the confederate's discernment; [and] informed the subject exactly how the confederate's behavior might reflect either high or low discernment . . ." (Aronson, Ellsworth, Carlsmith, & Gonzales, 1990, pp. 223–224). Not all manipulations require this degree of emphasis, but experimenters do need to ensure that the participants in their research notice the manipulation.

Controlling Extraneous Variance

The experiment is characterized not only by manipulation of the independent variable, but also by procedures used to control factors that cause extraneous variance in the dependent variable. Some of this variance is due to random factors, such as slight variations in the way that the experimenter treats research participants. Other variance is due to factors that are systematically related to the dependent variable, but are not of interest to the researcher. Such factors are often referred to as *extraneous variables*. For example, there are gender differences on many variables that sexuality researchers study (e.g., Basow, 1992), but these differences are not of interest to all researchers. Unless extraneous variables are treated as independent variables in the research, their effects form part of the error variance in the statistical analysis of the data (see the section on factorial designs later in this chapter). Experimenters must therefore take steps to control extraneous variance.

Holding Extraneous Variables Constant

Extraneous variables that are part of the research situation, such as the characteristics of the room in which the research takes place, are fairly easy to control: The experimenter holds these variables constant across conditions of the independent variable. Because these factors do not vary as part of the experiment, they cannot cause systematic variance in the dependent variable. However, individual differences in participants' responses to these controlled variables do form part of the error variance in the experiment.

Extraneous variables that are characteristics of the research participants, such as personality and background, are more difficult to control. Differences among people, unlike differences among rooms, cannot always be eliminated by the actions of the experimenter. Nevertheless, it is sometimes possible to hold participant variables constant. For example, if a researcher uses only men or only women as participants in an experiment, sex of participant can have no systematic effect on the dependent variable. However, this strategy can limit the generalizability of the results of the research if participants with only one aspect of the extraneous variable—for example, only men—are used in all research on a topic. As I discuss later, researchers can avoid this problem by treating participant characteristics as independent variables when analyzing data.

Experimenters most commonly control the effects of variance in research participants' personal characteristics by the ways in which they assign participants to conditions of the independent variable. In between-subjects designs (also called independent groups designs), a participant takes part in either the experimental or control condition, but not both. The researcher distributes the effects of extraneous participant variables evenly across the experimental and control groups by either randomly assigning participants to conditions or matching the participants in each condition on key extraneous variables. In within-subjects designs (also called repeated measures designs), each participant takes part in both the experimental and control conditions so that the effects of participant variables are perfectly balanced across conditions.

Between-Subjects Designs

Because between-subjects designs have different people in the experimental and control groups, a major consideration in using them is ensuring that participants in the two groups are equivalent in their personal characteristics. Two strategies can be used to attain equivalence: simple random assignment of participants to conditions and matched random assignment.

Simple Random Assignment. The strategy used most often to assign participants to groups is simple random assignment. When a participant arrives to take part in the experiment, the experimenter uses a random procedure, such as a table of random numbers or flipping a coin, to determine whether the participant will be in the experimental or control condition. For example, an even number or heads could mean the control condition, and an odd number or tails means the experimental condition. When one uses random assignment, one assumes that, because group assignments are random, members of the two groups will, on the average, have the same personal characteristics. For example, if some participants are unusually skilled at the research task and others unusually unskilled, then randomly assigning people to groups should put about half of the skilled and half of the unskilled people in each group. Consequently, the effects of their skill should cancel out when the groups' mean scores on the task are compared.

Similarly, random assignment results in preexperimental equivalence of scores in all conditions of the independent variable. For example, if participants are randomly assigned to groups, the mean sexual attitude score would be essentially the same for each group. Hence, when random assignment is used, pretesting on the dependent variable is not usually necessary, and the threats to internal validity entailed by pretesting (see chap. 4, this volume) can be avoided.

Random assignment of participants to conditions does not guarantee that the members of the experimental and control groups will be equivalent. Although equivalence or near equivalence is the most common outcome of randomization (e.g., Strube, 1991), there is a real, albeit small, possibility of the groups' being substantially different. For example, if a participant pool consisted of 10 men and 10 women who were randomly assigned to experimental and control groups, there is about a 1 in 2,400 chance of getting a group with 8 or more women in it. These odds are probably good enough for most research, but researchers could exercise more control over the characteristics of the members of the experimental and control group by matching the members of the groups on important personal characteristics.

Matched Random Assignment. With matched random assignment of participants to conditions, the researcher attempts to ensure that the members of the experimental and control groups are equivalent on one or more characteristics. The researcher does this by measuring the characteristic and balancing group membership accordingly. To continue with the example of participant gender, the researcher could guarantee that the groups were equivalent in gender composition by randomly assigning half the women to the experimental group and half to the control group and doing the same for the men. Each group would then be composed of five women and five men.

Matching on physical characteristics of participants, such as gender, is fairly easy; for other characteristics, such as personality, it is more difficult. For these kinds of characteristics, researchers must first pretest all potential participants to determine their scores on the variable. One must then rank order the people by their scores and then divide them into pairs from the top down. The first member of each pair is randomly assigned to either the experimental or control group; the other member of the pair is assigned to the other group. A major drawback of matched random assignment for psychological characteristics is the time and other resources necessary for pretesting. Matched random assignment is therefore normally used only when the control variable is known to have a strong effect on, or relationship to, the dependent variable and the researcher wants more control over it than is afforded by simple random assignment.

Within-Subjects Designs

In within-subjects (or repeated measures) designs, each research participant experiences both the experimental and control conditions of the independent variable. These designs have both advantages and limitations.

Advantages Relative to Between-Subjects Designs. Because participants in within-subjects designs take part in both the experimental and control conditions, these designs result in perfect equivalence of participants in both conditions. Because the same people are in each condition, the personal characteristics of the participants match perfectly. This perfect matching results in one of the primary advantages that within-subjects designs have over between-subjects designs: reduced error variance. This reduction in error variance means that within-subjects experiments are more likely than equivalent between-subjects experiments to produce statistically significant results. This advantage is stronger to the extent that participant characteristics affect scores on the dependent variable. A second advantage of within-subjects designs is that, because the same people participate in both the experimental and control conditions, a two-condition within-subjects design requires only half the participants required by the equivalent between-subjects design. This advantage can be especially useful when people are selected for participation in research on the basis of a rarely occurring characteristic.

The Problem of Order Effects. Despite these advantages, researchers use within-subjects designs much less frequently than between-subjects designs. This less frequent use results from a set of disadvantages inherent in within-subjects designs that are referred to collectively as *order effects*. An order effect occurs when participants' scores on the dependent variable are affected by the order in which they experience the conditions of the independent variable. For example, participants might do better in whichever condition they experience second, regardless of whether it is the experimental or control condition. There are four general categories of order effects: practice effects, fatigue effects, carry-over effects, and sensitization effects (Greenwald, 1976).

Practice effects are differences on the dependent variable that result from repeatedly performing the experimental task. For example, when people are faced with an unfamiliar task, they often do poorly the first time they try it, but improve with practice. The more often the experiment requires them to engage in a task, the better participants' performance becomes. Another kind of practice effect relates to the independent variable. Assume that a researcher is conducting a study on the effects of exposure to sexually explicit materials on sexual arousal. Over time, participants might habituate to, or become used to, the stimuli, so that it has less effect on their arousal. In contrast, fatigue effects result when participants become tired or bored from repeatedly performing the same task. In contrast to practice effects, fatigue effects lead to decrements in performance. For example, in the study of sexually explicit materials and arousal, participants might become bored with repeated exposure to the stimuli and become less aroused over time.

Carry-over effects occur when the effect of one condition of the experiment carries over to and affects participants' performance in another condition. Consider a hypothetical experiment on the effects of caffeine or some other stimulant on sexual response. In the experimental condition, the researchers give participants a standardized dose of caffeine, and in the control condition, the researchers administer an inert substance. If participants take part in the caffeine condition first, the effects of the drug might still be present in their bodies when they take part in the control condition. The effects of the caffeine can then carry over and affect response in the control condition. Yet the researchers would not want to give all participants the inert substance first because practice effects would be confounded with the effects of the caffeine in the experimental condition.

Sensitization effects occur when experiencing one condition of an experiment affects participants' performance in the other condition. For example, Wiederman and Allgeier (1993) studied college students' emotional responses to hypothetical situations in which they suspected that a dating partner was involved with another person. Participants read two scenarios: "One of the scenarios made reference to suspected sexual infidelity by the dating partner without loss of partner time, commitment, or emotional intimacy (hereafter referred to as the sex scenario). The other scenario described suspected loss of partner time, attention and love without loss of sexual exclusivity (hereafter referred to as the love scenario)" (p.

126). Wiederman and Allgeier found that participants who responded to the sex scenario before the love scenario rated the love scenario as less upsetting than did participants who responded to the love scenario first.

Sensitization can also induce demand characteristics when exposure to more than one condition of the independent variable allows research participants to form hypotheses about the purpose of the research or calls forth a social desirability response bias (see chap. 3, this volume). Consider a hypothetical experiment on the effects of physical attractiveness on how desirable a person is perceived to be as a dating partner. In one condition, the researchers show participants a picture of a physically attractive person and, in the other condition, a picture of a less attractive person. They ask participants to rate the person in the picture on the degree to which they would like to go on a date with the person. Participants will probably respond naturally to the first picture, giving their true estimate of likability, but when they see the second picture, problems could arise: Because it is socially undesirable to evaluate people solely on the basis of appearance, participants might deliberately manipulate their responses, giving the same rating to the person in the second picture that they gave to the person in the first picture even if their true responses are different.

Controlling Order Effects. In some cases, the researcher can design a within-subjects experiment in ways that control order effects. Practice effects can be controlled by counterbalancing the order in which participants experience the experimental and control conditions: Half the participants undergo the experimental condition first and the other half undergo the control condition first. This procedure is designed to spread practice effects evenly across the conditions so that they cancel out when the conditions are compared. Counterbalancing is easy to carry out when an experiment has only two conditions (Conditions A and B). There are only two orders in which participants can experience the conditions: A before B and B before A. However, experiments frequently have three or more conditions. Under these circumstances, counterbalancing becomes much more difficult because all possible orderings of conditions must be used: Each condition must appear in each position in the ordering sequence an equal number of times to balance the order in which participants experience the conditions, and each condition must follow every other condition an equal number of times to balance the sequencing of conditions. The number of orders increases dramatically with the number of conditions: A three-condition experiment requires that participants be divided into six groups to completely counterbalance the order of conditions, four conditions would require 24 groups, and five conditions 120 groups.

Because the number of condition orders required by complete counterbalancing can quickly become enormous as the number of conditions increases, partial counterbalancing is frequently used for studies involving more than three conditions. One way to partially counterbalance is to randomly assign a different order of conditions to each participant. A more systematic technique is to use a Latin square design. In this design, the number of orders is equal to the number of conditions, with each condition appearing in each place in the order. The basic Latin square design therefore balances the order of conditions but not their sequencing. For example, except when it comes first in a row, Condition B always follows Condition A and precedes Condition C. Sequencing can be partially controlled by using a balanced Latin square design in which each condition is preceded once by every other condition. Although the balanced Latin square design controls the sequencing of pairs of conditions, it does not control higher order sequences; for example, the sequence ABC precedes, but does not follow, Condition D. Many statistics textbooks provide details about conducting research using Latin square designs and analyzing the data they produce (e.g., Kirk, 1982).

Counterbalancing can also be used to distribute carry-over effects across conditions. However, it is better to insert a wash-out period between conditions. A wash-out period is a period of time over which the effects of a condition dissipate. For example, in the hypothetical study on caffeine and sexual response described earlier, the researchers could have participants undergo one condition one day and have them come back for the other condition the next day without consuming any caffeine in the meanwhile. This procedure allows the caffeine to "wash out" of the bodies of those participants who experienced the experimental condition first so that it does not affect their responses in the control condition. A wash-out period might last minutes, hours, or days depending on how long the effects of a condition can be expected to persist.

Sensitization effects are more difficult to control than are practice or carry-over effects. Although counterbalancing spreads these effects across conditions, it does not eliminate the effects of any demand characteristics produced. Therefore, it is best not to use a within-subjects design when sensitization effects are likely to produce demand characteristics, as in the physical attractiveness example given earlier.

The use of counterbalancing assumes that order effects are equal regardless of the sequence in which participants experience the conditions. For example, in a two-condition experiment, counterbalancing assumes that the order effect for participating in the experimental condition first is the same as the order effect for participating in the control condition first. A differential order effect occurs when participating in one condition first has a greater effect than participating in the other condition first. A differential order effect artificially increases the observed difference between the conditions, resulting in an overestimation of the effect of the independent variable. Differential order effects can be detected by using a factorial experimental design discussed further later.

QUASI-EXPERIMENTS

In a quasi-experiment, the researcher manipulates an independent variable in a field setting using preexisting groups of people as the experimental and control groups. The goal is to achieve greater naturalism than is possible in a laboratory experiment while maintaining a reasonable degree of control over the research situation. For example, Stevenson and Gajarsky (1990) studied the effect of taking a human sexuality course on attitudes toward homosexuality. They compared the attitude change (over the course of a semester) of the students in the sexuality course to the attitude change of students in a general psychology course who expressed an interest in taking the sexuality course. Individual participants in quasi-experiments cannot be randomly assigned to the experimental and control conditions, although the groups to which they belong often can be. The researcher is also not likely to have much control over extraneous variables in the natural setting used for the research. However, the researcher does manipulate the independent variable as in a true experiment. The most common design for quasi-experiments is the nonequivalent control group design (Cook & Campbell, 1979).

The Nonequivalent Control Group Design

In the nonequivalent control group design, the researcher studies two (or more) groups of people. The members of one group experience the treatment condition of the independent variable. The members of the other group, chosen to be as similar as possible to the experimental group, serve as the control group. This control group is considered to be nonequivalent to the experimental group because participants are not randomly assigned to conditions. Consequently, the confidence provided by random assignment that person-related extraneous variables are not confounded with conditions of the independent variable is absent.

The nonequivalent control group design is a useful tool in situations in which it is impractical to randomly assign research participants to conditions. However, use of the design poses two problems that limit the degree to which one can draw causal conclusions from the research: the possibility of preexisting differences between groups on the dependent variable and biased selection of people into the experimental and control groups.

The Problem of Preexisting Differences

Stevenson and Gajarsky (1990) included a pretest in their research designs to assess participants' attitudes toward homosexuality at the beginning of the semester. Researchers using nonequivalent control group designs should conduct such pretesting whenever possible to ensure that the experimental and control groups are similar on the dependent variable before the independent variable is introduced. Otherwise, preexisting differences between groups provide an alternative explanation for any effect of the independent variable. For example, consider the situation if Stevenson and Gajarsky (1990) had not included a pretest in their study and had found that, at the end of the study, the students in the human sexuality course had had more positive attitudes compared with the students in the other course. The difference might have been due to the effect of the course, but it also would have been found if the students in the human sexuality course had started out with more positive attitudes and the independent variable had no effect. Because Stevenson and Gajarsky conducted a pretest, they could determine whether the groups initially differed on the dependent variable.

When the experimental and control groups do not differ significantly on the pretest, researchers can proceed with the study and assess the effect of the independent variable with a posttest. The desired outcome is little change in the scores of the control group coupled with a statistically significant change in the scores of the experimental group. Of course, history, maturation, and other time-related effects frequently lead to some change in the control group's scores. The simplest nonequivalent control group design with a pretest is therefore a 2×2 factorial design with one between-subjects factor (the conditions of the independent variable) and one within-subjects factor (time). The desired outcome is an interaction between time of assessment and the independent variable, in which the groups are the same at the pretest but differ at the posttest (see the discussion of factorial designs later in this chapter).

If the experimental and control groups do differ on the pretest, the researchers have a problem: There is no way to directly determine the effect of the independent variable beyond any effects resulting from the preexisting difference between the groups. One approach to dealing with this problem is to use analysis of covariance (ANCOVA; e.g., Porter & Raudenbush, 1987); this is the approach Stevenson and Gajarsky (1990) took. ANCOVA provides a test of the effect of the independent variable adjusted for group differences in pretest scores. This adjustment is based on a regression analysis of the relation between the pretest and posttest scores. In essence, ANCOVA asks the question, "What would the posttest means look like if the experimental and control groups had not differed on the pretest?" Although ANCOVA can be a powerful statistical tool, it requires that the slopes of the relationship between pretest and posttest scores be equal in both groups, a requirement that must be tested before the analysis is conducted. In addition, ANCOVA does not always provide a precise answer to the research question being asked (see Porter & Raudenbush, 1987).

Why not simply match participants on pretest scores and only use the data for those in each group who have similar scores? Achieving equivalence by matching people in the experimental and control groups on their pretest scores is tempting, but it can result in invalid research results. Recall that the type of matching discussed previously was matched random assignment to groups: Members of matched pairs were randomly assigned to the experimental and control conditions. Random assignment of individual participants to conditions is not possible in a quasi-experiment.

As an example of the problem posed by trying to match participants when they cannot be randomly assigned to conditions, consider a hypothetical study similar to Stevenson and Gajarsky's (1990) research, in which the pretest shows that the average attitude scores of the students enrolled in the sexuality course were substantially more positive than those of the students enrolled in the general psychology course. The researchers therefore conduct the study using students from the two groups who have similar pretest scores; that is, they only analyze the posttest data from the general psychology students who had the most positive pretest scores and from the human sexuality students who had the most negative pretest scores. The problem is that, over time, extreme scores regress toward the group mean. Consequently, the scores of the human sexuality students chosen for the research would be more positive at the posttest because their pretest scores were extremely negative relative to their group's average score, and the scores of the general psychology students chosen for the research would be more negative at the posttest because their pretest scores were extremely negative relative to their group's average score. Therefore, it will appear that the intervention improved the attitudes of the human sexuality students and had a negative effect on the attitudes of the general psychology students. Trying to match members of nonequivalent groups that differ on the pretest will always lead to the possibility of a regression confound and so should not be done.

The Problem of Biased Selection

Participants in true experiments are randomly assigned to conditions of the independent variable to avoid any bias that would result from confounding personal characteristics of the participants with conditions of the independent variable. However, participants in nonequivalent control group designs are not randomly assigned to conditions. Therefore, it is possible that the personal characteristics of the members of the experimental group differ from those of the control group. For example, in Stevenson and Gajarsky's (1990) study, students chose which course they took.

The nature of research that uses the nonequivalent control group design makes it impossible to rule out differences in the characteristics of the experimental and control participants as an alternative explanation to the effect of the independent variable for differences between the conditions. Consequently, this design cannot determine causality with certainty. However, two steps can be taken to increase confidence that the independent variable was the cause of the difference. The first is replication: The more often an effect is replicated under different circumstances, the more likely it is that the independent variable was the causal agent. Second, it is sometimes possible to have multiple naturally occurring groups randomly assigned to experimental and control conditions. For example, in research on the effects of sexuality education, the schools in a school district might be randomly assigned as experimental and control sites for an educational intervention. Although students were probably not randomly assigned to schools, randomly assigning schools to conditions provides a limited degree of equivalence between the experimental and control groups. The data from such a study can then be analyzed using a nested analysis of variance design, which can separate the variance in the dependent variable due to the effect of the independent variable from that due to the effect of attending a particular school (Hopkins, 1982).

NONEXPERIMENTAL STUDIES

Sexuality researchers are frequently interested in variables that cannot be manipulated, such as gender, personality, and other characteristics of research participants. To investigate the relationships of these factors to other variables in group comparison designs, researchers use one of two strategies. The first strategy is to group participants on the basis of personal characteristics (such as gender or sexual orientation); the second strategy is to measure a continuous variable such as a personality trait and classify participants into high and low scorers on the basis of median splits of the variable or pretest cutoff scores. This section examines some issues related to these strategies.

When conducting or reading nonexperimental studies, it is essential to remember that, although group comparisons are being made, because the independent variable is measured or observed and not manipulated the research is correlational in nature. Consequently, it is never appropriate to draw causal conclusions from this kind of research. Although that warning may appear so basic as not to need stating, one nonetheless sees titles of research reports beginning with the phrase, "The Effect of Gender [or another measured variable] on," thereby implying a cause–effect relationship.

Grouping by Personal Characteristics

When research participants are classified on the basis of personal characteristics, an important consideration is the validity of the classification system. When the variable of interest is reasonably concrete, such as self-indicated gender, classification is not much of a problem. However, sometimes the variable is a hypothetical construct that can be operationally defined in many ways. For example, Sandfort (1997) noted that the term *homosexuality* has been operationally defined many ways, including "feelings of physical or emotional attraction, fantasies, actual behavior, and self-definition. . . . The various aspects do not necessarily overlap and may change during someone's personal development" (p. 262). Such diversity of operational definitions clearly contributes to inconsistencies among the results of studies. Therefore, researchers should be scrupulous in adhering to consensually agreed-on operational definitions when these exist and carefully describe any deviations from them and the reasons for those deviations. When no consensual operational definitions exist, researchers should clearly describe the criteria for classifying research participants into groups.

Another consideration that arises when research participants are classified into groups is the possibility of group membership being confounded with other variables, such as age, experience, and so forth, that might be related to scores on the dependent variables. As in quasi-experiments, it is necessary to assess any possible confounding variables and ensure that the average scores are the same in each group. Another strategy is to match participants in the groups on critical characteristics. For example, in a study of conflict resolution styles among heterosexual, gay, and lesbian couples, Metz, Rosser, and Strapko (1994) matched couples on age and length of relationship.

Creating Categorical Variables From Continuous Variables

Sometimes researchers measure hypothetical constructs on continuous scales, but convert the continuum into categories (e.g., high, moderate, and low scorers) for data analysis. This conversion can be accomplished by using median splits, dichotomizing multiple level variables, or using cutoff scores.

Median Splits.   When an independent variable is measured on a continuous scale, as are many personality traits, researchers sometimes transform the continuous variable into a categorical variable so that research participants can be placed into the discrete groups required by group comparison statistics such as the *t* test and ANOVA. This transformation is often accomplished using a median split: The median score for the sample being used is determined and participants scoring above the median are classified as *high* on the variable and those scoring below the median being classified as *low*. This procedure raises conceptual, empirical, and statistical problems. The conceptual problem is illustrated in Fig. 11.1, which presents the scores of four research participants—A, B, C, and D—on a continuous variable. As can be seen, use of a median split to classify participants on this scale makes the implicit assumptions that Participant A is similar to Participant B, that Participant C is similar to Participant D, and that Participants B and C

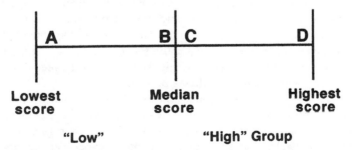

FIG. 11.1.   Use of median split to classify research participants into groups on a continuous variable. *Note.* From *Principles of Research in Behavioral Science* (p. 298), by Bernard E. Whitley, Jr., 1996, Mountain View, CA: Mayfield. Copyright 1996 by Mayfield. Reprinted with permission.

are different from each other. The problem is whether these assumptions are tenable for the hypothesis being tested; often they are not.

The empirical problem brought about by the use of median splits is that of the reliability of the resulting classification of research participants. Because classification cutoff scores are relative (changing from sample to sample as the median changes) rather than absolute, participants who are in different samples, but who have the same scores, might be classified differently. This problem is especially likely to occur in small samples, in which the sample median might be a poor estimate of the population median; comparability of results across studies is therefore reduced. Comparability can be further reduced when different studies use median splits on different measures of the same construct. For example, although scores on Bem's (1974) Sex Role Inventory and Spence, Helmreich, and Stapp's (1975) Personal Attributes Questionnaire (two measures of the personality variable of gender-role orientation) are highly correlated, agreement between category classification based on median splits is only about 60%, which is reduced to about 40% when agreements due to chance are taken into account (Kelly, Furman, & Young, 1978).

Median splits engender two statistical problems. The first is that of power, that is, the ability of a sample correlation to accurately estimate the population correlation. Bollen and Barb (1981) showed that given a population correlation of .30—the conventionally accepted level of a moderate correlation (Cohen, 1988)—the estimated r in large samples is .303, whereas a median split gives an estimate of .190, much less than the true size of the correlation. Although increasing the number of categories improves the sample correlation relative to its population value (e.g., three categories gives an estimate of .226), there is always some loss of power (see also Cohen, 1983). The second statistical problem is that the use of median splits with two or more correlated independent variables in a factorial design can lead to false statistical significance: A main effect or interaction appears to be statistically significant when, in fact, it is not (Maxwell & Delaney, 1993). This result can occur because dichotomizing two correlated independent variables confounds their effects on a dependent variable so that in an ANOVA, the effect for one independent variable represents not only its true relationship with the dependent variable, but also some of the other independent variable's relationship with the dependent variable. Consequently, the apparent effect of the first independent variable is inflated. The more highly correlated the predictor variables, the more likely false significant effects become.

These problems all have the same solution: Treat the independent variable as continuous rather than as a set of categories and analyze the data using multiple regression analysis (see chap. 13, this volume). One might argue, however, that sometimes a researcher wants to investigate both an experimentally manipulated (thus, categorical) variable and a continuous variable in one study. Because the manipulated variable in such studies is categorical, one might think it necessary to categorize the personality variable and use ANOVA to analyze the data. However, regression analysis can accommodate categorical variables, such as the conditions of an experiment, by assigning values such as 1 and 0 to the experimental and control conditions of the manipulated variable.

Dichotomizing Variables With Multiple Categories. Similar problems arise when researchers take a group of participants who could be placed into multiple categories of variable, such as different forms of childhood sexual abuse, and split the sample into two groups, such as presence or absence of abuse. As Roosa, Reyes, Reinholtz, and Angelini (1998) noted in their discussion of operational definitions of childhood sexual abuse:

> researchers ask women, often with a single question, whether they have had unwanted sexual experiences, such as touching or fondling, that made them feel uncomfortable . . . or sexual touching or intercourse that involved force. . . . These and similar approaches then dichotomize respondents into those who were abused and those who were not abused. In these studies, women who had been touched against their will are categorized along with women who had been raped as victims of sexual abuse with no consideration for differences in the severity of their experiences. (p. 226)

Such procedures not only incur a loss of information concerning the incidence of different types of abuse, but also affect the apparent magnitude of the relationship between abuse and other variables, such as psychological well-being. Roosa et al. (1998), for example, found that dichotomized measures of childhood sexual abuse underestimated the strength of the relationship of some specific forms of abuse, such as rape, to psychological well-being.

Cutoff Scores. Type theories of personality postulate the existence of discrete personality types or categories and assume that a person fits into one and only one of the categories. Consequently, measures used to assess the constructs on type theories usually provide preset, absolute criteria for classifying people as to personality type based on extensive validation research on the measure. Therefore, deviation from the established procedures threatens the construct validity of the classifications. In addition, deviation from established classification procedures means that people who have the same score on the measure may be classified into one category in one study but into another category in another study, thereby reducing the comparability of results across studies. Consequently, when established classification procedures exist, researchers should rigidly adhere to them.

MULTIPLE GROUP DESIGNS

Experiments, quasi-experiments, and nonexperimental studies often consist of more than the traditional experimental and control or comparison groups. Experiments and studies with more than two groups can be referred to as *multiple group designs*. Multiple group designs (as well as two-group designs) can involve either quantitative independent variables or qualitative independent variables. Quantitative independent variables vary by degree; the conditions of the independent variable (called *levels* in these cases) represent more or less of the independent variable. Qualitative independent variables vary by quality; the conditions of the independent variable represent different types or aspects of the independent variable.

Quantitative Independent Variables

When studying the effects of quantitative independent variables, researchers are usually interested in determining the effect on the dependent variable of adding more of the independent variable. For example, as part of a more complex experiment, Elliott and O'Donohue (1997) hypothesized that being distracted while listening to an erotic audiotape would reduce women's sexual arousal. They manipulated three levels of distraction (none, low, and high) and found that sexual arousal as measured by vaginal photoplethysmography (see chap. 7, this volume) was highest in the no distraction condition and lowest in the high distraction condition, with mean arousal level in the low distraction condition falling midway between the other two.

In a multiple group design using a quantitative independent variable, the relationship between the independent and dependent variable can take either of two forms. In a linear relationship, scores on the dependent variable increase or decrease constantly as the level of the independent variable increases or decreases, as was the case in Elliott and O'Donohue's (1997) experiment. In a curvilinear relationship, the relationship takes a form other than that of a straight line, such as rising then falling, falling then rising, rising to a peak and leveling off, and so forth. When studying the effects of a quantitative variable, it is important to use at least three levels of the variable because if there is a curvilinear relationship between the independent variable and the dependent variable, it can be found only if there are more than two levels of the independent variable. Consider the graphic presentation of the results of a study. If there are only two points on the graph (low and high levels of a treatment), one can draw only a straight line between them, which represents a linear relationship. If there are more than two points (e.g., low, moderate, and high levels), one can draw a curved line if that is what the graphic points represent. It would be appropriate to use just two groups only if there is a substantial body of research using multiple group designs that showed that only a linear relationship existed between the independent and dependent variables being studied.

When using multiple levels of an independent variable, one should ensure that the levels represent the entire range of the variable: *High, moderate,* and *low* are abstract terms, and their operational definitions could affect the results of a study. Consider two hypothetical teams of researchers who are investigating how the proportion of scenes in sexually explicit videos that depict sexual violence affects

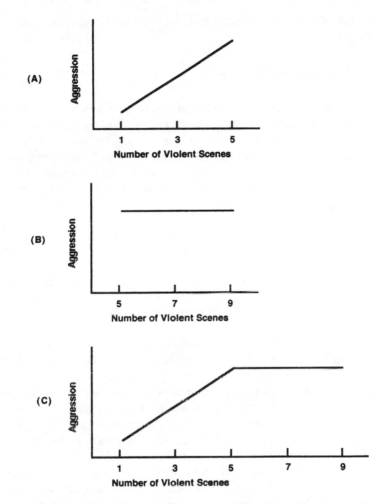

FIG. 11.2.   Only when the the full range of a quantitative independent variable is used does the true curvilinear relationship between the variables become apparent.

subsequent aggression. Each team constructs three videos consisting of 10 scenes each, one video representing a low amount of violence, another a moderate amount of violence, and the third a high amount of violence. However, Research Team A operationally defines low, moderate, and high violence as one, three, and five violent scenes, respectively, whereas Research Team B operationally defines low, moderate, and high violence as five, seven, and nine scenes, respectively. Research Team A gets the results depicted in Panel A of Fig. 11.2 and concludes that aggression increases linearly with violent content, but Research Team B gets the results depicted in Panel B and concludes that different amounts of violence have no differential effect on aggression. Panel C, which combines the results of the two studies, shows the actual effect: Aggression increases up to a point and then levels off.

Qualitative Independent Variables

Multiple group designs that use qualitative independent variables compare conditions that differ in characteristics rather than amount. Such comparisons can be made for either of two reasons. One reason is that a complete test of a hypothesis requires multiple comparisons. For example, based on a particular theory of persuasion, Bauserman (1998) proposed two hypotheses concerning male research participants' responses to sexually explicit videos that depicted an egalitarian, sexist, or aggressive scene:

> (1) both the sexist scenes and the sexually aggressive scenes would increase attitudes and beliefs accepting of inequality and male dominance in relationships because both types of scenes present implicit messages of inequality and male dominance, and (2) only the sexually aggressive scenes would increase attitudes and beliefs accepting of rape myths and sexual coercion because only the aggressive scenes would present implicit messages supportive of sexual coercion. (p. 245)

Although these hypotheses were not supported, Bauserman did find that the participants gave more negative ratings of the aggressive video than of the egalitarian video, with ratings of the sexist video falling between the other two.

Another reason for using a multiple group design is that more than one control or comparison group is needed to rule out alternative explanations for an effect. For example, watching sexually violent films can cause men to be aggressive against women (e.g., Donnerstein, 1983). Donnerstein wanted to determine whether the aggression was due to the sexual or violent content of the films. He had male research participants watch one of four films: aggressive erotic, nonsexual aggressive, erotic, and neutral. He found no difference in aggression against a female target in response to the neutral and erotic films, higher levels of aggression in response to the aggressive film, and still higher levels of aggression in response to the aggressive erotic film. He concluded that violence and the combination of sex and violence, not sexual content, were the primary instigators of aggression.

Interpreting the Results of Multiple Group Experiments

Multiple group designs are very useful to researchers, potentially providing a wealth of information unavailable from two-group designs and providing additional controls for alternative explanations for the effect of the independent variable. However, a potential pitfall exists in the interpretation of the results of the statistical analysis of these designs. The data from multiple group designs are analyzed using a one-way ANOVA, which was designed for this purpose. A statistically significant F value means that, out of all the possible two-group comparisons among the group means, at least one comparison is statistically significant; however, it does not indicate which comparison is significant. For example, Bauserman's (1998) data analysis revealed a statistically significant F value for affective responses to the sexually explicit videos, but did not indicate which of the three comparisons among group means was statistically significant: egalitarian versus sexist, egalitarian versus aggressive, or sexist versus aggressive.

To determine which difference or differences are statistically significant, one must conduct follow-up tests that directly compare the group means. When there are specific hypotheses about differences in means, the comparisons among those means are made with a priori (or preplanned) contrasts. If there are no specific predictions about differences in means, then post hoc (or after-the-fact) contrasts must be used; however, post hoc contrasts have lower statistical power than a priori contrasts. Bauserman (1998), for example, used post hoc contrast analysis to find the statistically significant differences among groups in his affective response data.

One should never interpret the results of a multiple group experiment solely on the basis of the F test; the appropriate post hoc or a priori analyses should always be conducted. Most statistics textbooks describe how to conduct these analyses.

FACTORIAL DESIGNS

Much, if not most, sexuality research uses two or more independent variables. Designs with multiple independent variables are called factorial designs; each independent variable is a factor in the design. This section discusses the information provided by factorial designs, the interpretation of interaction effects, and some of the uses of factorial designs.

Information Provided by Factorial Designs

Factorial designs provide two types of information about the effects of the independent variables. A main effect is the effect that one independent variable has independent of the effect of the other independent variable. The main effect of an independent variable represents what would be found if the experiment were conducted using only that independent variable and ignoring the possible effects of the other independent variable. For example, in a study of the effects of viewing a sexually explicit versus nonsexual film on aggression in men and women, the main effect for type of film is the difference in mean aggression scores between the group that viewed the sexually explicit film and the group that viewed the nonsexual film, ignoring the fact that both groups were composed of both men and women. An interaction effect (or simply interaction) occurs when two or more independent variables combine to produce an effect over and above their main effects. Interactions can be seen only when the effects of two or more independent variables are considered simultaneously. Consequently, interaction effects can only be found when a factorial design is used.

A study conducted by Kelley, Byrne, Greendlinger, and Murnen (1997) is an example of a factorial design. Kelley et al. were interested in gender differences in affective responses to heterosexual, lesbian, and gay male erotica. They had male and female research participants view one of the three types of films and rate their affective response to it. Table 11.2 shows participants' mean positive affect ratings by gender of participant and type of film. The column in Table 11.2 labeled *Gender Mean* shows the main effect for participant gender (ignoring type of film): Men's ratings were more positive than women's, and the difference was statistically significant. If this were a two-group study with gender as the independent variable, one would conclude that men respond more positively to erotic films. The row labeled *Film Mean* shows the main effect for type of film (ignoring participant gender): The heterosexual film was rated more positively than the lesbian film, which was rated more positively than the gay male film. Because the F test for this effect was statistically significant, if this were a three-group study with type of film as the independent variable, one would conclude that affective reactions vary as a function of type of film.

However, as can be seen from the individual condition means, both of these conclusions would be inaccurate. In actuality, men and women responded similarly to the heterosexual and gay male films, but men responded more favorably to the lesbian film. In addition, men's responses to both the heterosexual and lesbians films were more positive than their response to the gay male film, whereas women responded more positively to the heterosexual film than to either the lesbian or gay male film. Responses were determined neither by type of film alone nor by gender of participant alone, but by their unique combined effect or interaction.

Interpreting Interaction Effects

Factorial designs are quite common in sexuality research, and they frequently reveal interaction effects. When interpreting interaction effects, it can be useful to

TABLE 11.2
Mean Positive Affective Responses to Sexually Explicit
Films by Gender and Type of Film

Variable	Film Type			Gender Mean
	Heterosexual	Lesbian	Gay Male	
Male Participants	67.6	67.0	43.8	59.5
Female Participants	63.3	52.1	45.2	53.5
Film Mean	65.4	59.5	44.4	

Note. Based on Kelley, Byrne, Greendlinger, and Murnen (1997), Table 2.

think of a piece of research as a question: "Does the independent variable have an effect on the dependent variable?" When the outcome is one or more main effects without an interaction, the answer is a simple "yes." When the outcome is an interaction, with or without main effects, the answer is, "It depends." The answer for one independent variable depends on the condition of the other independent variable. For example, in the Kelley et al. (1997) study, one question was, "Is a person's gender related to his or her affective reaction to a sexually explicit film?" The answer, as shown in Table 11.2, is not a simple "yes" or "no"; it depends on the film's theme. Men had more positive reactions to the lesbian film, but there were no gender differences in response to the other two films. The other question Kelley et al. asked was, "Does the theme of a sexually explicit film affect affective responses to it?" Again, the answer is, "It depends," this time on the gender of the person whose reaction is assessed. For example, men responded equally positively to the heterosexual and lesbian films, whereas women responded more positively to the heterosexual film than to the lesbian film.

The "it depends" nature of interactions has an important implication for understanding the results of research. If the research reveals an interaction, any main effects found may be deceptive, representing a statistical artifact rather than a true main effect of the independent variable. Consequently, if the statistical analysis finds both a main effect and an interaction, the main effect for one independent variable may apply only to one condition of the other independent variable, not to both conditions. For example, Kelley et al. (1997) found a main effect for gender of participant, but that effect was limited to one type of film. Nevertheless, sometimes there can be both an interaction and a true main effect. This situation would occur when members of one group, say women, consistently score higher than members of the other group across all conditions of the second independent variable, but the rates of change differ across levels of the second independent variable.

When faced with a significant interaction effect in a factorial design, the researcher is in a position much like that which occurs when one finds a significant F value in a multiple group design: There is a significant difference somewhere among the means, but one does not yet know where the difference or differences lie. Again, the solution is to conduct post hoc comparisons if the hypothesis did not include prediction of a particular form of interaction. If the hypothesis did specify a particular outcome, then a priori contrasts should be used.

Design Complexity

The examples of factorial designs used so far in this discussion have been relatively simple 2 × 2 and 2 × 3 designs. However, in principle, there is no limit on the number of independent variables that one can have or the number of levels or conditions per independent variable. For example, Sprecher, McKinney, and Orbuch (1987) used a 2 × 2 × 2 × 2 design to investigate the factors that influence people's evaluation of other people whom they learn are sexually active. The independent variables were gender of the person being evaluated, age of the person (16 or 21), type of relationship in which the sexual behavior took place (casual or close), and gender of the research participant.

Although there is no theoretical limit on the number of independent variables or conditions, one rarely sees studies that use more than three independent variables or three conditions per independent variable. The reason for this limitation is practical: The total number of conditions in the study increases quickly as the number of independent variables and number of conditions per independent variable increase. For example, a 2 × 2 design has four conditions: all the possible combinations of the two conditions of each of the two independent variables. A 2 × 3 design (Kelley et al., 1997) has six conditions, and a 2 × 2 × 2 × 2 design (Sprecher et al., 1987) has 16 conditions. As the total number of conditions increases, the number of research participants one needs in a between-subjects design increases. With 20 participants per condition, a 2 × 2 design requires 80 participants, but a 2 × 2 × 2 × 2 design requires 320. In addition, the complexity of the data analysis and the interpretation of the results of that analysis increase. Consequently, most researchers limit themselves to relatively simple designs.

Uses for Factorial Designs

Factorial designs are fairly complex, requiring two or more independent variables and multiple groups of participants, one group for each combination of the independent variables. Why should one bother with this complexity when the effect of an independent variable can be determined with a simpler design? Factorial designs can be used to test hypotheses about moderator variables, detect order effects in counterbalanced within-subjects designs, and control extraneous variance by a technique called *blocking*.

Testing Moderator Hypotheses.   A moderator variable is one that is hypothesized to change the effect of an independent variable: The effect of the independent variable is different under different conditions of the moderator variable. Thus, in the Kelley et al. (1997) study, one could say that gender of participant moderated the effect that type of film had on affective responses. One could also look at it the other way and say that type of film moderated the relationship between gender and affective response. The variable that one considers to be the moderator variable depends on one's frame of reference; that is, which variable the researcher conceptualizes as the independent variable being studied and which is conceptualized as the moderator variable influencing the effect of the independent variable. If one is testing a theory, the theory will often provide the frame of reference, designating which variables are independent variables and which are moderator variables. However, because the effect of a moderator variable takes the form of an interaction, the hypothesis that one variable moderates the effect of another can be tested only with a factorial design and will be supported only if the predicted interaction is found.

Detecting Order Effects. Earlier I noted that order effects present a potential threat to the validity of the conclusions that can be drawn from the research. When the order of conditions is counterbalanced, the presence and size of order effects can be detected using a between–within factorial design, with the independent variable being tested as the within-subjects factor and order of conditions (experimental before control and control before experimental) as the between-subjects factor. Some possible outcomes of this procedure are shown in Table 11.3.

Panel A shows an outcome in which the independent variable had an effect and there was no order effect. In this case, there will be a main effect for the independ-

TABLE 11.3
Hypothetical Example of the Use of Between-Within
Designs to Detect Order Effects

(A) No Order Effect: There is a main effect for condition, no main effect for order, and no interaction.

	Condition		
Variable	Experimental (E)	Control (C)	Order Mean
Order E → C	40	30	35
Order C → E	40	30	35
Condition Mean	40	30	

(B) Equal Order Effects: There is a main effect for condition, no main effect for order, and an interaction.

	Condition		
Variable	Experimental (E)	Control (C)	Order Mean
Order E → C	40	40	40
Order C → E	50	30	40
Condition Mean	45	35	

(C) Differential Order Effects: There are main effects for condition and order, and an interaction.

	Condition		
Variable	Experimental (E)	Control (C)	Order Mean
Order E → C	40	40	40
Order C → E	60	30	45
Condition Mean	50	35	

Note. From *Principles of Research in Behavioral Science* (p. 469), by Bernard E. Whitley, Jr., 1996, Mountain View, CA: Mayfield. Copyright 1996 by Mayfield. Reprinted with permission.

ent variable (the mean for the experimental condition is 10 points greater than the mean for the control condition), no main effect for the order factor (the two order means are equal), and no interaction effect. Panel B shows the outcome for the same experiment when there is an order effect that is the same for both orders. There is a main effect for the independent variable, no order effect, but there is an interaction between the conditions of the independent variable and the order in which participants experienced the conditions. In this case, experiencing a condition as the second condition added 10 points to the participants' scores. Because the order effect happens to be the same as the effect of the independent variable, there is no difference between the means in the experimental and control conditions for participants who experienced the experimental condition first, and an exaggerated difference for those who experienced the control condition first. Note, however, that because the order effect was the same for both orders, the difference between the means for the experimental and control conditions reflects the true difference between the means.

Panel C shows the outcome for a differential order effect in which experiencing the control condition second added 10 points to a person's score, whereas experiencing the experimental condition second added 20 points. In this case, there are main effects for both the independent variable and order, as well as an interaction between the two. Note also that the difference in means in the experimental and control conditions is greater than the true difference shown in Panel A.

Although the presence of order effects contaminate the data, all is not lost. Note that order effects do not affect the condition that participants experience first. Consequently, one can analyze the experimental and control data from the experimental-first and control-first participants as a between-subjects design and still test the hypothesis. The cost of this procedure is the loss of the advantages of a within-subjects design, but the benefit is the ability to draw valid conclusions from the data. Order effects are always potential threats to the validity of within-subjects designs, so researchers should always test to see whether these effects are contaminating their data.

Blocking on Extraneous Variables.   Recall that, from a statistical point of view, any variance not attributable to an independent variable is error variance and that extraneous variables are one source of such variance. One way in which researchers can deal with the effects of extraneous variables is to include them as independent variables in a factorial design. A factorial ANOVA will remove the variance due to the extraneous variable and its interaction with the independent variable from the error variance and treat it as variance due to an independent variable and to the interaction of two independent variables. This procedure can reduce the error variance and so increase the sensitivity of the statistical test of the effect of the independent variable.

Consider the data presented in Panel A of Table 11.4, which come from a hypothetical experiment in which the researcher ensured that equal numbers of men and women participated in the experimental and control conditions. The experi-

TABLE 11.4
Effect of Blocking on an Extraneous Variable on Statistical Analysis

(A) Scores

	Experimental Group		Control Group
M1	13	M7	15
M2	21	M8	13
M3	17	M9	9
M4	14	M10	9
M5	15	M11	8
M6	11	M12	11
F1	16	F7	19
F2	16	F8	16
F3	22	F9	18
F4	20	F10	23
F5	21	F11	14
F6	19	F12	15

(B) Analysis of Two Group Design

Source of Variance	Degrees of Freedom	Mean Square	F	p
Conditions	1	45.37	2.71	NS
Error	22	16.75		

(C) Analysis of 2 (Condition) × 2 (Sex) Design

Source of Variance	Degrees of Freedom	Mean Square	F	p
Conditions	1	45.37	4.57	< .05
Sex	1	155.04	15.63	< .001
Interaction	1	15.05	1.52	NS
Error	20	9.92		

Note.   M = male participants, F = female participants, NS = *not significant*. From *Principles of Research in Behavioral Science* (p. 469), by Bernard E. Whitley, Jr., 1996, Mountain View, CA: Mayfield. Copyright 1996 by Mayfield. Reprinted with permission.

mental group had a mean score of 16.9 and the control group a mean score of 14.2. However, as shown by the statistical analysis in Panel B of the table, this difference was not statistically significant. The statistical analysis shown in Panel C of the table shows what happens when the participants are blocked on gender. The term *blocking* means that the participants are grouped according to an extraneous variable and that variable is added as a factor in the design. The new analysis reveals significant effects for both the independent variable and for participant gender, with women, who had a mean score of 18.1, performing better than men, who had a mean score of 13.0.

The numbers in the *Mean Square* columns in Panels B and C represent the amount of variance in the dependent variable attributable to each factor in the design, including error. Panel C shows that participant gender accounted for much more variance in the dependent variable than did the independent variable. This variance, along with the nonsignificant variance accounted for by the interaction, was treated as part of the error variance in the analysis shown in Panel B, increasing the size of that error variance. The variance attributable to the independent variable is the same in both analyses. Because the *F* test is the ratio of the variance due to an independent variable to the error variance, the *F* value in Panel B is smaller than that in Panel C. An experimenter who ignored the effect of participant gender as an extraneous variable would incorrectly conclude that the independent variable had no effect on the dependent variable.

When conducting the literature review for a research project, it is extremely important to identify extraneous variables so that one can take steps to control them. A major advantage of the use of an extraneous variable as a factor in a factorial design is that it becomes possible to determine whether that variable interacts with the independent variable. The alternative methods of control, such as holding the extraneous variable constant across conditions of the independent variable, ignore its possible moderating effects and limit the interpretations one can make about the generalizability of the results of the research: If there is no interaction between the independent variable of interest and the blocking variable, then the results for the independent variable generalize across conditions of the blocking variable However, blocking should be used with care: It only operates to reduce error variance when the blocking variable has a strong effect on or is highly correlated with the dependent variable. Under other conditions, blocking could actually increase the error variance by decreasing the degrees of freedom associated with the error term.

SUGGESTED READINGS

Aronson, Wilson, and Brewer (1998) provided an excellent introduction to the issues of experimental research, and Aronson et al. (1990) covered those issues in more detail. Greenwald (1976) presented the advantages and disadvantages of within-subjects designs. Cook and Campbell (1979) is the classic work on quasi-experimental research and included designs in addition to the nonequivalent control group design. Porter and Raudenbush (1987) presented a brief discussion of ANCOVA, and Tabachnick and Fidell (1996) provided a more detailed statistical presentation. Cohen (1983) and Maxwell and Delaney (1993) discussed the shortcomings of the use of median splits to form groups.

REFERENCES

Aronson, E., Ellsworth, P. C., Carlsmith, J. M., & Gonzales, M. H. (1990). *Methods of research in social psychology* (2nd ed.). New York: McGraw-Hill.

Aronson, E., Wilson, T. D., & Brewer, M. B. (1998). Experimentation in social psychology. In D. T. Gilbert, S. T. Fiske, & G. Lindzey (Eds.), *The handbook of social psychology* (4th ed., Vol. 1, pp. 99–142). Boston: McGraw-Hill.

Basow, S. A. (1992). *Gender stereotypes* (3rd ed.). Monterey, CA: Brooks/Cole.

Bauserman, R. (1998). Egalitarian, sexist, and aggressive sexual materials: Attitude effects and viewer responses. *The Journal of Sex Research, 35*, 244–253.

Bem, S. L. (1974). The measurement of psychological androgyny. *Journal of Consulting and Clinical Psychology, 42*, 155–162.

Bollen, K. A., & Barb, K. H. (1981). Pearson's r and coarsely categorized measures. *American Sociological Review, 46*, 232–239.

Cohen, J. (1983). The cost of dichotomization. *Applied Psychological Measurement, 7*, 249–253.

Cohen, J. (1988). *Statistical power analysis for the behavioral sciences* (2nd ed.). Hillsdale, NJ: Lawrence Erlbaum Associates.

Cook, T. D., & Campbell, D. J. (1979). *Quasi-experimentation.* Chicago: Rand-McNally.

Donnerstein, E. (1983). Erotica and human aggression. In R. G. Geen & E. I. Donnerstein (Eds.), *Aggression: Theoretical and empirical reviews* (Vol. 2, pp. 127–154). New York: Academic Press.

Elliott, A. N., & O'Donohue, W. T. (1997). The effects of anxiety and distraction on sexual arousal in a nonclinical sample of heterosexual women. *Archives of Sexual Behavior, 26*, 607–624.

Fisher, W. A., & Grenier, G. (1994). Violent pornography, antiwoman thoughts, and antiwoman acts: In search of reliable effects. *The Journal of Sex Research, 31*, 23–38.

Greenwald, A. G. (1976). Within-subjects designs: To use or not to use? *Psychological Bulletin, 83*, 314–320.

Hopkins, K. D. (1982). The unit of analysis: Group means versus individual observations. *American Educational Research Journal, 19*, 5–18.

Kelley, K., Byrne, D., Greendlinger, V., & Murnen, S. K. (1997). Content, sex of viewer, and dispositional variables as predictors of affective and evaluative responses to sexually explicit films. *Journal of Psychology and Human Sexuality, 9*(2), 53–71.

Kelly, J. A., Furman, W., & Young, V. (1978). Problems associated with the typological measurement of sex roles and androgyny. *Journal of Consulting and Clinical Psychology, 46*, 1574–1576.

Kirk, R. E. (1982). *Experimental design: Procedures for the behavioral sciences* (2nd ed.). Belmont, CA: Brooks/Cole.

Landy, D., & Aronson, E. (1968). Liking for an evaluator as a function of his discernment. *Journal of Personality and Social Psychology, 9*, 133–141.

Maxwell, S. E., & Delaney, H. D. (1993). Bivariate median splits and spurious statistical significance. *Psychological Bulletin, 113*, 181–190.

Metz, M. E., Rosser, B. R. S., & Strapko, N. (1994). Differences in conflict-resolution styles among heterosexual, gay, and lesbian couples. *The Journal of Sex Research, 31*, 293–308.

Porter, A. C., & Raudenbush, S. W. (1987). Analysis of covariance: Its model and use in psychological research. *Journal of Counseling Psychology, 34*, 383–392.

Roosa, M. W., Reyes, L., Reinholtz, C., & Angelini, P. J. (1998). Measurement of women's childhood sexual abuse experiences: An empirical demonstration of the impact of choice of measure on estimates of incidence rates and of relationships with pathology. *The Journal of Sex Research, 35*, 225–233.

Sandfort, T. G. M. (1997). Sampling male homosexuality. In J. Bancroft (Ed.), *Researching sexual behavior: Methodological issues* (pp. 261–275). Bloomington: Indiana University Press.

Spence, J. T., Helmreich, R. L., & Stapp, J. (1975). Ratings of self and peers on sex-role attributes and their relation to self-esteem and conceptions of masculinity and femininity. *Journal of Personality and Social Psychology, 32*, 29–39.

Sprecher, S., McKinney, K., & Orbuch, T. L. (1987). Has the double standard disappeared? An experimental test. *Social Psychology Quarterly, 50*, 24–31.

Stevenson, M. R., & Gajarsky, W. M. (1990). Issues of gender in promoting tolerance for homosexuality. *Journal of Psychology and Human Sexuality, 3*(2), 155–163.

Strube, M. J. (1991). Small sample failure of random assignment: A further examination. *Journal of Consulting and Clinical Psychology, 59,* 346–350.

Tabachnick, B. G., & Fidell, L. S. (1996). *Using multivariate statistics* (3rd ed.). New York: HarperCollins.

Wiederman, M. W., & Allgeier, E. R. (1993). Gender differences in sexual jealousy: Adaptionist or social learning explanation? *Ethology and Sociobiology, 14,* 115–140.

12

$$\text{\tiny vvvvvvv}$$

Regression Models

Alfred DeMaris
Bowling Green State University

Regression is easily the most frequently used statistical technique in the social sciences (Allison, 1999), and with good reason. The regression model is both flexible and robust. It can be employed for any response variable that is at least approximately interval or even binary. The independent variables can be characterized by any level of measurement. It can easily be adapted to handle many types of nonlinear and nonadditive relationships between the response and explanatory variables. A variety of mechanisms may be employed to get around violations of model assumptions. It affords a good first approximation to analyses requiring more complex statistical techniques. Additionally, software for estimating regression models is simple enough to be included in even the most rudimentary statistical packages.

This chapter is a survey of the major issues involved in using and interpreting regression in sexuality research. Because it is assumed that most readers have at least a passing familiarity with regression, this chapter is not written at the introductory level. Nevertheless, particularly technical details are confined to the endnotes. Readers not comfortable with this material may simply skip over it. Because regression coefficients are most frequently used to infer causal relationships, the chapter begins with a discussion of causality and its relationship to regression analysis. Next, the chapter reviews the model and assumptions required for estimation by ordinary least squares and discusses the interpretation of model parameters. The subsequent section is a discussion of inferential tests and assessment of model fit. Further sections address the problems of multicollinearity and influence, and how the model is adapted to address nonlinearity or nonadditivity in the relationships between predictors and response, or how one compares models across groups. The remaining section of the chapter focuses on more advanced issues, such as the problem of heteroskedasticity, using weighted analyses with complex sampling designs, and comparing coefficients across regression models. The chapter concludes with suggestions for further reading.

To give substantive flesh to the discussion throughout the chapter, I utilize an example drawn from my own research interests. The data are from the National Survey of Families and Households (NSFH). This is a panel study of a national probability sample of households in the coterminous United States based on surveys taken from 1987 to 1988 and from 1992 to 1994 (details of the design and implementation of the first survey are given in Sweet, Bumpass, & Call, 1988). As part of a larger study on changes in sexual activity over time in intimate relationships, I present several analyses of the predictors of sexual frequency. My subsample from the NSFH consists of 2,997 married and heterosexual cohabiting couples who had been together at most 20 years at the time of the first survey, who were still together in the second survey, and who had nonmissing data on the response variable *sexual frequency in the past month.* (Valid means were substituted for missing values on the independent variables.) This variable was based on a question asked of each partner about how many times the couple had had sex in the past month. In that the true sexual frequency for the couple can be considered a latent variable imperfectly tapped by each partner's recall, partners' responses were averaged. Values greater than 31 were recoded to 31 to avoid undue influence on the results produced by possibly bogus responses (see the discussion of influence farther on; analyses for this chapter are based primarily on data from the first survey).

REGRESSION AND CAUSALITY

Most researchers are interested in the causes of the phenomena they study. The strongest design for inferring causal effects, of course, is the controlled experiment. However, most of the interesting phenomena in sexuality research, such as sexual attitudes and behaviors in natural settings, are not often amenable to experimental manipulation. Much of the data, therefore, are nonexperimental, as exemplified by the NSFH. Regression is often seen as a technique for estimating causal effects in such situations. Consider the extent to which regression coefficients lend themselves to causal interpretations.

First, what is meant by the term *causal*? Bollen's (1989) definition of causality involves three components: isolation, association, and direction of influence: "Consider one variable, say, y_1, which is *isolated* from all influences except from a second variable called x_1. If a change in y_1 accompanies a change in x_1, then x_1 is a cause of y_1" (p. 41). For example, Model 2 in Table 12.1 shows a regression of sexual frequency on three predictors for the 2,997 couples in the sample. The

TABLE 12.1
Unstandardized Coefficients for the Regression of Sexual
Frequency on Sociodemographic Characteristics of Couples

Regressor	Model 1	Model 2	Beta	Model 3	Model 4
Intercept	8.171***	13.969***	.000	16.009***	16.006***
Cohabiting	3.314***	2.322***	.094	1.794***	1.798***
Female's Age		−.144***	−.183	−.179***	−.179***
Duration		−.010***	−.105	−.010***	−.010***
First Union				−.552*	−.553*
His Church Attendance				−.139*	−.139*
Her Church Attendance				.179**	.178**
His Health				.538**	.515***
Her Health				.493**	.515***
His Education				−.169***	−.174***
Her Education				−.180***	−.174***
Household Income				.002	.002
Children Under 5				−1.417***	−1.412***
F	54.646***	82.744***		29.767***	35.738***
ΔF				11.257***	.026
R^2	.018	.077		.107	.107
R^2_a	.018	.076		.103	.104
MSE	43.183	40.631		39.415	39.389

*$p < .05$. **$p < .01$. ***$p < .001$.

predictors are *cohabiting*, a dummy variable coded 1 if a couple is cohabiting un-married, 0 if they are married; the female partner's *age* in years; and *duration* of the relationship in months. The unstandardized regression coefficient for duration is −.01. It seems quite reasonable that duration in a relationship has a causal effect on sexual frequency. Over time, through routinization of sexual activity, or through boredom with each other, couples' sexual ardor appears to taper off (James, 1981). I might be tempted to interpret the effect of duration in the model as the drop in sex-ual frequency that is expected to occur with each passing month in a relationship.

There are several difficulties with this interpretation. The first is that the data are cross-sectional. No change is actually being observed in sexual frequency or duration. Rather, I am observing differences in sexual frequency for those who are a month apart in duration, net of the other two factors in the model. A more quali-fied interpretation might therefore be that −.01 is the expected difference in sexual frequency for those who are a month apart in duration. The second difficulty is that the association of duration with sexual frequency in my sample may not be causal at all. If couples maximized their sexual compatibility to the detriment of other aspects of fit, the most sexually intense relationships may also be the most short-lived. The association of longer duration with lower sexual activity might be an artifact of selection, with the most sexually intense relationships being selected out over time. Although I do not actually subscribe to this interpretation, the key is that nothing about regression precludes this possibility. It can only be ruled out based on information external to the analysis (e.g., theory, previous research). A third difficulty is the problem of isolation. There is no assurance that some omitted factor, call it Z, which is a correlate of duration, is not actually responsible for the apparent effect of duration. Only random assignment—an impossibility with nonexperimental data—engenders confidence that all extraneous influences have been controlled.

The point of all this is to emphasize the tenuousness of any causal inferences that result from regression with nonexperimental data. The best that the researcher can do is demonstrate that his or her results are consistent with a particular causal framework. Indeed, if sexual activity declines with the passage of time in relationships, then the researcher should find that longer duration unions exhibit lower levels of sexual frequency than shorter duration ones, net of other factors. Model 2 is therefore *consistent* with a causal effect of duration on sexual activity. However, is −.01 an estimate of this effect? Even assuming that the causal direction is correct and the impact of duration is isolated from all possible extraneous Zs, there are those who would say "no." Several scientists subscribe to a different definition of causality.

In this scheme, the causal effect of Treatment t over Treatment c for a given unit is the difference between what the value of y would have been at Time 2 if the unit had been exposed to t at Time 1, versus what would have happened if the same unit had been exposed to c at Time 1. This definition is called *counterfactual* because it is impossible, or contrary to fact, to observe what would have happened if a different treatment (or level of a regressor) had been given to the same unit. Accepting this notion of causality, it can be shown that an estimate of the true causal effect of some factor can only be estimated without bias if there is random assignment to the cause (see e.g., Holland, 1986). Because this rarely occurs with nonexperimental data, these scholars argue that regression coefficients should not generally be interpreted as causal effects (Sobel, 1998).

Although the counterfactual definition of cause has considerable intuitive appeal, not everyone agrees with this notion of causality (see e.g., Bollen, 1989). The researcher should simply be aware that the use of causal language is somewhat controversial. As mentioned earlier, the most cautious interpretation of a regression coefficient is that it is the estimated difference in the mean of the response for those who are a unit apart on the regressor in question (more on this later). Whether this represents a causal influence of X on Y depends on the research design that generated the data and what arguments the researcher can marshall to rule out alternative plausible interpretations.

MODEL AND ASSUMPTIONS

The multiple linear regression (MULR) model for some population of interest is:

$$Y_i = \alpha + \beta_1 X_{1i} + \beta_2 X_{2I} + \ldots + \beta_K X_{Ki} + \varepsilon_i, \tag{1}$$

where the betas (βs) represent constant weights for each case in the population, and the Xs represent each case's values on the independent variables, or regressors, in the equation. A particular collection of X values is referred to as a *covariate pattern* (Hosmer & Lemeshow, 1989). The mean of Y for all cases with a given covariate pattern is used to predict the individual Y values for those cases. That mean is called the *conditional mean* of Y, given a particular covariate pattern. The last term, ε_i, is called the *disturbance* or *error* in the equation. This represents the difference between the value of Y predicted by the part of the equation involving the parameters, $\alpha + \beta_1 X_{1i} + \beta_2 X_{2i} + \ldots + \beta_K X_{Ki}$—the conditional mean—and the actual value of Y for the ith case. The meaning of this model is very simple: If we could measure Y and the Xs for all members in the population, we should find that the relationship between these variables is described by the linear equation shown in Eq. (1). The task of regression analysis is nothing more than to estimate the parameters (α and the βs) of this equation. The assumptions for estimation of this model by ordinary least squares (OLS) are the following.

Y Is Approximately Interval. In theory, Y is supposed to be continuous, but measurement limitations result in Y never actually being continuous in practice. With large samples, Y can even be ordinal with at least five levels, or Y can be binary—coded 1 and 0. The latter results in what is referred to as the linear probability or discriminant analysis model. This model is not discussed in this chapter because logistic or probit regression are the preferred techniques for binary responses. A good introduction to logistic regression is DeMaris (1995).

No Regressor Is a Perfect Linear Combination of the Other Regressors in the Model. In other words, the regression of one of the regressors on all others in the model does not produce an R^2 of 1.0. If this assumption is violated, it is obvious. The regression computer program simply refuses to run.

The Conditional Error, E, Has a Distribution With Mean Equal to Zero and Variance Equal to σ^2 at Every Combination of Regressor Values; The Covariance of Errors for Any Two Different Observations Is Zero. These are very important assumptions and bear comment. The error term represents whatever affects Y other than the regressors in the model. In the interest of achieving isolation, or what Bollen (1989) referred to as "pseudo-isolation" (p. 43) of the impact of any regressor on Y, we require that the influences on Y that are left out of the model are uncorrelated with each of the regressors in the model. If this condition is not met, our parameter estimates will be biased (more on omitted-variable bias later). This assumption is encapsulated by positing that the conditional errors have zero mean. This means that the errors are linearly independent of the regressors or the correlations between the regressors and the error term are all zero. This assumption cannot be checked because an artifact of OLS estimation is that the residuals are always uncorrelated with the regressors. The only way to minimize the violation of this assumption is through correct model specification. That the error variance is a constant value, σ^2, at each combination of regressor values is the homoskedasticity assumption. (How to check on this assumption is explained later.) If this is violated, the best estimates are achieved with weighted least squares (WLS), rather than with OLS. (This is discussed later.) The assumption of zero correlation between errors for different observations is typically met with random sampling. However, it is usually violated with time series data. Tests for the violation of this assumption are available if the researcher is concerned about it (Greene, 1997).

In Small Samples (Fewer Than About 15 Cases per Parameter Estimated), the Errors Are Normally Distributed.   This assumption, required for valid tests of the coefficients, ensures that parameter estimates are normally distributed. In large samples, the parameter estimates tend to be normally distributed regardless of the distribution of the errors due to the central limit theorem.[1]

The Model Is Linear in the Parameters.   This means that the equation is a weighted sum of the parameters—the betas. This precludes models such as $Y = \alpha + X^\beta + \varepsilon$ because here beta enters the equation in a nonlinear fashion. This type of model can be estimated, but not with OLS (see Greene, 1997, for a discussion of nonlinear regression).

The Model Is Correctly Specified.   This is probably the most important assumption of all. It implies that, for each X_k, any other correlates of both X_k and Y are also in the model, and that the model reflects the correct functional form (e.g., linear, quadratic, interactive) of the relationships between these determinants and Y.

Provided these assumptions are met, OLS estimates are said to be Best Linear Unbiased Estimators (BLUE; i.e., they are unbiased estimators with the smallest variance in the class of all linear, unbiased estimators). When one or more of these assumptions is not met, the OLS estimators may still be unbiased, but there are better estimators to use. For example, when homoskedasticity is violated, WLS estimates have smaller variance.

That the OLS estimates are unbiased means that $E(b_k) = \beta_k$, where $E()$ is the expectation operator. In other words, the expected, or average, values of the sample regression coefficients, the b_k, are equal to the true population parameter values, the β_k. (*Average* refers to averaging over repeated sampling and repeated estimation of the regression equation.) The OLS estimates are also consistent, which means that as n tends to infinity the probability that the estimates are within any given distance, no matter how small, from the true parameters approaches one.[2] In other words, in large samples, consistent estimators can be relied on to be close to the true model parameters.

Estimation and Interpretation

Estimation of the model by OLS proceeds as follows. Consider any set of estimates of the model parameters. Call them a, b_1, b_2, . . . , b_K. The sample estimate of the population equation is then (dropping the subscript i for simplicity):

$$Y = a + b_1X_1 + b_2X_2 + \ldots + b_KX_K + e, \tag{2}$$

and the residuals for each observation are:

$$e = Y - (a + b_1X_1 + b_2X_2 + \ldots + b_KX_K).$$

We see here that the residuals are a function of the parameter estimates. The OLS estimates are those values that make the sum of squared residuals (SSE) as small as possible (hence the name, *ordinary least squares*). The a and the b_k are interpreted as follows: a is the estimate of the predicted value, or conditional mean, of Y when all Xs take on the value zero. This is readily apparent from setting all the Xs to zero in Eq. (2). This interpretation is rarely of interest unless the Xs are centered. The partial slope, b_k, is the estimated difference in the mean of Y for those who are a unit apart on X_k, holding all other Xs constant. This is also apparent from Eq. (2). Consider an equation with just two Xs. Suppose that we wish to compare the mean of Y for a case with value x_1+1, versus the value x_1, holding X_2 constant at the value x_2. Then the estimated difference in the mean of Y for those who are a unit apart on X_1, controlling for X_2, is (substituting for X1, X2 in Eq. [2] and leaving out the residual): $a + b_1(x_1+1) + b_2x_2 - (a + b_1x_1 + b_2x_2) = b_1(x_1+1) - b_1x_1 = b_1(x_1+1-x_1) = b_1(1) = b_1$.

The partial regression coefficient, b_k, shows the impact[3] of X_k controlling for all other Xs in the model. What is meant by *control*? In regression, control is accomplished by removing from X_k the linear association of X_k with the other Xs in the model and then regressing Y on this purged version of X_k. In this way, b_k represents the covariation of Y with a version of X_k that does not covary with other Xs in the model. It is as if X_k is made, in a sense, uncorrelated with the other Xs in the model so that its independent effect on Y can be assessed. The price that is paid in doing this is that this cleaned version of X_k has lower variance than before. The variance shared with other Xs has been subtracted out. How is this accomplished? Again, consider the model with two Xs: $Y = a + b_1X_1 + b_2X_2 + e$. If X_1 is first regressed on X_2, we have $X_1 = c + dX_2 + u_1$. U_1, the residual here, is equal to $X_1 - (c + dX_2)$. It is X_1 minus its linear association with X_2. Recall that, as an artifact of OLS, u_1 is uncorrelated with X_2. If we then regress Y on u_1, we have $Y = a^* + b_1^*u_1 + v$, and we find that $b_1^* = b_1$.

Omitted Variable Bias: Confounding, Mediation, and Suppression

Suppose that the researcher is primarily interested in the effect on Y of the variable X_1, which I refer to as the *focus variable*. Why do we need to control for other factors? The most pressing reason is that, without doing so, we run the risk of omitted-variable bias. To avoid matrix notation, I couch this discussion again in terms of very simple models. Suppose that the true model for Y is $\alpha + \beta_1 X_1 + \beta_2 X_2 + \varepsilon$, where ε is uncorrelated with each regressor. Instead, the researcher estimates $Y = \alpha + \beta_1 X_1 + \upsilon$. Notice now that $\upsilon = \beta_2 X_2 + \varepsilon$. Suppose also that there is either a positive or negative correlation between X_1 and X_2. What are the consequences?

First, notice that the pseudo-isolation assumption is violated because simple covariance algebra[4] shows that $Cov(\upsilon, X_1) = Cov(\beta_2 X_2 + \varepsilon, X_1) = \beta_2 Cov(X_1, X_2)$. This suggests that the pseudo-isolation assumption fails whenever predictors of Y excluded from the model are also correlated with one or more variables in the model. Second, the sample estimator of β_1, b_1 is no longer consistent for β_1. Rather, it is consistent for $\beta_1 + \beta_2 \rho_{12} \sigma_2 / \sigma_1$, where ρ_{12} is the population correlation between X_1 and X_2, and σ_2 and σ_1 are the population standard deviations of X_2 and X_1, respectively. In other words, in large samples, b_1 is close to $\beta_1 + \beta_2 \rho_{12} \sigma_2 / \sigma_1$, instead of β_1 alone. The bias due to the omitted variable is evident in this expression. The nature of the bias depends on the signs of β_2 and ρ_{12}, along with the sign of β_1 (note that the standard deviations are always positive). If β_1 is of the same sign as the product $\beta_2 \rho_{12}$, then we say that the relationship between X_1 and Y is *confounded* by X_2; that is, its magnitude is overestimated when X_2 is omitted from the equation. However, if the sign of $\beta_2 \rho_{12}$ is opposite to that of β_1, then the relationship between X_1 and Y is *suppressed* by X_2. Its magnitude is underestimated when X_2 is omitted. When the confounding variable is caused by X_1, so that the model is $X_1 \rightarrow X_2 \rightarrow Y$, then X_2 is said to *mediate* the impact of X_1 on Y. In this instance, X_2 is the mechanism by which X_1 affects Y.

To make the problem more concrete, suppose that β_1 is really 2, β_2 is 3, the correlation between X_1 and X_2 is .5, the standard deviation of X_1 is 1.5, and the standard deviation of X_2 is 1.8. Then the sample estimate of β_1 in a large sample is approximately $2 + (3)(.5)(1.8/1.5) = 3.8$. The estimate of β_1 is therefore biased upward by 1.8, compared with the true value.

An Example. The analyses in Table 12.1, referred to previously, are actually designed to examine the association between cohabiting status and sexual frequency. Do those who are cohabiting outside of marriage have a more active sex life than the married? The literature suggests that cohabitors, compared with married couples, are more unconventional in attitudes and behavior and enjoy a lifestyle that is more like singlehood than marriage (DeMaris & MacDonald, 1993; Rindfuss & VandenHeuvel, 1990). Freedom from the mutual obligations of marriage may prolong the honeymoon period of intimacy. Therefore, cohabiting couples might be expected to enjoy a heightened level of sexual activity compared with their married counterparts.

Model 1 in Table 12.1 shows the regression of sexual frequency on the dummy variable for cohabiting status. With only a categorical variable in the model, the analysis is equivalent to a one-way ANOVA. The intercept, 8.171, is the average monthly sexual frequency for married couples. The effect for cohabiting, 3.314, is the difference in average sexual frequency for cohabitors compared with marrieds.[5] Average sexual frequency is therefore about 3.3 more sexual acts per month for cohabitors. It would appear that cohabitors do have a more active sex life. However, cohabitors are also younger, on average, than marrieds and have shorter duration relationships compared with marrieds. Younger couples in shorter duration relationships have sex more often, regardless of marital status. We suspect, therefore, that the impact of cohabiting is confounded with both age and duration. Model 2 confirms this. Once the female's age and the duration of the relationship are in the model, the effect for cohabiting declines to an average difference of about 2.3 sex acts per month. As suspected, both duration and the female's age are negatively associated with sexual frequency.

Standardized Coefficients.   Researchers are frequently interested in which variable in their model has the strongest effect on Y. For example, from the magnitudes of the unstandardized coefficients in Model 2, it appears that cohabiting status has the strongest effect. The impact of age also appears to be quite a bit stronger than that of duration. This is misleading because these variables are all measured in different metrics. Age is in years, duration is in months, and the 0,1 metric for cohabiting is an arbitrary choice of numbers that has no real quantitative meaning. For comparison purposes, a more useful measure is the standardized coefficient, or beta, shown in Column 3 of Table 12.1. The beta for b_k is b_k (s_{xk}/s_y). It can also be thought of as the regression coefficient obtained when all variables are standardized before performing the regression. From the betas, it appears that it is female's age that has the strongest effect, followed by duration, followed by cohabiting. Except in covariance structure models (see chap. 13, this volume), I prefer unstandardized to standardized coefficients and almost never present the latter in regression tables. The unstandardized coefficient is much more interpretable. (The standardized coefficient is the expected standard deviation difference in Y for those who are a standard deviation apart on X_k, net of other factors in the model.) Moreover, the unstandardized coefficient can be compared in regressions across different groups of cases (e.g., males vs. females, Blacks vs. Whites). The standardized coefficients should never be used for this purpose because standard deviations for variables can vary across groups, although unstandardized coefficients remain the same. Standardization can therefore make it appear as if the same variable has different effects in different subpopulations purely due to changes in the distributions of the variables across groups.

INFERENCE AND ASSESSMENT OF MODEL FIT

Provided that the assumptions enumerated in the previous section are satisfied, a variety of inferential tests are of interest in regression. The researcher is usually interested first in which of the regressors in the model have important effects on Y. By *important* we typically mean nonzero. To test whether a particular regression coefficient, β_k, is nonzero in the population, we form a t statistic by taking the ratio of the coefficient to its estimated standard error ($\hat{\sigma}_b$). This statistic has degrees of freedom equal to $n - K - 1$ under the null hypothesis that β_k is zero. Hence, the test for a significant effect of cohabiting after controlling for age and relationship duration differences between cohabitors and marrieds is $t = 2.322/ .448 = 5.183$. With 2,993 degrees of freedom, this is a highly significant result ($p < .001$).[6]

Although testing individual coefficients is our primary interest, we usually precede these tests with a global test for whether any of the coefficients is nonzero. This affords some protection against the inflation of Type I error—significant findings through chance alone—that accrues to performing multiple tests. The global test is an F test, with degrees of freedom equal to K and $n - K - 1$ under the null hypothesis. This hypothesis is typically phrased as H_0: $\beta_1 = \beta_2 = \ldots = \beta_K = 0$. The alternative is H_1: At least one of the β_k is not zero. Actually, the test is more general. The null hypothesis is that every linear combination (weighted sum) of the coefficients is zero (Graybill, 1976). When it is rejected, we can conclude that at least one linear combination of the coefficients is not zero. (Note that a single coefficient is also a linear combination of the coefficients.) Thus, once in a while the researcher will not find any individual coefficients to be significant after rejecting the null. However, it is likely that some linear combination of the coefficients (probably one that is not of any interest to the researcher) would prove to be significant. The other instance in which a significant F test coincides with nonsignificant coefficient tests is under the condition of high collinearity among the regressors (discussed later). At any rate, the F of 82.744 for Model 2 has 3 and 2,993 degrees of freedom and is highly significant ($p < .001$). All of the coefficients are also individually significant.

Nested F Tests.   A variant of the global F that is very useful for comparing models is the nested F test. Model B is said to be nested within Model A if the parameters of Model B can be produced by placing constraints on the parameters in Model A. Model B is then a more parsimonious model, and may be preferred if one incurs no loss in fit compared with Model A. Only nested models may be compared using this test. Moreover, both models must utilize the same sample. The most common type of nesting is when the nested model results from setting one or more parameters of the parent model to zero. For example, Model 3 in Table 12.1 adds several variables to Model 2, including whether couples are in a first cohabiting or marital union for each partner (dummy coded $1 = yes$, $0 = no$); each partner's church attendance (from $1 = $ *never* to $9 = $ *more than once a week*), self-assessed health status (from $1 = $ *very poor* to $5 = $ *excellent*), and education; the couple's total household income; and whether the couple has children under age 5 in the household (dummy coded $1 = $ *yes*, $0 = $ *no*). Model 2 is therefore nested inside Model 3 by setting all of the added regression parameters to zero. Does this result in a significant loss in fit, or does adding these variables significantly enhance the fit? The test is:

$$\Delta F(\Delta df, n - K_A - 1) = \frac{(RSS_A - RSS_B)/\Delta df}{MSE_A}, \qquad (3)$$

where ΔF is the F statistic, Δdf is the difference in the number of parameters estimated in Model A versus Model B, K_A is the number of regressors in Model A, RSS is the regression sum of squares, and MSE is the mean squared residual. (This test can also be done with R^2 or SSE from each model; see Agresti & Finlay, 1997, for details.) For A $=$ Model 3, we have RSS $=$ 14,078.996 and MSE $=$ 39.415, and 13 parameters (including the intercept). For B $=$ Model 2, RSS $=$ 10,085.794, and there are four parameters. The test is therefore $[(14,078.996 - 10,085.794)/9]/39.415 = 11.257$, a very significant result ($p < .001$). It appears that the fit of the model is significantly enhanced when these additional factors are added. Except for household income, all of the new factors have significant effects on sexual frequency. The model suggests that sexual frequency is elevated among cohabitors, younger couples, those with shorter duration relationships, those who are in a first cohabiting or marital union for both partners, those among whom the male has infrequent but the female has frequent church attendance, healthier couples, less educated couples, and those with no children in the household under age 5.

It may be of interest to test whether regression coefficients are significantly different from each other. In Model 3 in Table 12.1, for example, the impacts of self-assessed health and education on sexual frequency seem to be about the same regardless of whether it is the male or female partner's attribute that is in question. To test whether males' and females' coefficients are different, we can again rely on the nested test.[7] The rationale for the test is as follows. For simplicity, consider just the following equation with four regressors:

$$Y = \alpha + \beta_1 X_1 + \beta_2 X_2 + \gamma_1 Z_1 + \gamma_2 Z_2 + \varepsilon. \qquad (4)$$

If $\beta_1 = \beta_2 = \beta$ and $\gamma_1 = \gamma_2 = \gamma$, then the equation is

$$Y = \alpha + \beta X_1 + \beta X_2 + \gamma Z_1 + \gamma Z_2 + \upsilon$$

$$= \alpha + \beta(X_1 + X_2) + \gamma(Z_1 + Z_2) + \upsilon. \qquad (5)$$

In other words, Eq. (5) is recovered from Eq. (4) by imposing restrictions on the coefficients in Eq. (4), which means that Eq. (5) is nested inside Eq. (4). The nested test in Eq. (3) applied to these two models tests the simultaneous restrictions $\beta_1 = \beta_2$ and $\gamma_1 = \gamma_2$. Equation (5) is estimated by summing scores for X_1 and X_2 into one scale, summing the scores for Z_1 and Z_2 into a second scale, and then regressing Y on these two scales (as shown in Eq. [5]). With respect to the prior substantive example, we need merely sum the scores for health and education for males and females in Model 3 and enter these sums in place of the separate variables. Model 4 in Table 12.1 shows the results. It estimates two fewer parameters than Model 3 because males' and females' slopes are assumed to be the same. These common values (the coefficients for the summated health and education variables) are shown in place of the separate coefficients in Model 3. The difference in fit of Model 4 versus Model 3 is nonsignificant ($df = .026, p > .97$), suggesting that the null hypothesis of equal effects should not be rejected.

Assessing Model Fit

Perhaps the most universally used measure of the fit of the model to the data in linear regression is R^2. There are many other ways to assess the adequacy of a model (see Myers, 1986, for a discussion). However, as a single measure, R^2 has much to recommend it. Nevertheless, its use has generated some controversy (Achen, 1982; King, 1985), so it is worth reviewing here in some detail. First, what population parameter does this statistic estimate? King maintained that there is no corresponding parameter in the population: "Thus, R^2 is not an estimator because there exists no relevant population parameter" (p. 676). Strictly speaking, this notion is accurate. Assuming that Y and the Xs are described by a multivariate normal distribution (a standard assumption in multivariate analyses), the distribution of Y, given the Xs, is completely described by the means, variances, and covariances of the variables (Greene, 1997). These are, in fact, the only parameters of the distribution.

However, it is a simple matter to define a new parameter, P^2 (Rho-squared), as the ratio of existing parameters. In particular, P^2 is the ratio of the variance of the conditional mean to the total variance in Y. This can be seen by considering the total variance in Y:

$$\text{Var}(Y) = \text{Var}(\alpha + \sum_{k=1}^{K} \beta_k X_{ki} + \varepsilon) = \text{Var}(\alpha + \sum_{k=1}^{K} \beta_k X_{ki}) + \text{Var}(\varepsilon). \quad (6)$$

(The partitioning of the variance of Y in the rightmost term in Eq. [6] is made possible by virtue of the assumption that $\text{Cov}(X_k, \varepsilon) = 0$ for all k.) Here it is evident that the variance in Y is composed of two parts. The first part of the rightmost term in Eq. (6) is the variance of the conditional mean of Y, which is modeled as a function of the regressors in the model. The second part is the variance of the conditional errors or the variance of the spread of points around the conditional mean. If all of the variation in Y is due to variation of the conditional mean with the regressors, and there is no variation around the conditional mean, we would have a perfect fit of the model to the data. That is, all of the variation in Y would be due to the variation of the regression function for the conditional mean; given the Xs, all Y values would be predicted perfectly. There would be no variation in Y once the regressor values were known. This would represent the ideal (but, of course, unrealistic) case in which our model correctly identified all of the causes of Y. However, if the conditional mean of Y does not change with the regression function, the variation of the conditional mean is zero. That is, if all of the βs are zero (all of the Xs have zero slopes), the conditional mean of Y, according to the model, is just α. This is a constant with no variation. All of the variation in Y would then be due to factors not in the model, represented collectively by ε. Dividing both sides of Eq. 6 by the variance of Y, we get:

$$1 = \frac{Var(\alpha + \sum \beta_k X_k)}{Var(Y)} + \frac{Var(\varepsilon)}{Var(Y)}, \tag{7}$$

where the index of summation has been suppressed for simplification. The first term on the right-hand side of Eq. 7 is P^2. It is the proportion of the variance of Y that is due to the variance of the conditional mean. In other words, it is the variance in Y accounted for by the regressors in the model, assuming that the model is correctly specified.[8] This expression can be further reduced:

$$1 = P^2 + \frac{Var(\varepsilon)}{Var(Y)}.$$

This provides another definition of P^2:

$$P^2 = 1 - \frac{Var(\varepsilon)}{Var(Y)}. \tag{8}$$

The sample analog of Eq. (6) is the partioning of the sum of squares in Y—a measure of the total variability in Y:

$$\sum (Y - \bar{Y})^2 = \sum (\hat{Y} - \bar{Y})^2 + \sum (Y - \hat{Y})^2$$

or TSS = RSS + SSE, where TSS stands for total sum of squares (in Y), RSS is the regression sum of squares, and SSE is the sum of squared errors (residuals). R^2 is then $1 - SSE/TSS$, which is analogous to Eq. (8).

R^2 is clearly seen to be an estimate of a population parameter, P^2, which has considerable intuitive appeal in terms of identifying the causal influences on Y. However, it does have some drawbacks. First, it is a biased estimate of P^2. In particular, the expected value of R^2 when $P^2 = 0$ is $K/(n-1)$ (Stevens, 1986). Assuming that $P^2 = 0$, a model with 10 regressors would still be expected to produce an R^2 of 10/50, or .2, with a sample of 51 cases. Therefore, one can easily inflate R^2 by adding more predictors to the model, especially in small samples, even when one's model is of no utility in the population. Moreover, R^2 is very sample dependent. The regression equation developed using a particular sample always produces the highest R^2 with that particular sample.[9] With a different sample, the prediction using that equation is not as good. A better estimate of P^2 is the adjusted R^2, R^2_a, defined as $1 - MSE/MSTO$, where MSE is the mean squared error and MSTO is the mean total sum of squares, or sample variance of Y. In that MSE is a consistent estimator of σ^2 (the variance of ε) and the sample variance of Y is a consistent estimator of the population variance of Y, R^2_a is a consistent estimator of P^2.

A second issue is that R^2 is typically of little interest in theoretical models. The goal of such models is not to maximize the variability accounted for in Y, but rather to investigate whether explanatory variables have the effects on Y that are predicted by theory. As a result, R^2s are typically quite low in theoretical research. For example, the maximum R^2 or R^2_a in Table 12.1 suggests that I have accounted for only about 10% of the variation in sexual frequency with the regression analysis. However, given the multifaceted determinants of sexual response, many of which are purely biological, why should we expect to account for most of its variation using only social variables? Rather, our interest is in examining how the interplay of social factors contributes to sexual response, acknowledging that many other factors also come into play. If the goal of the analysis is to produce a model for the accurate prediction of Y in a new sample, a high R^2 may be more important. In this instance, accurate forecasting is the primary goal. Factors are included in the model because they are good predictors of Y, regardless of whether their relationship to Y is truly causal.

Finally, larger R^2s do not necessarily imply a better model. As mentioned, a given model is likely to produce a larger R^2 in a small, compared with a large, sample. R^2s also tend to be larger when attitudes are used to predict other attitudes, which often only reflects the fact that people tend to be consistent in their answers to survey questions. R^2s also tend to be large in longitudinal studies of change, in which the Time 1 version of a variable is a control in models for the Time 2 measure. As an example, a model for sexual frequency in Wave 2 of the NSFH, using only Wave 1 sexual frequency, and two dummy variables representing cohabiting status—one flagging cohabitors who married between waves and the other flagging those cohabiting at both time periods (married couples are the omitted category)—results in an R^2 of .221. However, much of this predictive power is due to the strong relationship between sexual frequency at both times. In fact, the regression of Time 2 sexual frequency on Time 1 sexual frequency alone produces an R^2 of .218. In summary, R^2 is a good measure of the model's predictive power. Whether this is of much interest in an analysis is up to the researcher to determine.

DATA PROBLEMS: MULTICOLLINEARITY AND INFLUENCE

Frequently the analyst encounters problems in the data that interfere with good estimation of the population regression. The two most well known are multicollinearity and influence.

Multicollinearity

Recall that an assumption of estimation by OLS is that no regressor is a perfect linear combination of the other regressors in the model. This assumption may be literally satisfied—no regressor is an exact linear combination of the other regressors. However, there can be situations in which one or more regressors is almost a perfect linear combination of the other regressors. This is the situation referred to as *multicollinearity*. What are the consequences? First, it should be noted that multicollinearity has no effect on model fit. It is possible to have a high R^2 in the presence of substantial collinearity among the regressors. What is affected are the estimates of individual coefficients. Myers (1986) showed that both the magnitudes and variances of OLS coefficient estimates become upwardly biased in the presence of multicollinearity. Under these conditions, it becomes difficult to obtain good estimates of coefficients for the affected variables.

Severe multicollinearity presents certain classic symptoms that the researcher should learn to recognize: (a) A large R^2 or significant F test is accompanied by coefficients that are all nonsignificant; (b) magnitudes of coefficients are unreasonably large; (c) signs of coefficients are counterintuitive; and (d) standardized coefficients are outside the range of -1 to 1. Even in the absence of such symptoms, however, it is easy to tell whether collinearity poses any problems in estimation. The best indicator of the problem is the variance inflation factor (VIF) for each coefficient in the model. This value represents the factor by which the variance of b_k is inflated, compared with the ideal situation in which all regressors are uncorrelated with each other. The VIF for the kth coefficient is defined as $1/(1 - R^2_k)$, where R^2_k represents the R^2 for the regression of X_k on all other regressors in the model. R^2_ks over .9—that is, VIFs over 10—signal problems with collinearity (Myers, 1986). The VIF is a standard option in most regression software.

The problem of multicollinearity in multiple regression is often overrated. It is only likely to cause diffculties in models that employ cross-products among the predictors (discussed later). It typically presents no problems in main effects models—that is, models without cross-products terms. For example, consider the models in Table 12.1. One would think that Models 3 or 4 would be riddled with collinearity because they use both partners' scores on church attendance, health, and education. Because intimate partners tend to be alike in many respects, their values on the same variables tend to be at least moderately correlated. Nevertheless, the highest VIFs in either model are for male and female church attendance, and both are only 1.84. Clearly, collinearity does not present any difficulties here.

If multicollinearity is a problem in a main effects model, there are two good solutions: Drop one of the collinear variables or combine the collinear variables. In fact, the first solution has been practiced in all analyses in this chapter. Because partners' ages are highly correlated (around .9 in the current data), I use only female age as a proxy for the age of the couple. If one variable is almost perfectly correlated with another, then most of the information contained in the second variable is also contained in the first. Why include both? The second solution would have been to have combined the two ages, for example, by averaging them. If the researcher has several highly correlated items that tap the same underlying construct, then combining the items into one scale is an advisable practice.

An alternative approach is to abandon OLS and use biased estimators of the coefficients. This is the strategy of both ridge and principal components regression (Myers, 1986). In the presence of high collinearity, either approach provides estimates that are likely to be much closer to the true values of the parameters compared with OLS. However, the major drawback to these techniques is that there are no tests of significance for the coefficients. In that the coefficients are biased and the extent of the bias is not known, it is not possible to determine the expected value of the parameter estimate under the null hypothesis. This precludes the construction of a test statistic.

Influence

Occasionally, there are certain observations that exert undue influence on the analysis. This may or may not be problematic. It may simply be that only a few observations are really driving the results, that is, being responsible for producing the observed effects of the regressors. If these observations represent valid cases, there is little that the analyst can or should do to change the situation. However, these observations may represent either data points that have not been adequately accounted for by model parameters or, worse, bad data. Bad data can arise in several ways. Values may have been incorrectly entered into data fields. Conversely, values may represent bogus responses on the part of subjects who have not taken the study seriously or are purposely trying to sabotage it. Identifying high-influence observations is therefore often of interest to the researcher. The following discussion draws heavily on Myers (1986).

I discuss three statistics that are especially useful in this regard. All are available as optional regression output in both SAS and STATA statistical software. The first is called the R-student statistic. It is defined for the ith observation as:

$$t_i = \frac{y_i - \hat{y}_i}{s_{-i}\sqrt{1 - h_{ii}}}, \tag{9}$$

where s_{-i} is the root mean-squared residual estimated without the ith data point in the regression (a good measure of σ when there are influential observations), and h_{ii}, called the HAT diagonal for the ith observation, is the standardized distance of the ith data point's X values from the average of the X values. The HAT diagonal is a measure of how much leverage an observation has to affect the regression and ranges from $1/n$ to a maximum of 1, with an average value of $(K+1)/n$. Values greater than about twice the average are considered to have strong leverage. As is evident from Eq. (9), observations with considerable leverage (h_{ii} is large) and substantial residuals produce large t_i values. R-student values of 2 or more signify potentially influential observations.

The actual influence exerted by an observation is measured by how much regression coefficients would change if that observation were left out of the analysis. The amount of change exerted by the ith observation on the jth individual coefficient is tapped by the DFBETA statistic:

$$DFBETA_{ij} = \frac{b_j - b_{j,-i}}{s_{-i}\sqrt{c_{jj}}}, \tag{10}$$

where $b_{j,-i}$ is the jth coefficient estimated by leaving the ith observation out of the regression, and the denominator of Eq. (10) is an estimate of the standard error of b_j. This statistic indicates by how many standard errors the coefficient changes when the ith observation is left out of the regression. Although DFBETAs are useful, the researcher has to look at $n(K+1)$ of these for a given analysis. With large samples, that is a lot of output to peruse. Instead, a composite measure of the influence of the ith data point on the set of regression coefficients is Cook's Distance, or D_i. It represents the standardized distance between the set of regression coefficients computed with the ith observation and the set computed without the ith observation (see Myers, 1986, for its formula). D_i can be compared to an F statistic with K+1 and $n-K-1$ degrees of freedom to assess whether it indicates significant influence on the part of the ith data point. Also, the analyst can simply compare D_i across observations to see which D_i values stand out as unusually large.

An Example. In DeMaris (1997), I examined the relationship between sexual activity and violence in intimate relationships using a subsample of 2,435 married and cohabiting couples from the NSFH. I found sexual frequency to be greater among violent couples. I suggested that one possible explanation was that, when males had been violent, women were acquiescing to partners' sexual demands to avoid any further assaults. The data tended to support this interpretation. Only the male's violence was associated with elevated sexual activity. Moreover, theoretical considerations suggested that sex under conditions of fear should be associated with increased depression. I found that, although sexual frequency was not associated with women's depression overall, it did have a significant positive effect among couples in which the male had been violent. In other words, sexual activity was depressing to the female if the male partner (but not the female partner) had been violent.

To explore whether any influential observations were affecting these results, I examined all observations that had t_i greater than 2.5 in absolute value, h_{ii} values greater than .04 [equal to $2(K+1)/n$, where K was 45 and n was 2,435], and D_i values greater than 1.5 [an $F(46, 2389)$ of about 1.37 is significant at the .05 level]. I found one observation whose influence clearly stood out from the rest. This case had $t_i = -2.65$, $h_{ii} = .68$, and $D_i = .32$. Although D_i was not significant according to F criteria, this was the largest Cook's D value of any observation in the data. Also, the h_{ii} value suggested extremely substantial leverage. On closer examination, this case had a sexual frequency score (i.e., number of sex acts per month) of 93. Most likely, this was a bogus response, although the respondent could have been defining *having sex* in terms of any act of affection expressed by the couple (see e.g., the interpretation of this item by Donnelly, 1993). Nevertheless, I deleted this observation from the analysis and re-ran it. Before deleting the case, the coefficient for the interaction effect of male violence × sexual frequency on depression was .66, with a t value of 2.58. After deleting the case, the interaction term was .88, with a t value of 3.26. So, in this case, the effect of the influential observation was actually to suppress the interaction effect somewhat. Overall, however, deleting the errant case did not result in any substantive changes in the findings.

NONLINEARITY AND NONADDITIVITY

There are often times when the simple main effects model does not fit the data well. This section considers two departures from the simple main effects model: nonlinearity and nonadditivity. *Nonlinearity* refers to the situation in which the relationship between Y and X_k is other than linear. *Nonadditivity* refers to the situation in which another variable interacts with X_k in its influence on Y.

Nonlinearity

In Table 12.1, for example, I assumed that the association of female age with sexual frequency was linear. In fact, I found a significant linear effect of $-.144$ in Model 2. In actuality, I suspect that increasing age does not produce the same drop in sexual frequency at each level of age. Rather, it seems reasonable that, after a certain age, the drop is more gradual. Nevertheless, I start from a position of complete ignorance about the nature of any nonlinearity and simply explore it. One way to do this is to treat age as categorical and enter it into the model as a set of dummy variables that represent the number of categories minus one. I categorized age according to the quintiles of the age distribution. The resulting categories are (a) 26.5 or less, (b) 26.5 to 30.75, (c) 30.75 to 34, (d) 34 to 38.584, and (e) greater than 38.584. I then regressed sexual frequency on four age dummy variables, with the youngest age category omitted.[10] Model 1 is therefore:

$$E(\text{Sexual Frequency}) = \delta_1 + \delta_2 D_2 + \delta_3 D_3 + \delta_4 D_4 + \delta_5 D_5. \tag{11}$$

The results are shown in Model 1 in Table 12.2.

The dummy coefficients suggest that there is, indeed, a declining effect of age with increasing age. For example, the difference in sexual frequency between those in Category b versus Category a is -1.986, representing a drop of about two sex acts per month. However, Categories c, d, and e represent drops of only about .6 to .8 times per month compared with Category b. Is this degree of nonlinearity significant? A formal test of nonlinearity relies on the nesting concept. Model 2 is the simple linear regression of sexual frequency on Age Quintile, whose values represent the age categories (a–e): This is nested inside Model 1. Thus, a nested F test assesses whether we experience a significant loss in fit when we model the relationship as linear. The F value is 2.924, which is just significant ($p < .05$), suggesting significant nonlinearity in the relationship between sexual frequency and female age. In that the pattern of coefficients suggests a declining effect of age, I included Age Quintile Squared in Model 3. Does this effectively capture the nature of the nonlinearity? Again, because Model 3 is also nested inside Model 1, I can use the nested F test of Model 3 against Model 1 to assess this. The F value is 1.419, which is not significant. This suggests that the nonlinearity is adequately

TABLE 12.2
Unstandardized Coefficients for the Regression of Sexual Frequency
on Linear and Nonlinear Specifications of Female Age

Regressor	Model 1	Model 2	Model 3	Model 4	Model 5
Intercept	10.848***	11.344***	12.540***	18.175***	8.207***
Ages (26.5–30.75]	−1.986***				
Ages (30.75–34]	−2.666***				
Ages (34–38.584]	−3.431***				
Age > 38.584	−4.179***				
Age Quintile		−.984***	−2.011***		
Age Quintile^2			.172*		
Age				−.383***	
VIF (Age)				23.395	
Age^2				.003**	
VIF (Age^2)				23.395	
Centered Age					−.214***
VIF (Centered Age)					1.492
Centered Age^2					.003**
VIF (Centered Age^2)					1.492
ΔF		2.924*	1.419		

*$p < .05$. **$p < .01$. ***$p < .001$.

captured by a quadratic term. However, I prefer to use the continuous age variable, so Model 4 is:

$$E(\text{Sexual Frequency}) = \alpha + \beta(\text{Females' Age}) + \gamma(\text{Female's Age}^2). \quad (12)$$

The results of estimating Model 4 show that both the linear and quadratic effects are significant, but the VIFs for the coefficients are both way over 10, suggesting a collinearity problem. Whenever models include cross-products among variables, such as quadratic or interaction terms, main effects are highly correlated with the cross-products, producing multicollinearity. The degree of correlation can be minimized by first centering continuous variables and then constructing the cross-products (see Aiken & West, 1991, for a proof). Centering refers to deviating the variable from its mean. Model 5 shows the result of first centering the variable female's age, taking the square of the centered variable, and then reestimating Model 4. Notice that the collinearity is now well under control, with both VIFs under 1.5. The estimate of the main effect of female's age is now correspondingly deflated to a more accurate value of $-.214$.

Interpreting Quadratic Models. In Model 4, the effect of age is no longer constant. To see this, simply compute the mean difference in sexual frequency for a year's difference in female's age according to Eq. (12). If x is any value for female's age, we have $\alpha + \beta(x+1) + \gamma(x+1)^2 - \alpha - \beta x - \gamma x^2 = \alpha - \alpha + \beta(x+1) - \beta x + \gamma(x+1)^2 - \gamma x^2 = \beta(x+1-x) + \gamma[(x+1)^2 - x^2] = \beta + \gamma[x^2 + 2x + 1 - x^2] = \beta + \gamma + 2\gamma x$.[11] This is clearly now a function of x, or, in the example, the difference in sexual frequency for a year's difference in age depends on which ages are being compared. When X is centered, as in Model 5, it takes on the value 0 when the original variable is at its mean. The effect of X at its mean is then $\beta + \gamma + 2\gamma(0) = \beta + \gamma$. The estimate of the average difference in sexual frequency when the female is a year older than average, versus average age (33.429), is therefore $-.214 + .003 = -.211$. However, at age 53.429, a year's difference in age results in only a $-.214 + .003 + 2(.003)(53.429-33.429) = -.091$ difference in average sexual frequency (values in the rightmost parentheses reflect conversion of 53.429 to a centered age value).

Nonadditivity

Although cohabitors have more frequent sex, on average, compared with married couples, this difference may depend on the duration of the relationship. Over time, there is a tendency for sexual activity to become routinized regardless of marital status. Therefore, I expect that, among couples who have been together for considerable time, the difference between cohabitors and marrieds in average sexual frequency should be minimal. This suggests that relationship duration should moderate the impact of cohabitation on sexual frequency. Moderating effects are captured by including in the model the cross-product between the focus and moderator variables. In general, if X_1 is the focus variable and X_2 is the moderator, the interaction model is:

$$E(Y) = \alpha + \beta_1 X_1 + \beta_2 X_2 + \beta_3 X_1 X_2, \tag{13}$$

where $X_1 X_2$ is the product of X_1 and X_2.

In this model, the impact of X_1 is no longer constant across levels of X_2, but rather depends on the level of X_2. This can easily be seen by factoring the common multipliers of X_1 in Eq. (13) to isolate the partial slope with respect to X_1:

$$E(Y) = \alpha + \beta_2 X_2 + (\beta_1 + \beta_3 X_2) X_1. \tag{14}$$

Here it is evident that the partial slope for X_1 is $\beta_1 + \beta_3 X_2$. This expression should look familiar because it is a simple linear regression model. In other words, the impact of X_1 on Y is now modeled as a simple linear function of X_2. The main effect of X_1, β_1, is the effect of X_1 when X_2 is zero, which may or may not be of interest. As in the case of quadratic terms, introducing cross-product terms generates collinearity. Therefore, it is advisable to center the continuous variables involved in cross-product terms prior to computing cross-products. Centering not only reduces collinearity, but it has the added benefit of making the main effect of the focus variable more interpretable. If X_1 and X_2 are centered in Eq. (14), then β_1 is the effect of X_1 at the mean value of X_2.

Table 12.3 presents the results of the regression of sexual frequency on cohabiting, female age, and duration of the relationship, plus the cross-product of cohabiting with duration. Both age and duration were centered in the analysis, prior to computing age squared or the cross-product between cohabiting and duration. Model 1 presents the main effects model, with a quadratic term for female age, based on the analyses in Table 12.2. It is evident that, treating the effect of cohabitation as constant over durations, cohabitors have sex about 2.3 times more per month than marrieds—a statistically significant difference. However, Model 2 reveals a significant interaction between cohabitation and duration. The partial slope of cohabitation is .185 − .038 * duration. The main effect of cohabitation is nonsignificant. This means that at average duration of the relationship, which is 92.63 months, mean sexual frequency is no different for cohabitors as opposed to marrieds. However, for couples who have only been together for a year, the centered value of duration is 12 − 92.63 = −80.63, and the effect of cohabitation is .185 − .038(−80.63) = 3.249; that is, among couples together for 1 year, cohabitors are predicted to have sex about 3.2 more times per month on average.

Is this difference statistically significant? A test of the significance of the cohabitation effect at a particular duration is as follows. Let b_1 be the main effect of cohabitation, X_4 be duration, and b_5 be the interaction coefficient, as indicated in Table 12.3. Then the variance of the partial slope is the variance of $b_1 + b_5 X_4$,

TABLE 12.3
Unstandardized Coefficients for the Regression of Sexual Frequency
on Cohabitation, Female's Age, Relationship Duration,
and the Interaction of Cohabitation with Duration

Regressor	Model 1	Model 2
Intercept	8.165***	8.166***
b_1 (Cohabiting)	2.324***	.185
b_2 (Centered Age)	−.152***	−.150***
b_3 (Centered Age^2)	.001	.000[a]
b_4 (Centered Duration)	−.010***	−.009***
b_5 (Cohabiting × Duration)		−.038**
R^2	.077	.080

Partial Covariance Matrix of Parameter Estimates:

	b_1	b_5
b_1	.622979	.007595
b_5		.000136

[a]Coefficient is actually .000496.
*$p < .05$. **$p < .01$. ***$p < .001$.

which, by covariance algebra, is $V(b_1) + X_4^2 V(b_5) + 2X_4 Cov(b_1, b_5)$. To calculate the variance of the partial slope (whose square root is the standard error we are looking for), we need the covariance matrix of regression parameter estimates. This can be printed out in SPSS by requesting BCOV as part of the regression output (the comparable option keyword in SAS is COVB). From the covariance matrix of parameter estimates (partially reproduced in the bottom panel of Table 12.3), the estimates are: $V(b_1) = .622979$, $V(b_5) = .000136$, and $Cov(b_1, b_5) = .007595$. The value of X_4 (duration) is, again, −80.63. Thus, $V(b_1 + b_5 X_4) = .622979 + (−80.63)^2(.000136) + 2(−80.63)(.007595) = .282$. The standard error is the square root of this, or .531. A test of the partial slope of cohabitation at 1 year is then $t(2991) = 3.249/.531 = 6.119$, a highly significant result ($p < .001$).

Comparing Models Across Groups. A variant of interaction is the situation in which model coefficients might vary across groups. For example, does the same model of sexual activity apply to couples among whom both partners are in a first cohabiting or marital union versus other couples? Table 12.4 examines this issue. The model labeled *Combined Sample* presents the full model of sexual activity shown as Model 4 in Table 12.1, with the refinements shown in Model 2 of Table 12.3. However, the variable *First Union* has been omitted. There are two ways to explore whether the model is different for those in first unions versus others. One is to include the dummy variable *First Union* in the *Combined Sample* model, then to add in cross-product terms between First Union and all other predictors in the model and test whether this block of cross-products is significant

TABLE 12.4
Unstandardized Coefficients for the Regression of Sexual Frequency on
Sociodemographics: Overall, and by Whether the Couple Is in a First Union

Regressor	Combined Sample	First Union	Other
Intercept	9.439***	5.767***	10.093***
Cohabiting	−.154	1.651	−.602
Centered Age	−.156***	−.272***	−.174***
Centered Age^2	−.000^a	.004	−.000^a
Centered Duration	−.011***	.005	−.017***
Cohabiting × Duration	−.036**	−.000^a	−.040**
His Church Attendance	−.157**	−.276**	−.072
Her Church Attendance	.176**	.272**	.126
His Health	.481***	.690***	.348*
Her Health	.481***	.690***	.348*
His Education	−.183***	−.135***	−.167***
Her Education	−.183***	−.135***	−.167***
Household Income	.002	−.004	.002
Children Under 5	−1.382***	−1.474***	−1.328***
N	2,997	1,393	1,604
SSE	117,386.935	50,383.207	65,627.346
R^2	.109	.100	.132

^{a}Actual value is smaller than −.0005.
*$p < .05$. **$p < .01$. ***$p < .001$.

when added to the Combined Sample model. This is a somewhat cumbersome strategy. Aside from producing an unwieldy model, there is the added disadvantage of creating substantial collinearity and having to deal with both a nonlinear interaction and a second-order interaction.

The second strategy is to split the sample by First Union status to estimate the model separately for each group, and then test whether the model is different across groups. This test is called the Chow Test (Chow, 1960), and the null hypothesis for the test is that the collection of regression parameters is identical in each group. Table 12.4 presents the information necessary to do the test. The columns *First Union* and *Other* show the results of estimating the model separately for those in a First Union and Other couples, respectively. The test statistic is:

$$F(p, n-2p) = \frac{[SSE_c - (SSE_F + SSE_O)]/p}{(SSE_F + SSE_O)/(n-2p)},$$

where C, F, O represent the Combined, First Union, and Other samples, respectively, and p is the number of parameters in the model, including the intercept. (There are only 12 parameters because the effects for health and for education have been constrained to be equal.) In the example, the test is:

$$F(12,2973) = \frac{[117386.935 - (50383.207 + 65627.346)]/12}{(50383.207 + 65627.346)/2973}$$

= 2.939, which is quite significant ($p < .001$). Apparently, model parameters vary according to First Union status. In particular, there appears to be no difference in sexual frequency by cohabiting status for first unions. In other than first unions, the effect of cohabiting varies by duration, similar to the result found in Table 12.3.

SPECIAL TOPICS

Heteroskedasticity and Weighted Least Squares

A key assumption of OLS regression is that the error variance is constant at each covariate pattern in the model. If this assumption is violated, the errors are said to be heteroskedastic. One consequence is that the OLS estimates are inefficient. This means that there are other estimators that have smaller sampling variance. More important, however, the OLS estimates of the standard errors of the coefficients are biased, particularly if the heteroskedasticity is related to the regressors in the model, which is typically the case (Greene, 1997). This implies that tests of significance may be quite inaccurate when heteroskedasticity prevails.

There are two issues to consider: whether there is significant heteroskedasticity present in the model and what to do if there is. The first issue can be addressed by using White's (1980) test for heteroskedasticity. If this test statistic is significant, an alternative estimator can be used in place of OLS. The generalized least squares (GLS) estimator would be used in this case. Because the GLS estimator is implemented by applying OLS to variables that have been transformed by weighting,[12] this is also known as the weighted least squares (WLS) estimator. Both the test and WLS are relatively easy to implement using standard multiple regression software (see appendix for the program). Another alternative is to use OLS, but to employ another means of estimating the standard errors. One possiblity is White's heteroskedasticity-robust estimator of $V(\mathbf{b})$, where $\mathbf{b}$ represents the vector, or collection, of OLS estimates. This can be readily constructed with standard software, but requires some additional matrix programming (see appendix for the program).[13]

White's Test.   Suppose that the model of interest is $E(Y) = \alpha + \beta_1 X_1 + \beta_2 X_2 + \beta_3 X_3$. To perform White's test for heteroskedasticity, one first estimates the model using OLS and saves the residuals. One then regresses the squares of the residuals on all main effects in the model plus all nonredundant cross-products among the variables. If X_1, X_2, and X_3 are three different variables, their nonredundant cross-products are X_1^2, X_2^2, X_3^2, X_1X_2, X_1X_3, X_2X_3. White's test is then nR^2 for this analysis, where n is the sample size. This has a chi-squared distribution with degrees of freedom equal to the number of regressors in the model for the squared residuals under the null hypothesis of homoskedasticity.

Weighted Least Squares. The WLS estimates are the as and bs that minimize $\Sigma w_i e_i^2$, the sum of squares of the weighted residuals. The weight to be used is the reciprocal of the variance of the errors for the ith observation. Intuitively, this means that observations count more in building the fitted regression line if they have smaller variation at a given covariate pattern compared with others. These variances can be estimated by regressing the squared residuals from the substantive model on the substantive model's predictors. In other words, in a three-variable model, one first regresses Y on X_1, X_2, and X_3, to get e_i. Then one regresses e_i^2 on X_1, X_2, and X_3, plus possible additional effects as needed. From this regression, one obtains the predicted values and uses the reciprocals of these as the weights for the WLS analysis. The predicted squared residuals are estimates of the error variances as these vary with the regressors because $V(\varepsilon) = E[\varepsilon - \text{Mean}(\varepsilon)]^2 = E(\varepsilon^2)$ —Mean(ε) is zero, by assumption—and the predicted squared errors are estimates of $E(\varepsilon^2)$. Most statistical packages such as SPSS and SAS allow the analyst to request WLS simply by specifying the weight to be used.

An Example. Table 12.5 presents the results of OLS and WLS analyses of the effect of female's age, male's health, and female's health on sexual frequency for the 2,997 couples in my NSFH sample. Model 1 is the equation estimated by

TABLE 12.5
Unstandardized Coefficients for Ordinary and Weighted Least Squares
Analyses of Sexual Frequency, and Model for White's Test

Model (Response) Regressor	Model 1 (Sexual Frequency)	OLS $\hat{\sigma}_b$	Model 2 (e^2)	Model 3 (Sexual Frequency)	White's $\hat{\sigma}_b$
Intercept	12.298***	1.084	147.243	11.506***	1.085
Female's Age	−.181***	.014	−3.132	−.166***	.013
His Health	.335*	.171	−5.861	.365*	.166
Her Health	.179	.168	−11.179	.216	.169
Age²			.023*		
His Health²			−.084		
Her Health²			.295		
Age × His Health			.040		
Age × Her Health			.023		
His Health × Her Health			1.696		
R^2_{ols}	.05635		.01350	.06370	
R^2_{wls}				.05597	
Weight for Analysis	1.000		1.000	$1/\hat{e}^2$	

*$p < .05$. **$p < .01$. ***$p < .001$.

OLS. The next column shows the standard errors of the coefficients that are estimated by OLS. Female's age and male's health are both significant, but female's health is not once male's health is held constant. The R^2 is .05635, as shown at the bottom of the table. Model 2 regresses the squared residuals from Model 1 on the terms needed for White's test. The R^2 for this analysis is .0135, and White's test is therefore 2997(.0135) = 40.1598, which, with 9 degrees of freedom, is highly significant ($p < .00001$). This suggests that the errors for Model 1 are heteroskedastic. I next regressed the squared residuals on the main effects of female's age, male's health, and female's health, plus female's age squared (not shown). The quadratic term is needed to correctly model the squared residuals, as is evident in Model 2. Without this effect in the model, 10 cases have negative weights and would be omitted from the WLS run.

Using the reciprocals of the estimated squared residuals from this last run as weights produces Model 3, the WLS model. The WLS estimates are somewhat different from the OLS ones, and the WLS standard errors (not shown in the table) are uniformly smaller (.012, .161, and .163, for female's age, male's health, and female's health, respectively). In any case, substantive conclusions would be the same with either Model. The White heteroskedasticity-robust standard errors of the parameter estimates in Model 1 are shown in the last column of the table. These are relatively close to those estimated by OLS, so, in this case, we are not led too astray just using the OLS results. Two R^2s are shown for the WLS model. The OLS R^2 is .0637. This is the R^2 value that is reported as part of the output. The reader should notice something fishy about this value. In particular, it is larger than the value in Model 1, the OLS model, which is .05635. But OLS maximizes R^2. Hence, the variance explained in sexual frequency using the WLS estimates cannot possibly be higher. This anomaly occurs because the R^2 that is reported by the program is not the variation explained in sexual frequency per se. Rather, the program transforms the regressors and the response using the weights to accomplish WLS. Hence, this R^2 is the variation explained in the transformed version of sexual frequency using the transformed versions of the regressors. The correct R^2 for WLS is found by using the WLS estimates to compute a prediction error for each case, e*, and then computing

$$R^2_{wls} \text{ as } 1 - \frac{\sum e^{*2}}{SS_y},$$

where SSy is the sum of squares in Y. That value is .05597 for Model 3, which is slightly lower than the OLS R^2 as expected.

Complex Sampling and Weighted Ordinary Least Squares

Large-scale surveys of the general population, such as the NSFH, are usually based on complex sampling designs that oversample various underrepresented groups. For example, the NSFH oversampled minorities, one-parent families,

families with stepchildren, cohabitors, and recently married persons (Sweet et al., 1988). Case weights are therefore provided that adjust the proportions of these groups in the sample to their corresponding proportions in the population. Case weights are necessary for the unbiased estimation of univariate population characteristics; however, it is not clear that they should be used in multivariate analyses. In what follows, I draw heavily on Winship and Radbill's (1994) lucid discussion of this issue.

There are two main problems with weighting cases in regression analyses—a strategy that Winship and Radbill referred to as *weighted ordinary least squares* (WOLS). First, if errors in the unweighted sample are homoskedastic, sample weights will make them heteroskedastic. Second, estimates of the standard errors of coefficients produced by software packages for WOLS are typically incorrect. If the weights are a function of the Xs included in the model and the model is correctly specified, unweighted OLS is the preferred technique. Unweighted OLS will provide the most efficient estimates and will also produce unbiased estimates of the coefficient standard errors. If the parameter estimates from weighted and unweighted analyses differ, this is an indication that the model is not correctly specified; that is, it omits important predictors or nonlinear effects of predictors that are in the model. To discern whether weighted and unweighted analyses are significantly different, Winship and Radbill advocated using the test developed by DuMouchel and Duncan (1983). The test is performed as follows: If the model being estimated is

$$E(Y) = \alpha + \sum \beta_k X_k$$

and W is the case weight, then one also estimates the model

$$E(Y) = \alpha + \sum \beta_k X_k + \delta_0 W + \sum \delta_k W X_k,$$

where WX_k represents the cross-product of the weight with the kth regressor, and the δs are just the regression coefficients for effects involving the weights. A nested F test for the difference between these two models then reveals whether the weighted and unweighted analyses are significantly different. If they are not, then unweighted OLS should be used. If they are, the researcher could then attempt to respecify the model. If that does not fix the problem, he or she could then use WOLS and the White estimator of V(**b**) to correct the estimated standard errors of the coefficients.

An Example. I examine whether WOLS should be used for Model 2 in Table 12.1. That model is reproduced as Model 1 in Table 12.6. Model 2 shows the WOLS estimates using the case weights provided in the NSFH. The weights have been further adjusted to sum to the unweighted sample size. The estimates are slightly different, although the largest change is in the intercept. Are the estimates

TABLE 12.6
Ordinary Least Squares and Weighted Ordinary Least Squares Results for the
Regression of Sexual Frequency on Cohabitation, Female's Age, and Duration

Regressor	Model 1	Model 2	Model 3
Intercept	13.969***	13.913***	14.490***
Cohabiting	2.322***	3.086***	-1.186
Female's Age	-.144***	-.149***	-.131***
Duration	-.010***	-.009***	-.014**
Weight			-.819
Weight × Cohabiting			4.498***
Weight × Female's Age			-.012
Weight × Duration			.005
Weight for Analysis	1.000	Case Weight	1.000
R^2	.077	.087	.081
ΔF			3.945**

*$p < .05$. **$p < .01$. ***$p < .001$.

significantly different? Model 3 adds the weight variable plus all interactions of the weight with the predictors in the model. DuMouchel and Duncan's F test is 3.945, which is significant at $p < .01$. Therefore, the weighted and unweighted models are indeed different. In this case, the model is clearly misspecified because, as the Combined Model of Table 4 reveals, several other terms should be included to properly model sexual frequency.

Comparing Regression Coefficients Across Models

Frequently researchers compare regression coefficients across equations to see whether the effect of some variable changes when other variables are added. It is common practice to conclude that an effect has changed if it changes in value or if it is statistically significant at first but becomes nonsignificant when other predictors are added. These informal guidelines do not constitute a formal test. Such a test has been developed by Clogg, Petkova, and Haritou (1995). Suppose that the baseline model is:

$$Y = \alpha + \sum \beta_p^* X_p + \varepsilon \qquad (15)$$

and the analyst adds a set of q predictors so that the full model is:

$$Y = \alpha + \sum \beta_p X_p + \sum \gamma_q Z_q + \upsilon. \qquad (16)$$

Let $\delta_k = \beta_k^* - \beta_k$. The sample estimate of δ_k is d_k, the sample difference between the coefficients for the same variable in each model. The null hypothesis for the test is that $\delta_k = 0$, that is, there is no difference in the kth β between the model in Eq. (15) and the model in Eq. (16). The test statistic is $d_k/s(d_k)$, which is distributed as t with $n - (p+q) - 1$ degrees of freedom under the null hypothesis that δ_k is zero. The estimated variance of d_k, $s^2(d_k)$, is $s^2(b_k) - s^2(b_k^*)\dfrac{\hat{\sigma}_v^2}{\hat{\sigma}_\varepsilon^2}$, where s^2 is the estimated variance of a coefficient, and the MSEs from the models are used to estimate the error variances.

An Example.   Returning to Table 12.1, part of the cohabiting effect in Model 1 seems to be accounted for by the age of the couple and the length of time they have been together. When the latter variables are included in Model 2, the cohabiting effect is diminished. To test whether this coefficient change is significant, I apply the Clogg et al. (1995) test. The variance of the cohabiting coefficient is .201 in both models, so the variance of the difference between coefficients is .201 − .201(40.631/43.183) = .012. The standard error of the difference is just the square root of this value, or .11. The test is then .992/.11 = 9.018. With 2,993 degrees of freedom, this is a highly significant result ($p < .001$).

This chapter covered a variety of issues in both the theory and practice of the multiple linear regression model. Those wishing to further their expertise in this area are advised to pursue additional works on the topic, many of which are recommended later.

SUGGESTED READINGS

Those wishing an elemental but authoritative introduction to multiple regression will find Allison (1999) very accessible. The book by McClendon (1994) and the regression chapters in Agresti and Finlay (1997) are also excellent resources for those wishing a relatively nontechnical approach. Both works have solid treatments of the estimation of ANOVA and ANCOVA models using regression. Aiken and West (1991) is especially useful for those interested in modeling interaction. Those with more mathematical sophistication should read Hanushek and Jackson (1977) for a rigorous treatment of regression issues. Myers (1986) is especially good at explaining more advanced topics, such as collinearity and influence diagnostics, criteria for comparing models, and WLS. A rigorous and still more advanced treatment of regression can be found in Greene (1997). The two latter works are advised only for those who are conversant in matrix algebra.

APPENDIX: ANNOTATED SAS PROGRAM
FOR ANALYSES IN TABLE 12.5

The SAS code shown next was used to accomplish the following analyses shown in Table 12.5: (a) the OLS regression of sexual frequency on the predictor set, (b)

White's test for heteroskedasticity, (c) the WLS regression of sexual frequency on the predictor set, (d) R^2_{wls}, and (e) White's heteroskedasticity-robust estimate of V(**b**). The definitions of SAS variable names are as follows:

SAS Name	Variable Label
COITFREQ	Sexual frequency
FEMAGE	Female's age
MHEALTH	His health
FHEALTH	Her health
FEMSQ	Female's age-squared
MHESQ	His health-squared
FHESQ	Her health-squared
FEMHIM	Female's age × his health
FEMHER	Female's age × her health
HIMHER	His health × her health
ERROR	Residuals from OLS run
ERRSQ	Squares of residuals from OLS run
ERRHAT	Predicted squared residual (estimate of the heteroskedastic error variance)
WTVAR	Weight used in the WLS run
YHATWLS	Predicted sexual frequency according to the WLS estimates
EWLS	Prediction error (residual) for sexual frequency using WLS estimates
EWLSSQ	Squared prediction error for sexual frequency using WLS estimates

Program
    OLS regression of sexual frequency on the predictor set:
PROC REG; MODEL COITFREQ = FEMAGE MHEALTH FHEALTH;
OUTPUT OUT = WHITE R = ERROR;
    Creation of the squared OLS residual:
DATA WHITE; SET WHITE; ERRSQ = ERROR**2;
    Regression model for White's test for heteroskedasticity:
PROC REG; MODEL ERRSQ = FEMAGE MHEALTH FHEALTH FEMSQ
MHESQ FHESQ FEMHIM FEMHER HIMHER;
    Regression model for estimation of the heteroskedastic error variance, which forms the basis of the weight variable:
PROC REG; MODEL ERRSQ = FEMAGE MHEALTH FHEALTH FEMSQ;
OUTPUT OUT = WLS P = ERRHAT;
    Creation of weight for WLS:
DATA WLS; SET WLS; WTVAR = 1/ERRHAT;
    WLS regression model:
PROC REG; MODEL COITFREQ = FEMAGE MHEALTH FHEALTH;
WEIGHT WTVAR;
    Computing the correct R-squared for the WLS run:
DATA WLS; SET WLS;
YHATWLS = 11.506159 − .16608 * FEMAGE + .364585 * MHEALTH
+ .21605 * FHEALTH;

```
EWLS = COITFREQ - YHATWLS;
EWLSSQ = EWLS**2;
```

SAS code to obtain the sum of EWLSSQ across cases, and the variance of COITFREQ, for computing R^2_{wls}:

```
PROC MEANS N SUM VAR; VAR COITFREQ EWLSSQ;
```

SAS IML code to compute White's heteroskedasticity-robust estimate of V(**b**). The first four lines are duplicates of code shown earlier:

```
PROC REG; MODEL COITFREQ = FEMAGE MHEALTH FHEALTH;
OUTPUT OUT = WHITE R = ERROR;
DATA WHITE; SET WHITE;
ERRSQ = ERROR**2;
ONEVEC = 1;
IF COITFREQ = . THEN DELETE;
PROC IML; USE WHITE; READ ALL VAR {ONEVEC FEMAGE MHEALTH
FHEALTH} INTO X;
USE WHITE; READ ALL VAR {ERRSQ} INTO E;
XTX = X' * X;
XINV = INV(XTX);
DE = DIAG(E);
VARB = XINV * (X' * DE * X) * XINV; [Note: VARB is V(b), the White
```
hetcroskedasticity-robust covariance matrix of parameter estimates.]

NOTES

1. The central limit theorem says that a weighted sum of random variables converges in distribution to normal as n tends to infinity (Hoel, Port, & Stone, 1971). The b_ks are actually weighted sums of the Y_i, which is easily seen by considering the least squares estimator of the vector of partial slopes. The estimator is: $b = (X'X)^{-1}X'y$, or Gy, where $G = (X'X)^{-1}X'$, and y is the vector of Y scores for all observations in the sample. Therefore, each b_k is of the form $g^{i'}y$, where g_i is the ith row of G. This is clearly a weighted sum of the ys.
2. More formally, $\hat{\theta}$ is consistent for θ if $\lim_{n \to \infty} P(|\hat{\theta} - \theta| < \delta) = 1$, for every $\delta > 0$.
3. Throughout this chapter, the words *impact* and *effect* merely refer to the values of regression coefficients and are not necessarily meant in a causal sense.
4. See the appendix to chapter 13 for a brief tutorial in covariance algebra.
5. The model is: E(sexual frequency) = $\alpha + \delta$Cohabiting. When Cohabiting = 0 (i.e., the couple is married), E(sexual frequency) = α. For cohabitors, E(sexual frequency) = $\alpha + \delta$.
6. Standard errors of coefficients have been omitted from the tables in this chapter to conserve space. They should, however, be reported in substantive analyses, although they are rarely of interest. Nevertheless, some readers may want to see exactly how close to being significant one's nonsignficant results are. In my view, with large samples, coefficients that do not even reach the .05 level of significance are not worth investigating further.
7. The difference between any two coefficients b_j and b_k can also be tested by dividing the difference between sample coefficients by the estimated standard error of this difference. That is, $\dfrac{b_j - b_k}{\hat{\sigma}_{bj-bk}}$ is a

t statistic with $n - K - 1$ degree of freedom under the null hypothesis of no difference. The standard error of the difference between sample coefficients (the denominator) can be recovered from the covariance matrix of parameter estimates. The variance of this difference, by covariance algebra, is $V(b_j - b_k) = V(b_j) + V(b_k) - 2\text{cov}(b_j, b_k)$. The standard error is just the square root of this variance.

8. If the model is incorrectly specified, P^2 understates the variance accounted for by the regressor variables. Consider that the true model is $Y = \alpha + \beta X + \gamma X^2 + \varepsilon$, and one estimates $Y = \alpha + \beta X + \upsilon$. P^2 for the estimated model may actually be zero because nonlinearity in the nature of the relationship between X and Y has not been modeled. Therefore, it is more correct to describe P^2 as the variance accounted for by the model, rather than by X.

9. $R^2 = 1 - \text{SSE/TSS}$, and TSS is a constant in a particular sample. Therefore, in minimizing SSE, the OLS estimates also maximize R^2 for that sample.

10. To dummy up a five-category variable, I use four dummy variables. In this example, they are $D_2 = 1$ if the female is between ages 26.5 and 30.75, 0 otherwise; $D_3 = 1$ if age is between 30.75 and 34, 0 otherwise; $D_4 = 1$ if age is between 34 and 38.584, 0 otherwise; $D_5 = 1$ if age is greater than 38.584, 0 otherwise. The mean sexual frequency for the omitted category (those ages 26.5 or less) is just the intercept. Each dummy coefficient is then the difference in sexual frequency between those in the dummied category and those in the omitted category.

11. The partial slope of X in a quadratic model, using differential calculus, is actually $\beta + 2\gamma x$. However, this does not indicate the change in Y for a unit increase in X (the unit impact interpretation of the partial slope), as is commonly believed. Rather, it is the instantaneous change in Y with change in X at the point x. When the range of X is large, a unit change is envisioned to be an infinitesimal change, and the unit impact interpretation does little harm. Nevertheless, I prefer to use $\beta + \gamma + 2\gamma x$ to indicate the unit impact of X in the quadratic model because it is literally correct.

12. The OLS estimator of **b** is $(X'X)^{-1}X'y$. The generalized least squares estimator of **b** is $(X'\Omega^{-1}X)^{-1}X'\Omega^{-1}y$, where Ω is the variance-covariance matrix of the equation errors. Under heteroskedasticity, Ω is a diagonal matrix with σ_i^2 on the diagonal. The inverse of this matrix, Ω^{-1}, has the reciprocals of the error variances on the diagonal, and the square root of this inverse matrix, $\Omega^{-1/2}$, has the reciprocals of the error standard deviations on the diagonal. If y and the X matrix are premultiplied by $\Omega^{-1/2}$—equivalent to multiplying the ys and the Xs by the reciprocals of the error standard deviations—then applying OLS to these transformed variables leads to the estimator:

$$[(\Omega^{-1/2})X)'(\Omega^{-1/2}X)]^{-1}(\Omega^{-1/2}X)'\Omega^{-1/2}y =$$
$$(X'\Omega^{-1/2}{}'\Omega^{-1/2}X)^{-1}X'\Omega^{-1/2}\Omega^{-1/2}y =$$
$$(X'\Omega^{-1}X)^{-1}X'\Omega^{-1}y,$$

which is the GLS estimator (Greene, 1997).

13. The estimator is $(X'X)^{-1}X'D_{e i^2}X(X'X)^{-1}$, where X is the regressor matrix and $D_{e i^2}$ is a diagonal matrix with the squared OLS residuals from the substantive model on the main diagonal.

REFERENCES

Achen, C. H. (1982). *Interpreting and using regression.* Sage University Paper series on Quantitative Applications in the Social Sciences, 07-029. Beverly Hills, CA: Sage.

Agresti, A., & Finlay, B. (1997). *Statistical methods for the social sciences* (3rd ed.). Upper Saddle River, NJ: Prentice-Hall.

Aiken, L. S., & West, S. G. (1991). *Multiple regression: Testing and interpreting interactions.* Thousand Oaks, CA: Sage.

Allison, P. D. (1999). *Multiple regression: A primer.* Thousand Oaks, CA: Pine Forge.

Bollen, K. A. (1989). *Structural equations with latent variables.* New York: Wiley.

Chow, G. (1960). Tests of equality between sets of coefficients in two linear regressions. *Econometrica, 28,* 591–605.

Clogg, C. C., Petkova, E., & Haritou, A. (1995). Statistical methods for comparing regression coefficients between models. *American Journal of Sociology, 100*, 1261–1293.

DeMaris, A. (1995). A tutorial in logistic regression. *Journal of Marriage and the Family, 57*, 956–968.

DeMaris, A. (1997). Elevated sexual activity in violent marriages: Hypersexuality or sexual extortion? *Journal of Sex Research, 34*, 361–373.

DeMaris, A., & MacDonald, W. (1993). Premarital cohabitation and marital instability: A test of the unconventionality hypothesis. *Journal of Marriage and the Family, 55*, 399–407.

Donnelly, D. A. (1993). Sexually inactive marriages. *The Journal of Sex Research, 30*, 171–179.

DuMouchel, W. H., & Duncan, G. J. (1983). Using sample survey weights in multiple regression analyses of stratified samples. *Journal of the American Statistical Association, 78*, 535–543.

Graybill, F. A. (1976). *Theory and application of the linear model*. Boston: Duxbury.

Greene, W. H. (1997). *Econometric analysis* (3rd ed.). Upper Saddle River, NJ: Prentice-Hall.

Hanushek, E. A., & Jackson, J. E. (1977). *Statistical methods for social scientists*. New York: Academic Press.

Hoel, P. G., Port, S. C., & Stone, C. J. (1971). *Introduction to probability theory*. Boston: Houghton Mifflin.

Holland, P. H. (1986). Statistics and causal inference. *Journal of the American Statistical Association, 81*, 945–960.

Hosmer, D. W., & Lemeshow, S. (1989). *Applied logistic regression*. New York: Wiley.

James, W. H. (1981). The honeymoon effect on marital coitus. *The Journal of Sex Research, 17*, 114–123.

King, G. (1985). How not to lie with statistics: Avoiding common mistakes in quantitative political science. *American Journal of Political Science, 29*, 666–687.

McClendon, M. J. (1994). *Multiple regression and causal analysis*. Itasca, IL: Peacock.

Myers, R. H. (1986). *Classical and modern regression with applications*. Boston: Duxbury.

Rindfuss, R. R., & VandenHeuvel, A. (1990). Cohabitation: A precursor to marriage or an alternative to being single? *Population and Development Review, 16*, 703–726.

Sobel, M. E. (1998). Causal inference in statistical models of the process of socioeconomic achievement: A case study. *Sociological Methods & Research, 27*, 318–348.

Stevens, J. (1986). *Applied multivariate statistics for the social sciences*. Hillsdale, NJ: Lawrence Erlbaum Associates.

Sweet, J. A., Bumpass, L. L., & Call, V. (1988). *The design and content of the National Survey of Families and Households*. Madison, WI: The University of Wisconsin, Center for Demography and Ecology.

White, H. (1980). A heteroskedasticity-consistent covariance matrix estimator and a direct test for heteroskedasticity. *Econometrica, 48*, 817–838.

Winship, C., & Radbill, L. (1994). Sampling weights and regression analysis. *Sociological Methods & Research, 23*, 230–257.

13
▼▼▼▼▼▼▼

Covariance Structure Models

Alfred DeMaris
Bowling Green State University

A covariance structure model—also known as a structural equation model—is a mathematical model for the structure that underlies a covariance matrix. This nomenclature brings a variety of well-known techniques under the same umbrella, including path analysis, factor analysis, LISREL modeling, seemingly unrelated regressions, and simultaneous equations models. This chapter presents an introduction to covariance structure modeling, with particular attention to path analysis, factor analysis, and LISREL models. Because these are all variants of regression models, it is assumed that the reader has a solid understanding of multiple regression. To illustrate the paradigm of covariance structure analysis, I begin with traditional path analysis. I then turn to factor analysis, distinguishing confirmatory from exploratory approaches. Last, I consider the full covariance structure, or LISREL, model, which is a combination of path and factor analysis.

Substantive examples are based on data from the National Survey of Families and Households (NSFH). This is a panel study of a national probability sample of households in the coterminous United States based on surveys taken in 1987–1988 and 1992–1994 (details of the design and implementation of the first survey are given in Sweet, Bumpass, & Call, 1988). The subset of respondents employed for analyses in this chapter consists of cohabiting or married mothers with a child between the ages of 11 and 18 in 1987–1988, whose child was also interviewed in 1992–1994. At that time, the children were between the ages of 17 and 25. One goal of the analyses was to examine the degree to which modern gender role attitudes of mothers in 1987–1988 predicted children's sexual attitudes and behavior in 1992–1994. Hence, only cases in which the child had had sexual intercourse by 1992–1994 were included. Mothers' gender role attitudes were measured by their extent of agreement with seven statements, such as "Preschool children are likely to suffer if their mother is employed" or "When both partners work full-time they should share household tasks equally." Two summated scales were created from these items: *mother's endorsement of women working* (Cronbach's alpha = .78) and *mother's gender egalitarianism* (alpha = .42). *Childrens' sexual permissiveness* was measured with the sum of four items reflecting a permissive attitude toward sexual behavior (alpha = .69). A typical item was, "It is all right for an unmarried couple to live together even if they have no interest in considering marriage." *Children's sexual adventurism* (alpha = .46) consisted of the sum of four items reflecting permissive sexual behavior: age at first intercourse (reverse coded), lifetime number of different sexual partners, frequency of sexual intercourse in the past month, and number of different sexual partners in the past month. Because these items varied in metric, they were standardized prior to summing.

PATH ANALYSIS

Path models provide a good starting point for the chapter. A path model is a mathematical or graphical depiction of a causal system. (The term *causal* is used throughout the chapter in a guarded sense. See the discussion of causality in chap. 12, this volume, for clarification.) An example is shown in Fig. 13.1. In the figure, I propose that both mother's endorsement of women working (W) and mother's gender egalitarianism (E) affect a child's sexual permissiveness (S), and all three variables affect a child's sexual adventurism (A). The arrows show the direction

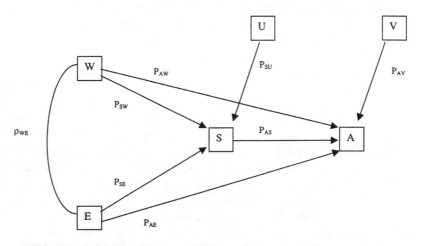

FIG. 13.1   Path model for relationships among mothers' endorsement of women working (W), mothers' gender egalitarianism (E), child's sexual permissiveness (S), and child's sexual adventurism (A).

of causal influence and, moreover, indicate linear relationships. The symbols on the arrows (e.g., "P_{AW}") are merely standardized regression coefficients—called *path coefficients*—that depict the linear effect of the causal variable on the effect variable. It is a convention in covariance structure models that the first subscript indexes the variable the arrow is pointing to, and the second subscript indexes the variable from which the arrow is coming. Two other variables appear in the system: U and V. These are typically referred to as *disturbances* and reflect all other variables that affect S and A but are left out of the model. They are equivalent to the error term in a linear regression. It is assumed that these omitted factors are uncorrelated with each other, as well as with other predictors that point to the same variable in the diagram. W and E are allowed to be correlated, as indicated by the curved line that connects them. It is also assumed that all variables are in standardized form; that is, they have means of zero and standard deviations of one. The variables S and A are called *endogenous* because they are determined by variables within the system. W and E are referred to as *exogenous* variables because their determinants lie outside of the system.

The model and the assumptions just delineated can also be represented by a set of equations, often called *structural equations*. These are:

$$S = P_{SW} W + P_{SE} E + P_{SU} U \tag{1}$$

$$A = P_{AW} W + P_{AE} E + P_{AS} S + P_{AV} V. \tag{2}$$

Also, $Cov(W,U) = Cov(E,U) = Cov(W,V) = Cov(E,V) = Cov(S,V) = Cov(U,V) = 0$. Each equation is a regression model in standard form. For example, the expression "$P_{SW} W$" means that the coefficient P_{SW} is multiplied by the variable W, just like βX represents a coefficient times a variable's value in ordinary regression models.

Understanding covariance structure models requires a slight reorientation compared with conventional regression analyses. In the latter, the focus is on accounting for values of a response variable for individual cases, using linear relations between the response and a set of regressor variables. In the analyses in this chapter, the focus is on accounting for variances and covariances in a covariance matrix. It is assumed in path analysis that all variables are standardized. Therefore, variances are all equal to one, and covariances are correlations. Hence, the focus in path analysis is on accounting for correlations among variables using the parameters of the structural model—Eqs. (1) and (2). The correlations among W, E, S, and A for the 357 mothers and their adolescents in my sample are shown in Table 13.1.

How are correlations attributed to the parameters of the model? To see this, we must use covariance algebra to decompose the correlation into its parts. (Readers unfamiliar with covariance algebra should review Appendix A before proceeding with the rest of the chapter.) For example, the correlation between S and W is (re-

TABLE 13.1
Correlation Matrix for Variables in Path Model of Children's
Sexual Attitudes and Adventurism Depicted in Fig. 13.1

	Mothers' Endorsement of Women Working	Mothers' Gender Egalitarianism	Child's Sexual Permissiveness	Child's Sexual Adventurism
Mothers' Endorsement of Women Working (W)	1.000			
Mothers' Gender Egalitarianism (E)	.142**	1.000		
Child's Sexual Permissiveness (S)	.134*	.024	1.000	
Child's Sexual Adventurism (A)	.015	−.000[a]	.210***	1.000

[a]Coefficient is less than .0005 in absolute value.
*$p < .05$. **$p < .01$. ***$p < .001$.

call that the covariance between standardized variables is the same as the correlation):

$$Corr(S,W) = Cov(S,W) = Cov(P_{SW} W + P_{SE} E + P_{SU} U, W) \text{ [substituting for S]}$$
$$= Cov(P_{SW} W, W) + Cov(P_{SE} E, W) + Cov(P_{SU} U, W) \text{ [by rules of covariance algebra]}$$
$$= P_{SW} Cov(W,W) + P_{SE} Cov(E,W) \text{ [Cov(U,W) = 0 and Cov(W,W) = Var(W) = 1]}$$
$$= P_{SW} + P_{SE} \rho_{WE}. \tag{3}$$

The expression in Eq. (3) reveals two important points. First, the correlation between S and W is shown to be a function of the parameters of the path model. These parameters are the path coefficients and the correlation between the exogenous variables. It is here that the structure underlying a correlation/covariance becomes evident. The correlation between S and W is produced, according to the model, by the sum of two components: P_{SW} and $P_{SE} \rho_{WE}$. The second important element here is the nature of the decomposition of the correlation. One component of the decomposition is causal: P_{SW} is the causal path from W to S. Hence, one reason for the correlation between S and W is that, according to the model, W causes S. The other reason for the correlation is noncausal. The compound path $P_{SE} \rho_{WE}$ reveals that part of the correlation between S and W is due to the fact that E and W are correlated and E also causes S. We say that this component of the S–W correlation is noncausal because it is not due to a causal impact of W on S, although it is associated with E causing S.

Let us next decompose the correlation between A and W:

$$\text{Corr}(A,W) = \text{Cov}(A,W) = \text{Cov}(P_{AW} \text{ W} + P_{AE} \text{ E} + P_{AS} \text{ S} + P_{AV} \text{ V, W})$$
$$= P_{AW} + P_{AE} \text{ Cov}(E,W) + P_{AS} \text{ Cov}(S,W)$$
$$= P_{AW} + P_{AE} \rho_{WE} + P_{AS} (P_{SW} + P_{SE} \rho_{WE}) \text{ [substituting (3) for Cov(S,W)]}$$
$$= P_{AW} + P_{AE} \rho_{WE} + P_{AS} P_{SW} + P_{AS} P_{SE} \rho_{WE}. \tag{4}$$

Here it is evident that, according to the model, the correlation between A and W is produced by four components. Two are causal: P_{AW} and $P_{AS} P_{SW}$. P_{AW} is called the direct effect of W on A. It is a causal effect that is not mediated by, or accounted for by, any other variables in the model. The other causal effect is the compound path $P_{AS} P_{SW}$. It is the product of the effect of W on S with the effect of S on A and is called the indirect effect of W on A. This effect represents an impact of W on A that is mediated by S. The sum of these two causal paths is $P_{AW} + P_{AS} P_{SW}$ and is called the total effect of W on A. The other components of the correlation between A and W are noncausal: $P_{AE} \rho_{WE}$ and $P_{AS} P_{SE} \rho_{WE}$. These represent components of the association between A and W that are not due to a causal effect of W on A. The zero-order correlation between A and W is referred to as the total association of A with W. We see in Eq. (4) that this total association is partitioned into total effects—both direct and indirect—as well as noncausal components. This decomposition of the total association between variables is one of the major goals of path analysis.

Once the correlation between exogenous variables and all paths connecting W, E, S, and A are known, the paths from the disturbances are given by the following equations (see Appendix A):

$$P_{SU} = \sqrt{1 - P_{S.WE}^2} \tag{5}$$

$$P_{AV} = \sqrt{1 - P_{A.SWE}^2}, \tag{6}$$

where $P_{S.WE}^2$ represents the population R-squared for the regression of S on W and E, and $P_{A.SWE}^2$ represents the population R-squared for the regression of A on S, W, and E. This means that there are only six unknown parameters in the model: ρ_{WE}, P_{SE}, P_{SW}, P_{AW}, P_{AE}, and P_{AS}. Once these are known, the error paths are given, as shown earlier. (It can also be shown that the R-squareds are functions of these six parameters; see Appendix A.) With four variables, there are six unique correlations to account for. Hence, the model shown in Fig. 13.1 is a saturated model: There is exactly the same number of parameters as there are cases (correlations) to account for. I say more about saturated models later.

Estimation

The model can be estimated using a variety of methods (see Bollen, 1989). However, classical path analysis, as described by Knoke and Bohrnstedt (1994) or Alwin and Hauser (1975), is estimated with ordinary least squares (OLS). There are two ways to perform the estimation, although these can be combined into one analysis if desired. The manner advocated by Knoke and Bohrnstedt (1994) is to regress each endogenous variable on all variables with arrows pointing to it in the model; that is, one uses OLS regression to estimate Eqs. (1) and (2). The Alwin and Hauser (1975) method is designed to render it easier to calculate indirect and total effects (discussed shortly). Their technique involves regressing each endogenous variable, first, on only the exogenous variables in the model. In subsequent regressions for a given endogenous variable, one adds in, in causal order, each variable mediating the impact of the exogenous variables on that endogenous variable. Because no variables mediate the impact of of W or E on S, both methods result in estimating the same equation—Eq. (1)—for the endogenous Variable S. However, for Variable A, the Alwin and Hauser (1975) method requires that we first estimate the regression of A on only W and E. In the next step, we estimate Eq. (2). Table 13.2 shows the results of these three regressions. Because it is assumed that all variables are standardized, standardized regression coefficients are presented.

Mothers' endorsement of women working has a significant positive effect on child's sexual permissiveness. This suggests that children whose mothers have favorable attitudes toward women's employment tend to be more sexually permissive than others. However, mother's gender egalitarianism has no significant effect on child's sexual permissiveness. Neither mothers' endorsement of women

TABLE 13.2
Standardized Regression Coefficients for Path Model of Children's
Sexual Attitudes and Adventurism Depicted in Fig. 13.1

	Dependent Variable		
Predetermined Variable	Child's Sexual Permissiveness	Child's Sexual Adventurism	Child's Sexual Adventurism
Mothers' Endorsement of Women Working (W)	.133*	.015	−.013
Mothers' Gender Egalitarianism (E)	.005	−.002	−.003
Child's Sexual Permissiveness (S)	—	—	.212***
R^2	.018	.000[a]	.044

[a]Coefficient is less than .0005 in absolute value.
*$p < .05$. **$p < .01$. ***$p < .001$.

working nor mothers' gender egalitarianism have significant effects on child's sexual adventurism; in fact, both effects are close to zero in either equation. However, not surprisingly, child's sexual permissiveness has a significant positive effect on adventurism: Those who are more sexually permissive are also more sexually adventurous. R-squareds tend to be low for each endogenous variable. The error paths are easily estimated from the R^2s. For example, the error path for sexual adventurism is the square root of $1 - .044$, or $.978$.

Of special interest in path analysis is the decomposition of associations between variables, with special attention to the causal effects. For example, let us use Eq. (4) to decompose the sample correlation between mothers' endorsement of women working (W) and child's sexual adventurism (A). Recall that, in terms of model parameters, that correlation is $P_{AW} + P_{AE} \, \rho_{WE} + P_{AS} \, P_{SW} + P_{AS} \, P_{SE} \, \rho_{WE}$. Its estimate is $-.013 + (-.003)(.142) + (.212)(.133) + (.212)(.005)(.142) = .015$. Notice that this is exactly equal to the sample correlation. In fact, the parameter estimates from saturated models always perfectly reproduce the sample correlations. I say more about this property later. At any rate, we can see how much of this association is causal and how much is noncausal. The direct effect of W on A is $-.013$. The indirect effect is $(.212)(.133) = .028$. Together, these sum to the total effect of $-.013 + .028 = .015$. Thus, virtually all of the association of W with A is causal. The reason the noncausal components are so miniscule is that the effect of E in the model—on either S or A—is virtually zero. Using similar algebra and the equations estimated for the Knoke and Bohrnstedt (1994) method of path analysis, all effects of predictors in the model can be so decomposed. Table 13.3 shows the decomposition of all effects in the model.

The Alwin and Hauser (1975) method of estimating path models obviates the need to compute compound paths to recover total and indirect effects. The total effect of any predictor is just the regression coefficient for that predictor in an

TABLE 13.3
Total, Direct, and Indirect Effects in Path Model of Children's
Sexual Attitudes and Adventurism Depicted in Fig. 13.1

Dependent Variable	Predetermined Variable	Total Effect	Direct Effect	Indirect Effect
Child's Sexual Permissiveness	Mothers' Endorsement of Women Working	.133*	.133*	—
	Mothers' Gender Egalitarianism	.005	.005	—
Child's Sexual Adventurism	Mothers' Endorsement of Women Working	.015	−.013	.028
	Mothers' Gender Egalitarianism	−.002	−.003	.001
	Child's Sexual Permissiveness	.212***	.212***	—

$*p < .05.$ $**p < .01.$ $***p < .001.$

equation that omits any mediators of the effect of that predictor on the outcome. Hence, the total effects of W and E on S are given in the first equation in Table 13.2. The total effects of W and E on A are given in the second equation in Table 13.2. The third equation in Table 13.2 shows the total effect of S on A. The indirect effects are recovered by subtracting coefficients in adjacent equations for the same endogenous variable. In particular, the indirect effect of W on A via S is just $.015 - (-.013) = .28$. Similarly, the indirect effect of E on A via S is $-.002 - (-.003) = .001$. The reader should consult Alwin and Hauser (1975) or Hasenfeld and Rafferty (1989) for more complex decompositions.

Caveats

Several caveats about path analysis are in order. First, because path analysis involves the estimation of a series of regression equations, all of the assumptions of regression apply. Thus, it is assumed, for each equation, that (a) the dependent variable is approximately interval, (b) no regressor is a perfect linear combination of the other regressors in the model, (c) the disturbance in each equation has zero mean and constant variance at each combination of predictor values, (d) disturbances are uncorrelated both within and across equations, (e) disturbances are normally distributed (for small samples), (f) the model is linear in the parameters, and (g) each equation is correctly specified.

Beyond these assumptions, however, path analysis is even more restrictive in assuming that the causal system is correctly specified to start with. That is, one begins with a causal system that one knows to be correct and then uses path analysis to estimate the parameters of that system. Path analysis cannot be used to test the correctness of a causal system except in the most limited sense. The real power of path analysis lies in its ability to help us understand the workings of a causal system that is known to be true. In this case, path analysis allows us to discern the extent to which the effects of the predictors on the response variables are nonzero, and, if so, the extent to which they are mediated by other variables. For the present example, this is revealed in Table 13.3.

Ultimately, all the researcher can show is that sample results are consistent with a hypothesized model being true. He or she must, at the same time, use established theory or other empirical results to rule out alternative explanations for the results. What path analysis cannot test is whether the causal system is correct. Recall that a saturated model will perfectly account for the sample correlations among all variables in the system. This means that we can randomly permute the order of, say, all variables in Fig. 13.1 and still account perfectly for all correlations in Table 13.1. We could, for example, set up the model so that S and A are the exogenous variables, E is the mediator, and W is the outcome (rightmost variable in the system). The fit of the coefficient estimates to the observed correlations would be unchanged from the current case. Nothing about the analysis allows us to choose between these models. Theoretically, of course, such a model would be implausible. Although children's behaviors have been shown to have some effect on mothers' attitudes (Axinn & Thornton, 1993), children's attitudes and behavior in 1992–1994 cannot affect mother's attitudes in an earlier period (1987–1988). Hence, this alternative model could be ruled out based on theoretical untenability.

I mentioned that path models can be tested in a limited sense. If one's variables are multinormally distributed—a fairly stringent requirement, by the way—it is possible to test whether certain overidentifying restrictions are correct. That is, suppose I set the paths from E to S and from E to A each to zero. This model would posit that E has no effects on S or A once W is controlled. Because there would be only four parameters to estimate and six correlations to explain, the model would be said to be overidentified (i.e., fewer parameters than observed covariances to account for). Once the model is no longer saturated, the correlations implied by the model estimates would no longer perfectly predict the observed sample correlations. I could then test whether the two overidentifying restrictions ($P_{SE} = P_{AE} = 0$) are valid by testing whether the model-implied correlation matrix is significantly different from the sample correlation matrix (see Bollen, 1989, for a development of the test). Notice, however, that the causal order of the variables is unchanged by setting these restrictions. Again, there is no test in path analysis to assess the plausibility of the model's causal order. In summary, path analysis is a powerful tool for using empirical data to understand the dynamics of causal systems that are known in advance to be true.

FACTOR ANALYSIS

Another type of covariance structure model is the factor model. These are also called *measurement models* in covariance structure analysis because they relate a set of observable measures to a set of underlying variables that they supposedly tap. All factor models posit that observed variable scores are linearly dependent on unmeasured, or *latent*, variables. Latent variables are abstract concepts in models that, although unobserved, are believed to drive attitudes and behavior in the social sciences. A concept is, according to Bollen (1989), "an idea that unites phenomena (e.g., attitudes, behaviors, traits) under a single term" (p. 180). Concepts are distinguished from manifest variables, such as annual salary, in that they are not directly observable. Rather, their presence is inferred from other observable entities. In fact, all of the variables in the model in Fig. 13.1 are really concepts, rather than directly observable variables. In path analysis, it is assumed that all variables are measured without error. With this in mind, I have formed scales to measure these concepts and treated these scales as if they were exact measures of each construct. It is obvious from the relatively low reliabilities (reported earlier) for these scales that each is characterized by considerable measurement error. To foreshadow what I later discuss, the full covariance structure, or LISREL model, is essentially a path model that takes account of measurement error in the concepts that drive the system. However, an understanding of factor analysis is required before we can consider such models.

Factor analysis comes in two basic varieties: confirmatory factor analysis (CFA) and exploratory factor analysis (EFA). The difference between the two depends on the degree to which the researcher knows or wishes to state ahead of time what the factor structure of a set of measures looks like. The factor structure refers to the number of factors, whether they are correlated, which variables they affect, and whether measurement errors covary. In CFA, the factor structure is posited ahead of time, and the researcher tests whether the data are consistent with this structure. In EFA, the researcher has no idea ahead of time what the factor structure looks like, and instead wishes to discover it. These, of course, are statements of two ideal types. In practice, many researchers begin with a hypothesized model, find that it does not fit, and then *tweak* it to achieve a better fit to the data. Once one begins to respecify a poorly fitting model by adding or dropping measures, changing the number of factors in the model, and so forth, the analysis becomes more and more exploratory. Or the researcher has a hypothesized structure in mind but uses EFA to see if that structure falls out of the analysis. Again, this strategy is somewhat of a hybrid between EFA and CFA.

Confirmatory Factor Analysis

Historically, EFA was the first to be developed and used extensively. However, I believe that CFA is easier to understand, so I discuss it first. Figure 13.2 presents a simple CFA model in LISREL notation. There are four observed variables: X1–X4. Observed, or manifest, variables are typically shown enclosed in rectan-

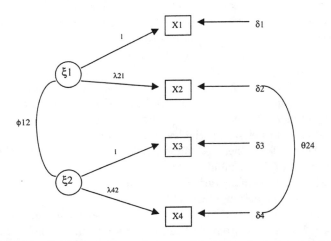

FIG. 13.2.   Confirmatory factor analysis model with two latent factors and four indicators.

gular boxes. These variables measure two latent variables, or factors: $\xi 1$ and $\xi 2$. Latent variables are typically enclosed in circles. There are two indicators of each latent variable: X1 and X2 measure $\xi 1$, whereas X3 and X4 measure $\xi 2$. The factors are also correlated: Their covariance is denoted $\phi 12$ in Fig. 13.2. Each indicator is also affected by a term reflecting measurement error. The measurement errors are denoted $\delta 1$–$\delta 4$. These terms are similar to the equation disturbances in Fig. 13.1 and represent everything that influences the measures other than the factors. It is assumed that these errors have means of zero. We see, moreover, that two of the measurement errors are correlated: Their covariance is $\theta 24$. In CFA and other latent variable models, the units of analysis are covariances, rather than correlations. Hence, this model is designed to account for the covariances among the variables X1–X4. Here, however, unlike in Fig. 13.1, the variables covary not because they are causally related to each other, but because they are mutually caused by other variables—the factors.

Once again, the model can be denoted by a set of structural equations plus additional assumptions. These are:

$$X1 = \xi 1 + \delta 1 \tag{7}$$

$$X2 = \lambda 21\ \xi 1 + \delta 2 \tag{8}$$

$$X3 = \xi 2 + \delta 3 \tag{9}$$

$$X4 = \lambda 42\ \xi 2 + \delta 4 \tag{10}$$

$\mathrm{Cov}(\xi_i, \delta_j) = 0$ for $i = 1,2$ and $j = 1, \ldots, 4$; $\mathrm{Cov}(\delta 1, \delta 2) = \mathrm{Cov}(\delta 1, \delta 3)$ $= \mathrm{Cov}(\delta 1, \delta 4) = \mathrm{Cov}(\delta 2, \delta 3) = \mathrm{Cov}(\delta 3, \delta 4) = 0$; $\mathrm{Cov}(\delta 2, \delta 4) = \theta 24$.

As we shortly see, the parameters of the model are (a) the variance of each latent variable, denoted $\phi 11$ for $\xi 1$ and $\phi 22$ for $\xi 2$; (b) $\phi 12$, the covariance of the latent variables with each other; (c) the factor loadings $\lambda 21$ and $\lambda 42$; (d) the variances of the error terms, $\mathrm{Var}(\delta 1)$–$\mathrm{Var}(\delta 4)$, and $\theta 24$, the covariance of $\delta 2$ and $\delta 4$. Thus, there are 10 parameters in the model. With four indicators, there are 10 covariances to account for (four variances plus six covariances among the four variables). In general, for K indicators, there are $K(K+1)/2$ covariances to account for in the covariance matrix.

Using Eqs. (7)–(10) in tandem with covariance algebra, it is possible to show that all of these covariances are functions of the model's parameters. For the model in Fig. 13.2, for example, $\mathrm{Var}(X2) = \mathrm{Cov}(X2,X2) = \mathrm{Cov}(\lambda 21\ \xi 1 + \delta 2, \lambda 21\ \xi 1 + \delta 2) = \lambda^2_{21}\ \phi 11 + \theta 22$, where $\theta 22$ is $\mathrm{Var}(\delta 2)$. Similarly, $\mathrm{Cov}(X2,X4) = \mathrm{Cov}(\lambda 21\ \xi 1 + \delta 2, \lambda 42\ \xi 2 + \delta 4) = \lambda 21\ \lambda 42\ \phi 12 + \theta 24$. Proceeding in this manner, we find that the full set of covariances is:

$$\text{Var(X1)} = \phi 11 + \theta 11 \tag{11}$$

$$\text{Var(X2)} = \lambda^2_{21} \, \phi 11 + \theta 22 \tag{12}$$

$$\text{Var(X3)} = \phi 22 + \theta 33 \tag{13}$$

$$\text{Var(X4)} = \lambda^2_{42} \, \phi 22 + \theta 44 \tag{14}$$

$$\text{Cov(X1,X2)} = \lambda 21 \, \phi 11 \tag{15}$$

$$\text{Cov(X1,X3)} = \phi 12 \tag{16}$$

$$\text{Cov(X1,X4)} = \lambda 42 \, \phi 12 \tag{17}$$

$$\text{Cov(X2,X3)} = \lambda 21 \, \phi 12 \tag{18}$$

$$\text{Cov(X2,X4)} = \lambda 21 \, \lambda 42 \, \phi 12 + \theta 24 \tag{19}$$

$$\text{Cov(X3,X4)} = \lambda 42 \, \phi 22. \tag{20}$$

Here it becomes clear that, if the model is correct, the covariances among the observed variables are produced by the parameters of the structural model. The task for the researcher is to estimate those parameters and then test whether the data are consistent with the model. However, in this simple example, once again we have a saturated model (10 covariances and 10 parameters). Such a model demonstrates a perfect fit to the observed covariances. Therefore, its fit to the data cannot be formally tested. Saturated models are rarely of interest. Next I present an unsaturated model to demonstrate how fit can be assessed.

Identification

Before estimating a model, the researcher must first confirm that it is identified. Because Eqs. (11)–(20) constitute a set of equations that are to be solved to find the model's parameter values, we must first ask if these equations have a unique solution. That is, is there a unique set of parameter values that will make these equations true, assuming that we know the covariances among the indicators? Although we do not really know the population covariances, we treat the sample covariances as estimates of these values. Because the sample covariances are consistent estimators of their population counterparts, they should be quite close to the population values in large samples. If, given actual values for the covariances, there is a unique set of parameter values that satisfies these equations, then the model is said to be identified. (Otherwise it is said to be unidentified.) It is possible, however, for individual parameters within the model to be identified although others are not. Nevertheless, the model as a whole is not said to be identified unless every parameter is identified (Bollen, 1989).

The identification problem is analogous to the simultaneous equations problem in algebra. In the equation $X + Y = 10$, X and Y are individually unidentified (although their sum is identified) because there are infinitely many X and Y values that make the equation true. For example, $X = 5$ and $Y = 5$ as well as $X = 4$ and $Y = 6$ are two sets of X,Y values that satisfy the equation. To make this analogy more relevant to causal models, think of 10 as a mental distress index for some individual and X and Y as depression and anxiety scale scores, respectively. From this equation alone, there is no way to know which are the correct X and Y values that produced a sum of 10 for this individual. However, if we add the equation $X - Y = 4$, we then have two equations and two unknowns, which can be solved for a unique X and Y of 7 and 3, respectively. The set of two equations renders X and Y identified because only the values of 7 and 3 make this set of equations true. If a model is not identified, it makes no sense to attempt to estimate its parameters. Because there is potentially an infinite number of parameter values that could have produced the same covariance matrix, there is no way to choose which set of values is the correct one.

Although the identification issue is being raised at this juncture in the chapter, it applies to all covariance structure models, including path models. To show that a model is identified, we must show that the set of equations relating the covariances/correlations to the model's parameters can be solved to provide a unique set of parameters. This means that each parameter must be able to be shown to be a function only of the covariances/correlations among the observed variables. Several identification conventions are used in covariance structure analysis to aid in model identification. For example, in path analysis, all variables are assumed to be standardized. Hence, their variances are all equal to one and need not be estimated. In CFA, it is conventional to set the scale for each latent variable to be the same as that of one of the indicators. Because the scale of a latent variable is arbitrary, it can be set to equal any of the indicators. Without doing so, the model is not identified. Setting the scale is accomplished by setting the factor loading for an indicator to equal one. In the model in Fig. 13.2, the scaling indicators are X1 for $\xi 1$ and X3 for $\xi 2$. Another convention is that the paths from the measurement errors to their respective indicators are also set to 1 (not shown on the figure).

Even with these conventions in place, model identification is not assured. Several rules have been developed that are either necessary or sufficient conditions for model identification. Often the researcher can draw on one or more of these to establish identification of his or her model. For example, all path analysis models that are recursive—that is, characterized by only unidirectional causal influences—are automatically identified by the recursive rule, provided that the disturbances are not correlated with each other (Bollen, 1989). A necessary condition for identification in all models is that the number of parameters does not exceed the number of covariances/correlations to account for. This is a necessary condition only. That is, models in which the number of parameters exceeds the number of observed covariances/correlations are known to be unidentified. However, a model that satisfies this condition is not necessarily identified. The model in Fig. 13.2 satisfies this condition, therefore it may be identified. Several additional rules are available to help identify CFA models (see Bollen, 1989; Davis, 1993; Reilly, 1995; Reilly & O'Brien, 1996).

If these rules do not apply, the researcher can always attempt to identify the model through algebraic means. I demonstrate this technique with the model in Fig. 13.2. I begin with Eq. (16), which shows that $\phi 12$ is identified because it is equal to Cov(X1,X3). Once a parameter is identified, mark it with an asterisk, or star, as in Cov(X1,X3) = $\phi 12^*$. Then mark the same parameter in every equation in which it appears. For example, Eq. (17) is Cov(X1,X4) = $\lambda 42 \ \phi 12^*$ and Eq. (18) is Cov(X2,X3) = $\lambda 21 \ \phi 12^*$. If there is only one unmarked parameter in an equation, then that parameter is identified because the equation can always be solved for that parameter in terms of the observed covariance and other identified parameters in that equation. For example, I can solve for $\lambda 42$ as Cov(X1,X4)/$\phi 12^*$, which equals Cov(X1,X4)/Cov(X1,X3). Thus, $\lambda 42$ is also seen to be solvable strictly in terms of the observed covariances. For the same reason, $\lambda 21$ is also identified. Moving to Eqs. (15) and (22), I star the lambdas and see that $\phi 11$ and $\phi 22$ are both identified. Also, starring the lambdas and $\phi 12$ in Eq. (19) identifies $\theta 24$. It is then a simple matter to use Eqs. (11)–(14) to identify all of the variances of the error terms. (Note that if a loading is identified, then its square is also identified.)

Measurement Error Covariances

The reader may wonder about the necessity of $\theta 24$, the covariance between measurement errors for X2 and X4. Correlated errors are commonplace when multiple measures are taken from the same individual. Recall that the error term represents anything that affects the score on an indicator other than the latent variable of interest. If there is some other factor that affects each indicator in the same fashion, a positive covariance between the measurement errors for those indicators is likely. This is easily seen using the covariance structure framework. Suppose that the true model for three indicators, X1–X3, is:

$$X1 = \xi 1 + \xi 2 + \delta 1$$

$$X2 = \lambda 21 \ \xi 1 + \lambda 22 \ \xi 2 + \delta 2$$

$$X3 = \lambda 31 \ \xi 1 + \delta 3,$$

where $\text{Cov}(\xi_i,\delta_j) = 0$ for $i = 1,2$ and $j = 1, \ldots, 3$; $\text{Cov}(\xi 1,\xi 2) = 0$; $\text{Cov}(\delta 1,\delta 2) = \text{Cov}(\delta 1,\delta 3) = \text{Cov}(\delta 2,\delta 3) = 0$; all loadings are positive; and $\lambda 21 = \lambda 31$.

The model as shown cannot be estimated because it is not identified: There are six covariances to account for, but seven parameters to estimate—the variances of $\xi 1, \xi 2, \delta 1, \delta 2$, and $\delta 3$, and two loadings: $\lambda 21 (= \lambda 31)$ and $\lambda 22$. Suppose, however, that the researcher estimates a model that omits $\xi 2$:

$$X1 = \xi 1 + \upsilon 1$$

$$X2 = \lambda 21 \ \xi 1 + \upsilon 2$$

$$X3 = \lambda 31 \ \xi 1 + \delta 3,$$

where $\upsilon 1 = \xi 2 + \delta 1$, and $\upsilon 2 = \lambda 22 \ \xi 2 + \delta 2$, and, once again, $\lambda 21 = \lambda 31$. If it is assumed that all error covariances are zero, this model is identified by the three-indicator rule (Bollen, 1989). In fact, it is overidentified: There are five parameters and six covariances to account for. Now, $\text{Cov}(\upsilon 1,\delta 3) = \text{Cov}(\upsilon 2,\delta 3) = 0$, but what is the covariance of $\upsilon 1$ with $\upsilon 2$? It is $\text{Cov}(\upsilon 1,\upsilon 2) = \text{Cov}(\xi 2 + \delta 1, \lambda 22 \ \xi 2 + \delta 2) = \lambda 22 \ \phi 22$. This term is typically positive unless $\lambda 22$ or $\phi 22$ is zero. Adding this error covariance as an additional parameter to estimate results in a saturated model, which can also be shown to be identified via algebraic means.

If the researcher is fortunate enough to have pure measures of his or her factors, error covariances may be nil. However, this is unlikely to be the case. Often indicators may be primarily affected by the factor of interest but also affected by some other factors that cannot be estimated, such as acquiescent response set, social desirability response bias, and so forth. As a result, positive covariances between error terms are to be expected. It has been my experience that article reviewers typically regard the specification of correlated measurement error with suspicion, as if the researcher is trying to use it to cheat the model into fitting the data. They then demand that the author or authors of an article using covariance structure modeling provide extensive theoretical justification for correlated errors. I argue that this approach is misguided. Correlated measurement error should be regarded as the default scenario. Otherwise, we have to believe in a purity of measurement that is unrealistic in the social sciences.

Estimation

A variety of methods can be used to estimate the parameters of CFA models. By far, the most commonly used technique is maximum likelihood. Maximum likelihood (ML) estimators have four very desirable properties in large samples. First, they are unbiased (on average, they are equal to the population parameter that they estimate). Second, they are consistent (in large samples, there is a high probability that they are close in value to the parameter). Third, they are efficient (no other estimator has a smaller sampling variance). Fourth, they are normally distributed, implying that the ML estimator divided by its asymptotic standard error provides a z test for the null hypothesis that the population parameter equals zero (Bollen, 1989). The drawback to ML estimation is that it must be assumed that the indicators are observations from a multivariate normal distribution. In actuality, the technique retains its properties under somewhat less stringent conditions, that is, that the multivariate distribution of the indicators has no excess kurtosis (Bollen, 1989). However, neither of these assumptions is likely to hold for many analyses. Later, I discuss one alternative to ML estimation for non-normal data. For now, suffice it to say that, at worst, ML estimates always retain the property of consistency, regardless of the distribution of the data. Again, this means that, at least in large samples, the estimates have a high probability of being close to the true population values.

The principle of all estimation techniques in covariance structure models is as follows. Suppose that we denote by θ the vector, or collection, of all parameters to be estimated for a specific model. For example, for the model in Fig. 13.2, the elements of θ are $\phi 11$, $\phi 12$, $\phi 22$, $\lambda 21$, $\lambda 42$, $\theta 11$, $\theta 22$, $\theta 33$, $\theta 44$, and $\theta 24$. The covariance structure hypothesis is that $\Sigma = \Sigma(\theta)$, where Σ is the population covariance matrix for the indicators and $\Sigma(\theta)$ is Σ expressed as a function of the model parameters. That is, the covariance structure hypothesis is that the population covariance matrix of the indicators is a function of the parameters in θ. (Equations (11)–(20) show how these covariances are functions of the parameters, for the model in Fig. 13.2.) To obtain the parameter estimates, we find those values of the parameters that minimize the difference between the covariance matrix implied by the models' parameter estimates, $\Sigma(\hat{\theta})$, and Σ, the population covariance matrix itself. $\Sigma(\hat{\theta})$ for the model in Fig. 13.2 would be found, for example, by substituting the parameter estimates for the model into Eqs. (11)–(20). Because we do not know Σ, we use S, the sample covariance matrix in its place, which is a consistent estimator of Σ. The difference between S and $\Sigma(\hat{\theta})$ is assessed by a fitting function, $F(S, \Sigma(\hat{\theta}))$. The maximum likelihood estimates are those estimates that minimize the maximum likelihood fitting function, F_{ML} (see Bollen, 1989, for its formula). For the model in Fig. 13.2, of course, $\Sigma(\hat{\theta})$ would equal S exactly, in that the model is saturated; hence, F_{ML} would be zero. The ML estimates of the parameters are those values that would have made the observed data most likely to have been observed, given that they came from a multivariate normal distribution.

Assessing Model Fit

Assuming that the data do, indeed, come from a multivariate normal distribution, ML estimation provides a test of the covariance structure hypothesis. The test statistic is $(N - 1) F_{ML}$, where N is the sample size. This statistic is distributed as chi-squared under the null hypothesis that $\Sigma = \Sigma(\theta)$. Its degrees of freedom are equal to the number of covariances to account for minus the number of parameters estimated. This is essentially a test of whether the data are consistent with the model. The greater the departure of the covariances implied by the model's parameter estimates, $\Sigma(\hat{\theta})$, from S, the larger this statistic's value. A significant value means that the model is not consistent with the data. Unlike the usual situation in which a researcher is looking for significant results, the ideal situation in covariance structure modeling is a nonsignificant chi-squared test. This means that one should not reject the hypothesis that the data were generated by the researcher's model.

The chi-squared test, like all significance tests, is affected by sample size. In large samples, therefore, even trivial departures of $\Sigma(\hat{\theta})$ from S may result in rejection of a model. For this and other reasons, several other fit indexes have been developed that do not depend as heavily on sample size. Unlike the chi-squared, these are not test statistics, but rather indicate the degree to which the data are consistent with a model. I discuss one such index here because it represents the manner in which many of them are constructed. The reader is referred to Bollen (1989) or Gerbing and Anderson (1993) for a more complete presentation of fit indexes.

Perhaps the easiest fit index to understand, for those familiar with linear regression, is Bentler and Bonnett's (1980) normed fit index, Δ_1 (see also Bollen, 1989):

$$\Delta_1 = \frac{\chi_b^2 - \chi_m^2}{\chi_b^2},$$

where χ_m^2 is the chi-squared value for the maintained, or hypothesized model, and χ_b^2 is the chi-squared value for a baseline model. The typical baseline model is called the *null* model and holds that no factors underlie the indicators, in which case all of the population covariances between indicators are zero in the population. This fit index reveals the proportionate improvement in fit of the maintained over the baseline model. It is analogous to R-squared in linear regression, which compares the hypothesized model to one in which the effects of all predictors are zero. In the case of Δ_1 and all of the fit indexes presented later in the chapter, however, only values of .9 or higher are considered indicative of an acceptable fit.

An Example. The model in Fig. 13.1 relies on a series of items to measure mothers' gender role ideology. Figure 13.3 depicts a CFA model for these items, which are described in the figure legend. The two factors are mothers' endorsement of women working and mothers' gender role ideology. A preliminary analysis suggested that one error covariance was substantial and should therefore be estimated. This is the covariance of errors for Items 3 and 4. The items use almost identical wording, except for the interchange of the terms *full time* and *part time*. Items with very similar wording are likely to be affected by some common re-

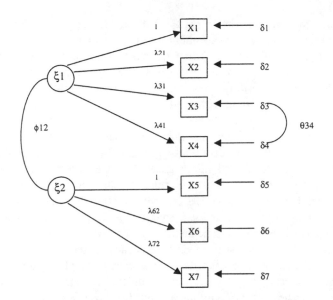

FIG. 13.3. Confirmatory factor model of mothers' gender role ideology. Notation: ξ1 = mothers' endorsement of women working; ξ2 = mothers' gender egalitarianism, X1 = mothers' disagreement that male should be sole breadwinner; X2 = mothers' disagreement that preschool children suffer when their mother is employed; X3 = mothers' endorsement of women working full time when their youngest child is under 5; X4 = mothers' endorsement of women working part time when their youngest child is under 5; X5 = mothers' agreement that daughters should be raised to be as independent as sons; X6 = mothers' agreement that when both partners work full time, each should share equally in household tasks; X7 = mothers' agreement that, in a successful marriage, both partners must have freedom to do what they want individually.

sponse factor in addition to the concept that is being measured. As I have shown, this usually results in a covariance between their error terms. The model can be shown to be identified using algebraic techniques, similar to the demonstration for Fig. 13.2. In this case, however, the model is overidentified. With 28 covariances to account for and 16 parameters, there are 12 degrees of freedom left for a chi-squared test of model fit.

Unstandardized ML estimates of model parameters are shown in Table 13.4. The covariance structure hypothesis is not rejected: The chi-squared statistic is 15.639, which, with 12 degrees of freedom, is not significant ($p > .2$). Statistically, at least, there is no reason to doubt the veracity of the model. Several fit indexes— Δ_1, as well as GFI, AGFI, Bentler's CFI, McDonald's Centrality, and Bollen's Δ_2— are well above .9, also indicating a high degree of fit of the model to the data. The t ratios (which are, in actuality, z tests) suggest that all parameter estimates are highly significant. All factor loadings are positive, as would be expected, given that all

TABLE 13.4
Unstandardized Parameter Estimates for Confirmatory Factor Analysis
of Mothers' Gender Role Ideology Depicted in Fig. 13.3

Parameter	Maximum Likelihood Estimate	t Ratio	Reliability
$\lambda 11$	1.000^{a}	—	.407
$\lambda 21$	1.055	8.513	.507
$\lambda 31$	1.531	8.417	.468
$\lambda 41$	1.171	7.269	.310
$\lambda 52$	1.000^{a}	—	.247
$\lambda 62$	.959	2.966	.226
$\lambda 72$	.897	3.054	.132
$\phi 11$	.587	5.510	—
$\phi 22$	.145	2.478	—
$\phi 12$	.066	2.180	—
Var($\delta 1$)	.857	9.641	—
Var($\delta 2$)	.635	7.649	—
Var($\delta 3$)	1.564	8.319	—
Var($\delta 4$)	1.792	10.344	—
Var($\delta 5$)	.440	7.274	—
Var($\delta 6$)	.455	7.865	—
Var($\delta 7$)	.767	10.683	—
Cov($\delta 3, \delta 4$)	.764	5.078	—
$\chi^{2}(12)$	15.639	—	—
Δ_{1}	.967	—	—
GFI	.988	—	—
AGFI	.971	—	—
Bentler's CFI	.992	—	—
McDonald's Centrality	.995	—	—
Bollen's Δ_{2}	.992	—	—

[a]Constrained parameter.

items were coded so that a high score reflects the more liberal response. The "Reliability" column lists the R-squareds for each indicator. This is the proportion of variance in the item that is accounted for by the factor. Were one to assume that the factors are, indeed, the true concepts the researcher is trying to measure, these would be validity coefficients. However, it is safer just to regard these as reliabilities. That is, they are the proportions of variance of the indicators attributable to some systematic attribute (Bollen, 1989). Whether that attribute is the concept that the researcher is trying to measure requires further demonstration of construct validity (see Mirowsky & Ross, 1991, for an example). As is evident from these values, the items are not particularly reliable indicators of the factors, with the highest reliability being only about .51. Otherwise, the model appears to be an adequate representation of these seven items tapping mothers' gender-role attitudes.

Exploratory Factor Analysis

The factor model that underlies a set of items does not depend on whether CFA or EFA is conducted. Whether CFA or EFA is used depends on how much the researcher is willing to hypothesize ahead of time about the factor structure. Up to this point, we have only been considering factor models in which the factor structure is specified in advance. Suppose, however, that the factor structure is unknown. The techniques of EFA are designed to help the researcher discover it. For example, the 357 mothers in my sample were asked a series of questions in 1987–1988 regarding how important it was to them that their children possessed certain traits or exhibited certain behaviors. These were "always follow family rules," "do well in school," "be independent," "be kind and considerate," "control their temper," "always do what you ask," "carry out responsibilities on their own," "do well in creative activities such as music, art, or drama," "keep busy by themselves," "get along well with other kids," "do well in athletics," and "try new things." It is reasonable that these items tap a smaller number of dimensions of childrearing values but how many? Which items tap which dimensions? Unsure of the answers to these questions, I use EFA to guide me.

EFA has a long and venerable tradition, as well as a vast literature. In many ways, it is more craft than science. I sketch out some commonly used principles for conducting the most prevalent form of EFA, principal factor analysis (PFA), and refer the reader to the authoritative books by Gorsuch (1983) and Harman (1976) for more detail on this and other approaches. In my view, EFA is much more difficult than CFA because so many subjective decisions must be made. Therefore, the reader should regard the following analyses as more heuristic than definitive.

In EFA, as in classical path analysis, the items are assumed to be standardized prior to analysis. Hence, the units of analysis are again correlations, rather than covariances. EFA differs from CFA in many respects, one of which is that model identification is no longer an issue. In fact, the parameters of EFA are typically unidentified because, as we see later, an infinite number of factor solutions can reproduce the item correlation matrix with the same degree of accuracy. Initial EFA solutions also assume that the factors are uncorrelated, and there is no provision for allowing measurement errors to covary.

The first step in a PFA is to determine the number of factors that underlie the items. This is usually accomplished by first conducting a principal components analysis of the correlation matrix. A component is nothing more than a weighted sum of the items. If there are K items, there are K uncorrelated components that can be extracted from the data. The first component is that weighted sum of the items that is most highly correlated with all of the items. The second component is that weighted sum of the items that is most highly correlated with the items, conditional on its being uncorrelated with the first component. Each succeeding component up to the Kth is extracted in like manner, being the weighted sum of the items that is most highly correlated with the items, conditional on being un-correlated with the already extracted components. The sum of squares of the correlations of the items with a given component is called the *eigenvalue* associated with that component. The eigenvalue is the variance in the items that is accounted for by a given component. As standardized items have variances of 1, the total variance in a set of K items is K. There are a total of K eigenvalues, and their sum is also equal to K. Their importance to factor analysis is in providing guidelines for the number of factors that underlie the items.

One general rule is that the number of factors is equal to the number of eigenvalues greater than one. Another way to use the eigenvalues is to plot their values against their order of extraction, as in Fig. 13.4. This is called a "scree" plot, after the term *scree* in geology, which refers to the rubble at the bottom of a cliff. The idea is that the eigenvalues decline steadily in magnitude from the first to the Kth. The point at which this decline first tapers off marks the number of factors in the data. This is often difficult to discern. However, the last several eigenvalues typically present a linear pattern of descent that can be represented with a straight line, as in the figure. Then, the first eigenvalue on the left that jumps off the line indicates the number of factors. According to the figure, both the eigenvalue rule and the scree plot suggest that there are three factors in the data.

The next step in an EFA is to estimate the proportion of variance of each variable attributable to the factor or factors underlying the items. These proportions are called the *communalities* of the variables in EFA. If a variable's reliability is known, this is the best estimate. If not, there are a variety of estimates that can be

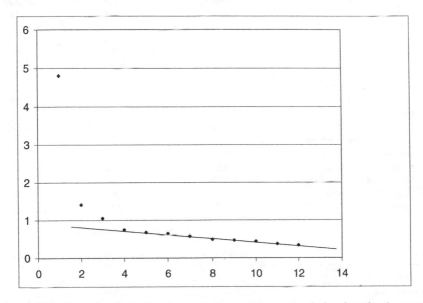

FIG. 13.4. Scree plot based on principal components analysis of mothers' childrearing values.

used. Two recommended by Gorsuch (1983) are (a) the absolute value of the largest correlation of a variable with all other variables in the set to be analyzed, or (b) the squared multiple correlation (SMC) of each variable with all other variables in the set. In the current example, I used each of these estimates and found the same factor solution with either one. The results presented (see Table 13.5) are those arrived at using the SMCs and then iterating twice (see Gorsuch, 1983, for an explanation of iteration). The communality estimates are then substituted for the ones (1s) in the diagonals of the item correlation matrix, and the principal components procedure is run again. This time, however, the analyst requests that only f com-

TABLE 13.5
Exploratory Factor Analysis of 10 Items Reflecting Mothers' Childrearing Values: Pattern Matrixes for Orthogonal and Oblique Rotations

	Orthogonal Rotation		
Item	Obedience	Achievement	Maturity
Always do what you ask	.736	.233	.195
Always follow family rules	.654	.154	.181
Control temper	.574	.222	.370
Do well in athletics	.184	.686	−.082
Do well in creative activities	.249	.601	.151
Try new things	.012	.551	.251
Keep busy	.300	.546	.257
Be independent	.118	.168	.653
Be kind and considerate	.294	.028	.630
Be responsible	.402	.235	.541

	Oblique Rotation		
Item	Obedience	Achievement	Maturity
Always do what you ask	.749	.074	.041
Always follow family rules	.673	.010	.048
Control temper	.541	.084	.261
Do well in athletics	.109	.690	−.163
Do well in creative activities	.155	.570	.075
Try new things	−.119	.560	.233
Keep busy	.202	.494	.180
Be independent	−.009	.104	.659
Be kind and considerate	.215	−.081	.606
Be responsible	.317	.122	.478

	Interfactor Correlations		
Item	Obedience	Achievement	Maturity
Obedience	1.000		
Achievement	.369	1.000	
Maturity	.375	.208	1.000

ponents be extracted, where f is the number of factors in the data. Substituting communalities for ones in the correlation matrix changes the extraction procedure so that only the variance accounted for by the underlying factors is being analyzed. The procedure is therefore no longer a component analysis, but is referred to instead as a PFA.

Of primary interest in EFA are the loadings of the variables on the factors; that is, the lambdas in Figs. 13.2 and 13.3. In EFA, these appear in the pattern matrix. Because the variables are assumed to be standardized, and because the factors are assumed to be uncorrelated—at least, initially—these loadings are simple correlations of the factors with the variables. The pattern of high and low loadings provides a guide to which variables are most strongly influenced by each factor. Ideally, each variable only loads on one factor, as in Fig. 13.3. This kind of structure is often referred to in the EFA literature as "simple structure" (Gorsuch, 1983). An infinite number of pattern matrixes for f factors can be constructed that will reproduce the sample correlations to the same degree of accuracy. The PFA procedure produces a unique pattern matrix by the manner in which factors are extracted. However, this solution is rarely of interest because all of the items typically have large loadings on the first factor. For this reason, we typically rotate the factors to achieve another, more desirable solution that more closely approximates simple structure. *Rotation* is a geometrical term that can be quite confusing. More simply, rotation involves finding another solution that (a) reproduces the correlations equally well, (b) preserves the orthogonality (uncorrelatedness) of the factors, and (c) comes closer to achieving simple structure.

There are several rotation procedures that accomplish these goals; however, the one most frequently used is called *varimax* rotation. It derives its name from the fact that it maximizes the variance of the loadings in a given column of the pattern matrix. When varimax was applied to the 12 childrearing items enumerated previously, two items were found that had roughly equal loadings on more than one factor: "do well in school" and "get along well with other kids." I therefore eliminated these items and reran the PFA, again requesting varimax rotation. The results are shown in the top panel of Table 13.5. The largest loadings for a given item are underlined, revealing which variables appear to be tapping each factor. Because of the nature of the items loading on each factor, I have named the factors "obedience," "achievement," and "maturity."

Has simple structure been achieved? If so, ideally there would be 20 zero loadings in the matrix in that all 10 items would only load on one factor. Gorsuch (1983) suggested that loadings in the range of $-.1$ to $+.1$ should be considered approximately zero, with compensation for sampling variability. This means that there are only 3 zero loadings (.012, .028, $-.082$). One way to improve the situation is to allow the factors to be correlated. This would be theoretically reasonable in that those who value achievement probably also value maturity, and so forth. Moreover, the alpha reliability for the original set of 12 items was .86. Gorsuch recommended allowing factors to be correlated when items are characterized by high alpha reliability. Another way to gauge whether factors are correlated is to check for significant correlations between the salient variables that load on each factor (Gorsuch, 1983). For the 10 childrearing items in Table 13.5, I examined the average inter-item correlation between items loading on each factor. For obedience and achievement, the average correlation was .279; for obedience and maturity, it was .360; and for achievement and maturity, it was .224. All correlations were highly significant.

I therefore re-ran the PFA, this time requesting the oblique, or correlated-factor, rotation technique known as *promax* (see Gorsuch, 1983, for a description of this procedure). This rotation algorithm has a power parameter that can be varied according to the desired degree of correlation among the factors. Gorsuch recommended allowing the factors to be correlated to the same degree as the inter-item correlations among the salient variables. Toward that end, I selected the lowest power of 2 for the rotation. The results are shown in the second panel of Table 13.5, along with the resulting interfactor correlations. The number of zero loadings has been increased from three to eight, showing some improvement in simple structure. The pattern of loadings is unchanged, although their magnitudes have been altered slightly. However, the correlated-factor model appears to be a closer approximation to the structure underlying the data and so represents the final factor solution for these items.

LISREL MODELS

The final type of covariance structure model considered in this chapter is the full covariance structure, or LISREL (LInear Structural RELations) model. This is essentially a path model that contains one or more latent exogenous or endogenous variables that are tapped by a set of indicators. It can also be thought of as a factor model that has been superimposed on a path model. As previously noted, the model in Fig. 13.1 is, in actuality, a model of relationships among latent variables. In the path analysis presented in Tables 13.1, 13.2, and 13.3, these have been treated as though they were precisely measured. In particular, I formed scales from the relevant items and then treated these measures as though they were identical with the concepts. However, there is considerable measurement error in these scales that is not taken account of in the path analysis. Measurement error frequently attenuates estimates of the relationships among latent variables, as well as estimates of the proportion of variance accounted for in the endogenous variables (Bollen, 1989). The LISREL approach allows a more accurate estimation of these effects by incorporating the impact of measurement error directly into the model.

Figure 13.5 is the LISREL version of Fig. 13.1. Mothers' endorsement of women working and mothers' gender egalitarianism are the latent exogenous variables ξ_1 and ξ_2, respectively, whereas child's sexual permissiveness and child's sexual adventurism are the latent endogenous variables, η_1 and η_2, respectively. The confirmatory factor model of Fig. 13.3 is now seen to be incorpo-

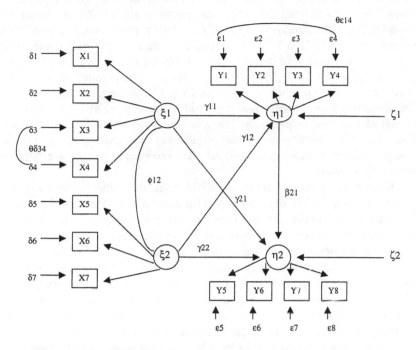

FIG. 13.5. Full covariance structure model for relationships among mothers' endorsement of women working, mothers' gender egalitarianism, child's sexual permissiveness, and child's sexual behavior. Notation: $\xi1$ = mothers' endorsement of women working; $\xi2$ = mothers' gender egalitarianism; X1 = mothers' disagreement that male should be sole breadwinner; X2 = mothers' disagreement that preschool children suffer when their mother is employed; X3 = mothers' endorsement of women working full time when their youngest child is under 5; X4 = mothers' endorsement of women working part time when their youngest child is under 5; X5 = mothers' agreement that daughters should be raised to be as independent as sons; X6 = mothers' agreement that, when both partners work full time, each should share equally in household tasks; X7 = mothers' agreement that, in a successful marriage, both partners must have freedom to do what they want individually; $\eta1$ = child's sexual permissiveness, $\eta2$ = child's sexual adventurism; Y1 = child's endorsement of others having children without being married; Y2 = child's endorsement of unmarried couples living together if they have no interest in marriage; Y3 = child's endorsement of unmarried 18-year-olds having sex without strong affection for each other; Y4 = child's endorsement of child's having children without being married; Y5 = child's age at first intercourse (reverse-coded); Y6 = child's number of different lifetime sexual partners; Y7 = child's frequency of sex in the past month; Y8 = child's number of different sexual partners in past month.

rated directly into Fig. 13.5, showing the measurement of the exogenous variables. The items tapping the exogenous variables are X1–X7. A similar factor model connects the items reflecting child's sexual permissiveness and child's sexual adventurism—Y1–Y8—to their respective factors. The path coefficients of Fig. 13.1 that linked the exogenous variables to the endogenous variables are the gammas (γ) in Fig. 13.5. The path from child's sexual permissiveness to child's sexual adventurism in labeled $\beta 21$ in Fig. 13.5. The two terms $\zeta 1$ and $\zeta 2$ represent the disturbances in the equations for child's sexual permissiveness and child's sexual adventurism, respectively. The goal here is to reestimate the path model of Fig. 13.1 while adjusting for the measurement error in each latent variable. In so doing, we hope to achieve a more accurate representation of the relationships among these factors.

Once again, we must begin by establishing that the model is identified. A necessary condition for identification is that the number of parameters in the model is less than or equal to the number of covariances in the covariance matrix of the indicators. There are now 15 indicators, which implies $15(16)/2 = 120$ covariances. There are 38 parameters to estimate in this model: 5 paths, 2 exogenous variable variances, 1 covariance between exogenous variables, 11 factor loadings (one of each of the four sets of indicators is used to scale each latent variable), 15 measurement error variances, 2 measurement error covariances, and 2 variances of the disturbances. Variances of the latent endogenous variables are not parameters to estimate, as they are accounted for by other parameters in the model. Similarly, their covariance is accounted for by $\beta 21$ and other model effects. Because this necessary condition for identification is satisfied, the model may be identified.

To complete the demonstration of identification, we use the two-step rule (Bollen, 1989). First, we distinguish the model linking the latent variables to each other from the factor model linking the concepts to their respective indicators. The first is referred to as the *structural* model, and the second is called the *measurement* model. In Step 1, we show that the measurement model is identified. In Step 2, we use the fact that the covariance matrix among the latent variables has been identified in Step 1 to further identify the structural model. Showing the identification of the measurement model involves ignoring the structural part of the model and treating the model as one big confirmatory factor model for the latent variables. This is depicted in Fig. 13.6. Here, $\eta 1$ and $\eta 2$ have been relabeled $\xi 3$ and $\xi 4$ to emphasize that the model is just a CFA for all of the indicators. The lines connecting the latent variables represent covariances, rather than path coefficients. All of the latent variables covary because there are causal relationships among them that lead to such covariance, as was previously demonstrated with respect to Fig. 13.1.

Attempting to identify this cumbersome model algebraically is tedious, although it can be done. Fortunately, the model can be identified more readily by drawing on the FC1 rule (see Davis, 1993, for a development of this rule). With the measurement model identified, the structural model is identified via the recursive rule, and the entire model in Fig. 13.5 is therefore identified.

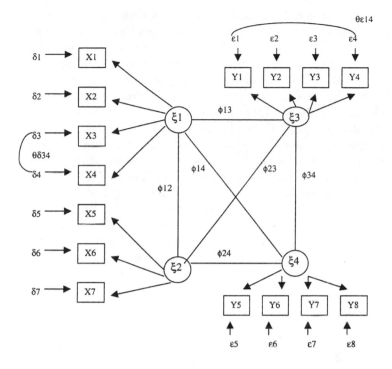

FIG. 13.6. Measurement portion of full covariance structure model for relation-ships among mothers' endorsement of women working, mothers' gender egalitari-anism, child's sexual permissiveness, and child's sexual behavior. Notation: $\xi 1$ = mothers' endorsement of women working; $\xi 2$ = mothers' gender egalitarianism; X1 = mothers' disagreement that male should be sole breadwinner; X2 = mothers' disagreement that preschool children suffer when their mother is employed; X3 = mothers' endorsement of women working full time when their youngest child is un-der 5; X4 = mothers' endorsement of women working part time when their young-est child is under 5; X5 = mothers' agreement that daughters should be raised to be as independent as sons; X6 = mothers' agreement that, when both partners work full time, each should share equally in household tasks; X7 = mothers' agreement that, in a successful marriage, both partners must have freedom to do what they want individually; $\xi 3$ = child's sexual permissiveness, $\xi 4$ = child's sexual adven-turism; Y1 = child's endorsement of others having children without being married; Y2 = child's endorsement of unmarried couples living together if they have no in-terest in marriage; Y3 = child's endorsement of unmarried 18-year-olds having sex without strong affection for each other; Y4 = child's endorsement of child's having children without being married; Y5 = child's age at first intercourse (reverse-coded); Y6 = child's number of different lifetime sexual partners; Y7 = child's fre-quency of sex in the past month; Y8 = child's number of different sexual partners in past month.

As before, the model was estimated with maximum likelihood, using the procedure CALIS in SAS (see Appendix B for the program). Table 13.6 presents the unstandardized ML estimates for the structural portion of the model, as well as several indicators of the fit of the model. Interestingly, substantive conclusions are the same as were reached in the path analysis. There are two significant structural effects. Mothers' endorsement of women working is significantly and positively related to child's sexual permissiveness. The effect is only slightly stronger than that shown in Table 13.2 (.14 as opposed to .13). Child's sexual permissiveness is again significantly and positively associated with child's sexual adventurism. In this case, the unstandardized effect is much larger than in Table 13.2 (1.12 vs. .21). Perhaps the most noticeable difference is in the R^2s for the endogenous variables. In treating the latent variables as exactly measured, only about 2% and 4% of the variance in child's sexual permissiveness and sexual adventurism, respectively, were accounted for by the model (see Table 13.2). When measurement error in the latent variables is accounted for, we see that these values have increased to 7% and 16%, respectively. Consistent with theoretical expectation (Bollen, 1989), coefficients of determination appear to be attenuated by measurement error.

TABLE 13.6
Unstandardized Parameter Estimates for Latent Variable Portion
of Full Covariance Structure Model of Child's Sexual Permissiveness
and Child's Sexual Adventurism Depicted in Fig. 13.5

Parameter	Maximum Likelihood Estimate	t Ratio
$\gamma 11$	.141	2.409
$\gamma 12$	.158	1.112
$\gamma 21$	−.007	−.045
$\gamma 22$	−.115	−.312
$\beta 21$	1.121	3.695
$\phi 11$	.583	5.515
$\phi 22$	.148	2.538
$\phi 12$	.066	2.182
$\text{Var}(\zeta 1)$	.245	3.461
$\text{Var}(\zeta 2)$	1.725	4.327
$R^2_{\eta 1}$	.069	
$R^2_{\eta 2}$	.158	
$\chi^2(82)$	85.542	—
Δ_1	.916	—
GFI	.970	—
AGFI	.956	—
Bentler's CFI	.996	—
McDonald's Centrality	.995	—
Bollen's Δ_2	.996	—

Estimation With Non-Normal Data

Maximum likelihood estimation, as mentioned previously, is based on the relatively stringent assumption that the data represent observations from a multivariate normal distribution. A necessary condition for multivariate normality is that each variable has a univariate distribution that is normal. This assumption is certainly not satisfied with these data, given that the indicators tapping mothers' gender role ideology and child's sexual permissiveness are only five- and four-category items, respectively. Additionally, a test for multivariate kurtosis (Bollen, 1989), as provided in CALIS (Hartmann, 1989), suggests that the data depart substantially from multivariate normality. When this condition is violated, ML estimators only retain their property of consistency. Chi-squared tests and tests for individual parameter estimates may be substantially biased. However, simulation work (Hu, Bentler, & Kano, 1992) suggests that if the data depart from normality, but the errors are still independent of the other latent variables in the model, the ML chi-squared test is still accurate in large samples. In small to moderate samples, it tends to be too conservative; that is, it too often indicates rejection of a correct model.

Often the data are non-normal and the researcher has no idea what distribution actually describes the data. An estimation technique that can be used in this case is weighted least squares (WLS). As this technique is asymptotically robust regardless of how the data are distributed, it is also called the arbitrary distribution function (ADF) estimator. When the model in Fig. 13.5 was estimated with WLS, the substantive conclusions remained the same, but the fit was noticeably degraded. The WLS chi-squared test, again with 82 degrees of freedom, was 136.3, a significant result ($p < .0002$). This suggests that the model should be rejected.

How reliable is the ADF estimator? Unfortunately, the same simulation study just cited found that the ADF estimator performed poorly under any distribution for the data unless N was 5,000 (Hu et al., 1992), in which case it gave accurate results regardless of the distribution of the data. With Ns as small as in the current sample (e.g., under 500), this estimator tended to markedly overreject correct models. What should the investigator do? The ML estimator appears to be robust to non-normality provided that the sample size is large and errors are independent of latent variables. In small samples, ML probably provides a conservative test of the covariance structure hypothesis. However, the ADF estimator requires very large samples before it is to be trusted. In the current example, the ML results are probably more accurate.

CONCLUSION AND SUGGESTIONS
FOR FURTHER READING

We have now considered some of the major varieties of covariance structure models: path, factor, and LISREL models. We have seen that all of these models attempt to account for observed covariances/correlations with the parameters of a structural model that underlies the data. This chapter is merely an introduction to a vast and complex topic. The reader wishing to deepen his or her understanding of these techniques is advised to pursue several additional sources. Those interested in path analysis will find Alwin and Hauser (1975) and chapter 11 in Knoke and Bohrnstedt (1994) especially useful. A thorough treatment of path analysis from the LISREL perspective can also be found in Bollen (1989). Although many treatments of exploratory factor analysis tend to be very technically advanced, the monograph by Gorsuch (1983) is especially accessible and informative. Those interested in EFA should also read the articles by Snook and Gorsuch (1989) and MacCallum, Widaman, Zhang, and Hong (1999). There are several good sources on LISREL models. Probably the most comprehensive is Bollen (1989). Other good treatments can be found in Long (1983a, 1983b), Hayduk (1987), and Loehlin (1987). Because these techniques are undergoing constant development, the serious student of covariance structure modeling may want to subscribe to journals that routinely feature articles on the topic, such as *Sociological Methods & Research* or *Psychological Methods*.

APPENDIX A: A TUTORIAL IN COVARIANCE ALGEBRA

Covariance algebra consists of a set of algebraic rules for finding variances and covariances involving variables and constants. These rules make it possible to find variances of terms, and covariances between terms, which appear at first glance to be quite complicated.

Definitions

Cov (X, Y) = $E[(X - \mu_x)(Y - \mu_y)]$. The population covariance is the expected value, or average, of the crossproduct of deviation scores in X with deviation scores in Y.

$$\text{cov(X,Y)} = \frac{\sum (X - \bar{X})(Y - \bar{Y})}{n - 1}.$$ The sample covariance is the average, in the sample, of the crossproduct of deviation scores in X with deviation scores in Y. The covariance of two variables is a quantitative measure of how two variables vary together. Positive covariance means that large values of X are associated with large values of Y, and small values of X are associated with small values of Y. Negative covariance means that large values of X are associated with small values of Y, and small values of X are associated with large values of Y.

$r_{xy} = \text{corr(X,Y)} = \text{cov(X,Y)}/(s_x s_y)$. The sample correlation between X and Y is the covariance between X and Y divided by the product of their respective standard deviations. The correlation is essentially a standardized covariance, standardized so that it falls in the range -1, 1. Another way to understand the correlation is to note that if you take the covariance between standardized variables, the result is their correlation. Hence, covariance algebra applied to standardized variables produces results that are in terms of correlations and standardized variances (which equal 1.0).

Basic Rules of Covariance Algebra

Let W, X, Y, and Z be variables in a particular data set, and let a, b, c, and d be constants. Then:

(a) $Cov(X,Y) = Cov(Y,X)$ Covariance is symmetric with respect to the order of the variables.

(b) $Cov(X, c) = 0$. That is, the covariance of a variable with a constant is zero. This makes sense because one of these variables is not varying at all.

(c) $Var(X) = Cov(X, X)$. The variance of a variable is the covariance of that variable with itself.

(d) $Var(cX) = c^2 Var(X)$

(e) $Cov(aX, bY) = ab\ Cov(X,Y)$

(f) $Cov(aX + bY, cW + dZ) = ac\ Cov(X,W) + ad\ Cov(X,Z) + bc\ Cov(Y,W) + bd\ Cov(Y,Z)$

Rule (f) shows a simple technique for finding the covariance of any two terms. Let us take that covariance again, to see how the technique works:

Step 1: multiply the terms on each side of the comma together using regular algebra:

$$(aX + bY)\ (cW + dZ) = aXcW + aXdZ + bYcW + bYdZ.$$

Step 2: separate the original terms in the resulting products with commas:

$$(aX + bY)\ (cW + dZ) = aX,cW + aX,dZ + bY,cW + bY,dZ$$

Step 3: take the covariances of the terms joined by commas:

$$Cov(aX,cW) + Cov(aX,dZ) + Cov(bY,cW) + Cov(bY,dZ)$$

Step 4: apply the appropriate basic rules above to reduce the result to an expression involving constants times covariances of variables or constants times variances of variables:

ac Cov(X,W) + ad Cov(X,Z) + bc Cov(Y,W) + bd Cov(Y,Z).

Notice that I have applied Rule (e) to each of the terms in this last expression.

Examples

Example 1. In linear regression, we regress Y on a set of Xs in a particular sample. Each b_k (i.e., each regression coefficient) has an associated standard error. Each pair of regression coefficients, like b_1 and b_2, say, has a covariance. These statistics only make sense when you understand the concept of repeated sampling. That is, the current sample is only one of an infinite number of possible samples of a given size from the population. Hence the current regression coefficients are only one set from an infinite number of sets of regression coefficients that could be obtained by regressing Y on the Xs in each of the infinite number of samples. The variance of b_k then is a quantitative measure of the variation in b_k one would encounter in performing all these different regressions, and the covariance of b_1 with b_2 is a measure of the extent to which the values of b_1 and b_2, from all these regressions, would covary.

Hence, suppose you have two coefficients in a particular sample, say b_1 and b_2, and you want to test a hypothesis that these coefficients are the same value in the population. Their population counterparts are β_1 and β_2. The null hypothesis is: $\beta_1 = \beta_2$ or $\beta_1 - \beta_2 = 0$. The test is $t = (b_1 - b_2) / SE(b_1 - b_2)$. $SE(b_1 - b_2)$, the standard error of the difference in regression coefficients, is the square root of $Var(b_1 - b_2)$. How do you find this variance? Realize first that b_1 and b_2 are variables over repeated sampling, and their difference is therefore also a variable, so we can use covariance algebra to find the variance of the difference between two variables:

$Var(b_1 - b_2) = Cov(b_1 - b_2, b_1 - b_2)$ [The variance of a variable is its covariance with itself]

$= Cov(b_1,b_1) - Cov(b_1,b_2) - Cov(b_2,b_1) + Cov(b_2,b_2)$

$= Var(b_1) + Var(b_2) - 2\,Cov(b_1,b_2)$.

Estimates of these variances and covariances can be found in the covariance matrix of parameter estimates that is an optional part of standard regression output.

Example 2. Suppose you run an interaction model: $E(Y) = a + bX + cZ + dXZ$. You are interested in whether the relationship between Y and X is significant at a particular level of Z, say, z. The partial slope for the effect of X on Y at a particular level of Z is, in fact, a function of Z. To see this, factor all multipliers of X in the regression equation:

$$E(Y) = a + bX + cZ + dXZ = a + cZ + (b + dZ)X.$$

Hence, the partial slope for the impact of X is the coefficient for X in this (rewritten) equation, or $b + dZ$. That is, the partial slope depends upon the particular value of Z at which it is evaluated. When $Z = z$, the partial slope is $b + dz$. The test for the significance of this partial slope is, like any test of partial slope, the partial slope estimate divided by its estimated standard error. This is a t test with $N - K - 1$ df, where K = the total number of regressors in the model (in this case K = 3). That is, the test is: $t = (b + dz)/SE(b + dz)$. How do we find $SE(b + dz)$?

You guessed it, we use covariance algebra. We have to find $Var(b + dz)$ and then take the square root of this term. Now, remember that if Z is fixed over repeated sampling—an assumption in classical regression—then z is a constant in this manipulation (i.e. it does not change over repeated sampling; only b and d change. Do not confuse b and d here with b and d in the covariance algebra rules. In that case, they were constants. Now they're estimated regression coefficients and, therefore, variables!). So:

$$Var(b + dz) = Cov(b + dz, b + dz)$$
$$= Cov(b,b) + Cov(b,dz) + Cov(dz,b) + Cov(dz,dz)$$
$$= Var(b) + 2 z Cov(b,d) + z^2 Var (d).$$

Again, these values are readily at hand (provided you request the covariance matrix of parameter estimates from your regression output).

Example 3. In path analysis, the variances of all endogenous variables and the correlations between all variables in a causal system can be decomposed in terms of the parameters of a structural model. Structural models can be represented either with equations or with path diagrams. Suppose we have two endogenous Variables S and A in a causal system, and two exogenous variables, E and R (from Knoke & Bohrnstedt, 1994, Fig. 11.3, p. 415). The path diagram for this model is shown in Fig. 13.7.

The population equations for these variables are:

$$S = Psr R + Pse E + Psv V$$
$$A = Pas S + Pae E + Par R + Paw W.$$

All variables are standardized (i.e., have means of zero and variances of 1.0). The Ps are path coefficients (i.e., standardized regression coefficients), subscripted by the effect variable, followed by the causal variable. It is a standard assumption of path analysis that the equation errors, V and W, are uncorrelated with the independent variables in their respective equations, and with each other. Now, let us

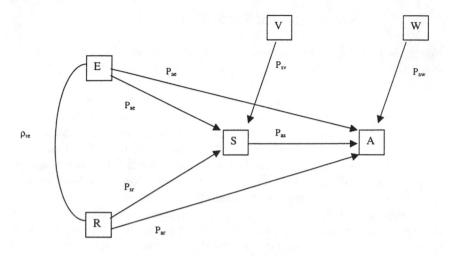

FIG. 13.7.   Four-variable path diagram from Knoke and Bohrnstedt (1994).

decompose the correlation between R and S in terms of the parameters of the first structural equation. Remember that since the variables are standardized, their correlations (symbolized by ρs in the population) are synonymous with their covariances. Hence:

$$\text{Corr(R,S)} = \text{Cov(R,S)} = \text{Cov(R, Psr R + Pse E + Psv V)}$$
$$= \text{Psr Cov(R,R)} + \text{Pse Cov(R,E)} + \text{Psv Cov(R,V)}$$
$$= \text{Psr} + \text{Pse } \rho\text{re (last term disappears since, by assumption, Cov(R,V)} = 0).$$

This decomposition reveals that the correlation between R and S is due to the sum of a direct effect of R on S plus a noncausal component of association due to the confounding of R with E. Now, let's untangle the variance in the endogenous variable S:

$$\text{Var(S)} = 1.0 = \text{Cov(S,S)}$$
$$= \text{Cov(Psr R + Pse E + Psv V, Psr R + Pse E + Psv V)}$$
$$= \text{Psr}^2 \text{ Cov(R,R)} + \text{PsrPse Cov(R,E)} + \text{PsrPsv Cov(R,V)} + \text{PsePsr Cov(E,R)}$$
$$\quad + \text{Pse}^2 \text{ Cov(E,E)} + \text{PsePsv Cov(E,V)} + \text{PsvPsr Cov(V,R)} + \text{PsvPse Cov(V,E)}$$
$$\quad + \text{Psv}^2 \text{ Cov(V,V)}$$
$$= \text{Psr}^2 + 2 \text{ PsrPse}\rho\text{re} + \text{Pse}^2 + \text{Psv}^2.$$

(Why? Recall that the variance of a standardized variable is 1.0, and covariances of the errors with predictors are assumed to be zero in the structural model.)

Here we see that one part of the variance of an endogenous variable consists of the sum of squared paths plus a term involving the correlation between exogenous variables. This part is: $Psr^2 + 2\ Psr\ Pse\ \rho re + Pse^2$. This expression is equal to the population R-squared for the regression of S on R and E, or $P^2_{S.RE}$. The remaining term is the squared error path. The error path is then easily recovered:

$$P_{sv} = \sqrt{1 - P^2_{S.RE}} \ .$$

Therefore, once the R-squared for the regression of the endogenous variable on all predetermined variables in its equation is given, the error path is also automatically given.

APPENDIX B: CALIS PROGRAM FOR ESTIMATION OF FIGURE 13.5

Here is the CALIS program that I employed to perform ML estimation of the model in Fig. 13.5. The reader should consult SAS Institute Inc. (1989) for a detailed description of CALIS and its associated programming instructions. The first starred statement is a comment. Following this, the CALIS program is specified via a PROC CALIS statement that requests the procedure plus any optional output, a LINEQS statement that defines the structural equations of the model, an STD statement that specifies which variances of latent variables are to be estimated, a COV statement which specifies which covariances among latent variables are to be estimated, and a VAR statement which specifies which observed variables are to be analyzed by the model.

Program

```
*  FULL LISREL MODEL OF CHILDRENS SEXUAL ATTITUDES AND BEHAVIOR;
PROC CALIS COV KURTOSIS MOD TOTEFF;
LINEQS
PERMIS1 = FPERMISS + E1,
PERMIS2 = LAM21 FPERMISS + E2,
PERMIS3 = LAM31 FPERMISS + E3,
PERMIS4 = LAM41 FPERMISS + E4,
FO373 = FBEHAV + E5,
FO374 = LAM62 FBEHAV + E6,
FO375 = LAM72 FBEHAV + E7,
FO376 = LAM82 FBEHAV + E8,
FLIVING = FWOMROLE + E9,
FPRESCH = LAMX21 FWOMROLE + E10,
FFULL = LAMX31 FWOMROLE + E11,
FPART = LAMX41 FWOMROLE + E12,
FDAUGHT = FEGAL + E13,
```

```
FSHARE   =  LAMX62  FEGAL  +  E14,
FFREE    =  LAMX72  FEGAL  +  E15,
FPERMISS =  GAM11  FWOMROLE  +  GAM12  FEGAL  +  D1,
FBEHAV   =  GAM21  FWOMROLE  +  GAM22  FEGAL  +  BET21  FPERMISS  +  D2;
STD
E1-E15   =  TE1-TE8  TD1-TD7,
D1  D2   =  PSI11  PSI22,
FWOMROLE  FEGAL  =  PHI11  PHI22;
COV
FWOMROLE  FEGAL  =  PHI12,
E1  E4   =  TE14,
E11  E12 =  TD34;
VAR  PERMIS1-PERMIS4  FO373  FO374  FO375  FO376  FLIVING-FFREE;
```

REFERENCES

Alwin, D. F., & Hauser, R. M. (1975). The decomposition of effects in path analysis. *American Sociological Review, 40*, 37–47.

Axinn, W. G., & Thornton, A. (1993). Mothers, children, and cohabitation: The intergenerational effects of attitudes and behavior. *American Sociological Review, 58*, 233–246.

Bentler, P. M., & Bonnett, D. G. (1980). Significance tests and goodness-of-fit in the analysis of covariance structures. *Psychological Bulletin, 88*, 588–600.

Bollen, K. A. (1989). *Structural equations with latent variables*. New York: Wiley.

Davis, W. R. (1993). The FC1 rule of identification for confirmatory factor analysis. *Sociological Methods & Research, 21*, 403–437.

Gerbing, D. W., & Anderson, J. C. (1993). Monte Carlo evaluations of goodness-of-fit indices for structural equation models. In K. A. Bollen & J. S. Long (Eds.), *Testing structural equation models* (pp. 40–65). Newbury Park, CA: Sage.

Gorsuch, R. L. (1983). *Factor analysis* (2nd ed.). Hillsdale, NJ: Lawrence Erlbaum Associates.

Harman, H. H. (1976). *Modern factor analysis* (3rd ed.). Chicago: The University of Chicago Press.

Hartmann, W. M. (1989). *The CALIS procedure extended user's guide*. Cary, NC: SAS Institute, Inc.

Hasenfeld, Y., & Rafferty, J. A. (1989). The determinants of public attitudes toward the welfare state. *Social Forces, 67*, 1027–1048.

Hayduk, L. A. (1987). *Structural equation modeling with LISREL: Essentials and advances*. Baltimore: Johns Hopkins University Press.

Hu, L., Bentler, P. M., & Kano, Y. (1992). Can test statistics in covariance structure analysis be trusted? *Psychological Bulletin, 112*, 351–362.

Knoke, D., & Bohrnstedt, G. W. (1994). *Statistics for social data analysis* (3rd ed.). Itasca, IL: Peacock.

Loehlin, J. C. (1987). *Latent variable models: An introduction to factor, path, and structural analysis*. Hillsdale, NJ: Lawrence Erlbaum Associates.

Long, J. S. (1982a). *Confirmatory factor analysis: A preface to LISREL* (Sage University Paper series on Quantitative Applications in the Social Sciences, 07-033). Beverly Hills, CA: Sage.

Long, J. S. (1982b). *Covariance Structure Models: An introduction to LISREL* (Sage University Paper series on Quantitative Applications in the Social Sciences, 07-034). Beverly Hills, CA: Sage.

MacCallum, R. C., Widaman, K. F., Zhang, S., & Hong, S. (1999). Sample size in factor analysis. *Psychological Methods, 4*, 84–99.

Mirowsky, J., & Ross, C. E. (1991). Eliminating defense and agreement bias from measures of the sense of control: A 2x2 index. *Social Psychology Quarterly, 54*, 127–145.

Reilly, T. (1995). A necessary and sufficient condition for identification of confirmatory factor analysis models of factor complexity one. *Sociological Methods & Research, 23*, 421–441.

Reilly, T., & O'Brien, R. M. (1996). Identification of confirmatory factor analysis models of arbitrary complexity: The side-by-side rule. *Sociological Methods & Research, 24*, 473–491.

Snook, S. C., & Gorsuch, R. L. (1989). Component analysis versus common factor analysis: A Monte Carlo study. *Psychological Bulletin, 106*, 148–154.

Sweet, J. A., Bumpass, L. L., & Call, V. (1988). *The design and content of the National Survey of Families and Households*. Madison, WI: The University of Wisconsin, Center for Demography & Ecology.

14

Analyzing Textual Material

Laura M. Carpenter
Johns Hopkins University

Mass media and their effects on behavior are topics of perennial interest among scholars in all areas of the social sciences; those who study sexuality are no exception. Many research questions motivate this interest, chief among them the conviction that mass media act as key agents of sexual socialization. For example, one frequently cited study (Strasburger, 1995) found that adolescents cite mass media as the third most important source from which they obtain information about sexuality, following peers and parents. A crucial step toward achieving a thorough understanding of mass media and their effects is analyzing the content of the media.

Content analysis is one of the oldest and consistently most popular methods for studying messages about sexuality, or any other topic, in mass media (Baxter, 1991; Krippendorff, 1980; Wimmer & Dominick, 1997). The techniques of content analysis enable researchers systematically to measure and track the topics and themes in selected mass media texts. Studies employing content analysis techniques are almost always comparative on some level and typically explore trends in media content and presentation over time, compare communication across cultures (i.e., social groups, societies, nation-states), or compare communication across different types of media (Berger, 1998).

Content analysis has been defined in numerous ways, virtually all of which share three elements. First, content analysis is systematic. Explicit rules are used consistently to identify and code the content to be analyzed. Second, content analysis is objective. Any researcher applying the same set of rules should obtain the same results, even if she or he interprets them differently. Finally, content analysis is at least partly quantitative, offering a way to establish the quantities and relative proportions of specified content categories in a given sample (Berg, 1989; Berger, 1998; Wimmer & Dominick, 1997). In effect, content analysis is a means for data reduction. It enables the researcher to condense large quantities of text into a finite number of categories, which are systematically comparable and can be analyzed efficiently.

With little adjustment, the techniques of content analysis can be applied to a wide variety of textual data sources, including interview transcripts, diaries, and ethnographic field notes. Nor are they limited to the analysis of textual data; many excellent studies have used these methods to examine visual materials ranging from photographs, magazine centerfolds, videotapes, television broadcasts, and films (see e.g., Bogaert, Turkovich, & Hafer, 1993; Ward, 1995; Whatley, 1994). The issues inherent in content analysis of visual material are addressed elsewhere (see chap. 16, this volume). This chapter concentrates specifically on the use of content analysis methods to study written texts in mass media.

MAJOR APPROACHES TO CONTENT ANALYSIS

For several decades now, scholars studying mass media and other texts have debated whether content analysis should be approached primarily as an enumerative or interpretive method. Analysts favoring the former approach confine themselves to tracking the numeric prevalence of key words or phrases in selected texts, whereas adherents to the latter approach emphasize the ways that audience members interpret and find meaning in the words, phrases, and texts they read. A researcher's position in this debate determines not only the avenues of analysis he or she pursues, but also the standards by which his or her research should be judged. Content analysts have also grappled over the closely related issue of whether they should limit their study to content that is physically present and countable (i.e., manifest content) or extend their domain to include content that requires more interpretation (i.e., latent content). For instance, whereas it is relatively simple to ascertain whether a newspaper article mentions homosexuality, it is somewhat more difficult to establish whether the article presents homosexuality from a positive, negative, or neutral perspective.

At times, researchers on either side of the debate have characterized their counterparts as missing the point of the social scientific enterprise. Scholars who are interested in causation and hypothesis testing have advocated the most stringently objective enumerative methods and have tended to criticize interpretive content analyses as nonsystematic and impressionistic. In contrast, researchers favoring the interpretive approach have argued that the complexities and symbolic nature of human communication preclude enumerating content in any simple fashion. Their critiques of quantitative content analysis include the charge that enumerating content assumes that the same words carry the same meaning regardless of context or rhetorical effect.

Although these characterizations and critiques each contain at least a grain of truth, the dichotomy so often drawn between the two branches of content analysis is partly false. True, practitioners of content analysis tend to favor one approach over another; however, most incorporate some elements of the alternative strategy in their own research. Furthermore, experts in social science methods have increasingly promoted content analyses that combine the most useful elements of both enumerative and interpretive approaches (e.g., Berg, 1989; Weber, 1985; for a thoughtful comparison of the two approaches, see Altheide, 1996).

Scholars who recommend a blended approach to content analysis typically contend that coding data is not an art, but rather a process that can be systematized (Baxter, 1991; Glaser & Strauss, 1967; Lofland & Lofland, 1984). Altheide (1996) offered a particularly comprehensive and useful guide to blended content analysis. Based on the symbolic interactionist position that all communication is symbolic at some level, Altheide developed the strategy he called *ethnographic content analysis*. This approach seeks to augment more traditional, objective content analysis methods by applying the techniques of participant observation to the study of inanimate texts. According to Altheide, the content analyst is engaged in an ongoing process of interaction with the texts she or he studies. This interactive process enables the researcher to guide and refine the analysis as it proceeds, achieving a progressively deeper understanding of the research question at hand. Altheide contended that, like traditional participant observation, ethnographic content analysis aims to be "systematic and analytic but not rigid" (p. 16). The techniques of content analysis described in this chapter conform closely to this ethnography-inspired method.

ADVANTAGES AND LIMITATIONS

Advantages

The advantages of the content analysis method are considerable. First, because documents survive long after the people who create and consume them, content analysis offers a superb means for studying historical phenomena. At the same time, the method allows the researcher to analyze a brand-new document, such as the morning's newspaper, the moment it becomes available. Consequently, content analysis techniques are extremely well suited to exploring change over time. Content analysts must, however, bear in mind that some textual materials survive over many years only because they have been favored by members of the elite; this tendency may introduce bias into a research project (Weber, 1985).

Another advantage of content analysis is that it is relatively inexpensive, at least when data are drawn from print sources. (Studying visual texts, especially film or television broadcasts, can be considerably more costly; see Wimmer & Dominick, 1997.) Typically, data are also easily available from sources such as library print media collections, archives, and computer databases.

In addition, because the researcher does not interact directly with the people being studied, content analysis reduces the extent to which the researcher influences the object of his or her study (Berg, 1989; Weber, 1985). Nonetheless, everyone studying social phenomena—content analysts included—may indirectly affect their research through the choice of topic, coding categories, research question, and so forth (Berger, 1998).

Limitations

As with any method, content analysis has its limitations; however, many of these limitations can be easily surmounted. For example, although some scholars find content analysis disagreeably painstaking and time-consuming, many contend that the time invested in the processes of coding and recoding yields exceptional familiarity with the data (Berg, 1989). A somewhat more intractable limitation stems from the fact that, in counting particular instances of content as having the same meaning, content analyses may ignore the unique ways that meaning emerges through social interactions in specific local contexts (Baxter, 1991). For example, a teenager might interpret an item in a magazine advice column as a joke if she or he reads it aloud among friends, but as a valuable source of serious information if read alone. The researcher cannot directly relieve this problem without collecting additional data through methods such as interviewing or participant observation; however, the researcher can compensate in part by taking these matters of meaning into account as he or she analyzes the data.

Another limitation of studies relying on content analysis techniques involves the degree to which their findings can be extended to the activities of mass media creators and consumers. At base, content analysis alone is not sufficient to reveal producers' intentions in creating mass media texts. For example, although editors of the fledging teen magazine *Sassy* wanted to provide more explicit information about sexuality than was available in competing magazines, they were compelled to reconsider when a conservative parents' organization threatened to boycott their advertisers (Larsen, 1990). A researcher who ascribed the relative paucity of explicit sexual information to the editors' conservatism would be severely mistaken. Yet Berg (1989) suggested that, interpreted judiciously, content analyses may help provide clues to producers' intentions. For instance, the particular terms creators opt to use may tell us something about them. In choosing to refer to surgery on the sexually ambiguous genitals of an infant as either a *correction* or *mutilation*, an author may reveal her or his own perspective on such operations.

Likewise, content analysis by itself cannot paint a comprehensive picture of the effects that texts have on the people who consume them. For instance, although Radway (1984) personally interpreted romance novels as oppressive to women, she found that the same texts inspired a community of habitual readers to resist fulfilling some aspects of the traditional roles of wife and mother, despite the demands and expectations of their husbands and children.

In short, we cannot assume that the patterns of conduct, attitudes, and values found in mass media materials reflect the conduct, attitudes, and values of their creators and consumers in a nonproblematic way (Berger, 1998). Scholars seeking to overcome this limitation have increasingly combined in single studies content analyses of mass media texts and research on audiences or producers. For example, Christian-Smith (1990, 1994) not only evaluated the content of 34 teen romance novels, but also interviewed 29 of the young women who read them (see also McRobbie, 1991; Radway, 1984). Researchers for whom such expanded studies are impractical can, however, rest assured that content analysis stands as an integral part of understanding media effects and production processes. Content analysis remains a central technique in media studies in large part because of its ability to provide a baseline for broader studies. Although every text can potentially be interpreted in more than one way, texts cannot be interpreted in ways that diverge utterly from their literal content (Griswold, 1987).

Finally, perhaps the least surmountable limitation stems from the reliance of content analysis on already recorded texts or messages. Quite simply, scholars may not always be able to locate data sources that are relevant to the research questions that interest them. For instance, a researcher wishing to chart changes over time in the sexual activities mentioned in pulp novels may find, to his or her frustration, that very few libraries collect, much less retain, ephemeral materials which are not only erotic, but also typically seen as lacking literary merit.

STEPS OF CONTENT ANALYSIS

The process of conducting a content analysis can be broken down into approximately 11 steps, generally undertaken in the following order (Altheide, 1996; Wimmer & Dominick, 1997):

1. Establish the research question or hypothesis.
2. Review the relevant literature.
3. Determine the universe of data from which the sample will be taken.
4. Identify several (6 to 10) examples of relevant documents from the data universe and read them repeatedly to decide on the appropriate unit of analysis.
5. List several (9 to 12) categories to guide data collection and draft the coding protocol.
6. Test the protocol by coding several (6 to 10) documents.
7. Revise and refine the protocol.
8. Settle on a sampling strategy and select the final sample.
9. Collect data, using preset codes and narrative examples.

10. Recode already coded items, using most recent protocol.

11. Analyze and interpret the data.

Assuming that readers are familiar with the fundamentals of conducting research in their respective fields, I limit my discussion to the steps in the process that are most specific to content analysis methods.

Steps 3 and 4: Defining the Data Universe and Determining the Unit of Analysis

After deciding on a research question and familiarizing him or herself with the relevant literature, the prospective content analyst must identify the pool from which his or her data will be taken. *Universe of data* is another way to refer to the broadest possible pool of documents or texts that are believed to contain information germane to answering the research question. This pool of data should be relevant to the research topic in terms of both subject matter and time period. For example, a scholar interested in the emergence of birth control as a suitable topic for public discussion would draw data from the universe of mainstream mass media starting from the publication of the initial articles on birth control (Flamiano, 1998). Table 14.1 compares four studies, showing the universes of data associated with the four research topics, as well as the choices researchers made about sampling and units of analysis.

In the primarily quantitative approach they outlined, Wimmer and Dominick (1997) recommended selecting a sampling method and drawing the complete sample at this point. Consistent with my advocacy of a more qualitative approach, I follow Altheide's (1996) recommendation that the selection of the final sample be postponed until the unit of analysis has been selected and a preliminary coding protocol established. According to this latter method, the researcher should next chose approximately 6 to 10 documents from the data universe and read them several times, with the goal of determining the appropriate unit of analysis for the project. Repeated reading is one of the best ways to become familiar with any body of textual data. It enables the researcher to develop a sense of the natural divisions—the sections in which potentially different topics, ideas, or themes are clustered—in the type of data that will be examined. Such familiarity positions the content analyst to select an appropriate unit of analysis given the research question at hand. During the coding process, the content analyst typically codes each unit of analysis separately, recording the relevant themes, topics, and so forth appearing in each one.

Content analysts have employed units of analysis including words and concepts (also known as *word sense*; Weber, 1985), sentences and paragraphs, themes, sections of text, and items (i.e., the whole unit of a sender's message, e.g., a chapter or entire book). Other possible units of analysis include characters (i.e., actors), writers, and semantics (i.e., the affective content of the message; Berg,

TABLE 14.1
Operational Definitions of Units of Analysis (following Wimmer & Dominick, 1997)

Researcher	Topic	Universe	Sample	Unit of Analysis
Christian-Smith (1994)	Teenage women's sexual socialization	All sexuality-related media consumed by teenage women	34 romance novels for teens, given positive reviews in 3 guides to children's literature, 1942–1982	Novels
McMahon (1990)	Links among gender, class, and women's sexual fantasies	All mass media containing women's sexual fantasies	Articles teased on covers of 38 issues of one magazine (*Cosmopolitan*), 1976–1988	Feature articles
Rind (1998)	Biased use of cross-cultural examples of homosexuality in sex education	All sex education curricula	18 most widely used college human sexuality textbooks	Historical and cross-cultural examples of homosexuality; textbooks
Garner et al. (1998)	Teenage and young adult women's sexual socialization	All sexuality-related media consumed by teen and young adult women	175 articles from 30 issues of 5 most popular magazines (April & October issues from 1974, 1984, 1994)	Feature articles, advice columns, letters to the editor

1989). In interpretive studies, the most commonly used units are sections of text (e.g., articles, editorials, book chapters, letters to the editor, and narrative episodes in larger texts) and entire items (e.g., textbooks, novels, and comic books). Many research questions necessitate considering more than one of these elements at a time. For example, in his study of the use of cross-cultural examples of homosexuality in college-level textbooks, Rind (1998) analyzed data at the levels of textbook and examples within textbooks. As with all stages in the analysis process, the researcher should develop and record a clear and easily followed rule for selecting the relevant units of analysis.

Steps 5 to 7: Developing the Coding Protocol

Once she or he has determined the data universe and settled on an appropriate unit of analysis, the content analyst can begin to develop a protocol for coding the data. The repeated readings of several sample texts done in Step 4 will prove useful in this process because they will have familiarized the researcher with the content of some texts eligible for the study.

Coding Categories.   The first step in this process is to list approximately a dozen categories that will guide preliminary data collection. Coding categories can refer to manifest content, such as whether sex between two males is depicted (Rind, 1998), or they can be broader and more thematic, such as opinions about birth control (Flamiano, 1998). In my own research on sexuality and romance in *Seventeen* magazine (Carpenter, 1998), I found it useful to think in terms of two broad types of categories: content and themes. Content categories in my study included specific topics such as sexual activities (e.g., kissing, petting, sexual intercourse) and themes such as stances toward women's sexuality (e.g., discourses of victimization, individual choice, and desire). When developing the protocol and coding the data, the researcher should bear in mind that the absence of certain theoretically relevant topics or categories may be as important as the presence of others. For example, if the virtual absence of oral sex in *Seventeen* magazine had led me to exclude that category from my coding protocol, I might have neglected the important findings that fellatio, a common practice among U.S. teens, was scarcely mentioned in the magazine, and cunnilingus received no mention at all.

Coding categories can be developed deductively, drawing on the existing literature on the topic in question. They can also be developed inductively, as meaningful categories become apparent to the researcher as he or she undertakes the processes of reading, rereading, and coding the data. The former method tends to be used by enumerative content analysts, the latter by their interpretive counterparts. Many researchers opt to use both methods for developing categories (Altheide, 1996). However they are derived, categories must be carefully defined or operationalized to ensure the consistency and objectivity of the research (Berg, 1989). For example, a content analyst interested in the presentation of sexuality in comic books must first decide what kinds of issues should be included in the category "sexuality." Although the depiction of sexual intercourse would clearly fall under this category, what about an ostensibly less sexual activity such as kissing, or a medical aspect of sexuality, such as sexually transmitted diseases?

Another important coding decision concerns the specificity of coding categories. One choice might be whether to use one category for "sexual activity" or several categories for specific activities such as "coitus," "fellatio," "masturbation," and so forth. Before beginning to code the data, the researcher must also decide whether coding categories should be mutually exclusive. On the one hand, because texts can be interpreted in more than one way, forcing units of text into mutually exclusive categories may do a grave injustice to the data and ultimately limit the value of the analysis. On the other hand, if the researcher plans to analyze the data using statistical techniques for which confounded variables present a major problem, the answer is probably "no" (Weber, 1985). The solutions to all of these issues are liable to differ depending on the research question and type of data at hand. Taking time to develop the coding protocol in a relatively flexible and reflexive manner ensures that the researcher can experiment with a variety of strategies before settling on a final approach (see Altheide, 1996).

As the coding protocol takes shape, the researcher should maintain a complete list of codes, along with their definitions and operationalizations. Particular care should be taken when operationalizing categories that require interpretation on the part of the coder (e.g., thematic codes). Interpretive operationalizations can often be made clear by providing extensive excerpts from texts as illustrations.

The Coding Protocol. Once preliminary coding categories have been selected, it is time to draft the coding protocol. Content analysts typically use standardized sheets or coding protocols for recording pertinent information about each unit of data in the sample. A generic coding protocol should include, at a minimum, the following categories: case number; medium (e.g., *The Washington Post*); date; item's location in the medium; length of item (in terms of space or duration); title (or emphasis if untitled); focus or main topic; themes; and format (e.g., editorial, feature article) if it varies across units of analysis (see Altheide, 1996). Figure 14.1 shows a sample protocol sheet. The protocol sheet should provide sufficient space for recording narrative examples of each code. One copy of the coding protocol should be used for each item coded. Researchers may find it helpful to make a blank copy of the protocol that can then be reproduced as necessary. Alternatively, researchers may opt to use computer-data-input programs in place of paper coding protocols.

Testing and Refining the Protocol. After the preliminary protocol has been drafted, the next step is to test the protocol by coding approximately 6 to 10 documents. Given a series of diverse texts, a well-honed protocol will enable the researcher to find and code all of the information relevant to the research questions. If the preliminary protocol does not pass this test (which is likely to be the case), the researcher should then refine the protocol and test it again on another handful of documents. This revision process may require several iterations before the protocol is complete enough to begin the coding process in earnest.

Step 8: Selecting a Sampling Strategy and Final Sample

Once these preliminary steps have been accomplished, the content analyst is ready to draw a sample of texts from the relevant universe. Any of the procedures conventional in the social sciences can be used. When the universe of texts is relatively small, the researcher may choose to analyze all of the relevant materials. For example, given her interest in a relatively brief period of time (1915–1917) during which print-based news media predominated, Flamiano (1998) was able to analyze every article covering birth control in the national news (although her choice to restrict the universe to national news does constitute a sample). When an

Case Number: _____   Date: _____   Magazine: *Seventeen*

Page(s): _____   Item Length: _____

Type of reference:

    feature article (Name/Topic: _____)

    regular feature (Name of Feature: _____; Topic: _____)

    Advice column segment (Name of Column: _____; Topic: _____)

Subject: Romance   Sexuality

               Romance & Sexuality   Other

Sexual Topics Mentioned: Narrative Examples:

  homosexuality

  masturbation

  "non-traditional" sexual practices

    (specify: _____)

  medical (STDs pregnancy abortion

    contraception menstruation other _____)

  violence against women (abuse stranger rape

    date rape incest other)

Sexual Themes: Narrative Examples:

  sexuality as violence

  sexuality as victimization

  sexuality as individual morality

  sexuality as desire

FIG. 14.1.   Portion of coding protocol used by Carpenter (1998).

analysis of all materials is not possible, the most basic methods for drawing a sample are simple random sampling and its close cousin, systematic sampling (in which a list of items in the universe is employed).

Content analysts interested in ensuring the representation of specific subgroups of data often employ stratified sampling, drawing simple random samples from segments or strata of the larger data universe. Depending on the research question, data can be stratified by time period (e.g., sources from before and after the U.S. Supreme Court's *Roe v. Wade* decision), intended audience (e.g., magazines for African-American, Latina, and Anglo-American women), editorial position (e.g., conservative, liberal, middle-of-the-road), or any other social division germane to the research question.

Purposive sampling (also called *theoretical sampling*), in which representative or especially appropriate texts are chosen based on the researcher's expertise, may be especially pertinent for some types of research questions. Using one such strategy, the researcher includes the widest range of messages expected, on a theoretical basis, to be relevant to the research question. This method in effect gives equal weight to typical and extreme cases (see Altheide, 1996). Another strategy involves using expert opinion to select the most appropriate texts. For example, from the vast number of teen romance novels published between 1942 and 1982, Christian-Smith (1990, 1994) selected those that had been reviewed positively in at least three guides to children's literature. Similarly, Rind (1995, 1998) limited his analysis to the most widely used human sexuality textbooks. Purposive sampling techniques are often used to guide stratified sampling (Altheide, 1996).

When choosing a sampling strategy, the content analyst should also consider the desired depth and breadth of coverage. Compare, for example, my study (Carpenter, 1998) and Garner, Sterk, and Adams' (1998) study of the content of teen magazines. Garner et al. sought breadth of coverage, drawing from five magazines every romance- and sexuality-related article from two issues per each of 3 years (1974, 1984, 1994). In contrast, I aimed for depth of coverage, electing to examine every sex- or romance-related article that appeared in every issue of a single magazine in the same 3 years. Finally, the researcher must determine an adequate sample size using the research question and precedents set by published research as guides (Berger, 1998). Interpretive analyses usually examine a relatively small sample in depth, whereas more traditional quantitative analysis use larger samples and rely on advanced statistical techniques for their analyses. Published articles offer practical guides to appropriate sample sizes. Another technique, generally used with purposive sampling, is to stop at the point of saturation; that is, when no new patterns are being discovered and no new relevant data sources have come to light (Altheide, 1996; Glaser & Strauss, 1967).

Steps 9 and 10: Coding the Data

With the sample chosen and a solid coding protocol in place, the researcher can turn her or his attention to the crucial task of data collection. The basic process of coding involves reading each unit in the sample and recording the relevant data on a copy of the coding protocol. For every code, especially ones involving interpretation of the text, a narrative example should be recorded. If resources permit, one or more people in addition to the main researcher can be employed to code the data. Using multiple coders not only provides a way to assess and achieve reliability in coding, but also ensures that someone familiar with the data is available to offer second opinions about tricky coding issues and other problems that might arise.

While coding the sample, the researcher inevitably notices potential new codes, categories, and themes and should keep track of these as coding proceeds. Then when between half and two thirds of the sample has been coded, the researcher should take the opportunity to refine and collapse existing categories, or even add new categories to the list (Altheide, 1996). If the researcher alters the protocol, he or she should code the remainder of the sample with the revised protocol and then go back and recode the previously coded items as well.

Step 11: Analysis and Interpretation of Data

As with other types of social scientific studies, data gathered through interpretive content analysis methods are typically analyzed using descriptive statistics such as percentages, means, medians, modes, cross-tabulations, and so forth. Researchers who adopt a more quantitative approach, especially those interested in testing specific hypotheses, may also use inferential statistical tests such as t tests and multiple regression analysis. Weber (1985) provided an excellent introductory discussion of analysis at the levels of word and concept frequency.

Assessing the proportion of units in which given categories appear—relative to one another, over time, or across types of sources—is a staple of content analyses. In addition to such numeric analyses, interpretive studies of media content also evaluate narrative data for patterns in meaning. The researcher should consider the range of data within categories as well as across them (Altheide, 1996). In my study of *Seventeen* magazine (Carpenter, 1998), for example, I first assessed the numeric prevalence of content and theme categories, which permitted a comparison of the relative prevalence of categories over time. I then compared narrative data within categories to explore changes or stability in the focus and meaning of those categories over time. Undertaking both types of comparison was invaluable because the numeric prevalence of a category did not indicate whether a topic was presented in a positive, neutral, or negative light.

As the analysis proceeds, the researcher may also wish to consider broader issues, such as the ways in which cultural and social context affect messages media texts. (This is especially important in studies that consider change over time; Weber, 1985, p. 420.) Altheide (1996) recommended knowing at least the basic steps involved in the production of the type of document to be studied; this helps the analyst better understand how particular types of producers select and insert meaning into texts. Another potential focus for analysis concerns the degree to which the depiction in mass media of the phenomena in question corresponds to or differs from the phenomena's prevalence in real life (e.g., Rind, 1995). Other topics of interest include the possible effects of texts on their consumers and ways in which the production of texts may have affected their content.

ENSURING RELIABILITY AND VALIDITY

Reliability

Reliability, that is, the extent to which repeated measurements produce the same results, can be assessed along a variety of dimensions. The most relevant to interpretive content analysis are stability and reproducibility (Weber, 1985). Stability refers to the consistency of results over time. A content analysis study is stable to the extent that the same researcher consistently codes a single body of data in the same way over time. A study is reproducible if different coders obtain the same results from a single data set, either within the same study (another term for this is *intercoder reliability*) or in a replication study. Studies in which more than one person codes the same data have a built-in test of reliability.

In small-scale or exploratory projects, it is not always feasible to have data coded by more than one person. Yet it is nonetheless possible to obtain a measure of stability for such a study. To do this, the researchers codes the same set of data (or a portion thereof) a second time, at a later date. For example, in my study (Carpenter, 1998), I recoded 30% of the sample, selected at random, after an interval of 3 months. Of course, stability can also be calculated for each coder in a multiple-coder study. Simple estimates of stability and intercoder reliability (for two coders) can be calculated as the percent of codes on which the two coders agree. Published studies usually have a minimum of 90% intercoder reliability (Wimmer & Dominick, 1997), although levels in the high 80th percentile are not unheard of.

Validity

Generally speaking, validity refers to whether a coding instrument measures what it is intended to measure (Wimmer & Dominick, 1997). Practitioners of interpretive content analysis are generally concerned with external validity, or the extent to which the analytic categories employed by the researcher carry the same meaning as that which would be imputed by others reading the same texts. (For an overview of other types of validity, see Weber, 1985.)

External validity in an interpretive content analysis study can be ensured by employing the technique used by other types of qualitative researchers: The content analyst should ask whether the analysis has captured the native point of view, whether the categorizations have captured the same meanings that would prevail in the community of people who typically consume the same texts (Baxter, 1991). The researcher can also assess the validity of the categories by comparing them with the opinions of their consumers, as did Christian-Smith (1990, 1994) in her study of teen romance novels. Another practical strategy for ensuring external validity is to use coding categories that closely resemble the exact wording in the messages (Berg, 1989). Finally, providing extensive excerpts from texts as examples enables readers to assess the quality of the scholar's analysis (Berg, 1989).

COMPUTER-ASSISTED DATA COLLECTION
AND ANALYSIS

Recent technological advances have improved the lot of the content analyst. Especially advantageous new technologies include sophisticated computer software designed for qualitative analysis (Atlas-TI and QSR NUD*IST are the most versatile in my experience), online data retrieval database services (e.g., LEXIS/

NEXIS, Academic Index), and optical character reader technology. For instance, a researcher may now identify relevant texts using an online database, download them to a desktop computer, and perform coding procedures with a qualitative analysis program. Alternatively, the content analyst may use optical character reader technology to upload selected texts (e.g., magazine articles) to a personal computer and proceed to analyze them with a qualitative software package. Researchers interested in conducting content analysis at the level of word or word sense frequencies may find especially computer software especially effective. (See Weber, 1985, for an early discussion of relevant techniques.)

The rapid pace of technological change ensures that published discussions of computer-aided social science analysis become outdated all too quickly. With that caveat, I direct the reader to the discussion in Altheide (1996), as well as to Kelle (1995) and Weitzman and Miles (1995).

CONCLUSION

In addition to introducing the reader to the basic steps involved in studies of textual mass media content, I have endeavored to sketch some of the possible avenues for investigations using these techniques. A brief overview of existing studies is presented in Table 14.2, including the purpose of each study, the choices researchers made about sample and units of analysis, and typical coding categories and the number of coders used in the studies. Content analysis methods offer tremendous potential for advancing research on sexuality, whether used alone or in combination with other types of data collection. Many textual sources of information about sexuality have yet to be tapped fully, if at all, by social scientists employing systematic content analysis methods. These sources include sex education curricula, sexuality advice manuals, sexual fantasy literature, and medical and public health pamphlets, to name only a few.

Beyond the materials suggested in this article, I encourage social scientists interested in content analysis to peruse two additional bodies of research. First, prospective analysts of textual materials can learn a great deal from a number of studies that have examined sexuality in visual media (e.g., a study of *Playboy* centerfolds, Bogaert et al., 1993; an analysis of sexual themes in prime-time TV programs, Ward, 1995). Second, because content analysis methods have yet to become a staple in sexuality research, a glance at the vast array of studies that have used content analysis techniques to examine nonsexual phenomena may offer researchers a more complete view of the possibilities of content analysis. Taken together, the high levels of popular and scholarly interest in mass media, the particular advantages of content analysis methods, and the relative absence of systematic studies of media content in the sexuality literature all indicate that the time is ripe for more research in this vein.

TABLE 14.2
Summaries of Studies (following Wimmer & Dominick, 1997)

Researcher	Purpose of Study	Sample	Units of Analysis	Representative Categories	Number of Coders
Flamiano (1998)	How birth control emerged as an acceptable topic for public discussion	118 articles from one newspaper and five national magazines, 1915–1917	Articles (editorials, features, letters to editor)	Stance on birth control; justification for promoting birth control	One
Rind (1998)	Reveal biased use of cross-cultural examples of homosexuality in college sexuality textbooks	18 most widely used college human sexuality textbooks	Historical and cross-cultural examples of homosexualiy; textbooks	Typology of homosexuality; appropriateness of examples	Four
Garner et al. (1998)	Assess patterns in teenage and young adult women's sexual socialization via mass media	175 articles from 30 issues of the 5 most popular magazines in 3 years (1974, 1984, 1994)	Articles (feature articles, advice columns, letters to the editor)	Appropriate settings for sexual relationships; women's duties as sexual partners	Five
Carpenter (1998)	Explore change over time in the depiction of romance and sexuality in teen magazines	244 articles from all 36 issues of most popular teen magazine in 3 years (1974, 1984, 1994)	Articles (feature articles, advice columns, letters to editor)	Sexual activities; stance toward women's sexuality	One

SUGGESTED READINGS

For social scientists interested in interpretive content analysis, Altheide (1996) provided a comprehensive and insightful introduction to conducting a study from start to finish. Another basic overview geared toward interpretive methods is Berg's (1989) chapter on content analysis. One classic text on qualitative analysis and the inductive development of coding categories more generally is Glaser and Strauss (1967). Researchers more inclined toward quantitative content analysis methods may wish to consult Wimmer and Dominick's (1997) chapter on content analysis, which features clear and practical step-by-step instructions. Weber (1985) also offered an invaluable overview of enumerative content analysis methods, particularly word and concept frequencies. Students in advanced undergraduate or early graduate courses may benefit from practice with Berger's (1998) exercise in the quantitative content analysis of newspaper comic strips. In their chapter on content analysis, Wimmer and Dominick (1997) provided detailed instructions for calculating inter-coder reliability when more than two coders are employed. Weber (1985) cited numerous sources about evaluating reliability and validity in the general social science literature on quantitative methodology.

REFERENCES

Altheide, D. L. (1996). *Qualitative media analysis* (Vol. 38). Thousand Oaks, CA: Sage.

Baxter, L. A. (1991). Content analysis. In B. M. Montgomery & S. Duck (Eds.), *Studying interpersonal interaction* (pp. 239–254). New York: Guilford.

Berg, B. L. (1989). *Qualitative research methods for the social sciences.* Boston: Allyn & Bacon.

Berger, A. A. (1998). *Media research techniques* (2nd ed.). Thousand Oaks, CA: Sage.

Bogaert, A. F., Turkovich, D. A., & Hafer, C. L. (1993). A content analysis of *Playboy* centerfolds from 1953 through 1990: Changes in explicitness, objectification, and model's age. *The Journal of Sex Research, 30*(2), 135–139.

Carpenter, L. M. (1998). From girls into women: Scripts for sexuality and romance in *Seventeen* magazine, 1974–1994. *The Journal of Sex Research, 35*(2), 158–168.

Christian-Smith, L. (1994). Young women and their dream lovers: Sexuality in adolescent fiction. In J. M. Irvine (Ed.), *Sexual cultures and the construction of adolescent identities* (pp. 206–227). Philadelphia: Temple University Press.

Christian-Smith, L. K. (1990). *Becoming a woman through romance.* New York: Routledge.

Flamiano, D. (1998). The birth of a notion: Media coverage of contraception, 1915–1917. *Journalism and Mass Media Quarterly, 75*(3), 560–571.

Garner, A., Sterk, H. M., & Adams, S. (1998, Autumn). Narrative analysis of sexual etiquette in teenage magazines. *Journal of Communication,* pp. 59–78.

Glaser, B. G., & Strauss, A. L. (1967). *The discovery of grounded theory: Strategies for qualitative research.* Chicago: Aldine.

Griswold, W. (1987). A methodological framework for the sociology of culture. *Sociological Methodology, 14,* 1–35.

Kelle, U. (1995). *Computer-aided qualitative analysis.* Newbury Park, CA: Sage.

Krippendorff, K. (1980). *Content analysis: An introduction to its methodology.* Beverly Hills, CA: Sage.

Larsen, E. (1990, July/August). Censoring sex information: The story of *Sassy. Utne Reader,* pp. 96–97.

Lofland, J., & Lofland, L. H. (1984). *Analyzing social settings: A guide to qualitative observation and analysis.* Belmont, CA: Wadsworth.

McMahon, K. (1990). The *Cosmopolitan* ideology and the management of desire. *Journal of Sex Research, 27*(3), 381–396.

McRobbie, A. (1991). *Feminism and youth culture: From* Jackie *to* Just Seventeen. Cambridge, MA: Unwin Hyman.

Radway, J. A. (1984). *Reading the romance: Women, patriarchy, and popular literature.* Chapel Hill: University of North Carolina Press.

Rind, B. (1995). An analysis of human sexuality textbook coverage of the psychological correlates of adult-nonadult sex. *The Journal of Sex Research, 32*(3), 219–233.

Rind, B. (1998). Biased use of cross-cultural and historical perspectives on male homosexuality in human sexuality textbooks. *The Journal of Sex Research, 35*(4), 397–407.

Strasburger, V. (1995). *Adolescents and the media: Medical and psychological impact*. Thousand Oaks, CA: Sage.

Ward, L. M. (1995). Talking about sex: Common themes about sexuality in the prime-time television programs children and adolescents view most. *Journal of Youth and Adolescence, 24*(5), 595–616.

Weber, R. P. (1985). *Basic content analysis*. Beverly Hills, CA: Sage.

Weitzman, E. A., & Miles, M. B. (1995). *Computer programs for qualitative data analysis*. Thousand Oaks, CA: Sage.

Whatley, M. H. (1994). Keeping adolescents in the picture: Construction of adolescent sexuality in textbook images and popular films. In J. M. Irvine (Ed.), *Sexual cultures and the construction of adolescent identities* (pp. 183–205). Philadelphia: Temple University Press.

Wimmer, R. D., & Dominick, J. R. (1997). *Mass media research: An introduction* (5th ed.). New York: Wadsworth.

15

Content Analysis of Visual Materials

Gloria Cowan
California State University, San Bernadino

Why analyze visual sexual material? In this age of TV, videocassettes, and the Internet, visual sexual materials may have a greater impact on sexual attitudes, values, and behaviors than do written material. Visual stimuli may be more memorable than the written word because they are encoded and more easily retrievable in memory. When I show students the antipornography film, "Not a Love Story," students frequently tell me that they cannot "get certain images out of their heads." Given the popular culture's devotion to visual media, the socialization process may be influenced strongly by exposure to visual materials. In particular, young people are exposed to visual media that contain sexual material that may ultimately affect their understanding of sexuality.

The issue of the impact of visual media on the general public and on young people has been hotly debated in public arenas and among professionals. Both sex and violence in media have been issues of concern particularly in terms of their effects on young people. Among the general public (*Attorney General's Commission on Pornography: Final Report*, 1986), social scientists (Linz, Donnerstein, & Penrod, 1987; Zillmann & Bryant, 1989), and even feminists (Russell, 1993; Vance, 1984), the issue of the impact of pornography on attitudes and behavior has been controversial and divisive. The question about pornography's impact has been a politicized, as well as scientific, issue.

To determine the effects of sexual material on viewers, one must first ask about the prevalence of sexuality in various visual media and what types of themes and messages are portrayed. Also, one needs to know the extent of exposure to these media. The most difficult question, however, has to do with the impact of sexual material on the attitudes and behavior of those who are exposed to it. It may very well be that sexual themes pervade certain media, and that the level of exposure is high, but a separate question (and one that is much more difficult to assess) is whether these sexual images and themes have an impact on attitudes and behavior.

Although the effect of visual material is the ultimate question, the first necessary task is to determine the type and frequency of sexual material available in media. If sexuality is not a primary content of media and if certain types of themes are relatively absent in visual media, the question of their influence becomes moot. For example, although a great deal of the debate on the influence of pornography has focused on violent pornography and its influence on sexual aggression, an important question is the extent to which current pornography portrays sexual violence. If sexual violence is not prevalent in pornography (Palys, 1986; Scott & Cuvelier, 1987; Winick, 1985), perhaps the questions need to be refocused. For example, some researchers (e.g., Donnerstein, Linz, & Penrod, 1987) have focused mainly on the effects of violent pornography, whereas others have examined the effects of dehumanizing pornography (Check & Guluien, 1989). Consequently, an important question, and one whose answer may change over time, is the extent to which violence, dehumanization, or neither are present in pornography. To answer this question, content analyses must be performed to assess the types and prevalence of specific themes in such sexual materials. Subsequently, the extent and effect of exposure are legitimate questions.

Some caveats are in order concerning the prevalence of types of content and the effects of such content. Certain types of non-normative sexual materials, such as child pornography, might not be readily available, but they are still a matter of concern regarding their effect and use by pedophiles. Also, it is possible that it is not the frequency of a particular kind of sexual material that is important but the context in which it occurs. For example, if one were to demonstrate that only 5% of *Hustler* or *Playboy* cartoons were violent, and that there is no increase in the frequency or percent of violent material (e.g., Scott & Cuvelier, 1987), does this mean that such violent images will have little or no impact on viewers? When non-normative material, such as sexual violence, is presented in an otherwise benign context, it may have a more subtle impact than when it is presented in the context of a medium clearly devoted to violent imagery.

Another example of the importance of context, rather than content alone, is in the area of research on exposure to violent images. Although not conclusive, research suggests that when violence is portrayed in a humorous context, the violence is trivialized (Wilson et al., 1997). A particular example relevant to sexuality would be the rape scene in the classic film "Young Frankenstein" by Mel Brooks. The scene in which Frankenstein's monster rapes the character played by Madeline Kahn and she breaks out in song is very humorous. It is only in retrospect and with a delayed reaction that we realize we are laughing at a rape. Material that may violate some normative standards may be assimilated to the prevailing imagery or mood of the scene. The most likely assumption made by researchers, however, is that increased prevalence of sexual imagery in media is associated with stronger effects on viewers' attitudes, behaviors, and values. Most content analyses that assess the frequency of sexual behaviors and themes are grounded in the assumption that frequency is important.

PURPOSES, STRENGTHS, AND WEAKNESSES OF CONTENT ANALYSIS

Weber (1990) described the many purposes of content analysis, and although much of his text was directed toward analysis of written material, some of these purposes clearly apply to content analyses of visual sexual material. The most straightforward purpose is to determine cultural patterns and the focus of societal attention. Clearly, examination of visual sexual media is intended to reveal cultural patterns with regard to sexual expression and to indicate the extent to which the mass media, as reflections of society, focus on sexuality. Content analyses of sexual visual material also document trends in communication about sexuality in public venues (i.e., media). Questions regarding increasing sexual communications over time, such as decades, have been a frequent focus in the examination of sexual material in specific media.

Two purposes Weber described as relevant to written text that may be less relevant to content analyses of sexual visual material are to identify the intentions of the communication and compare media or levels of communication. It is far easier to make inferences about the intentions of communications when a particular spokesperson is associated with a theme or statement than when the medium does not reflect the views of any particular person or group. Further, it is difficult to compare sexual content in various media when the content categories used in content analysis are typically developed to fit the sexual communications in a particular medium. However, if visual media are examined as sources of persuasion, then a purpose of content analysis would be to determine the content of those messages. In a typical communication paradigm, "who says what to whom with what effect," content analysis reveals the *what*. The *who* is the medium, the *to whom* are the viewers of the medium, and the *effect* cannot be addressed through content analysis.

Compared with other scientific methods, content analysis has both strengths and weaknesses. Its strengths include the opportunity to decipher and track cultural messages about sexuality in a way that does not rely on the cooperation and honesty of research participants, its nonreactive or unobtrusive manner of data collection (i.e., analysis of content does not change the content), and its status as a creative alternative to the use of questionnaires. One weakness of content analysis is its dependence on existing data (i.e., being tied to the type of data available in media), in contrast to other methods in which measures are designed specifically to answer a research question. Further, content analysis typically does not test relationships between variables other than the association of a particular form of expression or medium with the quantity and quality of sexual material contained in it. Also, because of its essentially correlational nature, content analyses cannot directly lead to causal conclusions.

Kolbe and Burnett (1991) cited several additional limitations of content analysis. They indicated that content analysis often yields categorical data, thus rendering it less sensitive to subtleties in communication that can be obtained from other research methods. Such data are also less amenable to the use of more advanced multivariate statistical techniques common today, such as structural equation modeling. Kolbe and Burnett (1991) also noted that researchers' biases can affect decisions made regarding the collection, analysis, and interpretation of data, biases in the selection of what categories of sexuality should be examined. Of course, biases are inherent in researchers' decisions throughout the process of research and are not unique to content analysis. However, the biases often are not as transparent in content analyses as in other forms of research. Many content analyses seem to have an implicit concern about the potential negative effects of sexuality in visual media. Few content analyses start with the premise that sexual content is beneficial for the viewer, or that the availability of content will enhance the viewer's personal development.

CONCEPTUAL ISSUES IN CONDUCTING A CONTENT ANALYSIS

Sexual content can be found in many, if not most, contemporary media. Some media are primarily sexually oriented, including sexually oriented magazine pictorials, movies, videos, and adult cable TV. Although these might be called *pornography*, a term less value-laden and individually interpreted is *sexually explicit media* (Harris, 1994). In these cases, the prevalence of sexuality is obvious, yet the more subtle meanings and content of the sexual themes is the issue at hand. Other less obviously sexual media have also been investigated. These include mainstream magazines (women's, men's, teen, and general magazines), TV (prime-time programs, talk shows, soap operas, advertisements, promos for shows), and films. Also, video games and music videos are particular venues of interest for teen audiences. Last, and most underresearched, is sexual material accessed through the Internet. Although the Internet does contain other than sexual content, the number of sexually oriented sites is large and continues to expand. According to Cooper, Scherer, Boies, and Gordon (1999), "sex is the number one search topic on the Internet" (p. 154); these authors cited a report by Goldberg indicating that, in April 1998, the five most frequently accessed sexual oriented adult web sites had around 9 million visitors.

The most elementary question for content analysis is the extent to which any given visual media has sexual content. The answer to this question is obvious when it is asked about material that is explicitly sexually oriented; of course, media designed for sexual arousal consist of almost all sexual content. However, the question of extent of sexuality is not as obvious when applied to media that are not typically considered primarily sexually oriented, such as prime-time TV, soap operas, advertisements, and general magazines.

Generally, sex in media may include "any representation that portrays or implies sexual behavior, interest, or motivation" (Harris, 1994, p. 249). The investigator can define a wide variety of behaviors as "sex," and yet the content that is analyzed is strongly influenced by the medium examined. The focus must necessarily vary with the medium investigated. For example, in sexually explicit media intended to produce sexual arousal, specific and explicit sexual behaviors, as well as the contextual messages and variables surrounding the sexual behaviors, are likely targets of investigation. In mass media, such as TV, sexual behaviors that are rare in sexually explicit media, such as kissing and flirting, are more likely to be included in content analyses.

Content analyses vary in the extent to which they test theory. It could be said that all content analyses of sexual material have the underlying theory that viewers are affected in some way by viewing sexual content and sexual socialization is influenced by exposure to media. This assumption is held most strongly with regard to the impact of exposure to sexual stimuli among young people; yet, it also applies to adults who may incorporate new norms and behaviors as a result of exposure to sexual material (e.g., Zillmann, 1989).

Some content analyses are intended only to document the prevalence of sexuality in visual media. However, even content analyses that are seemingly atheoretical may have a theory embedded in them based on the perspective the researcher takes while conducting the research. For example, the decision to include themes of sexual responsibility, precautions, and consequences as themes for analysis (e.g., Lowry & Towles, 1989a, 1989b) suggest that sexual activity can be dangerous and sexual expression in media should be accompanied by warnings about sexual expression and its consequences. The simple categorization regarding whether sexual intercourse is more likely to occur among married or unmarried couples in soap operas reflects an emphasis on traditional sexuality as occurring between married couples.

Clearly, to at least some extent, one's theoretical perspective guides the selection of both the medium or population to be examined and the selection of content to be analyzed. For investigators interested in the juxtaposition and combination of sex and violence, the categories explicitly focus on the presence of sex, violence, and sexual violence (e.g., Malamuth & Spinner, 1980; Yang & Linz, 1990), whereas investigators interested in sexual objectification examine evidence of inequality and other indexes that indicate objectification (e.g., Cowan, Lee, Levy, & Snyder, 1988).

Rather than testing theory, a major focus of many content analyses is simply to document the prevalence of various sexual behaviors and themes in the medium over time (e.g., Brosius, Weaver, & Staab, 1993; Greenberg & Busselle, 1996; Lowry & Shidler, 1993; Sapolsky & Tabarlet, 1991; Soley & Kurzbard, 1986). Thus, researchers have conducted studies on changes over time in sexual content in TV, advertising, soap operas, and pornography. Investigators are often specifically interested in whether the sheer amount of sexual material in a medium varies over time and whether a particular type of sexual expression (e.g., sexual violence or portrayal of intercourse) increases or decreases. More recently, content analyses have focused on sexual imagery in the context of the AIDS epidemic, unplanned pregnancies, and sexually tranmitted diseases (STDs; e.g., Kunkel et al., 1999; Lowry & Shidler, 1993; Lowry & Towles, 1989a, 1989b). From a time perspective, these changes may be used to document cultural changes in sexual themes and behaviors. It seems important to document changes over time in connection with changes in cultural beliefs and attitudes about sexuality. In general, it would be more meaningful if there were some theoretical, or at least stated, reasons for documenting specific sexual activities at various points in time.

In some analyses, a broad range of behaviors are assessed (e.g., Kunkel et al., 1999), whereas in others, only a few indicators are assessed, such as physical attractiveness and characters' wearing of skimpy or sexy clothing (e.g., Signorielli, McLeod, & Healy, 1994). The use of a broad or narrow range of indicators depends on the investigator's purpose. Some content analyses are intended to document a broad range of sexual behaviors, whereas others are intended to examine just one or several elements (e.g., the combination of sex and violence).

Another difference among content analyses is the extent to which the social context of the sexual behavior is analyzed. Several examples illustrate the range of possibilities. Matacin and Burger (1987) examined four themes in *Playboy* cartoons: (a) who is doing the seducing, (b) exploitation or taking advantage of an inequitable power relationship, (c) sex with an innocent, virginal female, and (d) whether female models have excessively attractive bodies. The content analysis of contemporary pornography conducted by Brosius et al. (1993) emphasized the social roles in sexually explicit movies and the context in which sexual activity takes place. In accord with their purpose, Brosius et al. analyzed the nature of the relationships, the persuasive efforts used to initiate sex, dominance and subordination in institutional relationships, the characters' motives or reasons for engaging in sex, and the types of sexual activity. Although the judgment of motives is more subjective, this category may be important for focusing on the social context of sexual expression in pornography. Cowan and Campbell's (1994) content analysis of interracial pornography videos included evidence of racism in the videos as well as aggressive physical and verbal behaviors. In the Kunkel et al. (1999) analysis of sexual behavior on TV, in addition to coding specific scene-level variables, these analysts also coded two program-level contextual variables: (a) emphasis in the program on sexual risks or responsibilities, and (b) consequences of sexual intercourse that are portrayed.

Content analysis can also examine the portrayal of the characters in the media associated with sexuality beyond the typical coding of gender, ethnicity, and occupation of the characters. This may appear to be a more subjective judgment than counting behaviors; however, in many portrayals, the characters are clearly designated or stereotyped in terms of their personal attributes. For examples, in studies of gender-role stereotyping on Music Television (MTV), Seidman (1992, 1999) included character behaviors and traits such as anger, adventuresomeness, and dependence. In the study of slasher films by Cowan and O'Brien (1990), the presence of positive and negative traits of female and male survivors and nonsurvivors was compared. Both positive and negative gender-typed traits were also coded.

Most content analyses of sexual material include only one medium in the analysis. Some analyses of sex on TV compare the amount of sex in different types of programs, but studies across media are rare. An example of the comparison of sexual content across program genres is the study by Kunkel et al. (1999). They compared the percent of programs and average number of scenes with sexual content in comedy series, drama series, movies, news magazines (e.g., *Dateline*), soap operas, talk shows, and reality programs. Two studies compared R-rated (typically for violent content) with X-rated (typically for sexual content) videos (Palys, 1986; Yang & Linz, 1990). Because Yang and Linz (1990) wanted to compare sexual violence in adult (R-rated) and sexually explicit films, behavior was coded for the presence of sex, violence, sexual violence, and prosocial activity.

An interesting debate that revolved around whether a content analysis of a particular genre can stand by itself or whether a control or comparison genre is needed occurred between Linz and Donnerstein (1994) and Molitor and Sapolsky (1994). Molitor and Sapolsky (1993) found that females in slasher films were no more likely to be victims than when males. Cowan and O'Brien (1990) and Weaver (1991) also found no difference between the number of female and male victims in slasher films. Previously, Linz et al. (1984) claimed that slasher films contain "explicit scenes of violence in which the victims are nearly always female" (p. 137). Linz and Donnerstein retorted by arguing that, had Molitor and Sapolsky (1993) compared the percentages of women and men killed in slasher films to the respective percentages killed in other film genres, including other types of R-rated films, they would have found that men are killed more often than women in these other genres. They argued that other film genres serve as "control points," and that a particular genre of film needs to be "systematically compared to some other genre" (p. 244). Molitor and Sapolsky (1994) agreed that Linz and Donnerstein made an interesting point, but also asked what genre would be the relevant comparison. As a non-neutral observer of this debate, having been the first author to demonstrate no difference in the percentage of men and women killed in slasher films, I agree with Molitor and Sapolsky. The content analyses stand as they are—consistent in their findings. Women are *not* killed more often than men in slasher films.

This debate raises a broader question. Are content analyses of one genre deficient if they exclude other genres in their research design or if they do not directly compare their findings to other genres? This is not an easy question to answer. An obvious problem pointed to earlier is that different types of sexual content are coded in different genres or media. A content analysis across media would have to establish a common denominator of sexual acts (or violent acts) to code so as to make the findings comparable. Perhaps media at similar levels of sexual explicitness could be compared, such as slasher films and other types of R-rated films, or the Internet and sexually explicit films. However, there would still be other dimensions that vary and would be unaccounted for in the analyses.

PRACTICAL ISSUES IN CONDUCTING A CONTENT ANALYSIS

The Research Problem

As with any type of research, the first step in a content analysis is identifying the research problem. Ideally, the research problem will reflect a theoretical model regarding communication. This can be a broadly based theory of communication, such as cultivation theory (Gerbner, Gross, Morgan, & Signorielli, 1994), social learning theory (Bandura, 1971), a feminist perspective (MacKinnon, 1985), or some other model, or the theory can be more specifically related to sexuality in that it presents a point of view about cultural views of sexuality (e.g., Durham, 1998). Because the researcher's biases about sexuality and theoretical focus can influence the content categories chosen for analysis, the researcher should make explicit his or her position in reports of the findings of content analysis.

Typically, published content analyses do not include specific hypotheses or tests of relationships between variables. More often, the research question concerns the particular domain that is the target of the content analyses (e.g., television, teen magazines, the Internet). Therefore, the usual first practical step is deciding the domain for study or the source of the data.

Choosing a Category System

The second step in content analysis is developing a coding scheme for the content of the material. A major step in content analysis is selection and definition of categories. The coding scheme can be based on theory or driven by the nature of the data itself. For example, if the research is based on feminist analysis concerned with the objectification of women in media, then categories reflecting this theory will be selected. If the theory involves the idea that sexuality in media reflects irresponsibility, the categories will involve assessment of responsibility and irresponsibility in sexual behavior. If the researcher is interested in sex and violence, the categories should obviously capture both sexual expression and violence. In other words, the categories should reflect the issues of concern in the research problem.

It is important that the researcher be familiar with the medium of interest so that the categories developed will accurately capture the content present. For example, it does not make sense to include a category of fellatio in analyzing prime-time TV programming. Fellatio is a form of sexual expression that is unlikely to occur on TV. In slasher films, there is little explicit sexual activity, so the concept of *sexual behavior* encompasses a broad range of activities, including kissing, fondling, foreplay, sexual teasing, provocative clothing, partial or full nudity, voyeurism, and intercourse (Molitor & Sapolsky, 1993). Some of these behaviors are less likely to occur in mainstream media (nudity, voyeurism, and intercourse), and others are less likely to occur in pornography (teasing, kissing, foreplay).

Further, other categories may emerge as the investigator examines the material being analyzed. For example, in the Cowan and Campbell (1994) analysis of interracial pornography, the category of "performs fellatio while on one's knees" emerged after viewing a number of videotapes and noticing that fellatio can occur in different positioning of bodies and contexts. Thus, content categories can emerge from theory, from the research problem as specified, and from the types of sexual expression in the particular medium to be analyzed. Lowry and Shidler (1993) suggested that scholars use a consistent set of definitions, categories, and procedures in a given area to track changes in the rates of sexual behaviors; yet as new issues regarding sexuality emerge in the culture, future content analyses will need to include indicators that identify the new issues.

A category system can be broad or narrow. Whitley (1996) defined a broadly focused coding system as a system that uses high-level categories and does not make fine distinctions. A narrow category system makes fine distinctions between behaviors or images. For example, a broad category might be "talk about sex," whereas narrow categories reflecting talk about sex might include "talk about past sexual experiences," "talk about present sexual behavior," and "talk about future sexual experiences." Holsti (1969) suggested that the costs of research will increase as coders have to make finer judgments. However, fine categories can be aggregated if that proves useful, whereas broad categories cannot be disaggregated once coding has taken place.

The coding system can be inclusive of all sexual behaviors or can more narrowly limit the type of content analyzed; that is, the system can be developed to code every type of sexual behavior and speech or it can be more narrowly focused on specific types of content. If the researcher is interested in assessing all evidence of sexuality, then a broad system makes sense. If the research problem is focused on a more narrow set of behaviors, then a limited set of categories is more appropriate. If the domain is limited (e.g., *Playboy* magazine centerfolds), then only so many categories can be constructed compared to an analysis of a more diffuse domain, such as mainstream TV programming. A factor that may be relevant in deciding how many behaviors to code is the efficiency of conducting the study.

It is difficult and tedious for coders to categorize a great number of variables across different levels (e.g., behaviors, scenes, films). Research that requires a fine-grained analysis with many categories is expensive to conduct. It requires more coders and coding time, more training, and a more complex coordination of effort.

The coding system can vary in the degree of inference required (Whitley, 1996). Systems that require decisions about the meaning of a behavior introduce subjectivity into the process. In a sense, the coders are research instruments; the more objective the categories, the more reliable the coding and the more valid the measures. The coding system typically should consist of specific behaviors and indicators, rather than coder interpretations. However, less behaviorally specified categories may prove to be interesting and important. In these cases, the researcher needs to provide specific indicators to assess the category. For example, if a researcher wants to assess objectification of women in pornography, the categories have to include indications of the specific content that will be coded as objectification, rather than depending on the coder to decide how objectification is demonstrated. For example, in Bogaert and Turkovich's (1993) examination of *Playboy* magazine centerfolds, coding of objectification included the degree to which characteristics indicative of the model's individuality were deemphasized, such as the clarity with which her eyes and face were shown, and her position relative to the camera (facing directly, side view, or turned away). Admittedly, objectification is ambiguous and subjective, but if a researcher wants to test dehumanization in sexual portrayals, some aspect of objectification needs to be included in the categories.

When video or Internet material is coded, the coding can occur as the material is accessed (concurrent) or the material can be recorded and the coding can occur at a later time. In the case of static material, such as magazines, this distinction is not necessary. The material as it exists can be catalogued and coded. In the case of videos or TV programs, researchers record the material and the record is then coded. This not only allows the coder to go back and review the material a number of times, but it also provides a repository of the data to be coded. As with researchers retaining questionnaires after the data have been analyzed, so too the coded material can be retained indefinitely. In the case of the content analyses I have conducted on videos, the material was coded from videotapes; however, the videos were rented. If another researcher wanted to review the material, the titles can be retrieved and the material is available through commercial means.

Each of these decisions can affect inter-coder reliability. Crano and Brewer (1986) suggested that the reliability of a coding system will be highest when (a) the system has a broad rather than narrow focus, (b) the unit of behavior is objectively defined rather than left to the discretion of the coder, (c) the coding system has a small number of categories, (d) coding is conducted after the fact rather than concurrently with the behavior, and (e) little or no inference is required.

A basic requirement of coding systems is that categories be mutually exclusive; otherwise, variables are confounded (Weber, 1990). Therefore, one piece of data should not be put in more than one category. This requirement is crucial when categories are compared. If a particular behavior is put in more than one category, it is double-counted. However, if there is more than one level of analysis, and the levels of analysis are not compared, it is possible to code a behavior in more than one category. For example, as in our content analysis of X-rated videos (Cowan et al., 1988), if one set of judgments includes the overall relational quality of the scene (e.g., reciprocal, dominant, exploitative) and another category system involves the coding of specific behaviors, a given behavior (e.g., an act of physical aggression) may be coded as an individual act and may also contribute to the overall tone of the scene. However, these two sets of categories cannot be directly compared. As Holsti (1969) noted: "The rule that each category must be derived from a single classification principle stipulates that conceptually different levels of analysis must be kept separate" (p. 100).

The Coding Manual

In developing the coding manual or the rules for coding, the categories need to be both conceptually and operationally defined. Investigators should first define what they mean by *sex*. For example, Kunkel et al. (1999) defined *sex* as "any depiction of sexual activity, sexually suggestive behavior, or talk about sexuality or sexual behavior" (p. 8). Further conceptual delineations are necessary. In the same study, Kunkel et al. (1999) defined *intercourse implied* as occurring when "a program portrays one or more scenes immediately adjacent (considering both place and time) to an act of sexual intercourse that is clearly inferred by narrative device" (p. 9). This definition would not suffice without detailed elaboration for coders. Further elaboration of *intercourse implied* involved "a couple kissing, groping, and undressing one another as they stumble into a darkened bedroom, with the scene dissolving before the actual act of intercourse ensues" (p. 9). If a kiss is to coded as sexual, an operational definition must distinguish a sexual kiss from an affectionate or perfunctory kiss. Some investigators have a "3-second rule;" if a kiss lasts longer than 3 s in an ambiguous context, it is classified as sexual (Lowry & Towles, 1989a). Others may code the kiss more subjectively in terms of its passion or the implied feelings behind the kiss.

The investigator needs to clearly lay out for the coders, and ultimately to the readers of the study, the precise nature of each category. During the coder training process, the coding manual frequently has to be revised to enable the coders to be accurate. When coders cannot agree, it is likely that the categories are ambiguous and more clarification is needed. Ultimately, the reader has to decide whether the categories and content of each reflect the conceptual definitions—a matter of validity. For example, some readers might argue that flirting is not sexual behavior, especially when flirting is included in the estimate of the extent of sexual behavior in a general audience medium. Another example that some readers might challenge comes from the research by Cowan and Campbell (1994) who included "penis slapping" as one of a number of indicators of physical aggression. Readers might believe that "penis slapping" is a playful rather than aggressive act. Experts may disagree on the definition and elaboration of a category, and it is critical that the experts or readers are able to discern how the investigator defined each category.

Unitizing the Categories

After, or concurrent with, defining the categories and in advance of analysis, the researcher must unitize the categories. Unitizing involves identifying the unit to be measured, the specific segment of content that is to be categorized, whether it is the actor or character, the behavior, an interpersonal interaction, the scene, or the entire program or film. For a content analysis to be reliable and valid, coders must operate within the identical unitizing system, and the unit must be clearly defined. For example, a scene is typically defined as an uninterrupted sequence of activity with the same characters in the same setting. Reliability estimates are often made of the unitizing itself, as well as the specific content. Do the coders, for example, identify the same number of scenes and the identical scenes as containing sexual content? Investigators should report how both the categories and units were defined.

Some investigators code at different levels in the same study. For example, although the scenes comprising a production may be coded, the results can be reported at both the scene and program levels such that the proportions of both scenes and programs containing sexual themes are reported. In the study conducted by Cowan et al. (1988), the percentage of scenes containing physical aggression was much lower (23%) than the number of films containing physical aggression (73%). In reporting the findings, it may make a difference if the results are reported in terms of the percentage of certain sexual behaviors relative to all scenes in the film or to the scenes that included sex, aggression, or sexual aggression (Palys, 1986) versus the percentage of these activities relative only to the sexual scenes (Cowan et al., 1988).

Decisions about unitizing can affect the results. If characters are the unit and two characters are kissing, the behavior will be counted twice, once for each character. If, instead, the interaction is the unit of analysis, the kiss will be counted only once. If specific behaviors are counted, an erotic kiss that includes an embrace may be counted as two instances of erotic touch (Lowry & Towles, 1989a). Ultimately, the decision about unitizing is left to the discretion of the investigator. One method of unitizing is not necessarily better than another, although smaller units may be more reliable than larger units. The important element of unitizing is that the unit needs to be clearly defined, operationalized, communicated to coders, and reported in the scientific product or publication.

Scaling the Categories

The categories used in content analysis are most often dichotomous, although some content analyses include ordinal scales that reflect the degree of a type of behavior. For example, Kunkel et al. (1999) created ordinal scales of the level of sexual behavior depicted (from flirting to intercourse) and the explicitness of the sex depicted. However, these ordinal scales may not capture the sexual activities portrayed as well as dichotomous reporting. The mean level of explicitness may carry less meaning than the number or percentages of specific behaviors. Dichotomous scales are easier for coders to use and involve less subjective judgment than do ordinal scales. Reliability is likely to be higher when the coders make dichotomous decisions rather than finer discriminations (Holsti, 1969) because the coders can focus on a single decision at a time.

Additionally, dichotomous scales can be combined into aggregate measures or used to create ordinal scales. For example, in our study of interracial pornography (Cowan & Campbell, 1994), dichotomous categories were used by the coders indicating presence or absence of a behavior; however, categories were then aggregated into indices of physical aggression, verbal aggression, intimacy, inequality, and race stereotyping to test the relationships of the race and gender of the actor to the frequency of occurrence of these aggregated categories. Aggregated categories may be less reliable than specific behaviors (Weber, 1990), but specific behaviors may be less conceptually interesting than aggregated categories. One problem with dichotomous measures is that material of differing intensity or degree is not often differentiated within the same category (e.g., degree of passion in a kiss).

A question may arise regarding the use of a qualitative approach to content analysis. Content analysis typically involves counting within categories—a quantitative task. Few content analyses involve qualitative analyses alone, although some content analyses combine quantitative and qualitative methods. For example, Cowan et al. (1988) included a qualitative description of a typical scenario in pornographic movies based on notes kept by the coders. An excellent example of qualitative analysis that involved coding of both visual and verbal content is Durham's (1998) study of representations of adolescent sexuality in two teen magazines. Durham analyzed written text and images in terms of broad themes, such as "rhetorical imperative of defending girls' virtue."

Qualitative research tends to focus more on the meaning of material than its frequency. As Taylor and Bogdan (1998) indicated, qualitative research is an inductive and intuitive process that depends on the analysis of themes. The advantage of qualitative content analysis is that it may identify broad themes and meanings or latent content of the material and it may be richer. For example, Durham's (1998) qualitative analysis of the representation of girls' sexuality in teen magazines reflects on the contradictory nature of the messages about sexuality aimed at teen girls, such as being sexy yet controlling sexuality. On the negative side, qualitative analysis is more subjective than quantitative analysis. The results from qualitative analysis may reflect the investigator's biases to a greater degree than results from quantitative analysis, although investigators' biases still affect quantitative content analyses.

Sampling the Content

Sampling is an important issue in selection of material for content analysis. Occasionally, researchers are able to analyze the entire population of materials. Bogaert and Turkovich (1993) were able to obtain the entire set of *Playboy* magazines from 1953 through 1990 for their analysis of *Playboy* centerfolds. More frequently, sampling has to be performed to reduce the amount of data to a manageable proportion. Assuming that the investigator is not able to analyze the total population of materials in a given domain, random sampling should be used. The sample should be representative of the population for generalizations from the sample to be valid. In their examination of contemporary pornography, Brosius et al. (1993) were fortunate in having available an archive of all heterosexually oriented pornography registered in Germany from 1979 to 1988 from which to sample.

Sampling may be a special problem when examining Internet content because there is no clear directory or catalogue of such material. The important aspect of sampling is that the selection of materials is not biased in any particular direction. In one content analysis of explicit videos (Garcia, 1991), coders were told to select the first film they saw in the erotic film section of a video rental store regardless of the title or description. This method of selecting material is not random and can be systematically biased by the interest value of the video cover. Sampling pornography videos is best done from catalogues, rather than leaving it to the coders to select the material from the shelves of a video store. How many programs or types of program are selected depend on the investigator; however, within that universe, random selection should occur.

Researchers may randomly select dates of programs or media to analyze. Content analyses of TV content typically specify the dates of data collection and how the sample was selected. Some researchers may only sample programs from the major networks (e.g., Lowry & Towles, 1989a), whereas other researchers may sample major networks, basic cable channels, public broadcasting, and premium cable channels (Kunkel et al., 1999). The Kunkel et al. (1999) analysis of sexuality on TV created a composite week sample across the 10 channels studied over a 5-month period. They used a random selection process so that each program that aired had an equal chance for inclusion in the sample.

Using a limited time sample may selectively bias the selection of material when programming reflects social events. For example, after a widely publicized shooting, it is likely that many programs on TV, including talk shows and news programs, contain a large amount of depicted violence. Similarly, during and following the Clinton–Lewinsky situation, TV programming may have contained a disproportionate discourse on sex. Signorielli and Bacue (1999) reported that a week of television programming is sufficient to accurately describe TV content. However, if a researcher is interested in changes over time, sampling may occur across several years.

Generalizability will depend not only on proper sampling, but also on the extensiveness of the programs selected. For example, if only MTV music videos are analyzed, the findings cannot be generalized to other networks that air music videos. Networks may vary in the genre of music videos aired. For example, Brown and Campbell (1986) found differences between music videos aired on an African-American channel and those on MTV. A larger selection provides a more representative sample of the genre. Analysis of 10 soap operas permits more generalizability than analysis of 3 soap operas. The issue of extensivity of sampling hinges on the resources of the investigator. An extensive study requires many coders and sufficient financial support. This is not to say that more limited content analyses are useless. Some content analyses are not intended to track changes over time or to generalize to a large universe of content. More limited analyses may be fascinating in and of themselves and may offer an in-depth understanding of some aspect of sexuality.

Selecting Coders

Coders can be screened on attitudes if the material to be coded is emotionally charged, such as explicit pornography. Yang and Linz (1990) prescreened coders of R- and X-rated videos on the basis of their responses to several measures, including attitudes toward women, acceptance of interpersonal violence, and sexual opinions. Only those applicants who scored close to the median on the three instruments were retained. An alternative approach to producing an attitudinally homogeneous set of coders is to select coders with a variety of relevant attitudes and beliefs. Consistency in coding is better produced by the clarity of the codes and training of the coders than the homogeneity of preexisting views of the coders.

Certainly, the investigator has to be cognizant of the possibility that coders may bring to the study certain background factors that lead to emotional responses to the material being coded. In one of my studies (Cowan et al., 1988), a coder had been a victim of rape. Although she found the task of coding explicit sexual videos difficult, she was strongly motivated to participate and be objective. In this case, she remained on the project. Using male and female coders to code sexually explicit behavior is preferable to using coders of only one gender because males and females may have differing responses toward sexually explicit material and differing thresholds for judging explicit material. In one of my studies (Cowan & Campbell, 1994), only female coders were used primarily because we spent a lot of time discussing the content and reviewing videos during training, and some of the female coders would have been uncomfortable had male coders been involved. The one male coder in one of our projects (Cowan et al., 1988) was less involved in the project possibly because he felt uncomfortable being the only male.

This last situation raises the question of coder motivation. In large studies involving sufficient funding, coders may be paid for their work. When coders are paid, such as is likely when many hours of training are required in addition to the hours spent coding (e.g., Kunkel et al., 1999), it is especially important that their work is monitored throughout. In my experience with small-scale studies, the motivation of the coders is critical. If they do not think the study is important and they are making a valuable contribution, they may be careless. Coding is a difficult and tedious task, especially when the medium is visual and the number of categories is relatively large. Motivation of coders is essential to accuracy and, hence, the validity of a study. The content analytic studies I have conducted have involved student coders, some from a research methodology class and others who volunteered. (In fact, all coders should be volunteers in that they do not view the task as imposed on them.) Both the study on slasher films (Cowan & O'Brien, 1990) and the study on dominance and inequality in pornographic videos (Cowan et al., 1988) used student coders from a laboratory course in social psychology. The students who participated in the pornography content analysis were committed to the project, and some of them became co-authors of the published research report as a result of their high level of input and commitment. The project was more a cooperative study than one imposed by the principle investigator, as the students contributed a great deal to the decisions about the categories. In another case, the content analysis failed because the particular coders in the project were not willing to put in the time and effort to successfully complete the project. In that instance, we were attempting to categorize whether women and men in slasher films were killed through different means and how much stalking preceded the killing of men versus women.

Another quality of coders that seems important is their meticulousness. Coders have to be precise and careful in their work. Some coders have more perfectionist personalities. More perfectionistic coders are better able to pay attention to the task at hand; creative types may be less successful at coding content.

Training the Coders

Training the coders is an essential component of content analysis. The number of coders may range from 2 in small studies to as many as 27 in large-scale studies (e.g., Kunkel et al., 1999). To assess reliability of coding, there should be at least 2 coders. Each coder is analogous to a measuring instrument and, like a tape measure, the instruments should be consistent, both with one another and over time. To produce a set of reliable codings, it is important to prepare as complete a coding manual as possible, including definitions of the variables and examples. Weber (1990) suggested that unreliability in individual coders over time can come from ambiguities in the material coded, cognitive changes within the coder, or simple errors. Failure to achieve satisfactory inter-coder reliability may stem from cognitive differences among coders, ambiguous coding instructions, or random recording errors. High inter-coder reliability or reproducibility is an essential requirement for a quantitative content analysis. When certain categories fail to achieve sufficient inter-coder reliability (e.g., at least 70% agreement), more training is required. After the coders are trained and have demonstrated a satisfactory level of reliability initially, reliability should be assessed at various points during the coding stage to determine whether there is "coder drift" and to identify problems as they arise.

Sometimes coders simply cannot agree on a category, especially when the category is subjective. For example, the coders in our study of interracial pornography (Cowan & Campbell, 1994) could not agree on two dimensions we believed were important to investigate: the darkness of the skin of the African-Ameican actors and the presence of animal-like sounds. Collins (1993) suggested that people of color are depicted more animalistically than are White people. Thus, this category was an important one theoretically. It would have been useful to determine whether darker African-American actors are treated differently in pornography than are lighter ones. Because these categories were inherently ambiguous, we decided not to use them. If the coders could not agree, it is likely that the viewers would not perceive those stimuli consistently either. Of course, as noted by Weber (1990), coder differences should be resolved after an index of reliability is calculated.

The length of training depends on the difficulty of the task. An example of minimal training is found in the study of erotic videos by Garcia (1991). The author reported that he "chose not to do a lengthy training procedure because we wanted the films analyzed, as much as possible, through the eyes of 'everyday persons' " (p. 97). However, coders are not expected to perform as everyday persons. They should be adequately trained and tested for the consistency and accuracy of their coding. In the Kunkel et al. (1999) study of sexuality on TV, coders were trained for approximately 8 hours per week for 8 weeks. If the levels of analysis are few and the number of categories are limited, a much shorter training period is necessary. Ideally, inter-coder agreement should be assessed throughout training and corrections made during that time. Weber (1990) suggested that the development of a coding scheme and training of coders may involve several iterations of defining the coding categories, coding, and assessing accuracy or reliability. When a particular coder is inconsistent with the other coders, that coder may need special training and practice. If one coder is careless or idiosyncratic in his or her coding, that coder should be dropped from the pool of coders.

Although some studies may involve coders working continuously for long periods of time, the coders in my studies were constrained to coding no more than two explicit videos on 1 day. Attending to the wealth of information is a difficult task, and the mind wanders. Coders cannot perform well for long, especially when coding visual media. For films and TV programming, it takes longer to scan and identify scenes and themes than when analyzing print materials. It may be possible to code more material when the operational definitions are very clear and the number of categories are small than when there is ambiguity (in either the categories or the material itself) and the number of categories is large.

With content analysis, ethical considerations are less obvious than with methods that utilize human participants. There are no issues of informed consent from research participants, issues of invasion of privacy, or protection of research participants from potential harm. Still, care has to be taken to protect the rights and choices of coders. Informed consent in the case of coders requires that the coders are informed of the nature of the task, including both the potential distress caused by viewing large amounts of certain types of material (e.g., sexually violent material) and the knowledge of what is required for accurate coding. Regardless of whether they are paid for their work, coders should be able to leave the project at any point.

Additionally, coding large amounts of sexual material, and especially sexually violent material, may contribute to coder desensitization. The coders who have worked with me on projects coding sexually explicit material have told me that they became desensitized to sexual behaviors after viewing the same behaviors repeatedly. On a personal note, I can attest to the desensitization that occurs with repeated exposure to sexually explicit materials. Similar to Zillmann's (1989) findings in his research on prolonged exposure to pornography, I found that watching sexual behaviors repeatedly to select instances of specific types of sexual stimuli (Cowan & Dunn, 1994) became boring. The only types of scenes that elicited my interest were those in which the sexual behavior was more atypical or extreme. Before coders begin their task, they should be informed about possible desensitization to sexual and violent material. Also, the primary researcher should be available to coders to discuss aversive reactions and experiences of desensitization.

Reliability and Validity of the Coding System

In their review of content analysis in consumer behavior research, Kolbe and Burnett (1991) offered criteria for judging the objectivity of the content analysis. As indicators of objectivity, they included whether (a) rules and procedures were reported, (b) coder training was reported, (c) pretesting of measures was reported, (d) coders were independent of the authors, and (e) coders worked independent of one another. These are relevant criteria to report in a content-analytic study, although in qualitative research, often the investigator also analyzes the content. Although an argument might be made for pairs of coders working together (provided that there are numerous pairs), more traditionally coders work alone.

As noted previously, an index of the reliability of both the coding units and specific categories should be calculated. Further, reliability assessment should be performed at various points in the research process, not only at the competition of training. Reliability of all categories used in the analyses should be reported, whether that involves individual categories or aggregated categories. Pooled reliabilities may hide low reliability of individual measures (Kolbe & Burnett, 1991). At the minimum, the range of reliabilities should be presented.

Several statistical indexes are used to calculate reliability. The simplest index is the coefficient (or percent) of agreement. It is easy to calculate and the statistic is intuitively understandable; that is, the percentage of the codings that show agreement between coders. One problem with percentage agreement is the lack of correction for the number of categories. As the number of categories decreases (as in present–absent dichotomous categories), the likelihood of agreeing by chance is larger than when there are more categories. Kolbe and Burnett (1991) also suggested that agreement is inflated by adding categories that are seldom present. Among categories that rarely occur, most coders agree on the absent coding. This is especially a problem when the reliability reported is the average of all individual reliabilities. In an ordinal system, it is possible to use the correlation coefficient as an index of reliability.

Certain measures of reliability adjust for change agreement among judges. Cohen's *kappa* (Cohen, 1960) adjusts for the number of judgments for which agreement is expected by chance. Other variants of Cohen's *kappa* for nominal data have been reported (e.g., Brennan & Prediger, 1981). A commonly used reliability coefficient that adjusts for chance expectations and for the number of categories in the category set is Scott's *pi* (Scott, 1955). In this formula, the percentage agreement expected by chance depends on both the number of categories in the dimension and the frequency with which each of them is used by coders (Scott, 1955).

The validity of a content analysis depends on the validity of its measures— are the categories measuring what they are intended to measure?—as well as the adequacy of the sampling design and reliability. According to Holsti (1969), adequate sampling and reliability are necessary, but not sufficient, conditions for validity. Much of what is considered valid in sexual content analysis involves the extent to which others agree that the category can be described as sexual. A category that measures sexuality should comprise commonly agreed on definitions and content that can be considered sexual. Some might argue that an analysis of sexuality on TV that includes flirting and skimpy clothing does not validly estimate the extent of sexual behavior on TV as the definition of sexual behavior is too broad. A category of sexual violence should reflect what the community of experts agree on as sexual aggression. These aspects of construct validity are more a matter of judgment than fact in content analyses. External validity should be demonstrated by the adequacy of the sampling and coverage of the medium. Generalization from an unsystematic analysis of nonrandomly selected TV shows about sexual content on TV in general would not be valid.

UNDERRESEARCHED MEDIA AND TOPICS

The most underresearched medium is the Internet. All Internet users are probably aware of the great extent of sexually explicit material available on the Internet. Even those of us who have no intention of exploring sexuality via computers are deluged with sexually explicit come-ons from unsolicited e-mail messages or "spam." The Internet is a fertile genre for content analyses; yet surprisingly few content analyses of Internet sexuality have been reported. One example is Mehta and Plaza's (1997) study of "Pornography in Cyberspace: An Exploration of What's in USENET." Mehta and Plaza suggested that other computer venues should be explored, such as bulletin board services, file transfer protocol servers, pornographic software, virtual reality games, and commercially available software on CD-ROM and diskettes. They anticipate that changes in direction and growth of the Internet and possible regulatory forces will require repeated assessment of pornography on the Internet. Cooper (personal communication, 1999), who has conducted questionnaire research on use of the Internet for sexual purposes through the cooperation of MSNBC, suggested that researchers who want to conduct content analyses of Internet sexual materials should limit their population to specific types of Internet outlets or groups, rather than try to assess a representative sample of all sexuality on the Internet.

Researchers should continue to examine the contextualization of sexual behavior. An example of a creative combination of imagery is the study by Pardun and McKee (1995) on the combination of sexuality and religious symbols on MTV. Also, more research should be conducted that focuses on the dehumanization or degradation of women (and men) in sexual material. It is important that future content analyses (as in the studies by Brosius et al., 1993; Cowan & Campbell, 1994; Cowan et al., 1988) explore themes, images, and behaviors that dehumanize or degrade before we can realistically assess the effects of such material. However, the attempts to perform content analyses that include degrading or dehumanizing categories are more difficult because the conceptual definitions and operational definition of such material are less precise and less universally acknowledged. What is degrading or dehumanizing to one viewer may not be to another.

Another relatively unexplored focus in content analysis is the investigation of the tone or direction of messages about sexuality targeted to adolescents. Do the media promote sexuality, condemn it, or present contradictory messages? For this purpose, qualitative analysis can be combined with quantitative analysis. In a creative use of content analysis to examine sexual themes in media directed toward adolescent females, Durham (1998) examined representations of girls' sexuality in two teen magazines, *YM* and *Seventeen*. Durham's content analysis was especially interesting from a methodological and theoretical perspective because it was framed in feminist thinking about female desire, analyzed both written text and visual images in terms of broad themes, and incorporated both quantitative and qualitative analysis.

CONCLUSION

This chapter might give the impression that content analyses are extremely difficult to conduct and should only be attempted with a great amount of resources. However, not all content analyses need to be extensive and expensive. For my own three content analyses, there was no funding available to pay for the coder's time, but we were still able to conduct relevant studies. In some ways, using extant data from communication sources is easier than obtaining a sample of motivated and honest research participants, but the process of systematic content analysis requires attention to a different set of tasks: selecting and adequately defining content categories, training coders, and attending to issues of inter-coder reliability and issues of validity.

A researcher with creative ideas can test theory and hypotheses with content analyses, rather than simply describing the amount and kind of sexual content in a particular domain. The large-scale content analyses that map an entire medium are important to track the amount and kind of sexual expression available to users of the media, but other kinds of limited content analyses, framed from a theoretical perspective, can be informative and stimulate ideas and further research. If the researcher chooses a limited domain, keeps the categories manageable, trains and motivates the coders, selects material randomly, and, most of all, asks relevant and interesting questions, the content analysis is likely to be of value. The Internet is entirely open for the application of content analysis. Finally, it may be more difficult to design a content analysis than to conduct a questionnaire study, but the process of conducting a content analysis is inherently interesting. Visual sexual material is such a pervasive part of contemporary culture that its exploration—its content and its messages—are an important piece of understanding current culture and its relation to sexuality.

SUGGESTED READINGS

At least three texts are available on content analysis (Holsti, 1969; Krippendorff, 1980; Weber, 1990). These texts describe the process of designing and conducting content analyses; however, most of the principles described and examples are designed for the analysis of text, not visual stimuli. A recent highly sophisticated study that extensively examined sexuality in TV programming was performed by Kunkle et al. (1999). Although on violence, not sexuality, the content analysis conducted by Wilson et al. (1997) provided detailed description of category construction, coder training, reliability assessment, and sampling of TV programming. For an example of a creative study that combined quantitative and qualitative data, see Durham (1998).

REFERENCES

Attorney General's Commission on Pornography: Final report. (1986, July). Washington, DC: U.S. Department of Justice.

Bandura, A. (1971). *Social learning theory.* New York: General Learning Press.

Bogaert, A. F., & Turkovich, D. A. (1993). A content analysis of *Playboy* centrefolds from 1953 through 1990: Changes in explicitness, objectification, and model's age. *The Journal of Sex Research, 30*, 135–139.

Brennan, R. L., & Prediger, D. J. (1981). Coefficient kappa: Some uses, misuses, and alternatives. *Educational and Psychological Measurement, 41*, 687–699.

Brosius, H., Weaver, J. B., & Staab, J. F. (1993). Exploring the social and sexual "reality" of contemporary pornography. *The Journal of Sex Research, 30*, 161–171.

Brown, J. D., & Campbell, K. (1986). Race and gender in music videos: The same beat but a different drummer. *Journal of Communication, 36*(1), 94–106.

Check, J. V. P., & Guluien, T. H. (1989). Reported proclivity for coercive sex following repeated exposure to sexually violent pornography, nonviolent pornography, and erotica. In D. Zillmann & J. Bryant (Eds.), *Pornography: Research: Advances and policy considerations* (pp. 159–184). Hillsdale, NJ: Lawrence Erlbaum Associates.

Cohen, J. (1960). A coefficient of agreement for nominal scales. *Educational and Psychological Measurement, 20*, 37–46.

Cooper, A., Scherrer, C. R., Boies, S. C., & Gordon, B. L. (1999). Sexuality on the Internet: From sexual exploration to pathological expression. *Professional Psychology: Research and Practice, 30*, 54–164.

Collins, P. H. (1993). The sexual politics of Black womanhood. In P. Bart & E. G. Moran (Eds.), *Violence against women: The bloody footprints* (pp. 85–104). Newbury Park, CA: Sage.

Cowan, G., & Campbell, R. R. (1994). Racism and sexism in interracial pornography: A content analysis. *Psychology of Women Quarterly, 18*, 323–338.

Cowan, G., & Dunn, K. F. (1994). What is degrading to women in pornography? *The Journal of Sex Research, 31*, 11–21.

Cowan, G., Lee, C., Levy, D., & Snyder, D. (1988). Dominance and inequality in X-rated pornography videocassettes. *Psychology of Women Quarterly, 12*, 299–311.

Cowan, G., & O'Brien, M. (1990). Gender and survival vs. death in slasher films: A content analysis. *Sex Roles, 23*, 187–196.

Crano, W. D., & Brewer, M. B. (1986). *Principles and methods of social research.* Boston: Allyn & Bacon.

Donnerstein, E., Linz, D., & Penrod, S. (1987). *The question of pornography.* New York: The Free Press.

Durham, M. G. (1998). Dilemmas of desire: Representations of adolescent sexuality in two teen magazines. *Youth and Society, 29*, 369–389.

Garcia, L. T. (1991). A content analysis of erotic videos. *Journal of Psychology & Human Sexuality, 3*, 95–103.

Gerbner, G., Gross, L., Morgan, M., & Signorielli, N. (1994). Growing up with television: The cultivation perspective. In J. Bryant & D. Zillmann (Eds.), *Media effects: Advances in theory and research* (pp. 17–41). Hillsdale, NJ: Lawrence Erlbaum Associates.

Greenberg, B. S., & Busselle, R. W. (1996). Soap operas and sexual activity: A decade later. *Journal of Communication, 46*(4), 153–161.

Harris, R. J. (1994). The impact of sexually explicit media. In J. Bryant & D. Zillmann (Eds.), *Media effects: Advances in theory and research* (pp. 247–272). Hillsdale, NJ: Lawrence Erlbaum Associates.

Holsti, O. R. (1969). *Content analysis for the social sciences and humanities.* Reading, MA: Addison-Wesley.

Kolbe, R. H., & Burnett, M. D. (1991). Content-analysis research: An examination of applications with directives for improving research reliability and objectivity. *Journal of Consumer Research, 18*, 243–250.

Krippendorff, K. (1980). *Content analysis.* Beverly Hills, CA: Sage.

Kunkel, D., Cope, K. M., Farinola, W. J. M., Biely, E., Rollin, E., & Donnerstein, E. (1999). *Sex on TV: Content and context. A biennial report to the Henry J. Kaiser Family Foundation, February 1999.* Menlo Park, CA: The Henry J. Kaiser Family Foundation.

Linz, D., & Donnerstein, E. (1994). Sex and violence in slasher films: A reinterpretation. *Journal of Broadcasting & Electronic Media, 38,* 243–246.

Linz, D., Donnerstein, E., & Penrod, S. (1984). The effects of multiple exposure to filmed violence against women. *Journal of Communication, 34*(3), 130–147.

Lina, D., Donnerstein, E., & Penrod, S. (1987). The findings and recommendations of the Attorney General's Commission on Pornography: Do the psychological "facts" fit the political fury? *American Psychologist, 42,* 946–953.

Lowry, D. T., & Shidler, J. A. (1993). Prime time TV portrayals of sex, "safe sex," and AIDs: A longitudinal analysis. *Journalism Quarterly, 70,* 628–637.

Lowry, D. T., & Towles, D. E. (1989a). Prime time TV portrayals of sex, contraception, and venereal diseases. *Journalism Quarterly, 66,* 347–353.

Lowry, D. T., & Towles, D. E. (1989b). Soap opera portrayals of sex, contraception, and sexually transmitted diseases. *Journal of Communication, 39*(2), 76–83.

MacKinnon, C. A. (1985). Pornography, civil rights, and speech. *Harvard Civil Rights-Civil Liberties Law Review, 20,* 1–70.

Malamuth, N. M., & Spinner, B. (1980). A longitudinal content analysis of sexual violence in the best-selling erotic magazines. *The Journal of Sex Research, 16,* 226–237.

Matacin, M. L., & Burger, J. M. (1984). A content analysis of sexual themes in *Playboy* cartoons. *Sex Roles, 17,* 179–186.

Mehta, M. D., & Plaza, D. E. (1997). Pornography in cyberspace: An exploration of what's in USENET. In S. Kiesler (Ed.), *Culture of the Internet* (pp. 53–67). Mahwah, NJ: Lawrence Erlbaum Associates.

Molitor, F., & Sapolsky, B. S. (1993). Sex, violence, and victimization in slasher films. *Journal of Broadcasting & Electronic Media, 37,* 233–242.

Molitor, F., & Sapolsky, B. S. (1994). Violence towards women in slasher films: A reply to Linz and Donnerstein. *Journal of Broadcasting & Electronic Media, 38,* 247–249.

Palys, T. S. (1986). Testing the common wisdom: The social content of video pornography. *Canadian Psychology, 27*(1), 22–35.

Pardun, C. J., & McKee, K. B. (1995). Strange bedfellows: Symbols of religion and sexuality on MTV. *Youth and Society, 26,* 438–449.

Russell, D. E. H. (Ed.). (1993). *Making violence sexy: Feminist views on pornography.* New York: Teachers College.

Sapolsky, B. S., & Tabarlet, J. O. (1991). Sex in prime-time television: 1979 versus 1989. *Journal of Broadcasting & Electronic Media, 35,* 505–516.

Scott, W. A. (1955). Reliability of content analyses: The case of nominal scale coding. *Public Opinion Quarterly, 19,* 321–325.

Scott, J. E., & Cuvelier, S. J. (1987). Violence in *Playboy* magazine: A longitudinal analysis. *Archives of Sexual Behavior, 16,* 279–287.

Seidman, S. A. (1992). An investigation of sex-role stereotyping in music videos. *Journal of Broadcasting & Electronic Media, 36,* 209–216.

Seidman, S. A. (1999). Revisiting sex-role stereotyping in MTV. *International Journal of Instructional Media, 26*(1), 11–22.

Signorielli, N., & Bacue, A. (1999). Recognition and respect: A content analysis of prime-time television characters across three decades. *Sex Roles, 46,* 527–544.

Signorielli, N., McLeod, D., & Healy, E. (1994). Stereotypes in MTV commercials: The beat goes on. *Journal of Broadcasting & Electronic Media, 38,* 98–101.

Soley, L. C., & Kurzbard, G. (1986). Sex in advertising: A comparison of 1964 and 1984 magazine advertisements. *Journal of Advertising, 15*(3), 46–54, 64.

Soley, L. C., & Reid, L. (1985). Baiting viewers: Violence and sex in television program advertisements. *Journalism Quarterly, 62,* 105–110, 131.

Taylor, S. J., & Bogdan, R. (1998). *Introduction to qualitative research methods: A guidebook and resource* (3rd ed.). New York: Wiley.

Umesh, U. N., Peterson, R. A., & Sauber, M. H. (1989). Interjudge agreement and the maximum value of Kappa. *Educational and Psychological Measurement, 49,* 835–850.

Vance, C. (1984). *Pleasure and danger: Exploring female sexuality.* Boston: Routledge & Kegan Paul.

Weaver, J. B. III. (1991). Are "slasher" and horror films sexually violent? A content analysis. *Journal of Broadcasting & Electronic Media, 35,* 305–312.

Weber, R. P. (1990). *Basic content analysis* (2nd ed.). Newbury Park, CA: Sage.

Whitley, B. E., Jr. (1996). *Principles of research in behavioral science.* Mountain View, CA: Mayfield.

Wilson, B. J., Kunkel, D., Linz, D., Potter, J., Donnerstein, E., Smith, S. L., Blumenthal, E., & Gray, T. (1997). *National television violence study: Vol. 1.* Thousand Oaks, CA: Sage.

Winick, C. (1985). A content analysis of sexually explicit magazines sold in an adult bookstore. *The Journal of Sex Research, 24,* 206–210.

Yang, N., & Linz, D. (1990). Movie ratings and the content of adult videos: The sex-violence ratio. *Journal of Communication, 40*(2), 28–42.

Zillmann, D. (1989). Effects of prolonged exposure to pornography. In D. Zillmann & J. Bryant (Eds.), *Pornography: Research: advances and policy considerations* (pp. 127–157). Hillsdale, NJ: Lawrence Erlbaum Associates.

Zillmann, D., & Bryant, J. (Eds.). (1989). *Pornography: Research advances and policy considerations.* Hillsdale, NJ: Lawrence Erlbaum Associates.

INTERPRETING RESULTS

16

vvvvvvv

Interpreting Research Results

Elizabeth Rice Allgeier
Bowling Green State University

This chapter begins with society-wide interpretations and misinterpretations of sexuality-related research findings. I then focus more narrowly on misinterpretations made by researchers as well as secondary and tertiary writers reporting the results of studies conducted by social scientists. In particular, I describe research on imputed sexism and several forms of sexual coercion and distortions that have crept into the language used to present results from research on this topic.

VARYING INTERPRETATIONS OF SEXUALITY
RESEARCH AT THE SOCIETAL LEVEL

Our American fascination with most aspects of sexuality is reflected in the percentage of jokes told by late night talk show hosts and stand-up comics devoted to sexuality, to stories reported in the popular media, to main themes in many movies and TV. Jones et al. (1986) conducted a major study of the relationship between the sexual openness of 37 different developed countries and their teenage pregnancy rates. Despite the apparent intense focus on sexuality in the United States, Jones et al. found that Americans are far less open about sex than most of the other countries and the United States leads all countries in teenage pregnancy rates. Jones et al. characterized the United States as having "an ambivalent, sometimes puritanical attitude about sex" (p. 230). Despite Americans' "sometimes puritanical attitude" toward sex, a half a century ago, the Kinsey group (Kinsey, Pomeroy, & Martin, 1948; Kinsey, Pomeroy, Martin, & Gebhard, 1953) found that some Americans either enjoy sex with animals (between 4%–17% depending on whether it is men or women or urban vs. rural populations being studied) or are erotically aroused by watching animals copulate (ranging from 5%–21%). While I was writing this chapter, a story was widely circulated in the media (and, jokingly, in talk shows) about a man sentenced to more than 3 years in prison for sexually assaulting sheep. He claimed that the sex was consensual, although how one determines that sheep are consenting was not specified.

Some may laugh at the jokes about the man–sheep story. However, societal misinterpretation of some empirical research on sexuality is not funny in that such misunderstanding may impede efforts to solve sexual problems. Much of the research described in this chapter demonstrates this issue. This section begins with the most recent major travesty in which the results of research on sexuality have been misrepresented.

Michael Wiederman and Bernard Whitley's invitation to contribute a chapter to this edited volume predated (as I write this) the fiasco involving the misinterpretation of an article by Bruce Rind and his colleagues (Rind, Tromovitch, & Bauserman, 1998). Their article involved a meta-analysis of 59 studies of the adult sequelae among college students of having experienced sexual contact with an adult when they were children or adolescents. Because I had published three articles by Rind and his colleagues during my tenure as the editor of *The Journal of Sex Research* (*JSR*), Rind had sent me a preprint of the article that was subsequently accepted and published by the American Psychological Association's (APA's) prestigious journal, *Psychological Bulletin*. I thought that the article by Rind et al. made a very important contribution. People who watch TV or encounter other popular media are regularly informed that sexual experiences by young people with adults cause a number of indelible effects throughout their lives. Supposedly, these people/women will:

1. Develop Multiple Personality Disorder.
2. Become lesbians.
3. Be sexually dysfunctional with their adult partners/spouses.
4. Lack self-esteem.
5. Lack assertiveness.
6. Lack trust.
7. Have low levels of psychological adjustment.
8. Be more likely to develop a learned helplessness attributional style that will render them unable to resist subsequent unwanted sexual approaches during childhood, adolescence, and adulthood than will nonmolested individuals.

A number of these assertions can be dismissed immediately. For example, experiences with sexual contacts during childhood are so common in North America that we could even consider them normative, as is documented later. In contrast, the clinical condition known as Multiple Personality Disorder or Multiple Personality Syndrome is exceedingly rare (American Psychiatric Association, 1994). A similar point can be made regarding the proportion of women who experienced sexual contacts during childhood versus the proportion of women in the population who are sexually intimate exclusively or primarily with other women (Laumann, Gagnon, Michael, & Michaels, 1994). Whether the other six characteristics are demonstrated depends on whether researchers study college student and community samples or samples of women who are in therapy (Wiederman, 2001). Among college students and community members, the other six supposed relationships have not been demonstrated.

In their meta-analysis, Rind et al. (1998) attempted to determine what reliable characteristics appeared among those women and men who had had sexual contacts with adults when the respondents were children and adolescents. The number of respondents in these studies ranged from 60 to 2,922, with the prevalence of self-reported child sexual abuse ranging from 3% to 71%. It should be noted that the definitions of child sexual abuse differed across the studies, with some researchers defining child sexual abuse as sexual contacts occurring before the age of 12 and others including unwanted sexual contacts with older persons up to the age of 17. Their analyses indicate that there was a great deal of variability in research participants' responses to surveys administered within and across the 59 studies: Self-reported reactions ranged from highly negative to somewhat positive. In addition, men were more likely to report neutral or positive reactions than were women. However, across the samples, the differences between the child sexual abuse and non-child sexual abuse groups on 18 different outcome variables (e.g., anxiety, depression, phobia, psychotic symptoms, sexual adjustment, social adjustment, etc.) were not strong for any of the psychological variables. The authors concluded that there was no support for the general belief that child sexual abuse always has long-term negative effects on victims. Further, the effects of such experiences were confounded by broader family characteristics. For example, in one of the studies included in the Rind et al. meta-analysis (Higgins & McCabe, 1994), any effects of child sexual abuse disappeared when the level of general family functioning was statistically controlled.

The audience for the Rind et al. article was intended to be advanced graduate students and scientists; it would be very difficult for the average layperson to understand the complex statistical analyses. However, the advanced level of training needed to comprehend accurately the findings did not stop various advocacy groups from interpreting the findings as supporting the acceptability of child–adult sexual contacts or from condemning the article as supportive of pedophilia. For example, on their website, the North American Man-Boy Love Association (NAMBLA) interpreted the Rind et al. findings as supporting the acceptability of sexual contacts between boys and men. On the other side of the advocacy spectrum, Dr. Laura Schlessinger, the radio talk show host, perceived the findings as supporting pedophilia, and she characterized the study as "severely flawed junk science." However, as pointed out in chapter 21 of this volume, Rind and his colleagues were not studying pedophilia or pedophiles per se. Instead, they were examining studies of the self-reported long-term sequelae of the experience of having had sex with an adult when one was still a child.

Dr. Laura, whose training is unlikely to have equipped her to understand the high-level statistical analyses employed in the Rind et al. article, apparently got her "information" from a letter sent by Paul J. Fink, associated with the right-wing Family Research Council (B. Rind, personal communication, July 22, 1999). She, in turn, sent the criticisms to members of the U.S. Congress. Various members of Congress joined the attack of the study, demanding that the APA repudiate the article, and in July 1999, the House of Representatives voted to condemn the study. This vote was reported as unanimous, but in fact, 13 of the Representatives simply voted present rather than voting for or against the condemnation. This condemnation occurred despite the careful statement by Rind et al. that issues of long-term harm are separate from issues of the wrongfulness of adults engaging in sexual contacts with children. In a four-page document refuting Fink's claims that the study was loaded in the direction of demonstrating "no harm" to children who have sex with adults, Rind demonstrated that he and his co-authors had actually made design and statistical decisions in a direction that would increase the likelihood of demonstrating damages of various kinds to the extent that such damages could be found among the studies sampling college students (Rind, personal communication, July 22, 1999).

THREATS TO THE INTERPRETATIONS
OF RESEARCH RESULTS

The intrusion of misinterpretations, based on political rather than scientific concerns, that followed publication of the Rind et al. study was not restricted to laypersons lacking the education to provide an accurate assessment of research findings. It also appeared among researchers who may confuse their theoretical beliefs or advocacy efforts with their empirical designs and results of their data analyses.

Researchers' Beliefs, Measurement Issues,
and Interpreting Statistical Results

During my tenure as editor of *The Journal of Sex Research*, I received a number of submissions on the topic of sex differences (or similarities, but it is rarely framed that way; see chap. 4 for discussion of the difficulty of publishing studies that support the null hypothesis) in perceptions of responsibility for date rapes that relied on responses to vignettes. In one of these studies, the authors hypothesized that women would be more likely than men to define a depiction of a forced sexual encounter as rape and to hold the man accountable. This basic paradigm, set of hypotheses, and dependent variables have been the core of a number of studies. This particular study had several additional interesting manipulations, but I do not describe them because I do not want to reveal the identity of the authors in the event that they published their study elsewhere. The point is that the authors did, indeed, obtain statistically significant differences using a preliminary multivariate analysis of variance (MANOVA) followed by a series of analyses of variance (ANOVAs). Essentially, the authors found that, on 5-point scales, women compared with men were more likely to agree that the man should have stopped (means of 1.12 vs. 1.40), that the man should be held legally accountable (1.50 vs. 1.95), that the woman should report the event (1.48 vs. 2.15), and that the encounter should be defined as date rape (1.22 vs. 1.50).

I noticed that the ratings of both men and women were on the *agree* side of the midpoint. There were also a series of statements in which men's and women's ratings were on the *disagree* side of the midpoint, but with women statistically significantly more so. In any event, the results of the analyses supported the authors' hypotheses that women and men significantly differed in their perceptions regarding date rape. However, a wonderfully alert reviewer computed the correlation between the men's and women's mean ratings and pointed out that the correlation was .99. What if the authors had posed their question differently? That is, what if they put their research volunteers through some kind of intervention aimed at sensitizing men and women to sexual coercion and hypothesized for their evaluation of the intervention that men's and women's ratings would be highly correlated demonstrating that the intervention had been successful? Obtaining a correlation of .99 with mean ratings toward the end of the scale that held the depicted rapist responsible would have thrilled them and led to very different interpretations of their data. The point is that we can be misled by the way we are thinking about our research questions into seeking confirmation of our beliefs.

We should also be alert to alternative interpretations and conduct analyses to see whether they could also be supported—in this case, that there appears to be very high agreement between men and women in their overall ratings of the acceptability of the behaviors in question. Although the authors obtained statistically significant gender differences, the difference in the means was very small. That is, the statistical effect size for gender would be slight, with gender predicting little of the variance in ratings. Specifically, although researchers may find a reliable difference between two groups (in this case, men vs. women), a statistically significant difference is not equivalent to the importance or magnitude of an effect because common probability estimates of differences depend on sample size. (For more details on this issue, see the *Publication Manual of the American Psychological Association*, 1994, p. 18).

Because of the difficulty we have in seeking disconfirmation of our hypotheses or confirmation of alternative hypotheses with which we do not agree, both as laypersons and scientists, I personally find it extremely useful to have others examine ideas that my students and I want to test before we even begin data collection. Our research group at Bowling Green State University contains faculty and students with a diversity of perspectives. If you do not have a diverse research group available to you, another strategy is to think of colleagues whom you believe might be highly skeptical about your ideas and run your ideas by those colleagues. Again, if you can do so before data collection, you may be able to build in measures that will allow you to test alternative hypotheses that had not occurred to you until your colleagues gave you their viewpoints.

Much research on gender-role stereotypes has been stimulated by concerns with sexism, specifically, the derogation of women's skills, personality development, and so forth. Many readers may be familiar with the classic studies by Inge Broverman and her colleagues (Broverman, Broverman, Clarkson, Rosenkrantz, & Vogel, 1970; Broverman, Vogel, Broverman, Clarkson, & Rosenkrantz, 1972; Rosenkrantz, Vogel, Bee, Broverman, & Broverman, 1968). I used to teach the Psychology of Gender, and I faithfully reported their conclusions with samples of college students and clinicians regarding characteristics of mentally healthy men, mentally healthy women, and mentally healthy adults of unspecified sex.

As represented in most of the textbooks that I used, the general conclusion was that college students and clinicians alike rated healthy adult men as very aggressive, very independent, not at all emotional, very objective, very dominant, very active, feelings not easily hurt, very ambitious, easily able to separate feelings from ideas, and so on. In general, healthy adults with unspecified sex were rated similarly to healthy men on the desirable traits. Women were also rated as having the desirable traits, but either by a slightly but significantly smaller proportion of participants in the Broverman et al. (1970) study or men were rated as slightly (but significantly) more likely to possess the desired attribute (Broverman et al., 1972). Broverman et al. (1970) concluded, "These results confirm the hypothesis that a double standard of health exists for men and women, that is, the general standard of health is actually applied only to men, while healthy women are perceived as significantly *less* healthy by adult standards" (p. 5; italics added). In secondary and tertiary sources (articles, texts, etc.), healthy adult women have been described as having been rated as relatively childlike, less independent, and so forth. For example, in an article entitled "Sexism and Psychiatry," Levine, Kamin, and Levine (1974) cited the work of Broverman and her colleagues as showing that "there is an obvious double standard of emotional health [and] healthy women were considered to be passive, submissive, emotional, excitable, dependent, etc. . . . . For a woman to be considered mentally healthy she must in fact show signs of behavior that no self-respecting male would want to manifest" (p. 329).

However, these studies by Broverman and her colleagues illustrate a classic misinterpretation of research findings. What did they actually measure and what did they find? Essentially, they found that healthy adult men and healthy sex-unspecified adults were rated as *more* likely to have various stereotypically masculine characteristics than were healthy adult women. As noted by Stricker (1977), "If on the 60-point bipolar scale [that Broverman et al., 1970, used] males received a score of 50 (scores for individual items were not given, and these scores are purely hypothetical), both of which are toward the logical pole, Rosenkrantz et al. would label logical as the male pole and label its bipolar opposite, 'illogical', as the female pole." (p. 17). In their 1972 article, Broverman et al. reviewed their earlier findings as showing that, relative to men, women are perceived as being more dependent, subjective, passive, illogical, noncompetitive, and so forth. However, Stricker (1977) pointed out that "stereotyping a woman as less logical than a man is quite different than stereotyping her as illogical" (p. 17).

Phillips and Gilroy (1985) conducted a replication and extension of the Broverman et al. (1970) study, and suggested that the Broverman et al. findings may have stemmed primarily from their use of a forced-choice methodology, or that clinicians may have moved to a less sexist position. However, readers who check their textbooks will see that women were described as perceived as childlike relative to men. If healthy adults—whether men, women, or sex-unspecified—are all perceived as possessing these desirable characteristics, it is inaccurate to describe their findings as indicating that clinicians and college students alike perceive women as childlike. To use an analogy from sports, the fact that Michael Jordan may be perceived as a more skillful basketball player than one of the current stars of the game does not imply that the current stars are lacking in basketball skill.

Regarding the Broverman et al. (1972) research, Stricker (1977) also pointed out that when individual means were examined, fewer than half differentiated healthy males and females. Further, of these, approximately half favored females. The real problem with the Broverman et al. interpretation involved the neutral point (or midpoint) of the scales that were used. For more than 90% of the items, the means for healthy males and females were on the same side of the neutral point. For example, on the scale anchored by *very intelligent* (1) to *not at all intelligent* (7), healthy females received a mean rating of 2.34, whereas healthy males had a mean of 2.56—a statistically significant difference. The appropriate conclusion, then, is not that men are seen as not at all intelligent, but that both healthy women and men are seen as intelligent, with women seen as even more intelligent.

More than a decade ago, Antonia Abbey (1982) published an article that continues to be widely cited in research articles and in texts in the social sciences. She posed a question in her title: "Sex Differences in Attributions for Friendly Behavior: Do Males Misperceive Females' Friendliness?" Essentially, she assigned college men and women volunteers to one of two conditions. They were either to engage in a conversation with a member of the other sex while being observed through one-way glass or to be observers of the conversants. After observing the dyads engage in the 5-minute conversation about their experiences that year at college, observers were asked to rate the man and woman regarding how each was "trying to behave." To measure sexual intent, "the key trait terms were the adjec-

TABLE 16.1*
Mean Scores for Ratings of the Female Actor on the
Sexuality Items as a Function of Sex of Participant

| | Sex of Participant | | |
Ratings of Female Actor	Male	Female	p <
Friendliness	5.7	6.0	ns
Promiscuous	2.2	1.7	.01
Seductive	2.3	1.9	.09
Flirtatious	2.9	2.8	ns

*Adapted from Abbey's (1982) text, p. 833 (friendliness ratings), and Table 1, p. 834.

Note: Ratings on all terms in Abbey's measure, including these three "sexual intent" terms, were made on 7-point scales, in which 1 indicated *absence of the characteristic*, 4 represented the *neutral point*, and 7 indicated *high levels of the characteristic.*

tives *flirtatious, seductive,* and *promiscuous.* These terms were selected because they were thought to measure the construct 'sexuality' " (p. 833). Abbey imbedded these three terms in a variety of trait terms using 7-point response formats. No sex differences emerged in volunteers' ratings of the women actors' friendliness, and the ratings were high (see Table 16.1).

Regarding her measures of sexual intent, Abbey (1982) reported that "as predicted, male subjects rated the female actor as being significantly *more promiscuous* than female subjects did ($p < .01$). Similarly, there was a marginal effect for males to rate the female actor as being *more seductive* [italics added] than did females ($p < .09$). However, there were no sex differences in subjects' ratings of the female's flirtatiousness" (pp. 833–834; italics added). Note that promiscuity, seductiveness, and flirtatiousness were rated on 7-point scales, with 1 indicating the absence of the behavior and 7 indicating its presence. Inspection of the means actually suggests that men and women alike gave low ratings on all three characteristics (refer to Table 16.1). Note that only one rating—promiscuous (or, more accurately taking into account the issue of the neutral point, not promiscuous)—reached statistical significance. Even so, the difference between 2.2 and 1.7, only half of one scale point, raises questions about effect size. Specifically, although a significant difference was found on this one variable, the meaningfulness of the difference—at the not promiscuous end of the scale—is small. That is, neither men nor women rated the stimulus as promiscuous, and women were slightly less likely to do so.

Now let's examine Abbey's abstract. Essentially, her interpretation of the answer to her question "Do Males Misperceive Females' Friendliness?" was "yes."

This investigation tested the hypothesis that friendliness from a member of the opposite sex might be misperceived as a sign of sexual interest. . . . The results indicate that there were sex differences in subjects' ratings of the actors. Male actors and observers rated the female actor as being more promiscuous and seductive than female actors and observers rated her. Males were also more sexually attracted to the oppo-site-sex actor than females were. Furthermore, males also rated the male actor in a more sexualized fashion than females did. There results were interpreted as indicat-ing that men are more likely to perceive the world in sexual terms and to make sex-ual judgments than women are. Males do seem to perceive friendliness from females as seduction, but this appears to be merely one manifestation of a broader male sex-ual orientation. (p. 830)

The likelihood of misinterpreting findings reported in abstracts of scholarly journals is increased by the hectic schedule under which popular press writers and textbook authors work. I could give a litany of how Abbey's data were reported in secondary or tertiary sources. Check the textbooks on your shelves. I give just one example. In the third edition of David Myers' popular social psychology text (1990), Myers uncritically reported the claims by Abbey (1982) that men are more likely than women to perceive a woman's friendliness as indicating "sexual intent." I know Dave Myers and wrote him about his rendering of Abbey's findings. Myers wrote back a very nice letter, essentially saying, "Oh, you are right, and I've made it worse in the fourth edition," which was already in press. Actually, all he did in the fourth edition was to add sexual harassment to the list of behaviors experi-enced by women as a function of men's "misattributions," including research by others in which the means were much closer to the "absence" than to the "presence" end of sexual intent. Here is his text description (Myers, 1993):

> Our conclusions about why people act as they do are profoundly important: They determine our reactions to others and our decisions regarding them. For example, Antonia Abbey (1987, 1991) and her colleagues have repeatedly found that men are more likely than women to attribute a woman's friendliness to sexual interest. This misreading of warmth as a sexual come-on (called "misattribution") can lead to be-havior the woman regards as sexual harassment (Saal, Johnson, & Weber, 1989). It also helps explain the greater sexual assertiveness exhibited by men across the world (Kenrick & Trost, 1987). Such misattributions contribute both to date rape and to the greater tendency of men in various cultures, from Boston to Bombay, to justify rape by blaming the victim's behavior (Kanekar & Nazareth, 1988; Muehlen-hard, 1988; Shotland, 1989). (p. 75)

It is easy to sound righteous on the issue of interpreting mean ratings relevant to the midpoint. However, I reexamined my own dissertation, completed in 1976. The relevant study was published in the *Journal of Consulting and Clinical Psy-chology* (Allgeier & Fogel, 1978). I showed slides of the same couple engaged in coitus in either the man-above or woman-above position. Students rated the man and woman in the slides along a number of dimensions and also completed a measure of gender-role identification. I expected that students who identified with traditional gender roles, compared to androgynous students, would rate both the man and the woman in the woman-above position more negatively than they would rate the couple in the man-above position. Gender-role identification was unrelated to ratings of the man and woman in the slides, but student sex was a strong predictor. Sex differences emerged on six of the nine ratings of the woman in the slides and on four of the nine ratings of the man in the slides. For example, on a scale ranging from *dirty* (1) to *clean* (7), mean ratings given by the women to the woman in the man-above versus woman-above condition were 6.17 versus 5.38, respectively ($p < .01$). Similarly, in ratings on the dimension from immoral to moral, the means by women for women in the man-above versus woman-above condition were 5.92 versus 4.88, respectively ($p < .005$). Similar judgments were made about the man in the man-above versus woman-above conditions, but here is what I wrote about the results displayed in the relevant table of my dissertation (Allgeier, 1976):

> Internal comparisons revealed that females consistently rated the couple in the woman-above position more negatively than they did the couple in the man-above position. Specifically, the woman was rated as dirtier, less respectable, less moral, less good, less desirable as a wife, and less desirable as a mother when she was on top than when she was beneath the man during intercourse. Females also rated the man as dirtier, less respectable, less moral, and less masculine when he was in the woman-above position than when he was in the man-above position. (p. 21)

Not one of those statements is accurate; in fact, women rated the woman in the man-above position as cleaner, more respectable, more moral, and so forth. With a neutral point of 4, the woman in neither set of slides was rated as dirty, unrespectable, immoral, and so forth. In retrospect, I would not recommend acceptance of my own study as I then wrote it, but my doctoral committee did, and the editor of the *Journal of Consulting and Clinical Psychology* did.

You may think that this issue is trivial, and with respect to my own study, I do not think that my error in interpreting my findings has made much of an impact. However, erroneous conclusions that men's "misattributions" contribute to date rape and to men blaming women for women's victimization are of considerable importance. We need to have accurate data and interpretations of findings if we are to plan effective interventions to reduce the likelihood of sexual assault and harassment. The point is that we can be biased by the way we think about our research questions into seeking confirmation of our beliefs and hypotheses.

Misunderstandings of the Meaning of the Mean

Another threat stemming from misinterpretation of results that may particularly affect laypersons is the perception that means or averages may be applied appropriately to oneself; that is, some individuals may believe that the mean or average response of a given group is either useful for making personal decisions or a goal toward which one should strive. This problem plagues interpretations of research findings in a variety of areas in the social sciences, but I mention just two: use of the hypothetical 28-day menstrual cycle to compute the date of ovulation, and self-evaluation in terms of average frequency of sexual intercourse or other sexual contacts with partners. Although relatively educated laypersons may understand intellectually that a mean is the average of a collection of scores on some variable, they may forget this when applying a finding to themselves.

I know of no studies employing nationally representative samples to determine the average length of women's menstrual cycles; it has long been conventional to describe women's cycles as lasting for an average of 28 days. In teaching parents of adolescents about adolescent sexuality with the goal of helping parents to increase their accuracy in, and degree of comfort with, communicating with their offspring about sexuality, I was initially surprised by the number of parents relying on the so-called *rhythm method* of birth control without having charted the woman's actual cycle on a calendar. They generally understood that ovulation typically occurs midway between one menstrual period and the next menstrual period, so avoided intercourse during the week surrounding the 14th day of their cycle. What they did not understand was the group and individual variations in lengths of the menstrual cycle. Many expressed surprise at the number of children they had ended up having despite their faithful use of the rhythm method. I explained that a particular woman may usually have a 25-day cycle or a 32-day cycle, for example, and be relatively consistent in the length of her cycle. Another woman may vary considerably in the length of her cycle from one month to the next. None of these women necessarily has anything wrong with them; it is just that they should not rely on the hypothetical 28-day average for birth control unless they have charted their own cycle for 6 months or so to determine the length and variations in their own cycles.

Another area in which many of the undergraduates in my sexuality course evaluate themselves using means or averages is the frequency with which they engage in sexual contact with their partners. Although students in my large course regularly ask questions in class, for questions about the normality of their frequency of sexual contact, they either ask me privately or send me e-mail. Again, I explain that a mean or average is not a prescription for the frequency with which they and their partner should have sexual relations. Means typically contain a lot of normal variation, so that the average frequency for couples during the first few years of their relationship may be two to four times a week, but that average is a combination of reports from couples who may engage in sexual relations every day with reports from couples who may engage in sexual contacts once a week or less. In evaluating the health of a relationship by the frequency of sexual relations, the appropriate guide is whether both members of the couple are comfortable with their frequency, not whether it conforms to an average based on responses of a large number of people.

Measuring Attempted and Completed Sexual Coercion

Studies of various forms of sexual coercion, including harassment and assault, are rife with political controversy regarding the methods used to assess both forms of potentially coercive behavior. Some people who have attempted to increase the validity of measures in this area have been seen as undermining the feminist agenda. However, we need as much accurate information as possible if we are to develop intervention strategies to reduce the prevalence of sexual coercion.

In 1988, the Equal Employment Opportunity Commission (EEOC) provided the following description of sexual harassment in an attempt to clarify the legal definition:

> Unwelcome sexual advances, requests for sexual favors, and other verbal or physical conduct of a sexual nature constitute sexual harassment when: submission to such conduct is made either explicitly or implicitly a term or condition of an individual's employment; submission to, or rejection of, such conduct . . . is used as a basis for employment decisions . . . ; or such conduct has the purpose or effect of unreasonably interferring with an individual's work performance or creating an intimidating, hostile, or offensive working environment. (cited in Tamminen, 1994, p. 44)

This definition established the main planks of sexual coercion charges: the quid pro quo (exchange of sex for employment or educational favors) and the hostile environment claim. Even so, there are a number of vague aspects to the definition. For example, how do we establish (or, for that matter, defend ourselves against) implicit conditions? Who determines what is unreasonable? What about the effect of interfering with a person's work performance? And what constitutes an intimidating, hostile, or offensive environment? What you might perceive as interference or an intimidating, hostile, or offensive working environment, I might enjoy (e.g., off-color jokes, sexually suggestive or explicit drawings or photos, etc.).

Broader definitions of *sexual harassment* have been offered by some researchers in the area. For example, in Sandler and Shoop (1997; cited in Patai, 1998), the following are included:

> "Sexual innuendoes, comments or bantering" through "humor or jokes about sex or females in general," "asking for sexual behavior," "touching a person," "giving a neck or shoulder massage," "leering or ogling such as 'elevator eyes,' " calling women "hot stuff" or "sweetie pie," "sexual graffiti," "laughing or not taking seriously someone who experiences sexual harassment," right up to "attempted or actual sexual assault or abuse." (p. 229)

Depending on how broadly harassment is defined, comparisons across studies of sexual harassment are difficult, and different researchers have obtained different prevalence rates of the behavior. The very wide net of acts used to measure and charge sexual harassment led Daphne Patai (1998) to write a superb book: *Heterophobia: Sexual Harassment and the Future of Feminism*. In the book, Patai described what she terms "The Sexual Harassment Industry," in which a large variety of accusations are used to terminate men's and women's jobs—with little or no due process. Many of these hinge on the perception of the accuser rather than the intent of the accused. The contents of her book underscore the importance of developing valid measures of sexual harassment. True sexual harassment does exist, of course, but it is imperative that we develop valid measures of the phenomenon if we are to understand the dynamics of the process and how to reduce the likelihood of it occurring.

Although the phenomenon of sexual assault (i.e., rape) seems easier to assess, there are also problems with measures of that behavior (Wiederman, 2001). In 1990, an advertisement from the Rape Treatment Center of Santa Monica Hospital had bold headlines and was widely distributed to colleges:

Think of the six women closest to you.
Now guess which one will be raped this year.

This headline was followed by text claiming that one out of six college women would be sexually assaulted that year. Advice was provided regarding safety precautions. When interviewed, personnel at the Rape Treatment Center acknowledged that its statistic was too high (Schoenberg & Roe, 1993). Behaviors included in the statistic ranged from unwanted touching to rape. The statistics were based on a survey conducted by psychologist Mary Koss and sponsored by *Ms.* magazine. In the Koss, Gidycz, and Wisniewski (1987) study, students at 32 colleges were given the Sexual Experience Survey (SES), a 12-item measure of unwanted sexual behaviors. The SES, originally designed by Koss and Oros (1982) and subsequent modifications of it, is the most widely used measure of sexual coercion (Porter & Critelli, 1992).

My students and I were investigating various forms of unwanted sex, and we began to wonder about the validity of 4 of the 12 items on the SES. Specifically, Ron Ross and I were interested in men's interpretation of a third of the items in Koss and Oros' 12-item measure of sexual coercion. Ross obtained a release from the federal government that allowed him to question volunteers without having to report their responses or identity to authorities, and he told our male volunteers about that release. The 102 men first responded to Koss and Oros' (1982) measure. Ross then interviewed each man about his interpretations of the four items that appeared to us to be ambiguously worded items (2, 3, 5, and 6), and those pilot data had indicated that many respondents found vague.

In presenting the categories of interpretation for the four ambiguous items, we attempted to distill the intended meanings of each item into a prototypic interpretation. Because of space limitations, I only report responses to Items 2 and 3 (see Ross & Allgeier, 1996, for full results)—Interpretations of Item 2: *"Have you ever had a woman misinterpret the level of sexual intimacy you desired?"* Overall, SES Item 2 was endorsed affirmatively by 42% ($n = 43$) of the sample; 58% ($n = 59$) responded "no." However, men's interpretation of the meaning of the item varied. "Underestimation" (the woman underestimated the level of sexual contact that the man had desired) was endorsed by 37% of the men. But "overestimation" (the woman overestimated the degree of contact desired by the man) was reported by 25% of the men. Both categories were endorsed by 20% of the men. Smaller percentages of men reported other interpretations, none of which involved sexual assault. The main result when considering this item is that 63% of the entire sample interpreted the item as having a meaning other than the meaning intended in Category 1 (man overestimated).

Similar problems exist with the other three items we investigated. For example, there were a number of interpretations of the meaning of Item 3: *"Have you ever been in a situation where you became so sexually aroused that you could not stop yourself even though the woman did not want to?"* Overall, SES Item 3 was endorsed affirmatively by 6% of the sample (94% responded "no"). Following the interviews, a group of three categories of interpretations emerged for this item including "vaginal penetration" (60% of the sample), "any sexual behavior excluding forced vaginal penetration" (34% of the sample), and "other" (i.e., interpretations that fit into neither Category 1 nor Category 2, such as becoming aroused visually while watching a woman dancing from across a room, but not approaching her).

Although others had attempted to assess the "validity" and "accuracy" of men's SES responses (e.g., Gavey, 1991; Koss & Gidycz, 1985; Koss et al., 1987), Ross and Allgeier (1996) provided the first published account of direct assessments of men's interpretations of SES items. Because interpretations necessarily affect a man's decision regarding a response to a true–false questionnaire item, understanding the meanings men attribute to such items is a necessary step in attempting to clarify the validity of SES self-reports.

The SES and altered versions have been used in several major ways. Some researchers have examined SES responses and categorized men into various groups based on the perceived level of sexual coercion that men admitted to by their number of "yes" responses. In contrast, some have chosen only one item, such as Item 3, and dichotomized men into "coercive" versus "noncoercive" groups according to whether a man responded "yes" or "no" to the item. Others have used the SES, or an alteration, and computed coercion "scores," whereby a "yes" response to any item earns a man a "point" toward a total index of his "coerciveness" (e.g., Malamuth, 1986; Peterson & Franzese, 1987). The results of Ross and Allgeier (1996) have implications for these uses of the SES. Specifically, men may be potentially categorized inaccurately regarding their level of sexual "coerciveness."

Although Item 3 ("could not stop") was dropped from at least one researcher's analyses because he perceived it as too "vague" (e.g., Malamuth, 1986), it continues to be used in the assessment of coercive sexual behavior. In fact, that one item was used as the basis for the assignment of men to "coercive" ("yes" responses) and "noncoercive" ("no" responses) groups (Craig, 1993). In the published report of her research, Craig wrote "[have sexual intercourse]" in brackets after the item (p. 420). We called to ask her if the bracketed material had also been on the measures to which her volunteers responded, and she candidly acknowledged that it was not. Our data provided statistical evidence that men's "yes" responses on item 3 were significantly more likely among men who reported interpretations not related to a coercive incident. Specifically, of the six "yes" responders in our sample, five of the six men interpreted the item as referring to a situation devoid of reported coercion. The lack of a behavioral referent in this item leaves open to interpretation just "what" a given man "could not stop."

Researchers' Language in Sexual Coercion Research

With the growing power of the feminist movement in the 1970s, rape was reconceptualized as an act of violence and humiliation, as opposed to earlier views of rape as largely due to psychodynamic factors (e.g., Cohen, Garofalo, Boucher, & Seghorn, 1971) or "victim precipitation" (Amir, 1971). Feminist approaches have had some irreplaceable, enduring, positive effects in terms of bringing the seriousness of male-perpetrated sexual violations to the forefront as a societal and individual problem. However, sexual coercion research has become deeply embedded within a political context of "violence," "victims," "survivors," "abusers," and "perpetrators" without adequate attention to men's (or women's) experiences beyond the realm of yes–no questionnaire responses. For example, Hull and Burke (1991) referred to any man's "yes" response on the original SES as an "abusive act." Others have labeled affirmative SES responses as representing "victimization" (e.g., Gavey, 1991) or "aggression" (Sawrer, Kalichman, Johnson, Early, & Ali, 1993). The use of such language has served to smooth research outcomes and ignore the item interpretations and behavioral referents that critically define the nature of a given sexual interaction.

Attempts have been made to develop a unified theory of sexual aggression capable of accounting for both the similarities and differences among all sexually aggressive males by identifying key motivational factors in men's coercive behavior (e.g., Hall, 1990; Hall & Hirschman, 1991; Knight & Prentky, 1990; Malamuth, 1986; Malamuth, Sockloskie, Koss, & Tanaka, 1991; Prentky & Knight, 1991; Shotland, 1989). Following the assumptions underlying this model has led researchers such as Malamuth et al. (1991) to approach all SES items as reflecting an underlying level of aggression toward women, whether it be verbal or physical attempts to gain sexual access. If a man interprets an SES item as asking if exaggerated flattery has been "used" on a woman, then his response may be grouped with other "yes" responses and collectively referred to as "coercive" in the present climate of methodology and language. On the basis of our data, Ross and I believe that it is inaccurate to equate flattery, exaggerated emotional investment, and talking a person into a sexual interaction with forcibly removing a person's ability to consent. Doing so appears to assume an unreasonable definition of what *consent* represents. A person who is sweet-talked home from a bar cannot be seen as "victimized" in the same way as a person whose ability to consent has been taken by physical force.

To extend conclusions from our findings, researchers should attempt their own investigations based on their own interpretations and understandings of interview material and questionnaire responses. Just as an SES item may be subject to various interpretations by a respondent, a given interpretation may be interpreted by various researchers in very different ways. Therefore, it is necessary that the results of our research be extended and replicated, insofar as this is possible, given the interpretive impact that other investigators may bring to various data.

For a number of reasons, many researchers continue to use paper–pencil measures of sexual coercion. Researchers who continue to select the original SES (Koss & Oros, 1982) for the assessment of sexual coercion now have as a reference several potential interpretations of four SES items. Therefore, in an attempt to assess more clearly the intended meanings that men may be conveying through a given response, researchers may wish to include our list of potential interpretations following each item. Following each survey item, respondents can be instructed to indicate the interpretation which most resembles what they thought the item was asking. In this way, researchers can potentially gain a clearer idea of what a man intended to relate by a "yes" or a "no" response. Such data likely allow researchers to more carefully categorize men's level of sexually coercive behavior.

Although a number of interesting and meaningful "noncoercive" interpretations emerged from the Ross and Allgeier (1996) sample, questions might be raised about the truthfulness of the respondents attributing such meanings to an item in an interview setting. Koss and Gidycz (1985) reported a tendency among their male participants to deny behaviors during interviews that they had revealed on paper–pencil measures. There is the possibility that men who gave "noncoercive" interpretations of "yes" item responses were simply attempting to cover up what they perceived to be inappropriate behavior. However, relatively large numbers of "no" responders, in comparison to "yes" responders, offered "noncoercive" interpretations. These "no" responders had nothing to lose, in that they had no discernable reason to alter an interpretation for fear of appearing coercive. This provides evidence that noncoercive interpretations were given by men who had little reason to fabricate an interpretation, from the standpoint of attempting to appear socially appropriate. If noncoercive interpretations had only been offered by "yes" responders to a given item, more caution would be necessary in interpreting the results of this study.

The SES, in addition to its use with men, has historically been used to classify women as to levels of "victimization." For example, an item worded for women states: "Have you had sexual intercourse when you didn't want to because a man gave you alcohol or drugs?" A woman's affirmative response to this item in the

Koss et al. (1987) study resulted in her being categorized as having been "raped." The meaning of having sex "because" a man gave you drugs is unclear. Gilbert (1993) observed that an affirmative response says nothing about duress, intoxication, the woman's judgment or control, or whether a man purposely got a woman drunk for the purpose of sex. He also suggested that the item might be interpreted to mean that a woman traded sex for drugs or that a small level of alcohol lowered a woman's inhibitions and she consented to an act she later regretted. If the interpretations given in this study offer any foreshadowing of women's experiences with similar items, such a scenario would not be surprising. As a next step in clarifying the meaning of SES items, such a project is crucial.

Are Men Always the Perpetrators and Women Always the Victms of Sexual Coercion?

There has an underlying assumption in research on sexual coercion that men are always the perpetrators (never the victims) and women are always the victims (never the perpetrators). Thus, the version given to men asked about their coercive behavior. The version administered to women inquired about their victimization experiences. That assumption was demonstrated to be false in three studies, published in 1988, in which men reported having been forced to have sex, and women reported having used coercion to obtain sexual contact with men (Aizenman & Kelley, 1988; Muehlenhard & Cook, 1988; Struckman-Johnson, 1988). Interestingly enough, 10 years later, the FBI's *Uniform Crime Reports* continued to define attempted or completed rape as "carnal knowledge of a *female* forcibly and against her will" (p. 25; italics added).

Nonetheless, some researchers have demonstrated that both men and women are victimized, and both men and women use coercive methods to obtain sex from a reluctant or unwilling partner. For example, Larimer, Lydum, Anderson, and Turner (1999) modified the Koss and Oros (1982), combined the male and female versions of some items on their SES, and rewrote them to make them gender neutral to create a 10-item questionnaire (see p. 300). Thus, both men and women could respond to the same form. Larimer et al. administered the measure to almost 300 undergraduates. Overall, 21% of the men and 28% of the women in their sample reported having been the recipients of one or more of the five types of unwanted sexual contact. Initiation of unwanted sexual contacts was reported by 10% of men and 6% of women. I still question retention of several sets of the five types (use of alcohol of drugs to obtain sex from an unwilling person; pressure because of continued arguments to have sex). Unless a drug such as Rohypnol ("roofies") is snuck into a person's drink without his or her knowledge, presumably adults should be able to decline the offer of unwanted drugs or alcohol. Similarly, an adult should be able to persist in declining sex with someone who verbally argues for sex or even leave the venue where the arguments are going on.

Significant gender differences did not emerge regarding the strategies in reported prevalence of unwanted intercourse because the partner was too aroused to stop, pressure from partner's arguments, or from being given alcohol or drugs. However, a significantly greater percentage of women than men reporting having had physical force used in rape attempts or in receiving alcohol or drugs by a partner for the purpose of obtaining intercourse (but intercourse did not take place). Although both findings were signficantly different, the magnitude of the difference (effect sizes) appear to be small. Regarding instigating unwanted sex, very few significant differences emerged. The major point I wish to make is that, if we want to increase our knowledge of the dynamics involved in sexual coercion, it is important that we follow the lead of the 1988 pioneers, who were the first to include both men and women as potential instigators and recipients of coercive methods to obtain unwanted sex, and of those studies such as the one by Larimer et al. (1999) to continue to try to reduce biases in this research area.

Unwanted Consensual Sexual Contacts

I have been struck for years by the apparent redundancy in the phrase "forcible rape" as used by the FBI's *Uniform Crime Reports* and by various researchers. Conversely, readers, particularly those who have not been in a relationship of much duration, may perceive the phrase "unwanted consensual sex" as oxymoronic. However, O'Sullivan and I (O'Sullivan & Allgeier, 1998) questioned if all unwanted sexual activity involves coercion; that is, does a "yes" answer to a "when you didn't want to" always imply that the other person forced you to engage in sexual interaction? Is it possible that many of us experience unwanted *consensual* sex from time to time? Most of us who have been in an ongoing relationship for extended periods of time will probably recognize that there are instances in which our partner desires sex with us when we are not feeling sexual desire. However, we may comply with our partner's interest in getting together sexually and may not indicate our relative disinclination for sex at a particular time. O'Sullivan and I wondered whether our speculations about unwanted sex would hold with unmarried college students who were involved in committed dating relationships. We wanted to avoid retrospective reports because if the sexual contact ended up being pleasurable, the initial disinterest might be less likely to be remembered. Thus, we used a diary approach in which we asked 80 college men and 80 college women to monitor their sexual interactions over a 2-week period. We were astounded to find that more than one third (38%) reported consenting to unwanted sex during just this 2-week period. The most common self-reported reasons for engaging in unwanted consensual sex were wanting to satisfy a partners' needs, promote intimacy, and avoid relationship tension. Supporting our expectations, most of these young people who reported unwanted consensual sex reported positive outcomes from these initially unwanted sexual interactions. Further, those who reported an unwanted consensual interaction could not be distinguished from those who did not on the basis of traditional gender-role endorsement, compliance with subjective norms, nor enactment of relationship-enhancing behaviors.

As might be expected with samples from this age group, there was a significant gender difference in reporting unwanted consensual sexual interactions. Specifically, half the women reported having had this experience during the 2-week period, whereas one fourth of the men (26%) reported unwanted consensual sex. Our findings were consistent with the findings of Sprecher, Hatfield, Cortese, Potapova, and Levitskaya (1994) with samples of college students in the United States, Russia, and Japan, although O'Sullivan and I were unaware of their study when we designed our research. Their overall rates were quite similar to ours, although there were variations among the countries. In their American sample of nonvirgins, 35% of men and 55% of women reported consenting to unwanted sex. The somewhat higher rates for their American sample may stem from the fact that Sprecher et al. asked respondents for retrospective reports of *ever* having consented to unwanted sex, whereas O'Sullivan and I used a prospective diary method over a 2-week period. The corresponding rates for Russians were 34% of men and 32% of women, and for Japanese, 30% of men and 25% of women.

An important issue is that the results from Sprecher et al. (1994) and O'Sullivan and Allgeier (1998) suggest that researchers classifying people as victims or rapists on the basis of questions about unwanted sex may have confounded the prevalence of unwanted nonconsensual sexual contacts with unwanted, but consensual, sexual interactions. It should be obvious at this point that I believe that our measures of coercive sex need to be phrased such that it is abundantly clear that the unwanted sex was actually coerced by the perpetrator from the recipient against his or her will.

Varying and sometimes imprecise definitions of a number of sexuality-related phrases such as "sexual harassment," "sexual assault," "sexual dysfunction," "child sexual abuse," "sexual precociousness," and so on, may ultimately reduce the ability of researchers, clinicians, and educators to design programs to decrease the likelihood of unwanted consequences for participants in these activities. Thus, from both a scientific standpoint and for humane reasons, it behooves us to be as accurate as possible in our measurement and evaluation of sex research results.

SUGGESTED READINGS

In her book, *Heterophobia: Sexual Harassment and the Future Feminism*, Patai (1998) described her transition from being a strong supporter of feminism to a gradual disenchantment with the movement as some of its advocates have become increasingly hostile toward men and toward women having sexual relationships with men. As noted in this chapter, Patai portrayed some of the injustices wrought by what she termed "The Sexual Harassment Industry." For people who support equal rights for both women and men, this book is a breath of fresh air. Whereas Patai's focus is primarily on alleged sexual harassment cases, Young's (1999) book is more broadly concerned with what some have called the *gender wars*, and the emphasis is on political action to the exclusion of treating individuals as individuals rather than as members of a particular group. I recommend reading Patai's and Young's books as a pair. Abelson's (1995) book is a good general introduction of the logic and philosophy of using statistical analyses to attempt to test hypotheses. It would be a good book to read before tackling the article by Rind et al. (1998) regarding the use of meta-analyses to attempt to answer some questions about the long-term sequelae for children of having sexual contact with adults.

REFERENCES

Abbey, A. (1982). Sex differences in attributions for friendly behavior: Do males misperceive females' friendliness? *Journal of Personality and Social Psychology, 42*, 830–838.

Abbey, A. (1987). Misperceptions of friendly behavior as sexual interest: A survey of naturally occurring incidents. *Psychology of Women Quarterly, 11*, 173–194.

Abbey, A. (1991). Misperception as an antecedent of acquaintance rape: A consequence of ambiguity in communication between women and men. In A. Parrot & L. Bechhofer (Eds.), *Acquaintance rape: The hidden crime* (pp. 96–111). New York: Wiley.

Abelson, R. P. (1995). *Statistics as principled argument*. Hillsdale, NJ: Lawrence Erlbaum Associates.

Aizenman, M., & Kelley, G. (1988). The incidence of violence and acquaintance rape in dating relationships among college mand and women. *Journal of College Student Development, 29*, 305–311.

Allgeier, E. R. (1976). *The influence of sex roles on heterosexual attitudes and behavior*. Unpublished doctoral dissertation, Purdue University, Lafayette, IN.

Allgeier, E. R., & Fogel, A. (1978). Coital positions and sex roles: Responses to cross-sex behavior in bed. *Journal of Consulting and Clinical Psychology, 46*, 588–589.

American Psychiatric Association. (1994). *Diagnostic and statistical manual of mental disorders* (4th ed.). Washington, DC: Author.

American Psychological Association. (1994). *Publication manual of the American Psychological Association* (4th ed.). Washington, DC: Author.

Amir, M. (1971). *Patterns in forcible rape*. Chicago: University of Chicago Press.

Broverman, I. K., Broverman, D. M., Clarkson, F. E., Rosenkrantz, P. S., & Vogel, S. R. (1970). Sex-role stereotypes and clinical judgments of mental health. *Journal of Consulting and Clinical Psychology, 34*, 1–7.

Broverman, I. K., Vogel, S. R., Broverman, D. M., Clarkson, F. E., & Rosenkrantz, P. S. (1972). Sex-role stereotypes: A current appraisal. *Journal of Social Issues, 28*, 59–78.

Cohen, M., Garofalo, R., Boucher, R., & Seghorn, T. (1971). The psychology of rapists. *Seminars in Psychiatry, 3*, 307–327.

Craig, M. (1993). The effects of selective evaluation on the perception of female cues in sexually coercive and noncoercive males. *Archives of Sexual Behavior, 22*, 415–433.

Gavey, N. (1991). Sexual victimization prevalence among New Zealand university students. *Journal of Consulting and Clinical Psychology, 59*, 464–466.

Gilbert, N. (1993). Realities and mythologies of rape. In O. Pocs (Ed.), *Annual editions: Human sexuality (1993/94)* (pp. 211–217). Guilford, CT: Dushkin.

Hall, G. C. N. (1990). Prediction of sexual aggression. *Clinical Psychology Review, 10*, 229–246.

Hall, G. C. N., & Hirschman, R. (1991). Toward a theory of sexual aggression: A quadripartite model. *Journal of Consulting and Clinical Psychology, 59,* 662–669.

Higgins, D., & McCabe, M. (1994). The relationship of child sexual abuse and family violence to adult adjustment: Toward an integrated risk-sequelae model. *The Journal of Sex Research, 31,* 255–266.

Hull, D., & Burke, J. (1991). The religious right, attitudes toward women, and tolerance for sexual abuse. *Journal of Offender Rehabilitation, 17*(1), 1–12.

Jones, E. F., Forrest, J. D., Goldman, N., Henshaw, S., Lincoln, R., Rosoff, J. I., Westoff, C. F., & Wulf, D. (1986). *Teenage pregnancy in industrialized countries.* New Haven, CT: Yale University Press.

Kanekar, S., & Nazareth, A. (1988). Attributed rape victim's fault as a function of her attractiveness, physical hurt, and emotional disturbance. *Social Behavior, 3,* 37–40.

Kenrick, D., & Trost, M. (1987). A biosocial theory of heterosexual relationships. In K. Kelly (Ed.), *Females, males, and sexuality* (pp. 59–100). Albany, NY: State University of New York Press.

Kinsey, A. C., Pomeroy, W. B., & Martin, C. E. (1948). *Sexual behavior in the human male.* Philadelphia: Saunders.

Kinsey, A. C., Pomeroy, W. B., Martin, C. E., & Gebhard, P. H. (1953). *Sexual behavior in the human female.* Philadelphia: Saunders.

Knight, R. A., & Prentky, R. A. (1990). In W. L. Marshall, D. R. Laws, & H. E. Barbaree (Eds.), *Handbook of sexual assault: Issues, theories, and treatment of the offender* (pp. 23–52). New York: Plenum.

Koss, M., & Gidycz, C. A. (1985). Sexual Experiences Survey: Reliability and validity. *Journal of Consulting and Clinical Psychology, 53,* 422–423.

Koss, M , Gidycz, C. A., & Wisniewski, N. (1987). The scope of rape: Incidence and prevalence of sexual aggression and victimization in a national sample of higher education students. *Journal of Consulting and Clinical Psychology, 55,* 162–170.

Koss, M., & Oros, C. (1982). Sexual Experiences Survey: A research instrument investigating sexually aggressive men. *Journal of Personality and Social Psychology, 50,* 455–457.

Larimer, M. E., Lydum, A. R., Anderson, B. K., & Turner, A. P. (1999). Male and female recipients of unwanted sexual contact in a college student sample. Prevalence rates, alcohol use, and depression symptoms. *Sex Roles, 40,* 295–308.

Laumann, E. O., Gagnon, J. H., Michael, R. T., & Michaels, S. (1994). *The social organization of sexuality.* Chicago: University of Chicago Press.

Levine, S. V., Kamin, L. E., & Levine, E. L. (1974). Sexism and psychiatry. *American Journal of Orthopsychiatry, 44,* 327–336.

Malamuth, N. M. (1986). Predictors of naturalistic sexual aggression. *Journal of Personality and Social Psychology, 50,* 953–962.

Malamuth, N. M., Sockloskie, R. J., Koss, M. P., & Tanaka, J. S. (1991). Characteristics of aggressors against women: Testing a model using a national sample of college students. *Journal of Consulting and Clinical Psychology, 59,* 670–681.

Muehlenhard, C. (1988). Misinterpreting dating behaviors and the risk of date rape. *Journal of Social and Clinical Psychology, 6,* 20–37.

Muehlenhard, C , & Cook, S. (1988). Men's self-reports of unwanted sexual activity. *The Journal of Sex Research, 24,* 58–72.

Myers, D. G. (1990). *Social psychology* (3rd ed.). New York: McGraw-Hill.

Myers, D. G. (1993). *Social psychology* (4th ed.). New York: McGraw-Hill.

O'Sullivan, L. F., & Allgeier, E. R. (1998). Feigning sexual desire: Consenting to unwanted sexual activity in heterosexual dating relationships. *The Journal of Sex Research, 35,* 234–243.

Patai, D. (1998). *Heterophobia: Sexual harassment and the future of feminism.* Lanham, MD: Rowman & Littlefield.

Peterson, S., & Franzese, B. (1987). Correlates of men's sexual abuse of women. *Journal of College Student Personnel, 28,* 223–228.

Phillips, R. D., & Gilroy, F. D. (1985). Sex-role stereotypes and clinical judgments of mental health: The Brovermans' findings reexamined. *Sex Roles, 12*, 179–193.

Porter, J. F., & Critelli, J. W. (1992). Measurement of sexual aggression in college men: A methodological analysis. *Archives of Sexual Behavior, 21*, 525–542.

Prentky, R. A., & Knight, R. A. (1991). Identifying critical dimensions for discriminating among rapists. *Journal of Consulting and Clinical Psychology, 59*, 643–661.

Rind, B., Tromovitch, P., & Bauserman, R. (1998). A meta-analytic examination of assumed properties of child sexual abuse using college samples. *Psychological Bulletin, 124*, 22–53.

Rosenkrantz, P., Vogel, S., Bee, H., Broverman, I., & Broverman, D. (1968). Sex-role stereotypes and self-concept in college students. *Journal of Consulting and Clinical Psychology, 32*, 287–295.

Ross, R. R., & Allgeier, E. R. (1996). Behind the paper/pencil measurement of sexual coercion: Interview-based clarification of men's interpretations of Sexual Experiences Survey items. *Journal of Applied Social Psychology, 26*, 1587–1616.

Saal, F. E., Johnson, C. B., & Weber, N. (1989). Friendly or sexy? It may depend on whom you ask. *Psychology of Women Quarterly, 13*, 263–276.

Sandler, B. R., & Shoop, R. J. (Eds.). (1997). *Sexual harassment on campus: A guide for administrators, faculty, and students.* Boston: Allyn & Bacon.

Sawrer, D. B., Kalichman, S. C., Johnson, J. R., Early, J., & Ali, S. A. (1993). Sexual aggression and love styles: An exploratory study. *Archives of Sexual Behavior, 22*, 265–275.

Schoenberg, N., & Roe, S. (1993, November 17). Erroneous statistic on rape stands uncorrected. *Toledo Blade*, pp. 1, 7.

Shotland, R. (1989). A model of the causes of date rape in developing and close relationships. In C. Hendrick (Ed.), *Close relationships* (pp. 247–270). Beverly Hills, CA: Sage.

Sprecher, S., Hatfield, E., Cortese, A., Potapova, E., & Levitskaya, A. (1994). Token resistance to sexual intercourse and consent to unwanted sexual intercourse: College students' dating experiences in three countries. *The Journal of Sex Research, 31*, 125–132.

Stricker, G. (1977). Implications of research for psychotherapeutic treatment of women. *American Psychologist, 32*, 14–22.

Struckman-Johnson, C. (1988). Forced sex on dates: It happens to men, too. *The Journal of Sex Research, 24*, 234–241.

Tamminen, J. M. (1994). *Sexual harassment in the workplace: Managing corporate policy.* New York: Wiley.

Wiederman, M. W. (2001). *Understanding sexuality research.* Pacific Grove, CA: Wadsworth.

Young, C. (1999). *Cease fire!: Why women and men must join forces to achieve true equality.* New York: The Free Press.

17

Integrative Literature Reviewing[1]

Bernard E. Whitley, Jr.
Ball State University

As of mid-1996, 121 empirical studies had been conducted investigating the psychosocial correlates of heterosexual condom use, producing 660 correlations involving 44 variables (Sheeran, Abraham, & Orbell, 1999). A reasonable question to ask is: What have all these studies told us about those correlates? Given that not all the results of the studies investigating a particular correlate were consistent—some supported the existence of a relationship with condom use, others did not—another reasonable question is: What caused these inconsistencies? An integrative literature review attempts to answer questions such as these by (a) collecting all of the available information on a topic, (b) organizing it to show the current state of knowledge on the topic, and (c) identifying gaps in knowledge that need to be filled.

The purpose of the integrative literature review is to summarize the research evidence on a hypothesis or set of related hypotheses. Such summaries have several goals. One goal is evaluating the validity of the hypothesis, determining how well it is supported. Although the outcome of a single study could be the result of its flaws rather than the effect of the independent variable, if several studies of a hypothesis, each with its own flaws but each also having strengths that compensate for the weaknesses of the others, all come to the same conclusion, then it is unlikely that the overall result is an artifact resulting from design flaws (Salipante, Notz, & Bigelow, 1982). The consensus of a number of studies, as shown by a literature review, therefore provides the best estimate of the effect of an independent variable.

[1]Adapted from *Principles of Research in Behavioral Science* by Bernard E. Whitley, Jr., Mayfield Publishing Company, 1996. Adapted with permission by Mayfield Publishing.

Nonetheless, some studies in a set will find support for the hypothesis and others will not; therefore, a related goal of literature reviewing is determining the causes of inconsistencies in research results. Sometimes the cause will be methodological, such as the use of different operational definitions in different studies, and sometimes the cause will be a variable that moderates the effect of the independent variable, such as when men respond differently than women. In such a case, the use of all-male samples in some studies and all-female samples in other studies apparently lead to conflicting results. Once the summary is completed, the literature reviewer can draw implications for theory, research, and application. For example, the discovery of moderating variables might require modification to theories, the literature review might show that a commonly used operational definition has validity problems, or the review might indicate that an intervention works better for some types of people or in certain situations than it does for other people or in other situations.

The results of literature reviews can be used in several ways. Literature reviews provide background information for new research studies, providing their scientific context, avoiding unnecessary duplication of effort, and identifying problems that might be encountered in conducting the research. Literature reviews also provide information about the current state of knowledge about a theory or topic and identify gaps in knowledge that need to be filled by research. Literature reviews can also address the generalizability of research results by determining their consistency across such factors as research strategies, operational definitions, research settings, and participant populations. Finally, reviews of evaluation studies can provide information that can be used in making policy decisions by identifying what programs work and the conditions affecting the quality of program outcomes.

Researchers who conduct integrative literature reviews usually start with a specific hypothesis (or a more general research question) and want to test the validity of that hypothesis. However, rather than using data collected from research participants, their data consist of the results of a set of studies testing the hypothesis. As in empirical research, there are five steps to literature reviewing: defining the research question, data collection, data evaluation, data analysis, and interpretation of results. This chapter discusses each of these steps. The principles discussed here can be used as general guidelines for conducting literature reviews (see the Suggested Readings section for specific methodological guides) and for critically reading published literature reviews.

DEFINING THE RESEARCH QUESTION

Literature reviews, like all research, start with a question. There are three issues to consider in formulating a literature review question: type of question one wants to answer, scope of the question, and approach to take in answering the question.

Types of Questions

Literature reviews can address three questions: What is the average effect of an independent variable on a dependent variable? What factors moderate that effect? Is the effect found under specific sets of conditions?

What Is the Average Effect of an Independent Variable? This question concerns what, in analysis of variance (ANOVA) designs, is called a main effect. That is, ignoring differences among studies in research strategies, participant populations, operational definitions, settings, and so forth, what effect does an independent variable have on a dependent variable and how large is that effect? Although this is a rather simplistic way of looking at the effect of a variable, this main effects approach to literature reviewing can serve two purposes. One is to guide social policymaking, which is often more interested in the overall effect of a variable than in the factors that moderate its effects (e.g., Light & Pillemer, 1984). For example, consider a hypothetical policy question such as, should public funds be used to pay for AIDS education? Because the question is one of whether the services should be funded at all, policymakers want to know whether AIDS education in general is effective and therefore deserving of funding. Questions concerning moderator variables, such as whether some types of education are more effective for some types of people, are too narrow to form the basis for a broad social policy. Paraphrasing Masters (1984), Guzzo, Jackson, and Katzell (1987) framed the issue in this way:

> Policy makers voice a need for "one-armed" social scientists who give straight, unqualified answers when asked for advice. Instead, they too often encounter a response such as, "Well, on the one hand thus and so is the case, but on the other hand this and that may hold." Unlike scientists, who often prefer to dwell on the contingencies that make global generalizations impossible, policy makers must seek to find the most justifiable generalizations. (p. 412)

A second purpose of main effects literature reviewing is to identify general principles that can guide research. For example, a general finding that there are sex differences in attitudes toward sexual behavior (Oliver & Hyde, 1993) implies that the gender of a research participant should be controlled in such studies to minimize extraneous variance.

What Factors Moderate That Effect? This is the question of the generalizability of an effect: Does the independent variable have the same effect under all conditions? In ANOVA terms, this is the question of whether an interaction exists between the independent variable whose effect is being reviewed and some other variable. Ideas for the potential moderator variables to consider in a literature review can come from a number of sources, including theories that deal with the independent variable. These theories might postulate the existence of moderator variables and so predict that researchers should find certain interactions. For example, Fisher, Byrne, White, and Kelley's (1988) theory of erotophobia–erotophilia holds that sexuality and contraceptive education programs will be less effective for certain types of people (i.e., those high in what Fisher et al. called *erotophobia*) than for others. Reviews of the literature on the effectiveness of sexuality and contraceptive education programs could therefore compare the outcomes of studies conducted with people high in erotophobia with studies conducted with people high in its polar opposite, erotophilia. This procedure would both test the theory and examines its impact under the conditions that it specifies as crucial to its effectiveness.

Potential moderator variables can also be identified from the reviewer's knowledge of research on the topic and from prior literature reviews. For example, the reviewer might know that the results of research on a topic vary as a function of research setting. Similarly, potential moderators may emerge from the studies being reviewed: As the reviewer reads through them, he or she may see patterns of relationships between factors such as study characteristics and the magnitude of the impact of the independent variable. Finally, one can apply "one's intuition, insight, and ingenuity" (Jackson, 1980, p. 443) to the problem: The reviewer might have hypotheses of his or her own to test in the review.

Is the Effect Found Under Specific Conditions?   This is the question of the ecological validity of an effect; that is, how well can a broad principle be applied to a specific type of situation? The answer to this question can be used to assist in deciding if an intervention should be implemented under a given set of circumstances; that is, has previous research shown it to effective or ineffective under those, or similar, circumstances?

The Scope of the Question

The issue of scope deals with how narrowly or broadly the question is defined. For example, is the review to be limited to just one operational definition of the independent variable or will multiple operational definitions be considered? Will the review be limited to one dependent variable or will the independent variable's effects on several dependent variables be assessed? Will the review include just one or more than one operational definition of each dependent variable? Will it include only one research strategy or will all strategies be included? The answers to questions such as these depend to some extent on the purpose of the literature review. For example, only experiments can test causality, so a reviewer who asks a causal question might be limited, or give more emphasis, to experiments. A review that is too narrow in scope, for example, one limited to one operational definition each of the independent and dependent variables, may lead to conclusions with little generalizability. In contrast, a review that is too broadly defined might become impossible to complete, with the reviewer overwhelmed by a huge number of studies. Defining the scope of the review is a judgment call that must be guided by the reviewer's knowledge of the topic under review.

Approaches to Answering Questions

There are three broad approaches to conducting literature reviews, although any review can involve a combination of the three. With the hypothesis-testing approach, the reviewer starts with a specific hypothesis about the relationship between an independent variable and a dependent variable and tests the hypothesis against the results of research. For example, Rind and Tromovitch (1997) tested three hypotheses about the psychological correlates of childhood sexual abuse by integrating the results of seven studies that used national probability samples of respondents. They found that childhood sexual abuse was not associated with pervasive psychological harm, that the harm that did occur was not severe, and that men reported fewer negative effects than did women. Reviewers taking this approach can also start with a theory and test a set of hypotheses derived from the theory to evaluated the overall validity of the theory (e.g., Sheeran et al., 1999).

The second approach compares predictions derived from competing theories to determine which theory is best supported by the evidence. For example, Murnen and Stockton (1997) compared predictions derived from social influence and sociobiological theories about gender differences in sexual arousal in response to sexual stimuli. They concluded that their results provided better support for social influence theories.

The third approach is exploratory, in which the reviewer focuses on an outcome and searches the relevant literature to determine which independent variables consistently produce the outcome. For example, Whitley and Schofield (1986) asked what variables predicted the use of contraception by adolescents. Their review revealed 25 reasonably consistent predictors for young women and 12 for young men. One drawback of the exploratory approach is that the predictors found can be intercorrelated, so that controlling for one or more might remove the effects of others. Therefore, any relationships found using an exploratory literature review should be confirmed by collecting new data. When Whitley (1990) did this, he found that only three of the variables independently predicted contraceptive use by young women and only one predicted contraceptive use by young men.

The choice among the three approaches to literature reviewing depends on the purpose of the review and the nature of the research being reviewed. For example, the hypothesis-testing approach can be used only when the reviewer has a specific hypothesis in mind, derived either from theory, prior empirical work, or personal insight or experience. Similarly, the theory-comparison approach is most appropriate when different theories make competing predictions about a phenomenon. In contrast, the exploratory approach can be used to identify important independent variables from which to develop new theories or, as Whitley and Schofield (1986) did, to catalog independent variables in an area of research that has been generally unguided by theory and so determine which appear have effects and which do not.

DATA COLLECTION

Data collection for a literature review consists of locating studies that address the hypothesis or topic of interest. Because most researchers are familiar with this process, I only briefly discuss means for locating studies.

There are several ways of locating information on a topic. Almost all professional journals are covered by indexes, such as *Psychological Abstracts* and *Sociological Abstracts*, that allow one to locate articles by topic or author. There are also indexes to some unpublished sources. *Dissertation Abstracts International* and *Masters Abstracts International* index doctoral dissertations and masters theses, respectively. Dissertations and theses can sometimes be borrowed on interlibrary loan and microfiche or paper copies can be purchased from University Microfilms, the company that publishes the indexes. The Educational Resources Information Center (ERIC) database indexes and provides abstracts for selected journals, convention papers, and technical reports in education and related fields. Finally, the *Monthly Catalog of US Government Publications* lists and indexes publications, including research reports, published by the Government Printing Office. Many academic libraries include selected government publications in their collections, usually in a special department.

Because research reports, theoretical articles, and literature review articles cite the studies on which they are based, a second source of studies is the bibliographies of these publications. If one or a few articles are central to the topic under review, one can conduct a citation search. *Social Sciences Citation Index* (SSCI) indexes all the sources cited in articles published in major journals in the social and behavioral sciences. Therefore, if Smith and Jones have written a particularly important article on a subject, you can look up all the subsequent journal articles that cited Smith and Jones' work; these articles probably address the same topic and so are likely to be relevant to your literature review.

Although these methods provide useful starting points for collecting data for an integrative literature review, they do not provide a complete listing of relevant research. M. Rosenthal (1994), for example, discussed what she called *the fugitive literature*—research reports in the form of technical reports, unpublished manuscripts, papers presented at conventions, and dissertations and theses—that are often not covered by the more commonly used indexes; several strategies for locating these kinds of studies are provided.

Modern computer technology has made literature searching seductively easy: Sit down at the terminal, type in your search terms, and the computer lists your sources. However, designing an effective computer search of a database can be difficult; Joswick (1994) provided an excellent overview of the process and identified a number of common pitfalls. For example, it is essential to use the correct search terms in searching computerized databases. Each index and related database has a book called a thesaurus that lists the terms that the index uses to categorize articles; if you do not use these official terms, you might not find what you are looking for. The thesaurus might also suggest synonyms, related terms, or broader terms under which to search. This problem is illustrated by a meta-analysis of gender differences in attitudes toward homosexuality, conducted by Oliver and Hyde (1993). Their literature search located 16 studies on the topic. However, Whitley and Kite (1995) noted that Oliver and Hyde had used inappropriate search terms for their search of computerized databases. Using thesaurus-derived search terms, Whitley and Kite located an additional 50 studies.

In addition, computerized searches can turn up large numbers of studies irrelevant to the literature review, but that happen to be indexed under the search terms used, and can overlook a large number of relevant studies that happen not to be indexed under those terms. As Durlak and Lipsey (1991) described their experience, "We discovered . . . that only one of every three entries appearing in our computer-generated study lists was relevant [to the literature review] and approximately two-thirds of the relevant studies were not picked up via the computer search" (p. 301). Supplementing a computer search with other means is slower, but in the long run more productive, than relying on the computerized indexes alone. People doing literature reviews, therefore, often find it useful to conduct what Green and Hall (1984) called a source-by-source search: Identify all of the journals that are likely to carry research reports on your topic and examine every issue of every journal for relevant articles. Such a procedure is laborious and time-consuming, but Green and Hall suggested that it is the best way of being certain to have located all relevant published studies.

DATA EVALUATION

Once you have collected the studies relevant to your hypothesis, you have to decide which ones to include in your literature review. Although one's initial impulse might be to include all of the studies, there are other options, the two most common of which are including only published studies, or including only highly valid studies. Each approach has advantages and disadvantages.

Include All Studies

Including all of the relevant studies in the literature review has the distinct advantage of completeness: all the available data will be used in drawing conclusions. There are, however, several potential disadvantages to this approach. First, it might be difficult or impossible to locate all relevant studies. For example, few unpublished studies are indexed, making it very difficult to locate them, and the benefit derived once they are found might not be worth the effort. Second, including all studies in the review will give equal weight to highly valid and poorly designed research. Conclusions drawn from the latter studies should be qualified by consideration of the alternative explanations for their results posed by the threats to their validity. However, if all studies are lumped together, valid results are confounded with potentially invalid results. Finally, if there is a very large number of studies on a topic, it might be impossible to include all of them, especially if the time available for conducting the review is limited.

Include Only Published Studies

Most literature reviews include only published studies or make only limited attempts to locate unpublished studies, such as through the use of the ERIC database. Published studies are easy to locate because they are indexed. In addition, the peer review process provides some screening for methodological validity, although the process is not perfect. Considering only published studies also limits the number of studies one has to handle.

The disadvantage of including only published studies in the review is that it brings into play the bias against publishing null results (Greenwald, 1975): Journal reviewers and editors prefer studies that find a relationship between two variables over studies finding no relationship. Because studies finding no statistically significant effect of the independent variable (i.e., those that typically find only small relationships between the independent and dependent variables) are unlikely to be published, those that are published may overestimate the true effect of the independent variable. Including such studies in a literature review can give a distorted picture of the relationship between the independent and dependent variables. Another form of publication bias is in favor of studies whose results are consistent with accepted theory (Greenwald, Pratkanis, Lieppe, & Baumgardner, 1986). Studies that produce findings that challenge popular theories tend to be evaluated more strictly than studies that support the theory and so are less likely to get published. Consequently, a literature review aimed at evaluating a theory is less likely to turn up data that challenge the theory if it includes only published studies.

Include Only Valid Studies

Including all studies in a literature review, or even only all published studies, may result in using studies that have threats to their validity. Consequently, literature reviewers frequently attempt to assess the validity of the studies conducted on a topic. Reviewers are generally most concerned with internal validity, theoretical validity, and ecological validity; they assess generalizability with analyses of the effects of moderator variables.

Internal Validity.   Because the results of studies that suffer from internal validity problems might not accurately reflect the true relationship between the independent and dependent variables, including them in a literature review could threaten the validity of the conclusions drawn from the review. White (1982), for example, conducted a literature review of studies of the relationship between socioeconomic status (SES) and IQ scores and found that the studies that he thought were of low internal validity produced an average correlation of .49 between SES and IQ scores, whereas the highly valid studies revealed an average correlation of .30. Consequently, literature reviewers usually evaluate the internal validity of the research that they review and give more weight to those considered to be more valid. Some reviewers completely exclude from consideration studies that they consider to be of low validity.

Theoretical Validity.   One can also evaluate studies on their theoretical validity (Cook & Leviton, 1980); that is, some theories specify conditions that must be met in order for predictions made by the theories to be fulfilled. A true test of the validity of a theory can take place only if the conditions that it sets for itself are met. Cook and Leviton (1980) cited the example of research on the "sleeper effect" in persuasion, the finding that attitude change is sometimes delayed until well after the persuasive message is received:

> If all past studies of the sleeper effect were included in a review without regard to how well the necessary conditions for a strong test of the effect were met, one would probably conclude from the many failures to obtain the effect that "it is time to lay the sleeper effect to rest." . . . And the number of failures to obtain the effect would be psychologically impressive. Yet the very few studies that demonstrably met the theory-derived conditions for a strong test of the effect all obtained it, . . . and one can surmise that these studies should be assigned greatest inferential weight because of their higher theoretical relevance. (pp. 460–461)

Ecological Validity.   Finally, when the literature review is aimed at determining the applicability of a principle to a specific situation, the reviewer will want to assess the ecological validity of the studies relative to that situation. The studies that were not conducted under conditions reasonably similar to those in the situation to which the principle is going to be applied could be eliminated from, or given less weight in, the review.

Evaluating Validity.   Excluding studies from consideration in a review on the basis of their validity raises the question of what constitutes a study that is sufficiently valid to be included in the literature review. No study can be perfect; as a result, even experts can disagree about the degree of validity of a study. Therefore, selecting studies for inclusion in a literature review on the basis of their validity might be overly restrictive: A methodological flaw in a study does not necessarily mean that its results are biased, only that the conclusions that one can draw from it are less certain than the conclusions that can be drawn from a better study (Jackson, 1980). In addition, as R. Rosenthal (1990) pointed out, "Too often, deciding what is a 'bad' study is a procedure richly susceptible to bias or to claims of bias. . . . 'Bad' studies are too often those whose results we don't like or . . . the studies [conducted by] our 'enemies' " (p. 126).

What, then, should one do when faced with a set of studies that vary as to validity? Mullen, Salas, and Miller (1991) suggested a three-step approach. First, exclude those studies that are so flawed in terms of internal or construct validity that no valid conclusions can be drawn from them. For example, a study might use a measure that later research has shown to be invalid. Because the wrong construct was measured, the study does not really test the hypothesis under review. Second, establish an explicit set of criteria for judging the degree of validity of the studies under review. For example, a study that randomly assigned participants to conditions of the independent variable would be considered of higher internal validity than a study that allowed participants to self-select into conditions. Criteria could also be established for ecological or theoretical validity. Third, classify the studies as to their degree of validity, being sure to check the reliability of the classification system, and then analyze the results of the studies within validity categories. Using this approach, one can determine if degree of validity affected the results of the studies. If there are large discrepancies in results on the basis of degree of validity, one might want to give more weight to the more highly valid studies when drawing conclusions.

DATA ANALYSIS

Once the studies are selected for inclusion in the literature review, the reviewer must synthesize or combine their results. This synthesis has two aspects. First, the reviewer must determine the overall effect of the independent variable as shown by the results of the studies: On the average, does the independent variable have an effect? Second, the reviewer must determine the factors that moderate, or lead to differences in, the results of the studies. For example, does the independent variable have an effect in one situation, such as a laboratory environment, but not in another, such as field settings? To accomplish these tasks, the reviewer must make several sets of decisions: how to operationally define the outcomes of studies, how to classify studies on possible moderating variables, how to assess flaws in research designs, how to broadly define the independent and dependent variables, and how to conduct the data analysis.

Operationally Defining Study Outcome

A literature review combines the outcomes of studies to draw conclusions about the effect of an independent variable. The first step in this process is operationally defining study outcome in a way that allows the reviewer to directly compare the results of different studies even though those studies might have used different operational definitions of the independent and dependent variables. For example, studies of the psychosocial factors related to condom use have used a wide variety of operational definitions of both condom use and of the factors studied (Sheeran et al., 1999). How can one compare the results of studies and draw overall conclusions in such circumstances? One must develop an operational definition of study outcome that can be applied to all the studies under review. Three operational definitions are commonly used: effect size, multiple outcome categories, and a dichotomous categorization based on whether the results of the study supported or did not support the hypothesis.

Effect Size.   Jackson (1980) recommended effect size as the ideal operational definition of study outcome because it provides a precise index of the impact of the independent variable on the dependent variable variable. Two effect size measures are commonly used in literature reviews: d and r. When the independent variable is categorical, such as the experimental versus control conditions in an experiment, the standardized difference in the means of the two conditions, indicated by the symbol d, is used as the operational definition of outcome. d is computed as the mean of the experimental condition minus the mean of the control condition divided by the pooled standard deviation of the conditions. d therefore indicates the number of standard deviation units that separate the means of the two conditions. Typically, d is given a plus sign if the results are in the direction predicted by the hypothesis being tested in the review and a minus sign if the results are opposite to the prediction. When the independent variable is continuous, such as scores on an attitude questionnaire, then the Pearson product–moment correlation, r, is used as the effect size indicator. Given an effect size for each study, one can answer the question of the overall effect of the independent variable by computing the mean effect size across studies (e.g., Hunter & Schmidt, 1990; R. Rosenthal, 1991). Both d and r require that the dependent variable in the study be continuous; however, there are also effect size indicators for categorical dependent variables that can be mathematically transformed to d and r (e.g., R. Rosenthal, 1991).

Multiple Outcome Categories.   One problem with the use of effect size as an operational definition of study outcome is that studies do not always report an effect size or the statistical information required to compute one. This kind of nonreporting is especially likely when the independent variable did not have a statistically significant effect. When exact effect sizes are not available, multiple outcome categories can be used as a secondary tactic (Jackson, 1980). A study would be put into one of five categories depending on the statistical significance of its outcome:

1. The results were statistically significant and supported the hypothesis.
2. The results were not statistically significant but did support the hypothesis.

3. The independent variable had no effect.
4. The results were not statistically significant and contradicted the hypothesis.
5. The results were statistically significant and contradicted the hypothesis.

Once all studies have been categorized, one can examine the distribution of outcomes to draw conclusions about the effect of the independent variable.

Two Outcome Categories. Unfortunately, not all studies provide sufficient information to allow the reviewer to use five outcome categories. Sometimes the best the reviewer can do is categorize studies as either supporting or not supporting the hypothesis, based on the statistical significance of the results, and draw conclusions about the effect of the independent variable by counting the "votes" for and against the hypothesis. This vote-counting approach to literature reviewing has a serious drawback: It is highly susceptible to Type II errors—incorrectly accepting the null hypothesis (Hedges & Olkin, 1985). Statistical significance is strongly affected by sample size. Consequently, two studies could find identical effect sizes for an independent variable, but the study using a large sample could have a statistically significant result while the study with a small sample could have a statistically nonsignificant result. For example, an r of .25 would be statistically significant with a sample size of 100, but not with a sample size of 50. Although the outcomes are identical in terms of effect size, the first study would be classified as supporting the hypothesis and the second as not supporting it.

Rossi (1990) described an example of this problem. He reported the results of two literature reviews of the same set of studies, one using the vote-counting method to operationally define study outcome and one using effect sizes. The vote-counting review concluded that the research was inconsistent, sometimes finding an effect for the independent variable and sometimes not finding an effect; however, the effect size analysis concluded that the independent variable did have an effect, albeit a small one, equivalent to a correlation of about .18. The five-category approach is also susceptible to Type II errors, but is less susceptible than the vote-counting method because it uses more categories.

Classifying Studies

In addition to identifying the overall effect of an independent variable, most literature reviewers want to identify the factors that moderate that effect. To achieve the latter goal, one must first identify possible moderator variables, such as participant population and research setting, and then classify each study on each variable. For example, one study might use a college student sample in a laboratory setting and another might use a noncollege-student sample in a field setting. Because a study might not clearly fall into only one category, classifying studies can sometimes involve relatively subjective judgments (Wanous, Sullivan, & Malinak, 1989). Consequently, one must be careful to check the reliability of the classifications, just as one would check the reliability of behavioral observations or the reliability of the classifications made in a content analysis. Once the studies have been classified, one can compare the typical outcome in one category with the typical outcome in another. For example, an independent variable might have an effect for college students but not for older adults (e.g., Murnen & Stockton, 1997). However, one must also be alert for confounds among moderator variables, such as a confound between participant population and research setting. These comparisons of outcomes between categories of studies can identify limits on the generalizability of an effect.

Analyzing Patterns of Flaws

In addition to establishing the degree of validity of each study in a literature review as discussed earlier, it is also important to look for patterns of design flaws within the set of studies being reviewed. A set of studies might all point to the same conclusion, but if the studies have one or more validity threats in common, the consistency in their results could come from the shared flaw rather than from the effect of the independent variable (e.g., Salipante et al., 1982). Salipante et al. recommended conducting a design flaw analysis by creating a matrix, such as that shown in Table 17.1, in which the rows represent the studies being reviewed and the columns represent potential validity threats. The columns in Table 17.1, for

TABLE 17.1
Sample Matrix for Assessing Validity Threats

Study	History	Maturation	Testing	Statistical Regression	Selection	Mortality
A			x		√	
B	√	√	x	x		
C	√	√	√			
D	√		√	√	√	
E			x		√	
F					√	
G					√	
H			x	√	√	
I	√		x	x		
J	√		x	x		
K	√		x	x		

Code: "x" = design precludes threat; "√" = study included control for or assessment of threat.
Note. From *Principles of Research in Behavioral Science* (p. 469), by Bernard E. Whitley, Jr., 1996, Mountain View, CA: Mayfield. Copyright 1996 by Mayfield. Reprinted with permission.

example, represent some of the internal validity threats identified by Cook and Campbell (1979); of course, the matrix could be expanded to include other threats to internal validity, threats to ecological, construct, and theoretical validity, and possible confounds.

In Table 17.1 an "x" indicates that the threat did not arise because the research design precluded it; for example, pretest sensitization is not a threat if the study did not use a pretest. A "√" indicates that the study included a specific control for or an assessment of the effects of the threat. A large number of blanks in a column, therefore, indicates that the entire set of studies suffered from a common flaw; consequently, conclusions drawn about the effects of the independent variable must be tempered by consideration of the flaw as a possible alternative explanation for the effects found. For example, Table 17.1 shows that the research reviewed (a set of quasi-experiments) generally did not control for the effects of maturation and mortality. Literature reviews are important because they allow researchers to draw conclusions from a set of studies each of which has strengths that compensate for the weaknesses of the others. A design flaw analysis lets researchers be sure that all weaknesses are compensated, that none affect all or most of the studies.

Level of Analysis

An important decision that literature reviewers must make is determining the the appropriate conceptual level of analysis at which to define the independent and dependent variables. Suppose that a researcher wants to conduct a literature review on the effectiveness of sex therapy. The concept of sex therapy could be operationally defined at different levels of abstraction. For example, the researcher could simply define sex therapy as a general concept and not investigate whether different types of therapy, such as individual and couple therapy, have different effects. Alternately, the researcher could decide to compare the relative effectiveness of individual and couple therapy but not investigate the relative effectiveness of specific therapeutic techniques within these general categories. Still another option, the researcher could conduct a very fine-grained analysis comparing the effectiveness of specific techniques within each of the categories. Similarly, dependent variables can be defined at various levels of abstraction.

The inappropriate combining of effect sizes or other definitions of outcome across different independent variables, dependent variables, and operational definitions of the variables is sometimes referred to as the problem of "mixing apples and oranges" (Cook & Leviton, 1980). This criticism was directed initially at a review of psychotherapy outcome studies (Smith & Glass, 1977), which combined effect sizes across different types of therapy (e.g., mixing the apples of behavior therapy with the oranges of psychodynamic therapy) after initial analyses indicated no difference in outcome by type of therapy. Glass (1978) defended this approach by noting that both behavior therapy and psychodynamic therapy are subcategories of the general concept of psychotherapy and that this higher order concept was the independent variable of interest in the review. In short, Glass argued that it is permissible to mix apples and oranges if one is interested in the effects of fruit. Such higher order combination of effect sizes is generally considered appropriate as long as two cautions are borne in mind. First, such "mixed" independent variables can at times be somewhat artificial or remote from real applications (Bangert-Downs, 1986). Second, effect sizes should be examined within types of independent variable to determine if effect sizes differ as a function of the type of independent variable or if moderators affect different independent variables differently (Shadish & Sweeney, 1991). For example, in their review of the research on gender differences in attitudes toward homosexuality, Kite and Whitley (1996) found that attitudes varied as functions of both the gender of the research participant and the gender of the attitude target (lesbians or gay men).

It is more difficult to justify combining results across different dependent variables as did Smith and Glass (1977), who held that in psychotherapy, an outcome was an outcome regardless of whether it was defined in terms of clinicians' judgments, clients' self-reports, or independent assessments of behavior. This is a risky tactic because any one independent variable can have greatly divergent effects on different types of dependent variables. For example, Kite and Whitley (1996) found that (a) the largest gender difference in attitudes toward homosexuality was in attitudes toward homosexual persons, (b) a smaller gender difference in attitudes toward homosexual behavior, and (c) no gender difference in attitudes toward the civil rights of lesbians and gay men.

Averaging outcomes across different operational definitions of a single independent or dependent variable is less controversial: If each operational definition is a valid indicator of the construct under investigation, the studies being reviewed should reveal the same pattern of results regardless of the operational definition used. It is extremely useful, however, to check this assumption of equivalence of operational definitions by treating operational definition as a moderator variable in the literature review. If no difference in outcome is found as a function of operational definition, the outcomes of the different operational definitions can be combined for further analysis; if differences are found, one must assess the implications of those differences for the validity of the research being reviewed. If, for example, there is evidence that one operational definition is more valid that another, then research using the more valid definition should be given more weight when drawing conclusions.

Choosing a Technique: Narrative Review or Meta-Analysis

The growing popularity of meta-analysis has led to disagreements between advocates of the narrative literature review, who see meta-analysis as being an overly mechanistic and uncreative approach to literature reviewing, and the advocates of meta-analysis, who see the narrative literature review as too subjective and impre-

TABLE 17.2
Comparison of Narrative Literature Review and Meta-Analysis

	Narrative	Meta-Analysis
Can analyze quantitative studies	Yes	Yes
Can analyze qualitative studies	Yes	No
Precision of conclusions	Low	High[a]
Vulnerability to Type I errors through publication bias	High	High
Vulnerability to Type II errors in studies reviewed	High	Low
Needs statistical information about outcome of studies	No	Yes
Number of studies required	Few	Many
Efficiency for large number of studies	Low	High

[a]Within the limits described in the text.

Note. From *Principles of Research in Behavioral Science* (p. 469), by Bernard E. Whitley, Jr., 1996, Mountain View, CA: Mayfield. Copyright 1996 by Mayfield. Reprinted with permission.

cise (Greenberg & Folger, 1988). However, a comparison of the techniques shows that they tend to be complementary, the strengths of one compensating for, rather than competing with, the shortcomings of the other. Table 17.2 summarizes some of the most important strengths and weaknesses of each technique.

Types of Studies That Can Be Reviewed. The narrative literature review can consider the results of both qualitative and quantitative studies in coming to its conclusions. Meta-analysis, as a quantitative technique, can only consider the results of studies that provide quantitative results. Consequently, meta-analysis must ignore research that makes use of case studies and other qualitative research methods. The exclusion of such studies from a literature review can severely limit the conclusions that one can draw, especially if qualitative and quantitative studies come to different conclusions about the effect of an independent variable. Such conflicts are not unlikely given the differences in philosophy, data collection, and data analysis evidenced in the two approaches to research (Guzzo et al., 1987).

Meta-analysis faces a similar problem of data exclusion when quantitative studies do not provide the information necessary to compute an effect size. This situation is especially likely to occur when the effect of the independent variable is not statistically significant; researchers often simply note that the difference between conditions was not significant and move on to report the (presumably more important) statistically significant effects. The number of studies that must be excluded from a meta-analysis can sometimes be substantial; for example, Murnen and Stockton (1997) could compute effect sizes for only 46 of 69 studies (67%). The exclusion of such no-difference studies can have substantial effects on the conclusions drawn from a meta-analysis. In another example, Marks and Miller (1987) described a meta-analysis that concluded that there was no support for one theoretical explanation of a particular phenomenon, but they noted that several studies supporting that explanation were excluded from the meta-analysis because effect sizes could not be computed. It is therefore important to use extreme caution when drawing conclusions from meta-analyses that had to exclude a substantial number of studies due to lack of data.

The dependence of meta-analysis on effect sizes can also limit the ability to evaluate interactions. As Mullen et al. (1991) pointed out, it can be difficult to find the data required to test theory-based interactions. If the interaction was tested as part of the original research, then the research report must provide the data necessary to compute the a priori contrast for the interaction predicted by theory. Such data are less likely to be available than are main effects data, especially as only a subset of studies testing the theory is likely to include any one moderator variable. If the interaction was not tested as part of the original research, one would have to find studies that were characterized by different conditions of the moderator variable and compare the mean effect sizes in the two groups of studies, just as one would test for the effects of a methodological moderator. However, it is often impossible to determine if a study was conducted in a way that represents one or another condition of the moderator variable. Lacking the data needed to evaluate interactions, all one can do is look at main effects; this problem would also apply to narrative literature reviews.

Shadish and Sweeney (1991) pointed out that meta-analysis gives almost no attention to the role of mediating variables (i.e., those that come between an independent and dependent variable in a causal chain) from either a theoretical or methodological perspective. As with moderating variables, the problem is often that there is not a sufficient number of studies that include all the important potential mediators to allow a good test of their effects. However, a few meta-analyses have attempted to test mediational hypotheses (e.g., Kite & Whitley, 1996).

Objectivity Versus Subjectivity. Advocates of meta-analysis generally view it as a more objective means of drawing conclusions about the effects of an independent variable compared to the narrative literature review (e.g., Green & Hall, 1984). This view is based on the use of statistical tests in meta-analysis to determine the overall effect of an independent variable and the effects of any potential moderator variables. The conclusions of narrative reviews are not based on a predefined criterion of whether an effect occurs, such as the probability values used in statistical analyses, but rather on the subjective judgment of the literature reviewer. This judgment can be affected by the theoretical and other biases of the reviewer; statistically based decisions are free of such biases.

Although it is true that the mathematical aspects of meta-analysis are relatively free of bias, the meta-analyst, like the narrative literature reviewer, must make a number of subjective decisions before getting to the data analysis stage of the review. Wanous et al. (1989) listed 11 decisions that must be made in a meta-analysis, 8 of which are subjective judgments that also must be made by narrative literature reviewers. Different decisions made at such choice points can easily lead to contradictions between the conclusions drawn from a meta-analysis and narrative literature review of a hypothesis, to contradictions between the conclusions drawn by two meta-analyses, and, of course, to contradictions between the conclusions of two narrative literature reviews (Cook & Leviton, 1980; Wanous et al., 1989). Also bear in mind that the interpretation of the results of research—what it means in theoretical and practical terms—is always a subjective judgment open to the influence of the personal and theoretical biases of whoever is making the interpretation. It would appear, then, that meta-analysis has only a narrow advantage in objectivity over the narrative literature review, limited to conclusions about the statistical significance of the effects of the independent and moderator variables.

Precision of Results.   The advocates of meta-analysis also believe that it provides more precise information about the magnitude of the effect of an independent variable—expressed as a mean effect size—than does the narrative literature review, which generally provides only a broad yes-or-no conclusion. In addition, the use of effect sizes in meta-analysis reduces the likelihood of making a Type II error; that is, deciding that the independent variable had no effect when there was insufficient statistical power to detect an effect. The vote-counting approach taken by most narrative literature reviews, on the other hand, must depend entirely on the statistical power of the studies being reviewed to avoid Type II errors.

There are, however, a number of factors that limit the precision with which meta-analysis can estimate the size of the effect of an independent variable. First, publication biases might inflate the Type I error rate present in the studies reviewed. Although this is also a problem for a vote-counting approach, it may be a greater problem for meta-analysis because it will lead to an inflated estimate of the mean effect size. To the extent that the effect size is used as an indicator of the importance of the effect, its importance will be overestimated, perhaps leading to faulty policy decisions (Bangert-Downs, 1986). Second, the mean effect size can be very sensitive to values that are unusually large or unusually small, especially when only a few studies are included in a meta-analysis. Light and Pillemer (1984) gave the example of a meta-analysis that revealed a mean d of .63 based on the results of seven studies. However, one study had an unusually large d of 4.01; with this value dropped, the mean d became .33, which might be a better estimate of the true effect size. Finally, as I have already noted, it might not be possible to compute effect sizes for all studies. Consequently, these studies cannot be included in the meta-analysis, and their exclusion reduces the precision with which the mean effect size found in the meta-analysis estimates the true effect of the independent variable.

The degree of precision gained by meta-analysis over the narrative literature review comes at the cost of requiring effect sizes from a relatively large number of studies. The precision with which a mean effect size estimates the population effect size depends on the number of observations. Although a meta-analysis cumulates results over a large number of research participants and thereby gains statistical power, the studies are also likely to vary widely in their operational definitions, participant populations, settings, and other methodological characteristics, which will lead to variance in effect sizes, thereby reducing the precision of the estimate of the true effect size (Cook & Leviton, 1980). To determine how much of this variance is attributable to these methodological factors, they must be treated as moderator variables in the analysis. The power of a meta-analysis to detect the effect of a moderator variable depends on both the number of studies and the average sample size of the studies (Hunter & Schmidt, 1990). For example, a power of .80 requires 33 studies in each condition of the moderator variable when the average sample size of the studies is 20 participants, 13 studies in each condition when the average sample size is 50 participants, and 7 studies in each condition when the average sample size is 100 participants. A narrative literature review can be conducted on fewer studies because it does not aspire to the higher degree of precision desired by meta-analysts, although this lesser precision should be reflected in more tentative conclusions.

Meta-analysis attains precision by focusing on numbers—effect sizes and statistical significance levels—which has led some observers to caution against mindless number-crunching in meta-analysis. Paying so much attention to effect sizes, their mean, and their statistical significance can cause analysts to lose sight of the meaning of the numbers (e.g., Wanous et al., 1989). It is easy, for example, to become so entranced by the seemingly precise bottom line provided by a mean effect size as to overlook the limitations that moderator variables might put on the accuracy of that statistic or the degree to which the mean might be influenced by publication and other biases (Cook & Leviton, 1980). Analysts must therefore always pay careful attention not only to the numbers produced by meta-analyses but also to the substantive meaning of those numbers, the limitations of the studies that produced them, and limitations of meta-analysis as a method. It is for this reason that Wanous et al. (1989) recommended doing a narrative literature review before conducting a meta-analysis. The narrative review will provide an overview of the important issues on the topic and sensitize the reviewer to the limitations of the studies under review and to factors that require attention as potential moderator variables.

"Best Evidence" Literature Reviewing. As discussed earlier, meta-analysis gains statistical precision at the cost of inclusiveness and the narrative review gains inclusiveness at the cost of statistical precision. The ideal literature review would therefore use the strengths of each technique to balance the weaknesses of the other by using both qualitative and quantitative elements in a review of the best evidence bearing on a hypothesis, providing what Slavin (1986) called *best evidence* research synthesis. As Light and Pillemer (1984) observed in the context of program evaluation:

> Both numerical and qualitative information play key roles in a good [literature review]. Quantitative procedures appeal to scientists and policy makers who experi-

ence feelings of futility when trying to develop a clear statement of "what is known." But using them does not reduce the value of careful program descriptions, case studies, narrative reports, or expert judgment, even though this information may be difficult to quantify. We cannot afford to ignore any information that may provide solid answers. For most purposes, a review using both numerical and narrative information will outperform its one-sided counterparts. For example, formal statistical analysis is often needed to identify small effects across studies that are not apparent through casual inspection. . . . But qualitative analyses of program characteristics are necessary to explain the effect and to decide whether it matters for policy. (pp. 9–10)

Best evidence synthesis would first use the narrative approach to provide an overview of the theoretical, applied, and empirical issues that have guided research in the field. This overview would identify potential theoretical and methodological moderator variables that would have to be taken into consideration in drawing conclusions about the effect of the independent variable and would identify appropriate criteria for deciding which studies should be included in the review. For example, studies that used operational definitions that were subsequently shown to be invalid would be excluded. Once studies have been located, they can be put into three categories: those for which an effect size can be computed for a meta-analysis, those that used quantitative procedures but for which an effect size cannot be computed, and those using qualitative procedures. Design flaw analysis can then be used to identify patterns of flaws (if any) across studies. This information can be used to categorize studies to see if outcomes vary as a function of design flaws and to determine the limits of the conclusions that can be drawn from the studies. The reviewer would then synthesize the results for each category of studies, using quantitative or qualitative methods as appropriate. Quantitative studies that report no effect for the independent variable, and for which no effect size can be computed, can be subjected to an analysis of their statistical power to see if that might be a problem (e.g., Kite & Whitley, 1996). The reviewer would next compare the results of the syntheses across categories of studies to see if they are consistent. If they are not, the reviewer would need to see if there were any apparent reason for the inconsistencies. Finally, the reviewer would interpret the results of the literature review in terms of the theoretical, applied, and empirical implications of its results.

DATA INTERPRETATION

Because the literature review is a form of research, the final stage of the literature review is the same as that of all research: drawing conclusions from the data and laying out the implications of those conclusions for theory, research, and application. Because Allgeier discussed that process in chapter 16, this volume, I only discuss a few limitations on the interpretation of the results of literature reviews.

The Effects of Judgment Calls

First, literature reviewing is a process that involves a fairly large number of judgment calls, decisions that one person may make in one way and another person may make in another (e.g., Wanous et al., 1989). For example, if two people were to review the research on the same hypothesis, they might make different decisions about which studies to include in their reviews. One person might choose to include only published studies, whereas the other might also include any unpublished research that could be found. One consequence of such differences in judgments in literature reviewing is the possibility of different results and different conclusions being drawn about the hypothesis being tested. Wanous et al. (1989), for example, described four pairs of literature reviews that came to opposite conclusions and showed how different decisions at various judgment points could have led to those conflicting conclusions.

Because differences in judgment calls can produce such large differences in conclusions, it is extremely important for literature reviewers to clearly specify the decisions that they make at each point in the review process (Halvorsen, 1994). Literature reviewers should report the operational definitions of variables included in the review. For example, in a review of the effects of sex therapy, reviewers should specify exactly what kinds of treatments were considered to be therapies for the purpose of the review and the kinds of therapies put into each subcategory used, such as individual or couple therapies. Similarly, one should specify the operational definitions of the dependent variables, such as sexual functioning or sexual self-efficacy.

Reviewers should also report the criteria used for including studies in the review or excluding them from consideration. Reviewers should also tell readers the methods they used to locate studies, such as computer searches of indexes (in which case the key words used should be reported), bibliographic searching, and source-by-source searching (specifying the sources searched). Finally, the reviewer should report the methods used to analyze the data, including the specific statistical techniques used for a meta-analysis. This information should be detailed enough that another person could exactly replicate the literature review. Such information allows readers to judge the adequacy of the review procedures and the validity of the conclusions that the reviewer draws.

The Correlational Nature of Moderator Variable Analyses

A second point to bear in mind when interpreting the results of a literature review is that any relationships found between moderator variables and study outcomes are correlational, not causal. That is, a literature review can, at best, only demonstrate that there is a relationship between a moderator variable and study outcomes, not that the moderator variable caused the difference in outcomes. For example, if the results of a literature review tended to support a hypothesis when it was tested in laboratory settings, but not when tested in natural settings, the only way to determine if type of setting caused the difference in outcomes would be to conduct an experiment with type of setting as an independent variable. In addition, conditions of a moderator variable might be confounded with other characteristics of the studies. For example, the research participants in the laboratory settings might have been college students and those in natural settings, older adults. The only way to determine which variable actually moderated the effect sizes would be through an appropriately designed experiment.

Publication Biases

Finally, it is important to temper the conclusions draw from literature reviews with consideration of the possible effects of publication biases. Publication bias in favor of statistically significant outcomes may lead the literature reviewer to overestimate the impact of an independent variable. Conversely, insufficient statistical power in the studies reviewed might lead to an underestimation of the independent variable impact. Finally, one must be aware of any design flaws that are common to the studies reviewed and to interpret the results of the literature review with these flaws in mind. A set of studies might point to a particular conclusion, but a common flaw would cast doubt on that conclusion.

UNDERSTANDING META-ANALYSIS

Meta-analysis has been increasingly used as a literature-reviewing tool over the past 30 years, especially in applied areas of the behavioral sciences, which account for about 78% of meta-analyses (Cooper & Lemke, 1991). Because of the increasing importance of meta-analysis as a means of reviewing research literature, it is important to have clear understanding of the technique's strengths and weaknesses to be able to correctly interpret the results of published meta-analyses. Therefore, I offer a brief "guided tour" of a meta-analysis conducted by Murnen and Stockton (1997).

Defining the Research Question

Murnen and Stockton (1997) noted that two competing viewpoints exist concerning why men are more likely to report greater sexual arousal in responses to sexual stimuli, such as visual depictions of sexual activity, than are women. The sociobiological perspective holds that the gender difference is innate: "While females have a great deal of parental investment in individual offspring because they produce few egg cells and are responsible for pregnancy and lactation, males have little investment in offspring since they do not bear children and they produce many sperm cells" (p. 137). In the simplest terms, because men are less invested in the care of children, their best reproductive strategy is to impregnate as many women as they can. Quick sexual arousal in response to a variety of stimuli would facilitate this reproductive strategy. In contrast, because of their parental investment, women need to attract men who can protect and provide for them and their children. Becoming sexually aroused quickly would be maladaptive for women because it would impair a woman's "ability to judge whether a potential mate had resources that could ensure the survival of her offspring" (p. 138).

In contrast to the sociobiological perspective, the social influence perspective holds that gender differences in sexual arousal derive from socialization experiences that are influenced by societal gender-role expectations and the ways in which sexuality is viewed in American society. From this perspective, men are more easily sexually aroused because as boys they were taught that that arousal is natural, whereas girls are taught that good girls have no interest in sex. In addition, American sexual culture is male-oriented, reinforcing the idea that men should be more interested in sex. For example, sexually explicit materials tend to emphasize male dominance and so may be less appealing to women (Murnen & Stockton, 1997).

Based on their analysis of these theories, Murnen and Stockton derived a set of hypotheses concerning gender differences in sexual arousal in response to sexual stimuli. They proposed that sociobiological theory would predict that gender differences in sexual arousal would be large and would be especially large in response to visual stimuli because visual clues make it easiest for men to identify potential sexual partners. Murnen and Stockton proposed that social influence theories would also predict that men would be more easily aroused than women (because most sexual stimuli are produced with a male audience in mind), but that because the difference arises from social influences rather than biology, the size of the difference would vary as a function of four factors:

1. Because pornography objectifies women to a greater extent than does erotica, there should be a larger gender difference in response to pornography.
2. Because gender similarity is emphasized more now than it has been in the past, the gender difference should be smaller in more recent studies.
3. Because younger research participants might be more influenced by social roles, the size of the gender difference would decrease with age of participants.
4. Because social role adherence is weaker under conditions of anonymity, participants would be more likely to behave according to gender-based social scripts under less anonymous testing conditions, resulting in larger gender differences.

Data Collection

Murnen and Stockton (1997) used three strategies to locate studies. First, they conducted computer searches of four indexes. Second, they looked through the tables of contents of journals that published research on sexuality. Finally, they checked the reference lists and bibliographies of the studies that they had located by other means. If a relevant research report did not include sufficient information to calculate an effect size for male–female differences in sexual arousal, they wrote the report's author requesting the information.

Data Evaluation

Because they were interested in gender differences, Murnen and Stockton (1997) excluded from their review any studies that used only male or only female participants. Because they were interested in normal sexual response, they also excluded studies that used criminals or people in treatment for sexual problems. They also limited their review to studies that used self-report measures of arousal because physiological measures of arousal are not comparable for men and women. "Further, only studies portraying both male and female actors were included to yield a more homogeneous sample. Finally, there were too few studies testing gay and lesbian participants to include sexual orientation as a variable, so only studies of assumed heterosexual participants were selected" (p. 142). The final sample for their meta-analysis was composed of 46 studies providing 62 effect sizes (some studies included more than one sample).

Data Analysis

Operationally Defining Study Outcome. Because meta-analysis is a set of techniques rather than a single method of combining results across studies (see Bangert-Downs, 1986, for a comparison of methods), Murnen and Stockton (1997) had to select a technique. They chose to define effect size in terms of d (they could, of course, have chosen r) and computed the mean effect size for the entire set of studies and within the conditions of the moderating variables. For each study, they computed d such that a positive value indicated that men reported more sexual arousal. In addition, they weighted the d from each study by the study's sample size, thereby giving more importance to larger samples in computing the mean value for d. This is a standard procedure in meta-analysis because a study using a large sample provides a more accurate estimation of the true effect size than does one using a small sample.

Classifying Studies by Moderator Variables. Murnen and Stockton (1997) classified the studies in their review by five moderator variables (k indicates the number of studies in a category):

> First, a visual stimulus was defined as a slide or film depiction ($k = 43$); while a nonvisual stimulus was a written vignette ($k = 19$). The erotic nature of a stimulus was as either [sic] erotica ($k = 46$) or pornography ($k = 19$). . . . [We defined a] stimulus as pornography . . . if it was described as such by the authors of the study. If a

stimulus was described merely as sexually explicit, it was assumed to be erotica. . . . The experimental setting was noted as either private (the person filled out the arousal scale alone or with only the experimenter, $k = 25$), small group (5 to 10 people, $k = 10$), or large group (more than 10 people present, $k = 8$). The age of participants was noted as either the typical undergraduate participant ($k = 54$), or an "older" group ($k = 8$). (p. 143)

Murnen and Stockton also recorded the year in which each study was published.

Results. Murnen and Stockton (1997) found a mean d for all 62 effect sizes of .31, indicating that men reported higher levels of sexual arousal than did women. However, an effect size of this magnitude is generally considered to be small to moderate in size (Cohen, 1992) rather than large as predicted by sociobiological theory. Furthermore, mean effect sizes did not vary significantly as a function of type of stimulus (visual or written), contrary to the prediction made by sociobiological theory. Contrary to the prediction made by social influence theory, year of publication of the studies was not related to effect size. However, the mean effect size was larger for pornography than for erotica and larger for college-age participants than for older participants; these results are consistent with the predictions made by social influence theory. Effect sizes also varied as a function of experimental setting, but not as predicted by social influence theory: The smallest difference was when participants were tested in large groups rather than privately. Note an important point illustrated by this set of results: An effect for a moderator variable in meta-analysis is equivalent to an interaction between the moderator variable and the independent variable being examined in the meta-analysis. That is, the relationship between the independent variable (gender of research participant in this example) and the dependent variable (self-reported sexual arousal) changes depending on the condition of the moderator variable (erotic or pornographic stimulus, age of participant, and testing condition). The meta-analysis that used testing condition as a moderator variable was therefore equivalent to a 2 (gender of participant) × 3 (testing condition) factorial design.

Interpretation

Based on these results, Murnen and Stockton (1997) concluded that the preponderance of the evidence supported social influence theory over sociobiological theory:

> In general, the small to moderate size of the gender difference in sexual arousal by sexual stimuli does not lend support to predictions of sociobiologists in this realm of sexual behavior. Moreover, the fact that whether or not the stimulus was a visual one did not affect variation in the effect size does not support sociobiological predictions. . . . On the other hand, social influence theories led to predictions that the type of stimulus would affect responses, as well as would the research setting, the year of the study, and the age of participants. All but one of these predictions was [sic] supported by the data. (p. 148)

Murnen and Stockton also pointed to several limitations of the research they reviewed, such as a confound between participant age and testing condition, with older participants being more likely to be tested in large groups. Because both of these variables were associated with smaller effect sizes, Murnen and Stockton could not conclude with confidence which variable was truly associated with magnitude of effect size.

Murnen and Stockton's (1997) findings provide an important lesson for the interpretation of meta-analyses and literature reviews in general. Their results illustrate the necessity of conducting thorough theoretical and methodological analyses of the hypotheses under consideration and the studies being reviewed to identify moderator variables. Notice that the conclusions that one would draw from the meta-analysis change as one moves from an analysis without any moderators to analyses that include moderators. A less thorough theoretical analysis might have overlooked a moderator variable and so led to incorrect conclusions.

EVALUATING LITERATURE REVIEWS

The integrative iterature review is an important tool for advancing scientific knowledge by summarizing, organizing, and evaluating the state of knowledge on a topic. However, care must be taken in conducting and using literature reviews because problems can arise at each step of the process. Table 17.3 lists some questions that can be used as guides to conducting and evaluating literature reviews, both meta-analyses and narrative reviews.

SUGGESTED READINGS

Light and Pillimer (1984) wrote one of the first books that treats literature reviewing as a form of research, and it provides an excellent overview of the review process. Because the statistical procedures for conducting a meta-analysis are fairly complex, I did not discuss them here. For those who are interested in con-

TABLE 17.3
Evaluating Literature Reviews

Question Formulation

---

1. What is the purpose of the literature review?
2. Was the hypothesis clearly stated so that the results of studies could be unambiguously classified as supporting or not supporting it?
3. Were all relevant theories thoroughly analyzed to identify variables that moderate study outcome and to identify the conditions required for an adequate test of the hypothesis?
4. Was all relevant research thoroughly analyzed to identify methodological variables (such as operational definitions, research settings, research strategies, participant populations) that might moderate study outcome?

(Continued)

TABLE 17.3
(Continued)

Data Collection

1. Was the scope of the search for studies clearly stated? That is, were there clear rules regarding the characteristics of studies that would be considered for inclusion in the review?
2. Were all relevant sources of studies checked? These include indexes, previous literature reviews of the hypothesis, reference lists and bibliographies from the studies already located, and a manual search of relevant journals.
3. Were the proper search terms used with indexes? Were all variants on the terms (such as both singular and plural) and synonyms checked?

Data Evaluation

1. Were the criteria used to include and exclude studies clearly stated? Were these criteria appropriate? What biases might these criteria bring to the conclusions drawn from the review?
2. How many studies were excluded from the review relative to the total number located? Is the remaining sample large enough to allow valid conclusions to be drawn?

Data Analysis

1. What literature review technique was used, narrative, meta-analysis, or best evidence? Was it appropriate to the purpose of the review and the nature of the research being reviewed, such as the number of quantitative and qualitative studies that have been conducted?
2. What was the mean (meta-analysis) or modal (narrative review) outcome of the studies?
3. How much variance was there in the study outcomes? Were there any outliers that increased the variance or skewed the mean?
4. Were moderator variables used to try to explain the variance in study outcomes?
5. Were clear rules established for classifying studies according the moderator variables? Were these rules applied reliably?
6. Were there enough studies within each category of the moderator variables to permit reliable conclusions to be drawn?
7. Were the studies analyzed to determine if there were any common design flaws that might call into question the validity of their overall results?
8. Was a list of studies that were used in the review included in the report? Did the list include how each study was classified on each moderator variable? In a meta-analysis, was the effect size for each study included?

Interpretation

1. Are the interpretations made appropriate given the scope of the review, the types of studies included in the review (such as restriction to one participant population), and the limitations of the review technique. For example, do the conclusions drawn from a narrative review reflect an awareness of the possibility of Type II errors? Does a meta-analysis acknowledge the possibility of inflated mean effect sizes due to publication biases?
2. Are clear implications drawn for theory, research, and application?
3. Are all possible interpretations of the findings considered? For example, does a review of correlational research consider both directions of causality and the possibility of third variable influences? Are all theoretical perspectives considered?
4. Is the impact of any common design flaws given full consideration?
5. Were possible confounds among moderator variables, such as having only college students participate in laboratory studies and non-college participants in field studies, taken into consideration in interpreting the impact of moderator variables?

Note. From *Principles of Research in Behavioral Science* (p. 469), by Bernard E. Whitley, Jr., 1996, Mountain View, CA: Mayfield. Copyright 1996 by Mayfield. Reprinted with permission.

ducting a meta-analysis, Hedges and Becker (1986) provided a readable overview of the statistical procedures, and Cooper and Hedges (1994) provided a very extensive review of the factors to consider in conducting meta-analyses. Many of the points made apply equally well to narrative literature reviews. R. Rosenthal (1991) and Hunter and Schmidt (1990) present more detailed how-to descriptions, with Rosenthal focusing on the use of d as an effect size indicator and Hunter and Schmidt focusing on r. Hedges and Olkin (1985) presented the statistical theory underlying meta-analysis. In addition, Johnson (1993) and Mullen (1989) wrote computer programs to analyze data for meta-analyses. Finally, Durlak (1995) wrote an extensive and extremely user-friendly guide to reading and understanding meta-analysis.

REFERENCES

Bangert-Downs, R. L. (1986). Review of developments in meta-analytic method. *Psychological Bulletin, 99*, 388–399.

Cohen, J. (1992). A power primer. *Psychological Bulletin, 112*, 155–159.

Cook, T. D., & Campbell, D. T. (1979). *Quasi-experimentation*. Chicago: Rand-McNally.

Cook, T. D., & Leviton, L. C. (1980). Reviewing the literature: A comparison of traditional methods with meta-analysis. *Journal of Personality, 48*, 449–472.

Cooper, H. M., & Hedges, L. V. (Eds.). (1994). *The handbook of research synthesis*. New York: Russell Sage Foundation.

Cooper, H. M., & Lemke, K. M. (1991). On the role of meta-analysis in personality and social psychology. *Personality and Social Psychology Bulletin, 17*, 245–251.

Durlak, J. A. (1995). Understanding meta-analysis. In L. G. Grimm & P. R. Yarnold (Eds.), *Reading and understanding multivariate statistics* (pp. 319–352). Washington, DC: American Psychological Association.

Durlak, J. A., & Lipsey, M. W. (1991). A practitioner's guide to meta-analysis. *American Journal of Community Psychology, 19*, 291–332.

Fisher, W. A., Byrne, D., White, L. A., & Kelley, K. (1988). Erotophobia–erotophilia as a dimension of personality. *The Journal of Sex Research, 25*, 123–151.

Glass, G. V. (1978). In defense of generalization. *Brain and Behavioral Sciences, 3*, 394–395.

Green, B. F., & Hall, J. A. (1984). Quantitative methods for literature reviews. *Annual Review of Psychology, 35*, 37–53.

Greenberg, J., & Folger, R. (1988). *Controversial issues in social research methods*. New York: Springer.

Greenwald, A. G. (1975). Consequences of prejudice against the null hypothesis. *Psychological Bulletin, 82*, 1–20.

Greenwald, A. G., Pratkanis, A. R., Leippe, M. R., & Baumgardner, M. H. (1986). Under what conditions does theory obstruct research progress? *Psychological Review, 93*, 216–229.

Guzzo, R. A., Jackson, S. E., & Katzell, R. A. (1987). Meta-analysis analysis. *Research in Organizational Behavior, 9*, 407–442.

Halvorsen, K. T. (1994). The reporting format. In H. Cooper & L. V. Hedges (Eds.), *The handbook of research synthesis* (pp. 425–437). New York: Russell Sage Foundation.

Hedges, L. V., & Becker, B. J. (1986). Statistical methods in the meta-analysis of research on gender differences. In J. S. Hyde & M. C. Linn (Eds.), *The psychology of gender: Advances through meta-analysis* (pp. 14–50). Baltimore: Johns Hopkins University Press.

Hedges, L. V., & Olkin, I. (1985). *Statistical methods for meta-analysis*. Orlando, FL: Academic Press.

Hunter, J. E., & Schmidt, F. L. (1990). *Methods of meta-analysis*. Newbury Park, CA: Sage.

Jackson, G. B. (1980). Methods for integrative reviews. *Review of Educational Research, 50*, 438–460.

Johnson, B. T. (1993), *DSTAT version 1.10: Software for the meta-analytic review of research literatures*. Hillsdale, NJ: Lawrence Erlbaum Associates.

Joswick, K. E. (1994). Getting the most from PsycLIT: Recommendations for searching. *Teaching of Psychology, 21*, 49–53.

Kite, M. E., & Whitley, B. E., Jr. (1996). Sex differences in attitudes toward homosexual persons, behavior, and civil rights: A meta-analysis. *Personality and Social Psychology Bulletin, 22*, 336–353.

Light, R. J., & Pillemer, D. B. (1984). *Summing up: The science of reviewing research*. Cambridge, MA: Harvard University Press.

Marks, G., & Miller, N. (1987). Ten years of research on the false consensus effect: An empirical and theoretical review. *Psychological Bulletin, 102*, 72–90.

Masters, J. C. (1984). Psychology, research, and social policy. *American Psychologist, 39*, 851–862.

Mullen, B. (1989). *Advanced BASIC meta-analysis version 1.10*. Hillsdale, NJ: Lawrence Erlbaum Associates.

Mullen, B., Salas, E., & Miller, N. (1991). Using meta-analysis to test theoretical hypotheses in social psychology. *Personality and Social Psychology Bulletin, 17*, 258–264.

Murnen, S. K., & Stockton, M. (1997). Gender and self-reported sexual arousal in response to sexual stimuli: A meta-analytic review. *Sex Roles, 37*, 135–153.

Oliver, M. B., & Hyde, J. S. (1993). Gender differences in sexuality: A meta-analysis. *Psychological Bulletin, 114*, 29–51.

Rind, B., & Tromovitch, P. (1997). A meta-analytic review of findings from national samples on psychological correlates of childhood sexual abuse. *The Journal of Sex Research, 34*, 237–255.

Rosenthal, M. C. (1994). The fugitive literature. In H. Cooper & L. V. Hedges (Eds.), *The handbook of research synthesis* (pp. 85–94). New York: Russell Sage Foundation.

Rosenthal, R. (1990). An evaluation of procedures and results. In K. W. Wachter & M. L. Straf (Eds.), *The future of meta-analysis* (pp. 123–133). New York: Russell Sage Foundation.

Rosenthal, R. (1991). *Meta-analytic procedures for social research* (rev. ed.). Newbury Park, CA: Sage.

Rossi, J. S. (1990). Statistical power of psychological research: What have we gained in 20 years? *Journal of Consulting and Clinical Psychology, 58*, 646–656.

Salipante, P., Notz, W., & Bigelow, J. (1982). A matrix approach to literature reviews. *Research in Organizational Behavior, 4*, 321–348.

Shadish, W. R., Jr., & Sweeney, R. B. (1991). Mediators and moderators in meta-analysis: There's a reason we don't let dodo birds tell us which psychotherapies should have prizes. *Journal of Consulting and Clinical Psychology, 59*, 883–893.

Sheeran, P., Abraham, C., & Orbell, S. (1999). Psychosocial correlates of heterosexual condom use: A meta-analysis. *Psychological Bulletin, 125*, 90–132.

Slavin, R. E. (1986). Best-evidence synthesis: An alternative to meta-analytic and traditional reviews. *Educational Researcher, 15*(9), 5–11.

Smith, M. L., & Glass, G. V. (1977). Meta-analysis of psychotherapy outcome research studies. *American Psychologist, 32*, 752–760.

Wanous, J. P., Sullivan, S. E., & Malinak, J. (1989). The role of judgment calls in meta-analysis. *Journal of Applied Psychology, 74*, 259–264.

White, K. R. (1982). The relation between socioeconomic status and academic achievement. *Psychological Bulletin, 91*, 461–481.

Whitley, B. E., Jr. (1990). College student contraceptive use: A multivariate analysis. *Journal of Sex Research, 27*, 305–313.-

Whitley, B. E., Jr., & Kite, M. E. (1995). Sex differences in attitudes toward homosexuality: A comment on Oliver and Hyde (1993). *Psychological Bulletin, 117*, 146–154.

Whitley, B. E., Jr., & Schofield, J. W. (1986). A meta-analysis of research on adolescent contraceptive use. *Population and Environment, 6*, 173–203.

V

SPECIAL ISSUES

18

Discovering the Value of Cross-Cultural Research on Human Sexuality

Suzanne G. Frayser
Colorado College

> *Discovery consists of seeing what everybody has seen and thinking what no-
> body has thought.*
>
> —Albert Szent-Byörgyi

Conducting research on sexuality is difficult at best. Conducting cross-cultural research on sexuality exacerbates conceptual and methodological issues that occur
within one cultural context. The sheer number and complexity of issues that
cross-cultural research raises expand to such an extent that the findings are
viewed with skepticism, if not outright rejection. Why, then, should we even embark on such an enterprise? What value for studying human sexuality does this research method offer? How do we go about doing it?

THE VALUE OF CROSS-CULTURAL RESEARCH

As Bolin and Whelehan (1999) stated, "We are a human community" (p. xiv). No
longer separated into socially segregated parts of the globe, humans are increasingly aware of their links with each other and the need to communicate across culturally diverse boundaries. Such awareness requires bridges to understanding,
connections that cross-cultural research can articulate; it translates from one
worldview or set of assumptions to another.

Cross-cultural research applies not only to research conducted in other countries or indigenous or tribal populations, but also to groups or subgroups that transcend geographical boundaries as distinct cultural units, such as genders, ethnic

425

populations, and age groups. Different cultures exist within the same geographical boundaries and within complex societies. Because such cultures are not spatially clustered or geographically identified, they may be more difficult to recognize. Therefore, cross-cultural research involves a shift in perspective to see the common attributes that define a group as cultural. This perspective requires us to closely examine what culture is and what it means to its participants and those who study it. This process attunes us to the subtleties of cultural diversity and expands our recognition of the cultural variables available for study. It allows us to discover the cultural dimension.

In an attempt to apply concepts and theories generated in one culture to the perceptions, beliefs, or behavior of people in another culture, researchers may find that the concepts do not comfortably overlap or dovetail. For example, the concept *homosexuality* may include different behaviors and psychological dimensions in different cultures. Although a behavior may be labeled homosexual, the sexual orientation of the person who engaged in it may not be; consider, for example, homosexual acts engaged in by people with a heterosexual orientation who are in prison. Consequently, researchers must rethink the concept and search for an operational definition that includes its attributes. This leads researchers to recognize how value-laden the concepts of one culture are, even when embedded in the scholarly scientific context of a discipline. It means that, to adequately define a concept, researchers must seek the range of variation of behaviors and the ideas that it includes. It also means that researchers must be aware of the personal and disciplinary biases that they bring to the definitional process.

The recognition of personal and disciplinary biases teaches the researcher how limited the theories and methods of one discipline are in trying to explain the range of variation in a domain as encompassing as human sexuality. This awareness can foster an interdisciplinary approach, enhancing cooperation among researchers who realize the power of other disciplines to explain dimensions of sexuality not emphasized by their own. Also, it can add clarity to the boundaries of a discipline and its methods, and pinpoint the areas where interdisciplinary cooperation is fruitful.

In addition, cross-cultural research has value because it forces us to remove our ethnocentric blinders. Although it can be uncomfortable for us to face a cultural home that is not our own, our participation in cross-cultural research requires that we confront our own biases and open ourselves up to other ways of experiencing and interpreting the world. This does not mean that we have to give up the way that we look at the world; rather, it means that we expand it. As Tafoya (1990) said, "A system of knowledge is also a system of ignorance." In other words, cultures differ in how they assign meaning; such differences entail emphasis on some types of knowledge and neglect of others. We never have complete knowledge and always have more to learn from groups in another culture.

Cross-cultural research requires that we view other cultures with a different set of eyes, allowing us to view behavior from the perspective of the participants.

Nevertheless, as we expand our horizons, Tafoya (1990) advised, "We should never give up our own eyes." This dance between the insider's experience and the outsider's interpretation poses some of the most difficult dilemmas of conducting cross-cultural research. As Herdt and Stoller (1990) noted, the classic problem of anthropologic epistemology is "knowing what to say about a culture and how to say it across cultural boundaries" (p. 87). Generalizing from a series of cultural studies makes this issue even more pressing. Whose eyes do we use—those of the researcher or those of the participant? Do we have to make a choice? These questions point to the promise and the shortcomings of the cross-cultural method in research on human sexuality.

HUMAN SEXUALITY AND THE CONCEPT OF CULTURE

The Dimensions of Human Sexuality

Before we can conduct cross-cultural research on human sexuality, we must have a clear idea of what the dimensions of human sexuality are and how they relate to culture. The term *human sexuality* indicates a search for more than *sex*, a concept limited to essential qualities of anatomy, physiology, and physical interaction. Because language, as a system of symbols, transmits much of the culture's meaning, the shift in terms is significant; it recognizes the broad range of life that sexuality encompasses. One of the major sexological organizations in the United States officially reinforced the significance of the concept *sexuality* when it changed its name from The Society for the Scientific Study of *Sex* to The Society for the Scientific Study of *Sexuality*.

Human sexuality consists of four major dimensions: biological, social, cultural, and psychological. Each of these dimensions incorporates significant components that elucidate its contribution to sexuality as a whole and that corresponds to a major disciplinary area of interest. Biologists focus on the anatomy and physiology of sexuality (evolution, cross-species comparisons); sociologists, on the social setting (institutions, regulations) and interpersonal dynamics (roles, behaviors) of sexuality; anthropologists, on the cultural context (shared beliefs, symbolic meaning) and expressions of sexuality; and psychologists, on the personal interpretation (processing) of sexuality (identity, perception, emotion, cognition, orientation). Disciplinary separation of the dimensions of sexuality highlights the complexity of sexuality and the biases inherent in only one perspective. Viewed one way, specialization shows how a system of knowledge can also be a system of ignorance; no one discipline can incorporate all dimensions in detail. Viewed another way, expertise in one specialty shows how an interdisciplinary approach to sexuality can enhance the perspective of each participating discipline; although each discipline has its boundaries, the researcher can remain open to the applicability of theoretical and methodological approaches from other fields. Taking culture into account deepens the research of each discipline; drawing on the concepts, methods, and findings of other disciplines enriches a cross-cultural approach to sexuality.

The Cultural Dimension of Human Sexuality

Identifying and researching the cultural dimension of sexuality is no small task. Anthropologists have different definitions of culture, and nonanthropologists often use the term *cultural* interchangeably with *social*, making little distinction between these attributes of human experience. How do we recognize and study what is cultural about human sexuality? What do we learn from it?

The key to finding the cultural dimension, implied but not specified in so many discussions, is to briefly examine what is human about human sexuality. Many biological and social aspects of sexuality are shared with other animals. For example, courtship characterizes all sexually reproducing animals; parenting, all mammals; and reliance on social life as an adaptive strategy, most primates. These are the broadest aspects of human sexuality and lend themselves to biological research (particularly cross-species comparisons, field studies, and experimental research) along with analysis in terms of adaptation, evolution, and sociobiology. However, the cultural and psychological dimensions of human sexuality do not clearly overlap as much with other animals. The development of culture channeled human sexuality into a distinctive direction, marked by a variety of social arrangements and psychological implications. Culture added shared meaning as a significant variable that interacted with biological and social dimensions of sexuality. As increased brain size became a major force in human evolution, learning (passed on from one generation to the next via symbols) became a dominant adaptive feature of humans. Cultural rather than physical adaptation became a distinctive human attribute, and a variety of beliefs and social arrangements based on learned rather than innate experience became the mark of human cultures and societies. Therefore, the diversity of sexual beliefs and behavior that we see within and across societies is an expression of the variety inherent in human adaptation via culture.

At its core, culture centers on shared, patterned meanings that people use to organize their behavior and interpret their experiences. Beliefs, values, and ideas, whether explicit or implicit, permeate behavior, interactions, and psychological responses and attitudes. Many of these beliefs, values, and ideas become codified in symbols, which synthesize many layers of meaning, particularly rational and emotional aspects of ideas. They derive their power from the ways in which they relate to both the social context and the individual. They receive additional strength because one generation teaches them to the next; they become part of a tradition that seems natural. Social interaction reinforces beliefs, values, and ideas shared by the wider social group as the individual learns them. Because the interplay between the cultural and social dimensions is so constant, it is often difficult to recognize the difference.

Language as Shared Meaning. Language is one of the clearest examples of how meaning can be shared and patterned. It is one of the major forms and transmitters of culture. People share a language and agree on its meaning. Words are symbols because they capture different levels of meaning when they are spoken or written. Individuals can use them according to agreed-on meanings in a social context (e.g., formal, informal, slang), and the social group can reinforce the value of the words by allowing people who use them to belong to their group, such as the use of slang among teens and jargon among academicians. People also can invest words with emotion and personal significance, thus linking to them in a more specific way. For example, *love* has these deeper dimensions of meaning for individuals. As such, it operates as a powerful symbol because the most powerful symbols draw on a variety of cognitive and emotional meanings that connect the individual to them and to the social context in which they occur. The difference between *making love* and *fucking* illustrates how words can invest the same behavior with very different meanings. Examining slang expressions for sexual anatomy or sexual activities can elucidate much about the meaning of sexuality. For example, in the United States, slang terms or euphemisms are the major means for talking about sexuality in everyday life. Reliance on slang terms and euphemisms highlights the culture's lack of commonly shared words for comfortably discussing sexuality and points to the ambivalence and negativity that cultural participants feel about it. Slang terms that are steeped with implications of danger, violence, and degradation (e.g., *prick, gash, penetration, the nasty, banging*) indicate and reinforce that negativity.

Behavior in relation to words breathes life into the cultural system of language. For example, men's culture reinforces the use of sexual slang, whereas women's generally avoids it. Swearing or cursing not only acknowledges an interest in sexuality but also indicates masculinity, thus confirming membership in the gender category of men. Women's sexual euphemisms distance them from directly acknowledging their interest in sexuality and confirm their membership in the traditional gender category of women.

Gender as a Cultural Concept. Beliefs about gender are structured and meaningful, operating like language as a patterned set of symbols, integral to any sexual system. The belief that there are two genders, man and woman, is a common cultural concept in the United States. Gender is assigned to babies when they are born based on the appearance of their genitals; thus, the physical body becomes a symbolic carrier of the belief in gender categories. People then respond to the child at least partly in terms of his or her gender, thus reinforcing the belief in what a boy or girl is. The child learns the role for a man or woman partly by observing others labeled *man* or *woman* and partly by gender lessons explicitly taught by family, peers, and others. In addition, the media transmit messages in words, images, and actions about men and women often in symbolic form. Ideas about masculinity and femininity are cultural messages that guide the perfor-mance of the gender role. These cultural messages, juxtaposed with social roles that the individual enacts, provide a shared framework to which the individual re-acts emotionally and cognitively. The private sense of the self as a particular gen-der is gender identity.

Thus, there are four aspects of gender that derive from four dimensions of be-ing human (and thus from human sexuality because gender categories are parts of a sexual system that occurs in every human culture):

1. *Biological:* gender assigned on the basis of anatomical and physiological characteristics.
2. *Social:* gender role, how a person behaves to demonstrate that he or she is a man or a woman.
3. *Cultural:* beliefs about gender, masculinity and femininity.
4. *Psychological:* gender identity, the private experience of gender.

Because these dimensions are learned together, their concordance with each other may seem natural. A person looks like a boy (biological), believes he should be masculine (cultural), acts like a boy (social), and feels like he is a boy (psycholog-ical). This sets the stage for a similar process in adolescence and adulthood. U.S. culture emphasizes that there are only two genders and that there should be coher-ence among the biological, social, cultural, and psychological dimensions. Devia-tion from any of these beliefs is labeled *abnormal*. Thus, a person who looks like a man, has a penis, and behaves in a masculine manner, but privately feels that he is a woman, is regarded as deviant. Consequently, many of these transsexuals have undergone hormone treatment and surgery to bring their bodies into conformity with their gender identity. Estrogens stimulate the development of fatty deposits in the breasts and buttocks, producing feminine contours. Surgery consists of re-moving the testes and penis and then using the skin of the penis to construct a va-gina. After these body-altering procedures, gender can be reassigned from man to woman; the reassignment gives the person permission to behave as a woman, con-forming to cultural messages of femininity and social rules of gender role. Reas-signment reinforces the culture's insistence on the concordance of biological, so-cial, cultural, and psychological aspects of gender.

Thus, labels such as *transsexual* are culture-bound and not usefully applied in cross-cultural contexts. Even within U.S. culture, most people do not understand the meaning of the term *transsexual* because they want to categorize sexuality solely in terms of male or female; variations from this dichotomy do not make cultural sense and confuse them. More productive is an examination of the quali-ties to which each term relates: breaking it down into its components and then reframing questions in a less biased way. Rather than assuming that biological, social, cultural, and psychological aspects of gender must be concordant, the cross-cultural researcher can ask how the culture deals with each dimension of gender. What are the gender categories? Are there only two? How are the genders supposed to behave? How do people think of themselves in terms of gender?

Cultural Dynamics

Kroeber and Kluckhohn's (1963) classic definition of culture illustrates how the social, behavioral, material, and symbolic aspects of cultural experience weave together:

> Culture consists of patterns, explicit and implicit, of and for behavior acquired and transmitted by symbols, constituting the distinctive achievement of human groups, including their embodiments in artifacts; the essential core of culture consists of traditional (i.e., historically derived and selected) ideas and especially their attached values; culture systems may, on the one hand, be considered products of action, on the other as conditioning elements of further action. (p. 357)

Drawing from Kroeber and Kluckhohn's definition of culture, what are some of the cultural dynamics of sexuality?

Explicit Patterns of and for Behavior. Explicit patterns of and for sexual behavior can include beliefs about gender (e.g., men and women are the only two genders); assumptions about how men and women should act (e.g., men should initiate sexual interactions); values (what is perceived as desirable); ethics (what is right to do); and morals (principles of right and wrong). Religions function as both cultural systems and social institutions, explicitly articulating their cultural principles as articles of faith, many of which are beliefs about the meaning of sexual behavior and gender. Many Christian churches stress the values of premarital chastity, marital sexual fidelity, heterosexuality, and men as the heads of families. Likewise, secular organizations, such as Planned Parenthood and Operation Rescue, have mission statements that articulate dominant beliefs, many of which take on the role of religious articles of faith.

These beliefs then guide people's behavior and shape the form of the institutions that derive from them. Churches, as social institutions, develop organizations and activities designed to uphold their beliefs. The close feedback between the cultural beliefs and the social behaviors that express them can lead to the conclusion that the social form replicates the cultural principles. Although that is often true in the beginning of a social movement based on central beliefs, it may not persist in institutional form (see Lawrence, 1989). When beliefs persist without enactment, we may call them *empty*; when rituals and other social behaviors persist without an overall commitment to the beliefs they were meant to express, we talk about "going through the motions" (e.g., saying we are religious when we only go to church at Christmas and Easter). Ideally, beliefs match behavior. In reality, they are more or less disjunct.

The disjunction between beliefs and behavior can be a source of great psychological distress, particularly in the area of sexuality. Understanding the source of the distress clearly shows that we must take the four dimensions of human sexuality into account to fully understand our own behavior. If a young woman has premarital intercourse, but has been taught all of her life that it is wrong to have intercourse before marriage, the conflict she feels may result in sexual arousal disorder, vaginismus, painful intercourse, or orgasmic disorder. Although she may regard this as a personal problem, the issue is not just an individual one. The immediate experience results from a conflict between cultural beliefs shared by many other people and her individual behavior in relation to them. The broader basis for this personal experience is the fit between the individual and the cultural belief system to which she subscribes.

Other cultural beliefs come into play in the definition of what constitutes a sexual disorder. It has only been since the publication of Masters and Johnson's *Human Sexual Response* (1966) that U.S. culture has validated women's sexual response, particularly orgasm, as acceptable. Coincidentally, reports of orgasmic disorders in women became more frequent. The therapeutic category of orgasmic disorders (then referred to as *orgasmic dysfunctions*) developed as a cultural construct based on the belief (substantiated by science, another belief system) that it was normal for women to have orgasms; therefore, women who did not have them had a disorder. This had ramifications at an individual level. If a woman believed that she should have orgasms and did not, she not only might feel inadequate but also might fake orgasms, further separating herself from her physical responses.

Other diagnostic categories are cultural in that they reflect the meaning of illness or disease at a particular time. The frequency of diagnosis of a problem can be regarded as a cultural indicator because the frequency indicates how often the patients and diagnosticians (e.g., medical doctor, therapist, psychologist, or the person with the problem) define themselves in these terms. For example, the basis for premature ejaculation occurs in very specific social contexts and with specific cultural beliefs about the respective roles of men and women in intercourse. In *Human Sexual Inadequacy* (1970), Masters and Johnson discussed social variables—such as amount of education, intercourse with prostitutes (where time means money), and initial sexual opportunities in semiprivate circumstances with concerns over surprise or observation (e.g., in cars, parents' home, friend's room, at drive-ins)—as some of the variables leading to premature ejaculation. Less education (a social variable) correlates with a belief in the importance of the man's sexual satisfaction (a cultural variable); the higher the education, the greater the concern with the woman's sexual satisfaction. The *beliefs* about the roles of men and women in the act of sexual intercourse affect concern about who should be satisfied. If a man ejaculates quickly but neither he nor his partner believe that it is important for the woman to be satisfied, then neither perceives a problem. Consequently, they do not seek treatment because the behavior is not labeled as a problem. In contrast, when the couple believes that both should be satisfied, then rapid ejaculation without the female partner's satisfaction is regarded as a problem. The meaning of the behavior by the partners, derived from beliefs about how men and women should respond (a cultural variable), determines whether they perceive it as a problem.

The cultural definition of a satisfactory sexual encounter shapes the diagnostic categories and therapeutic techniques used to deal with the problem. That is why Masters and Johnson (1970) said that "a definition of premature ejaculation should reflect sociocultural orientation together with consideration of the prevailing requirements of sexual partners rather than an arbitrarily specific period of time" (p. 92). Revisions of the *Diagnostic and Statistical Manual of Mental Disorders* (American Psychiatric Association, 1994), routinely referred to by clinical psychologists in labeling psychological disorders, provide another clear example of the ways in which diagnostic categories shift in response to changes in the social and cultural context; as beliefs change, so do these categories. (See Torrey, 1973, for an elucidation of the cultural principles that underlie psychotherapy in U.S. culture and others.)

Implicit Patterns of and for Behavior. Implicit patterns of and for behavior are no less important than explicit ones, but may be more difficult to discern because they are not tangible or observable. There are no explicit statements of belief to guide us. Nevertheless, similar principles operate in fashioning the interaction among cultural, social, psychological, and physical dimensions.

Beck (1989) considered the significance of beliefs for relationships by analyzing common marital problems (disappointment, frustration, and anger) as consequences of "unfortunate misunderstandings that result from faulty communications and biased interpretations of each other's behavior" (p. 12). He suggested dealing with the problems by examining beliefs and thoughts that precede problem behaviors. He even included a checklist of beliefs that spouses have that hinder positive changes in their relationship. His therapeutic approach included an examination of "troublesome situations and meanings you attach to them" (p. 255). He advised couples to alter the messages they gave themselves about troublesome behaviors so that their emotional responses were different. Beck assumed that thoughts precede emotional responses, which in turn lead to problem behaviors. The couple must bring these negative thoughts to light and then change them.

By adding the cultural piece to Beck's analysis, we ask where the troublesome messages originate. Psychologists often focus on the immediate and past contexts (e.g., childhood, family, previous relationships) that give rise to the messages. Cultural anthropologists articulate the cultural context that contributed to the individual message. The individual drew on these beliefs and ideas to interpret and give meaning to the social situation. By tying all of these dimensions together, we can see how each interacts with the other.

Cultural and social dimensions interact but do not coincide. The mutual reinforcement of belief and behavior influence the individual's perception of the situation as comfortable or as a problem; this perception, in turn, affects how the individual thinks about it, triggering an emotional response followed by a behavior.
Beck (1989) maintained that therapy for a troublesome situation consists of
changing the cognitions that followed the perception of the situation.
"Reframing" these cognitions affects the individual's emotional response and the
behavior. The ability to reframe cognitions, that is, rethink thoughts about a situation, is really substituting different beliefs about it—a process supported or de-
terred by other cultural influences, such as media images, parental teachings, and
peer beliefs. This is how the cultural dimension affects individual experience in a
very real and immediate way. These patterns are often implicit guides to behavior.
Beck's therapeutic approach encourages the individual to make these implicit
messages conscious. Researchers must make the implicit cultural context explicit
and then tie it to the individual messages.

Symbolism.   Some of the most powerful aspects of the cultural dimension are
symbolic. An earlier section discussed the force of language as a significant cultural form and transmitter of culture. What people talk about and what they do not
talk about are major indicators of culture. For example, talk about sexuality varies
considerably in different social groups. Sex talk at different ages carries different
meaning, an indication of cultural significance. Whereas adults may engage in
sexual behavior and talk about it, children are not supposed to behave in sexual
ways nor talk about sexuality. The belief in childhood sexual innocence is so
strong that verbal or behavioral sexual expression among children may be regarded as abnormal or an indication of child sexual abuse. These attitudes negatively affect funding for and research on normal childhood sexuality (e.g.,
Goldman & Goldman, 1982) possibly because they reinforce the belief that childhood sexuality does not exist. However, funding and support for research on child
sexual abuse or abnormal sexual behavior in children is more forthcoming; this
fits into the acceptable cultural model affirming the normalcy of childhood sexual
innocence.

People may become symbolic of major themes in the culture and thus come to
occupy the status of cultural icons. For example, Baty (1995) discussed why Marilyn Monroe persists as a cultural icon despite her death almost 40 years ago. Con-
trasting Gloria Steinem's, Norman Mailer's, and Thomas Noguchi's reconstruc-
tions of Marilyn's life, Baty explored the cultural meaning that each story tapped.
In so doing, she revealed how symbols become powerful; they are not tied to one
set of meanings, but relate simultaneously at cognitive and emotional levels to individuals within a culture. Thus, the reproduction of images about Marilyn in the
media means different things to different people. To some, she means sexiness,
vulnerability, and femininity; to others, she means the loss of innocence, and cor-
ruption by acting out an unacceptable sexual script; and to others, she illustrates

the consequences of living an image rather than an authentic life. The cultural significance of the stories has to do with how they reveal cultural themes, not the degree to which the story is true. The persistence of stories about and reproductions of Marilyn indicate her cultural significance beyond her personal history. Because symbols may encode many different meanings, we first identify them and then investigate the meanings they tap in different time periods. Although the symbol persists over time, its dominant meaning may change. Tracing the shift in meaning provides insight into the culture at the time.

Transmission. Transmission of culture from one generation to the next establishes important explicit and implicit patterns within the individual and in the society. Learning, some explicit (deliberately shown or said) and some implicit (inferred from behavior and messages in a variety of contexts such as family, school, or TV), occurs from an early age. The messages derived from enculturation (ways of learning beliefs about what behavior means) become so much a part of the individual's milieu that the messages seem natural, even though they are learned, not inborn. They constitute a cultural system within which the individual functions. They provide guidelines for how the individual should behave as well as interpretations for the way that the individual does behave.

Just as behavior and interactions may not conform to an individual's beliefs, the organization of the society may not synchronize with that of the culture. If individual behavior required by the society is not in line with deeply held personal values and beliefs, many of which are implicit, then the person is likely to feel personal stress of some kind. For example, problems of low sexual desire have developed hand in hand with the large-scale entry of women in the workforce, particularly mothers of small children. As the traditional division of labor changed, so too did aspects of intimacy. The sheer amount of energy required to deal with the organization of the home and children's activities, as well as work responsibilities, may lead couples to desire sleep rather than sex. The continuing belief that home and family are important responsibilities of women is the cultural contribution to the personal stress; many women retain most of the responsibility for the home and family despite added responsibilities outside the home. The conflict between the dual cultural demands of success at work with responsibilities to home and family engender stress sufficient to bring a high-powered career woman to tears at home; her energy for sexual interaction may suffer as a consequence.

Artifacts. Finally, artifacts—products of human activity—express culture. Archaeologists demonstrate the close link between artifacts and culture in their work. Based on material remains such as structures, domestic items, art, ornaments, ritual objects, and weapons, archaeologists try to reconstruct the context that produced them. After inferring the type of social organization of which the items were a part (e.g., a civilization, the common people), archaeologists turn to the task of inferring the meaning of the objects or material remains within that context—that is, inferring the cultural system. Despite concrete physical remains of past cultures, debates persist about the meaning of the objects and their relation to social organization at the time. Appraisers and antique dealers go through a similar process; value is based on reconstructing the context (e.g., who made it, when, under what circumstances) within which the object was produced. (Watch the "Antiques Road Show" on PBS for a popular illustration of the process.)

The significance of meaning becomes clear when we consider whether artifacts are considered suitable for public display. Kendrick (1987) noted that, as early as 1758, a selection of artifacts from Pompeii were regarded as *lascivious*; they were "placed under lock and key as being unsuitable to display to visitors, especially women and children. These artifacts were placed in a Secret Museum, [and] identified as pornography. . . . In England a similar museum was established at the British Museum to house such artifacts; also, erotic books were stored in a locked case in the library of the Museum" (Frayser & Whitby 1995, p. 611). The sexual taboos of the culture of the person who classified the artifacts channeled how they were labeled, selected, and presented, thus hindering an accurate portrayal of the role they played in an ancient culture. Therefore, the selection tells us as much about the culture in which the artifacts are presented as the culture from which they derive.

Many artifacts may be material symbols of "expressive culture," which deals with the expression of individual desires, needs, and stresses that are not satisfied by the social organization. Expressive culture is an outgrowth of the classic sociological issue of the relation between the individual and society. How does one accommodate the other? Expressive culture reflects and channels the tension between the individual and the society through stories and literature; music; art; fashion; religion, philosophy, and worldview; media; and fads and trends.

As societies increase in population size, so too do the ways in which culture is expressed. Although the question of whether there is an American culture remains debatable, we can point to consistent messages that the media communicate via TV, radio, print, and personal computers. Popular culture expresses many of the dreams, frustrations, and rationalizations of its participants. Jhally (1995b) pointed out that advertising "does not merely tell us about things but of how things are connected to important domains of our lives. . . . To understand the system of images that constitutes advertising we need to inquire into the definition of happiness and satisfaction in contemporary social life" (p. 79). Jhally's (1995a) video *Dreamworlds 2* showed how music videos express and promote specific beliefs about male sexuality, female sexuality, and sexual interaction. His narrative described how images of men as dominant, women as nymphomaniacs, and sex on demand reinforce sexual stereotypes and abuse in real life.

Expressive culture includes patterns of behavior linked to material objects because the use of the objects is an integral part of what the person who has them is trying to express. For example, people who use products found in the "Good Vibrations" catalogue of sex toys might share certain beliefs about sexuality that guide their behavior. Overall, games provide models for social behavior and express cultural beliefs. Whips and costumes used in sado-masochistic scenes are part of the sexual games people play.

Personal computers are objects that open another avenue into expressive culture. As we move into cyberspace, the possibilities for uses of the imagination expand. An examination of web pages (images presented, language used, and messages conveyed) can be a valuable source of information about cultural expression of the meaning of sexuality. Sexual behaviors generated through computer use are also part of expressive culture. What does it mean to have sex with someone on the Internet? What dreams and frustrations do people project about sexuality in chat rooms? What criteria do people use in selecting Internet contacts for in-person dates? What do they tell us about the culture as a whole and about sexuality in particular?

Conclusion

Researching cultural aspects of human sexuality depends on understanding the concept and dynamics of culture. Although biological, social, cultural, and psychological aspects of sexuality interact with each other, they need to be kept analytically distinct, particularly the social and cultural dimensions of sexuality. Sexual behavior and sexual interactions may appear to have similar meanings in different contexts, but explanations for their patterns can be very different. Conclusions about the meaning of these patterns depends on asking individuals for their interpretations of their behavior as well as examining beliefs and ideas that may have shaped them. For example, abortion may mean an affirmation of a woman's right to make choices about her own body or it may mean murder. Opposing sides of the abortion controversy have significantly different views about reproduction, women's roles, and the definition of human life; their cultural beliefs clash. The fact that cultural expressions of sexuality carry so much symbolic weight entails different, often highly emotional, interpretations of the same behavior. Once we are clear about what culture is and how it works, we are in a better position to research it, not only intraculturally but also cross-culturally.

CROSS-CULTURAL RESEARCH ON HUMAN SEXUALITY

Broadly construed, *cross-cultural research* refers to a variety of activities and findings. These types of research range from single case studies to cross-cultural surveys. While each approach has its advantages, the best method depends on what one wants to know.

The original meaning of the term *science*, a state of knowing, centers on selecting a domain for study. As a part of culture, science adheres to a set of assumptions that guide the search for valid knowledge. Scientific methods are procedures that follow specific rules for obtaining evidence that supports claims about knowledge. The important questions for the scientific researcher center on what one wants to know and how a method will facilitate the pursuit of that knowledge.

The types of cross-cultural research described in the next section demonstrate that researchers have different goals for their investigations. The single case studies examine one context in depth, plumbing it for the pattern of deeper meanings that guide people's behavior and give them a basis for interpreting their experiences. This type of research demands close interaction with the participants of the culture. Detailed descriptions of their experiences become rich data for interpretation and knowledge.

Survey approaches to cross-cultural research pursue a different goal: explaining underlying human constants and variants. The questions revolve around variables that transcend cultural differences. What are the general or universal principles that all humans share?

Types

Single Case Studies/Ethnographies.   Case studies or ethnographies focus in depth on one cultural group, such as a particular ethnic group within the United States or a community in another country. Cultural and social anthropologists, as well as sociologists, have typically conducted such research. Anthropologists often use *participant observation* (Spradley, 1980), a qualitative research method focused on developing an ethnography (i.e., a cultural description). The anthropologist not only participates in the social context selected for study but also observes its activities, interactions, and material organization. The goal is to understand the lens (i.e., the cultural principles) through which cultural participants see their world and to describe the world they see. What does the world look like viewed through the eyes of insiders? What is it like to walk in their shoes/boots/moccasins/sandals? Interviews and observations form the bedrock of this method. Sociological case studies may focus more on the organizational principles of the group than the cultural ones.

Ethnographies can take two approaches. One approach is the study of geographically based communities such as Gregor's (1985) description of the sexual lives of the Mehinaku in central Brazil, Herdt's (1981) description of sexual development of Sambian men in the Highlands of New Guinea, or Shostak's (1983) narrative about the !Kung San in northwestern Botswana, reflected in the life of a !Kung woman in her 50s. The other approach is to investigate specific cultural groups such as Bolin's (1987) description of the lives and gender transitions of transsexuals in the United States or Nanda's (1990) description of the world of people living in an institutionalized third role (*hijras*) in India.

Herdt and Stoller (1990) introduced the *clinical ethnography* as a variation of the single-case approach. Clinical ethnographies are "reports that study the subjectivity of the researcher and the people who inform him or her. What matters are our communications with real people, one to one or one to many; people creating and exchanging meanings with interpersonal relationships" (p. 29). Psychology, psychiatry, and anthropology cross paths in this method when Herdt and Stoller refer to psycholoanalysis as "a certain kind of microethnography" (p. xiii). In contrast to other field methods, including participant observation, which encourage an objective stance to avoid bias in the findings, clinical ethnography aims to engage researchers in the cross-cultural study of subjectivity, which "describes, interprets, compares ways people express feelings, beliefs, and motives" (p. 30); by so doing, it enriches and deepens observations. The goal of objectivity is elusive because "there is no hard and fast boundary between subjectivity and objectivity" (p. 3); "subjectivity edits observation" (p. 6). Clinical ethnography encourages the researcher to engage in deep dialogue with the participant(s) to explore the world of fantasy and meaning often kept private.

This method has much in common with that used by clinical psychologists, who elicit descriptions of clients' lives to understand how they experience their lives. However, unlike anthropologists, clinical psychologists do not directly participate in or observe the lives of their clients; they rely instead on conversations with the client to infer the psychological dynamics of their lives.

When ethnographic descriptions of one culture are compared and contrasted with those of another culture, then the research may be labeled *cross-cultural*. Ethnographic insights are often used to illustrate the variety of human behavior and beliefs and become examples of a cross-cultural perspective. Bolin and Whelehan (1999) made good use of ethnographies and other case studies in their book *Perspectives on Human Sexuality*, which attempts to integrate "evolutionary, cross-cultural and bio-cultural dimensions to human sexuality" (p. xiii).

Cross-Cultural Field Studies in Multiple Sites. Engaging in research that examines specific variables or topics in different field settings is another type of research referred to as cross-cultural. Rather than studying one case in depth and then making comparisons with the cases of other researchers, the researcher specifies the social contexts and consistent variables to be compared before the fieldwork begins. The structure of the research ensures that the variables of interest will be investigated and available for analysis, forestalling gaps in data that occur when comparisons occur ex post facto. The logic of the approach is similar to that of experimental research in which one or a few variables are examined under different conditions, keeping the other variables constant or controlled. However, comparing variables in different "naturally occurring" social contexts (i.e., "the field") expands the range of extraneous variables, making it more difficult to maintain an experimental model. The method's strength lies in examining variables in contexts that may suggest other relevant variables and routes to explanations not anticipated before the research was conducted. In short, researchers can take advantage of "extraneous variables," incorporating them into later research or drawing on them for the final analysis. However, as Minturn and Lambert (1994) pointed out, "The problem of cross-cultural research is to design measures that will reflect variation without losing the core meaning of the behavior studied that is necessary for meaningful comparisons" (p. 2).

Goldman and Goldman (1982) used this approach in their research on cognitive aspects of childhood sexuality. They interviewed samples of children ages 5 to 15, drawn from regional clusters of schools in four societies: Australia, North America, Britain, and Sweden. Surveys based on personal interviews rely on a more structured approach to crossing cultures in the field. The recent National Health and Social Life Survey (NHSLS) of sexual practices in the United States used a probability sample of 3,432 men and women in the United States between the ages of 18 and 59 to explore the influence of social context (e.g., demographic characteristics like gender, age, marital status) on sexual conduct and attitudes (Laumann, Gagnon, Michael, & Michaels, 1994). With the intent of designing and conducting the national survey according to "high standards of scientific rigor and replicability" (p. 35), the researchers gave particular priority to sample selection and questionnaire construction. They characterized the essence of survey research as asking "a large sample of people from a defined population the same set of questions" (p. 63). The focus of the method is consistency across contexts rather than the meaning of the contexts to the people interviewed. Consequently, the emphasis is on gathering comparable information on the same variables from each person interviewed. The structured set of questions in the questionnaires helps to ensure comparability of individual responses to the questions.

Cross-Cultural Surveys. Cross-cultural research has yet another variation—that of the *cross-cultural survey*. Using principles of survey research within one culture, this type of cross-cultural research tests hypotheses using cultures rather than individuals as the sample. After developing a sample of societies representative of the world's cultures, the researcher codes variables of interest from information in written sources. After coding the same variables for each culture in the sample, the researcher uses statistical measures to determine frequency distributions, correlations, and so forth, which he or she then uses to explore variations in variables to evaluate a hypothesis.

Murdock's (1949) examination of the relation of family and kinship organization to sex and marriage and Ford and Beach's (1951) cross-cultural, cross-species exploration of sexual behavior remain classic illustrations of the cross-cultural approach applied to human sexuality. Murdock organized his findings in terms of a series of hypotheses derived from a broader theoretical framework. Ford and Beach took a different approach, exploring the range of variation in sexual behaviors rather than using their data for testing hypotheses derived from theory. These and many more recent studies (e.g., Martin & Voorhies, 1975; Frayser, 1985; Reiss, 1986; Schlegel & Barry, 1991) drew on the findings of cross-cultural surveys to examine how aspects of sexuality are systematically related to each other.

What Can We Know?

Regardless of the method used, the researcher faces difficulties in establishing valid findings about sexuality. The nature of sexual expression may pose a barrier. As Friedl (1999) pointed out, it is almost universal that "sex acts are ordinarily hidden from view" (p. 91). Consequently, how do we know about the details of sexual interaction? Friedl contended that "the most significant value of participant observation—the ability to compare statements about behavior, attitudes, and values with observed actions—is not possible for ordinary sexual acts" (p. 93).

Another barrier to researching sexuality is the influence of the investigator's culture on his or her research. Every society regulates sexuality in some way, and every culture endows sexuality with its own particular brand of meaning. Relative to other cultures of the world, beliefs about sexuality in the United States are more restrictive than permissive (Frayser, 1985). These beliefs affect assumptions, research designs, and analyses by scientists who undertake research on sexuality. Fausto-Sterling (1985) provided many examples of cultural bias affecting scientific research on gender. Scientists do not necessarily take off their cultural glasses when they design and analyze their research. Similarly, lack of funding for sexuality research that does not relate to social problems (e.g., teen pregnancy or AIDS among heterosexuals) can discourage researchers from initiating studies on important questions about sexuality.

Political agendas of researchers may blind them to a balanced view of the cultural context of sexuality. For example, it is sometimes difficult to distinguish between a scientific perspective and a political agenda in discussions of the relationships between men and women or in debates about sexual abuse. The experience of the researcher may alter research despite the best methodological tools. As Herdt and Stoller (1990) commented, "Subjectivity edits observation" (p. 6).

Even when thorough research has been conducted on a sexual topic, the findings may not be accepted because of cultural constraints. More than a decade ago, a prominent author of trade books on gender conducted research on incest. When the research showed that not all consequences of incest were harmful, the person's publisher and colleagues warned the researcher not to present the findings because the public and professional response could ruin the researcher's career; the findings might be misinterpreted as a rationale for, or advocacy of, child sexual abuse. The findings were never published, and the manuscript of the book remains sequestered in the author's home, available for reading by a few trusted colleagues.

Other research on sexuality remains submerged for similar reasons. I have spoken with many anthropologists who have field notes or other data on sexuality from the societies where they conducted fieldwork, yet they say they did not publish the material because it was not likely to be regarded as a suitable topic for investigation in the profession. Vance (1991) described the drawbacks of pursuing a career with sexuality as its focus (also see chap. 21, this volume). With the prospect of not being taken seriously, encountering problems in advancing to tenure, and having difficulty in obtaining funding for research on sexuality, the potential sexuality researcher may choose another path strewn with fewer obstacles.

The negative impact of disciplinary and public perceptions of sexuality research may lead to the suppression of sexual information gathered in the field. Consequently, the position of the researcher, as well as the influence of his or her cultural beliefs about sex, are likely to produce bias or gaps in ethnographies. Information that one might assume would be there is not. For example, in my data collection for *Varieties of Sexual Experience* (Frayser, 1985), I wanted to include data on topics like who is present at a child's birth, attitudes toward menstruation, and the social role of homosexuals. However, the information was often absent or sketchy; there was not enough to include in a statistical analysis. In these cases, the absence of information can lead to more questions about the meaning of the void in data. Was the practice or belief absent, or was it absent because of the researcher's cultural biases? When relying on data derived from descriptions written by government officials, travelers, or religious functionaries, the biases are often more apparent. The more subtle biases of researchers who share a disciplinary paradigm, live in the same culture, or both may be less obvious.

Sometimes information that a researcher assumes would not be in a source is there. For example, I was surprised to find so much information on sexuality in the accounts of Christian missionaries in the 19th century. Although they condemned many sexual practices as sinful, they described in detail the behavior that contrasted with their own beliefs of moral conduct. When reading sources, it is important to scan an entire description for relevant information rather than search in familiar categories. The labels may vary significantly depending on the author's status, ethnicity, home culture, or role.

On What Basis Do We Know?

In addition to the constraints posed by the study of sexuality in general, the methods may confine the scope of knowledge gained from the research. Single case studies embrace an ideographic approach that focuses on "concrete descriptions of particular people, events, and things located in time and space" (Pelto & Pelto, 1978, p. 19). Surveys embrace a more nomothetic approach that searches for principles that "apply to domains of phenomena without regard to specific times or locations" (p. 19). Both are important. Yet as anthropologists Suggs and Miracle (1993) pointed out, "Situated within existing theories of culture, anthropological studies of sexuality primarily have been descriptive. There have been few attempts to explain the nature of human sexuality and its relationship to culture" (p. 5). Their conclusion encourages researchers to engage in more nomothetic approaches to the cultural dimension of human sexuality.

Generalizing cross-culturally is even more difficult than doing so with surveys within one culture because more variables come into play. When members of a research team are working simultaneously in different contexts with well-defined field guides and research objectives, their systematic approach and communication with each other in the research process can defuse potential problems of comparability of results. More often than not, however, large-scale cross-cultural research relies on the data of researchers who collected their data independently. This means the study design has to deal not only with questions raised about the validity of ideographic research, but also with additional ones that confront nomothetic research. Although some researchers regard ideographic and nomothetic approaches as mutually exclusive, they complement each other in the cross-cultural arena. Generalization depends on having detailed information available to test hypotheses about topics of interest, and cross-cultural research, with its systematic inquiries into different domains of life, can point out the gaps in ideographic accounts. The source of debate about each approach lies in assessing the validity of the results. Ideographic proponents argue that nomothetic approaches rob the findings of the context that give them meaning, thus rendering their results meaningless. Nomothetic proponents argue that a few cases, however well described, cannot be generalized without testing their applicability in a broad sample. However, pursuit of one does not invalidate the other because the goals of each are different. The issue goes back to the question of what the researcher wants to know. Ideographic researchers explore the details of context and meaning; nomothetic researchers explore the systematic patterns that underlie the array of meaning. One feeds into the other.

Understanding context and meaning allows the nomothetic researcher to better develop operational definitions that will apply to a variety of cultures. It fosters a human rather than an ethnocentric perspective by focusing on core principles underlying all human behavior. It also raises rather than suppresses questions of meaning because exceptions to generalizations provide as much understanding as do consistencies. To find out why a case is an exception, the researcher must examine the context. To say that there is a cultural or social-psychological pattern does not eradicate individuality, just as elucidating rules of grammar does not erase the rich array of specific languages and unique literary works. To oppose the two is a red herring, just as opposing nature and nurture are. They divert attention from the inherent interaction among different dimensions of human life.

An Ideographic Approach. Bolton (1992) suggested that the researcher may need to be a member of the culture that he or she is researching to gain valid data and insights about sexual behavior and experiences. Rather than maintaining distance for objectivity's sake in participant observation, the researcher participates more fully in the culture to find out what sexual behavior actually occurs and what its meaning is. This may mean participating in sexual activities with members of the group, carrying the participation part of participant observation to its extreme.

The fundamental question that Bolton (1992) raised is whether people outside of a culture or subculture can really know what occurs inside. A related question is whether we can ever really know the details of people's private sexual behavior and thoughts. Bolton's option allows for a closer look at behavior occurring in restricted settings. Talese (1980) adopted a similar strategy in some of his research on the changing sexual context in the United States from the post-WWII years until 1980. He actively engaged in some of the activities that he described, including managing a massage parlor, living at Sandstone (a 15-acre retreat in Topanga Canyon, CA, dedicated to exploring human sexual potential), and going to swing clubs.

Interaction with fellow participants opens communication about the meaning of a behavior in a way that an interview or questionnaire submitted from the outside does not. Cultural anthropologists routinely use participant observation in developing ethnographies and case studies. However, the standard of objectivity requires that the researcher not be so involved in the process that he or she is unable to impartially describe the experience. Intimate involvement in the culture, particularly sexual activities, would seem to violate that standard. Even if it transgresses this scientific principle, does it lead to more valid conclusions? Does the private nature of some aspects of sexual behavior call for a very different research approach?

Herdt and Stoller (1990) said that it does because an essential aspect of sexual experience is its subjectivity. Their method of clinical ethnography attempts to legitimize subjective descriptions as data for understanding sexuality and to provide a basis for richer observations about sexual behavior. Although this approach may cross the boundaries of traditional participant observation, it does not violate other guidelines for psychological or cultural understanding. Psychologists and psychiatrists routinely enter the private worlds of their clients, eliciting descriptions of their perceptions, cognitions, interpretations, and emotions. Cultural anthropologists have acknowledged the significance of subjectivity in interpretive anthropology, which explores the anthropologist's psychological position as well as the descriptions of the participants as cultural narrative, to be analyzed as a text. According to Herdt and Stoller, the difference between their approach and that of the interpretive anthropologists is they do not regard the text as the whole picture. They want to examine the interplay between the individual and the culture, the inner experience and public behavior. This emphasis channels their view of ethnography: "Ethnography is concerned mainly to use . . . private feelings and fantasies to better understand what shapes cultural institutions and public behavior" (p. 378). Although clinical ethnography probes subjectivity, it acknowledges the cultural patterning and social institutions with which it interfaces.

This leads us back to the original question: On what basis do we know about sexuality? According to Bolton (1992), we participate fully. According to Herdt and Stoller (1990), we investigate subjectivity and use it not only as a basis for understanding but also as a route to better observe and interpret public behavior. Even when we participate in the behavior directly, we do not know whether we share our experience of the behavior with others. What we do know is that there is a similarity in behavior, and being part of the group that accepts the behavior allows for a wider range of observations about sexual behavior than being outside of it.

Apart from direct participation and observation, we can ask people about their private experiences. Whether their descriptions accurately reflect the behavior that occurs in private is questionable (see chap. 3, this volume). This leads us back to another question: What does one want to know? If one's focus is to describe how people perceive their behavior and what they believe about it, then their descriptions may be enough. What do they include, and what do they leave out? Do they have a vocabulary to discuss these issues? If the goal is to make generalizations, then a more structured, systematic approach may be appropriate.

Nomothetic Approaches within the United States. The Kinsey Reports (Kinsey, Pomeroy, & Martin, 1948; Kinsey, Pomeroy, Martin, & Gebhard, 1953) and the recent National Health and Social Life Survey (NHSLS; Laumann et al., 1994) combined personal interviews with a systematic approach to survey sexual behavior and attitudes in the United States. Pomeroy (one of Kinsey's original collaborators and co-authors), Flax, and Wheeler (1982) described and explained Kinsey's pioneering sex interview technique. In the research for *Sexual Behavior in the Human Male* and *Sexual Behavior in the Human Female*, Kinsey took care in knowing the community from which the interviewees came and adapting his language and questions to the context within which he was working. Pomeroy et al. detailed the importance of knowing the respondent's background and social situation, how questions are asked, their sequence, and engendering the respondent's trust. This book remains a good guide to interviewing techniques for obtaining a sex history. Although an interview usually proceeds according to a specific sequence, the technique allows for flexibility in gathering information. The interviewer codes responses on one page, reserving specific spaces for different topics. If the conversation shifts out of the planned sequence, the form can accommodate the shift. This technique allows for a personal interview with a systematic way of recording the information.

The NHSLS design was more structured than Kinsey's, although it also used personal interviews rather than mailed questionnaires or telephone contacts as the basis to collect data. While the Kinsey interview allowed for flexibility in the wording and sequencing of the questions, the NHSLS used a questionnaire with a more formal protocol. As Laumann et al. (1994) noted, "The basic problem was to construct an instrument that would collect information in a way that would minimize reporting bias and error" (p. 65). "As much as possible, each respondent should be asked the same questions in the same words and in the same order. . . . An essential goal in survey interviewing, especially on sensitive topics like sex, is to create a neutral, nonjudgmental, and confiding atmosphere and to maintain a certain professional distance between the interviewer and the respondent" (pp. 63, 67, 68).

Despite their differences, both approaches had generalization of findings as their goal. Both attempted to take social and cultural variations into account in their research design, and both segmented their findings according to different social and cultural criteria, such as education, age, religion, and gender. Both showed that social contexts do affect patterns of sexual behavior and attitudes, even as they demonstrated consistencies within and across contexts.

The Process of Developing a Cross-Cultural Nomothetic Approach.   When I embark on sexuality research, I remind myself, "Do the best you can with what you have," especially when it is cross-cultural research. I illustrate this process with the research I conducted for *Varieties of Sexual Experience* (Frayser, 1985).

When I began to conduct cross-cultural research on human sexuality, I was a graduate student trained in symbolic anthropology by British social anthropologist Victor Turner. I then worked for 7 years as a research assistant to George Peter Murdock, the founder of the cross-cultural method in the United States. Turner provided me with principles to meticulously examine symbolism in context, whereas Murdock gave me the tools to systematically examine social and cultural variables in different cultural contexts. The initial cognitive dissonance of a very ideographic approach juxtaposed with a very nomothetic one gave way to an appreciation of the variety of social and cultural contexts worldwide. For 7 years, I read about the social organization of 186 cultures in the Standard Cross-Cultural Sample and coded information about them into categories. At first, I found it painful to code rich description; I had voluminous notes and qualifications beside my codes. After years of reading ethnographies, government reports, narratives by travelers, and descriptions by religious people, I could not deny that there were patterns across these contexts. I also realized that some of the theories that I had learned in graduate school were not applicable to *human* society and culture; rather, they applied more to *Western* societies. My work at this National Science Foundation-funded project became the second part of my education in anthropology because I learned about the wide range of social and cultural contexts to which the concepts and theories had to apply. Context was important, but so too was an examination of the patterns that underlay varying contexts that define another part of being human. Both are relevant because culture is a mainstay of human existence. As I explained in the first part of this chapter, it is human to have variable cultures and societies because symbolic learning plays such a large role in human adaptation.

I embarked on my first adventure into the world of human sexuality. I asked a series of questions in the process: What did I want to know? How would I go about finding out what I wanted to know? What conclusions and applications would my research have? My answer to the first question was that I wanted to know what is human about human sexuality. I wanted to find out if human sexuality is a system in and of itself. My answer to the second question flowed from my answer to the first. To know what is human about human sexuality is to ask how what is human applies to sexuality. This led to identifying the four dimensions of human sexuality: biological, social, cultural, and psychological. I assumed that if human sexuality were a system, then there must be consistent relationships among the components of the system. How would I go about finding them? I relied on cross-species research and evolutionary theory to define the similarities and differences of humans and other animals. I called this the *biological baseline* because it highlighted the physical variables that would play a role in any social or cultural context.

The result of this research led to my conceptualization of the sexual and reproductive cycles. Because intercourse does not necessarily coincide with peak fertility in humans, as it does in most mammals and many other primates, there is a disjunction between sexual and reproductive activity. Therefore, I wanted to find out the extent to which sexual and reproductive activities overlapped in human societies and how the cultures conceptualized their association.

This led to my identifying the variables to study. I decided to follow the phases of sexual and reproductive development throughout the life cycle. I then had to define what is sexual and what is reproductive and how I could clarify the difference. Conceptualization of variables and clear definitions of what to include and what not to include became a significant aspect of the research design. This was difficult because it seemed that I had to define in advance what I was trying to find out. I was not sure of the variations I would find and whether the variables I chose would be applicable across the 62 groups I would research. For example, I wanted to define marriage so that I could recognize its attributes in different cultures, despite how the researcher described it or the labels under which it appeared. What are the basic elements of a marriage? How do we recognize them? I reviewed theoretical formulations of marriage as well as notes from my previous years of cross-cultural research on social organization, paying close attention to how different cultures define the components of marriage. I realized that the social and cultural aspects of marriage were often merged in its definition, making it difficult to generate a single definition that applied across cultures. This prompted me to divide my consideration of marriage into its social and cultural aspects. I found that the behavior is easier to identify than the concept. What do people do in relation to what they regard as marriage? Is there a ceremony? Do the individuals comprising the couple live together? What activity finalizes the marriage? Following these questions, I asked what defines marriage. The definition I decided on was "Marriage is a relationship within which a group socially approves and encourages sexual intercourse and the birth of children" (Frayser, 1985, p. 248). Separating the social and cultural dimensions facilitated defining the attributes of the concept. I followed this principle throughout the study design, separating beliefs and concepts from behavior. This led to my developing ordinal scales of social involvement in each of the aspects of the sexual and reproductive cycles. For example, how extensive a group is involved in a marriage ceremony? To whom does the incest taboo apply? How extensively does harm radiate from incest? Who attends the birth of a child? Who celebrates the birth of a child?

After identifying variables and operationalizing concepts, I conducted a pretest of the coding manual. This meant that I read complete ethnographies and other accounts of six societies from different parts of the world: the Insular Pacific, North America, South America, Europe, Asia, and Africa. I selected each group from the Standard Cross-Cultural Sample, using the bibliography and pinpointing sheet (which described the time and place to which the information should pertain) as a guide. I found that some needed revision and that I had to add categories to the code that I had not anticipated. For example, one coding category was on grounds for divorce. Although I had anticipated illicit sexual relationships, physical violence, incompatibility, and desertion, I added reproductive problems and incompatibility with affines (relatives by marriage) after the pretest. I also decided to focus on shared aspects of sex and reproduction rather than investigate the psychological dimension. This was a practical rather than a theoretical consideration, as most sources would consistently describe public events related to sexuality, but not private, psychological aspects.

The next step was to finalize the coding manual and read ethnographies and other sources to find the information I was seeking. There were coding categories that I deleted due to the dearth of information about them, such as the meaning of menstruation or sexual techniques. The lack of information indicated biased presentations of information and pointed to neglected topics ripe for future research. Omissions of this sort particularly plague research on sexuality—a topic laden with negative value judgments from the Western world.

After completing the coding, I turned to the analysis of the results. I first looked at the frequency distributions for each of the categories, such as premarital and extramarital restrictiveness and permissiveness for men and women. Then I examined the links between the variables based on my initial question: Are there systematic links between aspects of the sexual and reproductive cycles? Are there patterns? I had developed hypotheses to guide my testing of the links. Logic rather than the array of frequency distributions led the search, although the frequencies sparked the development of more hypotheses. This process resulted in my developing models for understanding variations in the sexual and reproductive cycles. At one end of the continuum were societies that culturally defined and socially positioned sex as reproduction—the sexually restrictive cultures. At the other end were societies that did not require that sex be reproductive—the sexually permissive cultures. Clusters of variables would routinely correlate with others. For example, sexually restrictive groups, indicated by prohibitions of premarital and extramarital sex as well as difficulty of remarriage after the death of a spouse or divorce, usually had elaborate marriage ceremonies with extensive social participation, finalized the marriage with a ritual, a bride-price, or both, and focused on barrenness and illicit sex as grounds for divorce. When examined according to geographical region, most of these sexually restrictive cultures clustered in the Circum-Mediterranean area, and most of the sexually permissive ones, in the Insular Pacific.

What was the relevance of these findings? I had wanted to look at their applicability to the United States. Rather than viewing sexuality in the United States as a standard by which to gauge other cultures, I used the findings from the cross-cultural research to place U.S. trends in perspective. The models I derived from cross-cultural research proved useful in interpreting changes in beliefs about sexuality from the 19th to the 20th century, providing guidelines for demonstrating a shift from a restrictive to more permissive model. The conflict between the social and cultural dynamics of change account for much of the ambivalence that people in the United States feel about sexuality. Whereas the increase in premarital sexual behavior, especially among women, indicates a sexually permissive society, beliefs that support this behavior have lagged behind; the culture is slower to change. Similarly, homosexuality has become more visible, but acceptance of homosexuality has been slow to change over the last 30 years.

This research helps explain why certain sexual problems occur in different historical periods and how sexual theories relate to the larger culture. These findings point to ways that historical research can be incorporated into cross-cultural studies; in a sense, different time periods represent different cultural contexts and can be construed as cross-cultural. Cross-cultural findings that specific cultural patterns, such as sexual restrictiveness, correlate with specific geographic regions can prompt ecological research about the link between environment and sexual behavior.

A Bigger Picture. The four dimensions of sexuality discussed in the beginning of this chapter are critical for finding out what we want to know. Different cultural contexts may only reveal one or two pieces of the puzzle. Comparison of the four dimensions across and within different groups can lead to a fuller picture of human sexuality, despite all of the drawbacks in conducting sexuality research. The research I conducted on normal childhood sexuality illustrates the process.

Being asked to write an overview of research on normal childhood sexuality (Frayser, 1994) raised the question that Bullough (1990) once asked: How do you research a taboo topic? I defined my goal as follows: "To present an anthropological analysis of the scattered empirical data and theory on normal childhood sexuality and to integrate it into a coherent framework that researchers can use to guide their search for and assessment of relevant information on normal childhood sexuality" (Frayser, 1994. p. 175). I used the four dimensions of sexuality to organize my paper. I began with research on the evolution of human sexuality and identified what we would expect to find in childhood, given our human heritage of learning. I concluded that it would be "surprising if children did not have an interest in or express sexual behavior" (p. 180). I then reviewed the available theory and empirical evidence (mainly drawn from research in Western societies) on different developmental stages—prenatal, infancy, and childhood. I concluded that the process of sexual development begins in the prenatal stage and proceeds through infancy and childhood. This raised the question of whether these developmental studies could be generalized across cultures. I turned to the cross-cultural evidence and found a wide range regarding acceptance of and responses to childhood sexual behavior. Compared to other cultures, the United States is relatively restrictive in its beliefs about and acceptance of normal childhood sexuality. The belief in childhood sexual innocence overrides an examination of almost any sexual behavior during childhood as normal. I concluded with a politically unpopular statement: "It is clear that the current cultural emphasis on child sexual abuse and the paucity of balanced, comprehensive programs of sex education for children reveal a culture at odds with the bulk of evolutionary, developmental, and cross-cultural evidence demonstrating that children are sexual beings, whose exploration of sexual knowledge and play, is an integral part of their development as fully functioning human beings" (p. 210).

Investigation of such an emotionally charged and politically controversial topic was difficult. Nevertheless, it showed me how the social taboos and cultural silence in one society can be understood by relating them to the contexts of other groups. Because of cultural variability, what is observable and talked about in one culture may not be in another. Cross-cultural research can paint a more balanced picture of the nature of this variability and present options for explaining it.

CONCLUSION

Sexuality research is, at best, a marginal and risky enterprise. Cross-cultural surveys are not popular in anthropology, where more ideographic approaches are preferred. Putting sexuality and cross-cultural research together can be detrimental professionally (Vance, 1991). Nevertheless, the journey into this area of research is theoretically challenging, enriching, and stimulating. Also, it is extremely productive in putting one culture in perspective, particularly our own. The applications are endless in a culture that has difficulty confronting its sexual taboos.

I advise those who want to conduct cross-cultural research on human sexuality to become familiar with at least one other cultural group before embarking on this enterprise. Pay attention to how it feels to be in a context without understanding its assumptions. Spend time reading about a variety of cultural contexts and become aware of the extent of variability that a cross-cultural approach entails. Define a specific goal—understanding the dynamics of one context whose principles for life can be compared with those of another *or* looking for human principles that underlie variability across cultures. Regardless of their goal, I hope that future researchers will find an appreciation of the complexity that defines us as human and an understanding of the impact that culture has on the configuration of human sexuality.

SUGGESTED READINGS

Ideographic Methods

For a basic understanding of how to develop an ethnography, refer to Spradley (1979, 1980); although dated, the books provide step-by-step, easy-to-understand introductions to the anthropological methods of the ethnographic interview and participant observation. Pelto and Pelto (1978) provided a comprehensive introduction to research methods in cultural anthropology. The methodological sections of the Kinsey reports (1948, 1953) as well as *Taking a Sex History* (Pomeroy et al., 1982) provided some excellent suggestions for how to ask questions about sexuality in an interview. Herdt and Stoller (1990) provided a theoretical rationale and example of clinical ethnography, which melds methods from anthropology and psychiatry to study subjectivity in a cultural context. Case studies of sexuality include Bolin (1980), Gregor (1985), and Herdt (1981).

Nomothetic Methods

Laumann et al. (1994) provided detailed guidelines for a large-scale sexuality survey within the United States. Reiss (1986) showed how to use the cross-cultural method to develop theories about sexuality. Barry and Schlegel (1980) gathered a series of articles from *Ethnology* that explain the rationale behind the Standard Cross-Cultural Sample (SCCS); the articles also present findings from specific codes using the SCCS. The appendixes in Frayser (1985) explain the procedures to follow in developing a cross-cultural survey on sexuality. Frayser (1985) used the cross-cultural method to demonstrate the constants and variants of sexuality as a human system of behavior. Schlegel and Barry (1991) demonstrated the application of the cross-cultural method to adolescence. The last section of Frayser and Whitby (1995) gives informative abstracts of many cross-cultural studies on human sexuality.

REFERENCES

American Psychiatric Association. (1994). *Diagnostic and statistical manual of mental disorders* (4th ed.). Washington, DC: Author.

Barry III, H., & Schlegel, A. (Eds.). (1980). *Cross-cultural samples and codes*. Pittsburgh, PA: University of Pittsburgh Press.

Baty, S. P. (1995). *American Monroe: The making of a body politic*. Berkeley, CA: University of California Press.

Beck, A. T. (1989). *Love is never enough: How couples can overcome misunderstandings, resolve conflicts, and solve relationship problems through cognitive therapy*. New York: Harper & Row.

Bolin, A. (1987). *In search of eve: Transsexual rites of passage*. South Hadley, MA: Bergin & Garvey.

Bolin, A., & Whelehan, P. (1999). *Perspectives on human sexuality*. Albany, NY: State University of New York Press.

Bolton, R. (1992). Mapping terra incognita: Sex research for AIDS prevention—an urgent agenda for the 1990s. In G. Herdt & S. Lindenbaum (Eds.), *The time of AIDS* (pp. 124–158). Newbury Park, CA: Sage.

Bullough, V. L. (1990). History in adult human sexual behavior with children and adolescents in western societies. In J. Feierman (Ed.), *Pedophilia: biosocial dimensions* (pp. 69–90). New York: Springer-Verlag.

Fausto-Sterling, A. (1985). *Myths of gender: Biological theories about women and men*. New York: Basic Books.

Ford, C. S., & Beach, F. A. (1951). *Patterns of sexual behavior*. New York: Harper & Row.

Frayser, S. G. (1985). *Varieties of sexual experience: An anthropological perspective on human sexuality*. New Haven, CT: HRAF Press.

Frayser, S. G. (1994). Defining normal childhood sexuality: An anthropological approach. *Annual Review of Sex Research, 5,* 173–217.

Frayser, S. G., & Whitby, T. J. (1995). *Studies in human sexuality: A selected guide*. Littleton, CO: Libraries Unlimited.

Friedl, E. (1999). Appendix: Sex the invisible. In D. N. Suggs & A. W. Miracle (Eds.), *Culture, biology, and sexuality* (pp. 90–107). Athens, GA: University of Georgia Press.

Goldman, R., & Goldman, J. (1982). *Children's sexual thinking: A comparative study of children aged 5 to 15 years in Australia, North America, Britain, and Sweden*. London: Routledge & Kegan Paul.

Gregor, T. (1985). *Anxious pleasures: The sexual lives of an Amazonian people*. Chicago: University of Chicago Press.

Herdt, G. (1981). *Guardians of the flutes: Idioms of masculinity*. New York: McGraw-Hill.

Herdt, G., & Stoller, R. (1990). *Intimate communications: Erotics and the study of culture*. New York: Columbia University Press.

Jhally, S. (1995a). *Dreamworlds 2* (2dn ed.). Northampton, MA: Media Education Foundation.

Jhally, S. (1995b). Image-based culture: Advertising and popular culture. In G. Dines & J. M. Humez (Eds.), *Gender, race, and class in media: A text-reader* (pp. 77–87). Thousand Oaks, CA: Sage.

Kendrick, W. (1987). *The secret museum: Pornography in modern culture*. New York: Viking.

Kinsey, A. C., Pomeroy, W. B., & Martin, C. E. (1948). *Sexual behavior in the human male*. Philadelphia: Saunders.

Kinsey, A. C., Pomeroy, W. B., Martin, C. E., & Gebhard, P. H. (1953). *Sexual behavior in the human female*. Philadelphia: Saunders.

Kroeber, A. L., & Kluckhohn, C. (1963). *Culture: A critical review of concepts and definitions*. New York: Vintage.

Laumann, E. O., Gagnon, J. H., Michael, R. T., & Michaels, S. (1994). *The social organization of sexuality: Sexual practices in the United States*. Chicago: University of Chicago Press.

Lawrence, R. J., Jr. (1989). *The poisoning of eros: Sexual values in conflict*. New York: Augustine Moore Press.

Martin, M. K., & Voorhies, B. (1975). *Female of the species*. New York: Columbia University Press.

Masters, W. H., & Johnson, V. E. (1966). *Human sexual response*. Boston: Little, Brown.

Masters, W. H., & Johnson, V. E. (1970). *Human sexual inadequacy*. Boston: Little, Brown.

Minturn, L., & Lambert, W. W. (1994). *Mothers of six cultures: Antecedents of child rearing*. New York: Wiley.

Murdock, G. P. (1949). *Social structure*. New York: Macmillan.

Nanda, S. (1990). *Neither man nor woman: The hijras of India*. Belmont, CA: Wadsworth.

Pelto, P. J., & Pelto, G. H. (1978). *Anthropological research: The structure of inquiry* (2nd ed.). Cambridge, England: Cambridge University Press.

Pomeroy, W. B., Flax, C., & Wheeler, C. C. (1982). *Taking a sex history: Interviewing and recording*. New York: The Free Press.

Reiss, I. L. (1986). *Journey into sexuality: An exploratory voyage*. Englewood Cliffs, NJ: Prentice-Hall.

Schlegel, A., & Barry, H. III (1991). *Adolescence: An anthropological inquiry*. New York: The Free Press.

Shostak, M. (1983). *Nisa: The life and words of a !Kung woman*. New York: Vintage Books.

Spradley, J. P. (1979). *The ethnographic interview*. New York: Holt, Rinehart & Winston.

Spradley, J. P. (1980). *Participant observation*. New York: Holt, Rinehart & Winston.

Suggs, D. N., & Miracle, A. W. (Eds.). (1993). *Culture and human sexuality: A reader*. Pacific Grove, CA: Brooks/Cole.

Suggs, D. N., & Miracle, A. W. (Eds.). (1999). *Culture, biology, and sexuality*. Athens, GA: University of Georgia Press.

Tafoya, T. (1990, November). *A new way of seeing*. Plenary speech presented at the annual meeting of the Society for the Scientific Study of Sexuality, Minneapolis, MN.

Talese, G. (1980). *Thy neighbor's wife*. Garden City, NY: Doubleday.

Torrey, E. F. (1973). *The mind game: Witchdoctors and psychiatrists*. New York: Bantam.

Vance, C. S. (1991). Anthropology rediscovers sexuality. *Social Science and Medicine, 33*(8), 875–884.

19

▼▼▼▼▼▼▼

Conceptualizing Diversity
in Sexuality Research

Michael R. Stevenson
Ball State University

Racism, sexism, ageism, and other prejudices are among the major events and forces currently shaping the global community (Marsella, 1998). Critics (e.g., Brown, 1989) have long recognized the impact of these prejudices on social science, arguing that science is based on a set of normative assumptions that value the experiences of some (i.e., White, male, heterosexual, young, middle-class, able-bodied North Americans) over others. As Vega (1992) wrote, "Given the current practice, we operate as if Anglophone normative performance constitutes a 'gold' standard for all cultural groups" (p. 381). More recently, Marsella (1998) noted, "Much of what we teach and know is confined to limited sectors of the world's population" (p. 1287). Furthermore, Prilleltensky (1997) argued that promoting respect and appreciation for diverse social identities, that is, valuing human diversity, is of prime importance in the evaluation of the moral implications of psychological perspectives. In other words, in social science, certain characteristics have defined the norm against which all others' experience has been evaluated, but researchers can no longer ignore human diversity in the conceptualization, execution, and interpretation of their research.

Potential alternatives to the prevailing paradigms in social science have been discussed for some time. More than a decade ago, Brown (1989) asked what it would mean if the experiences of being lesbian or gay were taken as the normative definitions of reality rather than as a special, tangential topic. Riger (1992) wrote about the value of a women-centered approach that takes the behavior and characteristics of women as the standard against which others' behavior is assessed. Both Brown (1989) and Riger (1992), as psychologists, directed their critiques toward their own scientific discipline; however, sexuality research is no less guilty of reifying potentially biased paradigms. Neither Brown nor Riger argued that gay/lesbian-centered or women-centered approaches should replace the status quo; that would simply substitute one set of biases for another, ultimately producing science that is equally distorted. However, these examples raise the epistemological questions that are at the root of discussions of the role of diversity in sexuality research design.

Defining Diversity

In contrast to conventional conceptualizations of diversity, which are often restricted to issues of race and ethnicity or, in rarer cases, gender, Thomas (1996) argued in *Redefining Diversity* that "diversity refers to *any* mixture of items characterized by differences and similarities" (p. 5). In the context of management, this conceptualization covers differences and similarities across job titles and work styles, across branches or levels of an organization, and across an infinite number of employee characteristics, including race and gender. As the definition implies and Thomas emphasized, "diversity is not synonymous with differences, but encompasses differences and similarities" (p. 5). Furthermore, he stressed that "diversity refers to the collective (all-inclusive) mixture of differences and similarities along a given dimension" (p. 7).

From this perspective, diversity refers to the collective, not just the pieces. To illustrate, Thomas (1996) offered the image of a homogeneous jar of red jelly beans, to which some green and a few purple jelly beans are added. According to Thomas, diversity is the mixture, not the green and purple candies. This is reminiscent of what the Gestalt psychologists claimed long ago: that the whole is more than the sum of the parts. In other words, when certain aspects of the workforce change, the relationships among the parts change, and therefore the whole changes. When we include in the universe of human sexual expression the experiences of groups that have been defined as "other," our understanding of sexuality is enriched.

This chapter applies a broad conceptualization of diversity to the process of conducting sexuality research in an attempt to promote research that will facilitate a more relevant and inclusive understanding of human sexual behavior. To accomplish this, I describe a conceptual model of the research process to provide a framework within which to discuss diversity-related biases in the way sexuality research is conceived, designed, executed, and published. In addition, an analysis of diversity issues in research published in *The Journal of Sex Research* provides insight into the extent to which diversity-related bias is evident in the extant literature.

To be successful in this effort, the relevant diversity dimensions must be specified; otherwise, every similarity or difference ends up as part of the domain. Although a case could be made to include other variables (e.g., the extent of one's sexual experience or interest in sexual stimuli), this chapter is limited to the discussion of ethnicity, gender, socioeconomic status (SES), national origin, sexual orientation, age, disability, and religious viewpoint. Bear in mind that everyone involved in sexuality research—whether as a participant, researcher, or consumer—can be classified along each of these dimensions. The current majority culture in the United States has an ethnicity just as ethnic minorities can be ascribed to ethnic categories. Regardless of their level of awareness, heterosexual people have sexual orientations, just as gay, lesbian, and bisexual people have sexual orientations. Most humans are *temporarily enabled*; that is, they will experience, at some point in their lives, a temporary or permanent limitation in their physical capacities.

Diversity-Related Biases

In sexuality research, *diversity-related biases* refer to the extent to which various prejudices (e.g., racism, sexism, heterosexism) distort the way research is conceived, designed, executed, interpreted, and published. For example, to the extent that certain groups or perspectives are underrepresented in sexuality research, whether as participants or researchers, our knowledge of human sexuality may be distorted accordingly. If sexuality research has been dominated by heterosexual, male researchers of European descent who study White, heterosexual, male participants, to what extent are the results of that research relevant to humankind in general?

The various processes that determine who participates in research clearly demonstrate this important point. Tiefer (1991) argued quite convincingly that benchmark studies of human sexuality, which produced influential theoretical constructions, were based on data gathered from samples selected using criteria (e.g., women who reach orgasm easily) that do not reflect the experience of the broad population of women. Similar arguments can be made concerning potential biases that are created when using any self-selected or volunteer sample because people who volunteer for participation in sexuality research are different, often in unspecified ways, from those who volunteer for other research and those who do not participate in research at all (see chap. 5, this volume; Kazdin, 1998; Stevenson, 1990; Turner, 1999; Wiederman, 1999).

The important point here is to consider the relationships between who participates in sexuality research and a litany of diversity variables (e.g., ethnicity, age, disability, sexual orientation, religiosity, national origin, economic, ability status). Asked simply, are individuals with certain characteristics (e.g., Euro-American, middle class, Christian, male) more likely to participate in sexuality research than people with other characteristics (e.g., people of color; gay, lesbian and bisexual people; people with disabilities)? Whether questions concerning diversity-related biases are empirical, conceptual, or methodological, they are often overlooked in the extant literature on human sexuality.

THE RESEARCH PROCESS

Scholars often make a distinction between qualitative and quantitative research and differ in their assessment of whether one type of research is inherently less biased than the other (Peplau & Conrad, 1989). Marsella (1998) claimed that increased use of qualitative research would enhance our knowledge of context, meaning, and power asymmetries; reduce ethnocentric bias; and broaden global understanding. In contrast, when qualitative studies of homogeneous groups repeatedly sample from the same population, the diversity of human experience is ignored (Cannon, Higginbotham, & Leung, 1988). As Simon (1999) explained:

> The choice between quantitative methods and qualitative methods, both of which have been and remain sources of major contributions, is often a choice between knowing a little about a lot of persons or knowing a lot about relatively few persons. If one's interest requires being fully responsive to the marked pluralization of American social life, then being concerned with differences of age, gender, race, ethnicity, socioeconomic status, and education makes survey research, for all its limitations, extraordinarily useful. In the context of such relevant forms of diversity, the questions of age, variety of partners, and frequency of sexual activities can take on a powerfully suggestive significance. . . . If, on the other hand, it is the specificities of experience, such as meaning and emotion, that are the focus of interest, then a looser, more ethnographic or quasi-clinical approach is clearly called for. However, even at this level of inquiry the questions of representativeness cannot be ignored. (p. 213)

Determining whether one approach is more sensitive to diversity issues than another is not among the goals of this discussion. On the contrary, as Simon (1999) implied, different approaches to research provide different kinds of data and, to some extent, answer different questions that will be differentially influenced by diversity-related biases. Moreover, this nomenclature presents a false dichotomy to some extent (Crawford & Kimmel, 1999) and attempts have been made to bridge the two approaches in the study of sexuality (Tolman & Szalacha, 1999).

Although qualitative research has been underutilized, ideally sexual scientists would value each approach for its unique contributions to our understanding of human sexuality. The model presented in Fig. 19.1 is intended to provide insight into the importance of diversity issues in sexuality research regardless of the approach. In many respects the model is self-explanatory; however, it may be useful to briefly highlight its primary components.

As Fig. 19.1 shows, the research process can be loosely divided into three interconnected components. The first, the *content*, is the result of the interaction between the research questions, the purposes of the study, and the conceptual framework (Maxwell, 1998). The second, the *process*, includes the research design and methods. The third represents the *products* of these processes, the interpretation of the research results, the dissemination of those findings, and the incorporation of the research findings into the knowledge base.

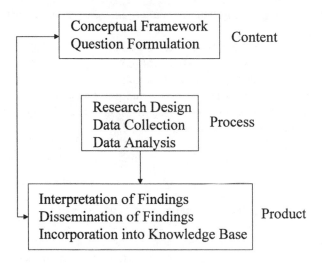

FIG. 19.1   A conceptual model of sexuality research.

Content

The conceptual framework of a study is constructed with ideas from a variety of sources (Maxwell, 1998). In addition to the formal theories that are in vogue at the time the research is initiated, much research on human sexuality springs from the rescarcher's own assumptions and personal experience, folk theories implicit in popular culture, attempts by the researcher to frame a social problem, or attempts by government agencies to seek answers to policy relevant questions (see chap. 2, this volume). A scholar's personal investment in his or her own research can be seen as a source of insight, theory, and data to exploit or as a potential source of bias to minimize. Qualitative researchers are more likely than quantitative re-searchers to explicitly acknowledge the interpretive role they play and to empha-size the reflexivity between themselves and their topic (Maxwell, 1998).

The historical context can also play a role. For example, the conceptual context of research on sexual behavior changed radically with the introduction of oral con-traception and the spread of HIV infection. The current ethnicity and age-related shifts in the demographics of the U.S. American population also signal changes in the historical context. As Maxwell (1998) suggested, published research should not necessarily be privileged over other sources in the construction of the conceptual framework because assumptions imbedded in the extant literature can potentially blind researchers to alternative conceptualizations of new data.

Some aspects of the conceptual framework are typically discussed in the intro-ductory sections of research reports when authors summarize and critique the extant relevant literature and discuss any theoretical underpinnings of the re-search. Others aspects of the conceptual framework, personal interests or motives, for example, are often left implicit, particularly in conventional reports of quantitative research.

Based on the more or less explicit conceptual framework, the researcher formulates the research questions. Unlike quantitative research which starts (ideally) with well-defined, testable hypotheses, research questions in qualitative research are refined as the process of data collection and interpretation proceeds. Whereas the process of quantitative research is sequential or linear, that of qualitative research is iterative or simultaneous (Maxwell, 1998).

Process

The research process includes several subcomponents: choosing a phenomenon, devising a way to measure it, determining who will participate in the study (whose experience will be assessed), and developing a research design (Hyde, 1985). Different kinds of research questions lead researchers to design studies in different ways. Theoretically, in quantitative research, specific methods are chosen because they provide the best avenue through which to answer predetermined questions. In contrast, qualitative researchers assume that the methods they choose may influence the questions that evolve over the course of the study. Thus, if Fig. 19.1 were to represent only quantitative research, an arrow would point from the content box to the process box; whereas to represent qualitative research, the arrow would point in both directions.

Most quantitative studies of human sexuality test hypotheses about linear relationships among variables or human qualities that are not easily brought under the researcher's control. As a result, most designs used in sexuality research are explicitly or inherently correlational or descriptive. Questions about cause–effect relationships require experimental designs. Because sexuality researchers have so little control over the experiences and behaviors of the people who participate in their studies, experimental designs are most often applied to questions concerning the effectiveness of a therapeutic or educational intervention or the effects of limited exposure to sexual stimuli.

Maxwell (1998) encouraged researchers to continually seek ways to test the veracity of particular interpretations of qualitative data, weighing them against potential alternatives. His discussion of *researcher bias* and *reactivity* is particularly relevant to our concerns about diversity-related biases. Researcher bias refers to the ways the researcher's theories, values, and so forth might distort data collection or analysis. Reactivity refers to the effect the researcher has on the setting or individuals studied. Rather than attempting to minimize or control for these effects (or simply deny their potential), qualitative researchers assume they influence their informants and attempt to understand how such influence affects the products of the research.

Product

Although qualitative and quantitative research are quite different in many ways, if the results are to affect the way we understand human sexuality, either within the research community or more broadly across a culture, these results have to be interpreted within the conceptual context and disseminated so they can be incorporated into the knowledge base. Major studies of human sexuality are often published as books (e.g., Kinsey, Pomeroy, & Martin, 1948; Kinsey, Pomeroy, Martin, & Gebhard, 1953; Laumann, Gagnon, Michael, & Michaels, 1994). Less comprehensive work is more likely to become part of the extant literature through publication in a journal or other periodical.

Sexuality research is now published in a wide variety of periodicals. Some are discipline-based journals (e.g., *Psychological Bulletin*) that publish articles on a wide variety of topics, whereas others publish only reports of research on sexuality (e.g., *The Journal of Sex Research*). Some are peer-reviewed; that is, articles are published only after undergoing some form of review by a panel of experts familiar with research on that topic. Using this process, elite journals reject the majority of the manuscripts that are submitted for consideration. Other journals publish virtually anything and may require subsidy by the author. Book publishers vary considerably in the way and extent to which the material is evaluated before publication. The Internet has provided yet another avenue for the dissemination of research findings, although norms have not yet been established for the evaluation of electronically published resources.

The point is that publication quality varies widely. However, once published, the research is more or less available to other scholars for incorporation into the knowledge base. A few scholars also attempt to disseminate their work to more general audiences in trade books, popular magazines, or on the Internet, and these, too, can have an impact on the conceptual context of future research.

SOURCES OF DIVERSITY-RELATED BIAS
IN SEXUALITY RESEARCH

Advice on avoiding bias in research is available from a variety of sources. For example, feminist psychologists and cross-cultural researchers have provided guidance on how to avoid sexist and ethnocentric bias (Denmark, Russo, Frieze, & Sechzer, 1988; Gonzáles-Calvo, Gonzáles, & Lorig, 1997; Hyde, 1985; McHugh, Koeske, & Frieze, 1986; Rabinowitz & Sechzer, 1993). Much of their advice generalizes to avoiding other forms of diversity-related bias and is included in the following discussion.

To provide substance to the discussion of potential sources of diversity-related bias in sexuality research, in general, and to assess its potential impact in the extant sexuality literature more specifically, each of the 208 empirical studies of human samples published in Volumes 25 (1988) to 35 (1998) of *The Journal of Sex Research* (*JSR*) were coded on a wide range of diversity-relevant variables. The coding process was executed over the course of an academic year (1998–1999) by two individuals who completed the work as part of their duties as graduate assistants.[1]

Published by The Society for the Scientific Study of Sexuality, *JSR* has been a leader in the publication of scholarly research on sexuality for more than 30 years. *JSR* was chosen for this project because it is the oldest and probably the most general sexuality journal. By 1999, circulation for the quarterly periodical had reached approximately 1,700. According to the masthead (1999), *JSR* is devoted to publishing

> articles relevant to the variety of disciplines involved in the scientific study of sexuality. *JSR* is designed to stimulate research and to promote an interdisciplinary understanding of the diverse topics in contemporary sexual science. *JSR* publishes empirical reports, theoretical essays, literature reviews, methodological articles, historical articles, clinical reports, teaching papers, book reviews and letters to the editor.

It is abstracted or indexed in nearly 40 print and electronic databases, including *Social Science Citation Index* and *Index Medicus*. I have served as book review editor for *JSR* since 1993. In the following sections, I illustrate the discussion of diversity-related bias in sexuality research with the results of our examination of empirical research disseminated through *JSR*.

Conceptual Framework

Feminist and other critical analyses of the epistemology and theory underlying social science research provide frameworks within which to evaluate the influence of sexism, racism, heterosexism, ageism, and the like on sexuality research. For example, the epistemological issues raised in the introduction to this chapter are relevant here; that is, there is value in using multiple paradigms (e.g., women-centered; gay/lesbian-centered) to interpret research findings. In-depth theoretical critiques are also helpful in identifying diversity-related biases. For example, Eagly and Wood (1999) critiqued two influential theoretical frameworks in their re-analysis of data on sex differences in mate-selection criteria. Although these data have long been used to buttress evolutionary theories, Eagly and Wood argued that they are better understood in the context of contemporary social structures.

In addition, many well-accepted theories concerning human sexuality have little or no cross-cultural validation. For example, Masters and Johnson's work has been criticized for being based on a culturally homogeneous group (White, heterosexual, well-educated, middle-class couples; Petrak & Keane, 1998). Given the differences among cultures, it is inappropriate simply to assume that sexological constructs are equally valid across cultural groups (see chap. 18, this volume). Both within North America and transnationally, basic research is needed to demonstrate that constructs have similar meaning in different cultural contexts (Petrak & Keane, 1998; Vega, 1992). Western concepts and methods do not adequately describe, explain, or value the culturally distinct experiences of the diverse groups of interest to sex researchers (Marsella, 1998). Petrak and Keane's (1998) description of Ayurvedic and Unani medical explanations for erectile dysfunction are illustrative in this context. More and more often, cultural groups and communities are refusing to accept research at face value when it is not sensitive to their interests (Vega, 1992). If cultural insensitivity is rooted in the procedural norms of research, as Rogler (1999) suggested, we need to develop culturally conscious norms.

The influence of ethnocentric and stereotypical thinking, implicit in some theoretical models, can be exacerbated by the use of imprecise terminology (Hyde, 1985). As central as they are to the understanding of human sexuality, potentially ambiguous terms, including *masculinity* and *femininity*, and *sex* and *gender*, when used without caution can contribute to diversity-related bias (Stevenson, Paludi, Black, & Whitley, 1994). Consider the term *sexism*, for example. Although technically the term refers to prejudice or discrimination based on sex, it is often used to refer specifically to discrimination against women. Eagly (1995) noted that stereotypes of women are currently slightly more positive than those of men. So, is it still *sexism* when men experience sex discrimination? Or is that reverse sexism? More specifically, is the sexual double standard simply sexism applied to sexual behavior or should the sexual double standard be understood as distinct from sexism? Similarly, to what extent is heterosexism simply sexism applied across sexual orientations (Stevenson & Medler, 1995)?

Stereotypes of ethnic minorities, such as machismo in Hispanic men (Gonzáles-Calvo et al., 1997) or sexual passivity in Asian women (Petrak & Keane, 1998), are also sources of potential bias in sexuality research. To complicate things further, group stereotypes may not apply equally to members of subgroups, as Eagly and Kite (1987) demonstrated with their findings that particular stereotypes of nationalities do not apply equally to men and women. If gender stereotypes contain a kernel of truth (Hyde, 1985), the same may be true for ethnic stereotypes; for example, Meston and colleagues (Meston, Trapnell, & Gorzalka, 1996, 1998) found that students of Asian ancestry held less permissive sexual attitudes, were less knowledgeable about sex, and were less sexually experienced than their North American counterparts. However, we must avoid letting stereotypical thinking dominate the conceptual context of sexuality research.

Race is an ambiguous construct with no explicit, agreed-on definition (Zuckerman, 1990). Although there have been attempts to debunk the concept as a biological fact since at least the 1950s, taxonomists have argued for as few as 3 and as many as 37 races (Yee, Fairchild, Weizmann, & Wyatt, 1993). This ambiguity applies to the group typically referred to as *White, Caucasian,* or, more recently, *Euro-American* as much as it does to other ethnic and cultural groups. Although these terms are often used synonymously, they have different origins and refer to distinct, albeit overlapping, groups. Although they currently account for the majority of the U.S. population, little attention has been given to the heterogeneity among those labeled *White*. The U.S. Census includes no subclassifications, although other U.S. government documents define White people as including those who have family origins in Europe, North Africa, or the Middle East (Bhopal & Donaldson, 1998). In contrast, considerable attention has been paid to the heterogeneity of other racial/ethnic groups. For example, the categories *Asian* and *Pacific Islander* have been subdivided into 28 groups of Asians and 18 groups of Pacific Islanders (Jenkins & Parron, 1995).

To add to the confusion, the terms *race* and *ethnicity* have been obfuscated in the policy arena, and this confusion has been adopted in social science (Yee et al., 1993). Although I cannot hope to resolve this ambiguity here, it is reasonable to suggest that racial groupings loosely based on observable physical features are of little use in understanding human sexual behavior. Ethnicity, as a culturally constructed concept, may prove more useful.

Diversity-related bias in the conceptual context of research can be so ingrained in the way research is conducted (Rogler, 1999), it is often difficult to detect. Implicit in the foregoing discussion, the language used in textbooks and research reports may provide clues to underlying diversity-related bias. Campbell and Schram (1995) found that, although textbook authors have been successful in avoiding sexist language, the majority of social science methodology books do not yet include discussion of feminist challenges to conventional research methods. If this is true, it is unlikely that they have dealt with diversity-related problems more generally.

In the 1994 edition of their *Publication Manual*, the American Psychological Association (APA) included guidelines for the reduction of bias in language concerning gender, sexual orientation, racial and ethnic identity, disabilities, and age. This is significant because journals in many disciplines require authors to prepare manuscripts according to the APA *Manual*. As part of our examination of studies published in *JSR*, the coders generated a list of examples of biased language based on the APA guidelines and subsequently coded studies for the use of biased language. In response to feminist critiques, the guidelines encourage writers to avoid use of the term *subject* to describe the people who contribute data, use parallel terms when describing groups of people (e.g., *men and women* rather than *men and girls*), and avoid using *man* in the generic sense. In *JSR*, 54.9% of authors used the terms *participant* or *respondent*, whereas 26.4% used *subject*. Only three cases of the use of unparallel terms were found. No examples of the use of *man* as a generic noun or at the end of a title (e.g., *chairman*) or other sexist language were located.

In contrast to a lack of sexist language in published sexuality research, considerable confusion remains concerning the labels for ethnic groups. The APA (1994) guidelines indicate that either multiword or color labels are appropriate, but that scholars should use the terms that participants prefer when possible. In *JSR*, multiword labels (e.g., Asian-American) were used slightly more often (23.6%) than color labels (e.g., Black; 18.8%), and the coders found only two cases where an outdated term was used to refer to an ethnic minority group.

Our relatively superficial coding scheme cannot produce a thorough assessment of diversity-related bias in the conceptual context of sexuality research. Indeed, raising researchers' awareness of widely held biases is, in some ways, akin to making fish aware of the water they inhabit. Regardless of the difficulty of the task, increasing awareness of these biases is of utmost importance if the knowledge produced by sexuality research is to be broadly applicable or relevant.

Question Formulation

Personal, institutional, and cultural biases can affect the kinds of questions researchers ask. For example, the vast majority of research on contraception focuses on women (Whitley & Schofield, 1985–1986). This implies that men have little responsibility for contraceptive decision making and is consistent with a cultural bias that blames women for unintended pregnancy. Research on public sexual behavior between adult men has often been based on the assumption that such behavior occurs primarily between men who identify as gay and in venues that cater specifically to this group (e.g., "dark-rooms" in gay clubs), although such behaviors often occur is other places (e.g., upscale, heterosexually oriented health clubs) between so-called *straight* men who insist they are not gay (Leap, 1999).

Considering the historical period in question, it is not surprising that empirical reports concerning HIV/AIDS were more common than reports on any other topic in our analysis of *JSR*. Of the 208 studies coded, 36 focused on HIV and an additional 13 considered risky sexual behavior or compliance with safer sex guidelines. Taken together, these studies accounted for nearly 24% of the total. Of the 20 topical categories that were generated during the coding process, only 3 additional categories accounted for more that 10% of studies. One category, general sexual practices, included 24 studies, but is not directly relevant to this discussion. However, the coding demonstrated that two diversity dimensions are of considerable interest to those who contribute to *JSR*. Gender-related issues were central to 26 studies, and 23 studies assessed attitudes toward lesbian and gay people or focused in some other way on sexual orientation.

In contrast to the attention given to gender and sexual orientation, only three studies were coded under the category *gender and race*. To their credit, the editors of *JSR* attempted to focus more attention on ethnicity by publishing two special sections on ethnicity—one in 1996 (Vol. 33, No. 4) and the second in the following issue (Vol. 34, No. 1). Categories corresponding to the other specified diversity dimensions were not salient during the coding process. However, *JSR* published a special issue entitled "Bodies Besieged: The Impact of Chronic and

Serious Physical Illness on Sexuality, Passion, and Desire" (1996, Vol. 33, No. 3) as a way to deal with certain aspects of the issue of disability.

Through special issues and sections on chronic illness and ethnicity, *JSR* has attempted to overcome some of the omissions in the scientific literature. However, these are only exceptions to the general rule that, when most researchers are from a homogeneous group, only certain questions get asked (Hyde, 1985). Solutions to this problem are obvious, but difficult to implement. Finding ways to increase both the heterogeneity and diversity awareness among researchers requires major changes in the way academic departments recruit, nurture, and train both students and new faculty. Given that most research on human sexuality is executed by scholars in narrowly defined disciplines, rather than interdisciplinary departments focused explicitly on sexuality, this is indeed difficult to achieve because it means working toward similar goals across an array of disciplines.

Design Choices

As suggested earlier, most studies of human sexuality are descriptive or correlational and more than 82% of those published in *JSR* fit this description. Only 34 (16.3%) studies were experimental, which leads to the inevitable conclusion that scholars can draw few legitimate conclusions about the causes of human sexual behavior. Historically, *JSR* has been closely associated with quantitative researchers, so it is not surprising that only three of the studies coded could be categorized as qualitative. In some ways, this preference for quantitative research reflects a greater interest in questions concerning "who does what"; questions that date to the origins of modern sex research and Kinsey's data (Kinsey et al., 1948, 1953). As researchers become more interested in what those behaviors mean to the people who engage in them, the need for qualitative research becomes more urgent.

Sample Selection. Potential sources of diversity-related bias are most readily apparent in the characteristics of the people who contribute data for sexuality research. The coding of studies in *JSR* showed that we know more about college students than any other definable group. College students were sampled in 43.3% (90) of studies, whereas only 13 studies (6.3%) were based on random samples and only 28 studies (13.5%) were based on what could be described as U.S. national samples.

Within a particular historical period, college students in the United States represent a distinct group with regard to national origin, age, SES, and ethnicity. The preponderance of college student samples undoubtedly affects the overall homogeneity of samples reported in *JSR*. Of the 208 studies coded, 49 (23.6%) were based on samples from outside the United States. Of the 148 (52.9%) studies reporting mean ages, the means ranged from 12 to 72.5 years, but the average mean was approximately 28 years. An additional 16 studies (7.7%) reported median ages with an average median (25 years) similar to the average mean. It is unfortunate that SES of participants was specified in only 25 studies (12%), with 21 studies (10.1%) reporting mean years of education (range 10 to 16.4; $M = 13.8$) and 13 studies (6.3%) reporting average annual income (range $12,686–$62,499; ($M = $34,485). Perhaps most surprising, the ethnic composition of the samples was described in only 51.8% of cases. Only 63 research reports (22.5%) included data on the percentage of African-American participants in the sample. Considering the other major ethnic groups, only 36 studies (17.3%) reported data on the percentage of Hispanic participants, with an additional 5 studies (2.4%) reporting Latino/a participation; 24 studies (11.5%) reported Asian-American participation; and 31 studies (14.9%) used an *other* category.

Ours was not the first attempt to examine the extent to which ethnicity is considered in sexuality research. Wiederman, Maynard, and Fretz (1996) examined this issue in their analysis of 25 years of sexuality research published in two prominent periodicals (i.e., *The Journal of Sex Research* and *Archives of Sexual Behavior*). Of the 1,123 research reports published between 1971 and 1995, only 26.4% reported the ethnic composition of the sample, and ethnicity was considered a relevant variable in only 7.3% of cases. In the 82 articles that focused explicitly on ethnicity, 44 compared one ethnic group to another, whereas 38 were based on a race homogeneous approach. Although it is not made explicit in the published report, studies exclusively sampling White or U.S. Americans, regardless of whether the results were interpreted within an ethnic context, were not included in this category. In other words, these 38 studies examined data gathered from individuals representing one definable ethnic group to which people of color could be ascribed.

We also need to question whether the genders have been equitably represented as participants in sexuality research. Of the 208 studies coded, 134 studies (64.4%) included female participants, whereas 165 studies (79.3%) included male participants. Only a single study explicitly included transsexual–transgendered participants. An extension of the Wiederman et al. (1996) study (Wiederman, Fretz, & Maynard, 1995) considered the status of women in sexuality research and demonstrated that, when participants in sexuality research were of a single gender, men were about 50% more likely than women to be the focus of the study.

In contrast to the recent reduction of sexist bias in studies published in *JSR*, heterosexist bias remains rampant. That is, researchers continue to assume that participants in their studies are heterosexual. The sexual orientation of the participants was specified in less than half (48.1%) of the studies despite that more than 11% of studies explicitly focused on sexual orientation in some way. Sexual orientation and sexual behavior were conflated (i.e., a person who has engaged in an act of heterosexual sex is assumed to be heterosexual, a person who has engaged in an act of homosexual sex is assumed to be homosexual) in 43 studies (20.7%). Only 59 studies (28.4%) reported the proportion of respondents who were heterosexual, 31 studies (14.9%) indicated the proportion of respondents who were gay or lesbian, and 23 studies (11.1%) reported the percentage of bisexual respondents.

With the exception of the special issue on illness and disability, research in *JSR* has ignored disability status. Attention to religious preference has also been negligible. Religious affiliation of participants was reported in only 15 studies (7.2%).

Taken together, these data suggest that research published in *JSR* is almost as likely to include women as it does men and that journal editors have been successful in avoiding some forms of biased language. Although Wiederman et al. (1996) reported that the attention given to ethnicity increased over the 25 years they examined, the results of our assessment show that, in general, authors of empirical articles still do not describe the diversity within their samples of participants nor do they adequately consider diversity variables in their analyses, particularly when diversity in broadly construed.

Operational Definitions. Much research in the social sciences can be described as culturally insensitive where concepts developed in the White U.S. middle class are applied to other groups without concern for cultural differences. As a result, concepts developed in one context do not always transfer productively to others. The concept of *family decision making*, although useful in understanding the dynamics of U.S. middle-class families, is not culturally salient among impoverished Puerto Rican families. *Major depression*, as it is conceived by the U.S. American dominant culture and echoed in the *DSM* (American Psychiatric Association, 1994), is not reflected in the way mental ill health is conceived among some Native American groups (Rogler, 1999; Vega, 1992). Conceptualizations of what it means to be gay or to have a gay identity vary across cultures and historical periods (Stevenson, 1995, 1998).

Typical procedures used to provide evidence of content validity (e.g., the judgments of a panel of experts) produce scales or questionnaires that may only be valid within the culture from which the experts were drawn. Research shows that "when instruments are based on the expert rational analyses model of content validity and used outside the American cultural mainstream, errors proliferate" (Rogler, 1999, p. 427). Similar problems arise when, in attempts to maintain standardization, questionnaires are translated word-for-word from one language to another (usually from English to another language) without regard to idioms and local word usage.

The central question here concerns the extent to which people who differ along various diversity dimensions interpret stimuli (e.g., questions in surveys or interviews) in the same way. For example, a sexual health intervention for African-American women led one group of practitioners to the realization that their clients did not share their conceptualization of masturbation (Cherry, Smith, & Robinson, 1999). Although the practitioners used the term *masturbation* to refer to any pleasurable, autoerotic activity, their African-American female clients used a much narrower definition. For the clients, masturbation referred only to behaviors that included vaginal penetration. O'Sullivan (1995) determined empirically that, among the college students at her institution, a high number of sexual partners for women was 7, whereas for men it was 13. Ford and Norris (1991) showed that data about sexual behavior could be successfully gathered from African-American and Hispanic youths in face-to-face interviews, but that members of some gender and ethnic groups (i.e., Hispanic females) have more difficulty than others understanding clinical terms such as *vagina* and *anus*.

Homogeneity among those who create the operational definitions used in research can also lead to bias. Eagly and Carli (1981) argued that researchers may choose operational definitions that reflect their own interests and areas of knowledge. As a result, ethnic or sex or other diversity-related differences may be artifacts of design; that is, they may be the result of different distributions of interests or knowledge, rather than reflections of sex, ethnic, or other diversity-related differences among groups of participants.

Data Collection. Diversity issues are relevant to data collection because measurement instruments are both devices to elicit information from respondents and sources of information respondents use to determine their task and arrive at a response (Schwarz, 1999). To what extent does self-report behavior interact with the diversity classification? Do members of some groups engage in more impression management (i.e., socially desirable responding) than do others either in general or in some circumstances (e.g., with different-ethnicity interviewers; Catania, 1999)? When Romer et al. (1997) compared responses to a computer-assisted interview to those in a person-to-person interview, they were careful to match the gender of the interviewer (or voice in the case of the computer) with the gender of the respondent, but their report does not indicate whether the same vigilance was used concerning other potentially important diversity variables.

The circumstances under which data are gathered can also influence respondents' behavior (see chap. 3, this volume). Catania (1999) described how the diversity-related status of both the interviewer and respondent can potentially influence data collection, yet data investigating these issues are scarce. Published reports of quantitative studies rarely include enough information on the data collection process to evaluate what some have referred to as *reactivity* (Maxwell, 1998) and others have called *experimenter effects* (Rosenthal, 1966). These effects have been demonstrated for gender and ethnic identity (Catania, 1999; Hyde, 1985; Kazdin, 1998). Sexual feelings may be more likely to be reported to a same-sex interviewer than one of the other sex (Walters, Shurley, & Parsons, 1962). Children may perform better with female experimenters, whereas adults may perform better with males (Rumenik, Capasso, & Hendrick, 1977). In sexuality research, cues concerning the experimenter's sexual orientation might be particularly important especially when sexual orientation or a related attitude is the topic of concern.

When data are collected in groups, the diversity composition of the group may also have an impact (Etaugh, Houtler, & Ptasnik, 1988). Unanswered empirical questions in this realm abound. Do respondents' reports of sexual behavior differ when data are collected in homogeneous rather than heterogeneous groups? Does the diversity dimension on which the group is homogeneous matter?

Diversity-related observer effects may also have an impact on data collection. Hyde (1985) indicated that "scientists are no more immune than lay people to having stereotyped expectations for the behavior of females and males. These stereotyped expectations might lead scientists to find stereotyped gender differences in behavior where there are none" (p. 11). It is reasonable to assume that the same could be true for other diversity dimensions given the prevalence of their associated stereotypes.

Eagly and Carli's (1981) data added yet another twist to experimenter and observer effects. They demonstrated that male and female authors describe results in somewhat different ways. In their meta-analysis of the persuasion literature, in studies published by male authors, females were more conforming and influenceable than were men, whereas studies with female authors found no sex difference. Making the (probably unrealistic) assumption that those who publish studies were the same sex as those who collected the data, one might hypothesize that sex differences occur in the presence of male experimenters but not when females collect data. It is more likely, however, that female authors more often report nonsignificant sex differences, whereas male authors only mention sex differences when they are statistically significant.

Although not intentionally distorting the data, Eagly and Carli argued that authors reported findings in a way that cast their own sex in the best light. Women authors might be more invested in demonstrating the absence of a sex difference, so they would include reports of no sex difference; in contrast, men authors might be more invested in showing women to be more easily persuaded and would neglect to report the absence of sex differences. Similarly, Hall (1978) reported that female researchers found men to be more inaccurate in decoding nonverbal cues than male researchers had.

Generalizing from these findings to other diversity dimensions and domains of research, one might hypothesize that when research is dominated by a homogeneous group, particularly in the presence of well-accepted stereotypes and widespread prejudices, the probability of diversity-related bias increases. In the 208 studies we examined, 54.8% of first authors had names usually given to males, whereas 42.8% had names usually used by females. Over the 25 years of sexuality research Wiederman et al. (unpublished) examined, 60.8% of first authors were men and 25.5% were women. Although men have contributed to sexuality research more often than women, it is impossible to determine from published reports the extent to which other specific groups are overrepresented.

Although qualitative researchers consider their impact on the data collection process as a matter of course, quantitative researchers do not. In either case, researchers need to be aware of how their status along various diversity dimensions may have an impact on data collection, whether with regard to reactivity or researcher bias.

Data Analysis

The point of applying statistical tests to the results of quantitative research is to determine the existence of statistically significant differences. In a very basic sense, the logic of the scientific method assumes that scientists are looking for differences. Such research cannot be adequately designed to demonstrate similarities. Even when research fails to produce evidence for a statistically significant difference, the logic of the scientific method does not allow the conclusion that the difference of interest does not exist. There is always the possibility that evidence for the difference would be found if only the study had more statistical power, if more samples were drawn, if the measures were of better quality, if a different operational definition was used, and so forth.

Whether researchers should routinely test for diversity-related differences is an open question. Under the assumption that evidence for differences is sought primarily when they are predicted by existing stereotypes, the absence of routine reporting of diversity-related differences decreases the likelihood of reporting null findings and reinforces stereotypes. As a result, it also hampers the use of meta-analytic and other techniques that allow researchers to consider diversity dimensions in their critiques of broad areas of research (Eagly, 1987, 1990, 1994, 1997). Furthermore, if a diversity variable is correlated with a dependent variable, including the diversity variable as an independent variable in the analysis increases the power of the test for the other independent variables, even if the diversity variable has no theoretical relevance to the research question. On the other hand, atheoretical testing for diversity differences can produce many incidental or artifactual findings that may further cloud our understanding of these differences.

Interpretation

Given the leap of faith it requires (Hyde, 1985), interpreting research results necessitates considerable awareness of diversity-related bias as well as considerable restraint. The degree to which sexuality research is based on homogeneous samples severely restricts the extent to which findings are relevant to our understanding of other groups. In other words, do conclusions based on samples of White, middle-class, Christian, college students from the United States generalize to other broader groups?

The epistemological questions raised earlier are particularly relevant to interpreting data because the interpretations a researcher offers about a finding reflect a particular perspective, and there are always multiple views from which to interpret findings. For example, based on a finding cited repeatedly in the sexuality literature, it can be stated (without interpretation) that, compared with heterosexual women, heterosexual men report having more sex partners, masturbating more frequently, engaging more frequently in extra-dyadic sexual behavior, and holding more permissive attitudes about a variety of aspects of sexuality (Oliver &

Hyde, 1993). How this constellation of findings is interpreted, however, depends on a point of view. Taking women's behavior as the accepted norm, men could be described as having above-normal levels of sexual interest, or as being promiscuous, licentious, or even uncontrollably libidinal. Conversely, if men's behavior is considered normative, women's behavior could be interpreted as prudish, provincial, or as evidence for a lack of normal levels of desire.

Rind's (1998) analysis of textbooks provides another example of how widespread interpretive practice camouflages implicit moral assumptions. He demonstrated that textbook authors often use examples of transgenerational sexual interactions (i.e., sexual behavior between men and boys) in cultures outside the United States and in earlier historical periods to demonstrate the normalcy and acceptability of sexual behavior between adult men in Western contexts. However, the same textbook authors present transgenerational sex (in the West) as pathological and unacceptable (i.e., sexual abuse).

Finally, caution must be used in interpreting any diversity-related difference because differences superficially associated with diversity-related variables may be confounded with other variables that have not been assessed in a study or in a research literature. To find a statistically significant difference between a group labeled *White* and another labeled *Asian American*, for example, tells us little about whether the difference has anything to do with ethnicity per se. Variation across individuals within ethnic groups has been shown to be greater than variation between such groups (Zuckerman, 1990). Whereas some apparent ethnic differences are better attributed to economic status, as in Jenkins and Parron's (1995) finding that poverty was more important than ethnicity in predicting adolescent pregnancy, other ethnic differences are not. For example, Weinberg and Williams (1988) found that differences in sexual attitudes and behaviors between African Americans and Whites can not be explained by social class. However, sometimes the data necessary for investigating such issues are lacking. My own work on the effects of divorce on gender-role development of offspring (Stevenson & Black, 1988) demonstrated that, among studies of boys where both ethnicity and economic status were specified, there were no studies of middle-class African-American samples. Without such data, it was impossible to attribute findings to either ethnicity or SES.

Dissemination and Incorporation into the Literature

In addition to funding agencies, publishing organizations act as important gatekeepers in the conduct and dissemination of research (Rogler, 1999). Simply adding women or representatives of ethnic or other minorities to those institutions does not necessarily change the way an organization functions (e.g., Howes & Stevenson, 1993). However, the absence of diversity on review panels and editorial boards undoubtedly increases the probability that diversity-related issues will continue to be ignored. In quantitative research, whether a manuscript gets published depends, in part, on finding a statistically significant difference of some importance. In the absence of efficient empirical ways to demonstrate similarities among groups, differences receive more attention in the published literature.

There are also political processes that shape what gets published and when. Eagly (1995) described how research on sex differences has been influenced by the historically recent political importance of demonstrating that women and men do not differ in significant ways. Furthermore, researchers are occasionally discouraged from publishing unpopular research results (see chap. 21, this volume). I was advised not to publish data concerning unwanted childhood sexual experiences (Stevenson & Gajarsky, 1991) because of the political implications of our finding that males were as likely as females to report such experiences. Similarly, Charlene Muehlenhard was pressured not to collect data on *token resistance* to sexual advances because it could potentially be used in court against women who have experienced sexual coercion. Even though the research eventually demonstrated that the overwhelming majority of women and men who say "no" to sex actually mean no (Muehlenhard & Rodgers, 1998), one critic argued that conducting this research was morally analogous to the development of the atomic bomb (C. Muehlenhard, personal communication, July 15, 1999).

As our reported data from *JSR* show, whether because of publication biases, lack of interest, or recruitment difficulties, the diversity of human experience is not yet represented in the published literature on human sexuality. Only a small percentage of published research reflects the interests of various groups. In addition, Hyde (1985) noted that if work by some members of the research community (e.g., women) is considered less authoritative than that of other groups, this will introduce bias as research findings are incorporated into the literature. Cases of mistaken identity and other misattributions provide indirect evidence of this phenomenon. Psyche Cattell went to her grave with her father, James McKeen Cattell, and another unrelated man, Raymond B. Cattell, often receiving credit for her work (Sokal, 1991). Similarly, bias results when scholars remember and cite studies that are consistent with their own views and ignore those that conflict.

CONCLUSIONS

A single chapter, such as this, cannot possibly provide a comprehensive analysis of diversity-related bias in sexuality research, nor can it avoid oversimplifying complex issues. Realistically, my goal was simply to discuss ways in which various forms of prejudice, evident in the world's cultures, can influence how sexuality research is conceived, executed, and interpreted. This discussion, however, leads to at least three interrelated recommendations that require explicit statement:

1. Sexuality researchers should develop diversity-conscious norms for the conception, execution, and interpretation of research. For example, researchers

should always provide evidence of cross-group validation when concepts and ter-minology developed from middle-class, U.S. American experience are used in other contexts. Data concerning demographic and cultural diversity of research participants should be gathered routinely, and editors should require authors to re-port these descriptive data even when diversity variables are not central to the spe-cific analysis and interpretation being described. The absence of this information limits the value of any research finding. Rather than asking *whether* they matter, perhaps the important questions have to do with *when* or *to what extent* ethnicity, gender, sexual orientation, and other diversity-related variables matter. It may be too much to ask a single study to consider all diversity dimensions simulta-neously. However, taken as a whole, there is no excuse for the glaring omissions now readily apparent in the sexuality literature.

2. Empirical research on human sexuality is susceptible to diversity bias re-gardless of its status as qualitative or quantitative, descriptive or experimental; no one approach is inherently free of bias. Methodology texts and courses should in-clude discussion of the influence of sexism, racism, ageism, and other forms of prejudice on the research process regardless of which methods are emphasized. Sexuality researchers should choose the research methodology that is best suited to the (diversity-sensitive) question at hand rather than privilege some methods over others.

3. Funding organizations, publishers, educators, researchers, and other institu-tional gatekeepers should develop ways to increase the heterogeneity among those who participate in the research process, whether as researchers, participants, or consumers. As sexual science begins to reflect human diversity and, in the pro-cess, becomes more relevant to larger segments of society, people from more di-verse backgrounds will be encouraged to pursue careers in research. Likewise, as sex researchers become more diverse, sexual science may become more diversity aware. This transaction will propagate a body of knowledge about human sexual-ity that will be more valuable than what is currently available to those who apply research findings for self-fulfillment, sex education and therapy, community de-velopment, or public policy.

As I made explicit in the introduction to this chapter, a sexual science that con-forms to conventional paradigms is of limited value in providing an understand-ing of the diversity of human sexual expression. Encouraging sexual scientists to attend to diversity-related biases represents progress toward that end. Put simply, good science, including sexual science, is diversity aware.

SUGGESTED READINGS

Few sources deal with the broad range of diversity issues covered in this chapter. One exception is APA's (1994) *Publication Manual*, which includes guidelines to reduce bias in language (pp. 46–60). A special issue of *Psychology of Women*

Quarterly on innovations in feminist research provides a context and commentary on the *Manual* (Landrine & Klonoff, 1999; Russo, 1999; Walsh-Bowers, 1999). A variety of authors have provided guidance on how to avoid specific diversity-related biases, particularly sexist and ethnocentric bias (Catania, 1999; Denmark et al., 1988; Gonzáles-Calvo et al., 1997; Hyde, 1985; Jenkins & Parron, 1995; McHugh et al., 1986; Rabinowitz & Sechzer, 1993). Much of their advice generalizes to avoiding other forms of diversity-related bias. Those interested in an extended discussion of the concepts *race* and *ethnicity* are referred to Jenkins and Parron (1995) and Yee et al. (1993). Finally, Eagly (1994) is the best source for arguments favoring the routine reporting of sex differences. In fact, that issue of *Feminism & Psychology* (Vol. 4, No. 4) includes articles describing a variety of positions on the issue of reporting sex difference. Again, these arguments generalize to other diversity dimensions.

NOTE

1. Marie A. Weakland and Cheryl Mullooly, both able-bodied female U.S. Americans of European descent, completed all the coding and data tabulations for this project while they were enrolled in graduate study in the Department of Psychological Science at Ball State University.

REFERENCES

American Psychiatric Association. (1994). *Diagnostic and statistical manual of mental disorders* (4th ed.). Washington, DC: Author.

American Psychological Association. (1994). *Publication manual of the American Psychological Association* (4th ed.). Washington, DC: Author.

Bhopal, R., & Donaldson, L. (1998). White, European, Western, Caucasian, or what? Inappropriate labeling in research on race, ethnicity, and health. *American Journal of Public Health, 88,* 1303–1307.

Brown, L. S. (1989). New voice, new visions: Toward a lesbian/gay paradigm for psychology. *Psychology of Women Quarterly, 13,* 445–458.

Campbell, R., & Schram, P. J. (1995). Feminist research methods: A content analysis of psychology and social science textbooks. *Psychology of Women Quarterly, 19,* 85–106.

Cannon, L. W., Higginbotham, E., & Leung, M. L. A. (1988). Race and class bias in qualitative research on women. *Gender & Society, 2,* 449–462.

Catania, J. A. (1999). A framework for conceptualizing reporting bias and its antecedents in interviews assessing human sexuality. *The Journal of Sex Research, 36,* 25–38.

Cherry, T. D., Smith, P. J., & Robinson, B. E. (1999, May). *Definitely safe sex: Masturbation among African American women.* Paper presented at the annual conference of the Society for the Scientific Study of Sexuality–Midcontinent Region, Madison, WI.

Crawford, M., & Kimmel, E. (1999). Promoting methodological diversity in feminist research. *Psychology of Women Quarterly, 23,* 7–39.

Denmark, F., Russo, N. F., Frieze, I. H., & Sechzer, J. A. (1988). Guidelines for avoiding sexism in psychological research: A report of the ad hoc committee on nonsexist research. *American Psychologist, 43,* 582–585.

Eagly, A. H. (1987). Reporting sex differences. *American Psychologist, 42,* 756–757.

Eagly, A. H. (1990). On the advantages of reporting sex comparisons. *American Psychologist, 45,* 560–562.

Eagly, A. H. (1994). On comparing women and men. *Feminism & Psychology, 4,* 513–522.

Eagly, A. H. (1995). The science and politics of comparing women and men. *American Psychologist, 50,* 145–158.

Eagly, A. H. (1997). Comparing women and men: Methods, findings, and politics. In M. R. Walsh (Ed.), *Women, men and gender: Ongoing debates* (pp. 24–31). New Haven, CT: Yale University Press.

Eagly, A. H., & Carli, L. L. (1981). Sex of researchers and sex-typed communications as determinants of sex differences in influenceability: A meta-analysis of social influence studies. *Psychological Bulletin, 90,* 1–20.

Eagly, A. H., & Kite, M. E. (1987). Are stereotypes of nationalities applied to both women and men? *Journal of Personality and Social Psychology, 53,* 451–462.

Eagly, A. H., & Wood, W. (1999). The origins of sex differences in human behavior: Evolved dispositions versus social roles. *American Psychologist, 54,* 408–423.

Etaugh, C., Houtler, B. D., & Ptasnik, P. (1988). Evaluating competence of women and men: Effects of experimenter gender and group gender composition. *Psychology of Women Quarterly, 12,* 191–200.

Ford, K., & Norris, A. (1991). Methodological considerations for survey research on sexual behavior: Urban African American and Hispanic youth. *The Journal of Sex Research, 28,* 539–555.

Gonzáles-Calvo, J., Gonzáles, V. M., & Lorig, K. (1997). Cultural diversity issues in the development of valid and reliable measures of health status. *Arthritis Care and Research, 10,* 448–456.

Hall, J. A. (1978). Gender effects is decoding nonverbal cues. *Psychological Bulletin, 85,* 845–857.

Howes, R. H., & Stevenson, M. R. (1993). *Women and the use of military force.* Boulder, CO: Lynne Rienner.

Hyde, J. S. (1985). *Half the human experience: The psychology of women* (3rd ed.). Lexington, MA: D. C. Health.

Jenkins, R. R., & Parron, D. (1995). Guidelines for adolescent health research: Issues of race and class. *Journal of Adolescent Health, 17,* 314–322.

Kazdin, A. E. (1998). *Research design in clinical psychology* (3rd ed.). Boston: Allyn & Bacon.

Kinsey, A. C., Pomeroy, W. B., & Martin, C. E. (1948). *Sexual behavior in the human male.* Philadelphia: Saunders.

Kinsey, A. C., Pomeroy, W. B., Martin, C. E., & Gebhard, P. H. (1953). *Sexual behavior in the human female.* Philadelphia: Saunders.

Landrine, H., & Klonoff, E. A. (1999). How often do you read the bible? *Psychology of Women Quarterly, 23,* 393–398.

Laumann, E. O., Gagnon, J. H., Michael, R. T., & Michaels, S. (1994). *The social organization of sexuality.* Chicago: University of Chicago Press.

Leap, W. L. (1999). *Public sex / gay space.* New York: Columbia University Press.

Marsella, A. J. (1998). Toward a "Global-Community Psychology": Meeting the needs of a changing world. *American Psychologist, 53,* 1282–1291.

Maxwell, J. A. (1998). Designing a qualitative study. In L. Bickman & D. J. Rog (Eds.), *Handbook of applied social research methods* (pp. 69–100). Thousand Oaks, CA: Sage.

McHugh, M. C., Koeske, R. D., & Frieze, I. H. (1986). Issues to consider in conducting nonsexist psychological research: A guide for researchers. *American Psychologist, 41,* 879–890.

Meston, C. M., Trapnell, P. D., & Gorzalka, B. B. (1996). Ethnic and gender differences in sexuality: Variations in sexual behavior between Asian and non-Asian university students. *Archives of Sexual Behavior, 25,* 33–72.

Meston, C. M., Trapnell, P. D., & Gorzalka, B. B. (1998). Ethnic, gender, and length-of-residency influences on sexual knowledge and attitudes. *The Journal of Sex Research, 35,* 176–188.

Muehlenhard, C. L., & Rodgers, C. S. (1998). Token resistance to sex: New perspectives on an old stereotype. *Psychology of Women Quarterly, 22*, 443–463.

Oliver, M. B., & Hyde, J. S. (1993). Gender differences in sexuality: A meta-analysis. *Psychological Bulletin, 114*, 29–51.

O'Sullivan, L. F. (1995). Less is more: The effects of sexual experience on judgments of men's and women's personality characteristics and relationship desirability. *Sex Roles, 33*, 159–181.

Peplau, L. A., & Conrad, E. (1989). Beyond nonsexist research: The perils of feminist methods in psychology. *Psychology of Women Quarterly, 13*, 379–400.

Petrak, J., & Keane, F. (1998). Cultural beliefs and the treatment of sexual dysfunction: An overview. *Sexual Dysfunction, 1*, 13–17.

Prilleltensky, I. (1997). Values, assumptions, and practices: Assessing the moral implications of psychological discourse and action. *American Psychologist, 52*, 517–535.

Rabinowitz, V. C., & Sechzer, J. A. (1993). Feminist perspective on research methods. In F. L. Denmark & M. A. Paludi (Eds.), *Psychology of women: A handbook of issues and theories* (pp. 23–66). Westport, CT: Greenwood.

Riger, S. (1992). Epistemological debates, feminist voices: Science, social values, and the study of women. *American Psychologist, 47*, 730–740.

Rind, B. (1998). Biased use of cross-cultural and historical perspectives on male homosexuality in human sexuality textbooks. *The Journal of Sex Research, 35*, 397–407.

Rogler, L. H. (1999). Methodological sources of cultural insensitivity in mental health research. *American Psychologist, 54*, 424–433.

Romer, D., Hornik, R., Stanton, B., Black, M., Li, X., Ricardo, I., & Feigelman, S. (1997). "Talking" computers: A reliable and private method to conduct interviews on sensitive topics with children. *The Journal of Sex Research, 34*, 3–9.

Rosenthal, R. (1966). *Experimenter effects in behavioral research.* New York: Appleton-Century-Crofts.

Rumenick, D. K., Capasso, D. R., & Hendrick, C. (1977). Experimenter sex effects in behavioral research. *Psychological Bulletin, 84*, 852–887.

Russo, N. F. (1999). Putting the APA *Publication Manual* in context. *Psychology of Women Quarterly, 23*, 399–402.

Schwarz, N. (1999). Self-reports: How the questions shape the answers. *American Psychologist, 54*, 93–105.

Simon, W. (1999). In search of the deeper truth. *The Journal of Sex Research, 36*, 213–214.

Sokal, M. M. (1991). Psyche Cattell (1893–1989). *American Psychologist, 46*, 72.

Stevenson, M. R. (1990). Tolerance for homosexuality and interest in sexuality education. *Journal of Sex Education & Therapy, 16*, 194–197.

Stevenson, M. R. (1995). Searching for a gay identity in Indonesia. *Journal of Men's Studies, 4*, 93–108.

Stevenson, M. R. (1998). Islamic homosexualities? *The Journal of Sex Research, 35*, 311–314.

Stevenson, M. R., & Black, K. N. (1988). Paternal absence and sex-role development: A meta-analysis. *Child Development, 59*, 793–814.

Stevenson, M. R., & Gajarsky, W. M. (1991). Unwanted childhood sexual experiences relate to later revictimization and male perpetration. *Journal of Psychology & Human Sexuality, 4*, 57–70.

Stevenson, M. R., & Medler, B. R. (1995). Is homophobia a weapon of sexism? *Journal of Men's Studies, 4*, 1–8.

Stevenson, M. R., Paludi, M. A., Black, K. N., & Whitley, B. E., Jr. (1994). Gender roles: A multidisciplinary life-span perspective. In M. R. Stevenson (Ed.), *Gender roles through the life-span: A multidisciplinary perspective.* Muncie, IN: Ball State University.

Thomas, R. R. (1996). *Redefining diversity.* New York: American Management Association.

Tiefer, L. (1991). Historical, scientific, clinical, and feminist criticisms of "The Human Sexual Response Cycle" model. *Annual Review of Sex Research, 2*, 1–24.

Tolman, D. L., & Szalacha, L. A. (1999). Dimensions of desire: Bridging qualitative and quantitative methods in a study of female adolescent sexuality. *Psychology of Women Quarterly, 23,* 7–39.

Turner, H. A. (1999). Participation bias in AIDS-related telephone surveys: Results from the National AIDS Behavioral Survey (NABS) non-response study. *The Journal of Sex Research, 36,* 52–58.

Vega, W. A. (1992). Theoretical and pragmatic implications of cultural diversity for community research. *American Journal of Community Psychology, 20,* 375–390.

Walsh-Bowers, R. (1999). Fundamentalism in psychological science: The *Publication Manual* as "Bible." *Psychology of Women Quarterly, 23,* 375–392.

Walters, C., Shurley, J. T., & Parsons, O. A. (1962). Differences in male and female responses to underwater sensory deprivation: An exploratory study. *Journal of Nervous and Mental Diseases, 135,* 302–310.

Weinberg, M. S., & Williams, C. J. (1988). Black sexuality: A test of two theories. *The Journal of Sex Research, 25,* 197–218.

Whitley, B. E., & Schofield, J. W. (1985–1986). A meta-analysis of research on adolescent contraceptive use. *Population and Environment, 8,* 173–203.

Wiederman, M. W. (1999). Volunteer bias in sexuality research using college student participants. *The Journal of Sex Research, 36,* 59–66.

Wiederman, M. W., Fretz, A., & Maynard, C. (1995). *Women in 25 years of Published Sexuality Research: 1971–1995.* Unpublished manuscript.

Wiederman, M. W., Maynard, C., & Fretz, A. (1996). Ethnicity in 25 years of published sexuality research: 1971–1995. *The Journal of Sex Research, 33,* 339–342.

Yee, A. H., Fairchild, H. H., Weizmann, F., & Wyatt, G. E. (1993). Addressing psychology's problems with race. *American Psychologist, 48,* 1132–1140.

Zuckerman, M. (1990). Some dubious premises in research and theory on racial difference: Scientific, social, and ethical issues. *American Psychologist, 45,* 1297–1303.

20

Institutional Review Boards and Conducting Sexuality Research

Michael W. Wiederman
Columbia College

Although sexual scholarship encompasses several different disciplines, sexuality researchers typically work in settings where approval of an institutional committee is a prerequisite to conducting their research. These committees are referred to as Institutional Review Boards (IRBs) or Human Subjects Review Boards or Committees. This chapter considers the history and functioning of IRBs, potential concerns IRBs have about sexuality research in particular, and specific ethical issues that sexuality researchers may have to address that may not apply to non-sexuality researchers. This chapter also offers suggestions on how to craft sexuality-related IRB proposals that address concerns IRB members commonly have about this research topic.

HISTORY AND FUNCTIONING OF IRBS

History of IRBs

Formal codes of ethics for research emerged in the United States in the 1960s. The "Ethical Guidelines for Clinical Investigation" were adopted by the American Medical Association in 1966, the same year that the Surgeon General decreed that any research financially supported by the Public Health Service had to undergo review by an institutional committee, which would ensure that risks to participants were minimized (Berg, 1992). Several revisions of this policy ensued and culminated in both publication of a formal guide to policy on the protection of hu-

479

man research participants by the Department of Health, Education, and Welfare (DHEW) as well as federal law (the National Research Act of 1974). The law extended the requirement of institutional review of research proposals to all research supported by DHEW funds that included human participants, including non-medical and nonexperimental research.

By the early 1980s, the mandate for institutional review of research was broadened to include all research involving human participants conducted at institutions receiving funds from the newly formed Department of Health and Human Services (formerly part of DHEW), even if a particular piece of research was not financially supported by such funds (Berg, 1992). It is this requirement that affects contemporary sexuality researchers. The federal regulations were subsequently expanded to stipulate that IRB review is required for all research conducted, supported, or otherwise subject to regulation by any federal department or agency that adopts a policy requiring such review (OPPR, 1996). Affected institutions include universities, prisons, and medical centers, each of which is required to form an IRB to review all research proposals and ensure minimization of risk to potential participants. Institutions may "share" IRBs, although most institutions entailing more than very minimal research activity have developed their own IRBs. As a result, there are probably 3,000 or more IRBs in the United States (Gillespie, 1999).

The guidelines governing contemporary IRBs were initially published in 1991 by the Office for Protection from Research Risks (OPRR) at the National Institutes of Health. This document, titled *Protection of Human Subjects* (OPRR, 1996), originates from Title 45, Part 46 of the Code of Federal Regulations. Additionally, an *Institutional Review Board Guidebook* (OPRR, 1993) has been published for use by members of IRBs. The information regarding IRB roles and regulations presented in this chapter are taken from these two documents.

Functioning of IRBs

Scope. The primary role of IRBs is to attempt to ensure that potential research participants are protected from harm. To accomplish this goal, IRBs review research proposals and evaluate both the potential risk to participants and the steps the researcher proposes to take to minimize and remedy harm from participation. I previously noted that the need for IRBs arose out of concerns regarding biomedical research, yet the scope of IRBs was broadened to include social science research, despite the lack of empirical evidence that participants had ever been harmed by involvement in social science research (Seiler & Murtha, 1980). At the same time, however, those who drafted the federal regulations recognized that some social science research presented minimal risk and should be deemed exempt from IRB review. The current federal regulations specify the categories of research considered exempt.

One category of exempt research is that carried out on instructional and curriculum issues in established educational settings (OPRR, 1996, p. 5). For example, research conducted on the comparison of instructional techniques, curricula, or methods of classroom management falls into this category. So, for the sexuality researcher, investigation of the effects of participation in a sexuality course is exempt from IRB policy.

A second category of exempt research involves the collection or study of existing data, records, or documents when those sources are publicly available or when the information is recorded by the investigator in such a way that participants cannot be identified (OPRR, 1996, p. 5). For the sexuality researcher, this category would entail data from marriage licenses (which are public records) or personal advertisements posted on the Internet (which are publicly available), as well as data collected as part of large surveys and subsequently made available to researchers at large (e.g., the General Social Survey conducted bi-annually by the National Opinion Research Center in Chicago). Similarly, data shared by a colleague would not require the most recent investigator to secure IRB approval if the data did not include information that identified the participants.

A third category of exempt research is broad in nature and holds the greatest implications for sexuality researchers. "Research involving the use of educational tests (cognitive, diagnostic, aptitude, achievement), survey procedures, interview procedures, or observation of public behavior" (OPRR, 1996, p. 5) are exempt from IRB policy unless the data are coded in such a way that participants could be identified and disclosure of the participant's responses could reasonably cause harm to the participant (e.g., harm his or her reputation). Certainly information about respondents' sexuality is sensitive and could conceivably cause harm if made known to particular others outside of the research context. However, as long as the data are collected anonymously, questionnaires and interviews asking for sexual information fall under this exempt category.

The federal regulations establishing IRB policy do not preclude additional policy enacted by individual institutions. For example, it is quite common for universities to require that all faculty and student research undergo IRB review, even if it is technically exempt according to the criteria in the federal regulations (Mosher, 1988). Such policy can be problematic with regard to using the federal regulations to anticipate how one should proceed as a researcher. For example, although an IRB's forms may provide an option for applying for exempt status, the actual IRB procedures may effectively nullify such a category. I am aware of IRBs that simply defer making any judgments regarding whether a particular research protocol meet the criteria for an exempt study until after all concerns and stipulations have been addressed! These stipulations, such as requiring a written informed consent form, are often similar to requirements for nonexempt research. So, even if a particular study is exempt from IRB policy according to federal regulations, particular IRBs may still require sexuality researchers to meet the requirements for nonexempt research prior to approving the study as exempt from IRB policy.

It is important to note that the federal regulations regarding IRB policy do not establish a mechanism for checks-and-balances or appeal by a researcher who believes he or she has been treated unfairly. An individual researcher may have the right to express concerns to high-level administrators, such as the provost or president of a university or a director of medical facility. However, that administrator may have little incentive to try to intervene on the researcher's behalf and has no formal authority to influence the IRB's decisions.

Membership.   Because the research that falls under the purview of an IRB may come from a variety of professionals and address a multitude of topics with different study populations, the federal regulations stipulate that each IRB comprises at least five members with varying backgrounds. The regulations strongly encourage diversity of IRB membership regarding sex, ethnicity, and profession. Accordingly, "each IRB shall include at least one member whose primary concerns are in scientific areas and at least one member whose primary concerns are in nonscientific areas" (OPRR, 1996, pp. 7–8) as well as "at least one member who is not otherwise affiliated with the institution and who is not part of the immediate family of a person who is affiliated with the institution" (p. 8). Note that it would be entirely possible that the majority (or even all but one) of the members of a particular IRB would not have experience or training in research methodology. One might argue that such training is unnecessary to make decisions on an IRB. However, without some training and experience regarding standard research methodology, IRB members may not appreciate what are considered to be routine and well-accepted research procedures.

Simply having training or experience in research, however, does not automatically qualify one as an adequate IRB member. Although it may sound strange, I am aware of some university faculty who, when appointed to an IRB, did nothing to prepare or educate themselves for the role. They were given a copy of the federal regulations and told how to access a videotape and written materials that would provide additional guidance. However, they did not see the need to read or view any of the materials because each had previous experience as a researcher. Their apparent belief was that, having been "on the other end," they were qualified to serve as a member of the IRB. Unfortunately, such thinking is liable to result in perpetuation of tradition, unofficial policies, and ways of doing things that may not follow the federal regulations. Berg (1992) noted that "the assumption that because a faculty member has managed to secure work in a university setting he or she is the best choice for an IRB is unacceptable if not naive" (p. 233).

Actions.   IRBs can take one of three actions with regard to each research proposal: approve, disapprove, or require modifications in the research protocol to secure approval (OPRR, 1996, p. 8). To arrive at an action, research proposals may undergo a full review (by several or all members of the IRB) or an expedited review (by the IRB Chairperson or one or more designated IRB members). The expedited option exists to ease the burden of IRBs by not requiring them to provide extensive review of protocols for studies unlikely to cause harm, and to speed the response to researchers regarding the disposition of their proposal. It is important to note that the federal regulations stipulate that the IRB members involved in an expedited review "may exercise all of the authorities of the IRB except that the reviewers may not disapprove the research" (p. 8).

Research is eligible for expedited review if it involves no more than minimal risk (defined later) to participants and falls into 1 of 10 categories (see OPRR, 1996). The categories applicable to sexuality researchers include existing data, records, or documents (presumably when participants are identified, as existing data recorded in such a way that participants are not identified is exempt from IRB policy, as noted earlier). The relevant categories also include "research on individual or group behavior or characteristics of individuals, such as studies of perception, cognition, game theory, or test development, where the investigator does not manipulate subjects' behavior and the research will not involve stress to subjects" (p. 17).

At first blush, this last category may appear to include anonymous questionnaires administered by sexuality researchers. However, recall that anonymous questionnaires fall into the exempt category. The expedited category described here entails observation or measurement of participants' behavior or responses to some stimuli, such as in investigations of perception, cognition, or in developing intelligence or aptitude tests. So, an analogous situation for sexuality researchers is when investigators expose participants to sexually explicit media and ask for responses to or ratings of such stimuli.

In conclusion, the large bulk of sexuality research involves self-reports and is, therefore, either exempt from IRB policy or is eligible for expedited review. Although studies involving psychophysiological measurement of sexual response (see chap. 7, this volume), or studies involving deception or a predictable degree of stress inflicted on participants, would indeed require a full IRB review, the typical sexuality study appears to fall under the categories initially created for research anticipated to pose little risk of harm to participants. Unfortunately, this does not mean that IRBs do not have concerns regarding sexuality research, even when such research simply entails completion of anonymous questionnaires. The primary IRB concerns are addressed in the next section.

IRB CONCERNS

Against a backdrop of social taboo and possible suspicion regarding a sexuality researcher's motives (see chap. 21, this volume; Brannigan, Allgeier, & Allgeier, 1997; Mosher, 1988), IRB members must make decisions regarding the ethical acceptability of proposed research. Accordingly, it should not be surprising that IRBs frequently consider sexuality research to be a sensitive research area fraught with more ethical concerns when compared to other research topics (Council,

Smith, Kaster-Bundgaard, & Gladue, 1999). Such concerns may lead to increased risk of having one's proposal rejected or substantially modified. Ceci, Peters, and Plotkin (1985) experimentally manipulated the topic of proposed research while maintaining the same treatment of participants within proposals sent to more than 150 university IRBs for evaluation. Interestingly, proposals addressing nonsensitive research topics were approved 95% of the time compared with the proposals addressing sensitive topics, which were approved less than 50% of the time.

It often seems as if IRB concerns over sexuality research have more to do with the topic than the research methods. To avoid such cases, the IRB guidebook repeatedly reminds members to avoid personal and subjective influences in arriving at decisions. For example:

> IRB members should guard against the inclination to approve or disapprove research based upon their personal feelings about the possible outcome of a research proposal [and] IRBs should resist placing restrictions on research because of its subject matter; IRBs should instead be concerned about research methods and the rights and welfare of research subjects. IRBs must differentiate disapproving a research proposal because of qualms about the subject being explored or its possible findings, such as genetic differences in intelligence, from disapproving research involving the performance of illegal or unethical acts. The former raises serious issues of academic freedom; the latter is quite different and appropriate. (OPRR, 1993, p. 5)

Unfortunately, personal perspective can color judgments that the individual believes he or she is making objectively.

What types of ethical concerns do IRBs have regarding sexuality research? The ethical principles underlying IRB decisions are based on the Belmont Principles for the Protection of Human Subjects (Gillespie, 1999; Mosher, 1988): beneficence, justice, and respect for persons. *Beneficence* refers to the principle that the researcher will refrain from harming the participants and will attempt to maximize the benefits of the research, both to the participants as well as the larger society. *Justice* refers to the idea that participants will be treated equally and fairly and that members of particular groups will not be discriminated against in the selection or treatment of participants. *Respect for persons* entails that the researcher will recognize each participant's capabilities and personal dignity and treat participants accordingly. This includes protecting the anonymity or confidentiality of participants' responses, minimizing risks to the greatest extent possible, and providing fully informed consent (as well as recognizing that some potential participants, e.g., children and those with diminished cognitive capacity, are unable to provide such fully informed consent).

To assess the extent to which a particular study meets the three ethical principles just elaborated, IRBs use specific evaluation criteria. For example, to cover the principle of justice, IRBs are charged with evaluating whether selection of participants is equitable, given the purposes of the research and the setting in which it will be conducted (OPRR, 1996, p. 8). Beneficence is addressed by assessing whether the risks to participants are reasonable given the potential benefits to the participants as well as the importance of the knowledge that may result from the research. Of relevance to some sexuality researchers, the federal regulations warn IRB members against considering "possible long-range effects of applying knowledge gained in the research (for example, the possible effects of the research on public policy) as among those research risks that fall within the purview of its responsibility" (OPRR, 1996, p. 8). Also, the guidebook for IRBs explains that "If only minimal risks are involved, IRBs do not need to protect competent adult subjects from participating in research considered unlikely to yield any benefit" (OPRR, 1993, pp. 3–9).

Accomplishing adequate respect for persons is handled through provision of informed consent, protecting privacy and confidentiality, and minimizing potential harm to participants (Gillespie, 1999). These three topics are also typically where IRBs raise concerns over proposed research in general (Gillespie, 1999; Sieber & Baluyot, 1992) and sexuality research in particular (Mosher, 1988; Wiederman, 1999a). Accordingly, I discuss each in some detail.

Informed Consent

In the context of a typical sexuality study, informed consent primarily involves the issue of making potential participants aware of the nature of the material they would encounter during the study (e.g., questions concerning sexual attitudes and behaviors, or sexual stimuli of some sort). Both researchers and IRB members would probably agree that providing adequate information to allow fully informed consent on the part of research participants is of utmost importance. Where disagreements might ensue is on the issues of the timing of such information, the level of disclosure provided, and whether a signed informed consent form is required. In other words, at what point will potential research participants be made aware that the study involves a sexual topic? To what degree will potential participants be made aware of the actual constructs measured in the study? Will participants be required to sign a form indicating their consent?

Timing of Informed Consent. Many university subject pools of which I am aware require researchers to post a brief description of the nature of the study along with the sign-up sheets for the study. For a sexuality study, the description may be as brief and generic as "Participation in this study involves completing several questionnaires regarding your attitudes and experiences with intimate relationships" or may be relatively more revealing such as "Participation in this study involves completing several questionnaires regarding your sexual attitudes and experiences." In either case, the researcher is liable to obtain a biased sample of college student participants.

Researchers have convincingly demonstrated that any indication that the study involves sexuality topics results in substantial self-selection on the part of students at the point of sign-up (e.g., Griffith & Walker, 1976; Jackson, Procidano, & Cohen, 1989). In general, college students who sign up for studies they believe to be sexual in nature are more likely to be male and relatively extraverted, sensation-seeking, and sexually experienced (Wiederman, 1999b). This form of selection bias also has important implications for researchers using the same participant pool, yet who do not conduct sexuality research. If studies on sexuality draw particular types of participants, then the remaining nonsexuality studies will draw more heavily from the remaining potential participants, who are liable to fall on the other end of the continuum with regard to such characteristics as extraversion, sensation-seeking, religious values, and so forth.

Ideally then, at least from the researchers' perspective, subject pool sign-up procedures would be such that participant self-selection would be minimized. Admittedly, regardless of the procedures used, such self-selection will never be completely eliminated, especially in relatively small subject pools. That is, some individuals will disclose to peers the nature of the research studies in which they participated, leaving some of those peers to seek out or avoid certain studies based on "word-of-mouth" information. Still, the self-selection problem would be minimized if potential participants were not aware of the research topic at the point of sign-up. However, without such awareness, how can researchers ensure informed consent to participate in particular studies?

One possible answer lies in the procedures currently used for the student subject pool in the Department of Psychological Science at Ball State University. One option students enrolled in introductory psychology courses have for meeting an activity requirement is involvement in research conducted by faculty and students supervised by faculty. Potential participants for such research are recruited through posted sign-up sheets, each of which contains a code number assigned to the research project, the names of the researchers, the time and location of the study, whether the study involves a survey or an experiment, the amount of research credit being offered for participation, and any restrictions on potential participants (e.g., only males, only those with corrected 20/20 vision, etc.).

On arriving at the testing site, potential participants are given much more detailed information about the nature of the project and what participation entails (i.e., they are provided with complete information about the study). Those students who decide not to participate are given an opportunity to leave and seek out other ways to earn participation credit, but still receive the minimum unit of participation credit because they showed up to the testing site. In this way, each researcher can at least monitor the extent to which students appear to be self-selecting to participate in his or her project (although it is always possible, especially in smaller subject pools, that the code numbers associated with sexuality studies leak out to other students through word-of-mouth communication from those students who have already participated).

What about the perception of coercion? It is possible that some students may feel too embarrassed to self-identify as someone uncomfortable with the research topic. It is also possible that some students might feel some (perhaps self-induced) pressure to participate after having signed up for a study and arrived at the testing site. To counter these concerns, one could inform potential participants that they are free to decide not to participate now that they have learned the nature of the study, but, if they are uncomfortable leaving without participating, another option exists. Because the questionnaires are anonymous and are not seen by the researcher until all participants have left the site, it is possible to pretend to participate, turn in a blank questionnaire around the time when others turn in theirs, and then collect the credit. Another option is to fill out the questionnaire without actually responding accurately or without much regard for the questionnaire items, yet provide indication at the end of the questionnaire that the respondent does not believe his or her data should be included in the study.

By making potential participants aware of these options, it is possible to defuse the sampling problem without causing an additional problem involving perceived coercion. As a side note, only about 1% of students in studies I have conducted left the testing session on learning the nature of the study or turned in a completely blank questionnaire.

Of course, there are instances in which complete informed consent cannot be obtained if the research is to be carried out effectively. In essence, these sexuality studies contain a degree of deception in that participants are not fully aware that they are participating in a research study, or that the particular behavioral response of interest to researchers constitutes their participation. Examples of such research are relatively rare in the area of sexuality. However, I am aware of a few published studies that illustrate the difficulty with obtaining informed consent in some instances.

Clark (1990; Clark & Hatfield, 1989) had male and female confederates approach students at Florida State University outside of classroom settings. The confederates approached each research participant and propositioned him or her for a date or for sex. The students' responses were the data of interest. Immediately after providing a response, students were debriefed in that they were informed that the proposition was part of a research study. In this context, the participants had not provided consent, informed or otherwise, to participate in research, yet to require such consent would have compromised the validity of the study. The reader is not told whether the research was approved by an IRB.

Mathes, Phillips, Skowran, and Dick (1982) examined romantic jealousy by having college students complete questionnaires. The more problematic aspect of their study, however, involved a follow-up telephone call made by a confederate of the same sex as the research participant. The confederate explained that he or she had met the participant's dating partner recently at the student union and was favorably impressed. The confederate supposedly found out through a friend that the partner was involved in a dating relationship with the research participant, yet the confederate wanted to ask the partner out "for a beer after class." The confederate was calling the research participant to ask permission to approach the partner for such a date. The telephone conversation was covertly recorded so that the research participants' responses could be subsequently coded for degree of jealousy expressed. The participants were debriefed immediately after giving their response, yet they clearly had not provided consent (nor had their dating partners) for such a ruse. Again, the reader is not told whether the research was approved by an IRB.

Finally, Goode (1996) examined responses to personals advertisements by placing several bogus ads himself and analyzing the responses (letters) each netted. Deception was used in that respondents were not aware that they were participating in research. Additionally problematic was that the respondents typically identified themselves, there was a small financial cost associated with replying to the bogus ads, and there was potential for the responses to contain personal information. In his study, the nearly 1,000 respondents were not subsequently informed of the research project. As in the other cases, the reader is not told whether the research was approved by an IRB.

In each of these examples, deception was used to examine participants' naturalistic behavior and responses; to require informed consent prior to participation would have invalidated the results. In this context, it worth noting that the IRB guidebook addresses fieldwork and the fact that such methodology involves "observation of and interaction with the persons or group being studied in the group's own environment. . . . Thus, while the idea of consent is not inapplicable in fieldwork, IRBs and researchers need to adapt prevailing notions of acceptable protocols and consent procedures to the realities of fieldwork" (OPRR, 1993, p. 5). Still, the ethical issues and potential solutions to problematic aspects of each study are debatable. As the Internet offers unforseen opportunities for empirical study of peoples' response to sexual and other stimuli, issues of deception and informed consent are liable to be salient. Regardless of the research context, if participants are to be informed of the nature of the research, there is also the issue of the degree to which the details and hypotheses involved in the research are disclosed.

Level of Disclosure.   Typically, researchers have no difficulty informing potential research participants that they will be asked to complete several widely used surveys designed to measure their sexual attitudes or will be asked several questions regarding their sexual relationships. However, with regard to some constructs or some studies, divulging what is being measured would be detrimental to the integrity of the research project.

As an example, consider a project submitted for IRB approval by a graduate student whose thesis committee I chaired (Maynard & Wiederman, 1997). Her proposed thesis project involved determining whether gender of the adult, gender of the child, or age of the child influenced perceptions that a sexual interaction involving an adult and child constituted child sexual abuse. Accordingly, each research participant would receive one version of a written narrative describing such a sexual interaction (a between-subjects design), and the age of the youth and the gender of the adult and youth would each be experimentally manipulated. The dependent variable was a rating by the research participant regarding the extent to which the respondent believed the depiction to be a case of child sexual abuse. Initially, the informed consent information to be provided to potential participants alerted them to the fact that participation involved reading a brief description of a sexual interaction and subsequently making judgments about it and about the characters in the narrative. The IRB refused to approve the research unless potential participants were warned that they would be reading "a description of child sexual abuse."

It should be obvious that informing potential participants that they would be reading a depiction of child sexual abuse, and then subsequently asking them whether the depiction they read was a case of child sexual abuse, entails some serious methodological problems. Here was a case in which providing too much disclosure in the name of informed consent would have resulted in invalid research (and hence a waste of time for both the researcher and participants). The IRB's initial refusal to budge on this issue caused the student and me much distress, given that much labor had been invested in the proposed project and it had been approved by her thesis committee (which comprised psychologists I believe to be of the highest ethical standards). In the end, a compromise was reached, although it did not seem particularly satisfying to either "side." The student conducted the study, informing potential participants that they would encounter a description of "a sexual interaction involving an adult and a minor."

In general, explicit disclosure of the constructs measured in, or the exact purpose of, a particular study severely compromises the validity of the findings. Previous research has demonstrated that respondents' presumed knowledge about what the researcher is examining or expects to find can bias responses accordingly (see chap. 3, this volume, for review). Explaining to potential participants that the purpose of the study is to "examine possible relationships between experiences of sexual coercion and attitudes toward sexuality" would almost surely result in responses that would confirm the expected association (at least the association respondents would expect between these two constructs).

Hopefully, explicit provision of the option of not answering any questions or responding to any items that the participant finds troubling (see previous section) would mitigate against having to provide explicit disclosure of measures to be administered or hypotheses to be tested. That is, if the expressed rationale for extremely explicit disclosure is to ensure that participants are not getting themselves into a situation that they subsequently find undesirable, then providing the "out" described in the previous section should accomplish the same end without jeopardizing the methodological integrity of the research.

Requiring a Signature.   Providing informed consent is a criterion on which IRBs evaluate proposed research. However, there is the additional issue of whether an IRB requires that a written informed consent form be signed by participants. Recall that paper-and-pencil questionnaires are exempt from the federal regulations regarding the protection of human subjects. Still, apparently because of the perceived sensitive nature of sexuality surveys, IRBs very often do not treat such studies as truly exempt and frequently require a signed informed consent form from participants. Even for research that does fall under the purview of IRB policies, however, such forms (or signatures) are not necessarily required by the federal regulations.

IRBs have the authority to waive the requirement of signed informed consent forms when either the research involves no more than minimal risk to potential participants and involves procedures that do not require written consent when they are performed outside of a research setting *or* when the only record linking the participants to the research would be the signed informed consent form and the primary risk from participating is a breach of confidentiality (OPRR, 1996, p. 10). What does this mean for the typical sexuality researcher? If one is administering an anonymous questionnaire, one could argue that participation involves no more than minimal risk and completing questionnaires does not require written informed consent when performed outside of a research setting. People are frequently called on the telephone or accosted in shopping malls by individuals who request that the person complete some questionnaire or interview (typically for gathering marketing information). These individuals do not seek written informed consent, nor do those who publish sexuality "surveys" in popular magazines.

The second instance in which an IRB may waive the requirement for a signed informed consent form is when such a signature links the participant to a study that may be sensitive or stigmatizing, even if there is no way to link the signature to a particular questionnaire or set of responses. Interestingly, particular types of sexuality studies are specifically used as examples of such research in the IRB guidebook (OPRR, 1993):

> In studies where subjects are selected because of a sensitive, stigmatizing, or illegal characteristic (e.g., persons who have sexually abused children, sought treatment in a drug abuse program, or who have tested positive for HIV), keeping the identity of participants confidential may be as or more important than keeping the data obtained from the participants confidential . . . Having the subjects of these studies sign consent forms may increase the risk of a breach of confidentiality, because the consent form itself constitutes a record, complete with signature, that identifies particular individuals of the group studied. (pp. 3–31)

It could be argued that this issue also applies to studies involving exposure to sexually explicit media or psychophysiological measurement of sexual arousal, as involvement in these types of studies might be considered stigmatizing by many participants (i.e., would participants want their friends and family knowing that they chose to take part in such a study?).

It is interesting to note that, even though there are many instances in which the requirement of signed consent forms can be waived by IRBs, those who administer IRB policy at the national level recognize that personal feelings of IRB members may cloud their judgment in making such decisions.

> Although consent requirements can be waived . . . this decision can easily be influenced by the extent to which IRB members approve of either the subject matter or what they expect may be the findings of the research. . . . IRB members should try to distinguish between qualms they may have about the subject matter (e.g., homosexuality or drug abuse) and qualms they may have about the research methods (e.g., covert observation, staged events, and so forth; (OPRR, 1993, pp. 3–18).

What does it matter whether IRBs require sexuality researchers to obtain signatures on informed consent forms? Apparently, even beyond any effects of the information conveyed in informed consent forms, the act of requiring participant signatures negatively affects both the willingness of people to participate (Singer, 1978) and the nature of their responses after deciding to participate (Adair, Dushenko, & Lindsay, 1985). Thus, the simple act of requiring a signature can influence research results both by introducing an additional form of selection bias and by altering the nature of participants' data. In addition, the act of signing an official-looking document may induce some participants to feel greater obligation to participate, even if they experience discomfort while doing so, because they made a formal "commitment" to do so (Adair et al., 1985). In this way, requiring a signature on informed consent forms may undermine the very purpose of the forms.

IRB members may explain that the rationale for a signature on the informed consent form is to ensure that participants have read and understood the content. Unfortunately, research on the issue actually points to the opposite effect. Mann (1994) presented Stanford (California) undergraduates with one of three informed consent forms (modeled after standard forms provided by the university IRB) for the same study. Long- and short-form versions of the consent form required signatures, whereas an "information sheet" version contained the same information as the long consent form minus the request for a signature. Students were "quizzed" about particular aspects of the study and the informed consent forms after having a chance to read (and possibly sign) the version each received.

Even though all forms contained explicit information indicating that the participant reserves the right to sue the investigator for negligence, only 28% of those in the signature conditions believed they could sue versus 63% in the nonsignature version. Apparently, the simple act of signing the form conveyed to many participants that they were "signing away" particular rights (although the form indicated otherwise). Similarly, although there were four things listed in the consent forms as to what the student's signature meant, only 20% of students correctly recalled any two of those four things. The majority of students failed to answer correctly other basic questions about the study or their rights as presented in the consent form.

One could argue that if standard informed consent forms do not seem to have the intended effects with Stanford undergraduates, their benefits when used with less-educated groups might be even more limited (see also Kent, 1996; Waggoner & Mayo, 1995, for data on participants' understanding of consent forms). Researchers and IRB members would likely agree that obtaining informed consent is important. However, they may disagree as to the means proposed to achieve this goal. Mann (1994) proposed verbal communication of the information needed for fully informed consent. In previous applications to IRBs, I proposed that potential participants be provided with an information sheet that provides essentially the same information as contained in a standard informed consent form, yet does not require a signature (for the reasons discussed earlier). IRBs were reluctant to accept my proposal, instead requiring signatures from participants.

Despite potential denial from IRBs, in many cases, IRB insistence on signed informed consent forms may have as much or more to do with reducing perceived liability on the part of the researcher, and thus the institution approving the research, than on protecting research participants per se. Indeed, Adair et al. (1985) speculated that a signed informed consent form "is more often used to protect the investigator than the research participant" (p. 61). Unfortunately, if this is true, we have an ironic situation in which procedures designed to protect from harm those who were seen as vulnerable (potential research participants) instead protect researchers and the host institution from harm (liability), even though the latter are the ones responsible for such harm (Mosher, 1988). As Mosher commented, " 'Cover your ass' is not an ethical principle" (p. 379).

Privacy and Confidentiality

Maintaining participant perceptions of privacy and confidentiality are important when conducting sexuality research because of the sensitive nature of the information requested. A researcher might go to great lengths to ensure privacy and confidentiality, yet if participants do not hold commensurate perceptions, they may be reluctant to participate or to provide accurate responses. Fortunately, issues of privacy and confidentiality are often relatively easy to address. For example, assuming for the moment that participation entails completing an anonymous questionnaire, issues of confidentiality can be addressed by emphasizing the anonymous nature of the questionnaire and requesting that respondents not provide any identifying information. Privacy can be enhanced by making sure that participants are not seated closely together and that they are not being scrutinized by research assistants or others during participation.

Although questionnaires may seem, and may actually be, anonymous from the researcher's perspective, there are instances in which particular respondents may question (at least to themselves) the degree of anonymity. For example, suppose that participants are college students recruited from a participant pool. Suppose further that the university IRB required the researcher to use signed informed consent forms. If there are only two or three people in a particular questionnaire session, respondents may believe that the researcher (or assistant) can easily discern which completed questionnaire belongs to each participant. Because of the signed informed consent forms, the participants may further believe that their questionnaire responses can then be linked to their name. To offset such a perception, I instruct research assistants to cancel such sessions, awarding research credit to the few individuals who show up.

A similar issue arises if a particular testing session contains only one member who is of a particular ethnic group, gender, or age group, and the questionnaire includes questions about such demographic information. In some such cases, these particular individuals may feel relatively self-conscious about participating because of the perception that their responses could be linked to them personally. As another example, suppose research assistants approached potential respondents in public places, such as airports, parks, grocery stores, and shopping malls. Although participation may involve a self-administered questionnaire, participants may perceive a lack of privacy or anonymity if they must hand their completed questionnaire to the researcher. In both examples, however, perceptions of anonymity can be enhanced by having participants return their completed questionnaire to a receptacle (e.g., box or large envelope) that contains several other previously completed questionnaires. That way respondents may perceive that their responses are being "mixed in" with those of other respondents (in addition to those in the current session).

What about when researchers need to know the identity of participants to match responses from two or more data collection sessions? In some cases, the researcher needs to know the names of participants so that they can be contacted for follow-up. These situations require keeping a list in which identifying information (e.g., name and address) is matched to identification codes that are used on the actual questionnaires or in the data (e.g., 001, 002, 003, etc.). In this way, the confidentiality of the participants' responses is not be compromised if someone gains access to the data, either in the case of unauthorized access or through necessary work as a research assistant, because he or she needs both the data and the list to match responses to particular participants.

In many instances, however, researchers need to simply be able to match two sets of responses, without necessarily needing to know the identity of the participants. For example, suppose a researcher was gathering data on the test–retest reliability of a scale. He or she could administer it to students in a classroom setting at two points in time. Of course, the researcher needs to be able to match each individual's responses. In this case, the researcher could request that the respondents generate a code number, known only to them, that has some inherent meaning to the participant but not to the researcher (e.g., the digits in one's street address, a particular loved one's birthday, the last four digits of one's telephone number). The likelihood of any two people in the group generating exactly the same number is low. Some individuals will forget, between administrations of the measure, the method they chose to generate a code number. However, these should represent only a small minority of the respondents.

Ensuring participant privacy and confidentiality goes a long way in reducing risk of harm from participation. Still, there are other forms of potential harm from participating in sexuality research that may concern researchers and IRB members. I discuss these concerns in the next section.

Potential Harm

At various points in the chapter, I use the term *minimal risk* of harm. This is a term that is used extensively in IRB documents. The relevant federal regulations define *minimal risk* as referring to instances in which "the probability and magnitude of harm or discomfort anticipated in the research are not greater in and of themselves than those ordinarily encountered in daily life or during the performance of routine physical or psychological examinations or tests" (OPRR, 1996, p. 6). This term, *minimal risk*, is open to interpretation as it is unclear in the definition what types of "physical or psychological examinations or tests" are being referred to, or whether the discomfort ordinarily encountered in daily life refers to that encountered in the daily life of the researcher, the participants, or members of the society at large.

In the context of sexuality research, the issue is whether reading questionnaire items, or perhaps being exposed to some form of sexual stimuli, constitutes a greater probability and magnitude of harm or discomfort than the stresses of daily life or taking other psychological tests. The issue of whose daily life is being used for comparison is a relevant one. For example, one could argue that college student participants encounter much more distress as a result of quizzes, exams, class presentations, and term papers, which are part of daily life as a college student, than they do from participation in sexuality research. Mosher (1988) noted that "in comparison to participation in most sex research, students are exposed to more sex and violence on prime-time TV and in the X-rated movies that routinely appear on campuses" (p. 379). Unfortunately, as objective criteria or data are sorely lacking, determining whether sexuality research constitutes more than minimal risk remains a judgment call and, thus, a possible point of contention between IRB members and sexuality researchers.

Overestimating Risk and Harm?   Empirically, compared to more invasive types of research, such as drug trials and hypnotic induction, IRBs appear to view sexuality surveys as posing relatively little risk of actual harm (Council et al., 1999). However, among survey research topics, sexuality surveys seem to raise more concern than do surveys on less sensitive topics. In other words, I believe there is frequently a contrast phenomenon that occurs within many IRBs, particularly those that typically assess questionnaire studies. It is possible that at institutions where the IRB routinely reviews proposals involving invasive procedures, drug trials, or both, all questionnaire studies (even those involving sexuality topics) are viewed as relatively benign in contrast to those studies that present a true risk of physical harm. At institutions in which nearly all proposals reviewed by the IRB are psychological in nature, the contrast is more likely to occur between those surveys addressing more mundane topics (e.g., food preferences, leisure pursuits, academic experiences) and those that address relatively sensitive topics (e.g., sexuality, experience of traumatic events, history of illegal behavior).

When the distinction is between relatively innocuous questionnaires and those that address sexual topics, it is possible for IRB members to view the latter as somehow "riskier." Still, there is the question regarding risk of what? Because reading questionnaire items cannot cause bodily harm, it appears that IRBs are concerned about emotional discomfort or psychological harm (Mosher, 1988; Wiederman, 1999a). Certainly that was the case with the graduate student whose interactions with the IRB were described previously in this chapter. The reason the IRB gave for requiring that the informed consent form contain disclosure that participation involved reading a description of "child sexual abuse" was concern for the psychological well-being of participants. The IRB expressed concern that some participants would have themselves experienced child sexual abuse, and that reading the brief description of a non-insertive sexual interaction between an adult and youth could cause substantial emotional discomfort or trauma to these individuals. I should note that (a) the depiction had been used in at least two previously published studies with college students, (b) the depiction did not include coercion or any type of response on the part of the youth, and (c) the IRB was aware of these points.

What is the probability that reading the depiction would result in psychological trauma for those students with a personal history of child sexual abuse? Unfortunately, despite that this is an empirical question, no data exist (to my knowledge) regarding whether encountering written material such as that used in sexuality studies causes psychological discomfort. In contrast, however, there are consistent findings that disclosure of emotional experiences results in both subjective and objective improvement in health and well-being (King & Miner, 2000; Paez, Velasco, & Gonzalez, 1999; Pennebaker, 1997). With a lack of empirical evidence as to possible negative effects of harm from participation in social science research, on what basis would an IRB member draw the conclusion that reading something in a sexuality questionnaire might result in harm? From the earliest federal regulations concerning social science research, the standard on which risk of harm seems to have been assessed rests on the possibility that a given research project could cause harm (Selier & Murtha, 1980). Is there a reason why IRB members may overestimate the risk of harm in sexuality studies?

One potential answer has to do with scenario thinking. Cognitive psychologists have documented that humans are prone to scenario (or representative) thinking in which clusters of events or characteristics that can be imagined as belonging together are subsequently overestimated with regard to actual probability of occurrence (Dawes, 1988). In other words, if I can imagine a scenario in which a student (my imagination tells me probably female) who had been sexually abused as a child unwittingly reads the narrative describing the adult–youth sexual interaction and subsequently flashes on her own personal experience, resulting in anxiety and tears, I will tend to overestimate the likelihood of such a scenario actually occurring. Indeed, participants themselves typically overestimate the degree of stress they might experience during participation in research (Aitkenhead & Dordoy, 1985). Accordingly, we should not be surprised if IRB members tend to overestimate the risk of harm when their role is one that places them in a relatively conservative position.

In actuality, given the relatively sensitive nature of sexual information in this culture, it is extremely difficult to anticipate how any particular individual will react to being asked certain questions about his or her sexual attitudes and experiences (even in an anonymous questionnaire). It is particularly difficult for any one individual to make such a determination, given that the individual has his or her own set of sexual attitudes and experiences and probably cannot help but be colored by them when making such a judgment. To make this judgment more problematic, the determination about effects of participation are often made by IRB members who differ significantly from the potential research participants with regard to generation, social group, ethnic heritage, religious perspective, sexual attitudes and experience, sexual orientation, or all of these.

Empirical data on harm from participating in sexuality research are scarce; however, the extant data point to a relative lack of harm. For example, consider the study described earlier in which college students were approached on campus by a confederate who propositioned each for a date or for sex (Clark, 1990). In that study, all respondents were provided with the "the author's name and telephone number in the event that they might be upset over the proposition or if they wished to discuss any aspects of the experiment. The author had two telephones on a single line, one ringing in his office and one ringing in the Psychology Department's main office as well. No calls were received from the subjects" (p. 775).

In addressing IRB concerns regarding possible harm from participating in sexuality research, investigators might try noting in their proposals that no data exist to demonstrate such harm. Indeed, researchers may point to the limited data on the potentially therapeutic and educational effects of research participation in certain cases. At the least, completing an anonymous questionnaire regarding sexual attitudes and behaviors affords the respondent the opportunity to learn how researchers attempt to measure sexuality constructs and may allow the respondent the opportunity to clarify his or her own attitudes. Still, sexuality researchers may be required by IRBs to provide direct remedy, or at least options for remedying, harm caused by participation in their research.

Remedying Harm?   To offset the perceived potential harm in the form of emotional discomfort, IRBs may require sexuality researchers to include in a written informed consent form a statement similar to the following: "Participation in this research project may cause you some anxiety or emotional discomfort. If you experience uncomfortable emotions as a result of participating in this project, you may wish to seek counseling services at _____." Typically in such cases, participants are then given the telephone number, location, or both of an appropriate agency providing mental health services. This warning and potential remedy are presented for the protection of participants, yet the effects of such a statement are unknown and apparently go unchallenged by researchers and IRB members alike.

It is conceivable that inclusion of such a statement actually causes some anxiety or sensitizes participants to the questionnaire material such that an emotional reaction of some sort is more likely. Packaged medications contain an insert in which potential negative side-effects of taking the medication are listed. These side-effects typically range from annoying symptoms to life-threatening events that have been documented in empirical research on the drug. Reading about their possible existence may cause substantial anxiety; however, the generation of such anxiety is apparently offset by the avoidance of serious medical complications, which could result if the patient took the medication, had an adverse reaction, and was not aware of the potential for the side-effect. With sexuality research, however, it is the anxiety or emotional discomfort itself that is apparently perceived by IRBs as the "harm" (Mosher, 1988; Wiederman, 1999a). In this case, does it make sense to warn potential participants of possible anxiety if such a warning itself causes anxiety?

To my knowledge, no one has empirically investigated the emotional impact of such warning statements and attempts at remedy through directing the participant to mental health services (nor has anyone investigated whether research participants ever seek out counseling as a result of participating in study involving sexuality). However, Smith and Berard (1982) experimentally manipulated the description of a classic psychological study to examine how labeling potentially negative aspects of the study would impact college students' judgments about the research. The described study included both deception and possible psychological "stress" to participants. Each college student respondent read the same basic, accurate description of the study; however, in addition to the basic condition, one condition included certain terms inserted in the description (e.g., *deception* and *stress*), whereas another condition included an addendum instead (in which it was stated that "to relieve stress, subjects will be debriefed at the end of the experiment"). The college student respondents then answered several questions about the study, including whether it should be allowed by the university IRB, whether each would participate in the study, and whether any harm would be likely. The large majority of students indicated that the study should be allowed, that they would participate, and that no harm would result. However, compared to the basic condition, students in the label and addendum conditions were significantly less likely to indicate that the study should be approved by the IRB.

The implication of Smith and Berard's findings are important. It may be that, by alerting research participants to the potential for emotional discomfort, the study will be viewed more negatively than if the same study was conducted without highlighting the potential for emotional harm. It is interesting to note in this context that labeling the experiment as *deceptive* or involving *stress*, or implying that such stress was likely through the need for debriefing, did not affect willingness to participate or degree of perceived harm associated with participation. In fact, the only effect of such labeling was with regard to judgments about the acceptability of the study to the IRB. It is possible that sexuality researchers, by trying to anticipate IRB members' concerns over perceived emotional harm, actually make their proposed studies less acceptable to IRBs by explicitly labeling the possibility for anxiety or discomfort. Of course, much more empirical study is needed to address the potential effects of warnings and references to the provision of counseling services on both participants' and IRB members' judgments of proposed sexuality studies.

When IRBs require warnings of anxiety that may result from participating in sexuality research, investigators may consider raising the issues presented here. IRB members may not be aware of the possibility that such warnings may themselves cause distress. Earlier I suggested pointing out in one's IRB proposal the lack of data indicating harm from research participation. In that regard, it is important to be aware of how participants view participation in sexuality research. I turn next to presenting the scant literature on that issue.

The Participant Perspective.   Determining the extent to which participating in a sexuality study causes participants some degree of emotional discomfort exceeding that encountered in daily living requires assessing the actual effects of such participation as perceived by the participants. Despite the important implications of such research, it is nearly nonexistent. I am aware of only a few instances of empirical data on the topic as it applies to the perceptions of research participants in sexuality research.

Abramson (1977) conducted a study involving 40 men and 40 women from an introductory psychology subject pool. Participation involved (a) completing an anonymous questionnaire regarding sexual experiences and sexual attitudes, (b) reading an erotic story and rating one's subsequent sexual arousal, (c) being secretly observed in a waiting room containing sexually explicit magazines, (d) responding to double-entendre words, and (e) being tested for retention of information presented on reproductive biology. Subsequent to participating in all phases of the study, participants were invited to attend a debriefing session in which a brief lecture was presented on correlational research, the measures used in the study were described, the distribution of participant responses to each measure were described, the procedures and deception was explained, and references for all pertinent previous studies were provided. Certainly, both the study and the debriefing procedure were extraordinary. Important for the current context, Abramson also had participants complete an anonymous questionnaire, after the debriefing, regarding their perceptions of having participated in the project.

Based on the results, Abramson (1977) concluded that "participation was viewed as an enjoyable learning experience which produced no negative aftereffects. In fact, the overwhelming agreement among subjects indicates that the measures employed to safeguard ethical requirements were sufficient to induce a very positive regard for the experimental procedures. It is also interesting to note that not a single subject felt that any part of this experiment was a serious invasion of privacy" (p. 189). The large majority of participants in Abramson's study judged their participation to be an important learning experience and a significant contribution to sexual science. These results are encouraging, but most sex researchers do not provide such an extensive debriefing/educational session. Also, one cannot generalize to the student subject pool at large because the participants in Abramson's study initially signed up to participate in a study advertised as having to do with sexual attitudes and behavior (p. 186).

Plaud, Gaither, and Weller (1998) asked college student volunteers to complete standard measures of sexual attitudes and experience, as well as to rate 400 words as to how "sexual" each was. Thirty of these words had potential sexual meanings (e.g., *prick, screw, bust*). After completing the study, respondents were asked to rate how comfortable they felt while completing the measures using a 5-point scale (1 = *very uncomfortable*, 5 = *very comfortable*). Although comfort ratings were significantly positively correlated with number of sexual partners and negatively correlated with religiosity and sex guilt, respondents generally indicated comfort during participation (the sample mean was 4.05). However, the reader is not told whether participants had volunteered knowing that the study entailed sexuality as the topic of focus.

Both studies discussed thus far leave unanswered the question of whether perceived comfort or discomfort during participation is related to likelihood of participating in a similar study in the future. If discomfort and likelihood of future participation are unrelated, perhaps participants are not placing much importance on emotional discomfort as the criterion for determining whether to participate in a particular study (as would be implied by IRB concerns over informed consent about potential discomfort). To address this issue in at least a rudimentary way, I conducted an assessment of college student participants' perceptions (Wiederman, 1999b).

The primary focus of the survey, administered to 310 men and 399 women recruited from the Department of Psychological Science subject pool at Ball State University, was experiences of extradyadic involvement during courtship (see Wiederman & Hurd, 1999). In other words, each respondent was asked extensively about instances in which he or she was involved in a serious dating relationship with one person, yet concurrently engaged in a variety of dating and sexual experiences with someone else. As potential correlates of such extradyadic experience, several other variables were measured, including demographic information, religiosity, self-monitoring, body satisfaction and self-rated physical attractiveness, sexual attitudes, sexual esteem, sexual sensation-seeking, and recent and lifetime sexual experience (sexual intercourse, oral sex, casual sex).

In many respects, the anonymous 10-page survey created for this study was very typical of those used in sexuality research with college student subject pools.

At the end of the survey, respondents were asked to self-rate the "comfort level while participating in this study" using a 5-point scale (1 = *very uncomfortable*, 2 = *uncomfortable*, 3 = *not really affected*, 4 = *comfortable*, 5 = *very comfortable*). Respondents were also asked to indicate yes or no to this question: "Would you participate in another sexuality study involving an anonymous questionnaire if given the opportunity to do so in the future?"

Given my earlier emphasis on possible self-selection at the point of subject pool sign-up, as well as potential effects of implying that participation may cause anxiety, it is important to note that participants in this study were unaware of the sexual nature of the study at the point of initial sign-up, and they were provided with verbal informed consent in which no mention was made of potential anxiety or provision of counseling services to combat any ill effects from participation. The two research assistants who conducted the study reported that no one left the numerous testing sessions on learning of the nature of the questionnaire. Also, it is important to note that, even though extradyadic involvement during courtship is considered a socially undesirable behavior, relatively large numbers of respondents in the current study reported such experience (Wiederman & Hurd, 1999). Thus, one might expect relatively high levels of discomfort responding to questions about a taboo topic, especially when respondents admit to socially undesirable behavior.

The mean rating of comfort was 3.48 for the sample as a whole. Taking a rating of 1 or 2 as indicative of some discomfort, a rating of 3 as neutral, and a rating of 4 or 5 as indicative of a positive response, 19.7% of the men and 24.3% of the women indicated some level of discomfort during the study. A positive response was most common (54.8% of men and 45.8% of women). Still, there was a sizeable minority of respondents who reported some discomfort during participation. One might imagine that if these respondents experienced discomfort, they would be hesitant to participate in a similar study in the future. However, 97.4% of the men and 94.7% of the women indicated that they would indeed complete an anonymous questionnaire regarding sexuality if given the opportunity in the future.

As one might expect, a smaller proportion (89.9%) of the respondents who were relatively uncomfortable would volunteer for a similar study in the future compared to respondents whose emotional reaction was neutral or positive (97.6%). Rates of volunteering for a future study were actually slightly higher for respondents who reported having experienced extradyadic dating (97.8%) compared to those who denied such experience (94.7%). The rates of volunteering among those respondents who reported extradyadic sexual intercourse and those who denied such activity did not differ significantly (95.5% vs. 96.1%, respectively).

RECOMMENDATIONS

From the inception of IRBs, critics have voiced concerns about their functioning (e.g., Adair et al., 1985; Hessler & Galliher, 1983; Mosher, 1988; Seiler & Murtha, 1980; Williams, 1984). Regardless of idiosyncratic or prevailing opinions regarding the usefulness of IRBs, they are a fact of professional life for most sexuality researchers. Unfortunately, sexuality research is frequently seen by IRB members as ethically riskier than research involving very similar methodology but focusing on a less sensitive topic. Despite the fact that the federal regulations regarding the protection of human subjects declare anonymous questionnaires as exempt from IRB policy (OPRR, 1996), sexuality studies based on such questionnaires are frequently seen as in need of greater IRB regulation than the federal guidelines necessarily dictate.

Conflicts are liable to ensue between sexuality researchers and IRBs with regard to issues of potential harm and steps needed to protect participants from such perceived harm (Mosher, 1988; Wiederman, 1999a). What can be done? My first suggestion is to obtain your own copy of the federal regulations regarding IRB policy and to take the time to read it. It is not very long and is surprisingly easy to understand. Sexuality researchers need to understand what the regulations stipulate to conduct research in a legal and ethical manner and to intelligently address IRB concerns that seem unreasonable or beyond the scope of the federal regulations.

After becoming conversant with the federal regulations, share them with students and supervisees. I am embarrassed to admit that my first direct exposure to the federal regulations stipulating IRB policy occurred as a faculty member. While a student, I was socialized according to local IRB policy and tradition. In retrospect, I realize that some of the policies and requirements inflicted by the IRB during my graduate school years were inconsistent with the federal regulations, as well as with sound research methodology, yet I was unaware of the standard against which the local IRB should have been compared. Indeed, even purported experts on IRB policy may not consult the federal regulations. For example, in a chapter on "effective faculty use of institutional review boards," Gillespie (1999) described the three types of IRB review: exempt, expedited, and full. However, she described questionnaire studies asking about sensitive topics such as sexuality or drug use as falling under the full review category (p. 165). I believe that relative ignorance leads to blind compliance on the part of researchers such that, after several years, tradition is established and no one (researchers or IRB members) questions the enacted policies.

Given the relatively sensitive nature of sexuality research and the potential reaction it may elicit from IRB members, particularly those who have not been exposed previously to such research, researchers should anticipate potential IRB concerns and address them in a proactive fashion. This is not the same as to say assume the most conservative stance from the IRB and comply before requested to do so. Rather, I encourage sexuality researchers to take an educative role in crafting their IRB proposals. Researchers do not need to be overly grim and foreboding with regard to issues of potential harm, yet researchers should demonstrate that each has given consideration to those issues and treats them seriously.

Do not assume that IRB members are aware of the standard practices in sexuality research, the potential for selection bias, how participants typically respond, and so forth. In making reference to judgments you make about the degree to which you are meeting ethical and federal mandates, quote from and cite the federal regulations in your proposals to IRBs (which is relatively easy to do if you follow my first suggestion). If done in a nondefensive manner, this can serve to communicate your knowledge of the requirements for protection of human subjects, demonstrate your concern about conducting ethical yet methodologically sound research, and remind IRB members what the regulations actually stipulate.

Along the same lines, providing rationales for your methodological choices can go a long way to securing cooperation, particularly when you are requesting that the local IRB departs from their traditional stance regarding a particular policy. For example, learning about and then explaining in your proposal the previous research on the effects of requiring a signature on informed consent forms can be used to argue against such a requirement in your particular case. Explaining potential concern over perceptions that respondents forfeit anonymity by signing such forms bolsters the position that such requirements may not be in the best interest of participants.

Although I suggest making reference to the empirical literature, I recognize that research is scarce. I urge researchers to take up the task of applying their empirical skills to understanding the experience of research participants (Adair et al., 1985; Stanley, Sieber, & Melton, 1987) as well as IRB members. Many of the issues raised in this chapter would not be debatable had previous investigators evaluated the effects of research participation and the attributions and judgments participants (and IRB members) make regarding the process. In many cases, these issues can be examined in the context of a larger study on whatever sexuality topic one is examining. At the very least, routinely reporting the proportion of participants who withdrew, indicated concerns, or took advantage of offers of remedy for harm caused by participation would allow subsequent researchers to cite data when petitioning IRBs to conduct similar research.

In the end, the ideal relationship between researchers and IRBs is a collaborative one in which the interests of participant protection and research integrity are paramount for both parties. Unfortunately, that does not always appear to be the case with sexuality research. It is time for sexuality researchers to address ethical issues proactively and empirically.

SUGGESTED READINGS

Of course, required reading in this area includes the federal regulations regarding IRB policy (OPRR, 1996). With regard to scholarly writing on IRBs and related issues, most research and commentary were published in the 1970s and 1980s. Mosher (1988) provided virtually the only commentary on ethical principles and IRBs as they apply specifically to sexuality research. For discussion and data regarding deception in psychological research generally, see Adair et al. (1985) and

Epley and Huff (1998). Stanley et al. (1987) provided a broad discussion of a research agenda regarding empirical study of ethical issues in psychological research.

REFERENCES

Abramson, P. R. (1977). Ethical requirements for research on human sexual behavior: From the perspective of participating subjects. *Journal of Social Issues, 33*, 184–192.

Adair, J. G., Dushenko, T. W., & Lindsay, R. C. L. (1985). Ethical regulations and their impact on research practice. *American Psychologist, 40*, 59–72.

Aitkenhead, M., & Dordoy, J. (1985). What the subjects have to say. *British Journal of Social Psychology, 24*, 293–305.

Berg, B. L. (1992). Institutional review boards: Virtue machines or villains? *Criminal Justice Policy Review, 6*, 87–102.

Brannigan, G. G., Allgeier, A. R., & Allgeier, E. R. (1997). *The sex scientists.* New York: Addison-Wesley.

Ceci, S. J., Peters, D., & Plotkin, J. (1985). Human subjects review, personal values, and the regulation of social science research. *American Psychologist, 40*, 994–1002.

Clark, R. D. (1990). The impact of AIDS on gender differences in willingness to engage in casual sex. *Journal of Applied Social Psychology, 20*, 771–782.

Clark, R. D., & Hatfield, E. (1989). Gender differences in receptivity to sexual offers. *Journal of Psychology and Human Sexuality, 2*, 39–55.

Council, J. R., Smith, E. J. H., Kaster-Bundgaard, J., & Gladue, B. A. (1999). Interactions concerning risky research: Investigators rate their IRBs (and vice versa). In G. Chastain & R. E. Landrum (Eds.), *Protecting human subjects: Departmental subject pools and institutional review boards* (pp. 183–199). Washington, DC: American Psychological Association.

Dawes, R. M. (1988). *Rational choice in an uncertain world.* New York: Harcourt Brace Jovanovich.

Epley, N., & Huff, C. (1998). Suspicion, affective response, and educational benefit as a result of deception in psychology research. *Personality and Social Psychology Bulletin, 24*, 759–768.

Gillespie, J. F. (1999). The why, what, how, and when of effective faculty use of institutional review. In G. Chastain & R. E. Landrum (Eds.), *Protecting human subjects: Departmental subject pools and institutional review boards* (pp. 157–177). Washington, DC: American Psychological Association.

Goode, E. (1996). The ethics of deception in social research: A case study. *Qualitative Sociology, 19*, 11–33.

Griffith, M., & Walker, C. E. (1976). Characteristics associated with expressed willingness to participate in psychological research. *Journal of Social Psychology, 100*, 157–158.

Hessler, R. M., & Galliher, J. F. (1983). Institutional review boards and clandestine research: An experimental test. *Human Organization, 42*, 82–87.

Jackson, J. M., Procidano, M. E., & Cohen, C. J. (1989). Subject pool sign-up procedures: A threat to external validity. *Social Behavior and Personality, 17*, 29–43.

Kent, G. (1996). Shared understandings for informed consent: The relevance of psychological research on the provision of information. *Social Science and Medicine, 43*, 1517–1523.

King, L. A., & Miner, K. N. (2000). Writing about the perceived benefits of traumatic events: Implications for physical health. *Personality and Social Psychology Bulletin, 26*, 220–230.

Mann, T. (1994). Informed consent for psychological research: Do subjects comprehend consent forms and understand their legal rights? *Psychological Science, 5*, 140–143.

Mathes, E. W., Phillips, J. T., Skowran, J., & Dick, W. E. (1982). Behavioral correlates of the interpersonal jealousy scale. *Educational and Psychological Measurement, 42*, 1127–1231.

Maynard, C., & Wiederman, M. (1997). College students' perceptions of child sexual abuse: Effects of age, sex, and gender-role attitudes. *Child Abuse & Neglect, 21,* 833–844.

Mosher, D. L. (1988). Balancing the rights of subjects, scientists, and society: 10 principles for human subject committees. *The Journal of Sex Research, 24,* 378–385.

Office for Protection from Research Risks (OPPR). (1993). *Protecting human research subjects: Institutional Review Board guidebook.* Washington, DC: Author.

Office for Protection from Research Risks (OPPR). (1996). *Protection of human subjects.* Washington, DC: Author.

Paez, D., Velasco, C., & Gonzalez, J. L. (1999). Expressive writing and the role of alexythimia as a dispositional deficit in self-disclosure and physical health. *Journal of Personality and Social Psychology, 77,* 630–641.

Pennebaker, J. W. (1997). Writing about emotional experiences as a therapeutic process. *Psychological Science, 8,* 162–166.

Plaud, J. J., Gaither, G. A., & Weller, L. A. (1998). Gender differences in the sexual ratings of words. *Journal of Sex & Marital Therapy, 24,* 13–19.

Seiler, L. H., & Murtha, J. M. (1980). Federal regulation of social research using "human subjects": A critical assessment. *American Sociologist, 15,* 146–157.

Sieber, J. E., & Baluyot, R. M. (1992). A survey of IRB concerns about social and behavioral research. *IRB: A Review of Human Subjects Research, 14*(2), 9–10.

Singer, E. (1978). Informed consent: Consequences for response rate and response quality in social surveys. *American Sociological Review, 43,* 144–162.

Smith, C. P., & Berard, S. P. (1982). Why are human subjects less concerned about ethically problematic research than human subjects committees? *Journal of Applied Social Psychology, 12,* 209–221.

Stanley, B., Sieber, J. E., & Melton, G. B. (1987). Empirical studies of ethical issues in research: A research agenda. *American Psychologist, 42,* 735–741.

Waggoner, W. C., & Mayo, D. M. (1995). Who understands? A survey of 25 words or phrases commonly used in proposed clinical research consent forms. *IRB: A Review of Human Subjects Research, 17,* 6–9.

Wiederman, M. W. (1999a). Sexuality research, institutional review boards, and subject pools. In G. Chastain & R. E. Landrum (Eds.), *Protecting human subjects: Departmental subject pools and institutional review boards* (pp. 201–219). Washington, DC: American Psychological Association.

Wiederman, M. W. (1999b). Volunteer bias in sexuality research using college student participants. *The Journal of Sex Research, 36,* 59–66.

Wiederman, M. W., & Hurd, C. (1999). Extradyadic involvement during dating. *Journal of Social and Personal Relationships, 16,* 267–276.

Williams, P. C. (1984). Success in spite of failure: Why IRBs falter in reviewing risks and benefits. *IRB: A Review of Human Subjects Research, 6*(3), 1–4.

21

Causes and Consequences of a Career in Sex Research

Paul Okami
University of California–Los Angeles

It is time to stop the nonsense—in both the science and scholarship within the organizations which support scholars and scientists who study this subject. We must admit that our progress has been slow. Admit that our methods are weak. Admit that our theories need considerable improvement. Admit that much of the work in our area is propelled by personal agendas. And admit that many "flakes" are attracted to, and thrive within, our field. . . .
—Abramson (1992, p. 450)

In the spring of 1999, I had the unpleasant and somewhat startling experience of tuning into my local a.m. talk radio station and hearing Dr. Laura Schlessinger, the highest-rated nationally syndicated midday talk show guru, vilify three of my colleagues in exceedingly harsh tones. "Dr. Laura," as she's called by her millions of fans, was focusing on a particular article that had appeared in the American Psychological Association (APA) journal *Psychological Bulletin* (Rind, Tromovitch, & Bauserman, 1998). The article was a meticulously thorough meta-analysis of outcome research among nonclinical samples of victims of child sexual abuse and other forms of sex between adults and minors. Indeed, this study was not merely carefully and competently conducted—it was among the most informative pieces on the topic of sexual abuse to have been published during the previous two decades. Nevertheless, Dr. Laura was claiming that the paper was *garbage*. With passion and certainty of moral rectitude, she impugned the characters of the authors, dismissed their work as a "defense of pedophilia," and, in a veiled manner, speculated about their sexual self-interest.

I was troubled about this broadcast for several reasons. First, the article did not defend pedophilia if *pedophilia* is defined in the medial or sexological sense as a paraphilic sexual interest in prepubertal children. Indeed, pedophilia was not even discussed in this article, which was concerned instead with the effects of sexual abuse on children. Thus, the broadcast misrepresented to the public the nature of important scientific research on an important topic. Second, I knew that, regardless of the lack of warrant for the various accusations, this sort of thing could potentially have serious consequences for my colleagues' professional and personal lives. This was particularly poignant given that each of the authors was more or less at the start of his academic career.

There was a third reason I felt uncomfortable listening to the broadcast. I also had published numerous articles on the topic of child sexuality, adopting an anti-alarmist viewpoint roughly similar to that taken by my besieged colleagues. As I listened to the radio, I wondered: Were people talking about me like this behind my back? Would I also end up as fodder for some talk show vulture?

By now, most of us in the field are aware of the upshot of Dr. Laura's crusade, which was also taken up by various religious zealots, right-wing politicians, and conservative groups such as psychotherapists. In the summer of 1999, the U.S. House of Representatives voted unanimously (with seven people abstaining from the voting process) to condemn my colleagues, the article they wrote, and the APA for allowing the article to be printed in their flagship journal. The APA in turn offered to have the article reevaluated by independent reviewers—this after the article had already passed competent review by *Psychological Bulletin's* referees (Ruark, 1999). The APA also announced their decision to enact a new process of special, additional review for articles considered potentially controversial. During this new review process, the public policy implications of publication would be considered. In other words, certain reports might not appear in print, regardless of their scientific merit, if their results were potentially upsetting to some people or if some people decided that social harm might result if they were published. There is no question that this represents an overt form of censorship on behalf of special interest groups.

Numerous commentators have explicitly argued that censorship and other restrictions on behavioral research are warranted when such research concerns sensitive topics (e.g., gender/sex, race/ethnicity, or childhood/motherhood). The rationale typically given is that research results may intentionally or unintentionally be used to the detriment of some demographic group (Seiber & Stanley cited in Whitley, 1996). In virtually all cases, it is feared that violations of democratic principles may be expressed in claims of fact based on such research.

Whitley (1996) noted two procedures suggested by critics of socially sensitive research to ameliorate potential problems. The first is cost–benefit analysis to be instituted prior to the conduct of research, taking into account potential beneficial and detrimental social effects of any particular study. The second procedure consists of limitations placed on publication through self- or editorial-censorship, again considering possible detrimental effects of publication on relevant demographic groups.

In contrast to these notions, Scarr (1988) warned that failure to conduct or publish such research may have negative impact on the very demographic groups protectionist commentators wish to shield. For example, accurate information is necessary to develop efficient sexual abuse prevention programs or counter destructive racial and gender stereotypes.

What seems to be ignored in both these perspectives is the simple fact that it is impossible to predict accurately the effects of the conduct or publication of any research. Indeed, it is foolish to claim otherwise. Thus, cost–benefit analyses and decisions to censor or not censor are splendid cases of garbage in, garbage out.

Clearly, this a not a climate in which to do scientific work. However, I have no right to complain. When I entered the doctoral program in psychology at the University of California, Los Angeles (UCLA) and decided to specialize in human sexuality, my eyes were wide open. I knew quite well (or thought I did) the magnitude of dues I would have to pay to remain a sexuality researcher in a hostile academic environment. I had read biographical material on the lives of Alfred Kinsey, Masters, and Johnson, and I was aware that they had made sure they were well established in *respectable* fields of research or medicine before they began their sex-related inquiries. I was equally and painfully aware that I would be treading on particularly sensitive toes with the research I was conducting on childhood sexuality. I had been advised by two highly respected, internationally known researchers not to publish my work (although, in private, they expressed admiration for it). One of my mentors at UCLA assured me (in a matter-of-fact tone) that the social science community would simply assume I was a pedophile if I published work that was critical of the social advocacy science then prevalent in sexual abuse-related research. Why else would I publish such criticism? Indeed, if I did not have some sort of sexual self-interest, why get involved in sex research in the first place?

CAUSES OF A CAREER IN SEXUALITY RESEARCH

Why does a person decide to study sexuality? After so deciding, why does he or she choose a particular topic? Are sexuality researchers motivated more by personal agendas than other types of behavioral scientists, as the Abramson quote opening this chapter suggests? If not, why do people presume that we are? If we are, does it matter?

These are interesting questions—I suppose. That is, they are not very interesting to me, but they are obviously of general interest in a tabloid sort of way. The reason that these questions do not particularly interest me is that their answers seem so self-evident. Why does a person decide to study orgasms? They're juicy! S/M? Definitely keeps you awake at conferences! Sexually transmitted diseases, sexual dysfunction, and rape? Important problems that elicit strong emotion and affect a great many people, including friends, relatives, and neighbors. There is perhaps no greater motivator of human behavior than sexuality. Indeed, I feel confident in proposing that if there were more money and prestige involved, if it did not put an ugly blot on a person's resume (particularly the resume of a beginning academic), if it did not make people snicker, if it did not make people angry, if it did not make people embarrassed, if it did not cause people to assume that you belonged to the sexual self-interest group you were studying—in short, if it were not sexuality research as it is currently viewed—a large number (perhaps the majority) of social and behavioral scientists would switch topics to sexuality.

Why does a person choose a particular topic within sexuality research? If we were honest, we would admit that stereotypes usually (although not always) have some factual basis. This is no less so as regards sexuality research. Many of us do choose topics because we identify directly with the group or event we are studying. Does this sort of thing occur more in sexuality research than most other forms of research? Although direct self-interest may be only one of many possible motivators to enter our field, I bet my complete set of Charlie Parker CDs that it appears more frequently in research on homosexuality and pedophilia than in research on affiliation and attribution. Nevertheless, personal agendas might not drive sexuality research any more often than they drive research on race and ethnicity, women's studies, clinical and abnormal psychology, social deviance and criminality, or a host of other things that trouble us or arouse our passions.

Perhaps self-interest does provide the motivator for sexuality research more frequently than it does the more so-called respectable fields listed earlier. Why might this be true? This question recalls a didactic technique utilized by the Southern California Gay and Lesbian Task Force when they sent representatives to speak to groups of university students about issues concerning homosexuality. When they got to the topic of whether homosexuality is a sexual choice or a sexual orientation, they asked the students to think of all the names for homosexuals they have heard throughout their lives. Of course, all the terms are highly pejorative—offensively so. They then asked, "Why on earth would a person choose to be thought of this way?" In the same sense, understanding the place that sexuality researchers have in the scientific community, one might well ask, "Why on earth would a person choose to be thought of this way?" The answer people arrive at may often be that the researcher must be motivated by something powerful—like personal agenda and self-interest.

Even if it were true that self-interest is present more often in sexuality research than in other fields, self-interest is only one of many possible motivators. Moreover, when people make judgments about sexuality researchers' self-interested motivations, *self-interest* is implicitly defined without much imagination. For example, a person such as myself, who has studied the topic of childhood sexual development, pedophilia, and child sexual abuse, might indeed have entered the field because he is a pedophile. However, consider that he might have entered because

1. his father, brother, or son turned out to be a pedophile;
2. he was sexually abused as a child or had a positive childhood experience with a pedophile;
3. he was aghast to learn that teachers at his children's day-care center were not permitted to hug or kiss his kids as a consequence of hysteria over pedophilia;
4. he had been a generally horny child and wanted to discover if he was exceptional;
5. he is a man in his early 50s who prefers women in their early 20s as wives or sexual partners, is fascinated with the way in which any form of intergenerational sex is socially denigrated, and understands that more data and opportunities to publish exist for intergenerational sexuality that involve children;
6. he has a generally perverse, anti-authoritarian streak, and data sets involving childhood sexuality fell into his lap as a graduate student and were self-perpetuating.

what about interaction effects? Perhaps it is a combination of any of these scenarios. Or maybe . . . maybe . . . maybe. This just covers possible self-interested motivations. It should go without saying that there are other types of motivations, including curiosity, feverish truth-seeking, and all the rest.

Suppose again that it is true that we chose our topics because of self-interested personal agendas. There is still the question: Does it matter? In an ideal scientific setting, it would not matter a bit because of peer review. Unfortunately, our peer review process, like our judicial process, is not ideal. When it comes to topics like sexuality, race, or drugs, all the potential problems in the publication process may be magnified. Flakey personal agendas may be shared by reviewers, editors, and researchers alike. If the topic is socially explosive or one on which received views are particularly entrenched or both, poor research may pass by sleepy or sloppy reviewers, or—as with the Dr. Laura–Rind et al. melodrama—very good research may be ignored or condemned in the halls of Congress and less auspicious venues. Therefore, although scientific truth prevails over time as the result of the self-correcting nature of our methods, this does not always happen in time to prevent significant damage—either to academic careers, the body of scientific knowledge, or society as a whole.

One consequence of the presence of personal agendas and self-interest that is usually not considered is that it has the potential of improving the quality of our work in several ways. Personal agendas or self-interest often fuel passionate involvement in our work. Although this obviously may introduce bias, it may also motivate us to put more effort into our research than others would. If we are well trained, this may translate into superior, not inferior, research and may stimulate more imaginative and productive theorizing.

Self-interest implies familiarity and experience with the subject matter. Although this can again introduce bias, it also may prevent our being misled by appearances in certain situations and may help us gain the confidence of research subjects. As an analogy, consider ethological research conducted among a preindustrial tribe by a member of the tribe who had been schooled in a Western university and earned his or her degree in anthropology. Now compare the usefulness of such a person to that of an anthropologist who has never left New Jersey.

In summary, there are proximate and ultimate causes of a career in sexuality research. For some of us, these causes may be apparent to ourselves, others, or both. For some of us, causes may be obscure or simply serendipitous. The important issue is the quality of our research, which is a dual result of our scientific imaginations and our scientific training.

CONSEQUENCES OF A CAREER
IN SEXUALITY RESEARCH

There are consequences to a career in sex research that do not exist in the careers of most other researchers. People—including university faculty and administrators—may assume that you belong to the group you are researching (Fisher, 1989) or they will simply assume that you are a pervert of the more general kind. Unpleasant consequences of these assumptions, be they accurate or inaccurate, are numerous and obvious. They may threaten one's livelihood or social standing, and may even put one in danger of false imprisonment or violence committed by various loonies.

If you begin studying sexuality in graduate school, you may find it difficult or impossible to get an academic job despite schooling at the finest academies, a strong record of publication, exemplary teaching evaluations, and exuberant recommendations from important people in the field. You will also find it difficult or, depending on your topic, impossible to get funding for your research. If you begin studying sexuality after you have secured a position, you may find it difficult or impossible to receive tenure or get promoted. Anecdotally, just this morning I received an e-mail from a well-published Ph.D. who works in a medical institution and will remain anonymous. The e-mail read, in part: "The sad thing is that 'well-respected sex researcher' is nearly an oxymoron—sex researchers, by definition, are not well respected (the head of my center just warned me to lay off studying orgasm because it won't get me promoted)."

As a sexuality researcher, you will also find it difficult to get your work published in the *better journals* unless this work is concerned with highly negative aspects of sexuality such as rape, sexual abuse, or disease. Even these topics are generally taboo for many psychology and medical journals. For all of these reasons, you will find precious few top-notch scientists and scholars working in sexuality-related areas. Consequently, you will discover that much of the research you are compelled to rely on for information is of poor quality relative to other fields.

Last, but certainly not least, you may be vilified on national radio or condemned in Congress. These fates in no way have been limited to the case of Rind, Tromovitch, and Bauserman. From Kinsey onward, sexuality researchers have found themselves in similar situations, albeit with perhaps less dramatic consequences.

Given all of this, is it any wonder that people make assumptions about our self-interest and personal agendas? Even we in the field make those assumptions! This is ironic given that we may know from *our own cases* that these assumptions are often completely unwarranted and inaccurate.

What is to be done? I suppose if a student wanted to minimize the more serious of these problems as they might affect her personally, he or she would do what the smart cookies who came before him or her have done: Do not mention sexuality to anyone while in graduate school, get a good job, publish a program of research in a nonsexuality-related area, wait for tenure or employment in the private sector, and then . . . sock it to 'em. Unfortunately, this may not be a very satisfying option for the individual researcher nor is it optimal for the growth of sexual science as a field.

What about these problems as they affect the field as a whole? Evolutionary theory as well as Freudian theory argue that, at bottom (excuse the word play), sexuality is the most important motivator of human behavior. If pressed, almost anyone will acknowledge that sexuality is, at least, one of the important motivators. How can it be that the social and behavioral sciences have turned their backs on the study of sexuality? It is foolish. Moreover, the entire cycle is self-perpetuating. When high-caliber scientists and scholars avoid studying sexuality because of personal and professional consequences, the field becomes fertile soil for Abramson's (1992) *flakes*. The more flakey work is published, the less attractive and respectable the field becomes and so attracts fewer high-caliber scientists.

It seems to me that the first step is to make the admissions suggested by Abramson (1992; quoted at the start of this chapter) and "stop the nonsense." Perhaps then we may begin to attract the more courageous souls from among the keener scientific minds. In the meantime, individual sexuality researchers need to be aware of the possible consequences of participation in their chosen field.

SUGGESTED READINGS

Brannigan, Allgeier, and Allgeier (1998) and Bullough, Bullough, Fithian, Hartman, and Klein (1997) each provided collections of personal accounts from sexuality researchers as to the perceived causes and consequences of their choice to study human sexuality. For a brief discussion of how political factors have affected sexuality research in the United States, see Udry (1993), who also described his personal experiences with having funding of his research blocked by political forces. As an illustration of how politics affects funding of sexuality research in places other than the United States, see Wellings, Field, Johnson, and Wadsworth (1994). Last, both Story (1993) and Williams (1993) discussed the intersection of self-interest and the topics they have chosen to study, and how these choices have affected both their research and their careers.

REFERENCES

Abramson, P. R. (1992). Adiós: A farewell address. *The Journal of Sex Research, 29,* 449–450.

Brannigan, G. C., Allgeier, E. R., & Allgeier, A. R. (Eds.). (1998). *The sex scientists.* New York: Longman.

Bullough, B., Bullough, V. L., Fithian, M. A., Hartman, W. E., & Klein, R. S. (Eds.). (1997). *How I got into sex.* Amherst, NY: Prometheus Books.

Fisher, T. D. (1989). Confessions of a closet sex researcher. *The Journal of Sex Research, 26,* 144–147.

Rind, B., Tromovitch, P., & Bauserman, R. (1998). A meta-analytic examination of assumed properties of child sexual abuse using college samples. *Psychological Bulletin, 124,* 25–53.

Ruark, J. K. (1999, June 11). Psychology association seeks review of article on child-adult sex. *The Chronicle of Higher Education.*

Scarr, S. (1988). Race and gender as psychological variables: Social and ethical issues. *American Psychologist, 43,* 49–55.

Story, M. D. (1993). Personal and professional perspectives on social nudism: Should you be personally involved in your research? *The Journal of Sex Research, 30,* 111–114.

Udry, J. R. (1993). The politics of sex research. *The Journal of Sex Research, 30,* 103–110.

Wellings, K., Field, J., Johnson, A. M., & Wadsworth, J. (1994). *Sexual behaviour in Britain: The National Survey of Sexual Attitudes and Lifestyles.* London: Penguin.

Whitley, B. E., Jr. (1996). *Principles of research in behavioral science.* Mountain View, CA: Mayfield.

Williams, W. L. (1993). Being gay and doing research on homosexuality in non-Western cultures. *The Journal of Sex Research, 30,* 115–120.

Author Index

Y

Subject Index